D1519778

THE WORKS OF JONATHAN EDWARDS

VOLUME 13

Harry S. Stout, General Editor

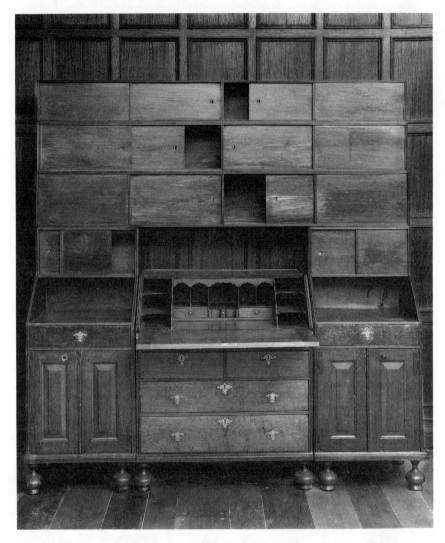

Jonathan Edwards' writing desk ("scrutore"), with matching cabinets supporting box shelves. Courtesy of Jonathan Edwards College, Yale University. Photograph by William K. Sacco.

JONATHAN EDWARDS

The "Miscellanies"

(Entry Nos. a–z, aa–zz, 1–500)

EDITED BY
THOMAS A. SCHAFER

PROFESSOR EMERITUS OF CHURCH HISTORY
McCORMICK THEOLOGICAL SEMINARY

New Haven and London

YALE UNIVERSITY PRESS, 1994

Funds for editing The Works of Jonathan Edwards
*have been provided by The Pew Charitable Trusts, The
Lilly Endowment, The Andrew Mellon Foundation, and*
The L. J. Skaggs and Mary C. Skaggs Foundation.

*Published with assistance from the Exxon Education
Fund.*

*Set in Baskerville type by The Composing Room
of Michigan, Inc., Grand Rapids, Michigan.*

*Printed in the United States of America by
Vail-Ballou Press, Binghamton, New York.*

*Library of Congress Cataloging-in-Publication Data
(Revised for volume 13)*

Edwards, Jonathan, 1703–1758.
    The works of Jonathan Edwards.
    *General editor, v. 3–6, John E. Smith; v. 7 edited by
Norman Pettit; v. 8 edited by Paul Ramsey; v. 9
transcribed and edited by John F. Wilson; v. 10 edited by
Wilson H. Kimnach; v. 13 edited by Thomas A. Schafer.*
    Includes bibliographical references and indexes.
    *Contents: v. 1. Freedom of the will — v. 2. Religious
affections — [etc.] — v. 13. The "miscellanies" (entry
nos. a–z, aa–zz, 1–500).*
    *1. Congregational churches—United States.
2. Reformed church—United States.   3. Theology.
4. Philosophy.   5. Ethics.   I. Miller, Perry, 1905–
1963.   II. Smith, John Edwin.   III. Pettit,
Norman.   IV. Title.*
    BX7117.E3   1957 vol. 13 230'.58   57-2336
    ISBN 0-300-06059-9

*A catalogue record for this book is available from the
British Library.*

*The paper in this book meets the guidelines for
permanence and durability of the Commmittee on
Production Guidelines for Book Longevity of the
Council on Library Resources.*

10   9   8   7   6   5   4   3   2   1

CONTENTS

ILLUSTRATIONS

TABLES

GENERAL EDITOR'S PREFACE

The Works of Jonathan Edwards began under the general editorship of Perry Miller in 1957 with Paul Ramsey's edition of *Freedom of the Will*. The following eight volumes, published under the direction of Miller and his successor, John E. Smith, contain most of the remaining treatises that Edwards published himself or that were published soon after his death. With volume 10, *Sermons and Discourses, 1720–1723*, edited by Wilson H. Kimnach, the *Works* entered a new phase in its history. Not only did the Edition acquire a new general editor, but it also began the systematic publication of the vast collection of Edwards' personal manuscripts. Alongside the sermons, the "Miscellanies" constitutes the major body of unpublished manuscript materials, and so this volume marks an important milestone in the edition's history of publication.

Prof. Schafer's edition of the first volume in this series of "Miscellanies" has been long-anticipated. His contributions to the study of Edwards, as epitomized by this volume, are immense. He has been with the edition since its beginning; indeed, his efforts predate the edition, since it was during his work on Edwards' manuscripts as a graduate student in the 1940s that he discovered the significance of the "Miscellanies" and began the arduous task of transcribing them. In the course of his work, he recognized that, in order to integrate the manuscripts fully into Edwards' intellectual biography, it was necessary to establish an accurate chronology of them. This difficult project, the work of several decades, resulted in the chronology from which several past editors have profited and which will be applied in forthcoming volumes of this edition.

An author-centered rather than an editor-centered approach to the texts naturally suits the transition from published treatises to manuscripts, an approach that for forthcoming volumes entails more succinct introductory and annotative apparatus in the interest of presenting more of Edwards' previously inaccessible manuscripts. In so doing, we seek to carry on the mission of this edition as formulated at its beginning. The result, we hope, will be the same that Perry Miller so eloquently identified four decades ago, namely, to "find today a new urgency to confront and reinterpret the historic philosophical and theological cruxes with which Edwards grappled so courageously."

Harry S. Stout

NOTE TO THE READER

Editorial Statement

The text of Jonathan Edwards is reproduced in this Edition as he wrote it in manuscript, or, if he published it himself, as it was printed in the first edition. In order to present this text to modern readers as practically readable, several technical adjustments have been made. Those which can be addressed categorically are as follows:

1. All spelling is regularized and conformed to that of *Webster's Third New International Dictionary,* a step that does not involve much more than removing the "u" from "colour" or "k" from "publick" since Edwards was a good speller, used relatively modern spelling, and generally avoided "y" contractions. His orthographic contractions and abbreviations, such as ampersands, "call'd," and "thems." are spelled out, though pronounced contractions, such as "han't" and "ben't," are retained.

2. There is no regular punctuation in most of Edwards' manuscripts and where it does exist, as in the earliest sermons, it tends to be highly erratic. Editors take into account Edwards' example in punctuation and related matters, but all punctutation is necessarily that of the editor, including paragraph divisions (especially in some notebooks such as the "Miscellanies") and the emphasizing devices of italics and capitalization. Regarding capitalization, pronouns referring to the deity are lowercase except in passages where Edwards confusingly mixes the "he" referring to God with that for man. Here capitalization of pronouns referring to the deity sorts out the references for the reader.

3. Numbered heads designate important structures of argument in Edwards' sermons, notebooks, and treatises. Numbering, including spelled-out numbers, has been regularized and corrected where necessary. Particularly in the manuscript sermon texts, numbering has been clarified by the use of systematic schemes of heads and subheads in accordance with eighteenth-century homiletical form, a practice similar to modern analytical outline form. Thus the series of subordinated head number forms, 1, (1), *1*, a, (a), in the textual exegesis, and

the series, I, *First*, 1, (1), *1*, a, (a), in Doctrine and Application divisions, make it possible to determine sermon head relationships at a glance.

4. Textual intervention to regularize Edwards' citation of Scripture includes the correction of erroneous citation, the regularizing of citation form (including the standardization of book abbreviations), and the completion of quotations which Edwards' textual markings indicate should be completed (as in preaching).

5. Omissions and lacunae in the manuscript text are filled by insertions in square brackets ([ ]); repeated phrases sometimes represented by Edwards with a long dash are inserted in curly brackets ({ }). In all cases of uncertain readings, annotation gives notice of the problem. Markings in the text designate whole word units even when only a few letters are at issue.

6. Minor slips of the pen or obvious typographical errors are corrected without annotation. Also, Edwards' corrections, deletions, and internal shifts of material are observed but not noted unless of substantive interest.

7. Quotations made by the editor from the Bible (AV) and other secondary sources are printed *verbatim ac literatim.* Edwards' quotations from such sources are often rather free but are not corrected and are not annotated as such unless significant omissions or distortions are involved.

Other conditions of textual preparation are related to differences of genre and factors unique to particular texts or manuscripts. For information on such matters please consult the note on the text in each volume or the first volume of each series within the Edition.

The Executive Committee
The Works of Jonathan Edwards

Acknowledgments

Anything like an adequate account of the various forms of aid and comfort I have received in over forty years of work on Edwards' "Miscellanies" and other manuscripts would fill several pages and amount to name-dropping on a grand scale. That is neither feasible nor desirable at this point. To those who do not appear in this necessarily highly selective note: please rest assured that I hold you also in grateful memory as I write.

Three people were intimately concerned in my decision to attempt an edition of the "Miscellanies." Through Albert C. Outler's generous hospitality I spent a month in 1945 at Sterling Library's Rare Book Room, where I became convinced that that notebook series was indispensable to all future Edwards scholarship. H. Shelton Smith, who had guided my dissertation on Edwards' metaphysics, encouraged me to attempt an edition of the manuscript and gave me much advice and counsel in the early years. Perry Miller confirmed my estimate of the "Miscellanies" by comments in his *Jonathan Edwards* and later incorporated my edition into the *Works.* He and other charter members of the Editorial Committee gave unstintingly of their time by discussing editorial problems with me, reading samples of edited text, and evaluating drafts of introductory chapters: Sydney E. Ahlstrom, David Horne, Norman Holmes Pearson, Paul Ramsey, and John E. Smith. After he succeeded Miller as General Editor, John E. Smith continued to offer enthusiastic support by correspondence, conversation, and critical reading of successive versions of the Introduction.

Other editors and members of the Editorial Committee have also patiently listened to my excited reports of discoveries in the manuscripts and shared their own findings, notably Wallace E. Anderson, George S. Claghorn, Stephen J. Stein, and Wilson H. Kimnach, most of whom read all or parts of my later drafts. I also greatly profited from many discussions with John H. Gerstner concerning knotty problems both in Edwards' manuscripts and in Reformed theology. George Claghorn, Douglas J. Elwood, and Kenneth Minkema discovered additional Edwards manuscripts that proved critical for the dating of the "Miscellanies." Many libraries and their personnel have aided my research, for which I am grateful, but I must mention especially the staff of Beinecke Library, who have offered continual support in the most friendly and efficient manner for so long a time.

Financial support for my research has come from several sources. The Duke University Research Council provided funds for microfilm and other supplies and services, as did the Bollingen Foundation through the budget of the Editorial Committee. During 1956–57 I was a John Simon Guggenheim fellow. A faculty fellowship from the American Association of Theological Schools enabled me to spend a semester in 1964–65 as a research fellow at Yale Divinity School, and McCormick Seminary's generous sabbatical leave policy made possible other seasons of concentrated study of the manuscripts. Through Robert W. Lynn, the Lilly Endowment made grants supporting my work. Upon the recommendation of Clyde Holbrook, generous contributions were also made by William Edwards Stevenson and his grandson, William Edwards Hunt. More recently, grants from the Pew Charitable Trust to the Yale edition of the *Works* have made possible the final preparation of this volume for publication.

The present Introduction and edited text would not have been accomplished so rapidly or so pleasantly without the labors of several people. The present General Editor, Harry S. Stout, shepherded my material through two readings by the Executive Committee of the Editorial Committee and made proposals for its further revision. At the office of *The Works of Jonathan Edwards,* Ava Chamberlain and Kenneth Minkema collaborated closely with me in that task by checking all the transcriptions with the manuscript and by drafting abridgments in text and notes. Ava did the lion's share of the technical work in preparing the finished copy for the Press, and Ken made the watermark tracings for Appendix B. At Yale University Press, James Mooney edited the copy, making valuable suggestions, and Editions and Series Editor Judith Calvert has directed the whole process of publication.

Finally, I wish to pay special tribute to some others without whom this volume of the "Miscellanies" would never have seen the light of day. Marjorie G. Wynne, through many years as Edwin J. Beinecke Research Librarian, saw to it that the Edwards editors had a place to work with easy access to the manuscripts. The directors and librarians of Andover-Newton Theological School lent Beinecke Library their considerable collection of Edwards manuscripts for about fifteen years, thus enabling for the first time in over a century the comparative and chronological study of nearly the whole Edwards corpus. For almost twenty-five years Robert and Harriette Balay of New Haven have given me a home away from home whenever I have been working on the manuscripts; without that and their supportive friendship I would have given up long ago. But my most fundamental enabler has been my wife Eudora Jones Schafer and four children who cannot remember a time when Dad was *not* working on Edwards. Her loyal support, sound advice, and willingness to keep home and family together during my sometimes long absences have gone quite beyond what I had any right to expect. There is really no way I can make it up to her and the children—but then, that's grace, isn't it?

Thomas A. Schafer

Chicago, Illinois
March 1, 1994

EDITOR'S INTRODUCTION

For students of American religious history, the publication of Jonathan Edwards' "Miscellanies" makes available a unique resource. Although other Puritan pastors in colonial New England kept theological notebooks or intellectual diaries, none surpasses that of Edwards in length, breadth of content, or depth of thought.[1] Edwards made his first entry in the "Miscellanies" in 1722 and regularly added to the series throughout his ministry. By the time he had made his final entries in the last year of his life it had grown to nine large volumes plus a separate index, which Edwards called the "Table."[2] For thirty-five years these notebooks trace the intellectual development and maturation of one of America's foremost theologians, providing valuable insights into his mind and spirit.

This edition of the "Miscellanies" is the first to present the complete text of Edwards' compositions in the order in which they occur in the manuscripts. This initial volume contains the Table and "Miscellanies" Nos. a–z, aa–zz and 1–500.[3] The remainder of the 1400-plus entries will be published in subsequent volumes of the Edition.[4] Nos. a–500, spanning the years 1722–31, are particularly important for understanding Edwards' early development as a scholar and theologian. Prior to 1731, although his intellectual production had been great, Edwards had had no audience for his work save the congregations to which he had preached and his fellow ministers in the Hamp-

1. Cotton Mather's "Biblia Americana" (Massachusetts Historical Society MS Collection) may rival the "Miscellanies" in length, but it is a work of scriptural exegesis, not an intellectual diary.

2. All volumes but one are in the Beinecke Rare Book and Manuscript Library, Yale University, New Haven, Conn. Book 6 is in the Trask Library, Andover-Newton Theological School, Newton Centre, Mass. Throughout the present volume it is assumed that all JE's MSS are at the Beinecke Library unless otherwise specified.

3. A capitalized "No." with numerals always cites "Miscellanies" entries; lower case is used for all citations of other MSS of JE.

4. No. 1069, "Types of the Messiah," has recently been published in *The Works of Jonathan Edwards, 11, Typological Writings*, eds. Wallace E. Anderson and Mason I. Lowance, Jr. (New Haven, Yale Univ. Press, 1993), 191–324. (After the initial citation, individual volumes in the Yale Edition are referred to as *Works*, followed by the volume number.)

shire Association. In July of that year he delivered the "Thursday Lecture" to the Boston clergy; it was published under the title *God Glorified in the Work of Redemption, by the Greatness of Man's Dependence upon Him, in the Whole of It.* Therefore, these youthful compositions in the "Miscellanies" preserve and reveal the genesis and incubation of Edwards' most characteristic ideas prior to their first exposition before a larger public and his entrance upon theological debate in a wider forum.

When Edwards made his first entries, his graduate study at Yale was drawing to a close, but his education was just beginning: a self-imposed discipline of reading and writing that transformed him from a precocious college student into an intellectual force that would strongly influence the course of theological debate in New England well into the nineteenth century. Edwards described his method of theological inquiry in a letter written near the end of his life:

> My method of study, from my first beginning the work of the ministry, has been very much by writing; applying my self in this way, to improve every important hint; pursuing the clew to my utmost, when any thing in reading, meditation or conversation, has been suggested to my mind, that seemed to promise light, in any weighty point—— Thus penning what appeared to me my best thoughts, on innumerable subjects for my own benefit.——— The longer I prosecuted my studies in this method, the more habitual it became, and the more pleasant and profitable I found it.[5]

In his 1765 biography of Edwards, Samuel Hopkins confirmed this characterization of his mentor's method: "Reading was not the only Method he took to improve his Mind; but he did this much by Writing . . . Every thought on any Subject, which appear'd to him worth pursuing and preserving, he pursued, as far as he then could, with his Pen in his Hand."[6] The nine manuscript notebooks that comprise the "Miscellanies" are tangible physical evidence of the truth of these accounts.

Piece by piece, number by number, the reader of the "Miscellanies" can look over Edwards' shoulder as he improved hints, pursued clues, and penned his best thoughts. It is not necessary to break down Edwards' mature views into their essential elements in order to arrive at their first formulations and trace the inner logic of his thought, for the

5. Letter to the Trustees of the College of New Jersey, Oct. 19, 1757, in Samuel Hopkins, *The Life and Character of the Late Reverend Mr. Jonathan Edwards* (Boston, 1765), p. 76.
6. *Life and Character*, p. 41.

"Miscellanies" does this for us. We can observe the seminal ideas already planted in the youthful entries and watch them emerge full-blown in his later essays, sermons, and published works. This privileged view is the genius of the "Miscellanies."

After some initial variations, Edwards settled on "Miscellanies" as the name for the series, and he used it for all citations of its entries.[7] He distinguished the "Miscellanies," as the repository for writings on various theological topics, from his notebooks devoted to particular themes, such as faith or the Trinity. Hence it may be called a "commonplace book," as it is by Ola E. Winslow, but not in the modern sense of "memorabilia" or "scrapbook," which she may have had in mind when describing it as containing "notations of many sorts under numbered topics."[8] But in comparison to the specialized notebooks, in which Edwards often wrote in a sketchy or outline form, his entries in the "Miscellanies" are remarkably well finished. There are no random fragments or jottings; the notes that he wrote at odd moments or brought back from a walk or ride into the woods were worked up at the first opportunity into outlines or drafts, which he copied in more complete form into the manuscript.[9] The entries do contain extracts from printed works, but until the 1740s they are few in number and well-integrated into Edwards' own discussion.[1] Most frequently, he used other authors to suggest or support his own composition without giving a clue as to what it was he was reading.

The "Miscellanies" would eventually become a storehouse of infor-

---

7. Early names he had used were "Reflections," "Miscellaneous Reflections," and "Rational Account." After 1729 he consistently wrote "Miscell." in his citations but never fully spelled the name. JE, Jr., our authority for "Miscellanies," studied theology for a while with Hopkins out of those very notebooks and must have known what JE had called them.

The word "Miscellanies" is not a plural but a collective noun, and "Miscellany" is not a singular but is identical in meaning with "Miscellanies." One cannot correctly call a particular piece in this collection a "miscellany." In this volume "Miscellanies" is always reserved for the whole series. To avoid excessive circumlocution or ambiguity, the lower-case plural "miscellanies" is sometimes used for a group of entries, e.g. "miscellanies in the 430s" or "these sermons and miscellanies." Each literary unit in the "Miscellanies" is usually referred to as an entry, an essay, or an article. If a specific manuscript is not indicated, it should be assumed that the citation is to a "Miscellanies" entry.

8. *Jonathan Edwards 1703–1758* (New York, Macmillan, 1940), p. 374.

9. JE's pages often have sets of pin holes where he had pinned scraps of paper. An example of the next stage of composition is the last leaf of the Bolton sermon on Rom. 12:18, which contains a draft for part of No. 87. It is printed below (p. 251, n. 7) unedited, as a specimen of JE's primary composition.

1. In the early 1740s JE began gathering material for a projected treatise against the deists; after that the extracts increased greatly in frequency and length.

mation, but at the outset Edwards had no clear idea of its character and no inkling of its ultimate usefulness. Several of the earliest entries are written in the disputational format to which he had become accustomed in college; others exhibit a more expository style. The earliest entries include, among other topics, a spiritual meditation, a scripture type, a comment on a text in Psalms, and a discussion of the atonement. After the first alphabet, however, Edwards generally discontinued making entries directly related to scripture exegesis and typology.[2] Later he began specialized notebooks on those subjects, including one on apocalyptic themes, which seldom appear in the "Miscellanies" after the second alphabet. Early entries apparently developed ideas suggested by reading, meditation, and sermon composition, but soon the entries themselves began to provide thoughts for sermons, further meditation, and additional entries. A fruitful interchange thus developed between sermons and miscellanies that was to continue throughout most of his ministry. From the time that he was a colleague of Solomon Stoddard, a sermon often became part of an inquiry that produced several related entries, or a sermon gathered up material from several entries to become a major discourse on some point of doctrine. His growing stock of sermons became so important to Edwards that he began to refer to them in the "Miscellanies," sometimes devoting a whole entry to the citation; later he wrote his sermon references directly in the Table. The same progression took place also with the Scripture notebooks and other manuscripts.[3]

Early in his career, Edwards established the habit of frequently rereading his "Diary," "Miscellanies," and other notebooks "to set me agoing again."[4] By the time he went to Yale as tutor in 1724, he had already written a sufficient amount in the "Miscellanies" and other notebooks to warrant the compilation of a list of projects on the "Cata-

2. There is a rather large exception to this statement in Nos. 891, 922, 1067, and 1068, which constitute a long treatise on messianic prophecy, and No. 1069, a shorter one on messianic typology.

3. Except for the Bolton sermon on Rev. 21:18 (below, p. 282, n. 4), the sermon series on John 16:8, written shortly after Stoddard's death in 1729, was the first to be cited in a contemporaneous entry (No. 398). No. 434, written in the latter part of that year, contains JE's first reference in the "Miscellanies" to the "Notes on the Scripture" (hereafter "Scripture") that is not a later addition.

4. Diary for Oct. 5, 1724; see also June 8 and Aug. 28, 1723 (Sereno E. Dwight ed., *The Works of President Edwards* (10 vols. New York, 1829–30 [hereafter Dwight ed.]) *1*, 104 and 87, 94.

logue" letter leaf for further development or even publication.[5] Even while at Bolton he had begun writing several entries close together on a topic or group of related topics, revealing what it was that received most of his attention at the time. Such clusters of entries, often related to sermons he was writing concurrently, became more frequent and took the shape of a mutually reinforcing process.

In order to keep control of so many entries Edwards developed three strategies. First was the cross-reference. The earliest of these were mostly back-references to his last entry on the same subject or a recent one on which he now wished to comment. As he read back over his essays, he frequently added to an entry citations of earlier or later articles that he considered relevant. Eventually he could (as one can now) read through a long succession of interconnected entries on a subject by simply following the cross-references.

The second of these practices was the direct augmentation of earlier entries. At first, Edwards made small revisions and insertions in an entry or in nearby spaces. But in the mid-1730s he began composing passages, both numbered and unnumbered, with instructions to add them to earlier entries, sometimes with a cue mark to indicate the point of insertion. No. 475, the first entry to receive large additions in this manner, illustrates the process. At the end of the third sub-section of this entry on "Sin Against the Holy Ghost," Edwards added a cross-reference to entry No. 703, with a cue mark indicating a passage at the end of the latter entry. The cued insertion further developed the point Edwards was making, that true blasphemy is a matter not only of thought and belief but of words and actions.

Edwards' third strategy was the Table, a sophisticated index in which he could find all that he had written on a given subject, not only in the "Miscellanies" but in other manuscripts as well.[6] After he began to add

5. JE used the leaf, derived from an envelope, to list books and reading programs during his first few months at the College but never sewed it into the "Catalogue" (below, pp. 15, 82–83). The "Catalogue" is a MS booklet of 24 quarto leaves, plus the letter leaf. At first JE recorded many books and other items in which he was interested; later he became more selective and gave information about the books he listed. Its entries have been assigned numbers by members of the Edition. The first three pages and the unnumbered letter leaf extend through the period presently under study; together they contain nearly half of the 720 entries in the booklet.

6. See the very revealing chart of what Kimnach calls "the functional relationships among the major notebooks and the sermon corpus in the reference cycles" (*The Works of Jonathan Edwards, 10, Sermons and Discourses, 1720–23,* ed. Wilson H. Kimnach [New Haven, Yale Univ. Press, 1992], 90).

citations of other authors, the Table became his chief means of assembling his materials for writing on any subject. This helps explain how it was possible for Edwards, in the midst of his labors and distractions at Stockbridge, to write *Freedom of the Will* in less than five months.[7] Through the Table and the corresponding entries in the "Miscellanies" one can see the architectonic quality of Edwards' mind and trace in sequence the complex and convoluted intellectual progression by which he marshaled his ideas into the comprehensive scope and incisive, well-buttressed arguments of his later treatises.[8] Initially, Edwards indexed his entries only after they had accumulated for a period of time. It was probably as he was bringing his indexing up to date that he decided to gather up the more than forty articles he had written on the Trinity into a treatise, which he did in the spring of 1730. Though he never completed it for publication, it was the first fully articulated composition of substantial length (other than sermons) that he wrote out of the "Miscellanies" using his Table and cross-references.

Over the years, there has been speculation concerning the nature of Edwards' unpublished manuscripts and the relation between their content and his published views. The delay of over two centuries in the publication of the "Miscellanies" and other manuscripts known (or at least believed) to exist has continued to pique curiosity about their contents and even generate suspicion that there may be a skeleton in the closet. For example, rumors flew in the nineteenth century about a treatise on the Trinity being held back because of supposed doctrinal indiscretions of Edwards.[9] Even some that defended his orthodoxy were prepared to concede that Edwards might have spun out theological speculations just to see where they would go and recorded "tentative" conclusions for which he would not, if challenged, have taken responsibility.[1]

One of the names by which Edwards referred to the "Miscellanies,"

7. Dwight ed., *1*, 532–33.
8. The textual notes identify several entries that JE used in later works. See also Note on the Table (below, pp. 113–17).
9. See below, Appendix A (pp. 548–49).
1. Edwards A. Park found it necessary to deal with this notion during the controversy over JE's trinitarian orthodoxy; he admitted the existence of a few provisional statements but minimized their importance ("Remarks of Jonathan Edwards on the Trinity," *Bibliotheca Sacra, 38* [1881], 149–57). Charles Hodge of Princeton insisted that JE was in almost total harmony with Old Calvinism, except for an "eccentric" view of imputation and an untenable theory of virtue as benevolence to being in general ("Jonathan Edwards and the Successive Forms of the New Divinity," *Biblical Repertory and Princeton Review, 30* [1858], 589–90).

at least up through his time as tutor, was "Rational Account."[2] This was one of the projects listed on the "Catalogue" letter leaf, where he later drafted a longer title for the proposed work. He also began an outline for such a treatise under the traditional doctrinal heads in mid-1729 but did little with it and finally abandoned it after 1740.[3] This is nearly all we know about the "Rational Account."

Perry Miller advanced the notion of a subterranean Edwards hidden even in his published works but surely lurking in the largely unpublished manuscripts.[4] He also identified Edwards' proposed "Rational Account" with the "Miscellanies." Although Edwards did construct rational defenses of Christian doctrines in his published works, Miller argues that "most of these thoughts he kept back, intending ultimately to put them into a monumental book which he provisionally entitled, "Rational Account of the Main Doctrines of the Christian Religion Attempted.'"[5] Miller believed that the answer to Edwards' secret lay, if anywhere, in the "Miscellanies," "the massive manuscript materials in which much of Edwards' most profound thinking and finest prose have been concealed."[6]

Publication of the "Miscellanies" should go far toward determining the extent to which Edwards kept back any of his views from public scrutiny. The truth in Miller's statements is twofold: most of the essays in the "Miscellanies" are in fact Edwards' efforts to add understanding to his faith or to defend it by rational methods; furthermore, Edwards

2. One of the few such references is found in "Beauty of the World," where Nos. 108 and 119 are cited under that name (*The Works of Jonathan Edwards, 6, Scientific and Philosophical Writings*, ed. Wallace E. Anderson [New Haven, Yale Univ. Press, 1980], 306).

3. JE made the last addition to his outline probably in the early part of 1739. No. 832, which may have been written in 1740, he wrote as a "Preface to the Rational Account." In it he castigates his own age as the most licentious and spiritually dead of any in Christian history and concludes that the "fashionable divinity" that accompanies it must also be in error. This preface may mark the point at which JE decided to lay aside the project of a single large-scale systematic work and instead defend the more threatened doctrines one at a time. The outline of the "Rational Account" is printed in *Works, 6,* 396–97.

4. After discussing JE's first two published sermons (*God Glorified* and *Divine and Supernatural Light*) Miller affirmed that the second sermon, "like his first—and his last—contains an exasperating intimation of something hidden." Indeed, "Edwards' writing is an immense cryptogram, the passionate oratory of the revival no less than the hard reasoning of the treatise on the will. . . .an occult secret. . . .His writings are almost a hoax, not to be read but to be seen through." *Jonathan Edwards* (New York, William Sloane Associates, 1949), pp. 50–51.

5. Ibid., p. 127.

6. General Editor's preface to *The Works of Jonathan Edwards, 1, Freedom of the Will*, ed. Paul Ramsey (New Haven, Yale Univ. Press, 1957), vii.

did plan a great exposition of Christian doctrine. In 1757, he described this project to the Princeton trustees as "a Body of Divinity in an entire new method, being thrown in the form of a history, considering the affair of Christian theology, as the whole of it, in each part, stands in reference to the great work of redemption by Jesus Christ; which I suppose is to be the grand design, of all God's designs, and the summum and ultimum of all the divine operations and degrees; particularly considering all parts of the grand scheme in their historical order."[7] Edwards did not, however, refer to the projected work as his "Rational Account."

The early entries in the "Miscellanies" show how, in the latter part of 1728, Edwards caught up his "Satan Defeated" theme into a new series of articles on "The Wisdom of God in the Work of Redemption"; many entries under this head (which he used through the 1740s) discuss various doctrines in terms of God's action in history. In 1739, Edwards incorporated much of his thinking on this subject into his lectures on the work of redemption, which were posthumously printed as *A History of the Work of Redemption*.[8] These lectures would have been part of a projected treatise, along with various miscellanies, especially those with the new title, "Progress of the Work of Redemption."[9]

It may well be significant that Edwards made his last addition to the outline for the "Rational Account" in 1739, about the time he was giving his lectures on the history of redemption and beginning to think of a new way of presenting Christian doctrine with a truly christological focus. Hence, though the "Miscellanies" cannot be identified with the "Rational Account," the "entire new method" that Edwards planned to use in his redesigned exposition of Christian theology was still based on the same intellectual appropriation of the faith he had earlier identified with the "Rational Account." If he had lived to write his great work, the "Miscellanies" would have provided much if not most of its content.

How is one to read the "Miscellanies"? If one simply reads it straight through, the subject changes kaleidoscopically at almost every new entry, resulting after a while in a sense of being lost in a labyrinthine

---

7. Hopkins, *Life and Character*, p. 77.

8. See *The Works of Jonathan Edwards, 9, The History of the Work of Redemption*, ed. John F. Wilson (New Haven, Yale Univ. Press, 1988).

9. Wilson discusses the "Miscellanies" in relation to the lecture series of 1739 in ibid., pp. 13–17.

complexity of ideas. The problem may be compounded by Edwards' frequent allusions to unfamiliar systems of thought and socio-political arrangements.

Another method is to take one or more topics and locate what Edwards has to say about them by means of his Table and system of cross-references. This procedure is often very rewarding, especially in these early entries, because it not only informs us about Edwards' earliest thoughts on a subject but on how his purview expanded to take in more and more of its aspects and connections with other topics. But this method, if pursued too narrowly, can separate the mind from the man, Edwards' thoughts from his biography.

What follows is an attempt to have the best of both approaches. The first section does indeed walk through the text, but it tries to show how Edwards' writings in each period of his early ministry were—at least to some extent—affected by his changing circumstances. It also treats the entries selectively in order to highlight dominant concerns and new developments in his thinking.

The second section attempts to look at Edwards' early thought systematically, not by tracing certain doctrines narrowly defined but by looking for certain fundamental convictions to which Edwards came early in his career, with some illustrations from the "Miscellanies" of their repercussions on his theology.

Finally, an effort is made to provide the reader with two kinds of tools. Section three (with illustrations from the appendices) hopes to justify some confidence in the chronological framework within which these early writings have been presented. The chart at its end provides further detail for those wishing to look more deeply into Edwards' biography or his other manuscripts.

This Introduction, with its appendices and textual notes, has achieved its purpose if it whets the reader's appetite for what is really a new way of studying Edwards, and then facilitates such a study.

1. The "Miscellanies" as a Theological Journal

The following narrative survey of Edwards' writings during the first nine years of his ministry is intended to illustrate the variety of topics on which he wrote, some of his dominant interests, and early intimations of theological positions for which he was to become well known. In these writings, Edwards sought to explore, appropriate, and defend "the things most surely believed" by his family, teachers, and peers; yet in doing so he was also responding to the intellectual stimuli provided by further reading and conversation, plus the demands of his successive positions as student, tutor, colleague, and pastor. Edwards' openness to new information and insights is nowhere more readily displayed than in the "Miscellanies." In the entries he wrote during those years, his eclectic mind ranged freely over an ever-increasing body of material. By returning time and again to a given topic, Edwards was able to pursue a line of reasoning that, while building on previous analysis, addressed each issue from a number of different angles. Later in life, this episodic method of investigation produced sustained arguments of impressive depth, complexity, and rigor.

NEW YORK, WINDSOR, AND BOLTON, 1722–1724

Edwards received his baccalaureate degree from Yale College in 1720. After two more years of graduate study, he spent the nine months from early August 1722 to the end of April 1723 ministering to a small Presbyterian congregation in New York City. Here, surrounded by warm Christian fellowship but in relative intellectual and ecclesiastical isolation, he began the series of theological notations that would in time develop into the "Miscellanies."[1] At some point during the fall of 1722, perhaps in November, Edwards folded a fresh sheet of foolscap in folio and headed the recto "Types of the Scriptures."[2] Before he had made a second entry in the list, however, he had begun recording on the outside verso thoughts that had come to him during seasons of meditation and prayer (Nos. a–d, f and h). The first of these, "Of Holiness" (No. a), he later quoted in the "Personal Narrative" as typical of his piety throughout the New York period. By the

1. During this period JE also began the "Resolutions & Private Diary," in which he recorded his personal struggles, and the "Catalogue" of books he had read or wished to acquire. Wilson H. Kimnach has treated JE's New York sojourn with special reference to his earliest sermons in *Works, 10,* 261–93. The recent biography by Iain Murray (*Jonathan Edwards: A New Biography* [Edinburgh, Banner of Truth Trust, 1987]) takes account of the revised dating of JE's early MSS contained in volumes 5 and 6 of the *Works.*

2. The following terminology is used in the present study. A sheet of foolscap (12" × 15") folded in half forms two folios (7.5" × 12"); a half-sheet forms two quarto leaves (6" × 7.5"); a quarto leaf forms two octavo leaves (3.75" × 6"). These are called double leaves. Several double leaves, when stitched together side by side, form a "gathering"; two double leaves sewed together prior to the stitching of the whole are called a "signature." Double leaves laid open in a pile and folded together (or "infolded" in 19th-century terminology) constitute a "quire." Such a quire is to be distinguished from a quire of blank sheets, which consisted of 24 or 25 sheets laid flat in a pile. A single leaf consists of a recto (the right-hand page, as in a book) and its back side, or verso. When describing a double leaf, its four pages are referred to respectively as the first recto and verso, and the second recto and verso.

time he had written Nos. e and g on Scripture passages that were not strictly types, Edwards must have realized that he did not have two clearly distinguishable kinds of subject matter but a variety of topics. He therefore opened the sheet flat and continued his entries as a single series on the inner and then the outer pages of the sheet. By the time he left New York he had probably written all the entries he later designated Nos. a–z, aa–zz.

Since the "Diary" was the main receptacle for reports of his religious experiences, Edwards' entries in the "Miscellanies" soon became more strictly theological and objective in tone, though they retained for some time a strongly meditative aspect. Several entries celebrate the beauty of holiness and the happiness of a life wholly devoted to God (Nos. a, f, x, z, tt) along with the related idea of personal victory in Christ (Nos. c, d, h, ff). The latter takes on a cosmic dimension as the victory of the saints in the millennium and resurrection (Nos. k, bb, cc, ii), for most of Edwards' Scripture expositions dealt with apocalyptic themes (Nos. k, hh, uu, ww, xx, yy). The happiness of a holy life, which was also a pervasive motif in the New York sermons, led Edwards to write a series of entries on happiness as God's end in creating the world (Nos. aa, gg, kk, ll, tt) and a correlative essay on God in which he first formulated his "idealism" (No. pp).

Edwards also pursued an interest to which much of his graduate study had been devoted, the rational explication and defense of the general doctrines of Christianity and the specific tenets of Calvinism. For example, he argued that "God has decreed all things that ever come to pass" (No. u); that sin is infinitely heinous (Nos. ll, nn), even the original sin that warrants the damnation of infants (No. n); that the atonement was intended only for the elect (No. t); that saving grace is instantaneous and irresistible (Nos. l, o, p); that the righteousness of faith is imputed (No. zz) and is a perfect righteousness won by Christ's perfect obedience, his death having only freed the believer from guilt (No. oo). The positions taken in most of these entries were directed against Arminianism.[3] Edwards was also concerned with the institu-

3. Arminianism took its rise from the Dutch theologian Jacobus Arminius (1560–1609) and the "Remonstrance" of 1610. The Arminians grounded predestination in the divine foreknowledge, denied that original sin had left the will unable to respond to the offer of the gospel, taught universal atonement, and denied that saving grace is irresistible and cannot be lost. The effect was to enhance the role of human freedom and action in the process of salvation. Arminianism had spread in England during the 17th century among Anglican divines and, especially after 1689, even among dissenters. For the "Remonstrance" of 1610 and the canons and decrees of the Synod of Dort, where these modifications of Calvinism were rejected, see Philip Schaff, *Creeds of Christendom* (3 vols. New York, 1877), *3*, 545–97.

tional church's government, creeds, ministry, and discipline (Nos. q, ee, mm, qq, rr).

Edwards spent the summer of 1723 with his parents in East Windsor. In spite of journeys to Boston, Norwich, and perhaps other places, he gave himself vigorously to his studies and may have written the first 25 or 30 numbered entries in the "Miscellanies" by mid-July. At first he pursued subjects that had been of special interest in New York—the happiness of heaven, God's end in creation, and the immortality of the soul (Nos. 1, 3, 5). His attention also returned to ecclesiastical matters with a series of seven more entries on the ministry, ceremonies, and church-state relations (Nos. 8–14), topics on which he continued to write at intervals during the summer and fall.[4] Two things in particular seem to have aroused his interest in these subjects. One was a controversy waged in the first two decades of the century over the requirement by the established Church of England that all ministers conform to its liturgy even in nonessentials.[5] The other was the defection to episcopacy of Rector Timothy Cutler and Tutor Daniel Browne of Yale, along with two neighboring ministers, in September 1722. This event had profoundly shaken Connecticut congregationalism and especially Yale College, for the books that converted the seceders were writings that they had found in the college library.[6] Edwards, like

4. E.g. Nos. 17 (creedal tests for ministerial candidates), 40 (the source of ecclesiastical authority), 65 (the pastor's power to admit and discipline members), 69 and 90 (aspects of Solomon Stoddard's proposal for a "national church"), and 70 (freedom of conscience).

5. The controversy began with Edmund Calamy's *Abridgment of Mr. Baxter's History of His Life and Times* (London, 1702), in the 10th chapter of which Calamy recalled the considerations that led so many dissenting ministers in 1662 to suffer ejection rather than conform. In answer to Calamy, Hoadly wrote *The Reasonableness of Conformity* (London, 1703), to which Calamy responded with *A Defence of Moderate Non-Conformity* (3 vols. London, 1703–05), which was answered in turn by two more books by Hoadly. John Ollyffe also wrote two books against Calamy.

In the second edition of his *Abridgment* (2 vols. London, 1713) Calamy expanded his 10th chapter with quotations from his opponents and his own replies; JE may have been reading this epitome of the controversy or possibly Hoadly's *Reasonableness of Conformity*. Some of the issues in the controversy are reflected in these entries: the right of the civil magistrate to compel religious conformity (Nos. 8, 9, 14), the right of a congregation to choose its own pastor (No. 10), the lawfulness of the Church of England's ceremonies and its right to require conformity in things indifferent (Nos. 11–13), and Hoadly's argument that those Dissenters who were willing to practice "occasional conformity" ought to go on to constant conformity out of concern for peace and harmony (No. 11).

6. Most of these writings had arrived in the Dummer collection, two large shipments of books solicited from well-known authors, including participants on both sides of the Calamy-Hoadly controversy (see above, n. 5); see Anne Stokley Pratt, "The Books Sent From England by Jeremiah Dummer to Yale College," in *Papers in Honor of Andrew Keogh . . . By the*

most other non-Anglican colonial clergy, feared an Anglican establishment not only because it meant episcopacy but because most Anglican
clergy were Arminians.

These considerations may have sharpened, if they did not initiate,
Edwards' decision to write his masters thesis on a complex of doctrines
disputed between Calvinists and Arminians with respect to the nature
and grounds of justification. He must have spent much of July and at
least the early part of August in this task, and the "Miscellanies" reflects this activity. Edwards made use of earlier entries, notably Nos. s,
nn, oo, and 2;[7] whether or not No. 27b had been written before Edwards began serious work on the thesis, that entry provided him with
both ideas and language for his definition of justifying faith. As he
worked at the thesis he wrote new entries of which he would make
direct use (e.g. Nos. 36 and 41, which he used in the earlier extant
draft) and others discussing related questions, notably Nos. 30, 32–33,
and 35–38. His final draft was probably completed by No. 45 around
the second or third week of August with the title: "A Sinner Is Not
Justified Before God Except Through the Righteousness of Christ
Obtained By Faith."[8] The doctrinal positions that Edwards articulated
in this and the related miscellanies would form the core of the lectures
on justification that helped usher in the revival of 1734–35.[9]

Edwards delivered his thesis at the Yale commencement in September 1723 and received the M.A. degree. During the month of October
he concluded negotiations with the nearby town of Bolton and on
November 11 signed the town book agreeing to settle as pastor. It is
likely that he preached at Bolton well into the spring of 1724.[1] This
was a highly active and creative period in Edwards' intellectual life. He

---

Staff of the Yale Library (New Haven, privately printed, 1938), pp. 7–44. The story of the crisis
at Yale is told in Richard Warch, *School of the Prophets: Yale College, 1701–1740* (New Haven,
Yale Univ. Press, 1973), pp. 103–08.

7. No. s contained an argument for the traditional distinction between Christ's active and
passive obedience which JE used in the thesis. Nos. nn and oo had already presented one of
his major contentions, that because of the infinite heinousness of the least sin against God no
repentance can bear the slightest proportion to the sinner's offense and that therefore a
satisfaction of infinite value must be secured; JE translated much of No. nn into the Latin of
the thesis. In No. 2 he had first expounded an underlying idea of the thesis, that calling faith
a condition performed by the believer inevitably puts it into the category of works, though in
the thesis itself he carefully avoided discussing the term "condition."

8. "Peccator Non Justificatur Coram Deo Nisi Per Justitiam Christi Fide Apprehensam."
The MS of the earlier draft is in the Trask Library, the final draft at Beinecke Library.

9. These lectures were published under the title: *Discourses on Various Important Subjects
. . . Viz. 1. Justification by Faith Alone* (Boston, 1738).

1. The length of JE's Bolton pastorate is discussed below, pp. 80–82.

was writing regularly in his "Natural Philosophy," where he had recently set forth his "idealism" in an addition to "Being," and on October 31 he sent his spider letter to Paul Dudley at Boston in hopes of its publication by the Royal Society.[2] His sermon on spiritual light (on I Cor. 2:14) was an important theological statement that contributed to the essay "Excellency" written shortly afterwards. Both of these echoed in sermons and miscellanies through much of his time at Bolton. He also commenced two new notebooks, one on the book of Revelation and the other on Scripture types (which eventually became a four-volume series on biblical texts in general), both of which he carried on for the rest of his life.[3]

Edwards wrote from fifty to sixty entries in the "Miscellanies" between his graduation M.A. in September and the beginning of his tutorship the following June. Many of these concerned ecclesiastical matters, and several others dealt with the divine decrees, free will, infused grace, and other issues of the Arminian controversy. The entries that give a distinctive character to this period, however, grew out of Edwards' writings on excellency, especially the essay by that name. In these ruminations, he expanded his thesis that God's goodness (God's desire to share his good) was the motive of creation and the creature's happiness its end, by identifying that happiness as delight in the excellency of God (Nos. 87, 92). These thoughts led in several directions, of which only examples can be given here. One was the immortality of the soul and the inexpressibly great happiness of heaven as the culmination of all things (Nos. 95, 99, 105, 114); another was Edwards' derivation of the Trinity from God's contemplation of and delight in his own excellency (Nos. 94, 96, 98) and even the extension of God's communicative goodness beyond the Trinity in the creation of the world to provide a spouse (the church) to be the peculiar object of the Son's love (Nos. 103, 104, 108). In that connection Edwards' view of the beauties and harmonies of the world as "shadows" of higher spiritual and divine excellencies (Nos. 42, 108) led to the first statement of his extension of typology not only beyond the Old Testament to the New but also to nature and human life (No. 119).

Nearly two years elapsed between the beginning of his New York ministry and the ending of that in Bolton. During that time the "Mis-

2. For "Natural Philosophy" (which includes "Being") and the spider letter, see *Works, 6,* 192–295, 163–69. Anderson discusses the spider letter in ibid, pp. 150–53.

3. Stephen J. Stein has edited the notebook on Revelation in *Works, 5, Apocalyptic Writings* (New Haven, Yale Univ. Press, 1977).

cellanies" became the centerpiece in a growing collection of manuscript notebooks. These entries contain his early efforts at the rational explanation and defense of his theological tradition, and they record the ways in which his own religious experience and speculative bent gave a distinctive character to his theology. They also show how Edwards was beginning to use his notebook both as a receptacle for his essays and as a sourcebook for other compositions.

TUTOR AT YALE, 1724–1726

Edwards' two years as a tutor at Yale made important contributions to his intellectual and professional growth. Through his renewed access to the college library he became much better acquainted with major authors in theology and philosophy, some of whose works he was still reading and citing years later. Long lists of titles on a loose leaf in his "Catalogue" testify to the many hours spent there during his first months as a tutor. There is also evidence of his increasing scholarly ambitions. He not only laid out a list of projects but made some progress on two of them: he enlarged the scale of his treatise on natural philosophy and made considerable additions in the manuscript, and he began collecting materials for a work in mental philosophy, "The Mind," by putting "Excellency" at the beginning of a new notebook and adding several essays in logic and metaphysics.[4]

It was not until early in the fall of 1724 that Edwards resumed composition in the "Miscellanies." The first entry he made at Yale was probably No. 126. By commencement in September 1725 he had reached No. 194, and by the end of his tutorship a year later, No. 235 (plus four other entries that he later renumbered). In the miscellanies of his tutorship he refined his thinking along several lines, such as ontology and epistemology, wrote what became for him a definitive study of the Lord's day, and gathered more biblical evidence for his conception of the Trinity.

Further reading in the college library on the deist controversy may account in part for the appearance of a new title, "Christian Religion," under which Edwards wrote about twenty essays during these two years, along with a few others of similar nature under different headings. Most of these early entries on the subject seek to prove the reasonableness and necessity of a divine revelation (e.g. Nos. 132, 204), the accuracy of the Bible's narratives and the sublimity of its content as

---

4. "The Mind" is printed in *Works*, 6, pp. 332–93.

proof that it is the needed revelation (e.g. Nos. 167, 196, 203, 204), and the truth of the accounts of Jesus' ministry in support of his claim to be a revealer of God (e.g. Nos. 131, 140, 152). With these entries, Edwards began more self-consciously to prepare to write a large-scale defense of the Christian revelation against rationalism in general and deism in particular.

Other new themes as well as extensions of earlier ones are to be found in these entries. In No. 126, Edwards applied to the understanding of Scripture the contention of No. 123, that one can have a true idea of a spiritual reality only if one already possesses an answering disposition: you can know what love or benevolence is only if you have a loving and benevolent disposition. No. 141 turns this argument around: a taste for holiness and the beauty of divine things enables one who possesses it to discriminate the genuine from the false: "the soul distinguishes as a musical ear."[5] This gift comes only by immediate divine communication, i.e. infused grace (Nos. 130, 138, 141). The fruition of this communication will be in heaven, where the true beauty of souls and their harmony with one another will be restored and their bodies made perfect receptors and vehicles of divine love (Nos. 137, 187, 188).

Edwards imagined the "new heaven and new earth" of the resurrected saints in very concrete terms, as can be seen from No. 149 and especially from No. 133, which speculates about the exact location of that place with respect to the universe.[6] Another apocalyptic theme, which had first appeared in No. 48, received a long essay entitled "Satan Defeated" (No. 156); here Edwards recounts various events in biblical and later world history to show how Satan's efforts to frustrate God's purposes in the work of redemption have been made the instruments of his own downfall.

Around the turn of the year 1725 Edwards wrote his longest entry to date, No. 160, "Lord's Day." In this entry he argues that Christians are commanded by the decalogue to celebrate the sabbath, but to do so on the first day of the week in honor of the new creation brought about by the work of Christ. Unlike the other topics of this period, which Edwards would continue to elaborate, this essay received only minor additions in occasional entries on the subject and, as largely repro-

5. In No. 201 JE explains this more fully, in language reminiscent of No. aa.
6. No. 133 was really the continuation of a discussion JE had initiated on a leaf intended for his "Apocalypse" notebook, where it is now no. 41 (see *Works*, 5, 140–42).

duced and expanded in his 1731 sermon on I Cor. 16:1–2, remains the single most complete exposition of his sabbatarianism.[7]

In the early months of 1725 Edwards made entries in the 160s and 170s on a variety of topics, but his main literary activity seems to have been in "Natural Philosophy" and "The Mind."[8] While he was writing one folio page containing "Miscellanies" Nos. 171–178, he filled over six in "Natural Philosophy" (US nos. 7–23), plus another page almost immediately afterwards (US nos. 24–26).[9] These investigations and certain metaphysical conclusions in "The Mind" doubtless lie behind Edwards' discussion of angelic influence on matter, the doctrine of providence, and the Spirit's operation in Nos. 176–178. By invoking the chain of being, No. 178 combines the two preceding entries with a view previously suggested in No. 64 to produce what is probably the first general formulation of Edwards' version of natural law as comprehending not only the regularities of nature but also miracles and saving grace.[1]

After No. 179, a brief reference to his idealism, Edward's attention suddenly shifted. Nos. 180–189 are devoted almost entirely to the themes of love, human as well as divine beauty, spiritual union, and communication between minds. The last of this group, No. 189, speaks approvingly of sexual love and the analogy between that and Christ's love for the church. These compositions surely reflect Edwards' courtship of Sarah Pierpont in the spring of 1725; the two became engaged in May or June of that year.

During his summer vacation at home in 1725 Edwards turned back to the blank space he had left after No. 123 and wrote three entries, Nos. 124, 125a, and 125b. No. 124 argues in *a posteriori* fashion that

---

7. This posthumously published sermon is printed in *The Works of President Edwards* (4 vols. New York, 1843, [hereafter Worcester rev. ed.]), *4*, 615–37.

8. JE resumed composition in "Natural Philosophy" in the late fall or early winter with a new series of unnumbered entries (printed in *Works, 6*, 261–95). The new notebook into which he had incorporated "Excellency" he now dedicated to metaphysical, epistemological, and logical subjects, leaving the continuing natural philosophy series exclusively to the examination of the physical world. He apparently wrote with some regularity in "The Mind" during the fall and winter, completing about 30 entries by the end of the summer in 1725 (text in ibid., 332–52).

9. Wallace Anderson's terminology for the three sub-series in "Natural Philosophy" is as follows: Short Series (SS), Long Series (LS), and Unnumbered Series (US).

1. Cf. "The Mind" nos. 3–4 with Nos. 176–177, and the last paragraph of the addendum to no. 13 with No. 178 (ibid., pp. 339, 343–44). The original location of the addendum in the MS cannot now be determined with certainty, but it may have been earlier than the one Anderson suggests in his note to no. 13.

there is as much evidence for "an universal mind in the world from the actions of the world" as there is for "a particular mind in an human body, from the observation of the actions of that." Thinking further about the world as a succession of God's actions, Edwards wrote No. 125a, his first full explanation of continuous creation as a radical moment-by-moment discontinuity of being. After his return to New Haven, he filled another blank space with No. 27a, an ontological proof that God is a necessary being because his "nonentity is a contradiction."[2] He then picked up the analogy in No. 124 with No. 194, where the omnipresence of God in the world is likened to the presence of the soul in the body.[3] These are all significant new statements on God's nature and relation to the world.

Edwards' study and writing were interrupted for three or four months by serious illness in the late fall of 1725. While convalescing at Windsor he probably wrote Nos. 195–205, a set of articles on the existence of God, the truth of the Christian revelation, the self-evidencing character of faith, and the epistemological problem involved in Jesus' claim to preincarnate knowledge. His entries from No. 206 to the original No. 239 cover the time from his return to New Haven in the winter of 1726 to his departure for Northampton at the beginning of August as a candidate for the position of assistant to his aged grandfather, Solomon Stoddard.

These entries are mostly quite short, in contrast to those immediately preceding them. One reason may have been the fact that during most of the time from April to July he was preaching to the congregation at Glastonbury, whose pastor had died in April. Two kinds of entries stand out during these months. Several are devoted to the Holy Spirit or to the Trinity with emphasis on the Spirit (nearly a third of the total). Of these, five in sequence (Nos. 223–227) were probably written while Edwards was composing a sermon on the Holy Spirit (of which only a fragment remains) for use at Glastonbury. The other group of entries are united in a different way: they are on topics related in one way or other to Stoddard's views and practices.[4] For example, No. 212 contains a highly intellectualistic account of how saving faith operates,

2. A very similar statement in "The Mind" no. 30 was probably written at the same time (*Works*, 6, 352).

3. No. 194 also is closely linked to the next two entries in "The Mind" nos. 31 and 32, which together express the same analogy (ibid., pp. 352–53).

4. JE almost certainly preached at Northampton at least once during the spring vacation; in any case he must have known for some weeks that he was a serious candidate for the position.

and No. 216 attempts to explain—by association of ideas—how saving faith might involve an experience of being personally "called" by Christ; both these seem, to some degree, concessions; on the other hand, No. 118 states clearly that an "agreeing or consenting disposition" is the source of and hence prior to explicit acts of faith and other virtues. No. 207 shows that Edwards saw no difficulty with Stoddard's practice of routinely admitting baptized youth to the Lord's Supper, and No. 232 contains his first attempt in the "Miscellanies" to explain (with reference to his conception of excellency) and make vivid the torment of hell, the importance of which in preaching was a strongly held conviction of his grandfather.

Two sets of dislocated entries seem to represent Edwards' transition from New Haven to Northampton: Nos. 311–314 were probably written at Windsor, and Nos. 267–274 during the first weeks at Northampton before he was fully settled into the routines of his new position. Like the essays composed during his convalescence some months earlier, they are primarily devoted to such larger topics as the existence of God, the end of creation, and the truth of the Christian revelation. Their tone is more speculative, and they contain some significant advances in his thought. A few examples may be given. Most of these proofs for the existence of God are *a posteriori*, stressing the beauty of the world and evidences of purpose; but one, No. 267, begins from "the mere exertion of a new thought" and ends by removing substance from the human mind and making it only a stream of ideas immediately created by God. Yet in the next entry Edwards speaks of innate ideas (of God, for example) as tendencies in the "natural powers" of the mind, such as "that natural inclination that persons have to excellence and order" and a "habit of the mind in reasoning . . . to argue causes from effects." No. 271 seeks to explain how God can create the world for the happiness of his creatures and yet be said to do it for himself (his answer draws on No. 104). Finally, No. 273 ("Election") offers a rational explanation of how "God's loving some and not others, antecedent to any manner of difference in them . . . may appear reasonable"—this from a champion of the absolute, inscrutable, and unconditioned will of God!

ASSISTANT AND COLLEAGUE, 1726–1729

Edwards arrived at Northampton in October; the town invited him to "settle" as Stoddard's colleague in November, and he was ordained on February 15, 1727. He and Sarah Pierpont were married on July 28 and set up housekeeping in the new manse on King Street. In spite of time spent providing a homestead and the pressure of his new duties (he preached half of the day on Sundays, gave other lectures, visited, and catechized the children) he managed to write 47 entries in the "Miscellanies" (Nos. 236–255, 279–305) by the end of October 1727. At that point a brief but frightening earthquake occasioned a religious awakening that probably extended into the first months of the following year.[5] By July or August 1728, when he resumed composition of his entries in regular sequence, he had reached No. 330, having written about 32 entries in the preceding eight or nine months. A period of intense activity in the notebook followed, and Edwards had probably written No. 386 by the time Stoddard died on February 11, 1729, leaving him sole pastor. There are concentrations of entries on certain topics at various points in this thirty-month period, notably on preparation and conversion in the weeks following the earthquake; however, the large number of entries that are not in chronological sequence make it more satisfactory to consider the period as a whole.

Edwards' writings in defense of theism and the Christian revelation were relatively few during his association with Stoddard, and most are extensions or restatements of previous entries. No. 365 repeats the proof, already offered in "Being" and No. 27a, for a necessary being from the inconceivability of nothing. No. 383 covers the same ground as No. 199 by arguing that the first principle must be like the human soul, the highest creature it has produced, and No. 333 follows a similar line by urging an analogy between deducing a soul from the actions of a human body and discerning God as its author from the contents of Scripture. Generally Edwards applies the test of rational necessity in predicting what a revelation from God must look like, then finds that the Scriptures contain just such a revelation (e.g. Nos. 358, 359, 378, 382). In No. 350, however, he insists that without the truths directly revealed to the patriarchs and the Jews, human reason would never have been able to answer any important questions about God and his will toward us.

Edwards continued the elaboration of his conception of the Trinity. Nos. 260, 309, and 331 infer from the biblical descriptions of Christ as word, image, and light that the Son is the perfect self-understanding, or idea, of God. No. 238 repeats the argument of No. 94 that the perfect idea of a thing is identical with the thing, but this time uses it of

5. For the dates of the awakening, see below, pp. 84–86.

"ideas of reflection . . . such as the ideas of thought, of choice, love, fear, etc."; such "spiritual ideas" are "the very same things repeated."[6] Descriptions of the Spirit as the river of water of life and other such metaphors show that the Spirit is the affection, love, and pleasure of God (Nos. 334, 336, 364); so does the fact that the Spirit is the content of the apostolic benediction (No. 341) and of our fellowship with the Father and the Son (No. 376). In Nos. 259 and 308 Edwards again tries to answer the objection that his scheme will result in an infinite number of divine persons.

In the fall of 1728, possibly as a result of seeking "shadows of divine things" for the notebook he had recently begun, Edwards wrote No. 362, in which he added natural images of the Trinity to the tripartite human analogy that was fundamental to his doctrine: the sun, with its light and its warmth, with emphasis on the constituent colors of sunlight as representing the various graces of the Spirit (Nos. 362, 370).[7] This led him, in the same entry, to explain more fully the conception of typology he had first stated in No. 119, that God has deliberately filled the world of nature and human society with types and images of spiritual things.[8]

Edwards also continued to worry the problem of God's end in creation: is it divine goodness and the happiness of the creature, or is it the divine glory, God as his own end? In No. 243 he affirms both as coordinate, but later in No. 247 he brings the two together in a restatement: goodness is the outflow of the divine being, glory its reflection and return.

In the winter or spring of 1725 Edwards had done some highly imaginative speculating about the Fall and its effects not only on the bodies and minds of our first parents (Nos. 173–174) but also on the natural world (No. 186). Now, two years later, he took up the question as to how Adam, being positively righteous, could have sinned; his answer was that God took away no grace Adam already had but only witheld additional "confirming" grace to keep him from sinning (No. 290). Then in No. 301 Edwards adopted enthusiastically Stoddard's explanation for the corruption of human nature as the inevitable

6. JE first derived this notion from his thinking about spiritual sight in No. 123; it has the same connection here, for his next entry (No. 239) applies it to spiritual knowledge.

7. For JE these colors are also biblical representations of the Spirit; he sees them reflected in the jewels of the high priest's breastplate (cf. No. 240), the stones of the temple, and the gates of the New Jerusalem.

8. JE's new notebook, "Images [originally Shadows] of Divine Things" and other typological writings are printed in *Works, 11*.

result of man's natural self-love without the love of God and the influences of the Spirit, which God withdrew after the first sin (No. 301; cf.
No. 374).

Edwards considered the chief battleground between Calvinists and
Arminians to be the question of whether the will is free to make
choices untainted by that corrupt inheritance. The axiom he laid down
in No. 342 is evidence that Edwards was already planning to join in
that debate. Then in No. 363 he advanced two propositions that he
would later defend in his treatise: *voluntary* evil actions are justly punished even though the will is determined, and objections to this are
caused by the misunderstanding of such terms as "necessary" and
"impossible."

Edwards' new relation with Stoddard and the necessities of preaching to and counseling those seeking conversion led him to give considerable attention to the morphology of conversion. One line that he
pursued was the different way faith was related to salvation in the
Mosaic covenant and in the covenant of grace, within which the Mosaic
covenant was included by Puritan theology (Nos. 246, 250, 252, 299).[9]
More important to him at the time was a double question, whether
there can be a habit of grace before the first gracious act, and whether
that first act must be an explicit act of faith. Stoddard denied the first
and affirmed the second.[1] Between the spring and fall of 1727 Edwards looked at these questions from several angles (Nos. 241, 284,
289, 302), conceding the force of Stoddard's views but expressing
reservations.

In spite of the unorthodox character of his own conversion, Edwards had earlier stated his belief that God's "ordinary" method was to
prepare sinners for grace by making them aware of their evil hearts
and danger of hell (No. 116b). During his first year at Northampton he
wrote several entries supporting that view by reason and Scripture
(e.g. Nos. 244, 245, 255, 283, 286, 295). But sinners must be "awak-

9. The "covenant of works" was the first covenant made with Adam. Immediately after
the Fall, God revealed the "covenant of grace," according to which, through the merits of
Christ yet to be revealed, the elect would be saved by the faith implicit in their obedience to
God's commandments. This covenant was renewed to Noah, to Abraham, and, in the Mosaic
covenant, to the children of Israel. It was called the "old" covenant in distinction from the
"new" covenant revealed by Christ. John von Rohr, *The Covenant of Grace in Puritan Thought*
(Grand Rapids, Eerdmans, 1986) contains a balanced and informative survey of the whole
covenant scheme, including its early continental and English representatives.

1. When JE admits that "a habit can be of no manner of use till there is occasion to exert it"
(No. 241) he is practically quoting Stoddard. See No. 27b, p. 214, n. 7.

ened" to their plight; this involves preaching about hell and providing the theological justification for such preaching.

Edwards had discussed hell torments in the "Miscellanies" for the first time in the summer of 1726 (No. 232), but now he began in earnest. No. 237 argues that hell torments will engender more hatred and thus guilt in the damned, which will merit more punishment, and so on for eternity. An *a fortiori* argument for the extremity of hell torments is the intensity of Christ's agony in the garden plus the despair that the damned will have in addition (No. 280). The infinity of both duration and degree is argued from the glory of God: his infinite majesty means that "his displeasure is infinitely dreadful" (No. 288). Edwards first stated his most notorious argument in No. 279: the eternity of hell follows from the eternity of the happiness of the saints in heaven, whose joy and thankfulness for their own salvation will be continually enhanced by contemplating the sufferings of the damned. During the awakening that followed the earthquake Edwards brought forward three more sets of biblical texts to support the use of extreme metaphors in sermonic descriptions of hell (Nos. 275, 316, and 318).

The awakening also turned Edwards' attention to questions related to preparation, conversion, and faith.[2] One fruit of this concern was No. 317, a long article on "humiliation," the last stage of preparation before actual conversion. He begins by presenting Stoddard's description of humiliation as a graceless state of mind, convicted of sin and helplessness to overcome it but still hard of heart.[3] Edwards allows that God may well work that way at times but not always (citing biblical examples), that there may be a habit of grace in the soul during a "preparatory" experience, and that sinners may not recognize the depth of their sinfulness until after they have been given a vision of God's glory. But No. 325 shows that he still affirmed the necessity of certain preparatory experiences for conversion.

In No. 317, and even more in No. 325, Edwards saw the main function of preparatory experiences as teaching the sinner God's hatred of sin and the depth of misery and danger from which Christ saves him, in order to "the proper and congruous exercise of grace" (No. 325). At the same time, he was comparing Christ's sufferings with those of the

---

2. It was probably during that time (late 1727 or early 1728) that JE began his notebook entitled "Faith," in which he explored various definitions and characteristics of faith.

3. Both JE's father and his grandfather Stoddard were unusually successful evangelists, and both adhered to the traditional Puritan "preparation" scheme, distinguishable steps by which conversion was believed ordinarily to come about.

damned to show how extreme the latter must be (No. 318). This led him in No. 319 to assert that Christ undertook the whole debt of punishment due the sinner in order to honor God's law and testify to God's hatred of sin. He then addressed the problem of how Christ's sufferings could equal those of the damned if he had no despair; his answer was that Christ's suffering was the same as that due the sinner "so far as a person of his nature was capable of it" (No. 321b), and the dignity of Christ's person and the infinite happiness he had lost—even though only temporarily—answered in his experience to the everlasting despair of the damned (No. 265).

These considerations led Edwards to give two main reasons for the work of Christ. First, "Christ came into the world to render the honor of God's authority and his law consistent with the salvation and eternal life of sinners" (No. 322). He did this not only by satisfying for the sinner's sin but also by subjecting himself to and perfectly obeying God's law, even the ceremonial law, thus honoring the law far more than Adam could have done. This obedience constitutes Christ's "active righteousness," without which the sinner would only have pardon but not merit eternal life (ibid.). Secondly, "the end of the incarnation and death of Christ" was to make a "bright and glorious manifestation" of "the infinite love . . . between the Father and the Son, [which is] the highest excellency and peculiar glory of the Deity": the love of the Father in forgiving an infinite debt for his Son's sake, the love of the Son "in his infinitely abasing himself for the vindicating of [God's] authority and the honor of his majesty" (No. 327a). Toward the end of 1728 Edwards returned to the work of Christ, developing the correspondence between Christ and Adam as surety (No. 357), as man subject to the law (No. 381), and as head of the human race (No. 385). What he had said in No. 322 he repeated more pointedly in No. 360.[4] In these writings during and after the earthquake awakening Edwards set forth the essentials of his doctrine of the work of Christ, which later entries would only elaborate.

These months of concentration on conversion and the work of Christ also influenced Edwards' cosmology. In terms of "Satan Defeated," he sees the devil frustrated in his campaign of temptation, for even the punishment of the damned contributes to the glory of God

4. Since "the very end of Christ's dying for sin was . . . that while God thus manifested his mercy, we might not conceive any unworthy thoughts of God with respect to his majesty and authority and justice . . . it seems therefore necessary that we should be made sensible of [God's hatred of sin] in order to our being brought into a state of salvation" (No. 360).

and the happiness of the saints (No. 344); the meek Lamb will eventually triumph over "his and our mighty, proud and cruel enemy" with martial pomp, as David did over Goliath (No. 347). These are almost the last entries under that title, but the dualistic theme is not abandoned; it soon becomes part of a much more extended view of cosmic history under the title "Wisdom of God in the Work of Redemption." The first of the new entries (No. 337) helps set the stage by showing how the linking of justice and mercy that Edwards sees in the atonement and in preparatory experiences has always been a part of the redemptive plan, from God's first revelation of grace toward fallen man soon after the defeat of the rebellious angels to the destruction of Antichrist before the full revelation of his grace on judgment day; it is even seen in the "legal awakenings before grace is bestowed."

Several familiar themes were restated with "wisdom of God" accents during the latter months of 1728. God's end in creation is still the communication of his glory and happiness (No. 332), but the shining forth of God's glory in his decrees must reveal his "goodness and love" and his "awful majesty . . . and justice and holiness" in equal measure (No. 348). Several entries stress the gradual, ever-unfolding character of divine revelation in history: in the superseding of old covenant and moral law by new covenant and gospel (No. 343), in the gradual unfolding of the mysteries of Scripture through the "pious wisdom and study" of the church (No. 351), and in the gradual arrival of the millennium (No. 356). Meanwhile, both angels and saints in heaven have their glory and happiness increased at each advance in the progress of the work of redemption and the advancement of Christ's kingdom, such as the incarnation, the resurrection and ascension of Christ, the Reformation, the fall of Antichrist, and the general resurrection (Nos. 371, 372).

While considering the nature of humiliation in the "Miscellanies," Edwards was writing on that and related subjects in both the "Faith" and "Signs of Godliness" notebooks. The latter he had begun probably in the summer of 1728 as an aid for counseling souls seeking assurance of salvation. Edwards had already stated (No. 314) that "it would be a grating, dissonant and deformed thing for a sinful creature to be happy in God's love," and in No. 374 he commented that it was necessary for God to take away original righteousness from man after he had sinned, for it would have been "improper" for God to continue a humble and loving disposition in one now become an enemy. Edwards turned this around in No. 375 ("Spirit's Witness") by concluding that when a person sees such dispositions and exercises in his soul "he sees that it would be utterly incongruous . . . that God should give them to him, if he did not accept of him." It may be that Edwards himself had had some such insight when seeking assurance of his own conversion.[5]

With respect to the church on earth, Edwards' entries during the latter months of his junior colleagueship suggest that he was, on the whole, comfortable with Stoddard's ecclesiology.[6] In No. 335 he says indeed that "visible Christians" means "appearing really Christians, true Christians" as a requirement for membership in the visible church; but it is visibility to "a public Christian judgment" based on Christian behavior and profession of belief in the gospel, not on accounts of "particular experiences . . . discoveries, illuminations, and affections," a judgment made with charity and the benefit of the doubt (No. 338). No. 377 asserts that "explicitly professing Christianity and the covenant of grace is the duty of everyone" as "part of instituted religion." In No. 339 Edwards applies the same criteria while seeking to define a "particular church."

Beyond the congregational level, No. 349 suggests that causes "too hard for a particular minister or a particular congregation" should be referred or appealed "to a higher judgment"; the supporting biblical texts imply much more than mere advice and counsel. This goes quite beyond the ultra congregational view Edwards had expressed in No. rr to Stoddard's high view of the power of ministerial associations.[7]

Edwards' years of apprenticeship to his grandfather were of crucial importance to his growth as minister and theologian. He had accepted, or at least come to terms with, Stoddard's distinctive views and customs, including a minatory sermon style in which he was becoming proficient; he had also increased his understanding of several doc-

5. This witness of the Spirit is the direct perception of holy dispositions, not a direct revelation to the soul of Christ's acceptance of the person, a notion Edwards had rejected in No. 329. In this he was in agreement with Stoddard: see Stoddard's *Defects of Preachers Reproved* (New London, 1724), p. 17; *Safety of Appearing* (Boston, 1687), pp. 225–26; and *Treatise Concerning Conversion*, (Boston, 1719) pp. 83–84.

6. Timothy Edwards accepted the children of baptized but unconverted parents for baptism and inclusion in the covenant, but he required a "relation of experience" and evidence of conversion for admission to full membership and the Lord's Supper. Stoddard admitted all such baptized children of the covenant to the Supper. Up through 1731 at least, Edwards seems to have had no serious reservations about following Stoddard's practice.

7. Timothy Edwards had supported the Saybrook Platform of 1708, with its provision for "consociations" of churches having mildly regulatory and disciplinary powers. Stoddard wanted a system of even higher ruling synods that he called a "national church." See his *Doctrine of Instituted Churches* (London, 1700).

trines, particularly the Trinity, the end of creation, the work of Christ, the process of conversion, and the afterlife.

NORTHAMPTON PASTORATE BEGUN, 1729–1731

Solomon Stoddard died on February 11, 1729, and Edwards assumed the whole round of duties belonging to the pastorate of a large congregation in the most important town in western Massachusetts. The standard biographies offer only a little information about the next two years of Edwards' life: an illness during the spring or summer of 1729 serious enough to keep him out of his pulpit for some time, the death of a sister in December of that year, the birth of a second daughter in April 1730, the fact that he was active in the Hampshire Association, and finally that in July 1731 he delivered the *God Glorified* sermon in Boston.

The effect of Edwards' new responsibilities is seen almost immediately in his manuscripts. The most obvious change is the larger number of sermons, many of which became theological treatises in themselves, accompanied by miscellanies providing summary or commentary. Furthermore, the sermons soon began to be written more hurriedly, with many abbreviations, more ellipses, and occasional resort to mere outline. With the exception of Scripture commentary, Edwards was writing very little in his specialized notebooks, and nothing at all in "Natural Philosophy" or "The Mind." His interest in publishing had shifted to theological subjects, such as the Trinity, on which he drafted a treatise in the spring of 1730, and faith, on which he already had a manuscript in process. Within the realm of theology his interest had also changed. Between early 1729 and mid-1731, Edwards wrote well over a hundred entries in the "Miscellanies" (Nos. 387–500), but none contains a proof for the existence of God and only five are entitled "Christian Religion." Edwards' interest concentrated on issues related to conversion, the basis for assurance of salvation, the means of grace, the living of the Christian life, and the saving work of Christ. Most of his more speculative essays have to do with such matters as the relation of habit to act or the future state of the soul. His debate with the Arminians continued, but this concerned sin, grace, and salvation.

When Edwards returned to the "Miscellanies" shortly after Stoddard's death, he left the rest of the page blank after No. 386 and devoted all of the next page to "Humiliation" (No. 393) in which he took up the question he had addressed in No. 317. The new entry begins with several passages of Scripture that he understood as proving that "humiliation is grace," and continues by analyzing the state of mind of the humbled sinner to show that "there is an exercise of faith in that humiliation." Three or four months later he added a long paragraph explaining why Stoddard had held that there was no grace in the soul before the first "explicit act of faith," which Stoddard had understood to be meant by faith as the only condition of salvation. Rather, said Edwards, "Persons are justified upon the first appearance of a principle of faith in the soul by any of the soul's acts." And faith itself, he added in No. 411, "arises from a principle of love." Edwards had finally stated in unambiguous terms his difference from Stoddard on this point.

"The prime alteration that is made in conversion," said Edwards in No. 397, "is the alteration of the temper and disposition and spirit of the mind; for what is done in conversion is nothing but conferring the Spirit of God, which dwells in the soul and becomes there a principle of life and action." This entry was a corollary to No. 396, which proved from Scripture that the word "spirit," when not used for the spiritual substance itself, "is put for the disposition, temper, inclination or will of that spiritual substance." In God it means the Holy Spirit, and for a human soul to have the spirit of God or the spirit of Christ is to be possessed by a divine disposition that is none other than the Holy Spirit.

When Edwards wrote these two entries linking conversion and the Trinity, he was also writing his longest lecture series up to that time, a three-sermon, seven-unit series on John 16:8 dealing with the work of the Holy Spirit. All his subsequent entries through No. 405 have some relation to that series, and No. 402 adds a further consideration to Edwards' view of the Trinity: the "exact equality in each person's concern in the work of redemption." It is also clear that he feels it necessary to exalt the Spirit's role ("The sum of all that Christ purchased is the Holy Ghost") against the notion that "more glory belongs to the Father and the Son because they manifested a more wonderful love, the Father in giving his Son . . . the Son in laying down his life; yet let it be considered, that the Holy Spirit *is* that wonderful love." Near the end of the original essay on the Trinity as he wrote it in 1730, Edwards included an expanded No. 402 in which he commented that "if we suppose no more than used to be supposed about the Holy Ghost [merely applying to us the blessing purchased by Christ] the concern of the Holy Ghost in the work of redemption is not equal with the

Father's and the Son's."[8] He clearly regarded his account of the Trinity as an improvement on standard Reformed theology.

In saying that faith "arises from a principle of love" Edwards was referring to the justifying faith that he had called in No. 218 "the same agreeing or consenting disposition that according to the divers objects, different state or manner of exerting, is called by different names," such as faith, love, or submission. Why, then, is faith the only act of the soul that is justifying? In the only entry he had written on justification since the completion of his masters thesis, No. 315, Edwards had simply asserted that though love and good works are also conditions of salvation, none of these in fallen man are acceptable to God; but "his believing does render it a fit and a worthy thing in God's esteem that he should be saved." Now, in No. 412, he explains that faith renders justification "fit" because, as "the heart's giving entertainment to Christ and the gospel," it makes it possible for the soul to be "looked upon as being in Christ." Love and obedience are conditions of salvation because of "their necessary and immutable connection with faith, as immediately flowing from the nature of it." Nevertheless, faith alone makes possible the imputation of Christ's righteousness to the soul, because receiving the gospel "is nothing else but the suitableness and agreement of the soul to the gospel Savior and salvation in actual exercise." Here and in No. 416, which repeats the thought of No. 412 more fully, Edwards laid down the distinction that later appears in the 1734 lectures on justification (though without the terms) between the moral fitness of good works and the natural fitness of faith. He made this clear in No. 455: "Believers ben't received for that reason, because they are so lovely, having the lovely qualification of faith, but because 'tis a receiving of Christ and a uniting the heart to him as Savior."[9]

Edwards defended this view of faith in No. 474 against allowing any justifying value to "sincere obedience" except as it is "a part of the reception of Christ and the gospel," and he named Arminians as his opponents. "As we do really depend on Christ for salvation and all spiritual blessings," Edwards says in No. 476, "so, if ever we truly believe, we must . . . see that it would not be condecent, not suiting

8. "An Essay on the Trinity," in *Treatise on Grace and Other Posthumously Published Writings*, ed. Paul Helm (Cambridge, England, James Clarke & Co., 1971), p. 125. JE made the same statement in his "Treatise on Grace," ibid., pp. 68–69. His comment applies to the Westminster Confession and catechisms as well as other Reformed creeds.

9. This entry illustrates the relationship between sermons and miscellanies. No. 455 is a summary of the main point of a sermon on justification (on Rom. 4:16), which in turn incorporated the thought of Nos. 315, 412, and 416.

with God's excellency, to bestow mercy upon us without Christ's mediation." The sinner as well as God must appreciate the fitness of reserving salvation for those only who are united to Christ by faith. This real dependence on God is further illustrated in No. 481, which affirms that grace (as the highest perfection, excellency, and happiness of the creature) is bestowed by God "according to his arbitrary will and pleasure, without any stated connection, according to fixed laws, with previous voluntary acts of men, or events in the series of natural things." Having thus denied human activity any causative value in procuring salvation, Edwards proceeded to write the sermon on I Cor. 1:29–31 that he afterwards preached at Boston, the doctrine of which he paraphrased in No. 486.[1] The only appropriate response to our real and total dependence for salvation upon God is what Edwards calls humiliation. When this is joined with repentance and faith it becomes "evangelical" or "gracious" humiliation: "Faith abases men, and exalts God, it gives all the glory of redemption to God alone."[2]

In spite of his insistence that God dispenses saving grace without being beholden to sinners for their utmost strivings, Edwards continued to urge them to prepare their hearts for the reception of grace, as in his multiple sermon on Hos. 5:15, whose doctrine is, "'Tis God's manner to make men sensible of their misery and unworthiness before he appears in his mercy and love to them."[3] One of his most important reasons is that love and grace reveal part, but only part, of the glory of God. As he says in No. 468, "If there was this love and grace without infinite majesty, sacred divine authority, infinitely dreadful hatred and wrath against sin, this love would be no part of God's glory: the manifestations of his love would be derogatory to his glory." Knowing God's love without his hatred of sin might lead the sinner to approach God, but with unseemly boldness. Even Christ had to experience the wrath of God before he was exalted and restored to the enjoyment of the Father's love (No. 469).

On the other hand, having only a conviction of God's greatness and one's desert of punishment without a revelation of God's beauty and grace will not carry a sinner beyond the quarrelsome disposition of devils (No. 470). The process of preparation could go awry at that

1. The sermon as preached at Northampton had this doctrine: "God is glorified in the work of redemption in this, that in everything belonging to the whole affair, there is so absolute and immediate a dependence of men on God."
2. "God Glorified in the Work of Redemption," Worcester rev. ed., *4*, 178.
3. The sermon was published in Dwight ed., *8*, 44–69.

stage and the sinner in revolt commit the unpardonable sin. Edwards was aware of this danger, but his most frequent pastoral problem in that connection was presented by anxious souls who feared that they had committed the sin against the Holy Ghost. Sermons and miscellanies addressed that fear, but Edwards' most extensive answer in the "Miscellanies" is contained in No. 375, a long essay with several addenda in which he lays down the conditions that must be met before one can be said to have committed the sin. The cumulative effect of these conditions must surely have excluded all of Edwards' congregation that were concerned enough to attend a sermon on the subject.

God's glory is manifested to the sinner in experiences preparatory to conversion, and God's sovereignty over the universe is manifested in his determinations concerning such matters as the Fall, election, and reprobation—otherwise things would be left to chance or control by creatures (No. 490). But it will be even more manifest throughout eternity to the inhabitants of heaven and hell. No. 491 and its continuation in No. 493 contain reflections on the misery of the damned. God's wrath must be infinitely dreadful because God is infinitely majestic, and therefore the sufferings of the damned must be great in the same proportion: "'Tis fit that those in heaven, that see the awfulness of God's majesty . . . should see answerable proportionable discoveries of it in the misery of those that bear his wrath; and this they can't do unless their present misery is in proportion." This proportionality extends also to the misery of the damned, which must be "extreme and amazing, and also eternal and desperate." For the damned exist only to suffer; "they are, on purpose that God may show the dreadfulness of his wrath upon them" (No. 491). These entries and the contemporary sermons show that Edwards remained faithful to the evangelistic sermon style he had learned from Stoddard and the theology that justified it.

There was, however, an important development in his thought in association with the sermons and miscellanies on the preparatory experience of God's wrath against sin. The sermon on Hos. 5:15 explains that God brings about that experience by means of natural conscience. In No. 471 Edwards assigns two functions to natural conscience: it gives an apprehension of right and wrong, and it suggests to the mind "the relation that there is between right or wrong and a retribution." But in No. 472 he virtually collapses the first into the second: natural conscience "gives no other notion to natural men of right and wrong, but only as it suggests the relation or adaptedness there is between such and such things and a being hated by others and having evil brought upon them," for "natural men in strictness see nothing of the proper deformity of wrong."

The Spirit works upon natural conscience by revealing the sinner's guilt, God's wrath, and the sinner's helplessness. In all of this there is an appeal to self-love, the sinner's love of happiness and aversion to misery. But how can we account for such natural virtues as love, gratitude, and benevolence among the heathen and unconverted Christians? No. 473 contains Edwards' first formal answer: self-love. It is "natural to the soul to exercise gratitude to persons that it conceives of as not only causes of pleasure, but also therein exercising respect"; and one may love another "as having those qualifications of mind that would enable him to do him good and minister to his profit or pleasure." Edwards then goes on briefly to derive love to other virtues and hatred of their opposite vices from the same principle. This view of natural conscience and the natural virtues is precisely the one Edwards later elaborated in *The Nature of True Virtue,* making use of No. 473 as a basic text.[4]

Throughout his first years as pastor Edwards was concerned about what he saw as the extremely low level of both piety and morality in his congregation, as his many sermons of castigation reveal. He was also aware that scrupulous souls needed help in reaching assurance that they had indeed received grace. Shortly before Stoddard's death, in No. 375 and contemporary passages in his "Faith" notebook, he had, like Stoddard, stressed the inner awareness of those holy dispositions and volitions that God would surely not grant to someone at enmity with him. But in No. 462, when discussing qualifications for church membership, he concedes that "these sensible exercises are not constant," and sometimes "the ideas can't be repeated at will. The principles of these are universal, but the lively actings are not so universal as those other signs." Those other signs, to which Edwards increasingly turned, had to do with what he often called "universal persevering obedience" to God and a consistently just and loving behavior toward others.

During his first three years as pastor Edwards wrote several sermons urging "universal and persevering obedience" and he began a note-

4. See No. 473, p. 514, n. 2. JE's definition of self-love in No. 473 has its background in No. 301 and "The Mind" no. 1 (*Works,* 6, 336–37); on his view of natural conscience see "The Mind" no. 45, § 14 (ibid., pp. 365–66).

book on "Signs of Godliness." Most of what he had to say on both subjects occurs in those manuscripts, but some entries are devoted to them in the "Miscellanies." Biblical warnings against falling away from righteousness, he says in No. 467, "don't at all argue, but that there is an essential difference in the very nature of the righteousness of those that persevere, and the righteousness of those that fall away . . . and so falling away or holding out are in those places respected as natural fruits or discoveries of the nature of the righteousness." And he concludes, "The promises in Scripture are commonly made to the signs, though God knows whether men be sincere or not without the signs whereby man knows." Indeed, as he says in a contemporaneous entry in "Signs of Godliness," "Men will be judged at the Great Day by their actions and not by the spirit of their actions, for the spirit of their actions is a thing that is to be made to apppear."[5]

Edwards' sermons constantly strike this note, calling on the saints to make their calling and election sure. Doing the will of God, taking on Christ's yoke, means keeping God's commandments, all of them, every day, for the rest of one's life.[6] For example, the doctrine of the sermon on I John 3:9 is, "Grace is in the hearts of the saints, in this world, as a seed." This can be a comforting thought to an over-anxious saint, but in this sermon it is a call to strenuous activity. If the seed is there it is alive, growing, and producing fruit; if there is no growth and no fruit, it is likely that no seed is there.

Persevering obedience to God's commands, Edwards says in No. 488, "is as directly proposed to be sought and endeavored by us, in Scripture, as necessary to salvation . . . as faith in Jesus Christ." Hence the unregenerate sinner as well as the saint may properly be exhorted to forsake all evil desires, commit no sins, and pursue a life of strict obedience. This cannot be done without regeneration, but "that is the way to obtain regeneration. 'Tis God's manner to give his Spirit in a way of earnest striving, and upon acts of notable self-denial, especially if repeated and continued in." At the level of everyday living there is a continuity between the preparatory striving of the sinner and the persevering striving of the saint.[7] Edwards does not stop with the

5. "Signs of Godliness," no. [29].
6. See, for example, the sermons on Matt. 7:21 and 11:29.
7. "We find the promises of God sometimes made to conversion and sometimes to perseverance; 'tis because perseverance is but the actual fulfillment of that which is virtually done in conversion" ("Signs of Godliness," no. [29]).

saints' completed perseverance; actualization of their souls' potential continues forever as one of the chief blessings of heaven.[8]

As thoughts of hell or humiliation inevitably reminded Edwards of the sufferings of Christ, so the call for "universal persevering obedience" led him to consider Christ's obedience to God's commands as part of his saving work. No. 483 begins with the role of love in the atonement: "The divine excellency of Christ and the love of the Father to him, is the life and soul of all that Christ did and suffered in the work of redemption." We are accepted into God's favor because of Christ's infinite worthiness and the Father's love to him, but "the foundation of our acceptance is Christ's love to us." This love, when risen to the height of willingness to suffer destruction ("that is, his own suffering equivalent to it") for the sinner, creates such an identity of the two that they are accepted as one by God. The second reason for the necessity of Christ's death is the expiation of sin, and the third is "as it was the main instance of Christ's obedience."

It was this third aspect of the atonement that Edwards addressed in his next entries on the subject, Nos. 496–498, which he wrote along with or immediately after the sermon on John 15:10, probably in June 1731. Much that he says in these entries was taken from the sermon, the doctrine of which is, "Jesus Christ kept all his Father's commandments." Following up on what he had said in No. 454, Edwards points out that Christ became subject to the Father as the human race's representative in the covenant of redemption, and therefore all Christ's acts of obedience, including his death, and all his excellency, are accepted for us. No. 497 draws the conclusion that Christ's death saves not only because it was a propitiation for sin but just as much because it was an act—his principal act—of obedience. That entry also cites the application of the John 15:10 sermon, in which, as in other sermons of the period, Edwards spells out in more detail the saving efficacy of Christ's sufferings and death as an act of honor to God and as a testimony to God's righteous hatred of sin.[9]

8. Sermon of March 14, 1731, on Rev. 22:3, the doctrine of which is that "the happiness of the saints in heaven consists partly in that they there serve God." As JE goes on to explain, "The well being or happy being of the creature and its perfect and excellent being evermore go together. But 'tis more excellent in the creature to be in action than in a state of inactivity. While men's powers of action lie dormant and inactive they are useless; they are as if men had them not . . . for the end of power is act. If it were not for the relation that power has to act, power would be no excellency at all."

9. E.g. the March 25, 1731, fast-day sermon on Num. 14:21 (II. 2 under the doctrine) contains a comprehensive summary of Christ's sufferings and death as a vindication of God's

When Edwards wrote No. 498 he was already deep in the composition of two sermons on Gen. 3:24 dealing with the Fall. Several passages in the sermons contrast the new covenant with the covenant of works, and No. 498 is an almost exact quotation from the application of the second sermon. It represents Christ as the tree of life, of which we may now freely partake; since Christ has "performed the term of obedience" we, unlike our first parents, have no probation to undergo.[1]

In the midst of his thinking about the work of Christ, Edwards made his first serious attempt at speculation on the relation between the divine and human natures of Christ, No. 487. He had recently written on the role of divine love in the atonement (No. 483), and that love, he had said many times, is the Holy Spirit. In No. 486 he had cited the sermon on I Cor. 1:29–31, which says, concerning the inherent good that the redeemed have in God, that "it is by partaking of the Holy Spirit that they have communion with Christ in his fullness. God hath given the Spirit, not by measure unto him, and they do receive of his fullness, and grace for grace."[2]

What might be called the paradigm of Edward's christological thinking in No. 487 is the Spirit as the bond of union between Christ and the believer, and between Christ and the church. "Perhaps," says Edwards, "the Spirit of the Logos may dwell in a creature after such a manner, that the creature may become one person [with the Logos], and may be looked upon as such and accepted as such." He suggests that the man Jesus became "one person" with the Logos "only by the communion of understanding and communion of will, inclination, spirit or temper." Edwards draws on Locke's conception of personal identity to explain this "communion of understanding": the man Jesus and the Logos shared "the same consciousness," including a memory of the relation between the Logos and the Father before the creation. Furthermore, every part of the life and work of Christ, from his conception to his resurrection, was by the Spirit of God. And since "all divine commu-

---

justice and majesty and a fulfillment of all God's threatenings against sin. It also restates the idea expressed in No. 463, that Christ's sufferings perform this function more successfully than do those of the damned, since his are now finished but theirs will never be completed.

1. The theological importance of these sermons in JE's eyes is suggested by the fact that No. 501 also is quoted from the second sermon (Prop. 1) and that No. 502 is probably a paraphrase of its application (Use 1, §4).

2. Worcester rev. ed., *4*, 175. JE had also been reading Mastricht's *Theologia* on "the economy of the persons of the Trinity and the church's communion with God," which he cited in No. 482 (see No. 482, p. 524, n. 1).

nion" is by the Holy Ghost, "the Spirit of God is the bond of perfectness by which God, Jesus Christ, and the church are united together."

The church of which Edwards wrote in this essay is, of course, the
church of the elect; but he was also concerned with aspects of the
visible church on earth. In the latter part of 1728, he had devoted four
entries to the subject of admission to church membership.[3] In the
spring of 1730, he again took up the matter with No. 462 ("Church
Order"). As before, he refuses to distinguish between full and half-way
covenant members; applicants must be either admitted as Christians
or rejected as not Christians. None are to be admitted to church privileges but those that come to the Lord's Supper. "And therefore all of
the congregation should be pressed and urged to come . . . But yet
they ought all to be sufficiently instructed, that they must be Christians
really, in order to come." Requiring a positive assurance of regeneration would exclude many of the "truly upright," so Edwards turns to
more visible evidences of belief and behavior. But the standard of
attitude and behavior he sets for an applicant's self-examination and
public profession is such as to imply the presence of grace in the soul.
Edwards is clearly following Stoddard in seeking to make the Supper a
"converting ordinance" in a very practical sense, as can be seen from
the educational and disciplinary steps he proposes in the rest of No.
462 and the combination of invitation and table-fencing to be seen in
his sacrament sermons.[4]

Edwards also addressed other ordinances of the church. Nos. 464
and 466 argue that the sabbath is to be celebrated on the day of Christ's
resurrection. About a year later, probably in May 1731, Edwards
wrote a lecture on I Cor. 16:1–2 with the same thesis but with all the
arguments he had used in No. 160, almost the whole of which he
incorporated into the lecture. He soon followed it with No. 495, the
theme of which, as of much that he wrote about the Lord's day, is the
supersession of creation by redemption. He returned to the subject in
No. 500, maintaining that the first-day sabbath is a type of both the
millennium and the church's eternal rest.

One other ordinance received direct attention in the "Miscellanies."
In the fall of 1730 Edwards preached a sermon on Acts 8:22 occasioned by an exercise of church discipline; it ends with a paragraph
warning that there is ordinarily no hope of salvation for persons who

3. The entries were Nos. 335, 338, 345, and 377.
4. E.g. the sermon on I Cor. 10:16 that he apparently wrote at the same time as No. 462,
and the sermon on I Cor. 11:28–29 that he preached about a year later in May 1731.

die under a just excommunication unless they have used proper means to be restored. Edwards must have moved directly to the writing of No. 485, which amplifies that paragraph and closes with the statement that "excommunication does as much mark out men as being in a damnable state, as if it made them so."[5]

The entries that have just been examined show that Edwards sought to make the visible institutional church approximate as closely as possible the real church that is the true spouse of Christ and the end of creation.[6] The tension in Edwards' thought between the earthly and the heavenly church was paralleled by an ambivalent attitude toward the church's "means of grace." These were of divine appointment and obviously used by God in the salvation of souls, but any confidence in them by humans seemed to smack of Arminianism or even Pelagianism. And yet they were part and parcel of the whole process of preparation and Christian growth.[7]

How critical this tension could be for Edwards in the cure of souls can be illustrated from a sermon and a "Miscellanies" entry. In the fall of 1730 Edwards wrote a sermon on the new birth from John 3:3. It is true that in conversion there is infused "a principle of spiritual understanding and spiritual action that is [as] far above any principles that man had before as the heaven is high above the earth," and therefore conversion is called a new creation. Nevertheless it is also a new birth, "because it is brought to pass by stated means . . . . 'Tis God makes men new. . . . But now 'tis in a certain stated way and according to a fixed law of nature. God could, if he pleased, convert men immediately without the use of means at all, but he doth not so; but there are stated means which are appointed and fixed by the law of grace, that are constantly made use of in producing this effect. Conversion is

5. Comparison with No. q, written at the beginning of JE's ministry, shows that he had not changed his mind on the subject at all.

6. A high view of the church is expressed in the doctrine of the sermon on Matt. 5:13, "The church of God is in this depraved and corrupted world as the salt that preserves it from utter ruin." The same is true of the five-sermon series Edwards preached in May 1731 on I Pet. 2:9, the first four of which deal respectively with the four metaphors for the church contained in the verse: "A chosen generation, a royal priesthood, a holy nation, God's peculiar people" (Dwight ed., *8*, 379–417). These sermons distinguish more sharply than does the sermon on Matt. 5:13 between the godly members of the church and all natural men, including the rest of the visible church.

7. E.g. the doctrine of the sermon on Ex. 20:24, "If we would be in the way of God's grace and blessing, we must wait upon him in his own way and in the use of his appointed means." No. 406 assures anxious sinners that "those that are willing to use the means of grace, have not committed the unpardonable sin."

wrought by the word and ordinances."[8] In the application he urges "the steady and diligent use of appointed means . . . the word . . . the law . . . the ordinances administered in the church, which is the mother. Believers are the children of the church."

Nevertheless, two or three months earlier Edwards had written No. 481, in which he made a sharp distinction between the gift of grace and all "common benefits":

> In grace not only consists the highest perfection and excellency, but the happiness of the creature: and therefore, although other things are bestowed on men by ordinary providence, that is, according to fixed laws of the succession of events from preceding events or preceding human voluntary acts; yet this has God reserved to be bestowed by himself, according to his arbitrary will and pleasure, without any stated connection, according to fixed laws, with previous voluntary acts of men, or events in the series of natural things. Common benefits . . . are statedly connected with preceding things in the creature, so that they are in a sense dependent on the creature; but this excellency and blessedness of the soul is connected only with the will of God, and is dependent on nothing else.

These two writings—and there are many more like both of them—start out from somewhat conflicting biblical metaphors and pursue different trains of thought. The sermon demands human activity; the entry (and the sermons it reflects) demands that no confidence be invested in that activity. The first relates the soul to God in some sense through the matrix of a human community; the second leaves the soul, in the moment of decision between life and death, alone with an inscrutable and arbitrary God.

By the time Edwards gave the lecture at Boston in 1731 he was able to speak with a tone of authority that was surely sensed by his listeners. This authority derived first of all from Edwards' own personal experience of the spiritual realities he described, secondly from nearly a decade of intense study and writing, and finally from his status as successor to Stoddard in one of the most important pulpits in New England. While he would not again be in the public eye for three more years, he was equipped for further growth in theological wisdom by adding to his writing in sermons and notebooks, especially the "Miscellanies."

8. The first and fifth sections, respectively, under the doctrine.

2. The "Miscellanies" as Repository for a System of Thought

Edwards not only accepted Reformed theology in its English Puritan form, he energetically defended it. He employed many traditional theological *loci* as titles for his essays, and he used them as subject headings in his Table. On the other hand, both the form and content of many entries suggest an openness to new ways of understanding the faith. His discussions of traditional topics often did not fit neatly into the formal theological categories, and he speculated freely on such subjects as angels and devils, heaven and hell, typology, and cosmology. He often seemed unsatisfied with his understanding of a doctrine; he raised objections to his own formulations and sometimes modified as well as defended them. There was also a certain fluidity or interconnectedness between doctrines. He frequently borrowed the implications of one doctrine while studying another and, beginning with No. 104, he occasionally wrote a synthetic essay weaving several doctrines together both in the main entry and in multiple corollaries and cross-references.[9]

Seventeenth-century Reformed theology provided a structural framework for Edwards' thought, and his adherence to its doctrines excluded contradictory options. Norman Fiering says, "His thinking was never open-ended and therefore subject to reversal."[1] "Never" is too strong, for in at least one case, the terms of communion, Edwards reversed himself on a matter that he considered of great importance and at great cost to himself. To speak of Edwards as a "thinker" is to imply that he modified the intellectual tradition he had received. He himself claimed to be going beyond the tradition of typology and expected to be criticized for doing so.[2] His orthodoxy was called into question in the nineteenth century, and the doughty conservative Calvinist, Charles Hodge, while asserting Edwards' orthodoxy, deplored such "speculations" as his means of conceiving human identity with Adam.[3]

In a "closed" system like the one Edwards inherited, each theological

9. For example, Trinity, incarnation, and church are often dealt with together; likewise the atonement, the Old Testament dispensation, preparation for conversion, and heaven and hell.

1. *Jonathan Edwards's Moral Thought and Its British Context* (Chapel Hill, Univ. of North Carolina Press, 1981), p. 10.

2. "I expect by very ridicule and contempt to be called a man of very fruitful brain and copious fancy, but they are welcome to it." "Notebook on Types," *Works, 11,* 152.

3. "Jonathan Edwards and the Successive Forms of the New Divinity," pp. 614–17.

topic received definitive treatment in relative isolation from the others and had its own niche in a structure set up according to logical or chronological relations among its main "heads" rather than emerging from dynamic relations and tendencies within the parts themselves. Such a system is often taken, especially by its inheritors, as literally descriptive of the transcendent realities with which it deals and as so complete and all-encompassing that it needs neither addition nor change but only commentary and application.[4]

Edwards does indeed have a system, but it is "open" in a sense that goes beyond his formal theological categories. Like all creative thinkers, Edwards could not contain his thought in pre-existent categories. As a result of his own religious experiences and his reading in theology and science, Edwards came to certain cosmological and epistemological positions in his earliest extant writings that greatly influenced his selection and interpretation of key biblical passages and affected his thinking on almost every topic. The result was a network of implicit relations and coimplications that imposes a unity on his thought beyond that provided by Reformed dogmatics and constitutes the truly distinctive element in his theology. The preceding survey of the miscellanies contained in the present volume has already pointed to recurrent motifs in Edwards' thought. The following is a more systematic treatment of these motifs that, while focusing on their genesis and expression in the early "Miscellanies," necessarily includes other of Edwards' early compositions.

GOD AND THE WORLD IN "ATOMS" AND "BEING"

Edwards' exploration of new conceptual categories antedates the beginning of the "Miscellanies." Early in 1721, while he was doing his Master's work at Yale, Edwards completed his last corollaries in "Atoms" and wrote the first essay in "Being." The dominant influence in these pieces was the Cambridge Platonist Henry More, who combated the materialism of Thomas Hobbes and the dualism of René Descartes, seeing in both a threat to belief in the existence of God and

---

4. In his Introduction to *Basic Writings of Saint Augustine* (2 vols. New York, Random House, 1948) Whitney Oates considers the systems of Epicurus, Aristotle, and Thomas Aquinas as "closed," but those of Plato, Augustine, and Whitehead as "open." (ibid., *1*, ix–x.) Of Augustine, Oates says that, strictly speaking, his thought is not a "system": "It is rather a world view or a 'universe view,' one which comprehends God and . . . all aspects of reality, one which recognizes the principle that 'life runs beyond logic,' and above all, admits the fact that human speculation on ultimate questions is always in process, and cannot in any final sense ever be completed." (ibid.)

the whole spiritual dimension of existence.[5] More had argued against Descartes that space as well as body has extension, that it is infinite in extent, and that the world of bodies is finite. Matter can be divided only to its ultimate units, atoms, which are impenetrable by any physical power. Spiritual substance is not defined merely as thought; it also has extension (though it is indivisible) and can penetrate and move matter, as souls do bodies. More also posited a "natural spirit" pervading all matter as the medium through which God directed all natural processes.

Edwards accepted More's main contentions but departed from them at certain points. Edwards' atom can be of any size and is defined as a body whose content is uniform and continuous; it is therefore absolutely full, a *plenum*. Such a body cannot be cracked or penetrated (which would amount to its annihilation) by any finite force. Hence there must be an infinite power that maintains that resistance to penetration, which resistance constitutes the solidity that is the essence of matter. That power can be nothing less than the omnipotent Deity acting in those parts of space where he sees fit, producing resistance (matter) or communicating resistance from one part of space to another (motion); the laws of nature are only "the stated methods of God's acting with respect to bodies."[6] Hence there is nothing that can really be called "matter," if by that is meant a "substance," i.e. a subject in which such properties as extension, mass, and color inhere. Since it is God's infinite power that keeps bodies in existence, creation was simply the first occasion on which God exerted that power.

The first three paragraphs of "Being" simply reproduce the *a priori* argument for the existence of God that follows from More's cosmology, a demonstration from the inconceivability of nothingness that "some being should eternally be" and that it "must be infinite and omnipresent." Since the nonexistence of space is also inconceivable, "I have already said as much as that space is God."[7]

While writing these two essays, Edwards came to a number of conclusions that strongly supported his Calvinism but subtly affected his

5. For the text of "Atoms" see *Works, 6*, 208–18, and for "Being" (first three paragraphs), see ibid., pp. 202–03. In his introduction Anderson discusses JE's college and graduate reading, including More (ibid., pp. 17–26), "Atoms" (pp. 53–68), and "Being" (pp. 68–75).

In *From the Closed World to the Infinite Universe* (New York, Harper, 1958) Alexandre Koyré discusses More's philosophy, especially in relation to that of Descartes, in a way that shows why More so instructed and stimulated JE (pp. 110–54).

6. "Atoms," prop. 2, corols. 11 and 15 (*Works, 6*, 215, 216).

7. Ibid., pp. 202–03.

theological thinking. One of these was the central contention of "Atoms": it is God's omnipresent power that holds every atom—and thus the world—in being at every moment. Edwards would have none of More's "natural spirit." There simply is no realm of even relatively autonomous "second causes" between God and the world. Not only humankind but all creation is immediately, totally dependent each moment on God's decision to continue both the fact and the manner of its existence. There are, of course, "natural laws" by which the world continues to operate; but what we call natural law is only the "method" or "rule" by which God has chosen to exercise his power.

The consequences for Edwards' theology are far-reaching. The infinitely powerful and omnipresent God of "Atoms" is the sovereign God of Reformed theology, whose "decrees" constitute the program by which everything occurs, from creation and fall to the day of judgment. The gravity that holds the heavenly bodies in their orbits, the sinner dangling over the pit of hell, and the soul suddenly infused with saving grace are alike forms of radical dependence on the will and power of God. This metaphysic explains at least in part Edwards' demand that the sinner be brought to "humiliation," an acknowledgment of absolute helplessness in the face of God's demands, and that the saint live in moment-to-moment dependence on God's grace. Paradoxically, the achievement of such humiliation seems to require the use of the means of grace; hence, as we have seen, Edwards can encourage, even demand, such use, and almost the next moment insist that God bestows his grace totally independent of those means.

As Edwards summed up the ontological implications of "Atoms," matter is "truly even nothing at all"; bodies "have no substance of their own . . . but all that is real, it is immediately in the first being." God is "*ens entium;* or, if there was nothing else in the world but bodies, the only real being."[8] This is Edwards' first reference—and that only by implication—to finite spirits in his extant papers, and it seems almost an afterthought. He was, of course, writing in natural philosophy, and he does conclude the entry by saying that "the nearer in nature beings are to God, so much the more properly are they beings, and more substantial; and that spirits are much more properly beings, and more substantial, than bodies."[9] Since Edwards defines a substance as a subject possessing qualities, it would seem that more and less cannot

8. LS no. 44 (*Works, 6,* 238). This was JE's last entry in the Long Series before he went to New York.
9. Ibid.

apply to finite spirits and that they either are or are not substances. Perhaps he had yet to make up his mind on that question.

In all his early writings in natural philosophy Edwards' primary purpose was to establish the priority of the spiritual, to prove that the only real world is the world of spirits. Nevertheless, there is another of his conclusions in "Atoms," i.e. continuous, moment-by-moment creation, that raises doubt about the reality—or at least integrity—of finite spirits as well as of bodies. Here we move to the "Miscellanies," where No. 18 proves in a dramatic way that Edwards understood continuous creation to apply to souls as well as bodies: "It is no more unreasonable that we should be guilty of Adam's first sin, than that we should be guilty of our own that we have been guilty of in times past. For we are not the same we were in times past, any other way than only as we please to call ourselves the same. For we are anew created every moment; and that that is caused to be this moment is not the same that was caused to be the last moment." And God, he adds, sets whatever conditions he pleases to constitute an identity between Adam and his posterity for the purpose of deriving guilt. When Edwards invoked this argument in *Original Sin* at the end of his career, he was only restating a position he had taken at its beginning.

Whether, when he wrote "Atoms" and the first part of "Being," Edwards had had his first experience of "that sort of inward, sweet delight in GOD and divine things" that he afterwards associated with his conversion,[1] it is true that these earliest essays concern only the being and omnipotent power of God. Edwards says nothing in them about God's goodness or beauty except to remark the divine wisdom manifested in creating and maintaining the harmonious relations among the atoms of the universe. God as sovereign power to destroy as well as to create filled Edwards' soul with awe and exhilaration, whether storming above the trees of Windsor, thundering from Sinai, or tormenting the damned.

RELIGION AND DEVOTION IN NEW YORK

The entries that Edwards made in his "Diary" and "Miscellanies" while he was in New York reflect his preoccupation with the cultivation of spiritual and moral discipline, and with the delights he experienced in seasons of Bible study and prayerful communion with God. It was a time in which the philosophical speculations and religious raptures of

1. Hopkins, *Life and Character*, p. 25.

his graduate years became more self-consciously interrelated as he meditated on the great themes of redemption by Christ. In his only back-reference to "Natural Philosophy" during the months in New York he affirmed that as "God . . . and other spirits are more substantial than matter," so "no happiness is solid and substantial but spiritual happiness" (No. f). The spiritual happiness of communion with God was now Edwards' dominant experience in spite of the struggles recorded in his "Diary." This experience he variously called "holiness," "religion," and "devotion." Religion, or devotion, is the single-minded pursuit of holiness, and its essence is the contemplation of the glories of the Creator in the works of nature and in the redemptive work of Christ. Holiness suffuses the soul with serenity and joy, and so assimilates it to the divine nature that if it were but holy enough it might "as it were naturally ascend from the earth in delight, to enjoy God as Enoch did!" (No. a).

In these early miscellanies Edwards revealed elements of his own piety that were to have repercussions in his later writings and indeed behavior. The "religion" he describes is a "lying low" before God like a flower in a garden, sweetly accepting whatever God sends upon it—though the weather in No. a is certainly benign. Here Edwards himself experiences the absolute dependence on God that he has discovered in the rest of creation, and his emotional horizon is filled with the divine in the way his intellectual had been filled in "Atoms." Religion is exceedingly pleasant, but its joy comes from spiritual things, not the pleasures of the world; its main occupation is contemplation, not social or ethical activity, which is only ancillary to "the *great* business" for which man was made.[2]

The very nature of this devotion is that it carries within it its own authentication. The "faith" Edwards is describing sees and feels in its object, in the experience itself, such marks of the divine as to produce an intuitive certainty that the object of faith and devotion is indeed the Deity. Such a direct experience of God is superior to the proof of God's existence and nature by discursive reasoning (No. aa). Edwards repeats this belief in a number of different ways in later miscellanies, and, as we have seen, for several years he placed the inner experience of grace above outward signs as the best ground of assurance.

Edwards was aware that the kind of religion he was describing and preaching (for it suffuses the sermons of the period) separated its

2. No. kk.

possessor not only from the heathen and the overtly wicked of the world, but also from the generality of professing Christians.[3] Several early miscellanies are directed against what he regards as the common view of those around him, that holiness is "a melancholy, morose, sour and unpleasant thing" (No. a), that religion makes its devotees melancholy killjoys (No. x), and that too much devotion renders people unproductive in the everyday affairs of life (No. tt). In his responses Edwards exhibits a certain defensiveness, an expectation of persecution, a sense of being among the remnant that have not bowed the knee to Baal. True saints are few and must expect to be "maliciously and spitefully used by this world" (No. d). When projected against a cosmic backdrop, this attitude led Edwards to visions of the saints participating in Christ's victory over the world and reigning over their erstwhile oppressors (Nos. d, k) and of the final and dramatic defeat of the devil at the end of history.[4] More serious consequences of this dualism will appear later.

INTELLIGENT BEINGS AND THE END OF CREATION

While he was in New York, Edwards continued to ponder the question of the reality of the external world and its meaning for human beings. But the new answers to which he came did not grow out of further analysis of the physical world but out of the metaphysical implications of his own contemplation of and communion with God. These meditations brought him to radical conclusions about the physical world that he expressed both in a group of lettered miscellanies and in the second stratum of "Being." No. gg, for example, records the speculation that without intelligent beings to observe it the world would have no end, purpose, or meaning. With all its grandeur and beauty, it would not even be of use to God, for without intelligent beings "God could neither receive good himself nor communicate good." Intelligent beings, then, are the end of creation, and "their end must be to behold and admire the doings of God, and magnify him for them, and to contemplate his glories in them." Without responding observers "the world would be altogether in vain."

Having become convinced that the world was created in order to be beheld and is inconceivable apart from its relation to a beholder, Edwards advanced a further step to the argument of No. pp, that the

---

3. For a discussion of the New York sermons, see *Works, 10.*
4. See the entries on "Satan Defeated."

being that has necessarily existed from eternity must be intelligent, must be conscious of its own existence. "For how doth one's mind refuse to believe, that there should be being from all eternity . . . and yet nothing know, all that while, that anything is." Can anything have a being if there is no one conscious of it? "Not at all more," he answers, "than there is sound where no one hears it, or color where none sees it." The things in an uninhabited room "have no being any other way than only as God is conscious [of them]."

In the spring or early summer of 1723, after his return home from New York, Edwards reread No. pp and pursued its line of thought further as an additional essay in "Being." Indeed, he started writing a direct continuation of No. pp that stated succinctly the new conclusion to which he had come: "Neither can be any such thing without consciousness. How is it possible there should something be from all eternity and there be no consciousness? It will appear very plain to everyone that intensely considers of it, that consciousness and being are the same thing exactly."[5] But then Edwards canceled that beginning and started over, this time greatly expanding the argument of No. pp point by point.[6] After referring to the objects in a room where no finite observer is present he supposes, for illustration's sake, a time when God's consciousness as well as that of all finite spirits was intermitted: "I say, the universe for that time would cease to be, of itself; and not only, as we speak, because the Almighty could not attend to uphold the world, but because God knew nothing of it."[7] After further illustrations based on the withdrawal of secondary qualities from matter, Edwards announced his conclusions in a corollary: "It follows from hence, that those beings which have knowledge and consciousness are the only proper and real and substantial beings, inasmuch as the being of other things is only by these. From hence we may see the gross mistake of those who think material things the most substantial beings, and spirits more like a shadow; whereas spirits only are properly substance."

Sereno Dwight's assignment of "Being" in its entirety to Edwards' early college years has encouraged later students to spend much time

5. *Works*, 6, 203, n. 5.
6. Ibid. 203–06 (through corol. 1). Dwight not only omitted these sentences but also interposed two later paragraphs between the first part of "Being," which Edwards had written in 1721, and the beginning of his continuation two years later (Dwight ed., *1*, 706–07).
7. Ibid., p. 204.

and effort trying to derive these conclusions from Locke or Berkeley. The beginning and degree of Locke's influence on Edwards' early thought is indeed an important question, but it seems clear that Edwards evolved his so-called "idealism" without the benefit of Locke's ideas, against the background of his own previous conclusions about matter and more directly from his own single-minded contemplation of God and his works. The three entries that lead directly to No. pp (Nos. gg, kk, ll) are all entitled "Religion." No. gg's argument runs: the world would be "useless," even to God, without intelligent beings to behold it, so they must be the end of creation; but they in turn are useless unless their end is to behold God's works and glorify him for them: "Wherefore religion must be the end of the creation." Those entries only assert that the world is useless without an observer. Then, in No. pp, he carries the argument further: there can be no being, either God or the world, without a consciousness of it. The addendum to "Being" simply elaborates that argument. It is noteworthy that the key word in No. pp is "conscious" and in "Being" is "consciousness." Only later did Edwards use the word "idea" when referring to this part of "Being."[8]

What Edwards had written in "Being" immediately became the dominant form of his immaterialism. That God's perfect idea of a material thing is the very thing became the basis for what Edwards in No. 94 considered his distinctive contribution to an understanding of the Trinity.[9] In No. 123 he uses the notion that the idea of a *spiritual* thing in some sense repeats it to explain the relation between grace and spiritual understanding, and later he substitutes this form of his idealism in his explanation of the Trinity (No. 238).

Many instances of Edwards' appeal to his idealism will be found throughout the "Miscellanies." To be conscious of something and to have an idea of it, Edwards considered forms of perception. Perhaps he used "perceive" and "perception" frequently because they could stand for both having physical contact with the solidity of matter and having an idea of spiritual as well as physical things. "All existence is perception," wrote Edwards near the end of his life while he was

8. In No. 94 JE introduces a reference to "Being" with "if nothing has any existence any way at all but in some consciousness or idea or other, and therefore those things that are in no created consciousness have no existence but in the divine idea. . . ."

9. "It the more confirms me in it," he writes in No. 179, "that the perfect idea God has of himself is truly and properly God, that the existence of all corporeal things is only ideas."

working on *Original Sin,*[1] and this conviction was a dominant motif in much of his theology. For example, Edwards quickly saw that if the creation is useless unless perceived by intelligent beings, it will be useless after those beings have ceased to exist; hence the soul must be immortal (Nos. gg, 1). It is also a fundamental conviction of Edwards that God created the world to manifest his glory in all aspects of it, what he calls God's manifestative, as distinguished from his internal, or immanent, glory. But the correlate of manifestation is perception: "There is no glory without perception" (No. 354). That perception must also be complete, and include both God's majesty and his mercy, his wrath and his love, his justice and his forgiveness. This was an important reason why Edwards accepted the doctrine of preparation in spite of his own relatively preparationless conversion, spent so much time balancing out the happiness of the saints in heaven and the misery of the damned in hell, and gave an account of the atonement that stressed the exhibition of divine love and the honoring of divine justice.[2]

Since intelligent creatures possess both understanding and will, Edwards describes the perception of God's glory as involving the response of the affections: "An understanding of the perfections of God, merely, cannot be the end of the creation; for he had as good not understand it, as see it and not be at all moved with joy at the sight" (No. 3). That joy, which is the happiness of the creature, was the end proposed by God's goodness. As these early (and many later) miscellanies illustrate, the relation between God's goodness and God's glory as the end of creation continued to perplex Edwards, and his final conclusions were recorded in his posthumously published *End for which God Created the World.*

Edwards was able to derive an argument for the immortality of the soul from the continuing necessity of a perceiver to render the universe "useful," indeed possible. But if "existence is perception," what about the existence of the perceiver? It is threatened by other elements in Edwards' developing world view. In No. 18, as previously mentioned, Edwards applied his doctrine of continuous creation—which is really discontinuous creation—to the moment-by-moment exis-

1. *Works,* 6, 398.
2. While JE never denied that Christ's suffering the punishment due to sin was a satisfaction of the inner justice of God, his emphasis on the *perceived* (and hence "public") justice led Joseph Bellamy and others of his disciples to accept the governmental theory of the atonement.

tence of the soul. The danger that his doctrine of perception could destroy the perceiving soul becomes clear in No. 267, where he is using it to prove the existence of God: "The mere exertion of a new thought is a certain proof of a God." There must be "something that immediately produces and upholds that thought." It cannot be "antecedent thoughts, for they are vanquished and gone . . . But if we say 'tis the substance of the soul (if we mean that there is some substance besides that thought, that brings that thought forth), if it be God, I acknowledge; but if there be meant something else that has no properties, it seems to me absurd." The removal of all properties from a "substance" leaves nothing.

That this conclusion was not an accidental aberration becomes clear in one of Edwards' last writings, a loose leaf on which he jotted some "Notes on Knowledge and Existence." After "How real existence depends on knowledge or perception," the next two items are: "From hence show how all union and all created identity is arbitrary" and "How God is as it were the only substance." He then confronts "that objection, that then we have no evidence of immaterial substance," and answers, "True; for this is what is supposed, that all existence is perception. What we call body is nothing but a particular mode of perception; and what we call spirit is nothing but a composition and series of perceptions, or an universe of coexisting and successive perceptions connected by such wonderful methods and laws."[3] One way of reading this metaphysical analysis is that, instead of guaranteeing the value and immortality of intelligent creatures, Edwards' doctrine of perception leaves God finally alone, talking to a reflection of himself in a mirror. That, of course, was not Edwards' intention, but it is curious that he never seems to have been aware of this potential objection.

SPIRITUAL LIGHT AND ITS IMPLICATIONS

Edwards' sermon on I Cor. 2:14 was one of the first new sermons he wrote for use at Bolton in the fall of 1723. It is a good example of how Edwards used sermon composition as an occasion for theological speculation and viewed his sermons, not as discontinuous from, but complementary to his private notebooks. There is no entry in the "Miscellanies" during the same general period that brings together so many aspects of Edwards' theology of conversion as does this sermon. Its doctrine is, "There is a spiritual understanding of divine things, which

3. *Works, 6*, 398.

all natural and unregenerate men are destitute of." The two parts of the doctrine embody Edwards' deeply held beliefs about conversion and its effects on the soul. In the first place he seeks to distinguish spiritual understanding from all merely "notional" knowledge, no matter how orthodox or sophisticated. It is a "taste" or "sense" of the beauty and excellency of divine things, a direct, immediate, intuitive and self-authenticating knowledge of their truth and reality. Edwards labors hard to describe this knowledge in experiential terms: it is a "lively apprehension," "a certain seeing and feeling" that is "deep intense and affecting." It is the difference between having a notion that honey is sweet and actually tasting its sweetness. But precisely because it is direct and immediate it is true knowledge; hence he calls it spiritual "light." There is also a "reflex knowledge" by which the soul can look inward and see the Spirit at work regenerating and renewing. In all these expressions Edwards is talking about the religion, devotion, and contemplation of God's glory that he had affirmed as God's end in creating the world.

This knowledge is "spiritual" because it comes from the Spirit of God. Those who lack the Spirit "have no principle of nature within them from whence this spiritual knowledge can be elicited; all that is within them despises it and is repugnant to it." Their minds are so gross, earthly, and filthy that they have no more comprehension of the affairs of the spiritual man than a beast or a worm has of human affairs. "There is such a contrariety that we may as soon expect to make friends of fire and water, or of light and darkness, as to make the natural man receptive of spiritual understanding." There seems no way to bridge the chasm, for "God will never give his Spirit and spiritual knowledge to natural men while they yet remain loathsome and filthy."

Yet God does indeed give his Spirit in regeneration: "he sanctifies and purifies the soul before he makes it the receptacle of things so pure and precious." In regeneration a "new nature" is given, new "principles" of action are infused, and the heart is utterly transformed, for with the new nature comes spiritual knowledge: "Just as if a new spirit were infused into that body, of an angel of darkness [it] has made an angel of light . . . has made him of an heavenly temper and an angelical mind, has sweetened and mollified his disposition, and of an heart of stone hath made a heart of flesh, of bitter has made sweet and of dark has made light."

Edwards is, of course, talking about irresistible grace, the "infused habit" (Nos. l, 73) that instantaneously transforms the governing disposition of the soul, the new "principle" without which no saving action, not even repentance, can be performed (No. 77). These descriptions of the reborn and sanctified soul are also similar to those by which he had characterized holiness, faith, devotion, and religion in his New York miscellanies—utterly alien in the degree of its ascetic discipline and single-minded contemplation of Deity to life as lived by most even of his pious neighbors.

This sermon is significant for several reasons, not the least of which is the fact that it contains the first full presentation of Edwards' doctrine of spiritual light and anticipates in almost every point the 1734 *Divine and Supernatural Light*. But three things may be noted in the sermon that express aspects of Edwards' developing theology.

1. Human understanding of divine things, so long as it is merely intellectual, consists only of "notions" that have no saving efficacy; it becomes a "spiritual" light only when it is accompanied by a "sense" or "taste" that is surely an affective response to the object of knowledge. Yet Stoddard, whose *Treatise Concerning Conversion*[4] is echoed more than once in this sermon, saw the saving vision of God's glory as an enlightenment of the understanding which then moves the will. Edwards sometimes uses this language, but when he speaks of the saving liveliness of the apprehension of good he always imports affective or volitional characteristics into the understanding.[5] In No. 489 he defines the "sense of the heart" wholly in those terms. Edwards was not totally satisfied with the traditional distinction of intellect and will, and he was strongly influenced by the Hebraic concept of knowledge as involving acknowledgment and intimacy.[6]

2. The "reflex knowledge" (Locke's term) by which one may discern the workings of grace in the soul, is akin to the intuition of divinity Edwards had spoken of in No. aa. This had been his own experience,

4. Chs. 7–15 especially are devoted to the converting action of spiritual light.

5. E.g. Nos. 27b, 123, and 126, where the key terms are "disposition" and verbal forms of "affection," and No. 489, where JE makes the same distinction as in the sermon on I Cor. 2:14 between purely intellectual knowledge and a sense of good and beauty that he specifically relates to the will. For the traditions of intellectualism and voluntarism in New England Puritanism before JE, see Norman Fiering, *Moral Philosophy at Seventeenth-Century Harvard: A Discipline in Tradition* (Chapel Hill, Univ. of North Carolina Press, 1981), pp. 104–46.

In No. 123 JE says that one can really have an idea of (i.e. understand) love or benevolence only to the extent one's disposition is loving or benevolent.

6. In what may have been a late entry in "The Mind" he writes, "How the Scriptures are ignorant of the philosophic distinction of the understanding and the will, and how the sense of the heart is there called knowledge and understanding" ("Subjects to be handled," no. 14 [*Works*, 6, 389]).

and it was his comfort when doubts arose because he had not undergone the "preparatory work" that Puritan divines had stressed. Writings during his last months with Stoddard suggest that this inward knowledge may indeed be the "Spirit's witness" to one's grace.[7]

3. Although Edwards had previously said as much in sermons and miscellanies, this sermon provides an opportunity to call attention to what the twentieth-century Protestant theologian, Karl Barth, might have described as an "infinite qualitative difference" between those who have received spiritual light and those who have not. The "loathsome and filthy" condition of the latter contrasts *toto cælo* with the "heavenly temper" and "angelical mind" of the former.[8] Religion is so contrary to natural men because "sin has brought them down nearer to the beasts, a sort of animals uncapable of religion at all" (No. ll). Edwards soon speculated further on the condition of the unregenerate, but some note should be taken of the regenerate, the spiritually enlightened, as he describes them here.

What Edwards came to regard as his conversion was not to the kind of Christian living that most Puritan pastors would have expected of their converts, but to what the medieval church would also have called "religion," a full-time pursuit of the counsels of perfection, the moral heroism of the monastic life and the mystic abstraction of the medieval saint. The "Diary" shows that Edwards himself could not live on that plane for long at a time, a fact that he admits in Nos. 123 and 126 and later allows to be true of others (No. 462). But the fact that he usually described the godly life in such absolute terms may help explain the difficulty many of his congregation experienced in gaining an assurance of grace and the fury with which his people turned on him when he began to demand what looked to them like the profession of a regenerate state.[9] Most of his entries in the "Miscellanies" on the visible church concern practical matters of ministry, polity, worship, admission, and discipline; generally, when he speaks of the church theologically, he has in mind only the saints, the church of the elect.

7. No. 375 and "Faith," in Worcester rev. ed., 2, 608–10; see above, p. 44. In 1729 and 1730, however, we find him placing greater emphasis on the more external and visible signs of grace (e.g. Nos. 462 and 488).

8. See JE's characterization of the "godly" and the "wicked" in No. 39.

9. Something similar happened among the clergy whenever an awakening began in a congregation; they expected the excitement and the conversions to continue indefinitely, since they were a work of the Spirit. When these phenomena subsided they attributed it to the machinations of Satan and berated their people for resisting the Spirit, as JE did in the period between the Northampton revival of 1734–35 and the Great Awakening.

EXCELLENCY AND THE CHAIN OF BEING

Very soon after writing the sermon on spiritual light Edwards drafted an essay entitled "Excellency."[1] Edwards had earlier used the term "excellency" in a general way for high quality, beauty, and attractiveness. But in No. 42 he contrasts the magnitude (expanse, bulk, motion) and beauty (harmony, proportion) of the physical world with the "true and real greatness and excellency" of the spiritual world. The former are "but shadows of greatness" and "shadows of excellency." The coordinate terms "excellency and greatness" (of God) occur again almost immediately in No. 44. In his sermon on spiritual knowledge, excellency is the distinguishing characteristic of divine things that is sensed or tasted by the spiritually enlightened soul. From all this it seems that Edwards has linked the being and excellency of God analogically with the understanding and will of man. One other indication of the direction of his thinking is found in No. 27b, where he describes faith, "a reception of Christ with the faculties of the soul," as not only "a believing of what we are taught in the gospel" but also "a consent of the will or an agreeableness between the disposition of the soul and those doctrines." When Edwards had finished the sermon on spiritual light he was ready to explore the excellency to which the will consents.

After stating that excellency is our prime, indeed only concern, Edwards begins his search for a definition of excellency from the notion that it is "harmony, symmetry, or proportion." After a series of diagrams presenting the classical view of beauty as balanced and proportional relationships, in which "particular disproportions" may be tolerable when they contribute to the more general beauty, he illustrates this from the beautiful relationships between the parts of plants and animal bodies, the harmony of music, and the impact of light, color, and odor on the sense organs. Above all these are spiritual harmonies, where "the proportions are vastly oftener redoubled, and respect more beings, and require a vastly larger view to comprehend them."

Edwards' explanation of why inequality and disproportion are disagreeable is a highly compact passage which the reader will recognize as relevant to Edwards' theology in more than one respect. This, he says, is

1. The essay, with its four addenda, is in *Works, 6,* 332–38.

> because being disagrees with being; which must undoubtedly be disagreeable to perceiving being, because what disagrees with being must be disagreeable to being in general, to everything that partakes of entity, and of course to perceiving being. . . . Disagreement or contrariety to being is evidently an approach to nothing, or a degree of nothing, which is nothing else but disagreement or contrariety of being, and the greatest and only evil; and entity is the greatest and only good. And by how much the more perfect entity is, that is, without mixture of nothing, by so much the more excellency.

Finally Edwards arrives at "an universal definition of excellency: The consent of being to being, or being's consent to entity. The more the consent is, and the more extensive, the greater is the excellency."

It is difficult to overemphasize the "degree and extensiveness" of the influence Edwards' conception of excellency (as developed in this and subsequent essays on the subject in "The Mind") had on his theology. The concept, in particular, contributes to the "openness" of Edwards' system. Only major "corollaries" can be noted here, however, for illustrative purposes.

1. Edwards' universe is a classical universe, in which, *ultimately,* all is order and harmony because it reflects the order and harmony of God's attributes (No. 38). Edwards is not a cosmic optimist in the sense of believing that all possibles must be actualized—both creation and election testify to God's freedom to choose—his universe is more like Leibniz' compossible universe, in which all things that God has chosen to exist fit together in total harmony. This becomes an explanatory principle; for example, sinners can be exhorted to strive, and saints to persevere, by pointing out that the means as well as the end were all decreed together as one harmonious whole (No. 29).

A correlate of Edwards' classical universe is his historical optimism. Christ as Mediator will rule until he has put all enemies under his feet, Antichrist will be overthrown, the saints will rule with Christ in the millennium over an enlightened and evangelized world, Satan will finally be defeated, and after Christ delivers up his mediatorial kingdom to the Father the glory of God manifested in the happiness of the saints will continue to all eternity. Hence Edwards' frequent insistence that the experience of evil is necessary to the knowledge of good, from mankind's first taste of the tree of knowledge to the glorified saints' contemplation of hell torments (Nos. 122, 172, 234, 279). More metaphysical are his attempts to prove the *felix culpa*, that the race is better off on account of the Fall (which brought redemption and restoration) than if Adam had never sinned (e.g. No. 158). Since happiness comes from consent to being and misery comes from dissent, there must finally be a surplus of happiness over misery, not a mere equality of the two.

It must further be noted that the actions of one being on another are all immediate divine acts and that a "cause is that, after or upon the existence of which, or the existence of it after such a manner, the existence of another thing follows."[2] This happens according to the "rules" by which God has chosen to act. But these rules all have to do with order, harmony, and beauty (No. 177). If one asks what, then, necessitates that this should follow rather than that, or why anything at all should follow, Edwards' answer is that this is more "fitting" or "condecent" than that. This is his explanation for why faith is the act that justifies: it unites to Christ and makes it therefore fit (*naturally* fit, not morally,) that God should impute the righteousness of Christ to the believer (Nos. 412, 416).[3] And though God makes sinners holy (in regeneration) before he confers happiness upon them, it is only because "it would be a grating, dissonant and deformed thing for a sinful creature to be happy in God's love" (No. 314). So there is a sense in which the only causal necessity in Edwards' system is aesthetic.

2. Edwards' universe is also ordered according to the great chain of being, which extends from inanimate objects to God (Nos. tt, 178). Only spirits are properly substance, and their excellency, their consent to being, is love.[4] The world of physical objects, including non-human animals, also has its beauty, but that is only a shadow or type of the beauty of spirits.[5] God is being in general, and in God being and excellency are one.

When excellency as well as substance is considered, the degree of consent to being introduces a further gradation, for it regulates the

2. "The Mind," no. 26 (ibid., p. 350).

3. The distinction between natural and moral fitness is made in JE's 1734 "Justification by Faith," where he explains natural fitness in purely aesthetic terms (Worcester rev. ed., *4*, 72–73).

4. "The highest excellency . . . must be the consent of spirits one to another. But the consent of spirits consists half in their mutual love to one another" (3rd addendum to "Excellency," *Works, 6*, 337). This is why JE can say that faith "arises from a principle of love" (No. 411) or from an "agreeing or consenting disposition" (No. 218).

5. Hence natural conscience, which sees only the "secondary beauty" manifest in the constitution by which good works are rewarded and bad ones punished, cannot lead to true repentance without supernatural grace (No. 472).

degree of the closeness creatures have to God. Dissent from being, the opposite of consent to being, diminishes excellency and therefore being. Though "particular disproportions" in bodies may be necessary when they add to the general beauty, they remain in themselves instances of dissent. The dissent of spirits, however, is a more serious matter, for the consent of spirits is love, love of God and other spirits. This love must be in proportion to the excellence of its object. God is most excellent, because he infinitely consents to his infinite being.[6] In "The Mind" no. 45, Edwards carefully delineates the conditions making for increasing degrees of dissent and thus of deformity. This produces "such contrarieties and jars in being as must necessarily produce jarring and horror in perceiving being." Therefore, "dissent from such beings, if that be their fixed nature, is a manifestation of consent to being in general; for consent to being is dissent from that which dissents from being."[7] And "if so much of the beauty and excellency of spirits consists in love, then the deformity of evil spirits consists as much in hatred and malice."[8] This is why God must hate the unconverted sinner temporarily and the reprobate eternally, and why the saints will hate and loathe those of the damned who have been most dear to them in this life.[9] Some of the most opprobrious aspects of Edwards' theology are direct extensions of his conception of excellency.

Since Edwards' dictum that dissent from being is "a degree of nothing" also applies to spirits, Edwards comes out with two hierarchies of being. In one, God and spirits (intelligent beings) alone have substance, i.e. real being, in contrast to the world of matter, which contains

---

6. "But yet a lower kind of love may be odious, because it hinders or is contrary to a higher and more general. Even a lower proportion is often a deformity" (*Works, 6,* 338). This is one reason why, in No. nn and elsewhere, the slightest sin against God is infinitely heinous and why, in *True Virtue,* no love is truly virtuous when given to any system of being less than God (*The Works of Jonathan Edwards, 8, Ethical Writings,* ed. Paul Ramsey [New Haven, Yale Univ. Press, 1988], 541–42). Something similar applies to JE's view of the natural world. One moment he can be ecstatic over its beauty (Nos. 42, 108), and at another lament "that the lower corporeal world has not its primitive beauty, but that only the ruins are to be seen" (No. 186).

7. *Works, 6,* 363.

8. Ibid., p. 338.

9. In his sermon of March 1733 on Rev. 18:20, JE not only describes such a judgment scene but points out that it is now our duty to love the wicked simply because we do not yet know which ones God loves as his elect. The sermon was posthumously published under the title, "The End of the Wicked Contemplated by the Righteous: Or the Torments of the Wicked in Hell, No Occasion of Grief to the Saints in Heaven" (Worcester rev. ed., *4,* 287–99; see esp. p. 293).

only shadows of being. In the other, the ontological chasm divides God and those spirits that consent to being in general from those spirits that dissent from being and, since they are good for nothing, *are* nothing.[1]

Not long after writing "Excellency" Edwards wrote his first entry on the Trinity (No. 94). It has already been noted that he made use of his idealism when explaining that the Son is the "perfect idea" of the Father as God the Father sees himself reflected in the Son. Using the analogy between the soul and God (in both there is the self, its knowledge, and its love), Edwards came to the same conclusion as did Augustine, that the Holy Spirit is the love whereby God loves himself, the love between the Father and the Son. This is God's excellency, for "his infinite beauty is his infinite mutual love of himself."[2] God must be a Trinity, for, as Edwards wrote in an addition to "Excellency," "One alone . . . cannot be excellent; for in such a case there can be no manner of relation no way, and therefore, no such thing as consent."[3] Edwards' "rational account" of the Trinity also derives from his meditations on excellency.

Shortly after writing No. 94, Edwards combined his views of Trinity and excellency to explain both the fact of creation and its end. Part of God's excellency is goodness, the desire to communicate happiness; since no finite being can receive all the goodness God is capable of communicating, God must have an eternal object, which is the Son (No. 96). Hence the creation is not necessary for God. "But yet the Son has also an inclination to communicate himself, in an image of his person that may partake of his happiness: and this was the end of the creation" (No. 104). As his body and his spouse, "the church is said to be the completeness of Christ (Eph. 1:23) . . . The Son is the fullness of God, and the church is the fullness of the Son of God." Given the

1. This duality in JE's ontology helps explain his often confusing use of the words "man," "men," and "mankind." Sometimes they simply mean the human race. But when he argues that mankind is happier for having fallen and been redeemed than would have been the case had there been no fall, the word is an empty abstraction (to all but a medieval realist), for the happiness to which the damned contribute by their misery belongs only to the glorified saints. The words often refer only to the elect or the saints or the church. "Man" or "men" sometimes refers to the fallen race or the unregenerate among them, i.e. the "natural man."

JE had, of course, inherited from early and medieval Christian philosophy the notion that sin as not-being diminishes an otherwise good nature; but there it was usually coupled with the proposition that, as Augustine put it, "whatever is, is good." So far as I know, JE never considered, as Origen did, whether the devil still has a good substance in which his evil inheres (Origen thought he did and was therefore redeemable).

2. "The Mind," no. 45, § 4 (*Works, 6,* 363). JE returned to this theme frequently in the "Miscellanies," as was noted in the preceeding section.

3. Ibid., p. 337.

permanence of the incarnation, this is a daring speculation, for it suggests an extension or unfolding of the Trinity: "In this also there is a trinity, an image of the eternal Trinity; wherein Christ is the everlasting father, and believers are his seed, and the Holy Spirit, or Comforter, is the third person in Christ, being his delight and love flowing out towards the church. . . .[and being received] flows out towards the Lord Jesus Christ" (No. 104).[4] That this is something more than a mere analogy appears in No. 487, where the union of Christ with the church by the Spirit is taken as the model for understanding the union of the Logos with the man Jesus by the same Spirit.

Since the original spiritual creation has been ruined by the fall, the creation of the spouse is accomplished by the work of redemption. This work also flows out from within the Trinity, from the eternal covenant of redemption between the Father and Son to the incarnation of the Son, his life, death, and resurrection, the gathering of the elect, Christ's final triumph over all his enemies, and the marriage supper of the Lamb. And the centerpiece of this drama, the atonement, is the supreme revelation of the love at the heart of the Trinity: "The divine excellency of Christ and the love of the Father to him, is the life and soul of all that Christ did and suffered in the work of redemption" (No. 483).[5]

The themes which have been discussed in this section interpenetrated, though they did not replace, the doctrines of Puritan Calvinism in Edwards' theology. Certainly they grounded those doctrines more securely in his personal religious experience and intellectual apprehension; they also enabled him not only to defend Calvinism for his own day but to modify it in subtle ways that left a decisive imprint on the theology of his successors. Even where these synthesizing ideas fail to achieve the complete harmonization of the doctrines among themselves and with reason that Edwards sought, or even point to unreconciled contradictions, they reveal a questing spirit and a speculative mind of high order. Edwards' distinctive ways of thinking about the ultimate issues of human existence led him to insights that make the "Miscellanies" and the other writings of his youth well worth reading today.

4. Sang H. Lee calls this outflow a "self-enlargement" of the Trinity. For Lee, JE's understanding of the relation between habit and act received its most significant application in his treatment of this doctrine. See Lee's *Philosophical Theology of Jonathan Edwards* (Princeton, Princeton Univ. Press, 1988), pp. 170–241.

5. No. 483, written in the fall of 1730, simply elaborates the view of the atonement that JE had succinctly stated in 1722 (No. b).

3. The Dating of Edwards' Early Manuscripts

Since Sereno E. Dwight published his biography of Edwards in 1829, chronology has had an inordinate influence on the interpretation of Edwards' thought.[6] Dwight was the first biographer to concern himself with the dating of Edwards' manuscripts, and his inaccurate chronology of the early scientific and philosophical writings became a venerable tradition for nearly a century and a half, taken for granted by practically all interpreters of Edwards' life and thought.[7] Dwight portrayed Edwards as a remarkably precocious child, composing sophisticated scientific and philosophical papers between the ages of ten and fourteen. Wallace E. Anderson, whose introduction to Edwards' scientific and philosophical writings contained the first systematic challenge to Dwight's chronology, points out the mischievous influence of this legacy:

> Subsequent accounts of Edwards' early life that are based upon the mistaken dates have consequently projected a distorted picture of his intellectual development. . . .Such recently debated questions as the sources of Edwards' thought, the relations between his scientific and philosophical interests and his theology, and the modernity of his thought, are all affected by assumptions concerning the order and dating of his private manuscripts.[8]

The outstanding example of how Dwight's chronology can be exploited is Perry Miller's well-known biography, in which Edwards is portrayed as a genius so remote from his own time that he is still ahead of ours today.[9]

Overcoming the weight of Dwight's legacy is the first difficulty that attends the effort to provide a chronology for Edwards' manuscripts. Other difficulties are of a more practical nature. Except for sent letters, sermons, and official documents, Edwards' early manuscript

---

6. Dwight ed., *1*.

7. There have been a few dissenters. Georges Lyon acutely criticized Dwight's dating of "Being" and "The Mind" in *L'Idéalisme en Angleterre au XVIIIᵉ siècle* (Paris, 1888), pp. 429–33. More recently, Alfred O. Aldridge raised questions about a childhood date for the insect and spider papers, though he accepted Dwight's dates for JE's early philosophical writings (*Jonathan Edwards* [New York, Washington Square Press, 1964], pp. 3, 8–10).

8. *Works, 6*, 2–3. Anderson's arguments challenging Dwight's dating of the early scientific and philosophical writings are presupposed in the present volume; see ibid., esp. pp. 1–37 and the notes to individual MSS.

9. *Jonathan Edwards*, pp. xii–xiii, 37–38 et passim.

corpus contains very few dates. Prior to 1733, Edwards did not date his sermons, and only two manuscript letters are extant from the period covered by the present volume.[1] Furthermore, in his private writings Edwards seldom identified the event, circumstance, or literary work that occasioned his choice of subject matter, though in later years he became more careful to document his use of printed works.

The absence of dates on Edwards' early manuscripts and the paucity of external evidence (which will be summarized later) means that internal evidence of another sort must be sought in the effort to determine approximate dates of composition for the "Miscellanies" and Edwards' other early writings, i.e. such physical evidence as the manuscripts themselves may offer. This comes mainly from four sources: the paper Edwards used, the ink with which he wrote, his handwriting in its successive styles, and his orthography.[2] None of these resources is by itself sufficient to establish a date, nor can the "Miscellanies" be dated in isolation from other manuscripts. If these four sorts of evidence are used in conjunction with one another, however, and if the "Miscellanies" is studied in relation to other manuscripts in the corpus, an approximate chronology can be arrived at for all of Edwards' early writings.

RESOURCES AND THEIR USES

1. Paper and Watermarks. The manufacturer's marks on the sheets of paper are the most basic source of evidence used in the dating of Edwards' manuscripts. Most research into the dating of documents by their paper does so by identifying, if possible, the paper mill from which a specific sheet came and then discovering, from mill records or dated samples of various kinds, the span of time during which the author in question is likely to have been using it. Even if this information could be obtained for any particular paper that Edwards used, it

1. These are JE's letter of Dec. 10, 1722, to the Bolton pulpit committee (MS, Connecticut Historical Society; printed in John A. Stoughton, *Windsor Farmes* [Hartford, 1883], pp. 84–85) and the Spider Letter, dated Oct. 31, 1723 (New-York Historical Society MS collection; printed in *Works*, 6, 163–69).

2. A helpful introduction to all these forms of evidence will be found in Joe Nickell, *Pen, Ink & Evidence: A Study of Writing and Writing Materials for the Penman, Collector, and Document Detective* (Lexington, University of Kentucky Press, 1990). This book addresses primarily the dating of discrete documents, however, not the establishment of a chronology for the entire manuscript corpus of a particular author. An example of a study of the latter sort is Thomas H. Johnson, "Establishing a Text: The Emily Dickinson Papers," in *Art and Error: Modern Textual Editing*, ed. Ronald Gottesman and Scott Bennett (Bloomington, Indiana University Press, 1970), pp. 140–54.

would only be accurate to within five to ten years.[3] For the closer dating attempted here, a method was used that depends upon identifying not the dates of a paper's manufacture or availability for purchase but the dates during which it appeared in Edwards' manuscripts.[4]

"Foolscap" was the standard writing paper and was used by Edwards for his permanent notebooks, sent letters, and all his sermons until the 1740s.[5] Until the latter 1720s most of his paper was of Dutch or Flemish manufacture; English papermaking began a period of rapid development only after 1713.[6] Each full sheet of standard foolscap contains both a watermark and a countermark.[7] The watermark proper is most

3. See Thomas L. Gravell and George Miller, *A Catalogue of Foreign Watermarks Found on Paper Used in America 1700–1835* (New York, Garland Publishing, 1983), pp. xiv–xv; and Dard Hunter, *Papermaking Through Eighteen Centuries* (New York, William Edwin Rudge, 1930), pp. 294–95.

4. Alan E. Shapiro used a very similar method to date the manuscript of Isaac Newton's *Optics*. See his article "Beyond the Dating Game: Watermark Clusters and the Composition of Newton's *Optics*," in *The Investigation of Difficult Things: Essays on Newton and the History of the Exact Sciences in Honour of D. T. Whiteside*, ed. P. M. Harman and Alan E. Shapiro (Cambridge, England, Cambridge Univ. Press, 1992), pp. 181–227.

5. For the characteristics of foolscap, see above, p. 10, n. 2. The writings of Dard Hunter on papermaking have been indispensable, especially his *Papermaking: The History and Technique of an Ancient Craft* (2d ed. rev. and enl. New York, Knopf, 1947). A more recent study is Bo Rudin, *Papermaking: A Look into the History of an Ancient Craft,* trans. Roger G. Tanner (Vällingby, Sweden, Rudins Publishers, 1990). E. J. Labarre, ed., *Dictionary and Encyclopaedia of Paper and Paper-Making* (2d ed. rev. and enl. Amsterdam, Swets & Zeitlinger, 1952) is a mine of information on paper and watermarks. Allan H. Stevenson's pamphlet, *Observations on Paper As Evidence* (Lawrence, University of Kansas Libraries, 1961) is an excellent general introduction, with illustrations. *Essays in Paper Analysis,* ed. Stephen Spector (London, Associated Univ. Presses, 1987), ranges widely over the field, but none of the pieces addresses the problem of a single MS corpus.

The books found most helpful for identifying the marks in JE's paper were W. A. Churchill, *Watermarks in Paper in Holland, France, etc. in the XVII and XVIII Centuries and Their Interconnection* (Amsterdam, Menno Hertzberger, 1935); Thomas L. Gravell and George Miller, *A Catalogue of Foreign Watermarks*; and Hendrick Voorn, *De Papiermolens in de Provincie Noord-Holland* (Haarlem, De Papierwereld, 1960). Two specialized studies have proved especially useful: David L. Vander Meulen, "The Identification of Paper without Watermarks," *Studies in Bibliography, 37* (1984), 58–81, and Allan H. Stevenson, "Watermarks Are Twins," ibid., *4* (1951–52), 57–91.

6. Donald C. Coleman, *The British Paper Industry, 1495–1860: A Study in Industrial Growth* (Oxford, Clarendon Press, 1958), pp. 18–100; Stevenson, *Observations on Paper As Evidence,* p. 9. Even paper bearing English marks was sometimes manufactured on the continent, imported at London, and re-shipped to the American colonies, for example, the London/PD and London/PvL papers in JE's MSS. No paper has been found among JE's MSS carrying marks from any of the fledgling colonial papermakers.

7. All the paper JE used was "laid" paper. Instead of the wire mesh on the paper mold being "wove," as gradually became common after 1755, it was made by stringing wires about an inch apart widthwise of the mold and, upon them (looking from underneath the mold) a mesh of fine wires placed lengthwise of the mold. On a sheet folded in folio the fine

often a heraldic device, such as the London, English, or Amsterdam arms. The countermark often served as a kind of trademark; it might be merely a decorative figure (e.g. a post horn), a set of initials (e.g. I V for Jan Villedary, P D for P. Dürring) or a monogram (e.g. PvL for Pieter van der Ley).[8]

The watermarks in the paper are the chief means for identifying Edwards' various paper purchases. However, because two different batches of paper may have the same set of watermarks, it is necessary to discern additional differentiating characteristics. An important variable is the position of the marks on the sheet. Both may be centered in their respective half-sheets, one may be centered and the other not, or both may be off-center to left or right. The location of marks vertically on the half-sheet and the space between a mark and the nearest chain lines are often significant. Within the marks themselves there are variations in the location and shape of elements within a mark owing to the design or execution of the figures or the presence of broken or skewed wires. Even the slightly jagged edges left by Edwards' knife may help in reconstructing a sheet or deciding the contemporaneity of the writing on two pieces of paper.

"laid" or "wire" lines are horizontal and the thicker "chain" lines vertical. To these were attached wires forming the watermark designs, one in the middle (usually) of each half-sheet.

The larger mark or "Watermark" proper (Wm) was usually in the right half-sheet and the smaller mark or "countermark" (cm) in the left half-sheet with the "right" or wire side facing the viewer and the marks reading correctly. Paper molds were made in pairs, the watermarks on one of the molds usually being mirror images of those on the other, so that the marks on half of the sheets from a vat read correctly only with the wire side away from the viewer. Hence in a batch of evenly mixed sheets the molds would be represented in multiples of two, the number of pairs depending on the number of vats from which the paper came.

8. The watermarks have been identified and standard nomenclature derived from the compilations listed in n. 3 above. For examples of watermarks found in JE's early MSS, see Appendix B. Short titles will be used for reference: the Wm (usually abbreviated), a slash [/], then the cm. Thus "Vreyheyt/horn," "London/PvL," "English/GR" (crowned GR for Georgius Rex); a "GR^{wr}" means that the crowned GR is enclosed in a wreath. When the cm is attached to the Wm it is called a "cipher"; this does not occur in any of JE's early MSS. There is a set of initials (probably CH) attached to the English Wm found on the first quire of "Natural Philosophy," but there is also a cm in the other half-sheet.

Close study and comparison of marks was greatly facilitated by the light table available in Beinecke Library. During 1973–74 the Library possessed a plastic plate of carbon-14 isotope by which several radiographs of watermarks were made. These have made possible the reading of marks in heavy or badly overwritten paper and greater accuracy in distinguishing between papers with similar marks but from different molds. Light pencil tracings, cheap but time-consuming, were also used for rough comparisons. Various new methods for reading watermarks have been developed since most of the present study was concluded; see, for example, Gravell and Miller, *A Catalogue of Foreign Watermarks*, pp. xi–xii.

Perhaps the most useful variable besides the watermarks themselves is the pattern left by the chain lines. These should match exactly for sheets made on the same mold; between these and sheets made on the mold's "twin" the match is likely to be slightly off but in a pattern recognizably the same. The feathery (or "deckle") edge left by the cover (deckle) that fitted on and framed the top of the mold helps identify the portion of a sheet from which an unmarked piece of paper comes. The deckle edges at the two ends of the sheet also provide the starting points for measuring the distance from them to the first chain line and from that to the next. These distances were often fairly uniform for paper from different vats but apparently from the same mill.[9] The pattern of the first two or three chain lines has been especially useful (though the others must match also) for assigning sermons to one or the other of contiguous batches of paper that have watermark or countermark in common; it is especially useful when a sermon or other manuscript can be approximately located by hand and ink but presents no watermarks at all.[1] (Fig. 1 illustrates the chain line pattern as well as the appearance and location of the watermarks on the half-sheets.)

2. Ink and Pen. In addition to their watermarks, Edwards' manuscripts can be identified by means of the appearance of the ink on the page.[2] Up through the eighteenth century, almost all permanent writing ink was of the iron-gall type, which in the eighteenth century was

9. The first chain wire from the deckle edge is called the "tranchefile"; unlike the other chain wires it was not laid on a wooden backing strip (which collected extra fibers that produced a contrasting "bar shadow") and hence usually left a fainter line in the paper. Its position varies considerably from one brand of paper to another.

1. JE cut his paper for duodecimo sermon booklets in such a way that a watermark occurs only on one double leaf out of three. In quarto booklets the marks are cut in two laterally and the halves occur in the spine at top or bottom. The same is true of octavo booklets, except that now each double leaf possesses only one-fourth of the mark. While the booklets remain sewn, close comparison of marks is well-nigh impossible—hence the great value of chain line patterns. These patterns also become increasingly important from the 1730s onward because of the near identity of watermarks between batches of paper sufficiently separated in time to have come from different mills, apparently because bought by different mills from the same watermark manufacturer. See the article by Vander Meulen (above, n. 5), also Gravell and Miller, *A Catalogue of Foreign Watermarks*, pp. xiv–xv.

2. Most of the descriptions of ink in this section refer to its appearance under a binocular microscope at 20-X magnification. Under the microscope, specimens that look identical to the naked eye may prove to be quite different in texture and even shade. Also, the depth dimension furnished by the binocular feature has made it possible to assess the effect of paper surfaces on the appearance of the ink. See below, Appendix D, for illustrations of different ink textures.

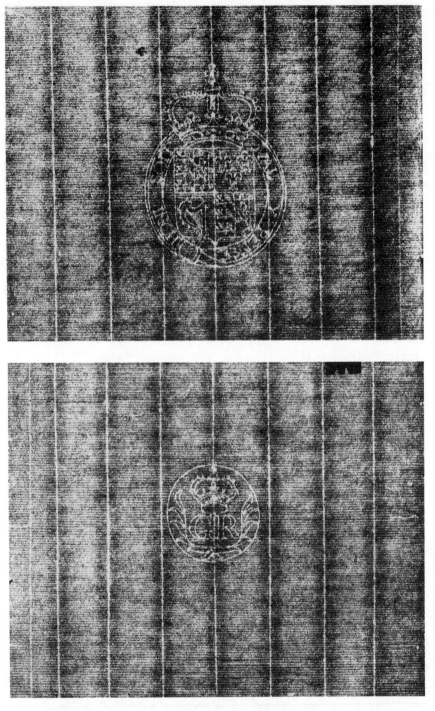

Fig. 1. Details of the first sheet of English GR^wr paper in the "Miscellanies," center portions showing the watermark (above) and countermark (below), along with the deckle eges and pattern of chain lines.

usually made at home by recipe.[3] This sort of ink was usually black when first applied, but as a result of oxidation its appearance now ranges from black or gray to various shades of brown. The factors determining these changes include the process employed in its manufacture, the proportions and purity of its ingredients, and the degree of its subsequent exposure to air and sunlight.[4] The ink was more of a suspension than a true solution; it colored the paper mainly by depositing its solids on the surface, though the action of the acid on the paper was also a factor. This deposit was vulnerable to abrasion, and faint-looking ink is often the result of wear rather than the original thinness of the ink.[5]

Texture is also helpful in distinguishing between inks. If the solids in an ink were fine, they formed a smooth coat, but if the coat was too heavy it might break off in spots, producing a mangy appearance. Sometimes the solids seem to have been deposited in large specks, causing a grainy texture. In some instances they caught on the rims of the pen strokes and the fibers of the paper in distinctive ways. Other variables include the amount of gloss, the apparent viscosity of the ink, its tendency to blot or bleed, and the presence of mold or other surface film.[6]

Not only did the ink vary from batch to batch, the same brewing might fluctuate in appearance with stirring, thinning, or addition of ink to the well. Furthermore, an ink that flowed onto smooth paper rather generously might skip over a rough surface, leaving unfilled holes and valleys; therefore the quality of the paper needs to be taken

3. A typical recipe called for two or three parts oak galls to one part copperas (ferrous sulphate), with about four parts gum arabic (to stabilize the mixture and improve the flow of the ink), steeped in water for two or three weeks with frequent stirring to hasten the "fermentation" that brought color to the salts. The mixture was then strained. Vinegar, wine, or other spiritous liquor was sometimes used as the vehicle, and sugar was sometimes added to produce a shine (it could also produce mold). By mid-century it was possible to buy an already ground mixture of the ingredients ready for soaking. Much information will be found in William J. Barrow, "Black Writing Ink of the Colonial Period," *American Archivist*, 11 (1948), 291–307. See also Nickell, *Ink and Evidence*, pp. 35–39.

4. Generally, the higher its acid content, the browner the ink now appears. Hence ink on paper that became watersoaked soon after writing usually did not turn brown, and the same is sometimes true of ink excessively thinned.

5. The kind of ink that was made in the East Windsor household, at least through the mid-1720s, had solids that easily eroded, a fact that sometimes helps in locating the place where JE was writing.

6. It should be noted that there are practically no signs that JE used sand for drying his ink; he apparently laid a fresh composition aside to dry. He also seems never to have made erasures with a knife (the usual method), but simply to have crossed out the rejected material.

into account when comparing ink on different manuscripts. The possibility must occasionally be considered that Edwards was using two different kinds of ink at the same time.[7]

The condition of the pen also affected the appearance of the ink. The goose quills that Edwards used were well suited to the ink and could be kept at the desired sharpness and flexibility by the use of a penknife.[8] The marks left by a pen of unusual character (for example a stiff stubby pen), especially if associated with a particular texture of ink, can point to contemporaneous passages in two or more manuscripts. The sharpening of the pen during the writing of a passage may subtly change the appearance of the ink and create the impression of a new sitting, but in such a case a change in the pen is usually accompanied by a noticeable change in the ink as well.[9]

3. Handwriting. Familiarity with the successive styles of Edwards' hand is a valuable asset for chronological study, although handwriting never stands alone as evidence for a date.[1] Since changes in Edwards' hand are seldom abrupt, it is only occasionally a decisive factor. Nevertheless, handwriting can often suggest the range within which, in conjunction with other means, closer dating can be accomplished.

Edwards' "public" writings, such as sent letters, minutes of meetings, and the rare "fair copy" of a treatise, are very legible and remarkably uniform in appearance over the last twenty years of his life. At the other extreme, manuscripts written carelessly or in great haste, such as letter drafts, memoranda, temporary notebooks, and most of the

7. Wallace Anderson uses a two-ink theory to date some of the manuscripts from JE's graduate years at Yale (*Works*, 6, 178, n. 1). After JE's student days, however, there is little evidence that he was writing out of two ink wells, for stretches of thinned ink most often precede the arrival of what appears to be a fresh brewing, suggesting that JE was stretching out his supply until a new ink became available.

8. Nickell (*Ink and Evidence*, pp. 3–8) describes in detail the making and maintenance of quill pens.

9. To say that a certain piece of writing was done at a "sitting" (a 19th-century term that is still useful), refers to a uniformity of appearance resulting from the precise color and density of the ink and the texture of the line left by the pen. For example, Sereno Dwight states that "the first twenty-one [resolutions] were written at once, with the same pen; as were the next ten, at a subsequent sitting" (Dwight ed., *1*, 67n.).

1. For handwriting styles in colonial America, see E. Kay Kirkham, *How to Read the Handwriting and Records of Early America* (Salt Lake City, privately published, 1961) and Laetitia Yeandle, "The Evolution of Handwriting in the English-Speaking Colonies of America," *American Archivist*, 43 (1980), 294–311. These works are very helpful in reading colonial manuscripts and suggest the kinds of variations to look for, but identification of the successive styles of an individual author's hand requires frequent study of the MSS over time.

Stockbridge sermon outlines, are difficult to decipher. Here the hand is often so formless as to defy reading, let alone close dating. Between these two extremes lie the vast majority of Edwards' manuscripts: the permanent notebooks such as the "Miscellanies," the fully written sermons, and various individual compositions. Manuscripts in this category are more legible than those intended only for temporary use, and changes in his hand are more discernible than in writings intended for eyes other than his own. Most of the manuscripts included in the present study are, fortunately, of this last type.

Edwards' earliest writing was rather print-like. In his late teens and twenties, as he strove for a more cursive style, his hand changed rapidly, making it especially valuable for dating purposes. In his graduate years it was often relatively large and sprawling; during the months in New York he brought down the size of the letters, but there was tremendous variation in their size and slant, even within a single word. In the year following Edwards' return from New York his handwriting remained very small but the individual letters gained in distinctness and in the "roundness" that Dwight considered a product of his undergraduate years. At the beginning of his tutorship his hand loosened up, and when it became more controlled it was slightly larger, more angular, and less well formed than before. These characteristics continued through his first year as Stoddard's assistant, with a slow but steady growth in speed, angularity, and the amount of space between words and lines of script. In his second year the hand picked up speed and accordingly lost in precision. For a while after Stoddard's death in February 1729 it became somewhat erratic in directionality, then settled down into a still more rapid script with less well defined letters. This trend continued into the early 1730s, with gradual modifications in the shapes of letters and a gradual increase in their size and in the spacing of words and lines.[2]

In the latter 1730s, Edwards still formed his letters with some care and spaced his words evenly. By the early 1740s his script had begun to take on the more acute slant to the right that characterized his later hand, and it soon became permanent. Letter formation was more spiky and angular and the words were more spread out. Edwards increasingly ran letters together, so that a stroke of the pen sufficed for two or more letters in commonly repeated groupings, usually at the

2. A selection of specimens illustrating the development of JE's hand to 1733 is found in Appendix C. Note that adjacent specimens may look a good bit alike, but as the time span increases differences become more apparent.

endings of words. In his last years the size of his hand increased, and his formation of individual letters became poorer since he less frequently picked up his pen between them. They also became more stretched out and looser, resulting in fewer words per line. Edwards' last hand was predominantly horizontal in appearance, with shortened vertical strokes and the loss of almost all roundness, even the backward loop of the lower-case *d*.

4. Orthography. Because Edwards quickly became a good speller, changes in his orthography are most useful in dating the manuscripts of his college and graduate years.[3] By the time he began the "Miscellanies" his spelling had become, with few exceptions, what it was to be for the rest of his life. In its early pages we still find "whither" (for "whether"), "wherin," "satisfie," and a few archaic forms like "restauration" and "smoak"; but the "att" and "verry" of the college letters are gone, and the doublet *ll* has disappeared from words like "eternal" and "natural." On the other hand, though Edwards spelled "deceit" correctly, he continued to use the spellings "concieve," "recieve," and "percieve," an error which he apparently never noticed until 1745 but which he then corrected after a short period of occasional backsliding.[4] In the late 1740s and 1750s Edwards' spelling of some words changed as he sought to imitate more elegant English models, e.g. from "rejoice" to "rejoyce," "virtue" to "vertue," and "ancient" to "antient." He also occasionally experimented with his method of scripture citations, abandoning arabic chapter numbers for capital roman numerals (e.g. Gen. XXVI. 1 instead of Gen. 26. 1).

The presence of abbreviations is sometimes significant. The archaic forms "y^e" and "y^t" appear almost exclusively in the earliest writings. After that only the ampersand and "X" for Christ are found, until suddenly, shortly after Stoddard's death in early 1729, Edwards introduced a plethora of radical abbreviations, first in his sermons and then in other writings. He began with "G." (God), "Sp.," (Spirit), "H. G." (Holy Ghost), and a few others, later adding the symbol ⊙ for "world" and abbreviations like "Gr." (grace) and "Righ." (righteousness).

---

3. See *Works*, 6, 149–50, 184–86. As with JE's handwriting, the following description of the evolution of his orthography is in large part the result of a dating of the MSS in which orthography was only occasionally a decisive factor.

4. JE's account book of 1733–57 documents the change; its precise beginning is not clear because of a missing leaf.

About the same time he began in the sermons to use a long dash to represent the rest of a Scripture quotation or a frequently repeated expression that he would fill out in the pulpit. These are all helpful when estimating the date of pre-1733 sermons and miscellanies. As for punctuation, there was a great increase in the frequency of commas in the New York sermons and miscellanies; probably meant to indicate pauses, these were very erratically placed and had mostly disappeared by the end of 1723. Thereafter, punctuation is sparse in Edwards' private writings and is of little or no chronological value.[5]

ESTABLISHING A CHRONOLOGY OF THE EARLY MANUSCRIPTS

Book 1 of the "Miscellanies," which contains all the entries in the present volume, originally consisted of separately folded sheets, written one at a time and later sewed together.[6] These sheets contain many different kinds of paper as evidenced by their watermarks. If the sheets of Book 1 are separated into groups according to their various watermarks, a pattern of paper use emerges. The first two sheets exhibit one set of marks, the next two another, the next six a third, and so on.[7] That this sequence of papers is not peculiar to the "Miscellanies" is shown by the fact that other manuscript notebooks made of separately folded double leaves have similar series of marks.[8] As will be seen, the undated sermons also contain papers having most of the same sets of marks found in the "Miscellanies" and in much the same order. This discovery led to a set of working hypotheses: for most of the period under study, Edwards was writing sermons and notebook entries with some regularity,[9] he drew on current stock for both, his

5. JE apparently did not discover the usefulness of the parenthesis until near the end of 1725. The first one in the "Miscellanies" occurs in No. 173, then one in No. 201, and thereafter with some regularity.

6. Dwight ed., *1*, 56. The folios of Bk. 1 had already been separated when the MS came to Yale in 1900. It was probably Dwight who took the book apart to facilitate its transcription.

7. See below, Fig. 2, pp. 71–72, where these are listed in the order of their occurrence in the "Miscellanies."

8. The first book of Scripture notes offers a good example. It begins with nine separately folded double leaves in 4to. The first two are London/PvL; the third is either London/PvL or London/GR. The fourth (in the order of its first entries) is London/GR, the fifth Amsterdam/MvL, and the last four English /GR[wr]. These are followed by a quire of four infolded double leaves made from a sheet of the London/GR paper JE bought in 1731.

9. The preparation of a chronological index to the dated sermons has revealed that there are sermons extant for almost every month from 1733 to 1750. Most of the new sermons after that date were written for the Housatonic (Mohican) and Mohawk Indians at Stockbridge.

paper purchases were of modest size (at least in his early years),[1] and he usually exhausted one supply before starting on another.

Of the various manuscripts in the corpus of Edwards' writings, the collection of sermons (over a thousand) is greatest in quantity, has the longest total time span, and, consisting of discrete units, is most manageable. Over 260 sermons are extant that were presumably written before 1733.[2] A preliminary sorting of these sermons reveals a dozen watermark-countermark combinations.[3] Hand and ink comparisons with the "Miscellanies" and other notebooks make it possible to distinguish more exactly the succession of watermarks in the paper Edwards used. For example, sermons on London/PvL paper appear in two different periods and sermons on English/GR^{wr} paper in three. There must have been three purchases of London/GR (countermark centered in the half-sheet), and another group of sermons with the same marks comprises two successive smaller sets, depending on whether the countermark is to right or left of the center of the half-sheet. As a result, around twenty different batches of paper can be found in the sermons prior to 1733. There are also a few sermons on mixed paper that were written during the transitions from one batch of paper to another.[4] These more numerous sets of watermarks can then be lined

1. Before he went to Northampton, JE's paper purchases (judging from the extant MSS) were small, seldom amounting to more than one or two quires (24 or 25 sheets per quire). Only at New York, and to a lesser extent at Bolton, had he needed a regular supply of paper for sermons. From 1727 onward his paper requirements increased greatly, especially after he became sole pastor in early 1729. His largest paper purchase before 1733 contained the London/GR and English/GR papers; it was probably made at Boston in the summer of 1731. Purchases from local suppliers were still limited to a quire or, at most, a quarter-ream (five quires), as invoices found in sermons of 1742–44 show. This paper was expensive; 24 sheets could cost as much as a spelling book or a sickle and twice as much as a pair of scissors.

2. Fifty others lacked dates for one reason or another but were found to belong among the post-1732 sermons.

3. These are Amsterdam arms, with either AAB or MvL countermark; English arms with GR (crowned GR) or GR^{wr} (in wreath) cm; English-CH with GR^{wr} cm; London arms with GR, IV, PD, or PvL cm; Maid of Dort with CAW cm; Seven Provinces with HVT cm; and Vreyheyt with horn cm. For examples of these marks see Appendix B, and for their occurrence in chronological order see below, Fig. 2 (pp. 71–72).

4. A "batch" and a "purchase" of paper are not necessarily the same thing. JE may have bought, say, two quires of paper having different marks at the same time but used up one before starting on the other. There are also three cases in which a purchase apparently contained paper of two different kinds that JE put into service at about the same time, one into sermons and the other into the "Miscellanies" and other notebooks. The first sheets of London/GR and London/PvL paper were probably part of one purchase in the fall of 1723. Most of the London/GR was used for sermons (also for the spider letter), whereas only one extant sermon was made wholly of London/PvL paper and the rest devoted to notebooks. A batch of London/PD and one of English/GR^{wr} paper begin at nearly the same time, the

up with the "Miscellanies" sheets, along with the number of sermons displaying each set of marks. (See Table 1.)

Table 1. Watermarks in the Early "Miscellanies" and Sermons through 1732

	Number of sermons	Number of sheets in "Miscellanies"
1. English-CH/GR^{wr}	1	
2. Vreyheyt/Horn	4	
3. Mixed paper[5]	1	
4. Amsterdam/AAB	18	2
5. Seven Provinces/HVT	2	2
6. London/GR	8	
7. London/PvL		6
8. London/PvL and English/GR^{wr}	3	
9. London/GR	3	2
10. Amsterdam/MvL	19	1
11. Mixed paper	7	
12. London/PvL	7	
13. Fleur de lis/EYD		1
14. English/GR^{wr}		8
15. London/PD	18	
16. Mixed paper	4	
17. London/GR (R)	9	
18. Mixed paper	1	
19. London/GR (L)	28	

(continued)

---

former in the sermons and the latter mostly in the "Miscellanies" and other MSS. The same is true of the last two papers before 1733, the English/GR going into sermons and the London/GR into the "Miscellanies." Differences in the behavior of pen and ink on different papers suggest that JE usually devoted the smoother paper to sermons.

5. Groups of sermons identified as mixtures contain leaves from both the preceding and the following batch of paper. In some cases they also contain leaves from miscellaneous sources, such as discarded scraps (the largest being the dismantled index JE had made for "Scripture" in 1726 [item 27]), unused paper he had laid up in a notebook (e.g. English/GR^{wr} paper, probably from the "Miscellanies," in item 16), and what may have been borrowed paper (e.g. the "Maid of Dort" paper in item 25).

Table 1. (*Continued*)

	Number of sermons	*Number of sheets in "Miscellanies"*
20. Mixed paper	3	
21. English/GR^wr6		1
22. London/IV	22	1
23. Mixed paper	4	
24. English/GR^wr	23	1
25. Maid of Dort/CAW and other paper[7]	6	
26. London/GR[8]		9
27. English/GR and "Scripture" index[9]	5	
28. English/GR[1]	66	

Once a tentative order of Edwards' "Miscellanies" sheets and sermon groups is established, certain things come to attention. The first two papers in the list do not occur in the "Miscellanies," and their sermons appear by hand, ink, and orthography to have been written earlier than the first pages of the "Miscellanies." The first sermon paper that is also found in the "Miscellanies" furnished the first large group of sermons, indicating a period of regular preaching such as Edwards engaged in at New York in 1722–23.[2] There is only one watermark combination in the "Miscellanies" that does not appear in the sermons (except for one probably unrelated scrap in a later ser-

6. Though it follows 8 sheets of English/GR^wr paper in the "Miscellanies," this sheet comes from the new batch of English/GR^wr that furnished both the sermons and another sheet of the "Miscellanies" in item 24.

7. Maid of Dort is the most prominent paper in this mixture, which also contains some of the previous English/GR^wr paper and several kinds of discarded paper.

8. These nine sheets carry the "Miscellanies" from mid-1731 to the end of 1732. Book 1 (which probably extends to 1735) also contains 13 more sheets beyond these: 7 London/GR (doubtless from the same batch as the preceding 9), 2 English/GR^wr, 1 London/GR, and 3 English/GR^wr.

9. See below, pp. 88–89.

1. These 66 sermons are the last undated sermons (JE began supplying dates in Jan. 1733). The English/GR paper continues in the dated sermons to mid-1733, but whether from the same paper purchase has not yet been determined.

2. The date of the first entry in the "Miscellanies" is discussed below, pp. 76–79.

mon), the Fleur de lis/EYD sheet. The same is true of the large batch of London/GR paper that begins in the "Miscellanies" at the same time as the long run of English/GR sermons that extends into the dated sermons of 1733; both are therefore considered the last papers Edwards was using before 1733.[3] Prior to these last papers, there are seven groups of sermons that correspond in hand and ink with sheets in the "Miscellanies" having the same marks; these provide a kind of framework around which the other groups can be tentatively located.

After the first large group of Amsterdam/AAB sermons there is a succession of different watermarks in both sermons and miscellanies but few sermons, doubtless representing the time between 1723 and 1726 when Edwards had less need to write new sermons. These are followed by another large group of sermons on Amsterdam/MvL paper, and much paper is devoted to sermons from that point on. The Amsterdam/MvL sermons thus probably begin in 1727, when Edwards would have begun to feel the need to write new sermons with some frequency.

When estimating the time occupied by these groups of sermons, it has been assumed that during periods of steady preaching Edwards wrote sermons regularly and that they have survived at a fairly uniform rate.[4] The proportion of sermons to miscellanies cannot be assumed to have been constant. As already pointed out, Edwards wrote

3. The sermons and miscellanies written in mid-1731 are discussed below, pp. 88–89.

4. Estimating the survival rate of the sermons is difficult. Only one or two of the New York sermons looks like a lecture (long doctrine, short application), and it is possible that JE preached there only on the two Sunday occasions each week. Dwight says that while JE was Stoddard's colleague he preached at one of the two Sunday services and gave a weekly lecture (Dwight ed., *1*, 110). Three sermons a week was the standard homiletical fare at the time. None of the early sermons is labeled as a lecture, and among the dated sermons the few that are so designated are usually very substantial compositions, such as might be delivered on special occasions.

JE had probably had about 60 preaching occasions at New York unless he gave a weekly lecture, and his extant sermons through April 1723 represent about 30. Except for 6 or 7 new sermons he repreached old sermons at Bolton, and only one and part of another sermon survive from his tutorship until near its end, when he was preaching at Glastonbury. From JE's arrival at Northampton to the end of 1732 he would have had something over 800 preaching occasions if he gave a weekly lecture, and about 500 if he did not. The 230 sermons extant for that period, when additional preaching units (installments) in multiple sermons are included, come to about 330 such units. In the first case the survival rate would be about two-fifths, in the second, three-fifths. A guess that about half have survived may not be far wrong. It is probable that proportionately fewer of the pre-Northampton sermons have survived, in view of the evidence that Edwards incorporated large sections from older sermons in new ones and even rewrote some, discarding the original sermons, during his first year at Northampton.

many more entries than sermons while a tutor; for well over a year after his arrival at Northampton and at times in later years he depended heavily on older sermons. The amount of writing he did in the "Miscellanies" also must have varied from time to time. These facts have to be taken into account when estimating the passage of time from the amount of Edwards' writing in sermons and notebooks.

When seeking to refine the rough chronology sketched above one can turn to the few external sources of information respecting Edwards' life and writings. The first biography of Edwards, the *Life and Character*, written only a few years after his death by his long-time friend and disciple, Samuel Hopkins, is generally reliable.[5] Where Dwight was not following Hopkins he sometimes had access to letters and other materials that have since disappeared, and his editions of the "Diary," "Personal Narrative," and other writings contain valuable information even though the manuscripts may no longer be extant. Contemporary letters and diaries occasionally make reference to Edwards or to matters that concern him in some way. A set of auditor's notes dates two sermons of September 1727, and another set dates several sermons in March-May 1731.[6]

Sermons at times include internal evidence that can serve as chronological indicators. One comes from the regular spring fast ("day of humiliation") and fall thanksgiving days set by the governor's proclamation and therefore dateable. Once the major groups of sermons are located in approximate time periods, enough of these fast and thanksgiving day sermons can be identified to sharpen considerably the accuracy of each group's time span. There are other such occasions, like the annual election day in May and, for Northampton, opening sessions of the county court.[7] Edwards himself identified one sermon as "upon the fast for the earthquake," which was held on December 21, 1727. To these should be added the sacrament sermons that came eight weeks

---

5. See above, p. 2, n. 5.

6. The first set of notes by an unidentified author occur in a few leaves folded in 8vo. in the Trask Library; the second were written on similar leaves by Lieutenant Joseph Hawley; they are now among the Major Hawley papers in the New York Public Library.

7. The focus of the election-day celebration was in Boston, and only *the* election sermon delivered there was printed. But there must have been local celebrations (as there were in Connecticut—see No. 193) and there are sermons of JE that have content as well as hand and ink that seems to fit the May event. At least one sermon is associated with a meeting of the county court. Other public addresses may be identified as the study of the sermons continues.

apart; several sacrament sermons have been approximately dated and a few sermons immediately preceding them identified.[8] Occasionally a sermon contains a dated or datable piece of paper, such as a marriage certificate or a prayer request mentioning a birth or death. The asterisks and shorthand notes of repreachings on sermons also at times yield information on Edwards' whereabouts and activities.[9]

Throughout his ministry, Edwards regularly wrote both sermons and miscellanies; hence the parallels between these two manuscript series are more extensive and complete than those between the "Miscellanies" and any other type of manuscript. This does not mean, however, that other manuscripts do not enter into the dating process. Several notebooks and manuscripts have contributed to the dating of the "Miscellanies." In turn, they have been assigned dates from their relation to various sermons or miscellanies through ink, paper, or content. The beginnings of "The Mind," "Notes on the Apocalypse," "Notes on the Scripture," "Faith," "Images of Divine Things," "Essay on the Trinity," and others have been located by these means, and successions of entries in most of them have aided in closer dating of the "Miscellanies."[1]

CHRONOLOGY OF THE EARLY "MISCELLANIES"

The following discussion illustrates how the procedures described above have been applied to the chronological problem. For this purpose, several biographical landmarks in Edwards' career between 1722 and 1731 have been chosen, and the technical procedures are described through which their approximate location in the "Miscella-

8. In his *Faithful Narrative* of the 1734–35 Northampton revival, JE stated that "our sacraments are eight weeks asunder" (*A Faithful Narrative of the Surprising Work of God*, in *The Works of Jonathan Edwards, 4, The Great Awakening*, ed. C. C. Goen [New Haven, Yale Univ. Press, 1972], 157). The second set of auditor's notes makes it highly probable that the sacrament sermon on I Cor. 11:28–29 was preached on Mar. 21, 1731. The substantial accuracy of forward projection by eight-week intervals is confirmed when it is extended into the dated sermons of 1733; calculation of sacrament days prior to the dated sermon is less successful but has turned up a few sacrament sermons, along with sermons containing an announcement of the forthcoming occasion.

9. For example, the shorthand annotations indicate that JE preached at least eight sermons at Glastonbury during the spring and summer of 1726 after the death of the pastor in April. Evidence gained from asterisks is discussed below in connection with the length of JE's pastorate at Bolton.

1. Parallel entries in these and other MSS are listed in "The 'Miscellanies' and Chronological Parallels," below, pp. 91 ff.

nies" manuscript has been determined. It should be noted that, as a result of efforts to ascertain a chronology of the early "Miscellanies," in some instances the dating of these landmarks differs from what is found in the standard biographies of Edwards.

1. First Entries in the "Miscellanies." Several lines of evidence converge on the beginning of the manuscript. Comparison with the "Natural Philosophy" shows that its first essays and the two numbered series through Long Series no. 44 and Short Series no. 21b, which Anderson places between late 1720 and the summer of 1722,[2] precede the first page of the "Miscellanies."[3] This is also true of Edwards' earliest extant sermons, the one written on English-CH/GR^{wr} paper and the four bearing Vreyheyt/horn watermarks. The Vreyheyt sermon on Matt. 16:26 may precede the summer of 1722, but the others, though still larger in hand, have a gray-brown ink that is closer to the preceding "Natural Philosophy" entries than to the first entries of the "Miscellanies."[4] The sermon on Zech. 4:7 is made of both Vreyheyt/horn and Amsterdam/AAB paper; there is less of a gray tinge in its light brown ink, which is very near in shade to some of the eighteen Amsterdam/AAB sermons that follow it and to the first entries in the "Miscellanies." Its hand is also similar in the size and shape of letters to the small script with which the "Miscellanies" begins. Since Edwards still had some Vreyheyt paper on hand in early December,[5] these sermons and others on the same paper (but now lost) may have lasted well into the fall of 1722!

Edwards' eight months in New York gave him his first opportunity for regular preaching. The Amsterdam/AAB sermons all have similar

2. *Works, 6,* 185–86.
3. The large hand with which "Natural Philosophy" begins had decreased in size and the orthography was nearly that of the first entries of the "Miscellanies" by that point in both series; the next entries in both have ink and hand contemporaneous with miscellanies in the 30s. Also, "Miscellanies" No. f was almost certainly written as an extension of Long Series nos. 26 and 44. See note to No. f.
4. Their orthography is also close to that of the "Miscellanies," except for the sermon on Heb. 9:27, in which JE was experimenting with a number of traditional abbreviations and organizational strategies; see Kimnach's note to that sermon (*Works, 10,* 352–53).
5. Letter to the pulpit committee of Bolton, Dec. 10, 1722 (Library of the Connecticut Historical Society, Hartford, Conn.). Both paper and ink are badly oxidized, but hand and ink seem compatible with those of the latter Vreyheyt sermons. That the MS of this letter was extant I learned only recently from Kenneth P. Minkema, whose help has also been of great value in estimating its relation to the New York sermons and notebook entries.

hand, ink, and orthography, and they treat themes Edwards later recalled as being prominent in his thoughts at that time.[6] There can be little doubt that they were written in New York.

In the "Personal Narrative" Edwards followed a generally chronological order, and he was explicit about his dependence on the "Diary" for his account of his experiences in New York.[7] He also mentioned in the "Personal Narrative" some "contemplations" on holiness that he had written while there:

> I remember the Thoughts I used then to have of Holiness. I remember I then said sometimes to my self, I do certainly know that I love Holiness, such as the Gospel prescribes. It appeared to me, there was nothing in it but what was ravishingly lovely. It appeared to me, to be the highest Beauty and Amiableness, above all other Beauties: that it was a *divine* Beauty; far purer than any thing here upon earth; and that every thing else, was like Mire, Filth and Defilement, in Comparison of it.
>
> HOLINESS, as I then wrote down some of my Contemplations on it, appeared to me to be of a sweet, pleasant, charming, serene, calm Nature. It seem'd to me, it brought an inexpressible Purity, Brightness, Peacefulness & Ravishment to the Soul: and that it made the Soul like a Field or Garden of GOD, with all manner of pleasant Flowers; that is all pleasant, delightful and undisturbed; enjoying a sweet Calm, and the gently vivifying Beams of the Sun. The Soul of a true Christian, as I then wrote my Meditations, appear'd like such a little white Flower, as we see in the Spring of the Year; low and humble on the Ground, opening it's Bosom, to receive the pleasant Beams of the Sun's Glory; rejoycing as it were, in a calm Rapture; diffusing around a sweet Fragrancy; standing peacefully and lovingly, in the midst of other Flowers round about; all in like Manner opening their Bosoms, to drink in the Light of the Sun.[8]

6. The first part of JE's "Diary" was written in New York; his "Personal Narrative," though written in the early 1740s, recalls his first converting experiences and pays special attention to his spiritual state in New York. Hopkins printed the first and best transcription of the "Personal Narrative" (*Life and Character*, pp. 23–39) but only excerpts from the "Diary." The Dwight ed. contains the "Diary" in Vol. 1 but breaks it into installments. Both MSS have since disappeared.

7. E.g. direct references to his entries for Jan. 12 and May 1, 1723.

8. Hopkins, *Life and Character*, pp. 29–30.

Although Edwards used the "Diary" as a source when writing the "Personal Narrative," this passage is not drawn from the "Diary" but from No. a, which Edwards later marked as the first entry in the "Miscellanies."[9] A comparison of the two texts reveals that he has copied in these paragraphs over 120 words from No. a.[1] Also notable is the frequency of his temporal references, e.g. "I remember the thoughts I used *then* to have of holiness. I remember I *then* said sometimes to my self. . . .Holiness, as I *then* wrote down some of my contemplations on it. . . ."[2] These and other such temporal references show that Edwards meant to contrast his new experiences and meditations with those that preceded his trip to New York.

There is other manuscript evidence that bears on the date of the first entry. It is almost certain that Edwards began his "Catalogue" of books after arriving in New York.[3] For several years he kept it on single quarto leaves and only later made it into a book by adding quires. The first leaf, though unmarked, has the chain line pattern of the Amsterdam/AAB paper. Its first dozen entries were probably made in one sitting, in hand and ink similar to those on the last three Vreyheyt sermons, and nos. 13–14 resemble the mixed sermon on Zech. 4:7. The next entry is very close in appearance to the first few entries in the "Miscellanies," and nos. 16–25 run parallel in ink and hand to the rest

9. No. a was probably not the first entry JE penned in the "Miscellanies." It now heads the first verso of the first sheet (what is now the second page) of Bk. 1. Nos. a–e on that verso and No. m at the top of the second recto all have a cursive style of heading and a full horizontal line after each entry, both of which were abandoned in subsequent entries. Also, No. l, which begins near the bottom of the verso, is concluded beneath No. m on the recto.

One or two double leaves have been discovered where JE accidentally began on a verso, but the most reasonable explanation for the present instance is that JE folded a sheet of Amsterdam/AAB paper and on its recto began a series entitled "Types of the Scriptures" (in larger script than any of the others on these pages) and made one entry under it. Before he had entered a second type, however, he had begun recording meditations, beginning with No. a, on the other side of the folded sheet. This must have happened shortly after the types entry. Having reached the bottom of the page, JE turned the sheet inside out, and filled the rest of the recto under the typological entry. He then filled the other side of that leaf and finally what is now the first recto. Hence No. m may actually have been his first entry; in any case it was written before No. f and subsequent entries. It would be another year before he began a new series of Scripture types.

1. This quotation by JE constitutes the main evidence Keith Reinhart offered for placing the beginning of the "Miscellanies" "sometime during the period of JE's stay in New York" ("A Comparison of the Writings of Jonathan Edwards Concerning God's End in Creation as Found in His Early Unpublished 'Miscellanies' and in a Dissertation Posthumously Published," [M.A. thesis, Eugene, Univ. of Oregon, 1941], p. 31).

2. Ed. italics.

3. On the "Catalogue," see above, p. 5, n. 5.

of the lettered entries. The first fifteen entries, coupled with the identity of the paper, suggest that the first entries in the "Miscellanies" and the first Amsterdam/AAB sermons began about the same time and shortly after the last Vreyheyt sermons. That the "Catalogue" was not commenced much earlier than August or September, and probably even later, is made likely by the fact that item no. 6 is Richard Blackmore's *Redemption,* a poem published in 1722.

The above factors support a date near the end of 1722 for the commencement of the "Miscellanies." "Diary" entries bearing on matters discussed in miscellanies and sermons suggest that the first entry was made in November or December of that year and put the beginning of the double alphabet shortly after the turn of the year 1723.[4] Several content parallels between Amsterdam/AAB sermons and miscellanies suggest that the later New York sermons were being written in tandem with entries in the double alphabet during the winter months.[5]

2. The Return to East Windsor. It is known that Edwards returned to his parents' home in East Windsor late on the last day of April 1723, but the event left no obvious mark on the manuscripts. Several factors make probable a location around the earliest numbered entries. Beginning with Nos. 8–14, Edwards shows an interest in ecclesiological topics; such topics would probably still have been under discussion in East Windsor because of Cutler's defection to Anglicanism in September 1722. Furthermore, the fact that several entries in the 30s are topics related to justification suggests mid-summer, when he was writing his M.A. thesis.

A consideration of the ink of the earliest numbered entries makes it possible to determine with greater precision the entry in the "Miscellanies" that corresponds to Edwards' move to East Windsor. With No. 1 the rich brown ink of the lettered entries takes on a slight gray tinge,

4. E.g. the Diary for Dec. 18 may be contemporaneous with No. r, that for Dec. 19 with No. s, and Resolution 38, made on Dec. 23, with Nos. w and x. JE made a visit home probably in the latter part of November—he mentions having recently returned to New York in his Dec. 10 letter to the Bolton Committee—and he may have begun the "Miscellanies" shortly before or after that trip. The first six entries were written close together, and less than a page of text separates them from No. r.

5. E.g. the sermon on Ps. 89:6 with Nos. ff, gg, and nn, that on Phil. 1:21 with No. oo. The sermon on Matt. 5:3 and No. ff are closely related in content, and JE's writing of several passages in the sermon praising poverty of spirit may have inspired the Diary for Mar. 2 (a Saturday, when JE would have been reviewing his next sermon).

which gradually increases; by No. 10 the surface becomes less uniform, by No. 17 the solids are more noticeably wearing off, and by the 30s the ink is clearly the same as that being used by his father. The same ink change as at No. 1 begins on the first page of the "Catalogue" at no. 26, and the following "Catalogue" entries to the end of that page exhibit the same successions of ink. All the Amsterdam/AAB sermons are written in the brown ink of the pre-No. 1 entries except one: the sermon on John 5:3 as extant (it lacks the first and last leaves) begins in ink like that on the last lettered entries but by its last pages has acquired the same gray tint as on No. 1.[6] This succession of ink changes is best explained by the supposition that Edwards brought home a small amount of ink he had been using in New York to which he gradually added ink from the household supply.

There is one other source of evidence supporting a date in May 1723 for the composition of entry No. 1. The front cover of the "Diary" survives, and on its back are various personal memoranda. Two of these memoranda are concerned with Edwards' keeping of his 47th resolution, as are the "Diary" entries for May 11 and May 19, 1723. The first of these cover memoranda has ink no later than "Miscellanies" No. 9 and the second probably no later than "Miscellanies" No. 16. Parallels in the wording of the memoranda and "Diary" entries make it likely that they were written at about the same time; if so, Edwards had written around fifteen numbered entries in the "Miscellanies" by the end of May 1723.

3. The Bolton Pastorate. According to Dwight, Edwards spent the period between September 1723 and June 1724 in New Haven, studying at the College.[7] After John A. Stoughton revealed that Edwards had negotiated with the town of Bolton in October and accepted a pastoral call on November 11, later interpreters harmonized that information with Dwight by assuming that when Edwards was elected to the Yale tutorship he "soon" (Alvord) or "immediately" (Winslow) resigned from Bolton and went to New Haven.[8]

Two facts militate against this view: Edwards was not elected tutor until May 21, 1724,[9] and the "Diary" entries for November 29 and

6. This sermon may have been started in New York and finished in East Windsor, or even begun in Windsor before JE added ink to his well.

7. Dwight ed., *1*, 95.

8. *Windsor Farmes*, pp. 81–82; Samuel Alvord, *Historical Sketch of Bolton, Connecticut* (Manchester, Conn., Herald Printing Co., 1920), p. 22; Winslow, *Jonathan Edwards*, p. 89.

9. F. B. Dexter, *Documentary History of Yale University, under the Original Charter of the Collegiate School of Connecticut 1701–1745* (New Haven, Yale Univ. Press, 1916), p. 252.

December 12 show that as late as December 1723 he was engaged in pastoral activities.[1] The manuscripts in fact support a ministry at Bolton that probably extended into the spring of 1724. In the fall Edwards began again to write sermons. The first two that we have were written on Seven Provinces paper; five more were written on London/GR paper from a new purchase.[2] Apparently Edwards was now engaged in regular preaching. There are not enough of these sermons to account for a ministry of the length suggested unless Edwards repreached most of his New York sermons, but there is evidence that he did. All but the last of the seven newly composed sermons (the Seven Provinces and London/GR sermons) each have an asterisk on the first page that is apparently in the same ink as the sermon; most of the New York sermons have the same asterisk, not in their own ink but in the ink of the newly composed sermons. The asterisk therefore seems to mean a preaching or repreaching at Bolton. There are enough marked sermons to allow for several months of preaching.[3]

The two Seven Provinces sermons were probably written in October 1723, while Edwards was negotiating with the town of Bolton. "Miscellanies" Nos. 27b–81 were also written on this paper. These sheets probably represent the last Seven Provinces paper to which he had access.[4] During October he was probably writing entries in the 70s of the "Miscellanies."[5] The next six sheets of paper in the "Miscellanies"

1. Dwight ed., *1*, 100.

2. One corroboration of this placing of these sermons is the presence in some of them of bits of shorthand. JE apparently devised his system in October, for on Nov. 1 he reminded himself to practice "writing *characters*" (ibid.; italics doubtless added by Dwight). Shorthand occurs in the first paragraph of the sermon on Rom. 12:18, and in a draft of No. 87 on the back of the booklet, as well as in No. 94. By Jan. 10 he was proficient enough to write a long diary entry in shorthand (ibid., p. 101), and during his years as tutor he used shorthand on the cover of "Natural Philosophy" for some of his rules on style and organization (*Works, 6*, 192–195). There are also occasional shorthand insertions in other manuscripts (usually in cramped spaces), but after he went to Northampton he employed it mainly for writing notes of repreaching on his sermons.

3. The lack of an asterisk on the fast-day sermon (preached April 15, 1724), if it is not an oversight, may mean that JE had either left Bolton by that time or, more likely, that he expected to do so soon and therefore had no further need to mark his sermons..

4. One of the sermons was made of a 12mo. quire (JE was using 8vo. booklets), but cut and folded in the shape Timothy often used, suggesting that there was no more uncut stock on hand. In September, after his return from commencement, JE had used three sheets to make the 4to. quire on which he had begun his "Apocalypse" notebook.

5. The draft of JE's spider letter, though written on a leaf of English-CH/GR[wr] paper, has hand and ink identical to the last page of the Seven Provinces sheet. The sent letter (dated Oct. 31, 1723) is a sheet of London/GR paper; its hand is more formal but its ink (judging without close comparison) has the same appearance as the first entries on the new London/PvL sheet in the "Miscellanies" (Nos. 82 ff.).

were marked London/PvL, but his next five sermons were written on the London/GR paper he had bought at the same time. The first four of these appear by hand and ink to be contemporaneous with Edwards' entries from No. 82 at the beginning of the first sheet of London/PvL to No. 106, which was written at the same time as the fourth London/GR sermon (on Rev. 21:18).

The hand and ink are relatively uniform from miscellanies in the latter 80s through No. 114. Beginning with No. 115, entries are made in very small sittings, with frequent changes in ink and even hand through No. 123 near the end of the second London/PvL sheet,[6] the last entry numbered at the time of writing. These ten entries may represent a span of time almost as long as that consumed by the previous thirty. The only suggestion of a date comes from the fast-day sermon of April 15, which is closer in appearance to Nos. 116b–117 than to any other of the later entries. It seems likely, then, that Nos. 82–114 extend from November to February or early March, and Nos. 115–123 from March to May.[7]

4. Beginning of the Yale Tutorship. The beginning of Edwards' two years as a tutor (June 1724–September 1726) has been assigned to the transition from the second to the third sheet of London/PvL paper in the "Miscellanies" for the following reasons:

Edwards left the lower half of the last page of the sheet blank after No. 123. When his entries resumed with No. 126 he began a new sheet with further change in the hand and a heavier ink than that of No. 123, and did not resume his practice of numbering his entries. A bit later he took up his "Natural Philosophy," but there also he ignored the space left on the last two pages of the quire, began on a fresh sheet of the same London/PvL paper, and left the new entries unnumbered.

The "Catalogue" provides evidence that a month or two must have elapsed between Nos. 123 and 126. The faint gray ink of No. 123 appears on several items at the bottom of "Catalogue" p. 2 and the first three items on p. 3. Edwards' next entries in the "Catalogue" are on a loose unpaged leaf, the envelope of a letter of Timothy Edwards ad-

6. E.g. Nos. 115–116a, 116b–117, 118; there is a change in appearance at almost every entry thereafter. One reason for the decreased incidence of miscellanies was almost certainly JE's new "Notes on Scripture." JE wrote its first entry on a 4to. double leaf of London/PvL paper somewhere between the latter part of No. 94 and No. 106; he wrote the next 34 entries while writing only Nos. 107–123 in the "Miscellanies."

7. Nos. 82–114 (33 entries) use almost six times as much space as do Nos. 115–123 (9 entries), but JE's hand changes considerably more during the latter group of entries.

dressed to his son at the College. It is unlikely that Edwards received this letter until at least a week or so after his arrival at New Haven near the first of June.[8] Edwards had made over 50 entries, requiring many sittings, on its clean inside surface before they reached ink that matches No. 126. Therefore, it appears that for several weeks after assuming his tutorship Edwards occupied himself in the college library browsing through books. After this period of adjustment to his new situation and its duties Edwards resumed composition in the "Miscellanies" with No. 126.

5. The Move to Northampton. There are several reasons for believing that the original Nos. 236–239 (later renumbered 261–264) were the last Edwards wrote before leaving for Northampton in August 1726. The ink had become more of a crusty brown on these entries; in that ink he wrote a new sermon on John 15:5 which is related in content to the original No. 238 (now 263). This sermon, however, is marked only as preached in Northampton.

The next datable specimen of Edwards' hand and ink is the sermon on Ps. 147:1, a thanksgiving sermon that must have been preached on November 10, 1726. This and a similar sermon on Job 14:5 are written on London/GR paper and have brown ink of a quite different texture from the last ink Edwards used at New Haven. It appears on the shorthand notes of repreaching that Edwards placed on some of his earlier sermons and on his shorthand for "Northampton" that he put on new as well as old sermons as he preached them there. He also used it on an index of his Scripture notes that he made at about the same time as the earliest shorthand notes. These activities probably belong to the first weeks after his move to Northampton in September. His earliest "Miscellanies" entries in this ink must have been the entries now numbered 267–274, which he wrote on the outside recto of the London/GR sheet on the verso of which he had inadvertently written the original Nos. 236–239. His next entries, which appear to have been written after the thanksgiving sermon, were Nos. 236 ff., with which the first London/GR sheet in the "Miscellanies" commences.

One other group of entries is associated with Edwards' move to Northampton. There is a sheet of Fleur de lis/EYD paper in the "Miscellanies" containing Nos. 311–328. The first four entries, however, are in a hand that looks earlier than that of the surrounding entries,

8. Diary for June 6 (Dwight ed., *1*, 103).

and their ink is a moderately light crusty gray that seems also out of place where it is. The best match for its hand is the one found on the last entries in New Haven and the first at Northampton, and its ink looks suspiciously like ink from East Windsor. The paper also seems to have had the same origin. The most likely explanation for these entries is that Edwards borrowed a sheet while visiting at home on his move to Northampton in the latter part of September 1726.[9]

The result of these discrete sets of entries was that for a while Edwards had as many as three unfilled sheets on hand at one time. He did not fill them all before going on to other sheets because he was evidently intending to fold his sheets into quires; upon his move to Northampton he started additional double leaves in the Scripture notebook and for a while wrote in one or another of them somewhat at random. Though Edwards carried out his plan in the Scripture series,[1] he finally abandoned it in the "Miscellanies" and after filling all his open sheets continued with separately folded sheets as before.

If the aforementioned explanations of the data are correct, Nos. 261–265 (original 236–238) were Edwards' last entries in New Haven, probably in July 1726; Nos. 311–314 were written at Windsor, probably in September; and Nos. 267–274 were his first entries in Northampton, probably in October-November 1726.

6. The Earthquake Awakening. On the night of October 29, 1727, a brief but sharp earthquake shook the New England coast, killing no one but bringing consternation and fear to thousands. Local days of humiliation were observed in many churches, and on December 8 the Lieutenant Governor proclaimed December 21 a day of fasting and prayer throughout the province.[2] There were awakenings at Boston, at Deerfield, and in several other places.[3] It can also be assumed that

9. There is no other paper with these marks among JE's manuscripts except for one sermon leaf of what may have been scrap from a letter, but there is a homemade notebook of Timothy Edwards' in the Trask Library that is made of the same paper and that Timothy was using in the middle and latter 1720s.

1. After filling eight double leaves and part of a ninth, JE formed them into a quire; after numbering his notes he removed the ninth double leaf and placed it between that quire and the next, so that there are no entries numbered 180–187. Dwight dismantled the quire and renumbered the entries in the original order of the separate double leaves. These are the "Scripture" numbers used in the Chart of Chronological Parallels.

2. *Boston Gazette*, No. 421 (Dec. 18, 1727). An account of the quake and early reactions to it was carried by the Boston *Weekly News-Letter*, No. 44 (Nov. 3, 1727).

3. Thomas Prince described the revival at Boston after the earthquake in "Some Account of the Late Revival of Religion in Boston" (*The Christian History . . . For the Year 1744* [Boston,

Edwards' account of "a considerable ingathering of souls" in North-ampton while he was Stoddard's assistant refers to an awakening sparked by the earthquake.[4] On the basis of these events one sermon can be dated with near certainty: Edwards wrote "Upon the fast for the earthquake" at the head of his sermon on Jonah 3:10; this sermon must have been preached on December 21, the day of the province-wide fast. The long double sermon on Ps. 102:25–26 also refers to the earthquake as though recent; it may have been preached at the session of the county court earlier in December.

"Miscellanies" Nos. 279–305 are written on a sheet of Amster-dam/MvL paper, but on Nos. 306–310 at the end of the sheet there is a break in the continuity of hand and ink: the hand suddenly becomes larger and more careless, and the ink takes on more of a grayish tinge. It is probable that Edwards intended to leave at least some of the page blank after No. 305, which is a collection of Scripture texts teaching "That the Holy Ghost is love," for the addition of more texts. For his next entries he took up the Fleur de lis/EYD sheet, which already contained the four entries now numbered 311–314.[5] No. 315 treats justification, and No. 316, on the torments of hell, uses an *a fortiori* argument for their severity based on the biblical account of the sacri-fice of children to Moloch in the valley of Hinnom. Edwards devoted the whole of the sheet's first verso to No. 317, a study of "humiliation," the final stage of preparation that loomed large in Stoddard's theol-ogy; another entry on hell (No. 318) heads the second recto of the sheet.

Four sermons have the hand and ink of the new entries on the Fleur de lis sheet: the two that directly mention the earthquake (Jonah 3:10 and Ps. 102:25–26) and two sermons on the future punishment of the wicked (Matt. 5:22 and Gen. 19:14). All of these sermons have a mina-tory, not to say imprecatory, character; furthermore, the Matt. 5:22 sermon uses the valley of Hinnom argument found in No. 316, with much the same language. Each of the new entries on the Fleur de lis

---

1745], pp. 377–78). He regarded it as rivaled in New England, before the Great Awakening, only by the Connecticut Valley revival of 1734–35. The awakening in Deerfield is mentioned in George Sheldon, *History of Deerfield, Massachusetts* (2 vols. Deerfield, 1895–96), *1*, 463.

4. *Works, 4*, 146.

5. The slight difference in hand and ink of the new entries probably represents the weeks immediately following the earthquake, when JE would have been devoting his time to sermon writing and counseling the awakened. Nos. 306–310, which he added at the end of the Amsterdam/MvL sheet after filling the Fleur de lis sheet, show further changes in the hand.

sheet shares general awakening themes with the four sermons, and they display a concern for the process of conversion.[6] "Miscellanies" entries around No. 300 have a September-October date,[7] and the Jonah 3:10 sermon was preached on December 21, 1727. Therefore, it seems evident that the earthquake occurred shortly after Edwards had written No. 305, that he became preoccupied with evangelism and the process of conversion during November and December, and that Nos. 315–318 at least on the Fleur de lis sheet grew directly out of that concern. It also seems likely that these and the rest of the entries on that sheet, Nos. 319–328, extended through the winter of 1728.

7. Solomon Stoddard's Death. "Miscellanies" No. 329 was the first entry Edwards wrote on the first sheet of a new supply of English/GR^{wr} paper, which furnished the next eight sheets of the "Miscellanies" and carried his entries through No. 462. No. 329 was written with the last of the (now considerably thinned) brown ink he had hitherto used at Northampton. The new ink was a darker, more intense shade of brown, quite distinguishable from the preceding ink. The transition from one ink to the other occurs in the first three sermons on London/PD paper, the paper on which he wrote all his sermons until the time of Stoddard's death. The new sermons and miscellanies probably begin in mid-summer. The only datable sermon, the thanksgiving sermon on Ps. 65:11, preached on November 7, 1728, was written in the vicinity of No. 362.

Solomon Stoddard died on February 11, 1729. The sermon on Jer. 6:29–30 is almost certainly the last extant sermon on unmixed London/PD paper. This sermon must have been preached shortly after Stoddard's death, for its references to Stoddard are such as to suggest that his decease had been very recent.[8] This sermon is also the last

6. While writing his first new entries on the Fleur de lis sheet, JE began a new notebook with a 4to double leaf of Amsterdam/MvL paper, entitled "Faith." The first pages of it he filled with definitions of faith, and those mainly in terms of its experiential content.

7. The first set of auditor's notes locates two sermons in the fall of 1727: Luke 13:24 in September and the three-installment sermon on Is. 1:18–20 in late September and October. The latter sermon makes use of No. 292, quotes part of No. 299, and has content parallels with Nos. 300–301. Hand and ink make it unlikely that the sermon was written after No. 305. Hence, these entries were probably written around the same time as the sermon on Is. 1:18–20.

8. For example, in the sermon's first use JE states, "There have [been] few places that have enjoyed such eminent powerful means of grace as you of this place have enjoyed. You have lived all your days under a most clear convincing dispensation of God's Word. The whole land is full of gospel light, but this place has been distinguishingly blessed of God with excellent means for a long time under your now deceased minister."

written in the ink that ends in the "Miscellanies" at No. 395. Edwards left almost half a page blank after No. 386, probably in order to devote the whole next page to a long entry on humiliation, an entry in which he expressed unambiguously for the first time his disagreement with Stoddard over whether there was grace in the stage of humiliation. This entry is numbered 393, for Edwards later placed six entries in the preceding blank space. He then reserved the next whole page for No. 394, a discussion of conversion. For No. 395, a short entry entitled "Christian Religion," Edwards did not go back to the space he had left after No. 386 but wrote it at the top of still another page. All three entries have ink almost identical with that of No. 386. Therefore, it is likely that No. 386 was the last entry that Edwards made before Stoddard's death, though his next three entries may have been written during Stoddard's last illness.

This judgment is supported by the characteristics of five other sermons that must have been preached within six weeks of Stoddard's death. One is the sermon on II Cor. 4:7, an Amsterdam/MvL sermon that Edwards had begun in February 1727 but now completed with an application relating to the close of Stoddard's pastorate and the beginning of his own. The new material is in ink similar to that of Nos. 386, 393–395. The next four are made of mixed papers. Of these the two earliest (on Titus 3:5 and Is. 53:3) have the same kind of ink as on those entries, but the other two, on Amos 8:11 and Jer. 42:20, record the transition to the new ink that begins in the "Miscellanies" with No. 396.[9] Furthermore, these two sermons are datable: that on Amos 8:11 must have been the fast-day sermon for March 20, and the Jer. 42:20 sacrament sermon was probably preached on March 23, 1729.[1]

8. *God Glorified.* Twenty-three sermons were written on English/GR^{wr} paper and extend from October 1730 to early May 1731. The sermon for thanksgiving day, November 12 (on II Chron. 32:25) is almost identical in hand and ink to the "God Glorified" sermon on I Cor. 1:29–31, which is cited in No. 486. This probably locates in No-

---

9. The paper of the sermons confirms this ordering. As JE was running out of London/PD paper he cut some of his notebook paper for sermons. The sermon on Titus 3:5 contains some London/PD but also English/GR^{wr} paper, and the last two sermons have English/GR^{wr} paper but also leaves from his new supply of London/GR(R). The first sermon containing all London/GR(R) paper is the long series on John 16:8, which parallels about a dozen entries beginning with No. 396.

1. JE must have been working on these sermons at the same time, for he wrote part of one on a double leaf he was using for the other; discovering this, he simply cut the double leaf apart and put one leaf into each sermon.

vember 1730 the first preaching of the sermon that Edwards delivered in Boston the following July.

Beginning with the sermon on Rev. 22:3, which was preached on March 14, 1731, precise or approximate dates are available in an auditor's notes for six of the English/GR^{wr} sermons. The fast-day sermon on Num. 14:21, which was preached on Thursday, March 25, provides an approximate date for "Miscellanies" No. 491, with which it shares both ink and content. The last sermon with a definite date is the one on Matt. 11:12, preached on May 2, 1731. It was probably the last of the English/GR^{wr} sermons and was written shortly before No. 494, which seems to be a comment upon its main theme.

In the auditor's notes one more sermon follows the May 2 sermon but it is undated; it is a long five-part sermon on I Pet. 2:9. Edwards' manuscript of the sermon has very little English/GR^{wr} paper in it and may be considered the first in a group of six sermons on mixed—very mixed—paper. It has been labeled a Maid of Dort group, since there is more of that paper than of anything else; the rest is mostly scraps. The sermon on Rom. 5:7–8 in this group was probably preached on May 16, the eighth Sunday after the previous sacrament day. Most of these sermons seem to have been written around Nos. 494–495, and the one with what appears to be the latest ink, the sermon on John 15:10, is intimately related in content to both No. 496 and 497. In addition, Nos. 498 and 499 look like meditations inspired by that sermon and the two preceding entries. Hence these six sermons parallel Nos. 494–499 and probably account for the rest of May and the month of June.

At this point Edwards was able to replenish his stationery, very likely when he went to Boston to give the Thursday Lecture on July 8. Perhaps out of exasperation at his long shortage, he purchased a relatively large quantity of foolscap in two batches, one bearing English/GR and the other London/GR watermarks. The first supplied Edwards' sermon booklets for two full years. The second he reserved for notebooks and other uses; the last English/GR^{wr} sheet in the "Miscellanies" is followed at No. 506 by several sheets of the London/GR paper. In the meantime Edwards had discovered another source of reusable paper, three London/PvL sheets containing the index to the Scripture series that he had begun in 1726 but abandoned in 1728. These he cut into sermon stock which he used up along with leaves cut from the new paper. The five sermons containing both papers were probably the earliest to carry the new English/GR watermarks. The earliest of these sermons may be that on Gen. 3:24, which incorporates

No. 498, is quoted by No. 501, and is probably alluded to in No. 502. Another, the sermon on Luke 10:38–42, is cited in No. 503. The uncompleted sermon on Rev. 22:17 seems to be interrelated with Nos. 504–507, and the sermon on Rev. 17:14 may have led to the writing of No. 508. No. 508, finally, is the first of four entries containing reflections on various aspects of the work of redemption; these must have been written while Edwards was preparing for the printer the "fair copy" of *God Glorified in the Work of Redemption* in July or August of 1731.[2]

THE "MISCELLANIES" AND CHRONOLOGICAL PARALLELS

Table 2 contains a summary of parallels among the manuscripts in Edwards' corpus from 1716 to mid-1731. It not only chronicles Edwards' writing habits and the products of his pen during this period but also illustrates the complex interrelationships among his sermons, notebooks, and other manuscripts. As such it provides, in schematized form, a reader's guide to the compositions of the young Edwards that record his intellectual, spiritual, and theological development. "Miscellanies" entries composed during a given period are listed in one column, sermons in the next, and other manuscripts in the third.

In this table the positioning of two items on the same line (e.g. a set of miscellanies and a sermon) does not imply that they were written simultaneously, but only that they have been assigned to the same time period, as indicated in the far left column. "Miscellanies" entries that are out of chronological order have been placed among the other entries in what appears to have been their order of composition.[3] "Miscellanies" entries and sermons are listed under the watermarks of the paper on which they were written.[4] In the "Miscellanies" between 1726 and 1728, two papers, London/GR and Fleur de lis/EYD, appear on the table in conjunction with more than one set of entries. This is because Edwards started on new sheets while leaving others incomplete and only later filling them.[5] Within periods sermons are listed, not by

---

2. The first sentence of No. 510 paraphrases and partially quotes the first and last sentences of the last paragraph before the application of the printed sermon, but the last sentence is not in the sermon MS and must have been printed from the copy JE prepared for the press (see the text in Worcester rev. ed., *4*, 177). The commendatory preface by the Boston ministers was dated August 1731.

3. A list of all the entries in their probable chronological order will be found in the Note on the Text, below, pp. 153–160.

4. For a list of these watermarks see above, pp. 71–72.

5. See examples from 1726–28, above, pp. 83–86.

date but by the order of their texts and are also identified by number ("Is. 3:10 [1]," etc.).[6] Short titles are used for some of the manuscripts in the right-hand column, mainly "Scripture" for "Notes on Scripture," and "Nat. Phil." for "Natural Philosophy"; the parts of the latter are also specified as "Being," "Atoms," the Long Series" (LS), "Short Series" (SS), and "Unnumbered Series" (US). Items in the "Catalogue" are cited by page and by the number of the item on the page. References to "Signs of Godliness" are by page number and location on the page. Entries in "Faith" have been assigned numbers by members of the edition. Other information about individual sermons and other manuscripts is provided in the notes.

A table of this sort may acquire a spurious magisterial quality simply by existing, because of its seemingly precise order and appearance of quantification. It is important to remind the reader that the chronological judgments offered here, as well as in the Introduction and notes, have varying degrees of trustworthiness.[7] The dating of a miscellanies entry, sermon, or other manuscript depends upon an accumulation of evidence. The cumulative weight of the evidence in a few instances establishes a date as a near certainty (e.g. the approximate time of the first entries in the "Miscellanies" and the identification of the entries and sermons near Stoddard's death). More frequently, however, a date can be shifted by a month or two, one way or the other, without violence to the available data. These less certain dates are approximations intended to suggest Edwards' rate of composition.

6. These numbers were assigned during my chronological study of the early undated sermons and have been adopted for those sermons by the Edition as part of the enumeration of the whole sermon corpus. For the undated sermons, these numbers merely follow the canonical order of the texts *within* watermark groups; the sets of numbers *between* such groups are intended to suggest a chronological order.

7. The chart summarizes the results of many years' study of all JE's early extant MSS. It is not, however, within the scope of this Introduction to provide documentation for every important event, but only (as in the immediately preceding sections) for major turning points in JE's early life and ministry. For the period 1716–June 1722, most of the evidence will be found in Anderson's introduction and notes to those writings (*Works, 6,* passim).

Table 2. The "Miscellanies" and Chronological Parallels: May 1719–August 1731

DATE	ENTRIES	SERMONS[8]	OTHER
1716			ALS to Mary Edwards, May 10
1718–19			Hebrew exercise on Ps. 1
1719			ALS to Mary Edwards, March 26 ALS to Timothy Edwards, July 24
1719–20			Of Insects Valedictory Oration, Sept. 1720
1720 Sept.–Dec.	*English-CH/GR^wr*	Is. 3:10 (1)	Letter draft, Nov. 1 Letter draft to Stephen Mix, n.d.
Jan. 1721– June 1722	*Vreyheyt/horn*	Matt. 16:26 (2)	ALS to Timothy Edwards, March 1, 1721 ALS to [Mary Edwards], Dec. 12, 1721 Natural Philosophy: Atoms, Being (3 pars.); Prejudices (through prop. 2); Long Series, nos. 1–44; Short Series, nos. 1–21 Of the Rainbow

8. Identified by text, paper batch, and sermon number (in parentheses).

(continued)

Table 2. (*Continued*)

DATE	ENTRIES	SERMONS	OTHER
Jan. 1721–June 1722			Of Light Rays
1722 Aug.–Nov.		John 8:34 (3) Heb. 9:27 (4) Frag. on seeking the Lord (5)	
	Amsterdam/AAB	*Vreyheyt/horn-Amsterdam/AAB*	
Nov. 1722–April 1723	a–z	Zech. 4:7 (6)	ALS to Bolton Committee, Dec. 10, 1722 Catalogue: p. 1, nos. 1–25 Resolutions and Diary (beginning)
	aa–zz	*Amsterdam/AAB* Job 1:21 (7) Ps. 98:6 (8) Ps. 95:7–8, (9) Prov. 29:25 (10) Is. 35:8 (11) Hag. 1:5 (12) Matt. 5:3(a) (13)[9] Luke 13:5 (14) John 6:68 (15) John 8:12 (16) Rom. 12:1 (17) Phil. 1:21(a) (18)	

		Phil. 1:21(b) (19) Heb. 9:12 (20) Jas. 1:12(a) (21) Jas. 1:25 (22) I John 5:3 (23) Matt. 21:5 (24)[1]	Catalogue: p. 1, nos. 26–36
1723 May–June	1–26		
1723 July–Aug.	27b–51	*Seven Provinces/HTV*	Catalogue: p. 1, nos. 37–46; p. 2, no. 1 Nat. Phil.: SS 22–23; LS 45–48 Prejudices, prop. 3; Being, second stratum Latin Thesis
Sept.	60–64		Catalogue: p. 1. nos. 47–55; p. 2, nos. 2–16
Sept.–Oct.	65–81	*Seven Provinces/HTV* Ps. 115:1 (25) I Cor. 2:14 (26)	Catalogue: p. 2, nos. 17–21 Nat. Phil.: SS 24–25 Excellency (The Mind, no. 1) Spider Letter, Oct. 23[2] Apocalypse: chs. 1–21; nos. 1–24

9. Written at the end of Feb. or the beginning of March 1723; contemporaneous with No. ff. See Diary for March 2, 1723 (Dwight ed., 1, 83).
1. Application only. It was combined with a new doctrinal section written at Northampton; see no. 49.
2. The draft of the Spider Letter is parallel with Nos. 80–81.

(*continued*)

Table 2. (*Continued*)

DATE	ENTRIES London/PvL	SERMONS London/GR	OTHER
Nov.–Dec.	82–94	Prov. 24:13–14(a) (27); Rom. 1:24 (28); Rom. 12:18 (29)	Catalogue: p. 2, nos. 22–23; Nat. Phil.: SS 26–27; LS 49–50; Prejudices, seven postulata; Apocalypse: nos. 25–29
1724 Jan.–Feb.	94–106	Rev. 21:18 (30)[3]	Catalogue: p. 2, nos. 24–34; Nat. Phil.: SS 28, LS 51; cover leaf memos: recto, [nos. 1–3]; Verso, nos. 1–4; Apocalypse: no. 30; Scripture: no. 1
Feb.–March	107–114		Catalogue: p. 2, nos. 35–36; Nat. Phil.: LS 52–55; cover leaf memos: recto, [nos. 4–5]; verso, no. 5; Apocalypse: nos. 31–33; Scripture: nos. 2–7
March–April	115–117	Ezek. 7:16 (31)[4]	Catalogue: p. 2, nos. 37–41; Nat. Phil.: LS 56–61; Scripture: nos. 8–11

April–May	118–123		Catalogue: p. 2, nos. 42–43; nos. 44ff.(?) Apocalypse: no. 41 Scripture: nos. 12–18
1724 June–Aug.		Ps. 119:60 (32)	Catalogue: p. 2, nos. 44–56(?); p. 3, nos. 1–3 (?); p. i, nos. 1–57, 106–126; p. ii, nos. 30–54 The Mind: nos. 2–11
Sept.	126–131		Catalogue: p. i, no. 58 The Mind: no. 13 Scripture: nos. 36–38
1724 Oct.–Dec.	132–146		Catalogue: p. i, nos. 59–105, 127–128; p. ii, nos. 1–17 Nat. Phil.: LS 62–64, US 1–4 The Mind: nos. 12, 24–26; notes in Brattle Logic Scripture: nos. 39–43
1725 Jan.	152–159		Catalogue: p. ii, nos. 18–26 Nat. Phil.: LS 64 (concl.), 65; US 5–6 Scripture: no. 43a (Is. 42:4)

3. See also no. 34.
4. Probably the fast-day sermon for April 15, 1724.

(continued)

Table 2. (*Continued*)

DATE	ENTRIES	SERMONS	OTHER
Feb.–March	160–169		Catalogue: p. 3, nos. 4–5
March–April	170–178		Catalogue: p. 3, nos. 6–7 Nat. Phil.: US 7–22 Scripture: nos. 44–49 Apocalypse: nos. 36–39
May–June	179–191	I John 3:2 (34)[5]	Catalogue: p. 3, no. 8 Nat. Phil.: US 23–26 Beauty of the World: pars. 1–4
July–Aug.	124–125b 192–193 27a 194		Catalogue: p. 3, no. 9 The Mind, no. 27 The Mind: nos. 28–31
1725–26 Dec.–Jan.	195–205		Miscellanies: a Table begun Catalogue: p. 3, nos. 9 (concl.)–11 Nat. Phil.: US 27; memos nos. 7–16 editorial notes to Being and Prejudices The Mind: nos. 40–45 (§§ 1–13) Beauty of the World: last par. and corol. Christ's Example: first essay

1726			
Feb.–March	206–214		Catalogue: p. 3, nos. 11 (concl.), 12
April–June	215–230	Rom. 12:1 (33, abandoned)[6] Frag. on Holy Spirit (34)[7]	Catalogue: p. 3, nos. 13–17 Scripture: nos. 50–56
		London/PvL-English/GR^{ur} Rev. 14:18–19 (35)	
1726			
June–Aug.	231–235	London/PvL I Pet. 1:15 (36)[8]	Catalogue: p. 3, nos. 18–21 Apocalypse: no. 40 Scripture: nos. 56 (addition), 57–58
	London/GR(2)[9] 261–264	English/GR^{ur} John 15:5(a) (37)[1]	
Sept.	Fleur de lis/EYD 331–314		Nat. Phil.: US 31 The Mind: no. 54

5. Only three leaves survive, inserted in no. 30.
6. JE stopped before he had filled one page (he already had a sermon on that text, no. 17). The sermon on Matt. 11:28 was begun on the second page in 1727 but not completed until 1730.
7. Along with the three leaves on I John 3:2(a) (34) inserted in the sermon on Rev. 21:18(a) (30) is a single tattered 8vo. leaf, probably from May or June 1726. Its contents suggest that it was part of a sermon on Eph. 4:30 or some such text.
8. Furnished with an additional application in a booklet of Amsterdam/MvL paper in 1727.
9. This and the London/GR sheet numbered "1" were made on twin molds. They are distinguished because the second (as now located in the MS) contains entries made in at least four different time periods as indicated in the chart.
1. Last sermon written at New Haven; contemporary with No. 262.

(continued)

Table 2. (*Continued*)

DATE	ENTRIES	SERMONS	OTHER
Oct.–Nov.	London/GR(2) 267–274	*London/GR* Job 14:5 (38) Ps. 147:1 (39)[2]	Scripture: nos. 59–63; index, nos. 1–63 posted
Dec.	London/GR(1) 236–237		Scripture: nos. 99–101
1727 Jan.–May	238–255	*London/GR- English/GR^{wr}* Luke 9:23(a) (40) *Amsterdam/MvL* Job 28:28 (43) Luke 2:14(a) (51) Luke 2:14(b) (52) II Cor. 4:7 (56)[3]	Nat. Phil.: US 32 Scripture: no. 102
June–Oct.	Amsterdam/MvL 279–305	Is. 1:18–20 (45)[4] Matt. 6:33(a) (48) Matt. 21:5 (49)[5] Matt. 24:35 (50) Luke 13:24 (53)[6]	Scripture: nos. 77–88

	Fleur de lis/EYD				
Nov.–Dec.	315–317	Gen. 19:14 (41) Jonah 3:10 (46)[7] Matt. 5:22 (47)		Scripture: nos. 103–110 Apocalypse: nos. 42–46 Christ's Example: p. 1, comment on Mark 10:21	II Cor. 6:10 (57) II Cor. 7:10 (58)
1728 Jan.–Feb.	318–322	Ps. 139:7–10 (44) Ga. 5:6(a) (59)			
	London/GR(2) 265, 275	Amsterdam/MvL- London/PvL Ps. 102:25–26 (61)		Faith: nos. 1–20	

(continued)

2. Preached for the thanksgiving of Nov. 10, 1726.

3. JE wrote between a third and two-thirds of this sermon early in 1727. One or more double leaves are missing from the center of the booklet. He completed and preached it in 1729, shortly after Stoddard's death.

4. Three units, the first probably preached on Sept. 24, 1727 (auditor's notes, Trask Library).

5. Incorporates the application from no. 24.

6. Only the last four pages are extant; the doctrine is taken from the auditor's notes (Trask Library), which place the sermon in Sept. 1727.

7. Preached for province-wide fast held on Dec. 21 following the earthquake that occurred on Oct. 29, 1727.

Table 2. (*Continued*)

DATE	ENTRIES	SERMONS	OTHER
1728 Feb.–March	*Fleur de lis/EYD* 323–328	*Amsterdam/MvL* Luke 17:9 (54) Acts 17:11 (55) *Amsterdam/MvL-* *London/PvL* Hos. 13:9 (62–63) Hab. 1:13 (a) (64)[8] *London/PvL* Jas. 1:17 (66)	Nat. Phil.: US 33–38 Apocalypse: no. 47 Scripture: nos. 89–94 Faith: nos. 21–28
April–June	*Amsterdam/MvL* 306–310 *London/GR(2)* 256–260 266 276–278	*Amsterdam/MvL* Deut. 32:4 (42) *Amsterdam/MvL-* *London/PvL* II Cor. 8:9 (65) *London/PvL* Ps. 90:12 (67) Dan. 4:35 (68) Matt. 10:28 (69) Luke 5:5–6 (70) Rom. 2:16 (71)[9] II Cor. 3:18(a) (72) Frag. C[1]	Catalogue: p. 3, nos. 22–30 Apocalypse: nos. 48–51 Scripture: nos. 95a–98 Faith: nos. 29–35
July–Aug.	*English/GR^{wr}* 330	*London/PD*[2] II Kgs 7:3–4 (74)	Catalogue: p. 3, no. 31

Faith: nos. 36–51
Miscellanies Table: Nos. 1–202 posted
Catalogue: p. ii, no. 27; p. 3, nos. 32–37
Scripture: nos. 64–73, 111–141
Christ's Example: pp. 1–2a (comment on Matt. 3:13)
Faith: nos. 52–58
Signs of Godliness: pp. 1–4a
Images of Divine Things: nos. 1–17
The Mind: nos. 57–59

Prov. 17:27 (77)
Cant. 1:3(a) (79)
Ps. 65:11 (75)[3]
Prov. 4:23 (76)
Eccl. 9:10(a) (78)
Is. 32:2 (80)[4]
Matt. 12:30 (82)
Matt. 13:22(a) (83)
Matt. 13:23 (84)
Luke 8:28 (85)
Luke 14:16 (86)[5]
Luke 16:24 (87)
Luke 17:34 (88)
Luke 19:42(a) (89)
I Cor. 16:22 (90)
Gal. 2:20 (91)
I John 4:19 (92)

Aug. 1728– Feb. 1729   331–384

8. The sermon is all Amsterdam/MvL paper except for a double leaf at the end. The leaf has no watermarks, but chain lines and knife marks show that it and a double leaf in no. 66 were cut from the same half sheet of London/PvL paper.
9. This sermon has no countermark, but ink and chain line measurements place it here.
1. The last ten pages of what may have been the doctrinal part of the election sermon for May 29, 1728. The two double leaves contain portions of a discarded table to the "Miscellanies," which was begun near the end of 1725 or early in 1726.
2. JE wrote "Northampton" in shorthand on his sermons from no. 37 onward as he wrote them, and on most of his earlier ones when repreaching them there. He placed the mark on the three following London/PD sermons (nos. 74, 77, and 79) before discontinuing the practice. Their ink confirms the presumption that they are the earliest in this watermark group.
3. Thanksgiving sermon for Nov. 7, 1728.
4. Printed in Dwight ed., 8, 355–78.
5. Sacrament sermon.

(continued)

Table 2. (*Continued*)

DATE	ENTRIES	SERMONS	OTHER
1729			
Feb.–March		*London/PD-*	
		English/GR^{wr}-	
		London/GR(R)	
		Titus 3:5 (begun) (96)	
	385–386	*Amsterdam/MvL*	
		II Cor. 4:7 (56)[6]	
	393–395	*London/PD*	
		Jer. 6:29–30 (81)[7]	
		London/PD-	
		English/GR^{wr}-	
		London/GR(R)	
		Is. 53:3(a) (93)	
		Jer. 42:20 (94)[8]	
		Amos 8:11 (95)[9]	
		Titus 3:5 (concl.) (96)	
		London/GR(R)[1]	
April–May	370	Ex. 20:24 (97)	
	396–405	Ps. 66:5 (98)	
	391–392	Ps. 82:6–7 (99)	
	406–409	Prov. 5:11–13(a) (100)	
	387–390	John 16:8 (101)	

June	410–417 (393, additions)	I Cor. 1:9 (103)[2] I Pet. 1:3 (104)[3] Rev. 3:15 (105) London/GR(R)- London/GR(L) Deut. 7:10 (106)	Scripture: nos. 74–76, 142–147, 148–150 Signs of Godliness: p. 4 (3 entries) Outline of Rational Account: first entries
July–Aug.	418–435	London/GR(R) Rom. 6:14 (102) London/GR(L) Num. 23:19 (107) Deut. 32:35(a) (108) Job 31:3 (110)	Scripture: nos. 151–158 Apocalypse: no. 52

6. Completed and preached during this time.
7. Preached shortly after Stoddard's death, possibly for a town fast day.
8. Sacrament sermon.
9. Preached on fast day of March 20, 1729.
1. When the watermarks read correctly on this paper, the Wm is to the left of center in the left half-sheet, and the cm is to the right of center in the left half-sheet. The next paper is exactly opposite. The two are distinguished here by the position of the cm, as (R) and (L).
2. Sacrament sermon.
3. The sermon is no longer extant but is located here because No. 409, which cites it, has the same ink as the London/GR (R) rather than the London/GR (L) group.

(continued)

Table 2. (*Continued*)

DATE	ENTRIES	SERMONS	OTHER
July–Aug.		Ps. 33:1 (112) Prov. 23:5 (116) Cant. 8:1 (118) Is. 3:1–2 (119)[4] Jer. 17:5–6(a) (122) Jer. 17:7–8 (123) Matt. 7:14(a) (124) Matt. 15:26 (125) Matt. 24:43 (126) John 8:44(a) (129) I Pet. 1:8(a) (131) II Pet. 1:16 (134)	
1729 Sept.–Oct.	436–449	Ps. 18:26 (111) Cant. 5:1 (117)[5] Jer. 5:9 (121) Luke 13:30 (127) Eph. 5:1 (130) I Pet. 2:2–3 (132) I Pet. 3:4 (133) II Pet. 2:14 (135)	Scripture: nos. 159–179, 188 Apocalypse: no. 52 Images: nos. 18–19

Nov.–Dec.	450–454	II Sam. 23:5 (109) Ps. 40:6–8 (113) Ps. 65:9 (114)[6] Prov. 14:34 (115)[7] Is. 45:25 (120)[8] *London/GR(L)-* *London/IV* Job 1:5 (136) Job 34:21 (137) Acts 17:31 (138)[9]	Scripture: nos. 189–191 Faith: no. 59
1730 Jan.–April	455–462	*London/IV* Deut. 32:35(b) (140) Ps. 14:1(a) (145) Is. 5:20 (147) Hab. 2:4 (149) Matt. 5:8(a) (150)[1]	Catalogue: p. 3, nos. 41–42 Scripture: nos. 192–193 Trinity Essay: pp. 1–8

4. Mentions Stoddard's ministry and death; possibly for a town fast day.
5. Sacrament sermon.
6. Preached on thanksgiving, Nov. 13, 1729.
7. For a public occasion, probably before the county court.
8. Sacrament sermon.
9. This sermon contains London/GR(L), English/GR^wr, Seven Provinces, and other scraps including some unmarked London/IV paper. Hand and ink place it clearly in this transitional group.
1. Printed in Dwight ed., 8, 280–304.

(continued)

Table 2. (*Continued*)

DATE	ENTRIES	SERMONS	OTHER
1730 Jan.–April	*English/GR^wr* 463–475	Mark 9:44 (152) Rom. 4:16 (153) Rom. 7:14 (154) I Cor. 10:16(a) (156)[2] Philip. 3:11 (158)	Apocalypse: nos. 55–56 Scripture: no. 194 Blank Bible: notes on Deut. 32:22 and John 4:14 Signs of Godliness: pp. 4d–5
May–Aug.	*London/IV* 475–480	Num. 14:22–23 (139) IISam. 22:26–27 (141)[3] I Kgs. 8:35–36 (142)[4] Job 36:22 (143) Ps. 10:6 (144) Ps. 119:2 (146) Is. 33:14(a) (148) Matt. 5:13 (151) Rom. 9:22(a) (155) I Cor. 10:22 (157) Jas. 3:16 (159)[5] Rev. 2:4–5 (160)[6]	
Sept.–Oct.	*London/IV–* *English/GR^wr* 481–483	Deut. 32:13 (161)	

Oct. 1730– May 1731		Hos. 5:15(a) (162)[7] John 1:14(a) (163) I Pet. 5:8 (164)	Images: nos. 22–28
	London/IV 484–487		
	English/GR^{wr} 488–494	English/GR^{wr} Num. 14:21 (165)[8] II Chron. 32:25 (166)[9] Job 33:6–7 (167) Ps. 73:18–19 (168) Prov. 19:21 (169)[1] Eccles. 2:26 (170) Eccles. 12:7 (171) Jer. 17:9 (172)[2]	

2. Sacrament sermon.

3. Contains a slip dated June 30, 1730, and so belongs to July; contemporary with miscellanies in the early to mid-470s.

4. Fast-day sermon, Aug. 16, 1730. There are no watermarks in this sermon, but chain line spacing, ink, and hand indicate its placement here. As the sermon was originally written, the text functioned as the doctrine, on which he made eight observations. When he preached the sermon again in 1749, he attached a slip of paper with a doctrine summarizing the observations.

5. Sacrament-day sermon, Aug. 9, 1730; contemporary with miscellanies in the latter 470s.

6. Probably the election-day sermon, May 27, 1730; contemporary with Nos. 463–467.

7. Printed in Dwight ed. 8, 44–69. The MS sermon contains three double leaves constituting a half sheet bearing a London Wm. Though the mark is not identical with that on the rest of the London/IV paper, the sheet may have come with that batch, and the ink is compatible with this location of the sermon. But the possibility must be kept open that JE wrote it later among the English/GR^{wr} sermons.

8. Fast day, March 25, 1731 (auditor's notes [Hawley Papers, New York Public Library]).

9. Thanksgiving sermon, Nov. 12, 1730; contemporary with No. 486.

1. MS not extant. Date of March 21, p.m. (auditor's notes [Hawley Papers]).

2. Probably March 28, 1731 (auditor's notes [Hawley Papers]).

(continued)

Table 2. (*Continued*)

DATE	ENTRIES	SERMONS	OTHER
Oct. 1730– May 1731		Ezek. 3:27 (173) Mic. 3:11 (174) Zech. 11:8 (175) Matt. 7:21 (176) Matt. 11:12(a) (177)[3] Matt. 11:29(a) (178) Luke 6:24 (179)[4] John 1:16 (180) John 3:3 (181) Acts 8:22 (182) Rom. 9:31–32 (183) I Cor. 1:29–31 (184)[5] I Cor. 11:28–29 (185)[6] I Cor. 16:1–2 (186)[7] Rev. 22:3 (187)[8]	

1731	English/GR*ʷʳ*	English/GR*ʷʳ*, Maid of Dort/CAW, odd pieces	
May–June	495–497	Eccles. 7:8 (188) Luke 11:27–28 (189) John 15:10 (190) Rom. 5:7–8 (191)[9] I Pet. 2:9 (192)[1] I John 3:9 (193)	Images: nos. 29–33
		London/PVL- *English/GR²*	
July–Aug.	498–505	Gen. 3:24 (194) Ps. 108:4 (195) Luke 10:38–42 (196) Rev. 17:14 (197) Rev. 22:17 (198)[3]	Faith: no. 60
	London/GR 506–510		

3. May 2, 1731 (auditor's notes [Hawley Papers]); written shortly after No. 494.
4. Probably early April 1731 (auditor's notes [Hawley Papers]).
5. Preached in Northampton in the fall of 1730; delivered with revisions at Boston on July 8, 1731 and published there as *God Glorified* the same year.
6. Sacrament sermon, probably March 21, 1731 (auditor's notes [Hawley Papers]).
7. Printed in Worcester rev. ed., *4*, 615–37.
8. March 14, 1731 (auditor's notes [Hawley Papers]).
9. JE removed the application and incorporated it into the May 1737 sermon on II Cor. 9:15.
1. Probably May 1731 (auditor's notes [Hawley Papers]).
2. The sermons in this batch are made either wholly or in part of discarded Scripture index paper (London [PvL]).
3. Incomplete as extant; possibly uncompleted.

TABLE TO THE "MISCELLANIES"

NOTE ON THE TABLE

THE Table to the "Miscellanies" was Edwards' chief means for controlling his writings in that series. Samuel Hopkins, in his biography of Edwards published in 1765, describes in detail his mentor's method of organizing the "Miscellanies":

> He *numbered* all his miscellaneous writings. The first thing he wrote is No. 1. and the second No. 2. and so on. And when he had occasion to write on any particular subject, he first set down the Number, and then wrote the Subject in capitals or large character, that it might not escape his eye, when he should have occasion to turn to it. As for instance, if he was going to write on the happiness of Angels, and his last No. was 148, he would begin thus——149. ANGELS, their HAPPINESS.——And when he had wrote what he design'd at that time on that subject, he would turn to an alphabetical table which he kept, and under the letter A, he would write, Angels, their Happiness, if this was not already in his alphabet; and then set down the Number, 149, close at the right hand of it. . . .The number of his miscellaneous writings rang'd in this manner, amounts to above 1400. And yet by a table contain'd on a sheet or two of paper, any thing he wrote can be turned to, at pleasure.[1]

This meticulous organization reveals a rigorous and disciplined mind, but the wide-ranging subject matter of the notebooks shows that his discipline was not a hindrance to creativity. On the contrary, compositions that Edwards could access through the Table provided not only finished materials ready to hand but also thoughts that became stimuli to further speculation. Without the Table, the vast bulk of the "Miscellanies" would have rendered its resources very difficult even for its own author to exploit.

The Table is in alphabetical order, and it served Edwards as an index. As such, the Table displays Edwards' theological system in its

---

1. Hopkins, *Life and Character,* pp. 83–84. In the "Miscellanies," however, JE went through two alphabets before getting to No. 1.

main loci and reveals his own view of the interrelationships among the various components of this system. It also exhibits his own special interests and the topics which were dominant in contemporary theological discussion. The Table, therefore, is far more than an ordinary index and deserves study as a theological document in its own right. It is also much less than an index as required by the modern reader; such an index is provided separately at the end of the volume.

Making the Table

Building and making use of his index gave Edwards opportunities to exercise his powers of logical analysis, a thing for which his college studies had prepared him and in which he took great delight.[2] Nevertheless, Edwards' method of organizing the "Miscellanies"—a system based upon consecutive numbering, alphabetical indexing, and cross-referencing of entries—developed gradually over a period of years. The earliest entries were distinguished by individual titles written in bold capital letters, but they were not numbered, much less indexed. That Edwards recognized from the outset the need to organize his writings is evidenced by a memorandum in his diary for July 25, 1723, "At a convenient time, to make an alphabet of these Resolutions and Remarks, that I may be able to educe them, on proper occasions, suitable to the condition I am in, and the duty I am engaged in."[3] The "Remarks" Edwards there had in mind to index were primarily those of the "Diary"; but in other diary entries during the summer he added "Reflexions" (his early name for the "Miscellanies") to the list of writings he wished on occasion to "read" and "peruse," for which an "alphabet" would have been equally useful.[4] About the time of the July 25 memorandum, while writing miscellanies in the latter 30s, Edwards took the first step toward an index by lettering and numbering his entries up to that point.[5] He also began, around No. 40,

2. See JE's tribute to "the old logic" in "The Mind," no. 17 (*Works, 6,* 345 and n. 4). For the influence of the logic books studied at Yale on some of JE's characteristic ideas and modes of thought, see William S. Morris, "The Genius of Jonathan Edwards," in *Essays in Ministry,* ed. Jerald C. Brauer (Univ. of Chicago Press, 1968), 5, 29–65. Incidentally, JE shows no sign of having been acquainted with John Locke's *New Method of Making Common-place Books* (London, 1706) or the method of indexing there proposed by Locke.

3. Dwight ed., *1,* 90.

4. The Diary for June 8 contains a reminder: "then to read my resolutions, remarks, reflections, etc."; a similar memorandum for Aug. 28 refers to "perusing resolutions, reflections, etc." (ibid., pp. 87, 94).

5. The ink JE used for the task, even on the lettered entries, is the same as that of entries in the 30s.

to number his entries as he wrote them. But there is no evidence that he attempted an "alphabet" at that time.

Edwards continued to number his entries as he wrote them until he assumed his tutorship in the spring of 1724, but he failed to maintain the practice during his first year at Yale. It was not until May 1725, during a vacation in Windsor, that he numbered these entries (Nos. 124–191). In the process he inadvertently skipped a whole page and as a result misnumbered the entries on three pages (Nos. 132–156).[6] Later, almost certainly during a convalescence at Windsor around the turn of the year 1726, he numbered the few entries of the preceding summer (Nos. 192–194 and 27a) and took up again the practice of numbering his entries as he composed them. He also laid out an alphabet in double columns on a single folio leaf but for some reason indexed the entries only down through No. q.

When Edwards moved his manuscripts from New Haven to Northampton in August or September 1726, he had completed entries through No. 235 plus Nos. 261–264 (the original 236–239). Again, as at Yale in 1724, he forged ahead without numbering his entries. In the late spring of 1728, doubtless realizing that his previous index was too small, he laid out a new alphabet on a full sheet, this time in single column format, and discarded the earlier index.[7] With his new Table in hand, Edwards turned immediately to the indexing of his previously numbered entries instead of numbering the newer ones. But he stopped indexing with No. 202 and allowed his unnumbered entries to accumulate for another year.

At this time, Edwards also introduced two innovations designed to give greater order to his entries. When he commenced his miscellaneous writings in 1722, to save paper he began each entry on the same line immediately after the preceding one, often leaving insufficient space for an entry number. In the spring of 1728 he abandoned this crowded format and decided to begin each entry at the left hand margin of the page, leaving space ahead of the title for the entry number. He also began dropping one or more line spaces after a

6. These entry numbers are corrected in this edition of the "Miscellanies" with explanatory notes; the corrected numbers appear in the Table with the MS numbers in parentheses.

7. JE later cut the discarded index into three pieces, two of which (and probably the third) he used in a sermon of May 1728, only ten pages of which are extant. The piece containing the watermark is missing, but the chain lines show that the leaf was from a sheet of the London/PvL paper JE used during most of his tutorship. The unused letters *Q–S* and *U–Z* are on extant leaves; these would have contained Nos. r ("Preparatory Work"), s ("Christ's Righteousness" [probably under "Satisfaction," as was No. b]), t ("Universal Redemption" [under *U* or *R*), and w ("Tone") had JE indexed them.

completed entry and drawing a horizontal line across the page, prior to the beginning of a new entry. Thereafter, with only minor exceptions, Edwards consistently followed these practices, although for some time he left the entry numbers to be inserted later and frequently omitted the horizontal dividing line.

Finally, during another convalescence in June or July 1729, Edwards tackled his backlog of entries with more success. First of all, he went back to No. 235 and brought his entry numbers completely up to date, i.e. through No. 410. He then picked up the indexing of his entries in the Table at No. 202, where he had left it in 1728, and, with one interruption that caused him to miss fifteen entries (Nos. 221–235), soon brought it up through No. 345. There he left it for at least several months, though he seems to have become current with his indexing by the time he was making entries in the early 500s. Beginning in mid-1729 Edwards indexed his entries at regular intervals and with only minor exceptions numbered them as he wrote them. He apparently reviewed and even cited his unnumbered miscellanies with some frequency; hence the fact that he allowed entries to accumulate unnumbered and unindexed for months and even years at a time is a bit puzzling. Perhaps he thought these tasks diverted him from more important duties, or perhaps he had a distaste for mechanical operations; even before his experiment of 1726–28 he may have toyed with the thought of making the sheets into quires. Whatever the explanation, these organizational tasks had become by the summer of 1729 sufficiently habitual for Edwards to maintain them with consistency.

The Table as Edwards set it up in 1728 took care of his indexing needs for almost a decade, certainly past the end of Book 1, in which No. 688 is the last entry. But as he indexed entries in the late 600s he found that the space allotted to some letters had been used up. And so, probably early in 1737, he took another sheet of paper and began a series of numbered supplements to the index,[8] carefully linking them to the parent index and when necessary to their own continuations.[9]

8. The sheet has the English/GR^{wr} watermarks. After 1735 (which is too early) the next paper from which this sheet might have been drawn appears only briefly among the sermons in March 1737. The sheet is not from any mold represented in these sermons, but similarities in marks and chain lines suggest that it is from the same mill. The earliest entries in the first four supplements are mostly of miscellanies in the very early 700s, and these probably began late in 1736 or early in 1737 (No. 698 refers to a sermon of Nov. 1736).

9. For example, the first three supplements are devoted to *S*, *C*, and *R* respectively. At the end of his original listings under *S* JE wrote, "See other paper No. 1," later adding "No. 11," and at the end of supplement no. 1 he referred to its continuation in no. 11. Subject listings that reached the end of a line he keyed to their continuations in the main index or subsequent supplements by pairs of matching symbols.

The second sheet contains 15 such supplements, which lasted into the early 1740s. Edwards found it necessary in mid-1743 to add another sheet, on which he wrote supplements 16–24.[1] A single folio contains the last of the supplements, nos. 25–27. Edwards probably put this leaf into service in late 1756 or early 1757.[2] It contains only a few entry numbers, which range from 1315 to 1336.

Indexing the "Miscellanies"

The indexing of the "Miscellanies" was, of course, dependent on Edwards' own identification and labeling of his entries. Some entries do not appear in the Table simply because they were not assigned numerals, and some numerals do not appear because no entries were written carrying those numbers. For example, Edwards not only skipped the numerals 52–59, as mentioned above, he also failed to make any entries for the numbers 881–883.[3] Many entries were not given numerals of their own but were designated as continuations of numbered entries; Edwards expected to locate them through his system of cross-references.

Several properly numbered entries were left out during the process of posting to the Table. Some omissions were simple inadvertences,[4] but others were intentional. Nine of the earliest entries (Nos. d, g, m, w, ss, uu, ww, xx, and yy) dealt mainly with Scripture types or with the Apocalypse and were written before the series was devoted more ex-

---

1. The third sheet also has the English/GR^wr marks. The mold on which it was made and its companion mold are distinctive in two ways at least: there is an unusually narrow distance between the deckle edge and the tranchefile, and the chain and watermark lines are crooked in several places. JE used some of this paper in a sermon of July 1743 and then again in sermons beginning in Dec. 1743. (At least two other molds represented in the batch have straight chain lines and a slightly different placing of the tranchefile.) During the 990s in the "Miscellanies" there was a transition in which a whitish coating, which had been present for a long time, disappeared from the surface of the ink. The first entries on paper no. 16 are of miscellanies in the late 990s and early 1000s in a brown ink that reflects this change in the ink, which occurs in the sermons around May 1743.

2. This leaf, which contains only the cm GR, is from the same mold as JE's letter to his son Timothy at Princeton dated Nov. 4, 1756.

3. JE began Bk. 4 with No. 884 while still composing No. 880, a long essay that exhausted the pages left vacant at the end of Bk. 3.

4. Some omissions were oversights caused by the crowded condition of many pages in the "Miscellanies" and the fact that several titles do not stand out sufficiently from the rest of the text. For this reason some essays failed to receive a number and hence were not posted to the Table. JE seems frequently to have indexed materials from Bk. 9 by page numbers before giving them entry numbers in the series; in the former operation some short entries were overlooked because they lacked numbers, and in the latter, numbers seem to have been given to a few items which he had originally meant to treat as parts of preceding essays.

clusively to dogmatic and philosophical theology; these were not included in the Table. Usually only the first in an uninterrupted series of entries with the same title was indexed, and some numbered items that were only corollaries to or continuations of other entries were omitted.[5] Occasionally entries whose sole function was to refer to other manuscripts were passed over. But considering the large number of entries in the "Miscellanies," the Table is surprisingly complete, and there are relatively few inaccuracies. At Edwards' death there were only three recent entries that he had not yet posted to the Table: the last entry in the "Miscellanies" is No. 1360, and the last one indexed by Edwards was No. 1357.

The heading under which an entry was indexed in the Table was usually its title, but the material in some entries, especially those of a synoptic character, was distributed under more than one heading.[6] In order to facilitate indexing as well as later retrieval, Edwards soon began to provide multiple titles for many of his essays. For example, No. 333 is entitled "Scriptures. Being of God. Christian Religion" and is indexed under each of these heads. In later entries he often introduced additional headings into subsections or raised the size of key words in important topic sentences. Such additional titles and subheadings provided the loci under which the entry was indexed and were occasionally used for cross-referencing.[7]

Edwards sometimes supplied variant forms of entry titles for multiple indexing, but in this he was not consistent. Entries entitled "Being of God" are sometimes found also under "Existence of God" and sometimes not. Those entitled "Righteousness of Christ," "Death of Christ," and the like were at first indexed not only by those titles but also by "Christ's righteousness," "Christ's death," and the like, but

5. Nos. 691–693 all carry the title "Sabbath. Lord's Day"; only No. 691 is entered in the Table. Similarly, Nos. 202–204 are each on the Christian Religion, but only No. 202 is entered in the Table. Also, No. 115 (an appendix to No. 104) and No. 1305 (an addendum to No. 1300) are not indexed.

6. No. 103 ("Incarnation") and No. 104 ("End of the Creation"), though relatively short, are early synoptic essays that are heavily indexed, having seven and six entries respectively. No. 103 is entered under these headings: Angels—End of the creation—Heaven—Incarnation—Redemption the greatest of God's works—Saints higher in glory than the angels (plus a variant of the last topic). No. 371 ("Resurrection") is indexed under five subjects. Some longer entries are found in ten or more places. The prize probably goes to No. 1351, a set of extracts from A.M. Ramsay's *Travels of Cyrus* that is listed 26 times in the Table.

7. No. 664b, an important synthetic essay, has nine topics listed in its title and is indexed under 16 heads, which are either the topics themselves or subjects related to them. Nos. 369 and 374 are among the first entries to contain subheadings.

Edwards soon gave up the practice. On the other hand, some procedures were begun early and never changed: all entries on the freedom
of the will are indexed under "Free will," not under "Will" or "Freedom," while those on free grace are listed throughout not only under
"Free grace" but also under "Grace, free."

In the early pages of the "Miscellanies" Edwards often used as the
title of an essay whatever aspect of the subject was uppermost in his
mind as he wrote. Later, both while composing and indexing, he
sought to bring these under more general heads. He indexed No. tt,
"Devotion," by placing it under "End of the creation," "Spirit's operation," and "Arbitrary divine operation"; "Devotion" does not appear
again in the "Miscellanies" as a title. Nos. 8 and 70 on "Conscience," 11
on "Discipline," 12 and 13 on "Ceremonies," 14 on "Civil Authority,"
and 17 on "Confession of Faith" all appear in the Table under "Liberty
of conscience," though Nos. 11–14 are also listed under their respective titles. No. 46, "Crucifixion," was entered under "Christ's death," a
heading later replaced by "Death of Christ." Similarly, "Theology," the
title of No. 83, was abandoned and the entry was indexed under
"Christian religion" and "Mysteries."

On the other hand, Edwards found some general headings too
broad. Three early entries were indexed under "Happiness,"[8] but
subsequent entries with that title or on that topic appear in the Table
under "Heaven," "Happiness of heaven," "Happiness of God," or "Incarnation." Other titles were rejected as headings because they were
too ambiguous. Nos. 68, 86, and 158 are all entitled "Kingdom of
Christ." Of these, Edwards entered the first under "Civil authority"
and "Discipline of the church," the second under "End of the world or
consummation," and the third under "Millennium"; he then ceased to
use the term as a title for entries in the "Miscellanies." The term
"Christian Religion," which Edwards first used as a title in Nos. 127–
129, became the Table heading for eight earlier entries having various
titles. Thereafter, articles in defense of the Christian revelation were
usually entitled "Christian Religion," often with the specific subject
(Scripture, miracles, mysteries, and the like) as a secondary title.

Edwards began the Table in order to be able to locate specific materials in the "Miscellanies" and to study in sequence his entries on a
given subject. But he soon began to use the "Miscellanies" itself for

---

8. I.e. Nos. f ("Spiritual Happiness"), x ("Pleasantness of Religion"), and ff ("Union with
Christ").

citing compositions of special theological significance in his other manuscripts and for quoting other writers on various doctrinal subjects.[9] With time, this coordinating function was transferred, in part at least, to the Table. After 1739 (i.e. about No. 800), Edwards began citing sermons and other manuscript compositions directly in the Table. He also entered in the Table many brief citations of publications by other authors; these appear to represent works which Edwards owned or to which he had easy access.[1] In this way the Table became Edwards' central apparatus for organizing not only his "Miscellanies" entries but the entirety of his theological thought and the growing body of compositions in which he expressed it. Only the "Blank Bible," begun about two years later than the Table, rivals it as a general index; but in that manuscript the materials are located only by scripture texts, not by subject.[2]

Editing the Table

The Table is a thin folio volume composed of three separately folded sheets of foolscap plus a single folio at the end, and paged 1–14 by Edwards. It is bound in a cover of soft heavy paper, on the outside surfaces of which Edwards wrote "Table" lengthwise in a very large cursive hand; the stitching (now missing) was placed in the exact centers of the folds so that the book would lie flat when open. Edwards' original index occupies the first four pages; the remaining pages contain the extensions added as the "Miscellanies" grew in size. Besides

9. No. 387 is the first to contain a sermon reference written at the same time as the rest of the entry; No. 434 is the first to contain such a reference to a "Scripture" note. JE also added references of both kinds to previous entries. There are brief quotations from printed works as early as No. 50, and the first long quotation occurs in No. 266; but it is the latter half of the "Miscellanies" that contains most of the long excerpts from other authors.

1. There are 55 citations, representing 17 titles. Of these the most frequently mentioned are Samuel Clarke's second series of Boyle Lectures (18 times), Matthew Poole's *Synopsis criticorum* (11 times), John McLaurin's *Sermons and Essays* (six times), and the second volume of Isaac Watts's *Works* (six times). William Warburton's *Principles of Natural and Revealed Religion* is cited twice, the other 12 works once each. From the character of the works most frequently cited and the nature of the citations, it is clear that JE's main interest was in identifying material for use in the apologetic work that he intended to write. Clarke and Poole, for example, are cited mainly for their discussions of theological "traditions" of the ancient heathen supposed to have been derived from Moses and the patriarchs.

2. There was, of course, much that was of value to JE in his other theological notebooks and writings which was not cited in the "Miscellanies" or the Table; he therefore supplemented the Table with indexes in other notebooks ("Images," for example) and by various other outlines and lists of subjects to be treated in projected works.

the index, the book contains only a few notes indicating the numbers with which successive volumes of the series begin and explaining abbreviations and symbols. The text is often very crowded, especially on the earlier pages, and complicated by many numerals and other marks left by copyists and editors. The leaves are badly worn and tattered at the margins, but very few entries are lost or totally illegible. (See the photograph of the first manuscript page facing the first page of the printed text.)

Although the Table is in alphabetical order, Edwards wrote individual subject headings as needed under each letter of the alphabet without regard to order. The supplements to the Table are in individual letter groups, but these groups were also added as demand dictated, and are therefore not in alphabetical order. In this edition, Edwards' original index and its supplements have been consolidated and the whole alphabetized under each letter. Entries under *I* and *U* were separated from those under *J* and *V*. As much as possible, headings beginning with the same word have been grouped together, as in a modern index; however, with one exception,[3] no item has been moved from the letter under which Edwards listed it. Hence, topics beginning with the word "Angels" are grouped together under *A*, but "Confirmation of the angels" remains under *C*.

Except for the very earliest entries, it is seldom possible to reproduce the order in which Edwards posted "Miscellanies" numbers and other items to the Table, nor would it be very useful. Hence a uniform sequence has been followed: under each topic or subtopic the "Miscellanies" numbers are listed first, then sermons, Scripture commentary, Scripture texts, other manuscripts, and printed works in that order.[4] Sermons and scripture notes have been listed in the canonical order of their texts unless there is a special reason for a different order, in which case the fact is noted. Edwards' slightly varying names for his own manuscripts have usually been allowed to stand, except for lengthening abbreviations, e.g. "SSS" to Poole's *Synopsis Criticorum* and "SS" to "Notes on Scripture" (the numbered series in four manuscript volumes). Edwards cites the notes in his "Blank Bible" by name

3. "Œconomy" has been changed to "Economy" and listed under *E*, with a cross-reference from "Œconomy."

4. JE frequently introduces non-"Miscellanies" items with "vid.," "see," or "see also." This practice (using "see") has been extended to all such additions to distinguish them not only from miscellanies but also from one another where, for example, a list contains sermons, Scripture notes, and biblical texts without other intervening material.

in only three references; the rest appear as "note(s) on" plus the biblical text.

Entry numbers not indexed by Edwards are supplied in brackets under the appropriate headings when it is clear that the omission was either inadvertent or not intended to exclude the entries, as when he indexes only the first in a series of entries having the same title. These are entered only under the subject or subjects most directly indicated by their titles, and in accord with Edwards' usual practice in dealing with items on those subjects.[5] Because Edwards himself varied considerably in the degree of completeness with which he indexed entries beyond their main subject headings, no effort could be made to achieve uniformity in this respect without greatly expanding the Table and changing its basic character. Several entry numbers have been inserted in the manuscript by a later hand, mostly by Jonathan Edwards, Jr., or Sereno Dwight; these have been ignored, except as helps in identifying omissions by Edwards to be supplied as indicated above.[6] In later years Edwards began to make cross-references to related topics; a few additional ones have been supplied in brackets.

Some of Edwards' devices for finding materials in his growing pile of "Miscellanies" volumes have been discarded. One of these is his practice of adding the book number to the entry number (e.g. "1152. B. 7"), mainly for Books 5–8; another is his listing entries from Book 9 by page rather than entry number (e.g. "P. 863," i.e. No. 1350).[7] Book numbers have been omitted, and page references have been converted to the corresponding entry numbers. Sometimes a "Miscellanies" number is accompanied by a page number (many long entries are separately paged); in such cases the passage is identified if it can be distinguished by some kind of recognizable internal division (space limitations have ruled out quotations and paraphrases). Sometimes the page number is accompanied by a symbol to indicate the place on a

5. JE occasionally ignored a main element in the title of an entry when indexing it. Wherever there seems reason to consider this an accident, the number has been supplied in brackets under that subject heading. For example, No. 860 has been added under "Signs of godliness" after the example of Nos. 800 and 868; all three appear under "Works, how proper signs of godliness."

6. These additions are most numerous under "Conversion," where 13 are added to JE's 22 entries, and "Conviction," where JE's 31 are joined by 22 others, all inserted by Dwight or his scribe. The vast majority are mistaken and show that Dwight had a defective understanding of JE's theological categories and style of indexing.

7. See JE's headnote to the Table.

column or page; these are explained in a note.[8] With these exceptions, Edwards' forms of citation have been retained.

"Miscellanies" entries through No. 500 are in the present volume. Previous printings of later entries will be found below in Appendix A. Those that have appeared in the Yale University Press edition are identified in a note. Whenever a printed text is available for a passage Edwards cites in one of his other manuscripts it is also identified. For the "Notes on Scripture" the Dwight edition is cited as the only available text; a few notes from the "Blank Bible" are printed in Grosart's *Selections* and in the Worcester revised edition.[9]

8. In JE's day it was common to specify the place on a page or column by the letters *a–e*, thus roughly dividing it into five sections. JE sometimes adds such letters to his citations.

9. Dwight ed., *9;* Worcester rev. ed., *3;* Alexander B. Grosart, *Selections from the Unpublished Writings of Jonathan Edwards, of America* (Edinburgh, 1865).

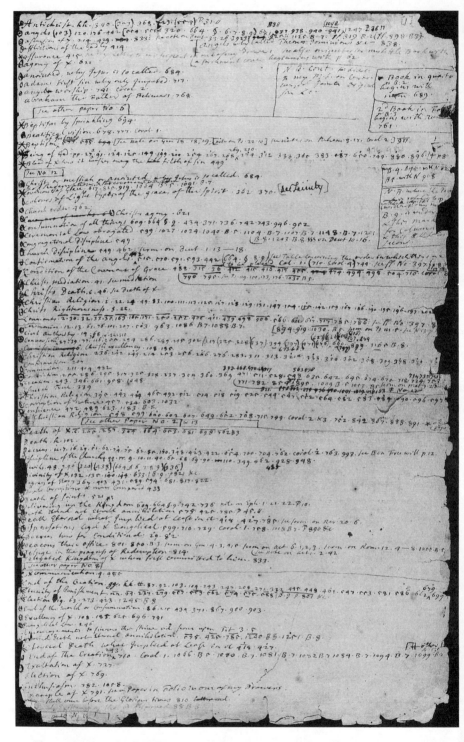

Fig. 2. Photograph of the first page of the Table to the "Miscellanies," showing Edwards'
headnotes, his alphabetical scheme, and the marks left by later transcribers and editors.
Courtesy of Beinecke Rare Book and Manuscript Library, Yale University.

TABLE[1]

FIRST book in quarto, or Book 2, begins with No. 689.
Second book in folio, or Book 3, begins with No. 761.[2]
Book 4 begins with No. 884, Book 5 with No. 958.[3]
N. B. Where the page is referred to with a capital P (without any n[umber][4]), Book 9 is understood; and this mark (⌐) for column [first], and this, ⌐, for column second.[5]
N. B. "Cont." directs to my MS on controversial points, original sin, etc.[6]

A

Abolishing the ceremonial law, 1027
Abraham, his calling in the progress of redemption, 814; the father of believers, 768
Adam, the head and representative of his posterity, *see* Ridgley, *Sermon on Original Sin*, pp. 25 ff.[7]
Adam's first sin, how far imputed to his posterity, *see* sermon on Gen. 3:11;[8] why only [it] imputed, 717

1. JE wrote the directions at the head of the Table at various times in unused space near the upper right corner of the first page and marked them off in little boxes from the rest of the text. They are here arranged in the approximate order of writing.

2. A similar note appears on the top of MS p. 5 at the beginning of the supplements to the original Table. It reads "Second Book in Folio begins No. 761."

3. JE regularly supplied the book number with Table entries from the latter part of Bk. 5 and from Bks. 6–8, which made further notes of this kind unnecessary. The book numbers are omitted in this edition of the Table.

4. Here and at the next two bracketed insertions a piece is broken from the margin.

5. All entries from Bk. 9 have been converted to "Miscellanies" entry numbers in this edition. In the body of the "Miscellanies" as well as in the Table, JE also uses these column symbols in citations of other MSS and printed works. Wherever JE's references to columns are preserved, his marks will be represented by "col. 1" and "col. 2."

6. JE is not consistent, however, and sometimes in the Table he also refers to it as "Contr.," "Controv.," or "Book on Controv."; the last two are the most frequent in citations found elsewhere in his papers. The MS, a large folio notebook from JE's last years at Stockbridge, now carries on its cover the title "Controversy Book," supplied by JE, Jr. "Book on Controversies" will be used as the title in this edition.

7. Thomas Ridgley, *The Doctrine of Original Sin Considered, Being the Substance of Two Sermons Preached at Pinners Hall* (London, 1725). The first sermon expounds the proposition "That all Mankind are concerned in *Adam's* first sin" under two heads. In the section to which JE refers Ridgley adduces the biblical proof of Adam's federal headship, a proof which consists mainly in a comparison of Adam and Christ as type and antitype.

8. The sermon on Gen. 3:11, dated Feb. 1738, has as its doctrine, "The act of our first father in eating the forbidden fruit was a very heinous act."

9. JE indexed this number but put it by mistake under "Justification." The error was probably made on an intermediate list used for indexing; no other explanation has been found.

1. JE inadvertently entered No. 353 and a duplicate listing of No. 554 under the heading "Antichrist," which immediately precedes "Angels" on the MS.

2. A citation in this form, except when otherwise stated, means that the comment is to be found in the "Blank Bible" The entry here cited is printed in Grosart, *Selections*, pp. 99–100.

3. All references to "Notes on Scripture" followed by a number designate the four-volume series of Scripture notebooks compiled by JE over the course of his ministry. No. 319, a note on Ps. 68, is printed in the Dwight ed., *9*, 346–50; no. 498 deals with John 16:8–11 and is printed in ibid., pp. 487–90.

4. This note is printed in Grosart, *Selections*, pp. 113–14.

5. The recipient was probably Rev. John Sergeant (Yale, 1729) who from 1734 until his death in 1749 was the first missionary to the Stockbridge Indians and JE's predecessor in that position. JE seems to have had some connection with the founding of the mission, and John Sergeant was one of his correspondents. While not officially an "opposer" of the revival, Sergeant became a strong critic of its excesses; see his *Causes and Danger of Delusions in the Affairs of Religion* (Boston, 1743).

A variety of evidence suggests that the letter draft to which JE refers is that written on the back of a fast day proclamation dated March 13, 1745 (Trask Library). The same handwriting and gray-black ink with which the Table entry was written (and which are characteristic of the middle and late 1740s) appear in a portion of the letter draft. Both the beginning and the ending of the letter are missing; however, the extant fragment consists for over half its length in a discussion of assurance. Whoever the recipient of this letter was, he had written in criticism of some statements JE had made about assurance, probably those in the *Religious Affections*, Pt. II, § 11 (*Works*, 2, pp. 167–81). At any rate, his other objections, which JE begins to answer in the latter part of the fragment, definitely concern the *Affections*, Pt. III, § 1, part of which is quoted in rebuttal. Hence this letter was probably written some time late in 1746 or within the next year. The draft has been printed, with an introduction by George S. Claghorn, in *Works, 8*, 631–40.

6. This booklet is no longer extant. It may have been one of those used in the preparation of the *Religious Affections*.

7. These three references were added at different times. The note on Gen. 18:18–19 is printed in Grosart, *Selections*, p. 65.

Beelzebub, *see* Satan

Being of God, *pp,* 27a, 91, 124, 125a, 134, 199, 200, 254, 267–269,[8] 274, 312, 333, 365, 383, 587, 650, 749, 880, 896, 976, 984

Blood of Christ: how it is mainly by that that we are justified, 381, 399, 447, 449, 452, 496, 913, 794, 845, *see* sermon on John 15:10 (last use), on Acts 20:28, and on Rev. 5:12;[9] how it washes away the filth of sin, 449

C

Calling of the Jews, the time when, *see* note on Luke 21:24[1]

Canon: of the New Testament, 1060; of the Scripture [is] complete, *see* sermon on I Cor. 13:8–13[2]

Ceremonial law abrogated, 599, 1027, 1034, 1040, 1104, 1107, 1148, 1201, 1203, *see* [Poole's] *Synopsis* on Deut. 10:16[3]

Ceremonies, 12, 13, 61, 76, 101, 207, 503, 963, 1086, 1088

Christ, or Messiah, or Anointed, why Jesus is so called, 684

Christ: had the Spirit of prophecy, 972,

1193, [1332b]; in what sense he suffered the wrath of God, 1005; no impostor, 1317, [1332a]; purchased faith and conversion, 1159; the true Messiah, 902, 972, 981, 1002, *see* Prophecies of the Messiah

Christ's: agony, 621; death, *c,* 46, *see* Death of Christ; excellency, 108, 185; glory increased after the day of judgment, 957; mediation, 41; righteousness, *s, zz,* [*see* Righteousness of Christ]

Christian religion, *i,* 22, 24, 49, 83, 100, 111, 113, 125b, 127–129, 131, 132, 139, 140, 152, 159, 167, 186, 190, 195–197, 202, [203], 214, [234], 236, 242, 249, 253, 256, 266, 276, 283, 311, 313, 321a, 333, 350, 352, 358, 359, 378, 379, 382, 395, 443, 444, 465, 492, 512, 514, 518, 519, 525, 544, 547, 552, 564, 582–584, 590, 596–600, 602, 607, 649, 652, 708, 715, 749 (corols. 2, 3), 752, 842, 867, 888, 891, 900, 902, 903, 912, 915, 922, 944, 945, 971, 972, 981, 983, 984, 1002, 1007, 1087, 1111, 1158, 1170, 1190, 1192–1194, 1228, 1290, 1299, 1306, 1312, 1314–1318, 1321, 1324, [1326, 1330, 1332a, 1341, 1342]; agreeable to reason, 1156,

---

8. JE inserted No. 270 at this point; this is an error, for No. 270 concerns the glory of God and is so indexed by JE.

9. The doctrine of the sermon on John 15:10 (spring 1731) is short: "Jesus Christ kept all his Father's commandments." Two sermons on Acts 20:28 are extant; the earlier of these, dated Dec. 1745, is the one meant here. Its doctrine is, "The church of God is purchased by the blood of God." The sermon on Rev. 5:12 (late 1731 or early 1732) has as its doctrine, "Christ was worthy of his exaltation upon the account of his being slain."

1. Of the two notes on Luke 21:24 in the "Blank Bible," the first one, which is intended here, comes to the conclusion that "Antichrist will fall and the Jews be called about the same time."

2. The burden of the sermon on I Cor. 13:8–13 (May 1748) is clear from its doctrine: "The extraordinary influences of the Spirit of God imparting immediate revelations to men, were designed only for a temporary continuance while the church was in its minority, and never were intended to be statedly upheld in the Christian church."

3. MS: "SSS on Deut. 10:16." On the first page of the "Blank Bible" JE wrote, "Note that this mark SSS is a reference to Pool's *Synopsis* in the place [i.e. the commented text], at a place marked in the margin." In the Table, however, JE more often uses the title. This work was an abridgment of the *Critici sacri* (9 vols., London, 1660) by Matthew Poole (or Pool) under the title *Synopsis criticorum aliorumque Sacræ Scripturæ interpretum* (4 pts. in 5 vols. fol. London, 1669–76). It was reprinted at Frankfurt in 1678–79, 1694, 1709, and 1712, and at Utrecht in 1684–86; all reprints were in 5 vols. In JE's writings there are references to at least three of the volumes; it is likely that he owned the whole set. His page references show that his copy had the same pagination as the London and Utrecht editions. JE's symbol will be rendered by "*Synopsis*" throughout the Table. Part and column numbers will be given; all the citations in the Table are to Vol. 1, which contains Pts. I and II paged separately. Poole's treatment of Deut. 10:16 ("Circumcise therefore the foreskin of your heart, and be no more stiffnecked") is found in Vol. 1, Pt. 1, cols. 780e–81a.

4. Isaac Watts' *Works* were collected and published in 6 vols. at London in 1753. Vol. 2 was also entitled *Sermons, Discourses, and Essays, on Various Subjects.* Included in the volume was "The Holiness of Times, Places, and People, under the Jewish and Christian Dispensations," originally published in 1738. Of this work Discourse V, which has the heading, "The holiness of the jewish and christian churches considered and compared," occupies pp. 453–67.

5. Only the first digit of the page number remains at the right margin, but it is probable that JE meant to refer to the same passage as in the immediately preceding entry (above, n. 4). The whole of Discourse V (pp. 453–67) deals with the Jewish and Christian churches as visible churches in relation to their invisible reality. JE found Watts supportive of his own position on requirements for church membership (ibid., p. 461).

6. The sermon on Deut. 1:13–18 (June 1748) carries the doctrine, "'Tis the mind of God that not a mixed multitude but only select persons of distinguished ability and integrity are fit for the business of judging causes."

7. This note is printed in the Worcester rev. ed., *3*, 552, with several changes.

8. JE also calls this MS notebook "Treatise on Faith" in the Table. "Treatise" describes JE's intention better than it does the MS itself, which is an accumulation of materials with a limited amount of continuity and structure. The section to which he refers was printed as § 46 in the *Remarks*, ch. 7, pp. 422–23 (Worcester rev. ed., 2, 614–15).

9. No. 515 contains a similar note, a later insert at the end of the third main argument: "See table concerning the order in which things in this miscell. are to be placed, col. 1." Dwight may have followed it in arranging the numbers on this subject which he printed in vol. 8 of his edition, for in his arrangement he goes beyond the directions contained in the cross-references attached to those miscellanies. But the table to which JE refers is now lost.

1. In no. 397 and its continuation in no. 469 JE derives a date for the confirmation of the angels (i.e. their being made unable to sin) from an ingenious speculation about the "tree of life" in Gen. 2:9, 3:22–24. Both notes are printed in the Dwight ed., *9*, 158–61.

2. This note is printed in Grosart, *Selections*, p. 172.

3. JE's number is 954, but in this case it refers to a continuation of No. 952 which was written after No. 954. The passage cited bears the heading, "Conflagration, whether a purifying fire."

4. Christoph Matthaeus Pfaff, *Institutiones dogmaticæ et moralis* (Tübingen, 1719). Pfaff was professor of theology at Tübingen. In the prolegomena to his dogmatics Pfaff discusses the role of reason in deducing doctrines from Scripture that are not expressly revealed there (pp. 25–32).

5. This sermon is no longer extant. The whole of No. 753 is a reference to it: "CONVICTION. Why it is necessary that a man should be convinced of his guilt in order to salvation. See sermon on Matt. 9:2, first direction under first use." In the Table, only the abbreviation "Direct." remains at the broken right margin, but the numeral was probably the same as in No. 753.

6. This sermon (a quarterly lecture, Aug. 1746) has the doctrine, "The excellency of this covenant and the great desirableness of an interest in its blessings is set forth here by two things: (1) that it is an everlasting covenant; (2) that the mercies promised in it are sure."

7. MS: "1075," which is surely a slip for 1074, since the two writings numbered 1075 are on original sin and free will respectively.

8. Note no. 397 (on Gen. 2:9 and 3:22–24) is printed in the Dwight ed., 9, 158–60, 160d–61 (corol.); for no. 398 (on Gen. 1:27–30) see ibid., pp. 157–58).

9. Only the first digit remains at the margin. There are but two numbers between 786 and 894 which are likely candidates. No. 825, entitled "Covenant of Grace and Redemption" is already indexed under each of those covenants, whereas No. 874, entitled "Covenants, Testaments," does not otherwise have a "Covenants" entry.

1. See the preceding n. 1.

2. This quarterly lecture (Aug. 1745) has the doctrine, "God never fails in any instance of faithfulness to the covenant engagements he has entered into on behalf of any of mankind."

3. See the preceding n. 6.

Creation, *continued*
on Deut. 33:26;[4] of the world, how the progress of redemption was begun in it, 833; of the world, why committed into the hands of Christ, 833, 1039, *see* notes on Eph. 3:9, 10[5]

D

Daniel, book authentic, 1309
Deacons, their office, 801, 850, 1055, *see* sermon on Gen. 4:3–5, on Acts 6:1–3, and on Rom. 12:4–8,[6] *see also* note on Acts 2:42
Death, *h*, 102, [235]; eternal, not eternal annihilation, 425, 575, 785, 1284; eternal, what implied at least in it, 418, 427, 785, *see* sermon on Rev. 20:6;[7] of Christ, *c*, 265, 287, 304, 653, 664b, 681, 698, 762; of saints, 521; threatened in the law, what is the proper notion of it, 785, 1056, *see* sermon on Ezek. 22:14 (the fifth thing proposed under the doctrine)[8]

Decrees, *u*, 7, 16, 29, 51, 62, 74, 75, 82, 85, 170, 348, 422, 423, 654, 700, 704, 762 (corol. 2), 763, 993, see Book on Free Will, p. 12;[9] how far conditional, 29, 82
Defects of the heathen morality, 1350, 1357
Degrees of glory, 367, 403, 431, 589, 594, 681, 817, 822
Delegated kingdom of Christ, when first committed to him, 833
Delivering up the kingdom, 609, 664b (§ 9), 736, 742, 1259, *see* note on Eph. 1:21–22
Deluge, in the progress of redemption, 814
Design of God in all his works [is] but one, 547
Destruction of Jerusalem, how a seal of Christ's mission, 1316, *see* Prophecy
Devil once the highest creature, *see* Satan
Devils, 48, 296, 320, 438, 664b (§§ 6–9), 936; have a sort of pleasure, 1272; their fall, the occasion of it, *see* Fall
Devils' corruption and men's compared, 433

4. See above, p. 126, n. 2.

5. The two verses were annotated separately but apparently at the same time. The note on v. 9 is JE's special interest here. At the end of the note on v. 9 is a later reference to "Miscellanies" No. 833, probably added when the note was listed in the Table.

6. These three sermon references occur in the Table between Nos. 850 and 1055, and were apparently all entered at the same time. Gen. 4:3–5 is a thanksgiving sermon of Nov. 1743, with the doctrine, "It has been a thing established in the church of Christ from the very beginning, that his people should publicly offer up a part of their worldly subsistence as a part of the stated public service of his visible church."

The other two sermons deal directly with the nature of the deacon's office. That on Acts 6:1–3 (June 1739) has the doctrine, "That the main business of a deacon, by Christ's appointment, is to take care of the distribution of the church's charity for the outward supply of those that need." It may have been preached near the time of an election of deacons, for it was followed not long afterwards (Aug. 19, 1739) by the sermon on Rom. 12:4–8, which was preached "On occasion of the ordination of the deacons." The doctrine of the latter sermon is, "The offices that Christ has appointed in his church do respect either the souls or bodies of men."

7. This sermon of Aug. 1742 uses the text, Rev. 20:6, as its doctrine. In its first half there are five propositions, of which the third is "that the future misery of the wicked is fitly called death." This is the material JE had in mind in making the reference.

8. The sermon on Ezek. 22:14 was preached in April 1741, with the doctrine, "Since God has undertaken to deal with impenitent sinners, they shall neither shun the threatened misery nor deliver themselves out of it, nor can they bear it." It was printed by JE, Jr., as sermons IX and X in *Sermons on the Following Subjects* (Hartford, 1780). The part to which JE refers is the last main doctrinal section (*Sermons*, pp. 158–60; Worcester rev. ed., *4*, 560–61).

9. This MS must be the "Gazetteer Notebook," so called because JE constructed it from pages of *The Gazetteer*, a Boston weekly newspaper. Though it has no "Free Will" title (it may lack an outside leaf) a large number of the entries in this notebook relate to the issue of free will, and on p. 12 begins a long section entitled "Decrees. Inability."

Discerning who is converted, 1112, *see* Notes on Scripture, no. 365[1]

Discipline of the church, *q, qq, rr,* 9, 10, 11, 40, 65, 68, 69, 90, 110, 349, 462, [485], 928, 948

Dispensation: no new one to be introduced, *see* sermon on I Cor. 13:8–13 (first inference, fifth argument in answer to the objection there);[2] old, gradually vanished and gave place to the new, 843

Dispensations, legal and evangelical, 599, 710, 729 (corol. 1), 758, [869], 1118, 1353a

Divinity of Christ, 142, 145, 150, 154, 633, 1349, [1358]

Divorces, *see* note on Matt. 5:32

E

Economy of the persons of the Trinity,[3] 482, 1062, *see* sermon on I Cor. 11:3, on I John 4:14, and on Gal. 3:13–14[4]

Efficacious grace, 73, 147, *see* McLaurin's *Essays,* pp. 232–63[5]

Elders, ruling, *see* sermon on Deut. 1:13–18[6]

Elect men beloved above all the rest of the creation, 1116

Election, 19, 63, 273, 423, 1245; how it is in Christ, 769 (latter end), 1245; of Christ, 769

Elias shall come before the glorious times, 810

Encouragements to sinners that strive, *see* sermon upon Titus 3:5[7]

End of the creation, *gg, kk, tt,* [3], 87, 92, 103, 104, [115], 208, 243, 247, 271, 332, 445, 448, 461, 547, 553, 581, 586, 662, 679, 699, 710 (corol. 1), 1066, 1080–1082, 1084, 1094, 1099, [1140], [1142], 1151, 1182, 1184, 1208, 1218, 1225, 1266a, 1275, 1277a, 1355b; that Christ might obtain a spouse, 104, 271

End of the world, or consummation, 86, 215, 434, 371, 867, 900, 903

End of the world spoken of as nigh by the

---

1. JE began no. 365 as a comment on Rom. 2:29 but continued it in nos. 367, 370, and 392 until it became a substantial essay with the title, "Judging and Discerning the State of Others' Souls." Ink, hand, and contents suggest a time in the early 1740s, in the aftermath of the Great Awakening. The whole essay, with some omissions and displacements, is printed as no. 365 in the Dwight ed., *9,* 499–505.

2. See above, p. 127, n. 2. JE's fifth argument is that "no writings that have been written since that time [the closing of the N.T. canon] have been acknowledged."

3. Stated as "Œconomy of the Trinity" in a continuation of the listings further down the MS page. Both headings, of course, were placed by JE under the letter *O.*

4. JE placed these three sermon references together in a parenthesis between Nos. 482 and 1062. The order in which the sermons are listed is deliberate, for together they form a series delivered in March and April 1746. The doctrine of the sermon on I Cor. 11:3 is, "God the Father acts as the head of the Trinity in all things appertaining to the affair of man's redemption." That of the sermon on I John 4:14 is, "The concern that the second person in this Trinity has in the affair of our redemption is this, that he is appointed of the Father to be the Savior of mankind." The sermon on Gal. 3:13–14 (Trask Library) has the doctrine, "The Holy Spirit, or the third person of the Trinity, in his operations and fruits, is the sum of the blessings that Christ purchased for us in the work of our redemption."

5. John McLaurin of Glasgow, one of the Scottish ministers with whom JE corresponded regularly, died in 1754. A volume of his *Sermons and Essays* was edited from his MSS by John Gillies and published at Glasgow in 1755. JE's reference is to the "Essay on the Scripture-Doctrine of Divine Grace," specifically the first section, "Concerning the Scripture-evidences of the doctrine of grace," which is really an exposition of the role of grace in every aspect of the Christian life.

6. See above, p. 128, n. 6.

7. The doctrine of this sermon (c. Feb. 1729) is short: "There are none saved by their own righteousness." In the fourth subsection of the application JE says that it is not self-righteousness for one to take encouragement from the fact that one is striving for salvation; but he warns that such encouragement is not to be taken as a promise from God.

8. This note on I John 2:18 is printed in Dwight ed., *9*, 556–57. No. 842, which precedes it in the Table, is cited at the end of the note.

9. JE must be referring to the MS entitled "Christ's Example," which he began while a tutor on a sheet folded into two folio leaves.

1. In his "Farewell Sermon" of July 1, 1750, JE had warned his erstwhile flock of the danger of Arminian principles prevailing among them (Worcester rev. ed., *1*, 79–80). Since he still occupied the pulpit, he immediately thereafter administered a heavy dose of doctrinal antidote in two long sermons on I John 5:1–4 (both dated July 1750). The first of these has the doctrine, "Saving faith differs from all common faith in its nature, kind and essence." This is obviously the one to which JE has primary reference here. Most of this sermon, from the statement of the doctrine to within a dozen or so pages of the end, was printed by JE, Jr., in *Remarks*, pp. 462–80 (Worcester rev. ed., 2, 631–41), as the last section in the chapter on faith.

2. MS: "1156, p. 9." Paged 1–10 by JE, this number contains essays on the reasonableness of various Christian doctrines. The last of these (pp. 9–10) is entitled, "The Reasonableness of the Doctrine of Faith as the Main Condition of Salvation."

3. I.e. the "Discourse on Faith"; see above, p. 128. n. 8.

4. See the preceding n. 2.

5. See above, p. 128, n. 8. The discussion to which JE refers is printed in the *Remarks*, ch. 7. However, because JE, Jr., misread his father's cue marks, it is there separated into two parts, § 46, from the third paragraph to the end, and § 51, from the second sentence to the end (pp. 423, 426–27; Worcester rev. ed., 2, 615, 616–17).

6. The essay here cited is entitled, "The Things wherein the Way of Justification by mere Law, and that by Grace through Christ, differ as to the Qualification of the Subject that primarily entitles him to Justification." It has eight sections, of which JE refers to the third. See above, p. 125, n. 6.

7. No. 1258 is entered on the MS under "Future state, its evidence from the Old Testament," which is separated by only one line from the heading, "Future state proved"; JE's eye apparently caught the wrong one. There is no mention of the O.T. in No. 1258.

8. See above, p. 127, n. 2.

9. The sermon is dated Feb. 1746, and its doctrine is, "'Tis the duty of God's people to be much in prayer for that great outpouring of the Spirit, that God has promised shall be in the latter days."

1. JE's reference is to a paragraph on pp. 110–11 at the end of a series of writings on perseverance. JE, Jr., apparently guided by this entry in the Table, printed the paragraph in ch. 4 of the *Remarks* as § 97 (pp. 285–86; Worcester rev. ed., 2, 597, misnumbered § 96). On the MS, see above, p. 125, n. 6.

2. John Owen, *A Practical Exposition on the CXXXth Psalm*. There were only two editions in the 17th century, the original London, 1669, edition, and a reprint by the same publisher in 1680; I have been unable to discover any other editions before 1772. JE's topic and page reference (MS: "p. 319 &c.") will not fit either edition. The first edition offers little hope, but the pagination of the 1680 reprint is close enough to suggest the passage which JE probably had in mind. On p. 324 there is a discussion of "two different estates whereunto all men belong," and on p. 325 the marginal heading reads: "Saving Grace specifically distinct from common Grace." On p. 329 begins a section entitled, "Difference between the State of Grace and Nature Discernable [sic]," and on pp. 229–30 mention is made of "common Graces" which a hypocrite may have. Probably the best guess is that JE meant to cite pp. 329 ff. of the 1680 ed., and that "319" is a simple slip of the pen. It is also possible that p. 324 was the first page of the material he intended to cite, but that his finger slipped back to p. 319, which is also a verso in this edition (the page numbers 318 and 319 are reversed).

3. William Warburton, *The Principles of Natural and Revealed Religion Occasionally Opened and Explained; in a Course of Sermons* (Vols. 1–2, London, 1753–54; Vol. 3, London, 1767), *1*,

H

Habit of grace, 655, [818]

Hades, 60, 67, 499, 556, 667, 746, 952,[4] 1281

Happiness, *f, x, ff;* of God in himself only, no objection against a proper delight in his creatures, 679

Happiness of heaven: after the resurrection, 95, 182, [233], 263, 721, 743; beyond any that would have been by the first covenant, 710 (corol. 11), 809 (and corol. 1), 1072, *see* sermon on John 10:10;[5] degree of it, 741, 886, 893 (corol. 1), 934; how perfect, 822; its absolute eternity, 1004; the nature of it, 938, 1137; progressive and increasing to eternity, 105

Happiness of saints and angels in heaven in its present state consists much in beholding and contemplating God's perfections as manifested in his providence towards the church on earth, 776–778, 804, 811, 744 (corol. 5), 1059, 1061, *see* Notes on Scripture, nos. 381, 391 (corol.)[6]

Head of the visible church, 1011

Heathen, their salvation, 1153 (corol. 2)

Heathen philosophers: their inspiration, 1162; their vices, *see* Watts, [*Works*], 2, 291e ff.[7]

Heathen world, things that happened therein that were attestations to Christ's divine mission, 981

Heathens had much from ancient tradition, 953, 959, 962, 969, 973; and from the Jews, 953, 959, 962, 969, 973, 983, [1350][8]

Heaven, *h, ff, ii,* 5, 95, 103–106, 108 (corol. 2), 112, 122, 137, 149, 153, 182, 188, 198, 206, [230, 233], 263, 272, 371, 372, 413, 421, 430–432, 435, 477, 499, 529, 546, 555, 565, 571, 576, 585, 639, [666, 678], 679, 681, 701, 710, 721, 741, [743, 775], 1072; its situation, 1222; not promised in the first covenant, 809; perfected after the day of judgment, 1126, *see* note on Job 26:13;[9] the eternal abode of the church, 743, 745, 889, 1134; the place of God's eternal abode and special glorious pres-

---

184–202. Vol. 1 at least was also printed in Dublin in 1753, and both volumes were reprinted in both London and Dublin in 1755. Neither of the 1755 sets agrees with JE's pagination; I have not seen the 1753 Dublin edition. JE may have read only the first volume; he does not use a volume number in the Table, and no references to Vol. 2 have been encountered in his MSS. The passage JE cites occurs in Sermon VI on "The Office and Operations of the Holy Spirit," in the first part of the first main section, concerning the gift of tongues.

4. MS: "954, p. 8." This material belongs to the concluding portion of No. 952; JE placed it after No. 954 and paged it separately (10 pp.). The passage thus indicated is a paragraph near the end of that addition and is entitled, "Hades. Paradise."

5. The sermon, doubtless on the words, "I am come that they might have life . . . more abundantly," is not extant.

6. This reference to the two notes occurs immediately after the No. 811 entry. The first note, no. 381 (Dwight ed., 9, 449–50) is an addition to no. 379, a comment on Matt. 22:31–32. At the end of the note (and integral to it) is written, "See 'Miscellanies' No. 811 at the latter end of that number."

"Scripture" note no. 391 is a simple continuation of no. 389 (they are printed together in the Dwight ed., 9, 400–07), and the whole is a note on the first chapter of Ezekiel. At the end several miscellanies are cited: Nos. 776–778, 804, 805, 811.

7. Watts' *Works,* 2, 205–316, contain his "Strength and Weakness of Human Reason: or the Important Question about the Sufficiency of Reason to Conduct Mankind to Religion and Future Happiness, Argued between an Inquiring Deist and a Christian Divine"; this work was first published at London in 1737. In Conference III Logisto the deist makes points by citing Cicero, whereupon Pithander the minister points out Cicero's own moral lapses, especially his vanity and his complying with the polytheism and idolatry he had previously condemned (pp. 291–93).

8. Conjecture for the entry number; JE entered the symbols for Bk. 9 and col. 1 but failed to indicate the page. It is possible that he meant to refer to an entry on this subject in the index at the back of No. 1350, a set of extracts from Philip Skelton's *Deism Revealed* (2nd ed., 2 vols. London, 1751).

9. The note is printed in Grosart, *Selections,* pp. 113–14.

ence, 743; the place shall be altered at the end of the world, 952, 957, 1122, *see* note on John 14:2;[1] the saints higher in glory there than angels, *ii*, 103, 104, 710 (corol. 2); whether the saints there are acquainted with what is done on earth, 372, 421, 529, 555, *see* Separate souls of saints

Hell, [232], 258, 275, 280, 282, 316, 318, 407, 418, 425, 427, 441, 456, 478, 480, 491, 493, 499, 505, 509, 527, 545, 546, 550, 558, 572, 579, 592, 646, 656, 690, [730], 805, 863, 866, 870, 886, 901, 905, 906, 910, 916, 921, 924, 926, 927, 929–931, 933, 944, 985, 987, 995, 1097, 1270, 1294, *see* sermon on Ex. 9:12–16, on Deut. 32:20, on Deut. 32:23, on Job 19:21, on Job 21:19–20, on Job 41:9–10, on Ps. 18:35, [on] Prov. 1:26–27, on Prov. 10:24, on Ezek. 22:14, on Luke 19:41 (the use), on Rom. 9:22 (these words, "vessels of wrath"), on I Cor. 10:8 ff., on I Cor. 11:32, on Heb. 12:29, on Rev. 6:16, on Rev. 14:14 (former part of sermon), and on Rev. 20:11,[2] *see also* note on Deut. 5:25,

---

1. The note on John 14:2 intended here is the one that deals with the words, "I go to prepare a place for you."

2. There are eighteen sermons in this list, most of which come from the early or middle 1740s:

Ex. 9:12–16 (July 1747). "They that will not yield to the power of God's Word shall be broken by the power of his hand."

Deut. 32:20 (March 1754). "The end that impenitent sinners will come to will be very remarkable."

Deut. 32:23 (July 1741). JE uses as his doctrine the text, "I will heap mischiefs upon them; I will spend mine arrows upon them."

Job 19:21 (Jan. 1748). "A touch of God's hand is enough to bring such an one as man into extreme distress."

Job 21:19–20 (Jan. 1741). "Wicked men have no reason to doubt of anything that is said in the Word of God concerning the future punishment of the ungodly, or to suspect whether it be true."

Job 41:9–10 (Jan. 1743). "We may in some measure judge how much more terrible the fierceness of God's wrath is than that of creatures', by the difference there is between him and them."

Ps. 18:35. This sermon, on the words "Thy gentleness hath made me great," was probably written in 1740 or early 1741. It is extant only in the application, but the first use is doubtless what JE has in mind; he there warns the sinner not to expect God's gentleness but only the violence of his anger.

Prov. 1:26–27 (March 1744). "Those that sin away their day of grace shall be wholly cast away by God as to any regard to their welfare." Because the words "sermon on" do not accompany the text in the Table, it is possible that merely the verse was intended.

Prov. 10:24. There are two sermons on this text to which JE may be referring. One is dated May 1737; its doctrine reproduces the words of the text, "The fear of the wicked shall come upon him." The other is dated Aug. 1747; it has no separately stated doctrine but expounds a series of propositions based on the text; because of its much more eschatological focus it is probably the one JE means to cite.

Ezek. 22:14. See above, p. 130, n. 8.

Luke 19:41 (May 1741). Its theme is Christ's weeping over Jerusalem; JE cites the application, which seeks to awaken Christless sinners to their miserable situation and prospects.

Rom. 9:22 (Nov. 1741). "God has no other use to put finally impenitent sinners to, but only to suffer his wrath." The parenthetical note in the Table is to distinguish this from an earlier undated sermon that treats the whole of v. 22.

I Cor. 10:8–11 (late 1731–32). "Those awful temporal destructions that we have an account of God's bringing on wicked men of old, are types and shadows of God's eternal judgments."

Hell, *continued*

Images of Divine Things, no. 128,[3] and a loose paper in one of my drawers (great bookcase at the right hand);[4] its eternity, *nn,* 44, 237, 279, 288, 557, 559, 562, 574, 575, 588, 1004, 1179, 1187, *see* sermon on II Cor. 4:18,[5] note on Matt. 3:12, *see also* Is. 45:23;[6] the justice of that punishment, *see* McLaurin's Essays, pp. 130–45[7]

History of the New Testament: early written, 1315; its truth, 1322, *see* Facts [of Christianity]

History of the Old Testament from Moses' time confirmed from heathen traditions and records, 983, 1015, 1020

Holiness: Adam's innocency and gospel holiness compared, 894; how secured in the covenant of grace, *see* Book on Controversies, pp. 202–07;[8] its excellency,

---

I Cor. 11:32 (Aug. 1741). "'Tis a dreadful thing but yet a common thing, for persons to go to hell."

Heb. 12:29. JE could have been referring to either or both of two sermons on the text. The first (late 1731–1732), has the doctrine, "God is a consuming fire." The second, dated May 1742, argues that "God himself is the fire that shall destroy and consume wicked men."

Rev. 6:16. There are two sermons on this text, each equally appropriate. One is dated Dec. 1745, and has the doctrine, "When gospel grace comes to [be] turned into wrath, that wrath is peculiarly dreadful." The doctrine of the other, dated Jan. 1747, is that "the weight of rocks and mountains is light in comparison of that wrath of God that shall hereafter come on ungodly men."

Rev. 14:14 (Sept. 1741). The theme is Christ's final ingathering of both elect and reprobate, developed in fourteen "observations" on the text. The first ten of these are relatively well written up, but the rest, along with much of the application, is in scanty outline. This probably explains JE's reference to the "former" part of the sermon. There is also a sermon of Oct. 1736 on the same text but with the doctrine, "Our Lord Jesus Christ is crowned with glory."

Rev. 20:11 (Aug. 1741). "When God shall appear at the day [of judgment], heaven and earth will flee away as though they could not bear his dreadful and wrathful presence."

3. *Works, 11,* 97.

4. This MS has not been identified. The entry itself is of some interest. Judging from the location, hand, and ink, it is clear that the first part was written about 1748 (no later than 1749 or early 1750) and that the words of the entry, "great bookcase at the right hand" were interlined around 1753 or 1754. This very likely reflects a change in the arrangement of the furniture in JE's study consequent on his move to Stockbridge.

5. There are five extant sermons on II Cor. 4:18. The last three (one for a private meeting in 1748 and two for the Stockbridge Indians) are excluded by the position and ink of the Table entry, which place it no later than 1743. Both of the other two sermons are topically eligible. The first, dated July 1733, has the doctrine, "The things of the unseen world are eternal things." However, JE must have meant the second sermon (April 1742), since he made the entry at about the same time it was written. Its doctrine is, "There is such a thing as eternity," and its application contains a section especially devoted to the eternity of hell.

6. "Is. 45:23" is probably a plain textual reference. No sermon on the text is extant, and the "Blank Bible" note on Is. 45:23, on the former part of the verse, does not deal with the eternity of hell.

7. JE's reference is to the first 15 pages of McLaurin's "Essay on Prejudices against the Gospel," printed in his *Sermons and Essays,* pp. 130–71. In this first section of his essay McLaurin seeks to answer prejudices against the doctrine of hell torments.

8. The "Book on Controversies" (see above, p. 125, n. 6) contains an essay in eight main divisions on the "*Ques.* Wherein do the two covenants agree as to the method of justification, and the appointed qualification for it?" (pp. 202–10, 236). In the long second division (pp. 202–07) JE seeks to prove that holiness is as effectually secured in the new covenant as in the old.

9. John Glas, the Scottish divine who became the founder of the Glassites (later Sandemanians, from his son-in-law Robert Sandeman), issued a series of *Notes on Scripture-Texts* in seven numbers (Edinburgh, 1747–60). The first four numbers were probably in the packet for which JE thanked John Erskine on July 5, 1750 (Dwight ed., *1*, 405); No. 5, published in 1750, must have arrived soon afterwards, for JE cited it in his *Misrepresentations Corrected* (see Worcester rev. ed., *1*, 256*n*.), which was published in 1752.

I have not been able to locate a single number of the first edition. Fortunately, the *Notes* were reprinted in Glas' collected *Works* (4 vols., Edinburgh, 1761–62), of which I have used the second edition (5 vols., Perth, 1782–83). The "Notes" are contained in *3*, 1–346, where the original dates of publication are also given. The passage in No. 5 to which JE refers is undoubtedly the second essay, a note on James 4:5–6 entitled, "The Spirit of Grace in the Church Called God" (ibid., pp. 123–24).

1. This note (Dwight ed., *9*, 267–69) deals with the golden calf incident and its aftermath in Ex. 32–34.

2. MS: "1156, p. 8"; the reference is to a quotation from Jean Alphonse Turretin which JE copied out of Johann Friedrich Stapfer's *Institutiones Theologiæ Polemicæ* (5 vols., Zurich, 1743–47) 2, 1172, under the heading, "The reason and fitness of Christ's appearing in the world in so low and mean a condition."

3. JE is probably referring to two different notes, one on v. 18 only, the other on vv. 18–19. Both are printed in Grosart, *Selections*, pp. 123–24.

4. Edward Young, *The Complaint: or, Night-Thoughts on Life, Death, and Immortality*. The nine "Nights" were issued successively and in various single or combined "editions" at London, 1742–45. The first collected edition which contained Night 7 in a continuous pagination apparently came out in 1746, followed by one in 2 vols., separately paged, 1747–48. The "7th ed." of 1747 contains only Nights 1–6. On the assumption that JE intended to give the page on which Night 7 began or a page within Night 7, his page reference does not agree with any edition I have seen or for which I can obtain a reliable pagination. Henry J. Pettit's *Bibliography of Young's Night Thoughts* (Boulder, University of Colorado Press, 1954) provides information about a few inaccessible editions. The most likely edition is that of London, 1755, in which Night 7 begins on p. 136. Although the immortality theme runs through Night 6 also, there is nothing especially notable on p. 130 of that edition which would make it a suitable beginning point for a citation. It seems more probable that "130" is a slip for "136."

5. The sermon on Deut. 29:4 (Sept. 1745) has the doctrine, "Persons are not at all excused for any moral defect or corruption that is in them, [for the fact] that God don't help 'em to be otherwise."

6. This note is printed in Grosart, *Selections*, p. 106.

7. JE here refers to two different notes, one on Ps. 59 and one on Ps. 59:13; both, however, have much the same content. At the end of the first note, "Miscellanies" Nos. 600 and 640 are cited; at the end of the second note, JE refers to his comment on David's lament in II Sam. 1:17 (see preceding n. 6). The note on Ps. 59:13 is printed in Grosart, *Selections,* p. 116.

8. This note is printed in ibid., p. 128.

9. The third section of McLaurin's "Essay on Prejudices against the Gospel" (*Sermons and Essays,* pp. 146–52) deals with prejudices against the doctrines of substitution and imputa- tion. JE's reference is to the latter part of that section, where McLaurin seeks to answer objections against the imputation of Christ's active righteousness or obedience to the be- liever.

1. There exists an undated (fall 1730) sermon on the latter part of the verse, with the doctrine, "That our Lord Jesus Christ is full of grace and truth"; but its structure and contents show that it is not the one cited by JE. A substantial sermon on the incarnation seems to have been lost.

2. [Joseph Moody], *Meditations on Several Divine Subjects . . . by a person unhappily taken off from his ministry by bodily disorders* (Boston, 1748). "Meditations upon the Humanity of Christ" occupy pp. 1–18 of the volume. On pp. 12–14 Moody discusses two advantages of the incarnation: it qualifies Christ to be judge of the world, and it enables the saints to enjoy God in their own nature.

The author was the eccentric "Handkerchief Moody" (1700–53) of York, Maine, who went about for years in a severe depression, wearing a handkerchief over his face even while preaching; see William B. Sprague, *Annals of the American Pulpit* (9 vols. New York, 1857– 69), *1,* 248–49. It was he who was presiding at Job Strong's ordination in June 1749 when JE belatedly arrived to preach the sermon. The story is told by James DeNormandie in "Jon- athan Edwards at Portsmouth," *Proceedings of the Massachusetts Historical Society,* 2nd ser., *15* (March 1901), 16–20.

3. MS: "1129, p. 5," i.e. the last two pages of the entry, where JE discusses the special case of elect infants dying in infancy.

4. This note consists of a quotation from John Owen, ΠΝΕΥΜΑΤΟΛΟΓΙΑ: *or, a Discourse Concerning the Holy Spirit* (London, 1674), Bk. 2, ch. 1, § 10 (p. 105).

5. *Sermons and Essays,* pp. 170–71, contain the eighth and last section of the "Essay on Prejudices against the Gospel." In his second reference JE probably means to include the whole last section of the "Essay on Christian Piety" (ibid., pp. 223–31).

6. See above, p. 127, n. 1.

7. See above, p. 131, n. 1.

8. MS: "1156, p. 5, 6, 7." No. 1156 (paged 1–10 by JE) contains essays on the reasonableness of various Christian doctrines; as indicated by the heading on p. 5, pp. 5–7 deal with "Another World, and a Day of Judgment, and Heaven, and Eternal Life".

9. John Taylor (1694–1761), *A Paraphrase with Notes on the Epistle to the Romans. To Which is Prefix'd A Key to the Apostolic Writings* (London, 1745), pp. 353–56. Taylor was the minister of Norwich, England, against whom JE wrote his *Original Sin*. Three editions of the *Paraphrase* were issued in JE's lifetime (a second in 1747 and a third in 1754), all with the same pagination.

1. Samuel Clarke (1675–1729) delivered the Boyle Lectures of 1704 and 1705. The first series was published as *A Demonstration of the Being and Attributes of God* (London, 1705), the second as *A Discourse Concerning the Unchangeable Obligations of Natural Religion, and the Truth and Certainty of the Christian Revelation* (London, 1706). Each of these works reached a second ed. in 1706, and by the third ed. of 1711 (if not before) the two were combined in one volume under the rather confusing title, *A Discourse Concerning the Being and Attributes of God, the Obligations of Natural Religion, and the Truth and Certainty of the Christian Revelation*. The second series often carried on its spine the title, *Evidences of Natural and Revealed Religion;* JE cites it by the short form *Evidences* throughout the Table. JE's page references to the *Evidences* in the Table match only one edition, the sixth, which was issued separately at London in 1724 and as part of the combined *Discourses* in 1725.

2. JE wrote this heading among his earliest entries in the Table but failed to add the number which was almost certainly the occasion for listing it.

3. Another "568" was also entered by mistake one line higher on the MS and thus under "Immortality of the Soul."

4. This note is printed in Grosart, *Selections*, p. 125.

5. The reference to this note follows No. 840a in the Table; No. 840a is a study of Scripture texts bearing on the same subject. The note is printed in ibid., p. 65.

6. Besides a comment on the meaning of the white garments, JE has three separate notes in the "Blank Bible" on the words, "for they are worthy." The third was written about the same time the Table entry was made; it concerns "the inherent graces and good works of the saints" as worthy of reward.

7. Meric Casaubon, *A Treatise Concerning Enthusiasme*, London, 1655. JE used the 2nd ed., rev. and enl., London, 1656.

8. No. 1068 is cited not by its numeral but by its title, probably because the entry itself is a separate treatise. At least two later hands (one that of JE, Jr.) have been at work on its section numbers. JE's § 149 is at the top of MS p. 120 and begins, "It is implicitly foretold that the Jewish sabbath should cease in the times of the Messiah's kingdom"; § 152 ends at the middle of p. 121.

9. The synopsis on Gen. 2:3 is found in Vol. 1, Pt. I, cols. 14–15, and that on Ex. 20:8 in cols. 405–06. (The MS lacks the chapter number because of a defective margin, but there can be little doubt in this case.)

1. JE's reference is to "The Holiness of Times, Places, and People," Discourse I, entitled "The perpetuity of a sabbath, and the observation of the Lord's-day," *Works*, 2, 395–423.

2. Friedrich Spanheim (1600–49), *Dubia evangelica discussa & vindicata* (3 pts. in 2 vols. Geneva 1634–39), 2, 564–80. In these "dubia" Spanheim seeks to prove, especially against charges brought by Jews, that while the seventh-day sabbath has been abrogated under the gospel, the sabbath law itself has not. The *Dubia evangelica* was reprinted at Geneva several times in the 17th century, apparently from the same type, and in 1700 a new edition was issued with different pagination. JE owned a 1639 printing of the work, which is now in the library of Tusculum College, near Greeneville, Tennessee.

3. See above, p. 132, n. 1.

4. The doctrine of this sermon (late 1731 or early 1732) is, "Christ was worthy of his exaltation upon the account of his being slain."

5. JE probably means ch. 20 in the comments on the successive chapters of Revelation at the beginning of "Notes on the Apocalypse" (*Works, 5*, 123–24). He may also have had in mind the note on Rev. 20:2 in the "Blank Bible." Each contains a list of "Apocalypse" entries on Rev. 20.

6. See above, p. 137, n. 5. Throughout the doctrinal part of the sermon JE tries to show that persons must bear the blame of their native corruption and evil actions. There is, however, no part of the sermon specifically on "the ground of moral evil," and it may be that JE had yet another sermon on the text that has since been lost.

7. This sermon is no longer extant. In "Miscellanies" No. 1304 JE refers to it as a "sermon on God's moral government," and in No. 1156 he speaks of it as "my sermons on this subject" (the agreeableness of the Christian religion to reason). Apparently it was a multiple sermon or series of sermons giving an extended treatment of the moral government doctrine.

8. Sermon II in *The Principles of Natural and Revealed Religion* (*1*, 45–70) is entitled "God's Moral Government" and is devoted to the proof of the doctrine. In the passage which JE cites (pp. 52a–53c), Warburton contrasts the realms of matter and mind as to essence, ends, and effects, in order to argue *a fortiori* from God's government of the natural order.

9. This discourse on Is. 51:8 is the series of sermons preached in March–Aug. 1739 and published posthumously in 1774 as *A History of the Work of Redemption*. Sermon 18, which was probably preached in late June or early July, 1739, introduces Period III, from Christ's resurrection to the end of the world. See *Works, 9*, 344–56.

1. This is a long sermon, preached in three or perhaps four installments, with the doctrine, "The work of redemption is as it were the creation of a new heaven and a new earth." The extant MS (Trask Library) commences near the beginning of the second main unit in the doctrinal part and is also defective at the end. The date is therefore missing. Given paper, ink, and hand, however, it is probably safe to place it in the first half of 1744. The sermon follows No. 1037 in the Table, and the two are very similar in content.

New heavens and new earth, *continued*
and Notes on Revelation, nos. 62, 64,
73a, 85²
New nature, 655

O

Obedience: how we are justified by it, 790,
819, 876, *see* Book on Controversies, p.
207d–e;³ of such as are entitled to salvation is from love, *see* sermon on I John
5:1–4⁴
Obedience, active, of Christ, 161, 381, 399,
794, 841; its trials, *see* sermon on Luke
9:51⁵
[Œconomy, *see* Economy]
Old Testament dispensation, 39, 49, 100,
250, 252, 300, 323, 326, 439, 440, 874,
1353a, *see* Luke 16:29–31, James 2:21 ff.,
see Dispensations
Old Testament saints redeemed by Christ,
874, Fulfillment of the Prophecies of the
Messiah [1068], § 169,⁶ 1283
One God, 651, 697, [*see* Unity of the God-
head]

Operative nature of grace the life and soul
of it, 868
Oracles of the heathen silenced after
Christ, *see* Clarke's *Evidences*, pp. 202–03⁷
Original sin, 18, 34, 78, 300, 301, 374, 384,
436, 459b, 605, 654, 788, 887, 960, 966,
997, 1049, 1073–1075a, [1147], *see* note
on Ezek. 9:5–6;⁸ sentiments of ancient
Jews concerning it,⁹ 1075, 1325, *see*
Poole's *Synopsis* on Gen. 8:21 (place
marked).¹ *See* Traditions of the heathen
Own righteousness, 637, 648

P

Paradise, 952²
Pentateuch written by Moses, *see* Notes on
Scripture, no. 416, etc.³
Perfection: of happiness, 822; of holiness,
437, 894
Perpetuity of the church, 852
Perseverance, *y*, 84, 171, [327b], 415, 428,
467, 695, 711, 726, 729, 744 (corol. 1),
750, 755, [773], 774, 795, 799, 823, 945,
see note on I John 3:[6]⁴ and sermon on I

---

2. This series of four items in the "Apocalypse" notebook really consists of three, since no.
85 is an addition to no. 73a. The three are linked together by cross-references, and each
contains at the end a reference to Miscell. Nos. 634 and 743 (no. 73a also cites No. 806). See
Works, 5, 158, 159, 166–67, 198–99.

3. See above, p. 125, n. 6. JE's point on p. 207 is that faith under the new covenant is no less
a justifying obedience than the keeping of the law was under the old.

4. See above, p. 132, n. 1.

5. The "subject" of the sermon on Luke 9:51 (June 1746) is "Christ's steadfastness in
going through with those labors and sufferings that he came into the world for."

6. See above, p. 140, n. 8. The section number has been deleted by a later hand, but JE's §
169 begins, as indicated, at the bottom of MS p. 134.

7. In Prop. XIII, § 11 of the *Evidences* (pp. 202–03) Clarke lists testimonies of heathen
writers to the facts surrounding Christ's birth, life, works, and death.

8. This note is printed in Grosart, *Selections*, pp. 129–30.

9. A duplicate entry reads: "Opinion of the ancient Jews concerning it."

1. On the words, "for the imagination of man's heart is evil from his youth," the *Synopsis*
(Vol. 1, Pt. 1, col. 105d) cites certain Jewish writers and teachers who interpret the phrase
"from his youth" to mean even the first beginnings of life in the womb.

2. See above, p. 129, n. 3.

3. This is an essay of over 32 folio pages entitled, "The Pentateuch Written by Moses,"
containing a closely reasoned argument for the Mosaic authorship of all but a small portion
of the Pentateuch (the account of Moses' death and a few alterations of place names). It is
printed in the Dwight ed., 9, 115–55. JE's "etc." at the end of the citation refers to the MS
notebook on the same topic which is a continuation of the original entry; nos. 417 ff. do not
deal with this topic.

4. The verse number is broken off at the margin, but v. 6 is the one upon which is written
the most appropriate note. There are several brief notes on v. 6, but the one JE surely has in
mind (ink and hand as well as content match the Table entry) concerns the words, "Whosoever sinneth hath not seen him, neither known him."

5. See *Charity and its Fruits*, sermons 11–13, in *Works, 8,* 313–50.

6. On the "Rational Account," see above, pp. 6–8.

7. JE's page reference is to a long unit in the middle of No. 1348, an "Argument" in ten numbered sections against the notion that the inhabitants of hell are still in a state of probation.

8. This note is a comment on Acts 17:26–27; it is printed in the Dwight ed., *9,* 494–97.

9. Like the long series on Is. 51:8 (which JE apparently felt it unnecessary to list here), these sermons all deal with the "history of the work of redemption."

Is. 9:7 (Aug. 1747) has as its doctrine: "God acts in the affair of man's redemption as one greatly engaged."

Is. 65:17–18. See above, p. 141, n. 1.

Ezek. 36:36–37. See above, p. 133, n. 9.

The doctrine of the sermon on Rom. 8:22 (Sept. 1737) is, "The whole creation does, as it were, groan under the sins of wicked men."

Eph. 1:10 (Jan.-Feb. 1739) has as its doctrine "Jesus Christ is the great mediator and head of union in whom all elect creatures in heaven and earth are united to God and to one another."

The doctrine of Heb. 2:7–8 (March 1743) reads "All works and dispensations of God, in all parts of the creation and in all ages of it, are such as show forth the infinite value God has for and delight he has in his Son."

Rev. 21:6 (Dec. 1744) has as its doctrine "There is a time coming, when God's grand design in all his various works and dispensations from age to age will be completed and his end fully obtained."

1. See above, p. 131, n. 7.

2. See the preceding n. 8.

3. I.e. prophecies each of which is fulfilled by more than one event or series of events.

4. This paper has not been identified.

5. MS: "954, p. 9," which occurs near the end of a long addition to No. 952 written after No. 954. The place referred to is an answer to an objection concerning the nature of the kingdom prepared for the saints from the foundation of the world, and it contains in large letters the words of the Table entry.

6. The note is printed in Grosart, *Selections,* pp. 99–100.

7. MS: "1156, p. 7, 8," i.e. a section headed, "[The] Reasonableness of the Doctrine of the Resurrection."

8. See above, p. 128, n. 4. Considering the general scope of the Table heading and the fact that p. 209 is the point at which the body of Watts' "The Strength and Weakness of Human Reason" begins, there can be little doubt that JE means here to refer to the whole of that work.

9. The pages cited are found in Conference I of "Strength and Weakness" (see the preceding note).

1. See above, p. 127, n. 2.

2. The plural "notes" was probably a slip, for the reference is to a single connected essay in the "Blank Bible" (entered, however, in more than one installment). It was probably written in 1733 and is printed in Grosart, *Selections,* pp. 168–69.

3. This note is printed in ibid., p. 66.

4. See above, p. 125, n. 6. On pp. 143–56 of this notebook there is a series of notes and short essays on justification. The longest of these (pp. 150e–55, 200–01) has as its running head "The Meaning of the words Righteousness, Righteous, etc. in the Old Testament."

5. See above, p. 128, n. 6.

1281, *see* catalogue of texts [in the] History of the Work of Redemption, pp. 29 ff.,[6] *also* note on Rev. 14:13;[7] meeting with former friends, 639; partake of Christ's own glory and happiness and the love of God to him, 1274

Sanctification from the womb, 78

Satan before the fall the highest of all creatures, 936, 980, 1264, 1266b

Satan defeated, 156, 298, 307, [320], 324, 344, 347, 560, 616, 618, 619, 809 (corols. 1, 2), 815

Satisfaction, *b, oo,* 113, 245, 265, 281, 306, 319, 321b, 357, 388, 398, 506, 516, 594, 764a, 779, [798], 898, 912, 915, 1005, 1035, 1076, [1083], 1145, 1173, 1206, 1208, 1212–1214, 1216, 1217, 1226, 1232, [1295], 1352, [1360], *see* note on Deut. 9:21[8] and sermon on Rev. 5:12 (application),[9] *also* Mr. Dickinson's *Five Discourses,* p. 182;[1] and merits of Christ different, 846; and righteousness of Christ, the fitness of accepting sinners for Christ's sake, 483; for sin, the necessity of it, 779, [798, 1295], *see* Mr. McLaurin's sermon on "God's Chief Mercy," p. 104[2]

Savior, why a particular Person should be appointed to that office, 1156[3]

Scripture, *dd,* 6, 61, 126, 195, [229], 303, 333, 351, 352, 359, 426, 760, 983, 984; the canon finished, *see* sermon on I Cor. 13:8–13;[4] consequences, 1291; history attested by heathen historians, 983; the manner of the inspiration of its penmen, *see* note on I Chron. 28:19[5]

Scriptures: interpretation of various distinct things, 851, 1172, *see* note on Dan. 5:25 ff., and paper in the drawer,[6] *also* Ex. 12:46; why constituted of such parts, 358, 359, 810

Searching the heart, God's prerogative, 777

Secret and revealed will of God, 7, 170

Self-determining power, [1075b], 1153–1155

Self-love, 473, 530, 821, *see* sermon on John 7:18;[7] the source of all sin, 1010

Self-righteousness, 610, 637, 648, 747, *see* sermon on Matt. 21:31[8]

Sense of the heart, 782, 1183

Separate souls of saints: acquainted with what is done on earth, 372, 421, 529, 555,

---

6. The words "History of the" are in shorthand, both here and in the title on the front of the notebook to which JE refers. (There is a second notebook with the same title, with the title entirely in shorthand.) On pp. 29–31 of the first notebook is a list of "Texts which intimate that the saints in heaven have communion with the church on earth in all that belongs to its prosperity, and [that] the sufferings of devils and damned spirits are proportionably increased."

7. MS: "SS p. 884." JE wrote the abbreviation for "Notes on Scripture," but he gave the page in the "Blank Bible," where this note is found.

8. This note is printed in Grosart, *Selections,* pp. 93–94.

9. See above, p. 127, n. 9.

1. Jonathan Dickinson, *The True Scripture-Doctrine Concerning Some Important Points of Christian Faith . . . Represented and Apply'd in Five Discourses* (Boston, 1741). The passage cited occurs in the "Discourse upon Justification by Faith" (pp. 177–217).

2. JE's reference is to McLaurin's third sermon, on Rom. 8:32 (*Sermons and Essays,* pp. 96–129); on p. 104 McLaurin seeks to answer those who ask why any person's sin can be so evil as to require eternal punishment or the satisfaction of Christ.

3. MS: "1156, p. 8," i.e. a discussion near the end of the number which contains the words of the Table entry in large letters for easy identification.

4. See above, p. 127, n. 2.

5. See above, p. 138, n. 4.

6. This paper has not been identified.

7. This sermon of March 1745 has the doctrine, "Men in the exercise[s] of true religion do make God and not themselves their highest end; or, men in the exercises of true religion do ultimately seek God and not themselves."

8. The theme of this sermon of Jan. 1748, is sufficiently indicated by its doctrine: "Self-righteousness is one of the greatest banes of the souls of men."

9. See above, p. 134, n. 6. These two citations occur immediately after No. 811 in this listing also.

1. John Owen, *Exercitations on the Epistle to the Hebrews . . . with an Exposition and Discourses . . .* (4 vols. London, 1668–84), 3, 27–28 (second pagination). Since both the "Blank Bible" and the "Miscellanies" (e.g. No. 1352) contain references to Vols. 3 and 4 at places marked in the margins, it is obvious that in his later years JE owned at least those volumes of the set. And though no references to Vols. 1 and 2 occur in the pages of the "Blank Bible" devoted to Hebrews, JE's memorandum in No. 1352 to "see various parts of Owen's *Exposition on the Hebrews*" may imply that the whole set was in his library.

2. See above, p. 135, n. 2. The application of this Nov. 1741 sermon has four uses, the first of which has three inferences. The third inference is "that in hell the wicked will be the subjects of every kind of suffering that their nature dreads."

3. MS: "1153, p. 10"; on that page begins the last large section of the number (before the corollaries), an essay headed "Sincerity."

4. Ibid.

5. See above, p. 131, n. 4.

6. This sermon, dated Aug. 1733, carries the doctrine, "There is such a thing as a spiritual and divine light immediately imparted to the soul by God, of a different nature from any that is obtained by natural means." Published at Boston in 1734, this is the best known statement of JE's doctrine of "divine and supernatural light."

7. This sermon of June 1746 deals with "Christ's steadfastness in going through with those labors and sufferings that he came into the world for."

8. MS: "1005, p. 4 of that number near bottom," i.e. the second of the two main divisions of the number, the second paragraph.

9. See the preceding n. 7.

1. "My design from these words," says JE in the doctrine, "is to consider Christ's expending his own blood for the salvation and happiness of the souls of men, in the view both of an inducement and a direction to ministers to exert themselves for the same end." JE preached the sermon on March 28, 1754, at the ordination of Edward Billings as the pastor of a new congregation at Greenfield, Massachusetts. Billings had been dismissed by his church at Cold Spring (Belchertown) in 1752 for espousing JE's cause in the communion controversy. JE had also preached a sermon on this text in Dec. 1745 with the doctrine, "The church of God is purchased by the blood of God."

2. See the preceding n. 7.

3. I.e. § 5 in the second set of numbered sections within No. 779.

4. "The nature of true virtue and the way in which it is obtained" is the entire entry. JE's dissertation is printed in *Works, 8*, pp. 537–627.

5. The wording of the first part of the entry varies with the form in which the latter part is stated. The topics that follow are listed alphabetically by the first word of the topic, except for the article and a few other introductory words.

6. See above, p. 139, n. 1. These pages occur in Clarke's defense of the rational and hence immutable "Moral Obligations in particular" (Prop. I, § 4). On the duty of self-preservation he quotes Plato, Cicero, and Arrian.

In the many citations of Clarke that occur under the heading of "Traditions" JE desires simply to locate bodies of heathen testimony that appear to support particular Christian doctrines. It is therefore unnecessary to annotate each citation.

7. Besides the Jewish writers cited in the *Synopsis* on Gen. 8:21, Seneca and Plutarch are also quoted as testifying to the ingenerate character of human wickedness even before the appearance of specific acts of vice (Vol. 1, Pt. 1, col. 105d–e). JE apparently marked both sets of material in his copy of Poole.

8. The *Synopsis* on I Sam. 28:11 (Vol. *1*, Pt. 2, col. 241) deals mainly with the words, "Bring me up Samuel." The chief source is Grotius, who cites Aeschylus and Herodotus for the widespread practice of necromancy in the ancient world and concludes with quotations from Virgil, Seneca, *et al.*

9. No. 1355a occupies MS pp. 939–63 in Bk. 9; JE here cites pp. 953–57.

1. The notes on Ex. 3:14 are found in the *Synopsis*, Vol. 1, Pt. 1, cols. 328–29.

2. At this point JE wrote a reference, obviously to Bk. 9, with "Miscell." at the right margin, and "col. 1. a" at the beginning of the next line; the "P." and page number have been worn off at the margin or, more likely, were accidentally omitted by JE. No passage has been found in an upper left column of Bk. 9 which unambiguously fits the topic.

3. On Ex. 20:4 (the prohibition of idolatry) Poole's authors cite Varro on the supposed imageless worship of the ancient Romans and mention Numa's removing the images from the temples (cols. 401–02). Most of the notes on Deut. 4:15 are devoted to quotations from Empedocles, Tacitus, *et al.* on the folly of idolatry (cols. 764–65).

4. Richard Kidder, *A Demonstration of the Messias* (3 vols., London, 1684–1700). In its complete form it incorporated Kidder's 1693 Boyle Lectures. By the latter 1740s JE owned the unabridged second ed. (London, 1726), which contained the three separately paged parts in one folio volume. In Pt. 3, ch. 6, pp. 122–25, Kidder quotes Plato and ancient poets relative to the Logos and the Trinity; he then (pp. 126–28) asserts the utility of these materials, especially for refuting the Socinian charge of "novelty" against Trinitarian Christianity.

5. Written "Unity of the Godhead" in the continuation entry.

6. See above, p. 128, n. 1.

7. This note (printed in the Dwight ed., *9*, 407–08) concerns Ezek. 1:4, in which "a whirlwind came out of the north, a great cloud, and a fire infolding itself," which JE understood to "represent the Deity before the creation," i.e. the divine essence interacting within itself.

8. See above, p. 131, n. 4.

9. Almost certainly, the place which JE marked in the margin of his copy was near the middle of Vol. 1, Pt. 1, col. 2, where the ancient Hebrews are said to have interpreted *Elohim* (*creavit Dii*) as implying a plurality in God; JE's pen must have marked at least the statement of Rabbi Simeon Ben Jochai that in the "mystery of the word *Elohim*" there are three ranks (*gradus*), each distinct but all joined together indivisibly. The commentary on Gen. 1:26 is found in Vol. 1, Pt. 1, cols. 11–12; those on II Sam. 7:22–23 and 23:2 are in Vol. 1, Pt. 2, cols. 298–99 and 391 respectively.

1. MS: "p 215 &c." Among the essays on justification in this notebook is one entitled, "Question. In what Sense did the Saints under the Old Testament believe in Christ to Justification?" (pp. 213–36). It contains thirteen sections, the second of which is devoted to proving that "the Jews understood their Savior to be a distinct person in the Godhead." The section is found on pp. 213–17; hence it is likely that JE meant to write 213.

2. See the preceding n. 9.

3. Entry No. 1069, entitled "Types of the Messiah," is printed in *Works, 11*, 191–324.

4. This is doubtless a reference to the "Types Notebook" (Trask Library). It consists of eight unpaged octavo leaves made of scrap paper (mainly letter wrappers). See *Works, 11*, 146–53

5. See above, p. 131, n. 5. The pages to which JE refers contain the "Essay on Prejudices against the Gospel," § vii, in which McLaurin deals with difficulties people have with the doctrine of the spiritual union between Christ and believers.

6. At the top of the first page of this sermon is written, "Fast for success in the expedition against Cape Breton, April 4, 1745." The text contains Solomon's petition that the Lord would hear his people's prayers for success when they went forth against their enemies. JE develops the theme in four propositions, of which the first is, "A people of God may be called of God to go forth to war against their enemies."

7. This sermon is the fifth in a series on the parable of the sower which was preached in Nov. 1740. The doctrine is an "Observation. That religion that arises only from superficial impressions is wont to wither away for want of root when it comes to be tried by the difficulties of religion." The fourth of the sermon's six propositions maintains that difficulties in religion are a proper trial of faith to prove whether it is sincere.

THE "MISCELLANIES,"
ENTRY NOS. a–z, aa–zz, 1–500

NOTE ON THE TEXT OF THE "MISCELLANIES"

T HE "Miscellanies" consists of nine manuscript notebooks plus a thin index volume or Table to the whole, all of which, with the exception of one book, are housed at Yale University's Beinecke Rare Book and Manuscript Library.[1] Edwards assigned numbers to these manuscript volumes, which he called "books," and in his own cross-referencing system often cited entries in the "Miscellanies" by both book and entry number. With the exception of the earliest entries in the "Miscellanies," to which Edwards assigned letters, the entries are numbered consecutively not only within but between books.[2] (See Table 3.)

Table 3. "Miscellanies" Entries By Books

Book 1:	a–zz, 1–688
Book 2:	689–760
Book 3:	761-880
Book 4:	884–958[3]
Book 5:	958–1066
Book 6:	1067–1068
Book 7:	1069–1155
Book 8:	1156–1253
Book 9:	1253–1360

1. In addition to the MS of Book 6, the Trask Library also holds a partial copy of the "Miscellanies" that was commissioned by Sereno Dwight when he was preparing his edition of JE's collected works. Consultation of this copy is at times valuable, especially in those instances where the tattered margins in the original MSS create lacunae in the text.

2. JE's numbering of the entries is described in the "Note on the Table," above pp. 113–23.

3. Book 4 was made of 25 sheets, which yielded 50 leaves and 100 pages. The front leaves of the two outside sheets are now missing. The copy of No. 884 in the Trask Library preserves the first part of that entry; the text thus preserved is just about sufficient to have filled the missing four pages at the rate JE was writing in the succeeding pages. There are no copies in the Trask Library MSS or references in JE's Table to entries numbered 881–883, so it can be assumed that no entries are missing between the books. JE apparently started No. 884 in the new book because of its length and allowed three numerals for entries he might make after No. 880, but never wrote them.

Each of the "Miscellanies" notebooks was constructed by Edwards himself, with the exception of the ninth, which had had a previous owner and was probably made by a commercial book binder. All but Books 1 and 9 are made of infolded quires.[4] Book 1 is a folio made from a gathering of separately folded sheets stitched together. Books 3–8 are in folio, Book 2 in quarto. Book 9 is also a quarto volume, but it is a collection of signatures stitched together and, unlike other volumes, has pages ruled in double columns. A few entries by its previous owner appear at the bottoms of some pages; Edwards turned the notebook upside down for his entries and repaginated the book. Though the physical condition of the "Miscellanies" manuscript is generally good, various kinds of damage have occurred. The ink is very faded in some places, either because it was low in pigment to begin with or because the surface has been subjected to an undue amount of weathering or abrasion, as on outside margins and on the outermost leaves of the notebooks. Perhaps because of age and repeated use, the first notebook is in the poorest condition: its pages are very fragile and the margins are tattered. A few loose leaves in other volumes are similarly damaged, but the majority remain in remarkably good condition. All notebooks are complete, except for the first four pages of Book 4 and a few leaves out of Book 7. The covers of Books 1, 4, and 9, and the original cover of Book 7 are also missing. The remaining original covers are each made of heavy paper, except that of Book 2, which is made from decorated oilcloth.

The folio volumes have an average of 78 leaves each. The quarto volume Edwards constructed himself has 96 leaves, and the one he obtained elsewhere, 315 leaves. The nine notebooks that comprise the "Miscellanies," therefore, have a total of 955 leaves or 1910 pages of text.[5] The earliest pages of the "Miscellanies" are extremely closely written, there is little space between lines, and the writing extends almost to the edge of the paper on all sides.[6] Edwards' handwriting gradually got larger and the amount of script on a page proportionally decreased. The length of the entries varies throughout the series; on average, they get longer as Edwards gets older. Book 1 contains 730

4. For an explanation of the paper terminology used in this study, see above p. 10, n. 2.

5. This calculation includes blank pages, but with the exception of Book 9, the notebooks have very few blank pages.

6. Most of these pages contain 100 to 125 lines of script, and many of the lines run to 30 or more words. Nos. a–zz occupy a scant 5 1/2 pp. in the MS. See the discussion of JE's handwriting in § 3 of the Introduction, pp. 66–68.

entries, more than all the other volumes combined. The shortest entries are one line citations of other texts; the longest entry, No. 1068, entitled "Fulfillment of the Prophecies of the Messiah," is, at 144 manuscript pages, the equivalent of a small treatise. The difference in length between the earlier and later entries results in part from a change in function, as Edwards combined material from earlier entries into larger, more complex essays.

There are a few places in Book 1 where the text runs in chronological order but entry numbers are omitted or out of order. The first of these is in the very first sheet of the "Miscellanies." What is now entry No. m, "Types of the Scripture," was probably written before—but only shortly before—No. a, and what is physically the first page is actually the fourth in the order of composition.[7] Another instance of misnumbering is a case of simple omission. No. 51 is at the bottom of a recto; when Edwards wrote the next entry at the top of the verso, he apparently misread the number of the last entry and numbered the new entry No. 60. Thus there are no Nos. 52–59 in the text. The final instance is more complicated. After Edwards went back to number entries Nos. 126–131 on the first recto of a sheet, he skipped the verso and began numbering entries on the second recto and verso of the sheet as Nos. 132–146. When he discovered his mistake, he merely numbered the entries on the first verso as Nos. 147–156, so that the numbers on the sheet run 126–131, 147–156, 132–146. In the text, the corrected numbers are used, with Edwards' original numbers following in parentheses.

Edwards generally kept his entries in chronological order, but there were occasions when he did not do so. There are instances where hand, ink, and other factors indicate that certain entries were written at a later time than those that precede and follow them. Such dislocations happened when, for one reason or another, Edwards left blank space in the manuscript which he afterwards filled in, sometimes months or years later. The most serious of these occurred during his first two years with Stoddard and for a few months after the latter's death in February 1729.[8] Table 4 indicates the probable chronological

---

7. What happened is described more fully above, p. 78, n. 9.

8. Information on these and other early dislocations is provided in the notes to pertinent entries. Later on, shorter breaks in chronological order sometimes occurred when JE moved ahead to begin copying a long entry or left space for its completion, later filling up the unused space.

Table 4. Chronological Order of "Miscellanies" *a–500*

Date	*Location*	*Entries*
Oct. 1722–April 1723	New York City	*a–zz*
May–June 1723	East Windsor	1–26
July–Aug. 1723	East Windsor	27b–51
Sept. 1723–May 1724	Bolton	60–123
June–August 1724	New Haven	Hiatus at beginning of tutorship
Sept. 1724–June 1725	New Haven	126–131 147–156
July–Aug. 1725	East Windsor and New Haven	124–125b 192–194 27a
Sept.–Nov. 1725	North Haven and East Windsor	Hiatus due to illness
Dec. 1725–Jan. 1726	East Windsor	195–205
Feb.–Aug. 1726	New Haven	206–235 261–264
Sept. 1726	East Windsor	311–314
Oct.–Nov. 1726	Northampton	267–274
Dec. 1726–May 1727	Northampton	236–255
June–Oct. 1727	Northampton	279–305
Nov.–Dec. 1727	Northampton	315–317
Jan.–Feb. 1728	Northampton	275 318–322 265
Feb.–March 1728	Northampton	323–328

(*continued*)

Table 4. *Continued*

Date	Location	Entries
April–June 1728	Northampton	306–310
		256–260
		266
		276–278
July 1728–Feb. 1729	Hiatus due to Stoddard's death	329–369
		371–386
Feb.–March 1729	Northampton	393–395
April–May 1729	Northampton	370
		396–405
		391–392
		406–409
		387–390
June 1729	Northampton	410–417
		393, additions
July 1729–Aug. 1731	Northampton	418–510

order of the composition of entries No. a–500 as determined by the methodology described in the Introduction.[9]

This edition of the "Miscellanies" was prepared from the autographs; manuscript copies and printed versions were used only in a supplemental way. The 1793 and 1796 editions prepared by Jonathan Edwards, Jr., have proved helpful in reading the originals, as also have the portions first published by Sereno Dwight in 1829. Even more valuable are the manuscript copies made by and for those editors, especially the massive (though incomplete) series of transcriptions prepared by Dwight's scribe and corrected by Dwight. Some items in Edwards' own hand have made small but important contributions. A few sermon booklets contain drafts of portions of early miscellanies. Other manuscripts, mostly sermons, quote or paraphrase portions of entries and have occasionally assisted in their reading or interpretation. Printings by more recent authors have suggested a few readings. All these are useful when employed judiciously. They preserve text

9. See above, pp. 60–69.

now missing from the autographs and furnish plausible conjectures where words are now illegible.

One vexing editorial handicap is a consequence of the editorial activity of Jonathan Edwards, Jr., for he made his revisions directly upon the autographs. Fortunately the son's handwriting, as well as the shade of the ink and the texture of the pen he used, can usually be distinguished from the original, but in some cases his insertions are easily confused with those of his father. Especially problematic are his cancellations of words and phrases, which sometimes obliterate the text. When their ink is close to that of the original, they are not only harder to identify but render suspect other deletions in the passage as possibly not made by Edwards himself. In many cases the task of sorting out the two hands can be accomplished only with the aid of a microscope.

There are many passages, especially in the earlier entries, that have the unadorned and provisional style that characterizes Edwards' manuscripts. Dropped words are common, the result no doubt of scribal errors or haste in composition on Edwards' part. Some entries contain awkward or provincial forms of speech, while others contain doublets of such words as "that," "its," and "will," caused not by a simple slip of the pen but by repetition later in the sentence. Double negatives sometimes occur in this way as well. Edwards often makes shifts in the person and number of pronouns and in the tenses of verbs, which can become very confusing. On occasion, the same pronoun has more than one referent and oscillates between them. The syntax of a sentence can change at any point, and grammatical constructions which today are considered solecisms are frequently encountered. Sometimes annotation or editorial insertion becomes necessary to make Edwards' meaning clear.

The unfinished nature of the text is most noticeable in its punctuation. Except for excessive and erratic use of commas in the earliest entries, the "Miscellanies" text is sparsely punctuated. On the rare occasions when they do appear, periods and commas are nearly indistinguishable from each other. Semicolons and colons almost never occur except in passages quoted from other authors; question and exclamation marks are practically nonexistent.[1] Confronted by these problems, a reader of Edwards' manuscripts must rely on other signs

1. JE apparently did not discover the usefulness of parentheses until near the end of his first year as tutor. The first set in the "Miscellanies" occurs in No. 173, then one in No. 201, and with some regularity thereafter.

to identify syntactical units. For example, a sentence sometimes does begin with a capital letter! Edwards often used space as punctuation, separating clauses and sentences by a longer space than usual. The beginning of a paragraph is indicated either by a very long space, a dash, a curved line between two words, or a horizontal line drawn from the left margin and extending partly or wholly across the page. Indented paragraphs begin to appear around No. 400 and occur regularly in the later entries. As indicated above in the "Note to the Reader," the editor assumes responsibility for all punctuation and paragraphing in the text. It must be noted, however, that even the longest and most complicated passages usually turn out to be perfectly articulated sentences or paragraphs once appropriate punctuation has been added.

The amount of deletion and interlineation both at the time of composition and in subsequent revision varies throughout the notebooks. Edwards' normal method for deleting material is a horizontal strike-through; for passages longer than a line or two he generally uses a large "X" mark. When the deleted passage is a numbered entry, it is printed in the text with an explanatory note unless Edwards used its numeral for the next entry; in that case it is treated like other deleted material, i.e. ignored unless it signals a change in Edwards' thought or assists in the interpretation of a contiguous passage.

In his later years Edwards began to mark passages in the "Miscellanies" that he had used elsewhere by drawing a line down the left margin beside the portions transferred.[2] It is also possible that a vertical line through a passage near the left margin or down the middle of the page has the same function. The presence of a vertical line on or beside an entry is indicated in the notes to the "Miscellanies" text, and the location of the transferred passage is given when known.

Edwards sometimes skips or repeats a numeral when numbering his entries, sometimes fails to number an entry, or overlooks an entry with the result that two entries on quite different topics share the same numeral. Edwards sometimes caught these repetitions himself and marked one or both of the entry numbers with the letters *a* and *b*. Where he did not, editorial brackets will be used with the supplied letters, but only at the heading of the entry and not in the Table or in citations.

---

2. JE's use of the marginal line is especially prominent in material incorporated into *End of Creation* and *Nature of True Virtue*.

Edwards often refers, usually at the beginning or end of an entry but sometimes within it, to biblical texts, other miscellanies, other manuscripts (especially Scripture notes), or printed works. When Edwards cites a note on a biblical text in the form "note on John 3:16," the Blank Bible is always meant. References to the "Notes on Scripture" and "Notes on Revelation" ("Apocalypse") are identified as such and the number of the note supplied if not already given by Edwards. He often began a new entry with a reference to an earlier entry and composed the new one as an obvious continuation of the previous one, and sometimes a cross-reference in one entry calls for its addition to a previous entry. Wherever possible, such cross-references are explained—or at least identified—in the notes.

In this connection, some editorial problems prominent in the "Miscellanies" may be mentioned here. Edwards' numbering is sometimes erratic in form. For example, he may introduce a series of three by "first," "2," and "in the 3 place" respectively, or even omit one of the numbers. His numbering has been regularized and corrected where necessary; the same holds for forms of citation and Scripture reference. Cardinal and ordinal numbers are sometimes interchangeable, and they are spelled out or left as numerals depending on the context. Edwards used "vid." and "see" to introduce citations, and "No." "numb.," or "num." for his entries; "see" and "No." are used uniformly in the edited text.

At various points up to mid-1729, Edwards left his entries unnumbered for long periods of time, making cross-referencing difficult. Sometimes he simply left a space for the entry number, usually but not always supplying it later; his citation sometimes took the form of "vid. last but two" or "see after the next but one." Since these were temporary devices superseded by the arrival of entry numbers, the entry Edwards intended is given as the citation and the circumlocutions ignored. Something similar happens with cross-references that specify some particular place in an entry, as in "see No. 412 this mark," followed by a cue mark. These references are all annotated at the places in the text designated by Edwards' marks, though the marks themselves are not reproduced.

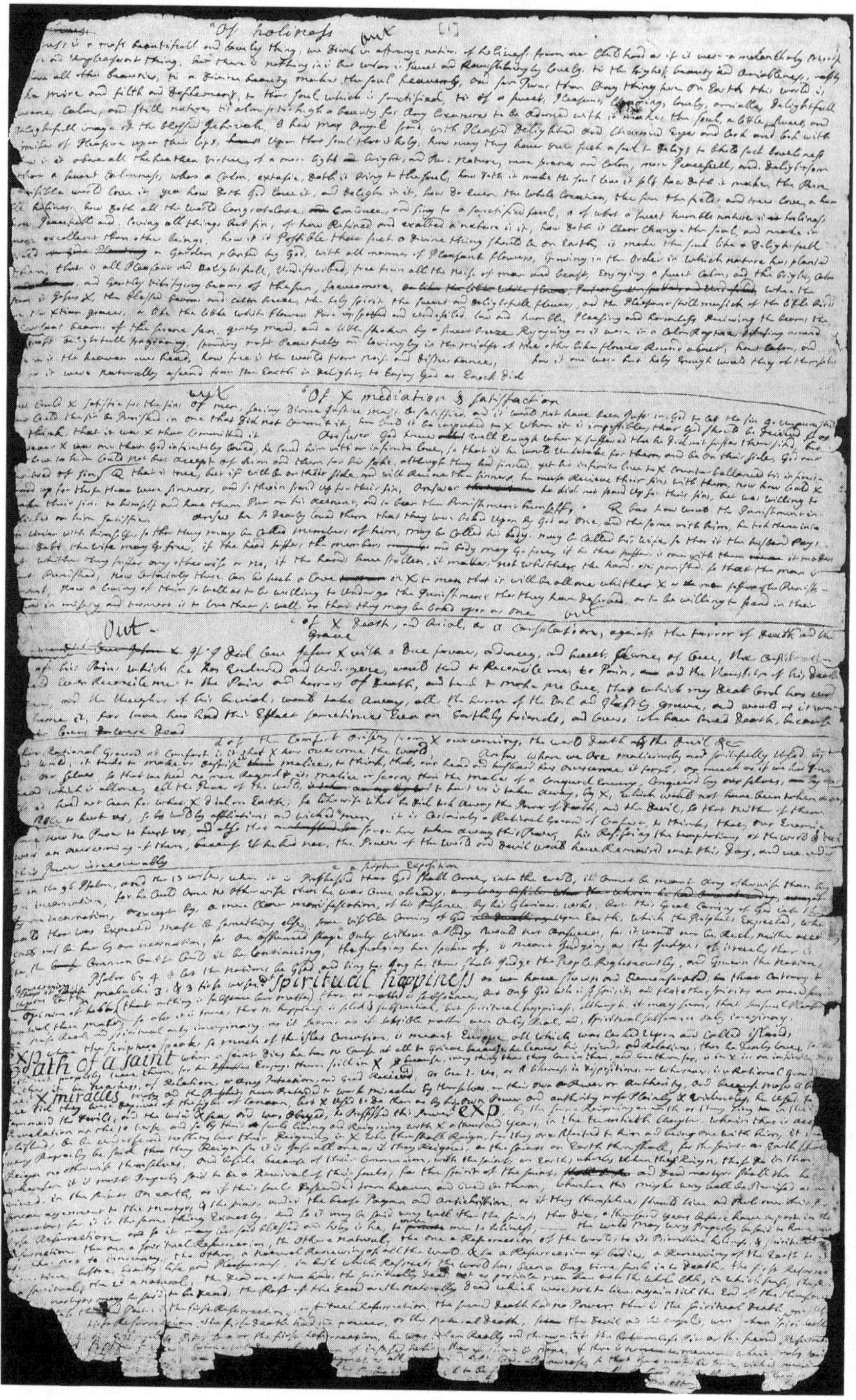

Fig. 3. Photograph of the first page of the "Miscellanies" text, showing entry nos. a–l. Courtesy of Beinecke Rare Book and Manuscript Library, Yale University.

THE "MISCELLANIES," ENTRY NOS. a–z, aa–zz, 1–500

a. OF HOLINESS.[1] Holiness is a most beautiful and lovely thing. We drink in strange notions[2] of holiness from our childhood, as if it were a melancholy, morose, sour[3] and unpleasant thing; but there is nothing in it but what is sweet and ravishingly lovely. 'Tis the highest beauty and amiableness, vastly above all other beauties. 'Tis a divine beauty, makes the soul heavenly and far purer than anything here on earth; this world is like mire and filth and defilement to that soul which is sanctified. 'Tis of a sweet, pleasant, charming, lovely, amiable, delightful, serene, calm and still nature. 'Tis almost too high a beauty for any creatures to be adorned with; it makes the soul a little, sweet and delightful image of the blessed Jehovah.

Oh, how may angels stand, with pleased, delighted and charmed eyes, and look and look,[4] with smiles of pleasure upon their lips, upon that soul that is holy; how may they hover over such a soul, to delight to behold such loveliness! How is it above all the heathen virtues, of a more light, bright and pure nature, more serene and calm, more peaceful and delightsome! What a sweet calmness, what a calm ecstasy, doth it bring to the soul! How doth it make the soul love itself; how doth it make the pure invisible world love it; yea, how doth God love it and delight in it; how do even the whole creation, the sun, the fields and trees love a humble holiness; how doth all the world congratulate, embrace, and sing to a sanctified soul!

1. The margins of the first several sheets in the "Miscellanies" are badly worn and sometimes tattered. This is especially true of the first leaf, and there is no copy of No. a in the Dwight copies. Not long after JE wrote the essay he copied a large extract from it into the sermon on Is. 35:8 (printed in *Works, 10,* 478–79), and about twenty years later he copied another into his "Personal Narrative"; both have been helpful in establishing the text. For the "Personal Narrative" passage and the date of No. a, see above, pp. 76–79.

2. MS: "astrange [sic] notions." In the sermon on Is. 35:8 JE read it as a plural: "Men are apt to drink in strange notions of holiness."

3. The first three letters are lost at the left margin, but the word is preserved in the sermon.

4. The second "and look" is a deliberate repetition; when JE copied this sentence into the sermon he interlined the second "and look" above a caret.

Oh, of what a sweet, humble nature is holiness! How peaceful and, loving all things but sin, of how refined and exalted a nature is it! How doth it clear change the soul and make it more excellent than other beings! How is it possible that such a divine thing should be on earth? It makes the soul like a delightful field or garden planted by God, with all manner of pleasant flowers growing in the order in which nature has planted them, that is all pleasant and delightful, undisturbed, free from all the noise of man and beast, enjoying a sweet calm and the bright, calm, and gently vivifying beams of the sun forevermore: where the sun is Jesus Christ; the blessed beams and calm breeze, the Holy Spirit; the sweet and delightful flowers, and the pleasant shrill music of the little birds, are the Christian graces. Or like the little white flower: pure, unspotted and undefiled, low and humble, pleasing and harmless; receiving the beams, the pleasant beams of the serene sun, gently moved and a little shaken by a sweet breeze, rejoicing as it were in a calm rapture, diffusing around [a][5] most delightful fragrancy, standing most peacefully and lovingly in the midst of the other like flowers round about. How calm and serene is the heaven overhead! How free is the world from noise and disturbance! How, if one were but holy enough, would they of themselves [and][6] as it were naturally ascend from the earth in delight, to enjoy God as Enoch did!

b. OF CHRIST'S MEDIATION AND SATISFACTION. *Ques.* How could Christ satisfy for the sins of men, seeing divine justice must be satisfied, and it would not have been just in God to let the sin go unpunished? How could the sin be punished in one that did not commit it? How could it be imputed to Christ, when it is impossible that God should be deceived so as [to][7] think that it was Christ that committed it? *Ans.* God knew well enough, when Christ suffered, that he did not suffer that sinned. But however, Christ was one that God infinitely loved. He loved him with an infinite love; so that if he would undertake for them and be on their side, God, out [of][8] love to him, could not but accept of him, and them for his sake. Although they had sinned, yet his infinite love to Christ counterbalanced his infinite hatred of sin.

Ques. That is true; but if [he] will be on their side and will receive the

5. The location of "most" on the MS shows that a short word is missing from the left margin.
6. A remnant of the last letter of a short word is visible at the left margin.
7. The word is broken off at the margin.
8. Ibid.

sinners, he must receive their sins with them. Now how could Christ stand up for those that were sinners, and so therein stand up for their sins? *Ans.* He did not stand up for their sins, but was willing to take their sins to himself and have them put on his account, and to bear the punishment himself.

Ques. But how would the punishment inflicted on him satisfy? *Ans.* He so dearly loved them that they were looked upon by God as one and the same with him. He took them into an union with himself; so that they may be called members of him, may be called his body, may be called his wife: so that if the husband pays her debt, the wife may go free; if the head suffers, the members and body may go free. If he that suffers is one with them, it matters not whether they suffer any otherwise or no; if the hands have stolen, it matters not whether the hands are punished, so that the man is but punished. Now certainly there can be such a love in Christ to men, that it will be all one whether Christ or men suffer the punishment. Now a loving of them so well as to be willing to undergo the punishment that they have deserved, as to be willing to stand in their stead in misery and torment, is to love them so well as that they may be looked upon as one.

c. Of Christ's Death and Burial, as a Consolation Against the Terror of Death and the Grave. If I did love Jesus Christ with a due fervor, ardency and sweet flames of love, the consideration of his pains which he has endured and undergone would tend to reconcile me to pain; and the thoughts of his death would ever reconcile me to the pains and terrors of death, and tend to make me love that which my dear Lord has undergone; and the thoughts of his burial would take away all the horror of the dark and ghastly grave, and would as it were consume it. For love has had this effect sometimes even on earthly friends, and lovers who have loved death because their lovers were dead.

d. Of the Comfort Arising from Christ Overcoming the World, Death and the Devil, etc. *Ques.* What rational ground of comfort is it that Christ has overcome the world? *Ans.* When we are maliciously and spitefully used by this world, it tends to make us despise its malice, to think that our Head and Husband has overcome it for us, as much as if we had done it ourselves; so that we need no more regard its malice or scorn than the malice of a conquered enemy, conquered by ourselves, [that is,] by our Head, which is all one. All the

power of the world to hurt us is taken away by Christ, which would not
have been taken away if it had not been for what Christ did on earth. So
likewise, what he did took away the power of death and the devil; so
that neither of them [is]⁹ able to hurt us so by worldly afflictions and
wicked men. It is certainly a rational ground of comfort, to think that
our enemies have now no power to hurt us, and also that our Spouse
has taken away this power. His resisting the temptations of the world
and devil was an overcoming of them; because if he had not, the power
of the world and devil would have remained unto this day, and we
under their power irrecoverably.

e. A Scripture Exposition. As in Ps. 96:13, where it is prophesied
that God shall come into the world, it cannot be meant any otherwise
than by an incarnation. For he could come no otherwise than he has
come already [but] by an incarnation, except by a more clear manifestation of his presence by his glorious works. But this great coming
of God into the world that was expected must be something else, some
visible coming of God upon earth which the prophets expected, which
could not be but by an incarnation. For an assumed shape only, without a body, would not answer, for it would not be real; neither, according to the common course, could it be continuing. The judging here
spoken of, is meant judging as the judges of Israel, that is, governing:
Ps. 67:4, "O let the nations be glad and sing for joy: for thou shalt
judge the people righteously, and govern the nations upon earth." Is.
9: [6–7]; Mal. 3:1–3.

f. Spiritual Happiness. As we have shown and demonstrated, that,¹
contrary to the opinion of Hobbes (that nothing is substance but matter), that no matter is substance but only God, who is a spirit, and that
other spirits are more substantial than matter; so also it is true, that no
happiness is solid and substantial but spiritual happiness, although it
may seem that sensual pleasures are most real and spiritual only imaginary, as it seems as if sensible matter were only real and spiritual
substance only imaginary.

9. Ibid.
1. MS: "demonstrated ~~in~~ that"; JE was refering to his "Natural Philosophy," for No. f is
based directly on two entries in that notebook. One is Long Series no. 26 (*Works, 6*, 235); the
other is no. 44 of the same series, the third corollary of which seems to be partially incorporated into No. f (ibid., p. 238).

g. EXPOSITION. Where the Scripture speaks so much of the isles' conversion, is meant Europe, all which was looked upon and called islands.

h. DEATH OF A SAINT.[2] When a saint dies, he has no cause at all to grieve because he leaves his friends and relations that he dearly loves, for he doth not properly leave them. For he enjoys them still in Christ; because everything that he loves in them and loves them for,[3] is in Christ in an infinite degree; whether it be nearness of relation, or any perfection and good received, or love to us, or a likeness in dispositions, or whatever is a rational ground of love.

i. CHRIST'S MIRACLES. Moses and the prophets never pretended to work miracles by themselves, on their own power or authority; and because Moses and Aaron once did, they were deprived of the sight of Canaan. But Christ used to do them as by his own power and authority, most plainly and evidently. He used to command the devils, and the wind and seas, and was obeyed. He professed this power.

k.[4] EXPOSITION. By the saints' reigning on earth (as they sing in the 5th [chapter] of Revelation at the 10th verse), and so by their souls' living and reigning with Christ a thousand years (in the 20th chapter, wherein that is accomplished), can be understood nothing but their reigning in Christ, who then shall reign; for they are united to him, and being one with him, it may very properly be said that they reign. For it is just all one as if they reigned, as the saints on earth then shall; for the saints on earth shall reign no otherwise themselves. And besides, because of their communion with the saints on earth, whereby when those reign, these[5] do in them. Wherefore it is most properly said to be a revival of their souls; for the spirit of the saints and dead martyrs shall then be revived in the saints on earth, as if their souls descended from heaven and lived in them. Wherefore this might very well be promised as an encouragement to the martyrs and the saints,

2. For a parallel passage in the sermon on Phil. 1:21, see *Works, 10*, 583–84.
3. MS: "that they love in them, and love them for."
4. There is no No. j.
5. JE apparently wrote "those . . . these," but on a rereading changed the former to "they"; this alteration, however, introduces an ambiguity. What seems to have been his original wording has therefore been restored, since it fits the context and expresses his thought clearly.

under the beast pagan and antichristian,[6] as if they themselves should live and rule over their persecutors, for it is the same thing exactly. And so it may be said very well, that the saints that die a thousand years before have a part in the first resurrection; and so it may be said, "Blessed and holy is he [that hath part in the first resurrection]" [Rev. 20:6], to move men to holiness.

The world may very properly be said to have two resurrections: the one a spiritual resurrection, the other a natural; the one a resurrection of the world to its primitive holiness and spiritual happiness (though not to innocency), the other a natural renewing of all the world, and so a resurrection of bodies, a renewing of the earth to its primitive luster, beauty, life and pleasantness, in both which respects the world has been a long time sunk into death. The first resurrection is a spiritual, the second a natural. The dead are of two kinds: [1] the spiritually dead (not as particular men but as to the whole church), in which sense the souls of the martyrs may be said to be dead; [2] the rest of the dead are the naturally dead, which were not to live again till the end of the thousand years. On those that had part in the first resurrection, or spiritual resurrection, the second death had no power, that is, the spiritual death. On those that were of the first resurrection, the first death had no power, or, the natural death. The devil and his angels were taken spiritually and thrown into the bottomless pit at the first resurrection; he was taken really and thrown into the bottomless pit at the second resurrection.

l. INFUSED HABITS.[7] This is certain, as to a demonstration of infused habits, that if there be none, if there is no moment wherein truly [saving][8] . . . infused . . . degrees . . . as all . . . habits gradually increase, so that there must be some wicked men in . . . perfection . . . to be . . . good, as to . . . good . . . to[9] inexpressible happiness.

Now it is certain that [in] every man that becomes good, there is a last moment of his being bad and a first moment of his being good, a last

6. I.e. the pre-Constantinian Roman government and the later papacy, which JE regarded as the two beasts of Rev. 13.
7. The first five lines of this entry are at the bottom of the MS page, which is badly tattered, and no copy is available. The few fragments of text that can be read with reasonable certainty are printed, since they help show the direction the argument is taking. Most of the gaps represented by ellipsis dots are several words long, and the last represents two whole lines in the MS.
8. Possibly "sanctified"; only the first two letters survive.
9. Or "for"; part of the word is missing at the margin.

moment of his being in a state of damnation and a first moment of his being in a state of salvation; or thus, there is a time before which if he had died but one moment, he would have gone to hell, and after which if he had died but one moment, he would have gone to heaven: this is self-evident. Or, which is all one, he is made immensely a better man in a moment than he was before; which being allowed, it is also self-evident that the notion of acquired habits is wrong. So that it is evident to a metaphysical demonstration, that one of these things is true of that man that is become good: either there was a time wherein if he had died he would neither have gone to heaven nor hell, that is, neither to great happiness nor great misery; or else the future state is not according to men's goodness or badness here; or else, there are infused habits.

m. Types of the Scriptures. How plainly is the investiture of Jesus Christ, Mediator, with the government of the church and world, typified by Pharoah's delivering to Joseph the government of Egypt (see Gen. 41:38–44).

n. Damnation of Infants. One of these two things are certainly true, and self-evidently so: either that it is most just, exceeding just, that God should take the soul of a new-born infant and cast it into eternal torments, or else that those infants that are saved are not saved by the death of Christ. For none are saved by the death of Christ from damnation that have not deserved damnation. Wherefore, if it be very just, it is but a foolish piece of nonsense, to cry out of it as blasphemous to suppose that it ever is [just], because (they say) it is contrary to his mercy.

Now such I ask, whether it is contrary to his mercy to inflict punishment upon any according to their deserts, and whether it was contrary to God's mercy to damn the fallen angels. There was no mercy showed to them at all. And why is it blasphemous to suppose that God should inflict upon infants so much as they have deserved, without mercy, as well as [upon] them?[1] If you say, they have not deserved it so much, I answer: they certainly have deserved what they have deserved, as much as the fallen angels; because their sin is not accompanied with such aggravating circumstances, so neither shall their punishment be so aggravated. So that the punishment of one is every whit as contrary

1. MS: "as they"; the reference is to the fallen angels, whereas the preceding "they" refers to infants.

to God's mercy as [that of] the other. Who shall determine just how much sin is sufficient to make damnation agreeable to the divine perfections? And how can they determine that infants have not so much sin? For we know they have enough to make their damnation very just.

0. IRRESISTIBLE GRACE. The dispute about grace's being resistible or irresistible is altogether perfect nonsense, for the effect of grace is upon the will. So that it is nonsense, except it be proper to say that a man can with his will resist his own will, or except it be possible for him to desire to resist his own will; that is, except it be possible for a man to will a thing and not will it at the same time. Or if you speak of enlightening grace, and say this grace is upon the understanding, it is nothing but the same nonsense in other words. For then the sense runs thus, that a man, after he has seen so plainly that a thing is best for him that he wills it, yet he can at the same [time] nill it. If you say, he can will anything when he pleases, that is most certainly true. For who can deny that a man can will anything that he wills, that he doth already will? That a man can will anything that he pleases, is just so certain as that what is, is.

Wherefore it is most enormous nonsense, to say that after a man has seen so plainly a thing to be so much best for him that he wills it, to say that he could not have willed it[2] if he had pleased. That is to say, he could not have willed [it][3] if he had willed not to have willed it; that is, if he had not *willed* it he could *not have willed* it.[4] That is certain, that a man never doth anything but what he can do. But to say, after a man has willed a thing, that he could not have willed it[5] if he had pleased, is to suppose two wills in a man: the one to will, which goes last,[6] the other to please to will. And so with the same reason we may say, there is ten

2. In this and the next three cases, the "not" is to be construed with "have" rather than with "could." As in the previous paragraph, JE is speaking of ability to nill (a now archaic term meaning "to be unwilling"), not inability to will, as he makes clear in "if he had willed not to have willed it." His argument would have been easier to follow had he written "could not-have-willed it" or (as JE, Jr. emended the MS at these points to read) "could have not willed it." See Paul Ramsey's introduction to the *Freedom of the Will* (*Works, 1,* 44–47), where an earlier transcription of No. o is printed and the meaning of its terms discussed.

3. Ibid.

4. Ibid.

5. Ibid.

6. JE, Jr. altered this word to "first," a very troublesome reading which I still accepted as JE's in the text furnished to Ramsey in 1956 (ibid., p. 45). The microscope has since made it possible to disengage JE's text from his son's emendations. JE, Jr.'s edition of this entry is reprinted in the Worcester rev. ed. (2, 566).

thousand: another to please to please to will, etc.[7] Wherefore, to say that the man could have willed otherwise if he had pleased, is just all one as to say (only a hundred times as nonsensically spoken) that if he *had* willed otherwise, then we might be sure he *could* will otherwise.

p. INFUSED GRACE. Those that deny infusion by the Holy Spirit, must of necessity deny the Spirit to do anything at all. "By the Spirit's infusing" is an unintelligible expression; but however, let be meant what will, those that say there is no infusion contradict themselves. For they say the Spirit doth *something* in the soul; that is, he causeth some motion, or affection, or apprehension to be in the soul, that at the same time would not be there without him. Now I hope, that God's Spirit doth, he doth; he doth so much as he doth, or he causeth in the soul so much as he causeth, let that be how little soever. So much as is purely the effect of his immediate motion, that *is* the effect of his immediate motion, let that be what it will; and so much is infused, how little soever that be. This is self-evident.

For suppose the Spirit of God only to assist the natural powers, then there is something done betwixt them: man's own powers do something, and God's Spirit doth something, but only they work together. Now the part that the Spirit doth, how little soever that be, is infused. So that they that deny infused habits own that part of the habit is infused. For they say, the Holy Spirit assists the man in acquiring the habit, so that it is acquired rather sooner than it would be otherwise. So that part of [the] habit is owing to the Spirit—some of the strength of the habit was infused—and another part is owing to the natural powers. Or if you say, not so, but it is all owing to the natural power assisted, how do you mean "assisted"? To act more livelily and vigorously than otherwise? Then that liveliness and vigorousness must be infused, which is a habit and therefore an infused habit; it is grace, and therefore infused grace. Grace consists very much in a principle that causes vigorousness and activity in action; this is infusion, even in the sense of the opposite party. So that if any operation of the Holy Spirit at all is allowed, the dispute is only, how much is infused. The one says, a great deal; the other says, but little.

q. EXCOMMUNICATION has great influence on the favor of God thus, because it is a great and dreadful sin to be justly excommunicated, that

7. For JE's later expansion of this infinite-regress argument, see *Freedom of the Will*, Pt. II, § 1 (*Works, 1,* 172–74).

is, to be obstinate even to the reception of excommunication, greater than obstinacy otherwise would be. And [it is] a greater sin to be actually excommunicated than intentionally, than to be in his own intention (and the intention of the church too, [if][8] some accident hinders), as much as actual murder is worse than intentional. So that thus it is that God punishes such more remarkably with manifestations of his displeasure in this. For certainly he punishes them upon no other account but for their sin; and it is as certain, that God is not displeased with any man upon any other account but his sin. Wherefore, excommunication is truly a dreadful punishment upon this account, as well as [a] sin,[9] and by this contrivance it is a punishment of God. So is it contrived that excommunication is a punishment from heaven, that it has great influence on the favor of God and manifestations of his favor. So excellently is this sort of punishment contrived, that when it is just it is exceedingly to be dreaded as a punishment from heaven, and [as] no punishment from heaven when it is altogether unjust, and all due care was taken by the person to avoid it.

Neither have men thereby the favor of God at all in their power; for God's displeasure is according to the greatness of men's sins, and not at all according to men's wills; but yet is much greater for just excommunication, and is justly followed with the marks of his anger: in the first ages sometimes by the actual bodily possession of the devil; and constantly by hellish horrors, and horrors of conscience, and a dreadful spiritual darkness and death, by reason of the inhabitation of the devil. And thus it is that whosoever sins are justly retained, are retained in heaven. What man doth is not at all by way of rule or government, but only for himself. He refuses communion, and will not acknowledge such an one to be a Christian, and refuses to grant him communion with him; whereby he is deprived of all the external privileges of believers. What man doth is only for himself, to keep himself free from sin; but the punishment is Christ's, who is the sole head of the church.

But, it may be queried, suppose a man were absent at the intended time of excommunication, and he really thought and was fully per-

8. Apparently the word, if JE wrote one, was already lost from the margin when Dwight's copy was made. Dwight supplied "when," but it is doubtful that the intact margin contained room for so long a word.

9. Or, "as well as [the] sin," i.e. the sin that originally rendered the person subject to excommunication.

suaded he was excommunicated, while his sin was not so great? I answer, no, his obstinacy is not so great, and his obstinacy don't remain with that aggravating circumstance of it. Neither can there be any instances given wherein his sin will be so great. But if there can, most certainly he is in the sight of God an excommunicate person, and His displeasure and the manifestations of it will be as great against him as if he were. Likewise it is said, "Whosoever sins ye remit, they shall be remitted in heaven";[1] because when he is[2] again received into communion, he don't continue to commit that sin of excommunication any longer.

r. PREPARATORY WORK. As to preparatory work before conversion, there is undoubtedly always, except very extraordinary cases, such a thing. For we have shown [No. l] that conversion is wrought in a moment. Now who can believe that the Spirit of God takes a man in his career in sin, without any forethought, or foreconcern or any such thing, or any preparatory circumstances to introduce it? We have no instance of such a thing without something preparatory, either preparatory thought or circumstances which prepared in some measure his thoughts. We do not determine how great a difference there may be[3] in this preparatory introduction of Christ into the soul.

s. CHRIST'S RIGHTEOUSNESS. 'Tis evident and certain that we are so much saved on the account of [Christ's][4] righteousness, that if he had not been righteous, as well as if he had not died, we should unavoidably [have] been damned. This further [is][5] also evident, that Christ by dying only removed the guilt of our sins, and makes us in that respect just as Adam was the first moment he was created. And it [would] be [no][6] more fitting that we should obtain heaven only on that account, than that Adam should be fixed in an unalterable state of happiness the first moment of his creation, without any probation. Now Adam was not to be made happy on the account of his being innocent—if so, he would have [had] his happiness fixed at once without probation— but he was to be fixed in happiness on the account of his activeness in

1. JE conflates John 20:23 and Matt. 16:19.
2. MS: "they are."
3. I.e. between one soul and another. See No. 116b for a discussion of the difference.
4. Broken off at the margin; no copy survives.
5. Ibid.
6. Ibid.

obedience; not on the account of his not doing ill, but on the account of [his][7] doing well. So for the same reason, we are not to be saved merely on the account of being free from guilt (as Adam was at the first existence) by the death of Christ, but on the account of Christ's activeness in obedience and doing well; he acted Adam's part over again. Now believers are so closely united to Christ that they are the same in the Father's account; and therefore what Christ has done in obedience is the believer's, because he is the same. So that the believer is made happy, because it was so well and worthily done by his Head and Husband. This is a great doctrine of Christianity.

But, you will say, if believers are saved wholly on the account of Christ's righteousness and not at all on their own, then all men must be equally happy in heaven, because Christ's righteousness is the same; he was as righteous for one believer as he was for another. I answer: although every believer has all Christ's righteousness made his own by his union with him, and by the same union is made partaker of Christ's glory as well as his righteousness; yet those that have a stronger faith are more closely united to Christ, and so shall enjoy him, his righteousness and his glory, more intensely, and so shall be more happy, because their sense of happiness will be greater and quicker.

t. UNIVERSAL REDEMPTION. Universal redemption must be denied in the very sense of Calvinists themselves, whether predestination is acknowledged or no, if we acknowledge that Christ knows all things. For if Christ certainly knows all things to come, he certainly knew, when he died, that there were such and such men that would never be the better for his death. And therefore, it was impossible that he should die with an intent to make them (particular persons) happy. For it is a right-down contradiction [to say that] he died with an intent to make them happy, when at the same time he knew they would not be happy. Predestination or no predestination, it is all one for that. This is all that Calvinists mean when they say that Christ did not die for all, that he did not die intending and designing that such and such particular persons should be the better for it; and that is evident to a demonstration. Now Arminians, when [they][8] say that Christ died for all, cannot mean, with any sense, that he died for all any otherwise than to give all an opportunity to be saved; and that, Calvinists themselves never denied. He did die for all in this sense; 'tis past all contradiction.

7. Ibid.
8. Ibid.

u. DECREES: whether God has decreed all things that ever come to pass, or no. All that own the being of a God own that he knows all things beforehand. Now it is self-evident, that if he knows all things beforehand, he either doth approve of them, or he doth not approve of them; that is, he is either willing they should be, or is not willing they should be.

w.[9] TONE. A tone is to be avoided in public, either in prayer or preaching, because it generally is distasteful; and a whining tone, that some use, [is][1] truly very ridiculous. But a melancholy musical tone doth really help in private, whether in private prayer, reading, or soliloquy; not because religion is a melancholy thing (for it is far from it),[2] but because it stills the animal spirits and calms the mind and fits it for the most sedate thought, the clearest ideas, brightest apprehensions and strongest reasonings, which are inconsistent with an unsteady motion of the animal spirits. Wherefore, this may be a rational account why a melancholy air doth really help religious thoughts; because the mind is not fit for such high, refined and exalted contemplations, except it be first reduced to the utmost calmness.

x. PLEASANTNESS OF RELIGION. It is no argument against the pleasantness of religion, that it has no tendency to raise laughter, but rather to remove it.[3] For that pleasure which raises laughter[4] is never great—everyone knows this by his own experience—and besides, it is flashy, external, and not lasting. The greater sort of temporal[5] pleasures don't raise laughter, as the joy of the sight and enjoyment of most dear friends, but only raises a smile, without any of that shaking laughter, which always arises from a mixture of pleasure and sorrow and never

9. There is no No. v.

1. Broken off at the margin; no copy survives.

2. At this point JE deleted the following words: "It raises to a pleasure clear above laughter, that is of an ex[ternal]." This thought probably suggested the writing of the next entry.

3. MS: "and rather to remove." JE corrected the wording, as above, when he copied the clause into the application of his sermon on I John 5:3 (*Works, 10,* 642).

4. MS: "which is raised by laughter." JE probably began the correction while copying the words into the sermon (which reads "that raises laughter" [ibid.]) but failed to carry it through by deleting "is."

5. The first three letters of this word and the top of the fourth are visible though not very distinct, but their shape and the preceding "not lasting" confirm the correctness of this reading. Dwight's scribe read "sensual," which Dwight changed to "earthly." JE wrote "worldly" in the sermon.

from pure pleasure, because it always arises from something[6] that is ridiculous. Now a thing that is ridiculous is a mixture of what is painful with what is pleasant; for[7] a thing is never ridiculous, except there be something in it that is deformed and contrary to beautiful, and therefore disagreeable to the soul. But that pleasure which is raised from the apprehension of something purely agreeable never causes laughter. The pleasure of religion raises one clear above laughter, and rather tends to make the face to shine than screw it into a grimace; though when it is at its height it begets a sweet, inexpressibly joyful smile, as we know only a smile is begotten by the great pleasure of dear friends' society. The reason why the pleasures of religion be not always attended with such a smile, is because we have so many sins and have so much offended God; and almost all our religious thoughts are unavoidably attended with repentance and a sense of our own misery. It is the pleasure of repentance alone that don't tend to a smile.

The reason why religious thoughts will cause one to sigh sometimes, is not from the melancholiness of religion, but because religious thoughts are of such an high, internal and spiritual nature as very much abstracts the soul from the body, and so the operations of the body are deadened; when arises a sigh to renew it, as a sigh will arise from weakness of body, whether by sickness or labor, whether one is melancholy or no. 'Tis this abstraction of the soul, in its height, leaves the body even dead; and then the soul is in a trance.

y. FALLING FROM GRACE. It is not reasonable to believe that a man may fall from grace, upon this account, because Christ has already acted the part of those that believe, and those merits are sure and certain that he has purchased. So that although Adam could fall, [it] is no argument that we may. For what Adam was to be made happy for was not yet performed; but ours is, and that fully.

z. LOVE OF GOD, as it is in the divine nature, is not a passion, is not such a love as we feel, but by the incarnation is really become passionate to his own, so that he loves them with such a sort of love as we have to him or to those we most dearly love. This was one great end of his

6. The words "because . . . something," now broken from the margin at the bottom of the page except for the first and last letters, are preserved in Dwight's copy. The copy also preserves other words in the entry that are not noted because their correctness is obvious from the context.

7. The words "mixture of what . . . for" survive only in Dwight's copy, but the space available and the letters that are wholly or partly visible support the accuracy of this reading.

incarnation, a merciful high priest. So that now, when we delight our-selves at the thought of God's loving us, we need not have that allay[8] of our pleasure which our infirmity would otherwise cause, that though he loved us, yet we could not conceive of that love. Now this passionate love of Christ, by virtue of the union with the divine nature, is in a sort infinite.

aa. FAITH. There may undoubtedly be such a thing as is called the testimony of faith, and a sort of certainty of faith that is different from reason, that is, is different from discourse by a chain of arguments, a certainty that is given by the Holy Spirit; and yet such a belief may be altogether agreeable to reason, agreeable to the exactest rules of phi-losophy. Such ideas of religion may be in the mind, as a man may feel divinity in them, and so may know they are from God, know that religion is of divine original, that is, is divine truth. Yea, this faith may be to the degree of certainty, for he may certainly intuitively see God and feel him in those ideas; that is, he may certainly see that notion he has of God in them. The notion of God, or idea I have of him, is that complex idea of such power, holiness, purity, majesty, love, excellency, beauty, loveliness, and ten thousand other things.[9] Now when a man is certain he sees those things, he is certain he sees that which he calls divine. He is certain he feels those things to which he annexes the term God; that is, he is certain that what he sees and feels, he sees and feels; and he knows that what he then sees and feels is the same thing he used to call God. There is such an idea of religion in his mind, wherein he knows he sees and feels that power, that holiness, that purity, that majesty, that love, that excellency, that beauty and loveliness, that amounts to his idea of God.

Now no man can say such a thing cannot be. A man may see a beauty, a charmingness, and feel a power that he can no way in the world describe. 'Tis so in corporeal beauties, in beautiful charming airs, etc., but more in those ideas that are very much abstracted from body. Then this is granted, that he may feel such an excellency that may amount to his idea of God.

8. Or "alloy," which was sometimes spelled "allay" in the 18th century. The two words were close in meaning: to diminish, either by subtraction (allay) or by admixture of baser elements (alloy).

9. These words furnish the earliest evidence in the "Miscellanies" of JE's acquaintance with the thought of John Locke. Locke expounds his doctrine of complex ideas in *An Essay Concerning Humane Understanding* (London, 1690), Bk. II, ch. 12. The edition used for refer-ence is that of Peter H. Nidditch (Oxford, Clarendon Press, 1975).

But then, you'll say, God and religion are the same! I say so much, that religion is tinged with a divine color and is of his air; and *there* is all the question, whether it has divine excellencies or no. There is a certain property is seen and felt in religion by faith, that is altogether ineffable, and can't be called either power, or beauty, or majesty (because neither of these half imply it), but rather *divinity*, which strongly certifies the mind that it is divine.

Now no man can deny but that such an idea of religion may possibly be wrought by the Holy Spirit. 'Tis not unphilosophical to think so. And if there actually is such a thing as we have shown may be, it may very significatively be called the testimony of the Spirit. This way of knowing or believing is very differing from all other kinds of knowledge or belief. It is not by discourse, neither is it by intuition as other intuition. Neither can this kind of faith, or this sort of knowledge, be exercised in any common objects; for there are [in them] no such distinguishing amiable properties, of such a force as to bear down the mind at such a rate as [do] the divine properties.

bb. RESURRECTION. How has the resurrection of Christ any influence on the bodies of believers and on their resurrection, by virtue of the union that is betwixt them? How shall we give a rational account of it? In order to answer this question, we must first show how can the bodies partake of this union, which are really no more than a stock or a stone. Indeed everything about a man besides the rational soul is no more than a house, ship or coach, but only this: the rational soul has power to affect the one and not the other, and the one and not the other has power to affect the rational soul. And how is it possible that a stock or stone should partake of the union to Christ?

To this I answer, that although the body be in itself no more than a stock, yet because God made the human soul with a design that it should be united to a body, therefore he has made it inseparable from its[1] nature, eternally inseparable (that is, by any but God), that it should strongly incline to a union to the body. So that this inclination to the body is part of the nature of the soul, which is just the same thing as if the body were part of the soul; so that with the soul it becomes partaker of the union with Christ in common with the rest of the soul. That is to say, to speak plainly and intelligibly: *that* part of the soul's nature, its inclination to the body as well as other parts of its nature, is

1. MS: "his."

united to Jesus Christ; which is the same thing as to say the body is united to him, and is most familiarly so expressed. If God had created the soul with the same inclination to some stone in the mountains as it has to the body, that stone, together with the soul, would be united to Christ. Thus we have shown how the body partakes of the union with Christ. So much for that.

Now it is by virtue of this inclination of soul to body, that the resurrection of the body becomes absolutely necessary in order to complete happiness. For how is it possible that the soul should be completely happy in the denial of an inclination that Almighty God, in the creation, has made inseparable from it? But then, you'll say, at that rate the separated souls of saints are not completely happy. I answer: they have a certain hope, a certain knowledge of the resurrection, that completely satisfies this inclination during the separation; so that they are so far completely happy before the resurrection, that they are without any uneasiness.

But to return to the question first proposed: suppose it be granted that the body partakes of the union with Christ; what rational account can be given how, by virtue of that, the resurrection of Christ's body influences the dead bodies of saints, though they are united? I answer, by virtue of the union between Christ and believers, it follows that believers must be partakers of all Christ's glorification. That is, they are so united that he, having them as parts of him, necessarily wills it (don't misconstrue necessity), John 17:22–24.

Thus it is that souls espoused to Christ must reign over the world, because Christ reigns over the world. This is frequently promised. They must sit down in his throne because he is set down on his Father's throne, Rev. 3:21. Because Christ has power over all the nations, and rules [them] with a rod of iron, and breaks them in pieces as a potter's vessel, so Christ says, Rev. 2:26–27, that they also shall have power over the nations, and "shall rule them with a rod of iron," and break them in pieces as a potter's vessel, too. Because Christ is God's Son and heir of all God's estate, believers must be sons and heirs of all God's estate too, Rom. 8:17. Because Jesus Christ is possessor of heaven earth and sea, sun moon and stars, so believers must be possessors of heaven earth and sea, sun moon and stars too (Rev. 21:7; II Cor. 6:10; I Cor. 8:22), and, as I could mention, in fifty other things. So, because Christ rose from the dead, which was a great part of his glorification, so shall saints rise from the dead too, which is a great part of their glorification.

cc. RESURRECTION. To deny that it is possible, after the body is dead, and burnt, and all carried away in smoke and vapor and exhalations—and suppose it be diffused clear round the globe, some of it mixed with clouds and rain water, and some into falling stars, some into the matter of thunder, and some drawn in by the breath of animals and so into the lungs, and thence part goes into the blood; and supposing it gets into the matter of all the plants on the globe, and part of the matter of it is propagated in the seed from plant to plant; and supposing some is in the constitution of every animal, some converted to earth, some to air, some to water and some to sunbeams, and by some means or other some shall get down into the center of the earth; and let some of it, if it will, be converted into the substance of some of the plants or animals in some of the planets of the star Alcor,[2] and in short, some of it be mixed in every inch square of matter in the great universe—let it be so, and then I say: 'tis just the same thing to deny the possibility of the resurrection of that body, as it is to say that Almighty God could not, if he never so much desired it, take three stones that lie together and separate them asunder, one in Europe, another in Africa, and another in America, and after that bring them together again to their old places and order. For the thing is exactly the same and there is no difference; only the atoms of man's body are less, and more in number, and more scattered; but we all know God can scatter, and again bring together and order in their same places, twenty bodies as well as three, small bodies as well as great, distant as well as near.

The resurrection of the same atoms is not absolutely necessary, but only for these two things, the order and pomp of the Day. So some shall rise out of the seas, some out of the earth, some out of the grave; some shall rise up in one place and some in another. If it be not so, doubtless all the bodies will be made out of one heap of ground at once without more ado, perhaps all out of one mountain.

Another reason [is that this] will be in compliance with human nature (and doubtless so is the nature of all intelligent beings), in compliance with that nature in him, whereby a murderer is more affected with the same knife with which he killed a man, more than he is at the sight of one exactly like it; and why the wicked will be more affected to think, "In this same body I committed sin," than "I committed sin in a body like it"; and the martyrs to think, "This same body was burnt at the stake," and "With this body I did and suffered such and such

2. A small star in Ursa Major.

things." Why is there not the same kind of reason why the same body shall arise, as that Eve should be made of Adam's rib?

As to the objection of man-eaters, it is no objection at all; for this is all that can be objected, put the case how you will, that an exceeding small part of the substance of one body that died, may again die the substance of another body. For if my body is devoured entirely, bones and all, by men, and it all digests as well as other meat, there will [be] but an exceeding small part of my body will convert into the substance of their bodies; and it is a thousand to one, if all of them shall die with the hundreth part of that which at first was converted into their flesh. And I believe never any man holds that the body should arise with exactly the same number of atoms to one, as were in him when he died (suppose it be of a man that died in a consumption, or of one that died with the dropsy), but that it should be the same body in general. That little part of Eve that was made of the atoms of Adam's rib, was suffi-cient to make it be said that *she* was made of the rib.

But we are only now disputing for the possibility of the resurrection of the same [body], and not that it will really be so. Everyone is left at his liberty of thinking as he pleases. I am not disputing for anything that is uncertain about it but that which is most certain, and that is, that there is no need of believing that the body that shall rise will not be the same that fell.

dd. SCRIPTURE. Some may ask why the Scripture expresses things so unintelligibly. It tells us of Christ living in us, of our being united to him, of being the same spirit, and many other such like expressions. Why doth it not call these things directly by the intelligible names of those things that lie hid under these expressions? I answer, then we should have a hundred pages to express what is implied in these words, "Ye are the temple of the Holy Ghost" [I Cor. 6:19]; neither would one word of it all be understood by the one-fortieth part of mankind. Whereas, as it is expressed, it serves as well to practice, if we will but believe what God says: that some way or other we are inhabited by the Holy Ghost as a temple, and therefore we ought to keep holy and pure; and we are united to Christ as much as members are to the head, and therefore ought to rejoice; seeing we know what it proceeds from, even his love to us, and the effects of it, [viz.] joy, happiness, spiritual and eternal life, etc. By such similitudes a vast volume is represented to our minds in three words, and things that we are not able to behold directly are represented before us in lively pictures.

ee. BELIEF. So many things are [conceived as necessary][3] to be known
and believed, as are necessary should be ever preached to a barbarous
and heathen nation, and is necessary in [order to their conversion to
Christianity],[4] whether there be one thing, or two, or three, or more.[5]
[There are those that say that in order to salvation there is no][6] necessity of more than one article of faith, that is, that Jesus Christ was a
person sent from God, and that all the rest, holiness of heart and life,
follows from that.[7] They don't explain themselves at all, and they need
somebody else to do it for them. That they may not be mistaken that
hear or read this their opinion, I shall endeavor [so] to do.

When they say that [it] is necessary only to believe that Jesus Christ
was a person come from God, they must be understood that it is
necessary to believe that he was a person come from a true being, that
is, from a being that would not send Jesus to tell the world nothing but
a parcel of lies. For they themselves will own, that he that believes[8] that
Jesus came from God on purpose to tell lies, is as bad as he that believes
that he did not come from God at all. They also mean that he came
from a merciful being, that did not send him to destroy mankind; for

3. This entry begins near the end of a page which is now badly frayed at the bottom, and
some words were illegible to Dwight's scribe. Only a letter or two are now visible at the right
margin where this lacuna begins. The scribe read "conceived" and left space for another
word or two before "to be." Dwight supplied "as necessary," but the three words probably
require more space than was available at the left margin. It is possible that "considered" was
the word the scribe was trying to read and that Dwight's "as" was editorial.

4. These words also were supplied by Dwight in space left by his scribe. The surviving
remnants of the last word or two are too faint for checking his accuracy.

5. The words "or more," though now broken off, must have been legible to the scribe, for
he inadvertently wrote them a second time.

6. The sentence up to this point constituted the last line of the MS page (the next page
begins with "-cessity") and is now almost entirely illegible. Dwight's scribe found it so difficult
that he left a long space, in which Dwight wrote, "There are those who deny the necessity, in
order to salvation, of more." Some of this may be conjectural or editorial. It does not account
for all the words that were probably on the line, it is rearranged in such a way as to move
"necessity" to the middle of the line, and it does not harmonize with the syntax of the rest of
the sentence. Little more than the tips of the letters is now visible in the last line. The location
of the visible words, "those that," makes it likely that the remaining words of the line were
"say that there is no ne[cessity]." But since other words Dwight supplied may be genuine
readings of words occurring earlier on the line, his version has been retained with minimal
alteration.

7. John Locke's *Reasonableness of Christianity* (1695) is usually credited with having
provided a focus for the deist attack on orthodox Christianity by stating that "the only
Gospel-Article of Faith" is the proposition that Jesus is the Messiah, his mission being
divinely attested by prophecy and miracles; see Locke's *Works* (3 vols. London, 1714), 2, 479–
87, 516–17.

8. MS: "they that believe."

they will own, that he that believes that Jesus came from God to destroy mankind, is as bad as he that don't believe that he came from God at all. He must also [believe] that that God he came from is wise, and that he knows how to profit mankind by sending Jesus; for he that believes that Jesus came from God to no purpose, is as bad as he that don't believe he came from God at all. And so it will be found, that they mean that it is necessary to believe God's other perfections.

So that, although they say it is only necessary to believe Jesus came from God, therein is implied that it is necessary to believe all these things: God's all-sufficiency, God's wisdom and omniscience, God's omnipotence, God's truth and faithfulness, God's mercy, God's holiness, God's justice, etc. They mean all these must be believed, or else we must be damned; and in saying that it is necessary to believe these things, is implied, that it is necessary that we should not believe any that necessitate a man to disbelieve any of these, if there can be any such in the world—and I believe anybody can think of thirty or forty presently. So that according to these men, a pretty many articles are necessary to be believed.

Furthermore, in this article is implied, that it is necessary to be believed that he came to do some good to mankind, and that the good that he came to do was that that he said he came to do. And in order to believing this last, it is necessary to believe, that he said he came to do that which the Scripture saith he said he came to do; wherefore the divine authority of the Scriptures is one of their necessary articles. 'Tis also necessary to believe that what he did had a tendency to obtain his end; and so, in short, they say the gospel scheme is necessary to be believed. And so it will be found, that they own almost all the articles to be necessary which good Protestants all along have said to be necessary. So that the difference is, that one expresses all in one comprehensive article, and others divide it to give us the meaning and full understanding of it.

ff. UNION WITH CHRIST. By virtue of the believer's union with Christ, he doth really possess all things. That we know plainly from Scripture. But it may be asked, how [doth] he possess all things? What is he the better for it? How is a true Christian so much richer than other men? To answer this, I'll tell you what I mean by "possessing all things." I mean that God three in one, all that he is, and all that he has, and all that he does, all that he has made or done—the whole universe, bodies and spirits, earth and heaven,[9] angels, men and devils, sun moon [and] stars, land and sea, fish and fowls, all the silver and gold, kings and potentates as well as mean men—are as much the Christian's as the money in his pocket, the clothes he wears, or the house he dwells in, or the victuals he eats; yea more properly his, more advantageously, more *his,* than if he [could] command all those things mentioned to be just in all respects as he pleased at any time, by virtue of the union with Christ; because Christ, who certainly doth thus possess all things, is entirely his: so that he possesses it all, more than a wife the share of the best and dearest husband, more than the hand possesses what the head doth; it is all his.

The universe is [his], only he has not the trouble of managing of it; but Christ, to whom it is no trouble, manages it for him a thousand times as much to his advantage as he could himself if he had the managing of all. Every atom in the universe is managed by Christ so as to be most to the advantage of the Christian, every particle of air or every ray of the sun; so that he in the other world, when he comes to see it, shall sit and enjoy all this vast inheritance with surprising, amazing joy. And how is it possible for a man to possess anything more than so as shall be most to his advantage? And then besides this, the Christian shall have everything managed just according to his will; for his will shall so be lost in the will of God, that he had rather have it according to God's will than any way in the world. And who would desire to possess all things more than to have all things managed just according to his will? And then besides, he himself shall so use them as to be most to his own advantage in his thoughts and meditations, etc.

Now how is it possible for anyone to possess anything more than to have it managed as much as possible according to his will, as much as possible for his own advantage, and for him himself to use it [as] much as possible according to his advantage? But it is certain, so much shall the true Christian possess all things; 'tis not a probable scheme, but absolutely certain. For we know that all things will be managed so as shall be most agreeable to his will. That can't be denied, nor that it shall be most for his advantage, and that he himself shall use [it] most to his own advantage. This is the kingdom Christ so often promised—they

9. Dwight's copy and its printed version (Dwight ed., *8,* 526) read "spirits, light, heaven." Of the second word, only the first two letters are visible at the right margin. The reading "ea[rth]" is not only more likely in itself than "li[ght]," but it fits the pattern of JE's list. There is also probably room on the missing margin for an ampersand, which occurs in the groupings both before and after it.

shall be kings with a witness at this rate! This is the sitting in Christ's throne and inheriting all things promised to the victors in the Revelation, and the like in many other places.

gg. RELIGION. 'Tis most certain that God did not create the world for nothing. 'Tis most certain that if there were not intelligent beings in the world, all the world would be without any end at all. For senseless matter, in whatever excellent order it is placed, would be useless if there were no intelligent beings at all, neither God nor others; for what would it be good for? So certainly, senseless matter would be altogether useless if there was no intelligent being but God, for God could neither receive good himself nor communicate good. What would this vast universe of matter, placed in such excellent order and governed by such excellent rules, be good for, if there was no intelligence that could know anything of it? Wherefore it necessarily follows that intelligent beings are the end of the creation, that their end must be to behold and admire the doings of God, and magnify him for them, and to contemplate his glories in them.

Wherefore religion must be the end of the creation, the great end, the very end. If it were not for this, all those vast bodies we see ordered with so excellent skill, so according to the nicest rules of proportion, according to such laws of gravity and motion, would be all vanity, or good for nothing and to no purpose at all. For religion is the very business, the noble business of intelligent beings, and for this end God has placed us on this earth. If it were not for men, this world would be altogether in vain, with all the curious workmanship of it and accoutrements about it.

It follows from this that we must be immortal. The world had as good have been without us, as for us to be a few minutes and then be annihilated—if we are now to own God's works to his glory, and only glorify him a few minutes, and then be annihilated, and it shall after that be all one to eternity as if we never had been, and be in vain after we are dead that we have been once; and then, after the earth shall be destroyed, it shall be for the future entirely in vain that either the earth or mankind have ever been. The same argument seems to be used, Is. 45:17–18. See No. 1292.

hh. ANTICHRIST. It is alleged against the Church of Rome being Antichrist—say they, how can he be Antichrist that professes Christ? To that it may be answered, that he is a great deal the more Antichrist for that, for he is a [great][1] deal the worse for it; and the worse he is, surely the more anti-Christ, against Christ. Now certainly, those wickednesses that are professed, est[ablished][2] and commanded by that church are much the worse for their profession of Christ, for their professing the fundamental articles of the Christian faith. They ever deny Christ, in being so contrary to him. So that now they are much more against Christ, because they profess him, than it is possible for any of those that do not profess Christ to be; more anti-Christ than it is possible for a heathenish, Jewish, or Mahometan church to be.

To illustrate it by example: thus the filthiness of a snake or toad is much more abominable for being joined with life, which is in itself excellent, than the same filthiness and shape would be in lifeless matter. Thus again, the hatefulness of the devil is much greater for its being united with an angelical nature. So there is as much difference [between] the Church of Rome and heathens, Jews, or Mahometans, as there is between a viper or some loathsome, poisonous, crawling monster, and lifeless filthy matter of the same shape.

ii. SAINTS. Is it not a very improper thing that saints in some respects should be advanced above angels, seeing angels are of more excellent natural powers? I answer, no more improper than it is for the queen in some respects to be advanced above nobles and barons, of far nobler natural powers.

kk.[3] RELIGION. *Corol.* on the former on this subject [No. gg]. Since the world would be altogether good for nothing without intelligent beings, so intelligent beings would be altogether good for nothing except to contemplate the Creator. Hence we learn that devotion, and not mutual love, charity, justice, beneficence, etc. is[4] the highest end of man, and devotion is his principal business. For all justice, beneficence, etc. are good for nothing without it, are to no purpose at all. For those duties are only for the advancement of the *great* business, to assist mutually each other to it.

ll. RELIGION. It may be said, if religion be really the very business of men, for which God made them, it is a wonder 'tis no more natural to

1. This word was almost certainly on the margin at a place now broken off.
2. Possibly "est[eemed]" or (if the last visible letter is *p*) "espoused." The margin is both torn and worn off at this point.
3. There is no No. jj.
4. MS: "are."

them. The world in general, learned and unlearned, say little about it; they are very awkward at it, as if it were contrary to their nature. I answer, 'tis no wonder; because sin has brought them down nearer to the beasts, a sort of animals uncapable of religion at all.

mm. MINISTERS. We know that [it] is necessary there should be teachers of men in Christianity; we know also that those that teach must be called of God and sent by Christ. Now what is this sending by Christ? We know that Christ has the managing of things relating to the church, that is, to Christianity. And we know that when he so manages and orders things that it becomes a man's duty to teach and administer sacraments, he is sent by Christ to do it; thus far is clear. And though you'll say, everyone may have the liberty of speaking his mind when he thinks it will do men good, yet it is clear that those that are in the New Testament called ministers are not every private Christian; and consequently, if any such remain now as are there spoken of, they are distinct from other Christians. 'Tis clear they are born undistinguished; from this 'tis clear they are distinguished afterwards. 'Tis also evident that they are distinguished some way or other by Christ, and that their distinction is known either by Scripture, or reason without Scripture. (I am willing the flaws of this reasoning should be discovered.) How their distinction is known I leave to be yet disputed.

nn. DEMERIT OF SIN. It is certain without dispute that an offense, injury or affront to God is greater than an offense, injury or affront in other respects equal, against any finite being that is or can be, however great. Now it is evident that an offense or injury, in other respects equal to the sin of man, committed against a finite being, may be of any finite degree of badness; because what is wanting in badness in other respects may be made up by the greatness of the person injured. Wherefore it follows, that the same injury against an infinite being is greater than an injury of any finite degree of badness; that is, is an injury of [an] infinite degree of badness, that is, of infinite demerit. By greatness we mean excellency, power, wisdom, loveliness, goodness, holiness, etc., which in God are infinite.

Again, 'tis evident that the injury increases in some proportion or other to the greatness of [its object]; that is, if you add greatness to the person injured, you add badness to the injury in some proportion or other. Now let this proportion be what it will—supposing it be but one degree of badness to ten degrees of greatness, or less if you please—an

infinite degree [of greatness] will have an infinite degree of badness.
(Let this be examined by the nicest mathematicians.)

oo. SATISFACTION. Now some may say, why could not God, of his
mercy, pardon the injury only upon repentance without other satisfaction, without doing himself any hurt? I also ask, why could not he of
his mercy pardon without repentance? For the same reason he could
not pardon with repentance without satisfaction. For all the repentance man is capable of is no repentance at all; or which is the same
thing, it is as little as none in comparison of the greatness of the injury,
for it cannot bear any proportion to it. Now I am sure, it would be as
dishonorable for God to pardon the injury upon repentance that did
not bear the least proportion to the injury, as for him to pardon without any repentance at all. Wherefore, we are not forgiven now because
our repentance makes any satisfaction, but because thereby we reject
the sin and receive the satisfaction already made.

pp. GOD. We know there was being from eternity, and this being must
be intelligent. For how doth one's mind refuse to believe, that there
should be being from all eternity without its being conscious to itself
that it was; that there should be being from all eternity and yet nothing
know, all that while, that anything is. This is really a contradiction; we
may see it to be so, though we know not how to express it. For in what
respect has anything had a being, when there is nothing conscious of
its being? For in what respect has anything a being, that angels, nor
men, nor no created intelligence know nothing [of], but only as God
knows it to be? Not at all more than there is sound where none hears it,
or color where none sees it. Thus for instance, supposing a room in
which none is, none sees the things in the room, no created intelligence: the things in the room have no being any other way than only
as God is conscious [of them]; for there is no color there, neither is
there any sound, nor any shape, etc.[5]

qq. MINISTERS. Although ministers are not properly governors but
only leaders, are not to make new laws but only to teach Christ's laws;
yet for the same reason as they may teach and instruct their flocks, they
may instruct the people who it is amongst them that doth those laws

5. The arguments from color, sound, and the furniture in an unoccupied room recur,
considerably elaborated, in the second stratum of "Being," and the case of the unoccupied
room also appears in "The Mind," no. 40 (*Works, 6,* 204–06, 356–58).

and who not; this is part of their[6] business and teaching. For the same reason, 'tis their business to instruct who are worthy of the name of Christians among them and who not, and the people are as much obliged to believe these instructions as they are the rest, and no more. If Christ has given to him the administration of the sacraments, he has given to him the administration of them to them that he thinks Christ would have him.

As for the power one church has over another, we know that adjacent churches have power, if they think they ought, to withdraw communion with them and to deny them the name of Christians amongst them. Now this is really a punishment, as well as [is] excommunication, and differs only in degree; because it is an advantage to have communion with other Christians. And the more of other Christians . . . [7]

rr. SYNODS. Who can deny but that ministers may take each other's advice, or may meet together for that purpose, and may [be] congregated together for the advancement of the kingdom of Christ? Whoever holds more than this does, holds that men have power to make laws for the conscience.

ss. EXPOSITION. Rom. 4:25, "He was delivered for our offenses, and raised again for our justification." That is, delivered for our offenses, and raised again that he might see to the application of his sufferings to our justification, and that he might plead them for our justifying.

tt. DEVOTION. It has been said that there may be too much of devotion, and this reason has been given for it: that one man was made to be useful to the rest of the universe, was made for the common good of the whole frame; and, that there may be a degree of devotion that may hinder one from their being so useful to the rest of the creatures as they might otherwise be—neither of which are agreeable to reason.

As for the first, that the highest end of a particular creature was to be useful to the common good of creatures in general. Which I think is the same thing as to say, that the world was made that the parts of it might be mutually useful to each other; that is, that the world was made to have all the parts of it nicely hanging together, and sweetly

---

6. MS: "his."

7. Except for "Christians" and part of "other," the beginning of this sentence has broken from the lower margin since Dwight's copy was made; even in his day the rest of the last sentence (about half a line on the MS) was illegible. There are several smaller lacunae in this entry which have also been supplied from the copy.

harmonizing and corresponding; that is, that the world might be nicely contrived, that the parts might nicely hang together; that is, that the world was nicely contrived, that when it was done it might be a nicely contrived world; that is, that the world was nicely contrived for nothing at all! So that it must be, according to that opinion of the highest end of every particular being to be useful to the whole; [it] is the same as to say that the whole, with all its parts useful to each other, is good for nothing at all. Who can't see this? For most certainly, if the highest end of the world be to have its parts useful to each other, the world in general is good for nothing at all.

To illustrate it by example: if the highest end of every part of a clock is only mutually to assist the other parts in their motions, that clock is good for nothing at all; the clock in general is altogether useless, however every part is useful to turn round the other parts. So, however useful all the parts of the world are to each other, if that be their highest end, the world in general is altogether useless. I am sure there is the same reason for one as for the other. Yea it is a contradiction and nonsense to say, the highest end of a particular part of the world is to be useful to the rest; for if that is the highest end, they are not useful. So it is nonsense to say of a machine whose highest end is to have one part move another, that the parts of that engine are useful to move the rest; for the whole is useless, and so every part, however they correspond together.

But as in a clock one wheel moves another, and that another, till at last we come to the hand, and there we end—the use of that immediately respects the eye of man—so it is in the world: some less perfect inanimate beings are useful to the more perfect, and they to beasts, one beast to another, and they to man. And what is man made for? where shall we go next? Surely man was not made for beasts; we must not go back again. Or is man good for nothing at all? The next immediate step is to the Creator. He was undoubtedly made to glorify the Creator, so that devotion must be his highest end. The hand of the clock was not made to move the wheels; we must not go back: after we are come from wheel to wheel, at last to the hand, the next immediate step is to the eye. In the creation, there is an immediate communication between one degree of being and the next degree of being (every wheel immediately communicates with the next wheel), but man being the top; so that the next immediate step from him is to God. Without doubt, there is an immediate communication between the Creator and this highest of creatures, according to the order of being. So that as the intelligent being is exercised immediately about the Creator, so without doubt the Creator immediately influences the intelligent being, immediately influences the soul; for 'tis but one immediate step from the soul to God. Those that call this enthusiasm talk very unphilosphically.

As for the other thing that is said, that there may be a degree of devotion that may hinder one from being useful to the rest of the universe: I suppose they will not dislike devotion if it only hinders one for but half a minute, and makes one much more useful ever after; I mean, if it only makes us useless during our life upon earth, and much more useful to eternity afterwards. Not that I believe that a man would be the less useful even in this world, if his devotion was to that degree, as to keep him all his lifetime in an ecstasy.

uu. APOCALYPSE. By not suffering the dead bodies of the witnesses to be put in graves [Rev. 11:8–10] must be understood a mocking, reviling, and venting hatred and malice against them after dead; for they could not satisfy their rage and cruelty upon them by only killing them. And we know that thus the Papists used always to do, very often venting their rage like fools upon their dead bodies, tearing and burning [them], sometimes digging them out of the earth on purpose to do those things to them, citing them to their bar after dead, and such like; also sometimes in not suffering any to bury them. Their anger and malice always used to be expressed so, that they used to curse and excommunicate them after dead, etc.

ww.[8] FOUR BEASTS. See Notes on Revelation, no. 70.[9] The meaning of the four living creatures mentioned in the beginning of St. John's visions [Rev. 4:6 ff.] may without [doubt be] easily understood, if they can be understood where they are mentioned elsewhere in Scripture. Now we know the four living creatures mentioned by Ezekiel are the same with these; that is, the faces of the living creatures were, one a man, another a lion, another an ox, another an eagle (Ezek. 1:10).

I think it is agreed on by all, that Ezekiel's first vision of the four

8. There is no No. vv.

9. This reference is a later addition, and the note to which it refers consists of material taken from Arthur Bedford's *Scripture Chronology* (London, 1730), pp. 459–61. Of special interest to JE was Bedford's support for the assertion made in No. ww that the standards of the four principal tribes stationed around the camp of Israel (Num. 3) bore respectively the faces of the four creatures described in Ezek. 1 and Rev. 4. JE had come across the notion elsewhere; see below, n. 2. See *Works,* 5, 162–65.

living creatures and the wheels full of eyes is an emblem of divine providence with which Ezekiel's prophecy is introduced, as likewise without doubt is St. John's. The wheels here mentioned [Ezek. ch. 1] are the wheels of providence, and the wheels were managed by the living creatures and by their spirit; so that these four living creatures are those four living creatures that have the management of God's providence, that managed it by their spirit. So likewise are the four apocalyptical living creatures. Very fitly are these wonderful prophecies of the great events of providence introduced by a vision: first, of God the great Beginning and Ending of all; secondly, of the church of God, represented by the four and twenty elders, the subject of all dispensations; thirdly, of the Spirit of God, the seven lamps, by whom God executes all; and lastly, of the four living creatures, who had the management of God's providence.

But what doth Ezekiel mean by four living creatures managing the wheel of providence? Certainly none have the management of God's providence but God himself. Angels sometimes may be sent out on some particular errands; but none but God do, and none but God can, manage the great wheels of God's providence. It is said, the wheels were managed by "the spirit of the living creature" [Ezek. 1:20–21]; but we know that the wheels are managed alone by the Spirit of God, by St. John's seven lamps burning before the throne. Wherefore we may certainly conclude, that these four animals are the emblems of something divine. It plainly appears by Ezek. 1:24 that they were something divine: it is said, the noise of their wings is as the voice of the Almighty, and as the noise of many waters, the same that is said of the voice of the Son of God (Rev. 1:15); and it further appears because they had the glory of God, the shechinah, upon them.

But what are these four in God that have the managment of providence? What four divine things are they that have the management of the world, that turn the wheel of providence and carry it just as they go? Answer this question, and the whole mystery will be unraveled at once. I answer, they are wisdom, power, goodness, and justice. These are the four attributes of God that have [to do] with the world, and these only; the rest concern himself. These are the four that manage all things; these are the four that have the management of the wheels of providence. Where these go, the wheels follow; when these stand still, the wheels stand still; when these are lift up from the earth, the wheels are lift up. That is, providence is always managed exactly according to these four, the divine wisdom, power, goodness, and justice: "the spirit of the living creatures is in the wheels."

These were the four beasts in the Revelation, that were in the midst of the throne and round about the throne. Very fitly are the prophecies of St. John introduced with these four managers of the wheels of providence. 'Tis the manifestation of these four in God's works and dispensations that do[th] continually praise and glorify him. The power and goodness, the wisdom and justice of God in his works, cease not to sing his praises day nor night: "they rest not day nor night, saying, Holy, holy, holy, Lord God Almighty, which was, and is, and is to come" (Rev. 4:8). And when these give glory, when God's glory is shown forth by these, then the church, the angels and saints, do also praise him; then the four and twenty elders do fall down before him and give glory to him (Rev. 4:9–11).

The first living creature was a lion, which is power. The second was a calf or ox, which was always, as I think, the emblem of goodness amongst the Israelites and the nations round about. The Egyptians used to worship a bull or ox in remembrance of Joseph, for the plenty that he foretold and for his preserving corn in the midst of a famine. 'Tis very probable that for this reason those nations worshiped golden calves as emblems of goodness; the oxen, they plow the fields, from whence we receive the goodness of God. The ox is observed to be the most compassionate of all creatures. It is said that the feet of Ezekiel's living creatures were calves' feet (Ezek. 1:7), because all God's paths are mercy and truth. 'Twas alone the goodness of God that moved him to make the world, that moves him to preserve it; and all God's providential proceedings are upon the feet of goodness, even his damning sinners (though not in them, yet in others, as I could show). The third beast had the face of a man, which is wisdom. The fourth was like a flying eagle, which, being the king and ruler of birds, the most just and exact of all creatures (how exact do philosophers observe they are in distributing meat to their young), also for their quickness of sight and swiftness of flight, is the emblem of justice. "Justice" and "eagle" in the Hebrew tongue are derived from the same root. See note on Ezek. 10:7 and on Rev. 4:6; note on Ezek. 10:5.[1]

But this matter will be abundantly enlightened by the consideration

1. These are successive later additions and all are references to JE's "Blank Bible." All citations of biblical notes refer to the "Blank Bible," except where they are otherwise identified.

of the four standards of the camp of Israel [Num. 2], which were the likenesses of those four living creatures.[2] How properly did God order the emblems of his power, wisdom, justice, and goodness to be set at the four corners of the camp of Israel, as standards of the church militant. Now we know the face of a man was upon the standard of Reuben, who is "the excellency of dignity and excellency of power," according to Jacob's blessing [Gen. 49:3]. A lion was Judah's standard, of whom Jacob says, "Thy hand shall be in the neck of thine enemies; thy father's children shall bow down before thee. Judah is a lion's whelp; from the prey, my son, thou art gone up. He stooped down, he couched as a lion, and as an old lion; who shall rouse him up? The scepter shall not depart from Judah," etc. [Gen. 49:8–10]. And accordingly, Judah, we know, was the most powerful tribe. Wherefore, I say, a lion in the Revelation signifies power. Dan had the standard of an eagle, by which at once it appears that an eagle is the emblem of justice, the signification of his name; and Jacob's blessing, "Dan shall judge his people" [Gen. 49:16], abundantly clears it. Ephraim's standard was an ox, and what was more remarkable in Joseph than goodness? He was a great means of God's goodness, and [a] means of the preservation of all Egypt, as well as his father's house; for which, as I said before, the Egyptians worshiped under that image of an ox. His own bounty and goodness were also very remarkable. How bountiful, how compassionate was he! It also appears by Jacob's blessing, Gen. 49:22, "Joseph is a fruitful bough, even a fruitfull bough by a well, whose branches run over the wall"; what better to set forth God's bounty? "Even by the God of thy father, who shall help thee, and by the Almighty, who shall bless thee; with blessings of heaven above, blessings of the deep that lieth under, blessings of the breasts and of the womb" (v. 25). Wherefore, I say, the standard of Joseph is God's goodness. It also appears by Moses' blessing:

> And of Joseph he said, Blessed of the Lord be his land, for the precious things of heaven, for the dew, and for the deep that coucheth beneath, and for the precious fruits brought forth by the

2. JE may have derived this notion from Matthew Poole's *Annotations upon the Holy Bible* (2 vols. London, 1683–85). Poole himself left it out of his notes on Numbers, but one of the men who completed the work after Poole's death states in the note on Rev. 4:7 that the four creatures of Revelation and Ezekiel were represented on the four standards of Numbers; he also matches up standards and creatures with the help of Jacob's blessing exactly as does JE in No. ww. A copy of the *Annotations* was in the Edwards household; it was much read by JE's sister Jerusha, according to Timothy's obituary of her in the Trask Library.

sun, and for the precious things put forth by the moon, and for the chief things of the ancient mountains, and for the precious things of the lasting hills, and for the precious things of the earth and fullness thereof, and [for the] good will of him that dwelt in the bush. Let the blessing come upon the head of Joseph, and upon the top of the head of him that was separated from his brethren. His glory is like the firstling of a bullock (Deut. 33:13–17).

Wherefore, I say, without doubt by the calf in the Revelation (the same with Joseph's standard) is meant the goodness of God.

xx. VIALS. That we may understand what those rivers are upon which the third vial was poured out [Rev. 16:4–7], we must consider what are those rivers by which the city of Babylon is watered, what are the fountains of waters at which they drink. Without doubt, they are those societies that are fountains of Popery, fountains of popish doctrines and doctors, fountains of teachers of Antichristianism; that continually send forth streams into every part to water the antichristian world, that water the stately cedars of their Lebanon, their trees that bring forth the grapes of Sodom and apples of Gomorrah; those fountains at which the Papists do continually drink. The water is the doctrine; the streams, or waterers, are the teachers. The teachers of true Christianity were said to water Christians (Paul planted and Apollos watered); so the teachers of Popery are the streams that water the popish world. And what are the rivers and fountains from whence these proceed but the societies from whence they issue forth, the universities, societies of Jesuits, and others? These are the rivers and fountains that continually keep the trees from withering and drying up, and the men from dying with thirst. Wherefore, I take the rivers here to be meant all such societies as are fountains of Popery, whether of one kind or another.

The kingdom of France has been the grand fountain of Popery. This has been the great river that has watered the antichristian world; this has been their market place, their great university, the seat and fountain of their learning and policy. Wherefore, the pouring out of the third vial may be the reformation of that kingdom and [its] casting off of Popery; then they shall no more drink at this river as they have done. At the same time shall also the other societies and universities be turned to blood; not that all the popish universities shall be reformed, but that all the most learned men everywhere shall begin to loath and scorn Popery when the learned nation of [France] rejects it. Thus, at the same time that France, the Nile of that city that is spiritually called Egypt, shall become loathsome to them as blood, so[3] also [shall] the lesser streams, brooks and pools of water; so that they shall have nothing but blood to drink, "for they are worthy." If France was but reformed, and the most learned men in other parts, the rest of Antichristendom will be but a miserable, dry, parched, withered, barren wilderness whose pleasant rivers are dried up. Some of those societies shall be reformed and others destroyed, as perhaps the societies of Jesuits. Whether this vial is not begun to be poured out already upon France in the dreadful judgments that have lately fallen upon that kingdom, I will not dispute.[4]

There han't been yet but two remarkable steps of the Reformation. The first [was] in Wicliff's, Hus's, and Jerome of Prague's days, and after, which was a vexing and grievous sore to them; which undoubtedly is too great to be left entirely out of prophecy and is, I am sure, great enough to answer the first vial. The second [was] the Reformation at and after Luther's days, when the sea was turned to blood; since which time all things have been at a stand, or at least have made slow progress. Nothing has happened since, that is any near great enough to answer the pouring out of one of the seven vials, especially the third; which is undoubtedly one of the greatest, or else there would not be such particular notice taken of it.[5]

yy. WOMAN IN THE WILDERNESS. One meaning of the "wilderness" [Rev. 12:6] may be the church of God in the valleys of Piedmont, where God always had an evangelical visible church; and the place prepared for her is that obscure, desolate, unknown, hidden place in the midst of those inaccessible mountains.[6]

3. MS: "and."

4. JE may have been referring to the losses France sustained in the War of the Spanish Succession, when by the Treaty of Utrecht in 1713 she was forced to cede to England considerable territory in America. But it is possible that he was thinking of the national humiliation, rioting, and widespread economic distress resulting from the collapse of the grandiose Mississippi Company in 1720; he would also have been aware that from 1720 to 1722 several provinces of southern France were devastated by a plague of incredible violence, which took about 100,000 lives.

5. I.e. by the comparatively large amount of space allotted to it in Rev. 16.

6. JE is speaking of the Waldenses, who were then widely believed to have had an uninterrupted existence from the earliest days of Christianity. This view is expressed, for example, by Samuel Morland in his *History of the Evangelical Churches of the Valleys of Piedmont . . . Together with a Most Naked and Punctual Relation of the Late Bloudy Massacre* (London, 1658). JE's interpretation of Rev. 12:6 is the same as that espoused by Morland, in language which suggests the possibility that the writing of No. yy was inspired by Morland's *History*.

zz. RIGHTEOUSNESS. By the righteousness of faith, God's righteousness, etc. is to be understood [not] *justitia,* but *justificatio*: not perfect holiness, but a justified state or freedom [from] guilt; and the imputation of righteousness, not so properly the righteousness imputed.

1. THE IMMORTALITY OF THE SOUL may thus be argued: man, or intelligent beings, are the consciousness of the creation, whereby the universe is conscious of its own being, and of what is done in it of the actions of the Creator and Governor with respect to it. Now except the world had such a consciousness of itself, it would be altogether in vain that it was. If the world is not conscious of its being, it had as good not be as be, as is very clear, for the Creator; for the creation was known as much in every respect from all eternity as it is now, to the Creator. Now it is as evident that the world is as much in vain, if this consciousness lasts but a little while and then ceases, as it would be if there was no consciousness of it; that is, after that consciousness ceases, and from that time forth forever, it is in vain that there ever was such a consciousness. For instance, when the earth is destroyed, if its consciousness don't remain, it is in vain that ever it has been.

2. COVENANT OF GRACE. Many difficulties used to arise in my mind about our being saved upon the account of faith, as being the condition upon which God has promised salvation, as being that particular grace and virtue for which men are saved. According to which there is no difference between the condition of the first covenant and the second, but this: before the fall man was to be saved upon the account of all the virtues; and since, upon the account only of one virtue or grace, even that of faith. For where is the difference? Adam was to be saved of grace; for if he was possessed of all graces, the Creator was not obliged to make him happy [but] only because he was pleased to make that the condition of happiness. So also, salvation now is of grace, for God is not obliged to save man because he has the grace of faith, but only as He has been pleased to make that grace the condition of salvation. Indeed there is more mercy, if this be so, in the second covenant, because of the circumstances of it; but yet the second is as much a covenant of works as the first. For now there is one virtue is the condition of happiness, as many virtues were then.

But, ye'll say, they explain themselves and say [that] though faith is the condition of salvation, yet they are not saved because of it as a work, but only a condition. But to this I say, I cannot think of any intelligible meaning of the word "work" in divinity, but something to be done as a condition; what Adam was to do was a work no otherwise. Talking thus, whether it be truly or falsely, is doubtless the foundation of Arminianism and neonomianism, and tends very much to make men value themselves for their own righteousness.[7]

But it seems to me, all this confusion arises from the wrong distinction men make between the covenant of grace and the covenant of redemption. It seems to me to be true, that as the first covenant was made with the first Adam, so the second covenant was made with the second Adam; as the first covenant was made with the seed of the first Adam no otherwise than as it was made with them in him, so the second covenant is not made with the seed of the second Adam any otherwise than as it was made with them in him. It was not one covenant that was made with Adam, and another, that he had nothing to do with, that was made with his seed; so neither was it one covenant that was made with Christ, and another, that Christ had nothing to do with, with believers. But then, in all respects wherein Adam was a common head and representative of men, so Christ is a common head and representative of believers; as Adam was only the first created of men, so Christ is the[8] eldest brother of believers.

As the condition of the first covenant was Adam's standing, so the condition of the second covenant is Christ's standing. Christ has performed the condition of the new covenant. There is nothing more to be done; all is done already. We have nothing to do, upon the account of which we are to be saved; we are to do nothing but only to receive Christ and what he has done already. Salvation is not offered to us upon any condition, but freely and for nothing. We are to do nothing for it, we are only to take it. This taking and receiving is faith. It is not said, "If you will do so and so you may have salvation, you may have the water of life," but "Come and take it; whosoever will, let him come" [Rev. 22:17].

It is very improper to say that a covenant is made with men any otherwise than in Christ, for there is vast difference between a free offer and a covenant. The covenant was made with Christ, and in him with his mystical body; and the condition of this covenant is Christ's

7. On the Arminians, see above, pp. 11–13. The word "neonomian" was used for those who stressed some aspect of the gospel as the "new law." JE was probably familiar with the controversy that raged among the dissenting ministers of London in the 1690s, in which Daniel Williams was accused of neonomianism by Isaac Chauncy and others. See Herbert S. Skeats and Charles S. Miall, *History of the Free Churches in England 1688–1891* (London, 1891), pp. 141–45.
8. MS: "is ~~only~~ the."

perfect obedience and sufferings. And that [covenant] that is made to men is a free offer; that which is commonly called the covenant of grace is only Christ's open and free offer of life, whereby he holds it out in his hand to sinners and offers it without any condition. Faith can't be called the condition of receiving, for it is the receiving itself; Christ holds out and believers receive. There was no covenant made, or agreement upon something that must be done, before they might receive. 'Tis true, those that don't believe are not saved, and all that do believe are saved: that is, all that do receive Christ and salvation, they receive it; and all that will not receive salvation, never do receive it and never have it. But faith, or the reception of it, is not the condition of receiving of it. It is not proper, when a man holds out his gift to a beggar that he may take it without any manner of preliminary conditions, [to say] that he makes a covenant with the beggar. No more proper is it to say, that Christ's holding forth life in his hand to us that we may receive it, is making a covenant with us.

But I must confess after all, that if men will call this free offer and exhibition a covenant, they may; and if they will call the receiving of life the "condition" of receiving of life, they are at their liberty. But I believe it is much the more hard to think right, for speaking so wrong. Christ and his church are one in law; that is, they are one in respect of the covenant. By Christ's performing the condition of the covenant, the condition is as if it were performed by them. If you divide Christ and the church in covenant, and say that one covenant is made with one and another with the other, you make them two in law. This making faith a condition of life fills the mind with innumerable difficulties about faith and works and how to distinguish them, tends to make us apt to depend on our own righteousness, tends to lead men into neonomianism, and gives the principal force to their arguments. Whereas, if we would leave off distinguishing the covenant of grace and the covenant of redemption, we should leave all these matters plain and unperplexed.

3. HAPPINESS IS THE END OF THE CREATION, as appears by this, because the creation had as good not be, as not rejoice in its being. For certainly it was the goodness of the Creator that moved him to create; and how can we conceive of another end proposed by goodness, than that he might delight in seeing the creatures he made rejoice in that being that he has given them?

It appears also by this, because the end of the creation is that the creation might glorify him. Now what is glorifying God, but a rejoicing at that glory he has displayed? An understanding of the perfections of God, merely, cannot be the end of the creation; for he had as good not understand it, as see it and not be at all moved with joy at the sight. Neither can the highest end of the creation be the declaring God's glory to others; for the declaring God's glory is good for nothing otherwise than to raise joy in ourselves and others at what is declared.

Wherefore,[9] seeing happiness is the highest end of the creation of the universe, and intelligent beings are that consciousness of the creation that is to be the immediate subject of this happiness, how happy may we conclude will be those intelligent beings that are to be made eternally happy!

4. MORALITY. The controversy about the morality of the sabbath, or the morality of the first day of the week, is founded on the great stress [that] is put upon the word "morality," and the arbitrary distinction that is made between moral duties and other duties, as much as if the morality of a duty were something given by God to us as a mark to know duties that are lasting from those that are but temporary; whereas morality is nothing but a mixed mode, or idea composed according to the will and pleasure of men, drawn only from one minute circumstance of a duty.[1] Whereas consider actions without circumstances, and there is no action is either moral or immoral; but consider things with their circumstances, and every duty whatever is a moral duty, a duty that the light of nature teaches and a duty of eternal reason, as much as any duty whatever.

Thus the action of killing of a man is nowise a moral evil abstracted from its circumstances; and the action of circumcision is a moral good, and what the light of nature teaches us, and a duty of eternal reason, considered with its circumstances, considered with that circumstance, that God has commanded it. For the light of nature teaches us as much that we ought to obey God, as that we ought not to do the grossest injury to our fellow creatures from revenge and malice; and there is as much eternal reason for the one as for the other. Circumcision is never the less a duty of eternal reason because it is a duty at one time and not

9. This paragraph is a later addition in space available at the end of the entry. Ink, pen, and hand show that it was written about the same time as miscellanies numbered in the 60s and early 70s.

1. See Locke's *Human Understanding*, Bk. II, ch. 22, §§ 1–4 (ed. Nidditch, pp. 288–90), where such ideas as obligation and murder are treated as mixed modes. JE later employed this category in "The Mind," no. 41 *(Works, 6, 359–60)*.

at another, any more than brothers and sisters marrying together is not an immorality of eternal reason because it is a sin at one time and not another.

There is no need to wonder why the command for the observation of the sabbath is put into the decalogue, because men call it "the moral law"; neither is there any reason to question whether baptism and the Lord's Supper are to be observed, because men say nothing but what is "moral" is duty under the gospel. Oh, how is the world darkened, clouded, distracted and torn to pieces by those dreadful enemies of mankind called *words!*

5. HEAVEN. There is no more reason why it should be a damp to the happiness of some in heaven that others are happier, than that their happiness should be damped by barely a possibility of greater happiness, supposing them to be all equal. For if they were all equal, and all full of happiness, yet everyone would know that greater happiness is possible absolutely, and possible for them if God had but enlarged their capacity; and why should not they, who are acted by pure reason, desire it as much as if it were actually enjoyed by some beings? For barely that, that it is enjoyed by other beings, cannot possibly cause those that are acted by pure reason, and whose desires in every respect are agreeable to reason, to desire it any more than if it was only possible to be enjoyed, and were not actually enjoyed by any.

But instead of the superiority of some above others in happiness its being a damp to the happiness of those that are inferior, there is undoubted reason why it should be an addition to their happiness, and why it would rather be a detraction from their happiness if it were otherwise. For most certainly there is a pure, ardent, even inconceivably vehement mutual love between the glorified saints; and this love is in proportion to the perfection and amiableness of the object loved. Therefore, seeing their love to them is proportionable to the amiableness, it must necessarily cause delight when they see their happiness proportionable to their amiableness[2] and so to their [own] love to them. It will [not] damp any to see them loved more than themselves, for they shall have as much love as they desire and as great manifestations of love as they can bear; and they themselves will love those that

2. I.e. the happiness of those who are superior in amiableness proportionable to the amiableness of those who are superior in amiableness. JE's use of the same pronouns for lover and loved becomes very confusing; a few editorial insertions have been introduced to make the meaning clearer.

are superior in holiness as much as [do] others, and will delight to see others love them as much as [they] themselves [do].

We are very apt to conceive that those that are thus, that are more holy and more happy than others in heaven, will be elated and lifted up above them; whereas, their being superior in holiness implies their being superior in humility, or having the greatest humility; for humility is a part of holiness that is capable of degrees in the perfect state of heaven, as well as other graces. Not that the holiest shall think more meanly of themselves than the less holy, for they shall all be perfectly humble and perfectly free from pride, and none shall think more highly of themselves than they ought to think; but yet as they see further into the divine perfections than others, so they shall penetrate further into the vast and infinite distance that is between them and God, and their delight of annihilating themselves, that God may be all, shall be greater.

And besides, those that are highest in holiness, and so necessarily highest in happiness (for holiness and happiness are all one in heaven), instead of anything like despising those that are less holy and happy, will love those that are inferior to them more than they would do if they [themselves] had not so much holiness and happiness, more than if they were but equal with them, and more than [do] those that are equal with them. This is certain, for the foundation of the saints' love to each other will be their love to the image of God which they see in them. Now most certainly, the holier a man is the more he loves the same degree of the image; so that the holiest in heaven will love that image of God they see in the less holy, more than [do] those that are equally less holy. And that which makes it beyond any doubt that their superior happiness will be no damp to them, is this, that their superior happiness consists in their greater humility and in their greater love to them, and to God and Christ, whom the saints look upon as themselves.

These things may be said of this, besides what may be said about everyone being completely satisfied and full of happiness, having as much as he is capable of enjoying or desiring, like a vessel thrown into the sea of happiness; and also [besides] what may be said about their entire resignation, for God's will is become so much their own that the fulfilling of his will, let it be what it will, fills them with inconceivable satisfaction.

6. SCRIPTURE. There is a strange and unaccountable kind of en-chantment, if I may so speak, in Scripture history; which, notwith-

standing it is destitute of all rhetorical ornaments, makes it vastly more pleasant, agreeable, easy and natural, than any other history whatever. It shines brighter with the amiable simplicity of truth. There is something in the relation that at the same time very much pleases and engages the reader, and evidences the truth of the fact. It is impossible to tell fully what I mean, to any that have not taken notice of something of it before.

One great reason why it is so, doubtless is this: the Scripture sets forth things just as they happened, with the minute circumstances of time, place, situation, gesture, habit, etc. in such a natural method, that one seems to be actually present; and we insensibly fancy not that we are readers but spectators, yea actors in the business. These little circumstances wonderfully help to brighten the ideas of the more principal parts of the history. And although the Scripture goes beyond other histories in mentioning such circumstances, yet there are no circumstances are mentioned but those only that wonderfully brighten the whole story and illustrate, nobody knows how, every part of it. So the story is told very fully, and without the least crowding or jumbling things together, or hastening one thing after another before one has fully taken up what was last related, and yet told in much less room than anyone else could tell it.

Notwithstanding the minute circumstances that are mentioned, which other historians leave over, it leads along one's ideas so naturally and easily, they don't seem to go too fast nor too slow. One seems to know exactly how it is from the relation, as if they saw it. The mind is so led that sometimes we seem to have a full, large, and particular history of a long time; so that if one should shut the book immediately, without taking particular notice, one would not suppose the story had been told in half so little room, but two or three negligent words and yet a long train of ideas. The story is so told that one's mind, although the things are not mentioned, yet naturally traces the whole transaction. And although it be thus cunningly contrived, yet things are told in such a simple, plain manner that the least child can understand it. This cannot be attained unto to the perfection of the Scripture, by any mortal or finite being; for there is need of an infinite understanding in order to it. I shall give a few instances of what I intend.[3]

7. WILL OF GOD. The Arminians ridicule our distinction of the secret and revealed will of God, or more properly expressed, our distinction

3. JE did not carry out his purpose but commenced No. 7 at the next line.

between the decree and law [of God], because we say he may decree one thing and command another; and so they say we hold contrariety and contradiction in God, as if one will of his contradicted and was directly contrary to another. But however, if they will call this a contradiction of wills, we do certainly and absolutely know there is such a thing, so that it is the greatest absurdity to dispute about it.

We and they [know it was] God's secret will that Abraham should not sacrifice his son, but yet his command was to do it. [We]⁴ do certainly know that God willed that Pharoah's heart should be hardened, and yet that the hardness of his heart was his sin. We do know that God willed that [the] Egyptians should hate God's people. Ps. 105:25, "He turned their heart to hate his people and deal subtilely with his servants." We do know that it was God's will that Absalom should lie with David's wives. II Sam. 12:11–12, "Thus saith the Lord, Behold, I will raise up evil against thee out of thine own house, and I will take thy wives before thine eyes and give them unto thy neighbor; and he shall lie with thy wives in the sight of this sun. For thou didst it secretly, but I will do this thing before all Israel and before the sun." We do certainly know that God willed that Jeroboam and the ten tribes should rebel. The same, we know, may be said of the plunder of the Babylonians; and other instances might be given. The Scripture plainly tells us that God wills to harden some men (Rom. 9:18), that Christ should be killed by men, [etc.].

8. CONSCIENCE.⁵ The dispute whether or no men may make laws to oblige the conscience [is nonsense]. For what nonsense is [it] for the world to be rent to pieces with a dispute, whether men are obliged to do that which at the same time they are obliged in the same sense not to do! It is the same thing precisely, for the dispute is this: whether men are obliged in conscience to go contrary to their consciences when men command them so to do; which implies that men's consciences may sometimes tell them that some things are right and ought to be done, which at the same time their consciences tell them it is wrong and ought not to be done.

9. SUPREMACY. To inquire whether or no everyone that is supreme civil ruler is supreme in ecclesiastical affairs, is nonsense. It ought to be

4. Several years later (probably in the late 1730s) JE interlined the words "God's secret will . . . to do it," but failed to integrate the insertion into the rest of his text. This has now been done by adding the bracketed words in this and the preceding sentence.
5. For the issues dealt with in Nos. 8–14, see above, pp. 12–13.

thus expressed: whether there be an indissoluble connection between supremacy in civil authority and supremacy in ecclesiastical authority, so that they must unavoidably be joined together in the same man. Or, whether or no the same reason that gives him a right to be ruler in civil affairs, necessarily and at all times gives him a right to be ruler in ecclesiastical affairs distinct from the civil, that one kind of power is so joined with the other that they forever refuse to be separate; that is, that it is impossible in nature that ever there should be a merely civil ruler that is supreme. So the question is whether it be possible for a man to possess just so much power and no more, just so much as the highest civil power and no more; or whether such a particular measure and degree of power be not impossible to be possessed by any, although higher power be possible.

10. PASTORS. This is certain and evident concerning its belonging to the people to choose their own pastor, that it is either the people's part to choose with what food they will be fed—let what will be offered them, 'tis their business to judge whether it be best for them to receive it in as their food—or else, that they in some cases are to receive that as their food, which they at the same [time] judge to be their poison; that is, they are to believe those things which at the same time they believe to be false, and are to think it best for them to do those things which they at the same time think it is best for them not to do: which are contradictions.

It [is] every man's business to choose that food which he thinks to be best for himself; that is, it is every man's business to choose that food which he thinks to be best for his eternal welfare, as certain as it is his business to get as much happiness as he can for himself in the other world; as all are fools that will not. And it is certainly the effect of folly, to suffer men to hinder us from it if we can help it. Wherefore, if it be the people's part to choose with what food they will be fed, it is also their business to choose with what feeders they will be fed. If I may choose my food, I may choose that feeder that will give the food that I choose, if I can obtain him. And I am a fool if I will be hindered by men, when I can help it, from being fed by such a feeder as I judge will be a means of my greatest eternal welfare.

11. DISCIPLINE. This is most certain, that if men have no power [and] authority to make ecclesiastical laws, then I am not obliged to obey them because of their power and authority. I am not obliged to obey them because of any power or authority they have; that is, I am not

obliged to obey them any more than I should be obliged to obey the meanest, most obscure private person in the kingdom if he should take on him to make laws. So that is proved, that I am not obliged to obey them because of their authority.

But then, if it shall be said that we are obliged to obey for the sake of peace, I answer: 'tis most certain that if the legislators have no authority to make such laws, I am no more obliged to obey them, merely for the sake of peace, than the people of England would be obliged to obey the Grand Turk, who has no authority, if he should make laws for them. Supposing that a breach of his laws would enrage all the people of Turkey and this should ensure every way as bad a breach of peace as by my disobeying those who have no authority in England; now indeed I say, the people of England would[6] be obliged, if the case were so, to obey the Grand Turk, if no worse thing would follow than the breach of peace; but it belongs to the people in England and not to the Grand Turk to judge whether there would or no. So it belongs to me to judge whether it will be best for me to obey those who have no authority, or no, and not the legislators.

12. CEREMONIES. If any ceremonies in divine worship are in any wise unlawful for this reason, because they are ceremonies of human invention, then human invention is a thing that makes ceremonies unlawful in the worship of God; and if so, then the ceremonies of the Church of England are unlawful. But if no ceremonies are unlawful because they are of human invention, then none of the ceremonies of the Church of Rome, nor all of them together, are unlawful upon this account, viz. because they are of human invention. But if it is said that the ceremonies of the Church of Rome are not unlawful upon that account, but because of their insignificancy or ill tendency; I say, who is to be judge in that case? Surely their legislators, as much as the legislators in England about the English ceremonies.

13. CEREMONIES. It is certain, if men have power to establish by law those things in the worship of God that are indifferent, they have power to establish whatever they think to be either good or indif-

---

6. It is not clear whether JE intended to write a "not" at this point, as seems to be required by what has gone before. The present sentence, as it stands, is in the form of a qualification ("now indeed I say . . . but") and seems to be saying that the people of England *should* obey the Grand Turk for the sake of peace if only that is at stake. For the issue JE is addressing, see above, p. 12, n. 5.

ferent; that is, the legislators are to be judges of what is good or indifferent, and not those for whom the laws are made. And if they have power of establishing by law whatsoever they judge to be good or indifferent in the worship of God, they also have power to punish according to the sanctions of those laws all those that break their laws. From whence it follows, that the Papists had full power to establish by law whatever they judged to be good or indifferent, and also had power to punish all that broke their laws; so that all they did in their persecutions was no more than they had full power to do. And if we grant that the Papists had such power, then it will follow that the Church of England have no power, because they are in subjection to Rome; so that I am not at all obliged to obey the Church of England, but the Church of Rome.

14. CIVIL AUTHORITY. The civil authorities' having nothing to do with matters ecclesiastical, with those things which relate to conscience and eternal salvation, or with any matters religious *as religious,* is reconcilable still with their having to do with some matters that in some sense concern religion. For although they have to [do] with nothing but civil affairs, and although their business extends no further than the civil interest of the people, yet by reason of the profession of religion and the difference that matters religious make in the state and circumstances of a people, many things become civil which otherwise would not.

Now by the civil interest or advantage of a people, as distinguished [from] those things which relate to conscience, the favor of God, and happiness in the other world, I think is commonly meant their general interest, or their interest as they are a people in this world, whether it [be] their general profit, or pleasure, or peace, or honor, etc. I say general interest, or interest as a people, because the pleasure, profit, peace or honor of a people in general, or taken one with another, may be advanced, yet[7] thereby the interest or pleasure of a particular person may be depressed; and so also, the interest of the whole for a particular time may be depressed, when yet, taken one time with another, it may be advanced.

Now I say, this interest of a people may be all that civil authority has to do with, and yet it may have to [do] with things in some sort religious for the beforementioned reason, because many things by reason of

7. MS: "may."

religion become their civil advantage, that is, their advantage in this
world, which otherwise would not be so; as also, many things become
their civil disadvantage. Thus it is for the civil interest of a people not
to be disturbed in their public assemblies for divine worship; that is, it
is for their general peace, quiet and pleasure, etc. in this world.

15. IRRESISTIBLE GRACE. To dispute, as more latterly they do,
whether the divine assistance is always efficacious or no, is perfectly
ridiculous. For it is self-evident that the divine assistance is always
efficacious to do that which we are assisted to; that is, it is always
efficacious to that which it is efficacious to. And it is no less certain, that
it is efficacious to all that God intends it shall be efficacious [to]; that is,
when God assists, he assists to all that he intends to assist to. But that
the divine assistance is always efficacious to all that it has a tendency to
in its own nature, is what nobody affirms.

16. FOREKNOWLEDGE. This is most certain, that if there are any
things that are so contingent that there is an equal possibility both of
their being or not being, so that they may be or they may not be; God
foreknows from all eternity that they may be, and also that they may
not be. All will grant that we need no revelation to teach us this. And
furthermore, if God knows all things that are to come to pass, he also
foreknows whether those contingent things will come to pass or no, at
the same time that they are contingent and that they may or may not
come to pass.

But what a contradiction is this, to say that God knows a thing will
come to pass, and yet at the same time knows that it is contingent
whether it will or no! That is, he certainly knows it will come to pass,
and yet certainly knows it may not come to pass. What a contradiction
is it, to say that God certainly foreknew that Judas would betray his
Master or Peter deny him, and yet certainly knew that it might be
otherwise, that is, certainly knew that he might be deceived! I suppose
it will be acknowledged by all, that for God certainly to know that a
thing will be, and yet certainly to know that it may not be, is the same as
certainly to know that he may be deceived. I suppose it will also be
acknowledged, that certainly to know a thing, and also at the same time
to know that we may be deceived in it, is the same thing as certainly to
know it and certainly to know that we are uncertain of it, or that we do
not certainly know it; and that that is the same thing as certainly to

know it and not certainly to know it at the same time. Which we leave to be considered, whether it ben't a contradiction.

17. CONFESSION OF FAITH,[8] with respect to declaring one's faith in Scripture expressions. This is certain, if there ought to be liberty of conscience, that every minister, every Christian, and every man upon earth is at liberty to declare or not to declare his consent to any man's being a minister, according as he does internally in his mind consent or not consent; that is, every man upon earth, if he may declare either way, may declare whether he thinks such a man is fit or unfit for the ministry, as he does really think him fit or unfit. 'Tis evident he has liberty of conscience to think about it; and if he has liberty of conscience, he has liberty of declaring according to his thoughts. This liberty every minister has, that is required to give his consent [to] a man's being a minister.

If so, 'tis also certain that if a minister believes that no man can be fit but what believes such and such things to be true, he has liberty of conscience to declare his consent or dissent, according as he thinks the person believes or disbelieves those things. And if so, 'tis absolutely certain that he has power to insist on those things which he shall think sufficient reasons to make him think that he does believe those things which he deems necessary, before he gives his consent to his being a minister; and if he thinks that speaking in the words of the Scripture be not sufficient to make him think so, he has power to insist on more. So likewise, every particular man and every congregation of men in the world have the same liberty to judge what man is fit to feed their souls.

Not but that creeds and confessions of faith have been some of the chief engines that Satan has made use of to tear the church of God in pieces; not but that if these were removed, the principal walls of sep-

---

8. In 1712, the General Association of Connecticut laid down five rules for the examination of ordinands, one of which provided that the candidate "give his assent" to the Savoy Confession (Benjamin Trumbull, *A Complete History of Connecticut* [2 vols. New Haven, 1818], *1*, 410, 416). In Oct. 1722, the Yale trustees enacted that all future rectors and tutors must "declare their Assent" to the Savoy Confession and Saybrook Platform (F.B. Dexter, *Documentary History of Yale University* [New Haven, Yale Univ. Press, 1916], p. 233). JE must also have been aware of the dispute over creedal subscription that had divided the London Dissenters at Salters Hall in 1719 and was beginning to appear among the colonial Presbyterians. For a brief account of these controversies, see Charles A. Briggs, *American Presbyterianism* (New York, 1885), pp. 194–208.

aration would at the same time be removed; not that 'tis right for men to insist upon subscription to any creeds, or confessions of faith, or any other particular ways of making known their faith. All that we plead for is that there be sufficient reasons to satisfy those whose business it is to declare their consent to their being ministers, that the candidate does believe what is thought necessary by them to be believed in order to his[9] fitness; not that they can demand any more than such satisfaction, which way soever they come by it.

18. ADAM'S SIN. It is no more unreasonable that we should be guilty of Adam's first sin, than that we should be guilty of our own that we have been guilty of in times past. For we are not the same we were in times past, any other way than only as we please to call ourselves the same. For we are anew created every moment; and that that is caused to be this moment, is not the same that was caused to be the last moment, only as there is such a relation between this existence now and a certain existence in time past as we call sameness; such as remembrance, consciousness, love, likeness, a continuation of being both as to time and place without interval, etc.: which relations the sovereign God has constituted stated conditions of derivations of guilt.[1] What relations he will constitute to be such conditions, is entirely at his will and pleasure.

19. FOREKNOWLEDGE, God's foreknowledge of the elect. As God is said to know those that are his own sheep from strangers, as Christ is said not to know the workers of iniquity; that is, he owns them not: in the same sense God is said to foreknow the elect from all eternity; that is, he knew them as a man knows his own things, he acknowledged them from eternity, he knew them as his children. Reprobates he did not know; they were strangers to God from all eternity.

20. IMMORTALITY OF THE SOUL. How doth it seem to grate upon one to think that an intelligent being, that consciousness should be put out forever, so as never to know that it ever did think or had a being! If it be put out as a punishment, it can never know that it is punished, never reflect on the justice of God, or anything of that nature.

9. MS: "their."
1. This notion of personal identity reappears much later in *Original Sin*, Pt. IV, ch. 3 (*Works*, 3, 397–407). The conceptions of created being and natural law on which JE builds in No. 18 are succinctly stated in "Atoms," prop. 2, corols. 8–9,14–15 (ibid., 6, 214–16).

21. UNIVERSAL REDEMPTION. This is certain, that God did not intend to save those by the death of Christ, that he certainly knew from all eternity he should not save by his death. Wherefore, it is certain that if he intended to save any by the death of Christ, he intended to save those whom he certainly knew he should save by his death. This is all that was ever pleaded for.

22. JEHOVAH. How plain is it to the mind in the least considerate, that it is impossible that ever men in those ancient and obscure ages of the world, in which it is most certain the books of Moses were written, could ever think of such names, which so wonderfully exhibit the essence and abstracted nature of God, according to and yet beyond the nicest, most abstracted, and yet most certain notions of the most penetrating metaphysicians. How certain is it, that the human inventions of those ages never gave to God such a name as I AM THAT I AM![2] Who should contrive that God should send Moses with such a message, "I AM hath sent me unto you"? Who can believe that those plain simple persons, in that most unphilosophical age, should so much surpass Socrates, Plato or Tully, as this most certainly doth? The third and sixth chapters of Exodus as strongly and as irresistibly prove themselves by their own powerful light to be of divine authority, as the meridian light of the sun proves it to be in our hemisphere.

23. RESURRECTION OF CHRIST. The resurrection of Christ is necessary in order to our salvation thus: if he had not rose again, it would have been because he could not get through his passion, could not get through that work that God required in order to satisfaction. The resurrection was the finishing of the work and the conquest of death, which was absolutely necessary.

24. MEDIATION. If we should suppose the Christian religion to be false (for it is lawful to suppose impossibilities, yea contradictions, for argument's sake), yet a mediation in every article like that of Christ's might be absolutely proved to be necessary, by the force of naked demonstration.

25. UNIVERSAL REDEMPTION. When Christ came into the world, he came with a design of doing that hard work and going through those

2. Cf. "Natural Philosophy," Long Series no. 44 (*Works, 6,* 238) and "The Mind" no. 15, corol. (ibid., pp. 344–45).

dreadful miseries which he endured. Now most certainly, there was something that he most ardently desired, that was the glorious end proposed by him when he undertook this work; now this end was salvation. Now can we suppose that Christ came down from heaven and went through all this upon uncertainties, not knowing what purchase he should get, how great or how small? Did he die only upon probabilities, without absolute certainty who, or how many, or whether any should be redeemed by what he did and suffered? Did he pay down such an exact price, that God required of him, at the same time that he knew not what or how much he was to have in return for it? And if he did know what he was to have for the price he paid, I suppose he paid the price for that and for no more.

If it is objected and said that Christ has that love for every particular believer that may be called "dying love," that is, such love as is sufficient to move him to die—but I answer, that it is inconsistent with the scheme of those that are for universal redemption [to say] that he did die with any view to particular persons that he loved, only from a love to the race of mankind in general, with a view to them as a race without any regard to particular persons.

26. MILLENNIUM.[3] How happy will that state be, when neither divine nor human learning shall be confined and imprisoned within only two or three nations of Europe, but shall be diffused all over the world, and this lower world shall be all over covered with light, the various parts of it mutually enlightening each other; when the most barbarous nations shall become as bright and polite as England; when ignorant heathen lands shall be stocked with most profound divines and most learned philosophers; when we shall from time to time have the most excellent books and wonderful performances brought from one end of the earth and another to surprise us—sometimes new and wondrous discoveries from Terra Australis Incognita, admirable books of devotion, the most divine and angelic strains from among the Hottentots, and the press shall groan in wild Tartary—when we shall have the great advantage of the sentiments of men of the most distant nations, different circumstances, customs and tempers; [when] learn-

3. This vision of the millennium is in harmony with the belief JE then held that the destruction of Antichrist would be accomplished by ideological rather than military warfare; see above, No. xx, and JE's comments (written about two months after No. 26) on Rev. 11:19 and 16:21 (*Works*, 5, 106, 117–18).

ing shall not be restrained [by] the particular humor of a nation or their singular way of treating of things; when the distant extremes of the world shall shake hands together and all nations shall be acquainted, and they shall all join the forces of their minds in exploring the glories of the Creator, their hearts in loving and adoring him, their hands in serving him, and their voices in making the world to ring with his praise.

What infinite advantages will they have for discovering the truth of every kind, to what they have now! There will continually be something new and surprising discovered in one part of the world and another [because of] the vast number of explorers, their different circumstances, their different paths to come at the truth. How many instructive and enlightening remains of antiquity will be discovered, here and there now buried amongst ignorant nations!

27a.[4] GOD is a necessary being, because it's a contradiction to suppose him not to be. No being is a necessary being but he whose nonentity is a contradiction. We have shown that absolute nothing is the essence of all contradictions;[5] but being includes in it all that we call God, who *is,* and there is none else besides him.[6]

27b. CONVERSION. 'Tis most certain, both from Scripture and reason, that there must be a reception of Christ with the faculties of the soul in order to salvation by him, and that in this reception there is a believing of what we are taught in the gospel concerning him and salvation by him, and that it must be a consent of the will or an agreeableness between the disposition of the soul and those doctrines; so that the disposition is all that can be said to be absolutely necessary. The act cannot be proved to be absolutely necessary; that is, it can't be proved that there is not the disposition before there is an act because it

---

4. This entry was written very close in time to Nos. 193 and 194, indeed probably between them; see above p. 18.

5. JE quotes almost directly from his essay "Of Being" (*Works, 6,* 206); but the occasion and proximate source of No 27a was probably the entries JE had been making in "The Mind," nos. 27–30, particularly no. 30 (ibid., pp. 350–52).

6. This or a similar ascription to Deity appears in several slightly varying forms in the Bible, notably in Deut. 4:35; Is. 45:5, 6, 22, and 46:9; cf. Zeph. 2:15. JE uses it elsewhere, e.g. "Natural Philosophy," Long Series no. 44, corol. 1 (ibid., p. 238) and "The Mind," no. 15 (ibid., p. 345).

is said by some[7] that [the fact that] a man can't be saved before he has actually believed, if he is come to years of discretion, is plain by Scripture. But I say, no plainer than that a man must actually live a holy life before he can be saved; for the Scripture in many places speaks as plainly about the necessity of a holy life as of believing. But by those expressions concerning a holy life, we can understand nothing else but a disposition that would naturally exert itself in holy [living] upon occasion; so we say of the believing disposition.

And as sometimes a person has this disposition within 'em who have in times past felt the quickest exercises of it, yet may not sensibly feel them for some time; so a man may have the disposition in him for some time before he ever sensibly feels them, for want of occasion and other reasons. 'Tis the disposition and principle is the thing God looks at. Supposing a man dies suddenly and not in the actual exercise of faith, 'tis his disposition that saves him; for if it were possible that the disposition was destroyed, the man would be damned and all the former acts of faith would signify nothing.

Those particular acts our divines describe may possibly be necessary thus, that it is impossible for such a disposition to be in the mind, in such circumstances, without its being exercised in such particular kind of actions; which must be determined by plain consequence of nature or else by Scripture. The Scripture indeed, in many invitations to Christ, doth make use of the words "come," "believe," "trust," "receive,"[8] which without doubt signify those actions that are aptly represented by these expressions. It need not be doubted but that many of the ancient Jews before Christ were saved without the sensible exertions of those acts in that manner which is represented as necessary by some divines, because they had not those occasions nor were under circumstances that would draw them out; though without doubt they had the disposition, which alone is absolutely necessary now, and at all times and in all circumstances is equally necessary.

This is furthermore certain and evident concerning conversion, or a true reception of Christ, if it be actual: there must be a dying unto sin

7. Among these JE could count his grandfather, Solomon Stoddard, who was vigorous in asserting that there is no gracious disposition prior to the explicit act of faith; see his *Safety of Appearing* (Boston, 1687), p. 101, and *Treatise Concerning Conversion* (Boston, 1719), p. 37.

8. JE left space on the line at this point, probably for the addition of other like terms. The order of these verbs, so far as this list goes, is identical with that of the corresponding Latin series found in the M.A. thesis.

and an emptying of self that Christ may be all in all, what in the Scripture is called "hating our own life."

28. SABBATH. The week of the children of Israel had its date from the day that the children of Israel went out of Egypt, and not from the first day of the creation. The day of their coming out was the seventh day of their week. Their week was not that which was the week in order of succession from the beginning of the creation, as we know of, but a week peculiar unto that nation; and there is no more reason why their week should be kept among all nations, than there is that all the customs of their law should be kept.

Their seventh day was the day wherein they were brought out of Egypt. Our seventh day, or first day—it's no matter by what name we call it—is the day that Christ brought *us* out of Egypt, out of bondage to sin and Satan; of which deliverance theirs was but a faint representation, between which and the thing represented there is as much difference as between a dim spark and the sun in the middle of the heavens, in the strength of his glory. They were commanded to keep that particular day because God then delivered them from Egypt, as is inserted in the fourth commandment in Deuteronomy, and the day was observed chiefly because their deliverance was a type of Christ's redemption. Their annual observation of the day, and the whole manner of it and all its rites and ceremonies, it is plain, were for nothing but to represent Christ. And must the antitype always give way to the type? How ridiculous is this!

God says, speaking of the redemption by Christ, that the days should come "wherein they shall no more say, 'The Lord liveth, who brought up the children of Israel out of Egypt'" [Jer. 23:7]. Now the days are come. 'Tis true the sabbath day used to be kept in remembrance of the creation of the world, but the first creation is spoiled; we have ruined it, and have reason to lament that ever we were created, except we are created again. We are truly to keep the sabbath in commemoration of the creation, but it is of the new creation. We are truly to keep the sabbath on the day wherein God rested from the creation of the heavens and the earth, but we are to do it in the day wherein God created the new heavens and the new earth, by which name God calls the restoration by Christ (Is. 65:17–18; 51:16; 66:22). God told us that when that was done we should no longer commemorate the first creation, but the second. Is. 65:17, "For behold, I create new heavens and a new earth; and the former shall not be remembered nor come into mind." But if we set apart one day in seven for this very end, to remember them and call them to mind, this is beside[9] the revealed will of God.

29. DECREES. The meaning of the word "absolute," when used about the decrees, wants to be stated. 'Tis commonly said,[1] that God decrees nothing upon a foresight of anything in the creature. This, they say, argues imperfection in God; and so it does, taken in the sense that they commonly intend it. But nobody, I believe, will deny but that God decrees many things that he would not have decreed, if he had not foreknown and foredetermined such and such other things. What we would[2] we completely express thus, that God decrees all things harmoniously and in excellent order; one decree harmonizes with another, and there is such a relation between all the decrees as makes the most excellent order. Thus God decrees rain in drought because he decrees the earnest prayers of his people; or thus, he decrees the prayers of his people because he decrees rain.

I acknowledge, to say God decrees a thing "because," is an improper way of speaking, but not more improper than all our other ways of speaking about God. God decrees the latter event because of the former, no more than he decrees the former because of the latter. But this is what we would: when God decrees to give the blessing of rain, he decrees the prayers of his people; and when he decrees the prayers of his people, he very commonly decrees rain; and thereby there is an harmony between these two decrees, of rain and the prayers of God's people. Thus also, when he decrees diligence and industry, he decrees riches and prosperity; when he decrees prudence, he often decrees success; when he decrees striving, then often he decrees the obtaining of the kingdom of heaven; when he decrees the preaching of the gospel, then he decrees the bringing home of souls to Christ; when he decrees good natural faculties, diligence and good advantages, then he decrees learning; when he decrees summer, then he decrees the growing of plants. Thus, when he decrees conformity to his Son, he

9. I.e. outside of, contrary to.

1. I.e. by Calvinists; the reference is to unconditional election. In the next sentence "they" are Arminians, who held that election is based on God's foreknowledge of the believer's faith and perseverance.

2. Here and in the next paragraph, "would" has the force of "intend" in the sense of "to mean." *Volo* is used in precisely the same way in the Latin thesis.

decrees calling; and when he decrees calling, he decrees justification; and when he decrees justification, he decrees everlasting glory.

Thus all the decrees of God are harmonious; and this is all that can be said for or against absolute or conditional decrees. But this I say, it's improper to make one decree a condition of another, [any]³ more than [the] other a condition of that; but there is a harmony between both.

30. COVENANT. With reference to what has been before spoken of the covenant [No. 2]. Covenant is taken very variously in Scripture, sometimes for a divine promise, sometimes for a divine promise on conditions. But if we speak of the covenant God has made with man stating the condition of eternal life, God never made but one with man, to wit, the covenant of works; which never yet was abrogated, but is a covenant stands in full force to all eternity without the failing of one tittle. The covenant of grace is not another covenant made with man upon the abrogation of this, but a covenant made with Christ to fulfill it. And for this end came Christ into the world, to fulfill the law, or covenant of works, for all that receive him.

31. FREE WILL.⁴ The freedom of will (to speak very improperly) don't infer an absolute contingency, nor is it inconsistent with an absolute necessity of the event that is to be brought about by this free will. For most certainly, God's will is free, or is no more bound than the will of his creatures; yet there is the greatest and most absolute necessity imaginable, that God should always will good and never evil. But if this instance will not be allowed, 'tis certain that the will of the man Christ Jesus was free, who was a man as well as we, one of the same faculties as we; yet as free as his will was, it was impossible that he should will sin.

32. MEDIATOR. To say that the covenant of works did admit of a mediator, is something improper. The covenant of works mentioned nothing about it; there is nothing in the covenant of works that opposes: but it is nature, and eternal reason, and the justice of God, and the immutable nature of order and harmony that admits [it]. And it

3. This word doubtless occurred on the defective right margin; what appears to be the lower tip of the *y* is still visible. The word must have been missing when JE, Jr. worked over the entry; he conjectured "as," misread "more" as "make," and altered the sentence to accommodate that wording.

4. This entry contains the thesis of two chapters in the *Freedom of the Will*, viz. Pt. III, §§ 1– 2 (*Works, 1*, 277–94).

would be mere superfluity as well as great impropriety, to go to stipulate and state anything expressly, and give a particular allowance, for that which is allowed by these and is highly agreeable to them.

33. FAITH. In order to one's being a representative of another, it is necessary either that there should be something in nature, and eternal reason and rectitude, and absolute justice that should constitute him so, or else it must be by voluntary delegation—the former our case with respect to Adam, the latter the case of believers with respect to Christ. Faith is our voluntary delegation of Christ to represent us, a hearty choosing of him as Mediator.

Corol. 1. Hence the reason why none are saved but those which believe, appears very clear.

Corol. 2. By this also appears, without any obscurity, the whole matter of justification by faith.

34. ORIGINAL SIN. There can be no question but that human nature, by some means or other (however it came about), is now in these days, all over the world, in every man that comes into the world, very much vitiated. Now the rectitude of human nature and of rational beings most certainly is, that they should be most highly affected with the highest excellencies, and less affected with lower excellencies; that the mind should have the sweetest taste and most quick and exquisite delight of those things that are truly most delightful, and a lower delight and slower relish of those things that in themselves are less delightful; that the things that are most beautiful and amiable, as soon as ever they are seen, should most ravish the eye, and those things which are less beautiful should less please the sight; that man should have the quickest and easiest, highest and most delightful perception of that which is best, and the slowest and dullest perception of that which is less good. This is the rectitude of human nature, and thus human [nature] once was; or else most certainly human nature proceeded from God an inconsistent, self-repugnant and contradictory thing.

But we know, as well as we know that have being, that this rectitude is not the present state of human nature, but the right contrary in all universally; till human nature, by some means after we are born, is wrought up into this rectitude again. We are the highest affected with the lowest excellencies; we have the easiest and greatest delight in things that in themselves are least delightful; things that are less beautiful and amiable in themselves, strike much quicker and deeper in with the sense and propension and constitution of the mind than things that have in themselves the highest excellence, most charming beauty and exquisite sweetness. Yea, we can hardly bring ourselves to be in any measure pleased with the beauty, or to taste any sweetness at all, in things that are infinitely the greatest excellencies. How much soever one has been out of the way of ill examples or from the practice of vice, set before his eyes or represent to his mind the brightest and most amiable instances of virtue, and his mind has very heavily at the perception; but bring before [him] beauty of body and some of the meanest perfections of mind, and the soul is immediately alive and in a mere rapture. And so in all other cases.

35. COVENANT. Towards the rectifying of what has been already said about the covenants [Nos. 2, 30]. The covenant of grace or redemption (which we have showed to be the same) cannot be called a new covenant, or the second covenant, with respect to the covenant of works; for that is not grown old yet but is an eternal immutable covenant, of which one jot nor tittle will never fail. There have never been two covenants, in strictness of speech, but only two ways constituted of performing of this covenant: the first constituting Adam the representative and federal head, and the second constituting Christ the federal head; the one a dead way, the other a living way and an everlasting one.

36. JUSTIFICATION. The question is not whether or not men are[5] [justified] by evangelical obedience. But the question is, whether we are justified by evangelical obedience because of the goodness that is in it, or whether it be merely because by evangelical obedience Christ is received, merely because it is a reception of him, merely because by this the believer is united to Christ and made one with him, and so is looked upon as the same by God; this is the question.[6] 'Tis a hundred pities that men don't think what the question is, about which they dispute.

37. FAITH. The soul is espoused and married unto Jesus Christ; the believing soul is the bride and spouse of the Son of God. The union

5. MS: "whether or men are not." In the M.A. thesis he translated the clause as "annon justificamur evangelica obedientia."
6. This was also JE's first formulation of the question debated in the M.A. thesis; see above, p. 13.

between Christ and believers is very often represented to a marriage. This similitude is much insisted on in Scripture—how sweetly is it set forth in the Song of Songs! Now it is by faith that the soul is united unto Christ; faith is this bride's reception of Christ as a bridegroom. Let us, following this similitude that we may illustrate the nature of faith, a little consider what are those affections and motions of heart that are proper and suitable in a spouse toward her bridegroom, what are those conjugal motions of soul which are most agreeable to, and do most harmonize with, that relation that she bears as a spouse.

Now it is easy to everyone to know that when marriage is according to nature and God's designation, when a woman is married to an husband she receives him as a guide, as a protector, a safeguard and defense, a shelter from harms and dangers, a reliever from distresses, a comforter in afflictions, a support in discouragements. God has so designed it, and therefore has made man of a more robust [nature], and strong in body and mind, with more wisdom strength and courage, fit to protect and defend; but he has made woman weaker, more soft and tender, more fearful, and more affectionate, as a fit object of generous protection and defense. Hence it is, that it is natural in women to look most at valor and fortitude, wisdom, generosity and greatness of soul: these virtues do—or at least ought, according to nature—move most upon the affections of the woman. Hence also it is, that man naturally looks most at a soft and tender disposition of mind, and those virtues and affections which spring from it, such as humility, modesty, purity, chastity. And the affections which he most naturally looks at in her are a sweet and entire confidence and trust, submission and resignation; for when he receives a woman as wife, he receives her as an object of his guardianship and protection, and therefore looks at those qualifications and dispositions which exert themselves in trust and confidence. Thus it's against nature for a man to love a woman as wife that is rugged, daring and presumptuous, and trusts to herself, and thinks she is able to protect herself and needs none of her husband's defense or guidance. And it is impossible a woman should love a man as an husband, except she can confide in him, and sweetly rest in him as a safeguard.

Thus also, when the believer receives Christ by faith, he receives him as a safeguard and shelter from the wrath of God and eternal torments, and defense from all the harms and dangers which he fears. Is. 32:2, "And a man shall be as an hiding place from the wind, and a covert from the tempest; as rivers of water in a dry place, as the shadow

of a great rock in a weary land." Wherefore, the dispositions of soul
which Christ looks at in his spouse are a sweet reliance and confidence
in him, a humble trust in him as her only rock of defence, whither she
may flee. And Christ will not receive those as the objects of his salvation who trust to themselves, their own strength or worthiness, but
those alone who entirely rely on him. The reason of this is very natural
and easy.

38. HARMONY OF GOD'S ATTRIBUTES IN THE WORK OF REDEMPTION.
The redemption by Christ is particularly wonderful upon this account, inasmuch as the justice of God is not only appeased to those
who have an interest in him, but stands up for them; is not only not an
enemy but a friend, every whit as much as mercy. Justice demands
adoption and glorification, and importunes as much for it, as ever it
did before for misery; in every respect that it is against the wicked, it is
as much for the godly. Yea, it is abundantly more so than it would have
been for Adam: for him it would be only because He graciously promised; but it is obliged to believers on the account of the absolute merit
of the Son of God, and upon the account of an eternal agreement
between God and his Son.

39. CONVERSION. I am now convinced, that conversion under the old
testament was not only the same in general with what it is commonly
under the new,[7] but much more like it as to the particular way and
manner, than I used to think. Among the children of Israel, there was
always without doubt two sorts of persons, wicked and godly, and there
used to be as manifest a difference between these two as there is now. It
appears that the wicked were the same as they are now: vain, profane,
light, proud, scornful, hating the godly. The righteous, by the descriptions we have of them, were also the same: humble, meek and lowly,
devout, full of fear, love and trust in God, just, righteous and charitable. And we can't question but that there were as frequent conversions
from one to the other as there is now.

This turning is very often spoken of in the Old Testament, frequently urged and encouraged; and we have no reason to believe that
what was said had no effect. And undoubtedly the first motives of their

7. The words "old testament" and "new testament" begin with lower-case letters when
"testament" is being used as synonymous with "covenant." The words are capitalized when
they refer to a portion of the Bible. When JE's meaning cannot be discerned from the
context, which is rare, the word is treated as referring to Scripture.

turning were a sense of the dangerousness of sin, and of the dreadfulness of God's anger; and [they] were convinced so much of their wickedness, that they trusted to nothing but the mere mercy of God, and then bitterly lamented and mourned for their sins. Wherever turning is urged, such a turning as this is urged; and what instances we have were of this kind. And thus it doubtless was, not only amongst the Israelites but also among the antediluvians, and from the beginning of the world.

40. MINISTERS. Relating to Nos. mm and qq. 'Tis a thousand pities that the words "church office" and "power" should so tear the world to pieces, and raise such a fog and dust about apostolic office, power and succession, [and about] popes', bishops' and prebyters' power. It is not such a desperately difficult thing to know what power belongs to each of these; if we will let drop those words that are without fixed meaning, the light of nature will lead us right along in a plain path.

Without doubt, ministers are to administer the sacraments to Christians, and that they are to administer them only to such as they think Christ would have them administer them. Without doubt, ministers are to teach men what Christ would have them to do, and to teach them who doth these things and who doth them not, that is, who are Christians and who are not, and the people are to hear them as much in this as in other things; and that so far forth as the people are obliged to hear what I teach them, so great is my pastoral, or ministerial, or teaching power. And this is all the difference of power there is amongst ministers, whether apostles or whatever.

Thus if I in a right manner am become the teacher of a people, so far as they ought to hear what I teach them, so much power I have. Thus if they are obliged to hear me only because they themselves have chosen me to guide them, and therein declared that they thought me sufficiently instructed in the mind of Christ to teach them, and because I have the other requisites of being their teacher, then I have power as other ministers have in these days. But if it was plain to them that I was under the infallible guidance of Christ, then I should have more power. And if it was plain to all the world of Christians that I was under the infallible guidance of Christ, and [that] I was sent forth to teach the world the will of Christ, then I should have power in all the world: I should have power to teach them what they ought to do, and they would be obliged to hear me; I should have power to teach them who were Christians and who not, and in this likewise they would be obliged to hear me.

41. MEDIATION. The Apostle says, Phil. 1:11, that "fruits of righteousness," or good works, are "to the glory and praise of God" by Jesus. Now how are good works to God's glory by Christ? What particular need of his mediation, to make good works to God's glory? We must consider, (1) that man never could have done any good works in a right manner, that is, never could have performed any good works without it. John 15:4–5, "Abide in me and I in you. As the branch cannot bear fruit of itself, except it abide in the vine; no more can ye, except ye abide in me. I am the vine, ye are the branches. He that abideth in me, and I in him, the same bringeth forth much fruit; for without me ye can do nothing." This is plain and needs no solution. But (2) if fallen man could perform a good work from hearty love and admiration of God without the intervention of Christ, yet it would not be to God's glory.

It cannot be but that the love and admiration of God, and the fruits of these, in any positive being, should be to the glory of God. By a positive being, I mean a being that is not so debased as to become as little or less, as bad or worse, than nothing. But if he is loved and admired by such, it is evident that he is glorified no more than if he were admired by nothing. Now fallen man is such a being. Sin, of which he is guilty, is an evil of infinite badness, as we have shown (No. nn); wherefore it follows that he is perfectly equivalent [to], or rather, less and worse than, no being. So that let him do what good works he will, yet if they are put in the scale with the evil, they bear absolutely no proportion at all; the scale of evil is not at all raised by it: the man taken together is every whit as bad in the sight of God as if he had no good works at all, because his evil infinitely outweighs it, and the good is perfectly adequate to nothing in comparison of it. And therefore, the man is a creature not at all actively to God's glory. But Jesus Christ blots out all the evil, and leaves that scale altogether empty; and so far are they from being as little as nothing, that they are members of the Son of God; and therefore, by his intercession, their good works become acceptable to God, and to his praise and glory.

Corol. 1. Hence we see of what large extent is the mediation of Christ, and how universally necessary in all matters of religion.

Corol. 2. Hence we see why it is that the Apostle says, Col. 3:17, "And whatsoever ye do in word or deed, do all in the name of the Lord Jesus, giving thanks to God and the Father by him"; and why it is, and in what sense, that such expressions as these are so often, upon all occasions, used in the New Testament: "by Christ," "through Christ," "in the name of Christ," "in the Lord," etc. See note on Col. 3:17, and No. 627.[8]

42. RELIGION. . . .[9] The greatness, distance and motion of this great universe, has almost an omnipotent power upon the imagination; the blood will even be chilled with the vast idea. But the greatness of vast expanse, immense distance, prodigious bulk and rapid motion, is but a little, trivial and childish greatness in comparison of the noble, refined, exalted, divine, spiritual greatnesses. Yea, these are but the shadows of greatness and are worthless, except as they conduce to true and real greatness and excellency, and manifest the power and wisdom of God.

When we think of the sweet harmony of the parts of the corporeal world, it fills us with such astonishment that the soul is ready to break. Yet take all that infinite variety of sweet proportions, harmonious motions, and delightful correspondencies there are in the whole compages of bodies, and they are all but shadows of excellency, in comparison of those beauties and harmonies there may be in one finite spirit. That harmony of the world is indeed a very true picture and shadow of the real glories of religion. This great world contains many millions of little worlds vastly greater than it. The glories of astronomy and natural philosophy consist in the harmony of the parts of the corporeal shadow of a world; the glories of religion consist in the sweet harmony of the greater and more real worlds with themselves, with one another, and with the infinite fountain and original of them.

43. SABBATH. Such is human nature, that man can serve God, *cæteris paribus*, much better at such a time, as he has frequently beforehand in his thoughts devoted and intended entirely for the service of God, than he can at another time. Anyone may observe that it is so in other things. Thus, if a man long beforehand devotes such a day for a particular study, he can devote himself to that study much the better for it when the time comes. If a man beforehand intends such a day for mourning, his grief will be much the more heavy; if he beforehand devotes a day to rejoicing, his joy will be higher when the time comes.

8. The note on Col. 3:17 is printed in Grosart, *Selections*, pp. 168–69.

9. The first line of this entry occurs at a broken upper margin and is illegible. The entire second line (with the possible exception of a "the" and two or three now illegible words at the end) was deleted by JE and rewritten as the latter part of the first sentence ("has almost . . ."), with which the legible text begins. It is therefore likely that most of the first line of the MS page similarly reappears in the former part of that sentence; if so, very little of the text is lost. No early copy of the entry is extant.

And such is human nature, that the consideration of its being the command and will of God, that we should be especially devoted to religion at such a time, it helps us to a higher exercise of religion than we can attain to, *cæteris paribus,* by the mere force of our wills.

44. ETERNAL TORMENTS. *Ques.* Seeing that the *malitia,* or evil principle, which is the essence of the sin, is not infinite, though the God against whom sin is committed be infinite, how can it be just to punish sin with an infinite punishment? I acknowledge, if man, at the same time that he injured God, had actually a full and complete idea of the infinite excellency and greatness of God whom he injured, he could not injure him without an infinite pravity of soul, and then infinite punishment would undoubtedly be deserved. But all finite beings are uncapable of this full idea. Wherefore, it is impossible for them to have this infinite restraint, nor [to be possessed] of pravity of infinite strength to break through [this] restraint. Thus[1] it seems that the pravity of an action is not to be measured by the real hidden excellency or greatness of the person offended, but by the understanding the offender has of his greatness; that which was hidden is no aggravation, because he did not know it. If his idea be finite, then a finite pravity of mind is sufficient to conquer that idea.

Ans. Eternal punishment is just in the same respects infinite as the crime, and in no other. Thus the crime or the injury done, in itself considered, is really infinite, yet is not infinite in the idea, or mind committing; that is, is in itself infinite, but is not committed infinitely. So it is with the punishment: it is really in itself infinite, but is never suffered infinitely. Indeed, if the soul was capable of having at once a full and complete idea of the eternity of misery, then it would properly be infinite suffering. But the soul is no more capable of having a full idea of that, than of the infinite greatness and excellency of God; and we should have as full and as strong an idea of God's infinite perfection as the damned have of the eternity of their torment, if it were not for sin. Eternity is suffered as an infinite God is offended, that is, according to the comprehension of the mind. Thus, if it were possible for a man eternally to be in pain, and all the while be deceived, and think that he had suffered not above half an hour, and was assured that he was not to suffer above half an hour longer; though the misery in

1. MS: "brake through. ⟨restraint⟩ th[ ]." The last word on the line is defective at the margin; Dwight's scribe read "but." "Thus" or "then" seems to be indicated rather than "that," since the point after "through" is clearly a full or nearly full stop.

God's idea would be infinite, yet in the suffering it is finite: in the suffering it is no more than if one should start out of nothing, and suffer one hour, and drop into nothing again. Sin against God in God's idea is infinite, and the punishment is infinite no otherwise but in the idea of God. For all that is past and all that is to come, that is not comprehended in finite ideas, is not anywhere else but in the divine idea. See where we have proved that nothing has any existence but in ideas.[2]

45. SABBATH. All the reason that can be pretended, why it is not as moral as anything else whatever that just a seventh part of time should be especially and entirely devoted to the worship of God, is the defect of human knowledge. For if we had so much natural reason as to be so fully acquainted with human nature, and the nature of other things with which we are concerned, as plainly and easily to see, that it was most agreeable to the natural constitution of things that just such a proportion of time should be devoted to God's worship, then it would be as moral as anything else; the light of nature would teach us that we ought to keep holy a seventh part of time.

46. CRUCIFIXION is perhaps the sort of death that men have ever been wont to suffer, whereby they die merely through the exquisiteness of the pain; and it must be very great pain indeed, which alone will kill a man in three hours. And it was the most ignominious of all deaths, chosen out by the Jews for him before any other kind of death, for the sake of the ignominiousness and painfulness of it. And then, hanging on a tree was the most cursed of all deaths.

47. RESURRECTION. Great stress seems to be put upon the resurrection of Christ everywhere in the New Testament, as if it were what had great influence unto our salvation. For if Christ were not risen, it would be an evidence that God was not yet satisfied for [our] sins. Surely it is very necessary, in order to our salvation, that God should declare himself satisfied for our sins. Whatever is done, all is good for nothing till God has manifested his approbation of it, and has set his seal to it. Now the resurrection is God declaring his satisfaction; he thereby declared that it was enough; Christ was thereby released from his work; Christ, as he was Mediator, is thereby justified. I Tim. 3:16,

2. See *Works, 6,* 203–06.

"God was manifest in the flesh, justified in the spirit." Whatever Christ did or suffered, there still wanted God's sanction or justification; so that except this had been done, we should be yet in our sins, and our faith would be vain (I Cor. 15:17). But now God has begotten us to a lively hope by the resurrection of Christ from the dead. See No. 23.

48. DEVIL. Seeing the devil is so cunning and subtile, it may seem a paradox, why he will endeavor to frustrate the designs of an omniscient being, or to pretend to counterwork him that is omnipotent, and will not suffer anything but what is for his own glory: seeing that God turns everything he does to the greater and more illustrious advancement of His own honor, and seeing he has experience of it, for so long a time, [that] all his deep laid contrivances have at last come out to his own overthrow, and the event has been directly contrary to his design.

To this I say, that although the devil be exceeding crafty and subtile, yet he is one of the greatest fools and blockheads in the world, as the subtilest of wicked men are. Sin is of such a nature that it strangely infatuates and bewitches persons: makes men deliberately choose eternal torments rather than miss of their pleasure of a few days, and to esteem a little silver and gold above eternal happiness; makes men choose a few minutes pleasure, though eternal flames be joined therewith, rather than not have it—thus do the cunningest of wicked men. Sin has the same effect on the devils, to make them act like fools, and so much the more as it is greater in them than in others. The devil acts not according to his deliberate judgment, but is driven on to his own inexpressible torment by the fury of sin, malice, revenge and pride; is so entirely under the government of malice, that although he never attempted anything against God but he was disappointed, yet he cannot bear to lie still, and refrain from exerting himself with all his might and subtilty against the interest of holiness; though he, if he considered, might know that it will turn to its advantage.

49. ISRAEL. See No. 597. The case is exceeding plain, why Christians in Old Testament prophecies should be called Israel; for they *are* Israel, in the same sense as the proselytes were called Israel; even in the Old Testament, they were then accounted as sons of Israel. In the same sense it is prophesied of gospel times, "And they shall bring thy sons from far, and thy daughters from the end of the earth" [Is. 43:6, 49:22]. And besides, there was a very great part of the Jews in Judea and dispersed over all the world that were Christians; whose posterity

we are not to suppose are extinguished, but only not distinguished from the Gentile proselytes, and it may be are as numerous as that nation that go by that name, considering their many slaughters.

And what if they are called by a new name? Was it not prophesied that they should? [Is. 62:2]. Perhaps the greatest part of Christians have some Jewish blood in them; it would be strange if they should not, considering how the Christian Jews were dispersed all over the world. And what if they have some Gentile blood in them too, must they not be called Israel? So had David by Ruth, and perhaps most of the rest of Israel in his time. And if they had no Jewish blood in them, they might be called Israel as well as the proselytes. And what if the Christians have more of Gentile blood in them than Jewish, and the proselytes be more than the rest of Israel? Was it not prophesied that the children of the desolate should be more than of the married wife? [Is. 54:1]. And besides all this, they have the essentials of Israelites, the circumcision of the heart, and are the spiritual Israel of God, of which the Israelitish nation are but a mere type and shadow.

50. LAW. The doctrines of the strictness and severity of the law appear to be the received doctrines in the early days of Christianity. Because as Tertullian writes, that Cerdon, a heretic (who appeared about 140), "introduced two beginnings, that is two gods: a good god and a fierce god, the good being the superior god, and the fierce one the creator of the world"; and Theodoret, "that he maintained there were two gods, the one a good god, the Father of our Lord Jesus Christ, the other a just god, the creator of all things."[3]

51. DECREE. It cannot be any injustice in God to determine who is certainly to sin, and so certainly to be damned. For if we suppose this impossibility, that God had not determined anything, things would happen as fatally as they do now. For such an absolute contingency and perfect chance which they attribute to man's will, calling of it the sovereignty of the will—if they mean by this sovereignty of will, that a man can will as he wills, 'tis perfect nonsense, and the same as if they

---

3. The first quotation is from § 16 of the Pseudo-Tertullian, *Adversus omnes hæreses*, which in turn is probably a Latin epitome of Hippolytus' *Syntagma;* see Robert M. Grant, *Second-Century Christianity, a Collection of Fragments* (London, S.P.C.K., 1946), p. 124 (trans. on p. 136). The second item is probably from Theodoret's *Hæreticorum fabularum compendium;* see *Dictionary of Christian Biography,* ed. William Smith and Henry Wace (4 vols. London, 1877–87), *4,* 917. The proximate source from which JE obtained this material has not been identified.

should spend abundance of time and pains, and be very hot at proving, that a man can will what he doth will; that is, that it is possible for that to be, that is. But if they mean that there is a perfect contingency in the will of man, that is, that it happens perfectly by chance that a man willed such a thing and not another; it's an impossibility and contradiction, that a thing should be without any cause or reason, and when there was every way as much cause why it should not have been. Wherefore, seeing things do unavoidably go fatally or necessarily, what injustice is it in the Supreme Being, seeing it is a contradiction that it should be otherwise?

60.[4] [HADES is said to be the separate souls of saints descending into hell as well][5] as the wicked, where they all are reserved in hidden [caverns under the][6] earth, not being yet judged till the day of judgment. [This] seems unreasonable, because it is altogether without foundation from Scripture, and is just like many other strange imaginations and dreams of the ancient writers.

Hades signifies the state of the dead, and not their place; 'tis a metaphorical expression and is used in the Revelation as a visionary representation. It is very common to represent states or conditions by places. Thus a state of affliction is called the wilderness, a pit, the depth of the sea, etc. So a state of light and joy is to be in [the] tabernacles of God; to be in a state of salvation is to be in Mount Zion. But if a state is represented by vision, it is commonly represented by places; 'tis the most natural visible symbol of it.[7] There are innumerable such instances in this book of the Revelation,[8] 'tis everywhere full of them. So when it was signified to John how persons came out of a state of death to a state of life, it was represented by their coming out of a place, hades, where all the dead were kept [Rev. 20:13]; and the meaning of

4. There are no Nos. 52–59, JE having accidentally omitted these numerals when numbering the entries.

5. The first two lines of this entry are now badly faded and broken at the top of the MS page. Except for a few letters, the text to this point is dependent on the Dwight copy. See below, n. 8.

6. These words also survive only in the Dwight copy.

7. JE originally wrote, "it is always represented by places, for there can be no other visible symbol of it." His revision was probably made in the early 1730s.

8. JE's "this book" and the fact that the rest of the entry contains commentary on Rev. 20:13 and 14 not only suggest that he was now writing chapter expositions for his new "Apocalypse" MS but raise the possibility that he began No. 60 with some reference to that chapter. It is very likely that not all the text lost from the first lines is preserved in the Dwight copy.

the vision is, that persons came out of a state of death. When persons entered upon that state, so dark and horrible to nature, it could not be better symbolized in a vision than by their descending into the dark and shady caverns of the earth; and when they came out of that dreadful state, [than] by their ascending again into the light and open air. So that hades signifies a state of death, a state of separation.

It seems to me ridiculous, that thereby is signified some one place in the creation where souls both good and bad are kept. But, they say, there is a division, to divide that part of hades where the happy souls are from that part where the miserable are kept. They say, there is a great gulf fixed. Well then, if there is a great distance between them, why must this hades needs be a particular place? If they are at a thousand miles' distance, and yet are called one hades, why may they not be one hades if they are twenty thousand miles distant? Or what if they are distant the semidiameter of the universe, why may they not both be one hades? What need they be both near together, so that they might be called by one name? Supposing one separate soul were at one end of the creation, and another at another, and some beyond the creation, and some in the middle; I can't see why they may not be all in hades, as well as if they were all together down in some great cavern of the earth, as long as their state is the same, to wit, a state of separation. What matter what place they are in? Or suppose that all the wicked are all in the bowels of the earth, and the happy in the highest heavens, why is it not as good as if there were but twenty miles' distance between them? Why may not their places be as far distant as their states are differing? It looks all just like a dream; it will do very well in a vision, but when it is taken for reality, it is childish.

When John says that after the day of judgment death and hades were cast into the lake of fire [Rev. 20:14], does he mean that all that place where separate souls used to keep, paradise and all, was taken up and thrown into the lake of fire? Why are they angry with paradise, that has done good service by affording many delights to the godly? And besides, it seems to me a very difficult thing, how they could throw a great cavern of the earth into the fire, along with death! But it is plain that the vision intends, that the state of separation was entirely and forever abolished. Hades here is the same hades that followed the pale horse in Rev. 6:8, where hades was represented as some moving creature.

But they say, that the souls of saints can't be in heaven before the resurrection, because that [is] the highest and most excellent place, which is reserved till afterwards. But what matter where their place? 'tis the highest state that is reserved till after the resurrection. But this opinion is unreasonable, for it keeps the souls of saints separate from Christ Jesus, their Head and Redeemer (they are kept also from the place of angels, and from the sight of God), and is against the whole strain of the Scripture. I suppose nobody doubts, but that Enoch and Elias are gone to some other place besides those dark caverns of the earth, and I can't conceive why the souls of saints should not go there too: why should we think that they alone[9] are in heaven? It is certain that Christ is ascended into the highest heavens, and shines gloriously as a Mediator, and is continually praised as such: and are there none of those that have been redeemed by him, to be visible instances of the efficacy of his mediation, and glory of his love? When we have an account of the angels praising the Lamb, we have also an account of the saints joining with them, Rev. 5:9–10; and so all over this book it is so represented, that the saints are with the Lamb. The Apostle says, if he should depart this life he should be with Christ (see notes on Phil. 1:23);[1] and why not other Christians? But the Apostle speaks of Christians in general, II Cor. 5:6, 8, "Therefore we are always confident, knowing that, whilst we are at home in the body, we are absent from the Lord . . . We are confident, I say, and willing rather to be absent from the body, and be present with the Lord."

They say, the saints will not be in heaven till after the resurrection, because that is their reward, and they are not to receive their reward till they are judged. But it is said in the Revelation that those who are dead in the Lord, they rest from their labors, and their works follow them. And they themselves say, that the departed souls of the godly shall have part of their reward, and the wicked part of their punishment, [that] the state of one is made happy, and of the other, miserable. But this cannot be without a judgment at death, for a determination of their state according to their works is a judgment: God gives sentence, by which their state is fixed forevermore. The Apostle, accordingly, after he had said in the 8th verse of this [chapter] of Corinthians [II Cor. 5], that to be absent from the body was to be present with the Lord, explains the matter more fully in the 9th and 10th verses: "Wherefore we labor, that, whether present or absent, we may

9. I.e. Enoch and Elias.
1. This note combines Phil. 1:23 with John 14:2–3 and concludes that "with Christ" means "in heaven." This and the other references to Scripture notes in No. 60 are later additions and all are in the "Blank Bible".

be accepted of him. For we must all appear before the judgment seat of Christ, that everyone may receive the things done in the body." This undoubtedly speaks of separate souls, because it is brought as explicatory of the 8th verse and because it says, everyone must "receive the things done in the body," which intimates that they are now out of the body. And it is expressly asserted in the four first verses of the chapter, that the house that departed saints are clothed with is "eternal in the heavens."

The innumerable company of angels, God the Judge of all, and the spirits of just men made perfect, and Jesus the Mediator of the new covenant, are represented as all together in Mount Zion, the city of the living God, the heavenly Jerusalem, Heb. 12:22–24. The Apostle meant heaven by Mount Zion, as is evident by the 25th verse (see notes).[2] There is no doubt but that this Mount Zion, where are the spirits of just men made perfect, is the same with the "Jerusalem which is above" spoken of, Gal. 4:26 (see note on Heb. 12:23 and on Gal. 4:25–26).[3] Shall we say that Stephen did not go to that place after death that he saw before death? And when he said, "Lord Jesus, receive my spirit," was not his spirit received to the man Christ Jesus, to that same appearance which he saw in heaven? Or that Saint Paul did not esteem it better to die than to live, that he might be where he had already seen ineffable things?

The church in Scripture is divided into the church in heaven and the church on earth, and we read not of a third. Eph. 1:10, "That in the dispensation of the fullness of times he might gather together in one all things in Christ, both which are in heaven, and which are on earth." Col. 1:20, "To reconcile all things to himself; by him, I say, whether they be things in earth or things in heaven." Eph. 3:15, "Of whom the whole family in heaven and earth is named." It would be endless to quote scriptures; they do everywhere intimate that departed saints are where God is, so that they see him. But where is he, but in heaven? we read of no other place where he unveils his glory, and where Christ is,

2. Heb. 12:25 contrasts "him that spake on earth" with "him that speaketh from heaven." The former spoke from Mt. Sinai (vv. 18–21), to which is opposed Mt. Zion, the heavenly Jerusalem (v. 22); therefore, JE concludes, by Mt. Zion heaven must be meant.

3. In the earlier of two notes on Heb. 12:23, JE gives several reasons for believing that "the spirits of just men made perfect" refers to "the saints in their separate state," especially the Old Testament saints, who can be said to have been "made perfect" since the ascension of Christ. The note on Gal. 4:25–26 contrasts "the literal Jerusalem, or the people of the Jews, and the spiritual Jerusalem, or the true church of God." The church is called "Jerusalem which is above" because "heaven is the proper city or dwelling-place of the church."

and where the angels are. That the apostles and prophets are in heaven appears by Rev. 18:20. See Nos. 67 and 556; see I Pet. 1:4.

Neither did the primitive Christians generally think otherwise, as appears by their hope in their martyrdom. They all expected, it is very plain, to be with Christ and to see him; as those who were frozen to death comforted each other with this, that they should be warmed presently in the arms of Christ.

61. SCRIPTURES. To say that the Scriptures contain all things that are necessary in matters of faith, and not of worship [or][4] practice, is to talk very unintelligibly. For if such a practice is necessary to salvation, the belief that that thing is the will of God is necessary to salvation. For practising of it without this faith is to no purpose in the world, for whatever is not of faith is sin.

62. DECREE. The dispute,[5] whether the decree of the means be part of the decree of election, [is][6] a very senseless one. For says the one,[7] that election is absolute, that such a person shall have eternal life, without any consideration by what means. I answer, that without doubt it is so, that eternal life is all that is included in the decree of election; but effectual calling, sanctification, faith, etc., they are the very eternal life that they[8] are decreed to. This and that in heaven be not different, but only in degree.

63. ELECTION. If God ever determined in the general, that some of mankind should certainly be saved, and did not leave it altogether undetermined, whether ever so much as one soul of all mankind should believe in Christ, it must be that he determined that some particular persons should certainly believe in him. For it is certain, that if he has left it undetermined concerning this and that and the other person, whether ever he should believe or not, and so of every particular person in the world; then there is no necessity at all, that this or that or any particular person in the world should ever be saved by Christ,

---

4. Or "[and]"; a short word is broken from the margin.
5. This entry originally began, "SUBLAPSARIANS. The controversy between the antelapsarians and sublapsarians, and the dispute." Subsequently, JE deleted everything before "the dispute" and supplied the new title. This must have happened before the entry was indexed, for it appears in the Table only under "Decrees" and "Predestination."
6. Broken off at margin.
7. JE originally wrote "For, say the antelapsarians."
8. The antecedent of "they" is "such a person."

for matter of any determination of God's. So that, though God sent his Son into the world, yet the matter was left altogether undetermined by God, whether ever any person should be saved by him; and there was all this ado about Christ's birth, death, resurrection, ascension and sitting at God's right hand, when it was not as yet determined whether he should ever redeem one soul, or have any mediatorial kingdom at all.

It is very nonsense to call such a conditional election as they talk of, by the name of election, seeing there is a necessary connection between faith in Jesus Christ and eternal life. Those that believe in Christ must be saved, according to God's inviolable constitution of things. What nonsense is it therefore, to talk of choosing such to life from all eternity, out of the rest of mankind? A predestination of such to life is altogether useless and needless. By faith in one that has satisfied for sin, the soul necessarily becomes free from sin; by faith in one that has bought eternal life for them, they have of unavoidable consequence a right to eternal life. Now what sense is it to say, that God from all eternity, of his free grace, picked and chose out those that he foresaw would have no guilt of sin, that they should not be punished for their guilt, as others were? when it is a contradiction to suppose that they can be punished for their guilt when they have none. For who can lay anything to their charge, when it is Christ that has died? And what do they mean by an election of men to that which it is in its own nature impossible that it should not be, whether they are elected to it or no, and so to say, that God chose them that had a right to eternal life, that they should have eternal life? What sense is it to say, that a creditor chooses out those out of his debtors to be free from debt that owe him nothing?

But if they say that election is only God's determination in the general, that all that believe shall be saved, in what sense can this be called election? They are not persons that are here chose; but mankind is divided into two sorts, the one believing and the other unbelieving, and God chooses the believing sort: 'tis not an election of persons, but of a qualification. God does, from all eternity, choose to bestow eternal life upon those that have a right to it, rather than upon those who have a right to damnation—is this all the election we have an account of in God's Word?

Such a thing as election may very well be allowed; for that there is such a thing as arbitrary sovereign love is certain, i.e. love not for any excellency, but merely God's good pleasure. For whether it is proper to say that God from all eternity loved the elect or no, it *is* proper to say that God loved men after the fall, while sinners and enemies: for God so loved the world, that he gave his only begotten Son to die. This was not for any goodness or excellency, but merely God's good pleasure; for he would not love the fallen angels.

64. Spirit. Thus the matter is, as to the Holy Spirit's gracious operations on the mind. We have shown in philosophy, that all natural operations are done immediately by God, only in harmony and proportion.[9] But there is this difference: these being the highest kind of operations of all, are done in the most general proportion, not tied to any particular proportion, to this or that created being; but the proportion is with the whole series of acts and designs from eternity to eternity, as miracles are, as the creation of the world, the birth and resurrection of Christ are. These operations are most arbitrary and bound to no knowable law, any more than any actions of the Deity whatever. Not but that there is commonly, in these spiritual operations, a respect to outward means; but they are not at all tied to them. That it is thus may be argued, because harmony argues it: lower operations are done by a more particular proportion, higher according to higher, and more general for the general . . .[1]

65. Ministers. See Nos. 40, mm, qq. There is no doubt (it is as natural and as easy as can be), those who are Christ's [servants] to baptize[2] and admit into the visible church, must baptize and admit into the church those that they think Christ would have them, and so, accordingly, excommunicate and cast out those who they think their Master would have them.

9. JE's primary reference is doubtless to "Atoms," prop. 2, corols. 8–16 (*Works, 6,* 214–16), though he may also be thinking of such essays in the Long Series as nos. 23a, 27, 44, and 47 (ibid., 234–42).

1. The concluding words of this entry (probably between five and ten) were already broken from the bottom of the MS page when Dwight's copy was made.

2. The words "and as easy . . . to baptize" are preserved only in Dwight's copy; the entry begins at the top of a page and much of the first line is now missing. The copy reads (insertions and deletions by Dwight): "t̶h̶o̶s̶e̶ ⟨that those⟩ who⟨m⟩ a̶r̶e̶ Christ's ⟨has appointed to baptize⟩." The scribe probably read "those who are Christ's" correctly, while Dwight's alterations were partially conjectural. The correctness of "to baptize" is clear from the context, but "has appointed" alters the scribe's text and requires more space than was probably available on JE's line. Since "Christ's" seems to demand a noun, the likelihood of a correlate to "Master" suggests "servants."

66. RIGHTEOUSNESS. See No. zz. Neither are we to understand by God's righteousness, in the New Testament, only a state of justification of God's mere grace, and in which man himself has nothing to do; but also that inherent holiness that is in the heart of the Christian, as being owing not at all unto man, to his own mere motion and natural power, but as being entirely communicated from God through Jesus Christ. The law requires that [we] obey the precepts of it, and supposes that we are to do it of our own natural power; but this way can never obtain righteousness. But the holiness of Christians is merely and entirely a reflection of God's light, or communications of God's righteousness, and not one jot of it is owing to ourselves. 'Tis wholly a creature of God's, a new creature; 'tis Christ within us. 'Tis not our holiness or our righteousness any otherwise than as a gift; not as our offspring or progeny, nor as our natural right, nor because we make any additions to it, or because it is of our preservation. Every motion and action of grace is Christ living in us, and nothing else.

67. HADES. See No. 60. It seems to me very evident that by paradise, in the 12th [chapter] of II Corinthians, is meant the third heaven. And I see no reason to believe that this paradise is not the same that Christ spake of upon his cross, when he promised the thief that that day he should be with him in paradise. See Rev. 2:7.

68. KINGDOM OF CHRIST.[3] [*Ques.*] How does it follow, that if men can give laws to Christ's subjects, that they are therefore so far kings in his kingdom, and Christ can't be sole King in his own kingdom? The governors commissioned by an earthly king may have power to make laws in their respective governments given them by their masters, provided they are not contrary to the king's laws and government, and yet not be distinct kings.

Ans. Yet if they have power to make what laws they please in their

---

3. This title was never adopted by JE as the name of a category or topic in the Table; the entry is indexed under "Civil Authority" and "Discipline of the church."

No. 68 is clearly based on Benjamin Hoadly's *Nature of the Kingdom, or Church, of Christ* (London, 1717), a sermon on John 18:36. Here, as in his *Preservative against the Principles and Practices of the Nonjurors* (London, 1716), Hoadly was concerned to vindicate the civil government and the rights of conscience against the claim of the Nonjurors to have the only legitimate and saving ministry. But the same weapon could be turned against the Church of England's laws by Dissenters and against all doctrinal norms by heretics; hence the extent, violence, and complexity of the ensuing Bangorian controversy (Hoadly was now Bishop of Bangor).

distinct governments, and themselves are judges whether they are not contrary to the king's laws and government, then they are distinct kings, and their governments are quite cut off from being parts of the king's dominions. For at that rate, they may make just what laws they please without any manner of limitation, however contrary they are to the king's government, if they do but say they are not contrary, and they have as unlimited a power as any distinct kings can have.

69. NATIONAL CHURCH.[4] See Nos. 9, qq, 65. This is evident by naked and natural reason, that those that live together are, if they have not overbalancing reasons on the other side, [to] worship God together. By the word "together" I don't mean as to place; for those that live within two rods may be further distant from me than he that lives five hundred. But I mean, those who are joined together in the same interest, have dependence one on another, and whose welfare more especially depends on a communication with each other, and whom the providence of God has[5] cast into such circumstances as that they subsist by communication; whatever those circumstances are, whether because they are under the same government, or live in the same place, or speak the same language, or whatever—thus families, societies, provinces, governments, kingdoms, nations, Christendom, world—and their obligation to worship together is in proportion to their nearness together. 'Tis evidently the duty of such to worship together, because they are united in one common interest, which they depend upon the object of their worship for, and because it is abundantly most convenient so to do.

70. CONSCIENCE. See No. 8. To say that a man ought not to be guided wholly and entirely by his own private judgment in what he ought to believe, is not only false, not only against the gospel and the plainest reason, and most absurd, but the thing itself—the supposition that a man is not entirely guided by his own private judgment in what he believes, whether it ought to be or no—is a direct, flat and immediate contradiction; and if it were never so much required, is an utter impossibility, and is the same thing as to say, that a man believes and yet believes not at the same time. For if he, in his own private judgment,

---

4. Solomon Stoddard strongly advocated a "national church," by which he meant that the Puritan congregations should adopt a system of synods after the Presbyterian manner; see, for example, his *Doctrine of Instituted Churches* (London, 1700), pp. 25–34.

5. MS: "have."

sees no apparent reason, nor don't think that he sees any reason, for the truth of such a thing, it is a contradiction to say that he believes; because not thinking in his own private judgment that he sees any reason for the truth [of a thing], is the same as not to believe it in his own private judgment.

The Papists, who really think that their church cannot teach anything but what is true, and so believe everything that their clergy teach, are guided entirely by their own private judgment, however dark and blind their judgment is; 'tis because they think, in their own private judgment, that they see some reason why whatever their clergy teaches should be true, to believe that their clergy are infallible. Let the reason of their believing so be their education or whatever, 'tis because then their education, or the opinion of their fathers, appears to their dark minds as a reason. Or if their judgment is swayed by their interest, they depend nevertheless upon their private judgment: 'tis because their interest has this influence on them, as to make them think in their own private judgment that they see reason for a thing, when in reality there is none. And if a man of a weak capacity, and sensible of it, had never so great a mind to depend entirely upon the judgment of his superiors, and truly to believe as they believed; he could not possibly do [so], except his own private judgment told him in the first place, that there was reason why what those his superiors believed should be true. Yea it is an absolute contradiction to suppose, that he should believe what *God* declared to him, for any other reason [than this], viz. that his own private judgment told him that God was omniscient, and could not lie, etc.

71. FREE WILL.[6] 'Tis very true, that God requires nothing of us as [a] condition of eternal life but what is in our own power; and yet 'tis very true at the same time, that 'tis an utter impossibility that ever man should do what is necessary in order to salvation, nor do the least towards it, without the almighty operation of the Holy Spirit of God, yea, except everything be entirely wrought by the Spirit of God. True and saving faith in Christ is not a thing out of the power of man, but infinitely easy. 'Tis entirely in a man's power to submit to Jesus Christ as a Savior, if he will; but the thing is, it never will be that he should will

6. This entry expands the argument of No. o with more emphasis on the concept of power. Locke's chapter on power (*Human Understanding*, Bk. II, ch. 21 [ed. Nidditch, pp. 233–87]) may have suggested this line of thought to JE, but No. 71 is quite independent of Locke in its use of terms and illustrations.

it, except God works it in him. To will it is to do it; [it] depends on a man's will and not on his power; and however easy the thing be, and however much in a man's power, 'tis an impossibility that he should ever do it except he wills it, because submission to Christ is a willing.

There are many things that are entirely in our power, of which things yet it may be said that 'tis an impossibility they should be, because of our dispositions. Perhaps some may say, that 'tis a contradiction to say that that is in our power, which yet 'tis an impossibility it should be. 'Tis according as what they mean by "being in our power." I mean thus, that that is in our power which we can do when we please; and I think those mean very improperly who mean otherwise. Now it is no contradiction to say, that we can do such a thing when we please, and yet that 'tis an impossibility that it should be when we don't please. And although it may be the easiest thing in the world, yet it is not contradictory to say, that it is impossible that we should please to do it except God works it in us. According as I have explained it, it is altogether in a man's power, when he has a cup of poison offered to him, whether he will drink it or no; and yet by reason of the man's internal disposition, the ideas and notions of things that he then has, it may be an impossibility that he should will to drink it. If a man who is a servant, exceeding wicked, debauched and licentious, who has it offered to him whether he will choose such a man, who is a man of most exemplary holiness and strict piety, for his master, and submit to his government; it is perfectly (in my sense) in the servant's power, whether he will take him for his master and governor or no: and yet it may be an impossible thing that it should be, as long as the servant has such and such inclination, desires, judgment and ideas.

The world has got into an exceeding wrong and confused way of talking about will and power, not knowing what they mean. Thus they say, man can will such a thing, and man can't will it; which is dreadful confusion. When we say a man can't will such a thing, the notion that is raised in our mind by such an expression is, that the man might heartily and truly desire to will it, but could not will it; that is, he truly willed to will it, but could not; that is, he truly willed it, but could not will it! I am sure that when we say a man can or cannot do such a thing, we don't mean that he wills or does not will it. We say (and truly, often) he can do such a thing, when yet he wills it not; and yet 'tis an impossibility that he should do [it] when he wills it not. But, you'll say, he could will it if he would. 'Tis most certainly true; if he *does* will it, he *can* will [it]. Yea, and you'll say, and if he does *not* will it, he can will [it]. I say, 'tis true things may so happen, circumstances or ideas may so fall, as to cause him to will it; but it is no act of his own power that he wills it (though it be necessary there should be a capacity), because will is the first spring of the voluntary exertions of active power in man, and the cause of it; and therefore 'tis impossible that active power should cause the will, its own spring, except the effect causes its own cause. However, we are compelled unavoidably thus to express it, that of ourselves we can do nothing, that we have [no] power,[7] etc. However, this manner of expression, as well as the contrary, carries often a wrong idea in the mind of such [realities].[8]

So that all that men do in real religion is entirely their own act, and yet every tittle is wrought by the Spirit of God. Neither do I contradict myself. By saying that all that men do in religion is entirely their own act, I mean that everything they do, they themselves do; which I suppose none will contradict: 'tis the exertion of their own powers.

72. FATHERS. Although it be said that weight ought to be laid on the testimony of the fathers, not indeed relying on their opinion as if they were inspired, but as testimony of matter of fact, of what was the received opinion of the church in their day; of which if they can be certain, they have very good reason to believe the truth of what was received, it being so near to the apostolic age that the doctrines which the apostles taught could not be lost; but yet it seems to me that rather too much weight is laid upon the testimony of the fathers on this account, by the Christian world in general. For it was not so impossible but that they might lose their traditions, and be very uncertain of them, even in a very little time.

Christians in the apostles' days were in such circumstances, that they were under no advantage to preserve the traditions of their teachers. There were not vast bodies and whole nations of them, cohabiting and united together; but there was here and there a Christian (most of the lower rank of men) and assembly of Christians, scattered up and down amongst the world of men. The assemblies of Christians here and there were not under such circumstances, as to occasion such a communication one with another as there [now is]. And whereas the tradi-

7. Or "that we have power"; but JE has been arguing that "it is no act of his own power that he wills it," and "as well as the contrary" in the next sentence implies that the clauses in the preceding sequence are synonymous.

8. Or "of such [as use them]"; JE squeezed this sentence in after the next paragraph had been written and ran out of space after "such."

tions of words and actions that are of importance to whole nations are preserved by whole nations, their[9] traditions were delivered down only by a particular assembly or city, for the most part, and they very much without other written records than the holy Scriptures. The children had no other tradition but what their fathers told them the apostles taught in that assembly or city; and the manner of the apostles' expression was exceeding liable, either to be wrong taken up at first, or to be forgotten and varied, even by the persons who heard them and were the first traditors. And except they did not vary the expressions, those who received it at second hand might be liable to mistake them, and take the doctrine in another sense from that in which it was delivered; and they again, either through a mistake of meaning or through defect of the memory, might vary the expression still more; yea so that if a man should come into one of those assemblies of Christians forty years after the apostles had been there, it would be but a weak foundation, to depend solely upon what the people said an apostle taught there forty years ago.

A much weaker foundation are the expressions found in writings seventeen hundred years after, that are but probably the writings, and possibly the uncorrupted writings, of a Christian that writ, suppose [A.D.] 200, or an hundred years after the apostles, not asserting that they are the doctrines that it is remembered the apostles taught, but only that it was their belief, or the belief of Christians where he dwelt at that time; therefore to depend upon it, that the apostles had taught that doctrine.

I suppose it will not be thought by any, that above half of the Christians in the apostles' times ever heard the apostles speak; and not a third of them that did hear any of them speak, ever heard them speak one quarter of the doctrine they taught. There were many even in the apostles' time (if I understand the matter right), that pretended and intended to build their belief upon what the apostles and evangelists taught, that yet believed very erroneous doctrines. I believe that the Christians, soon after the apostles' times, depended as entirely upon the holy Scripture, with relation to the doctrines they ought to believe, as we at this distance. I think that God never intended that we should ever have any other sure rule of faith but the holy Scriptures, and has left everything else uncertain, that we might prize and improve them.

9. MS: "but their," i.e. the Christians'.

73. INFUSED [HABITS].[1] To say that a man who has no true virtue and no true grace can acquire it by frequent exercises of [it], is as much a contradiction as to say a man acts grace when he has no grace, or that he has it [when][2] he has it not. For tell me [how] a man that has no true grace within him shall begin to exercise it: before he begins to exercise it, he must have some of it. How shall [he] act virtuously the first time? how came he by that virtue which he then acted? Certainly not [by] exercise of virtue, for it supposes that he never acted virtuously before, and therefore could not get it by acting of it before.

'Tis said that a sinful [man][3] begins to use himself to act the matter of virtue, and after a while it became habitual to him. I answer, that it may become habitual to him [if][4] he did;[5] but it can't become habitual to him to act as he never did before, by the means of his using of himself to it. When [was the][6] time when the man first began to act from a truly virtuous principle? I suppose that it was [the time] that the man first acted true virtue. But [what made][7] him so to act true virtue, or from a truly virtuous principle, then? Was it because he had used himself to it, when it is . . . [8]

[Perhaps you will say, the][9] man got the habit of acting from a virtuous principle from doing[1] . . . from a virtuous principle; that is, that a man by degrees got the habit of acting virtue by acting something that was [a good][2] practice. Supposing there is a person [of] most profligate and vicious life, who afterwards leaves his old courses and reforms, and [is][3] a very good [man]: I ask, how this man became better than he was before, in his first beginning to reform; how came he by that virtue from which he acted when he first began to reform? If you say he did not act virtue when he first began to reform, did it not from a virtuous principle; then I ask, how came he by his virtue by which he first did act from a virtuous principle? If you say that even the

---

1. The word is broken off at the margin. There are several lacunae in the text of this entry, and no early copy is available.
2. Broken off at margin.
3. Ibid.
4. Ibid.
5. I.e. act the matter of virtue.
6. Broken off at margin.
7. Ibid.
8. Three or four words at the bottom of the MS page are broken off, as well as about a third of the line at the top of the next page.
9. Conjecture for part of the missing words in the first MS line.
1. The next four or five words are illegible at broken margins.
2. Conjecture for text broken from the left margin.
3. Broken from the left margin.

worst have some sparks of virtue remaining in them, and by acting and exercising of them he strengthens them; if we allow it to be so, the case is the same. The man begins to reform today who did [not] begin yesterday. How comes he by more virtue at that time that he first begins to reform, than at that time when he did not begin to reform? Is it because he had strengthened his virtue before? But this is a contradiction, when we suppose that he now begins to exercise his virtue, and that it had been weakening, and vice increasing, till that time.

74. DECREE. Contingency, as it is held by some, is at the same time contradicted by themselves, if they hold foreknowledge. This is all that follows from an absolute, unconditional, irreversible decree, that it is impossible but that the things decreed should be. The same exactly follows from foreknowledge, that it is absolutely impossible but that the thing certainly foreknown should precisely come to pass.

75. DECREE. If it will universally hold, that no [one] can have absolutely perfect and complete happiness at the same time that anything is otherwise than as he desires at that time they should be; or thus, if it be true that he has not absolute, perfect, infinite, and all possible happiness now, who has not now all that he wills to have now: then God, if anything is now otherwise than he wills to have them now, is not now absolutely, perfectly and infinitely happy. If God is infinitely happy etc. now, then everything is now as God would have them to be now; if everything, then those things that are contrary to his commands. If so, it is not ridiculous to say, that things that are contrary to God's command are yet in one sense agreeable to his will.

Again, let it be considered whether it be not certainly true, that everyone that can with infinite ease have a thing done, and yet will not have it done, wills it not; that is, whether or no he that wills not to have a thing done, properly wills *not*[4] to have a thing done. For example, let the thing be this, that Judas should be faithful to his Lord: whether it be not true, that if God could with infinite ease have it done (if he would), but would not have it done (as he could if he would); whether it be not proper to say, that God would not have it be, that Judas should be faithful to his Lord.

76. CEREMONIES. Even circumstances that are in the general necessary may be made parts of divine worship. Then circumstances in the

4. Though he did not adequately deal with it, JE seems here to have been more aware of the ambiguity of his language than he had been in No. 0. See notes to that entry.

general necessary are made parts of divine worship, in my sense, when they are used as essentials of worship; i.e. when they are particularly as absolutely enjoined, regarded, and set as much by in worship, and the neglect of it in worship as much discountenanced, censured and punished, as the neglect of what is essential in or a constituent part of worship. As, if the particular place where the minister should stand, and the particular key and height of his voice, which are things in the general necessary—not with a moral, but a metaphysical necessity: that is, 'tis absolutely impossible but that the minister should be in some place or other when he is performing his ministry; so it is absolutely impossible, when he is speaking, but that he should speak in some key or other—yet I say, if the particular place and key should be as indispensably enjoined, and as much regarded in worship, and the neglect as much censured and punished as a neglect in worship, as what is an essential part of divine worship; then standing in such a particular place and speaking in a voice of such a pitch is made a part of divine worship, and there is properly an addition of parts of divine worship besides those parts He has instituted. And 'tis the same thing,[5] whether they are in themselves circumstances or distinct actions, if they are added as new parts of worship. I think that that is not used as an indifferent circumstance, that is, indifferent with relation to the rewards or privileges of a Christian, which is made necessary in order to the enjoying the rewards or privileges of a Christian.

It may be very true, that nothing is to be done in the worship of God more or less but what God has instituted. Notwithstanding, it is absolutely impossible but that the acts of worship will be attended with some particular circumstances which are not instituted, because these circumstances are not pertaining to the worship, they are not *in* the worship. Therefore 'tis not proper to say they are something in the worship which God has not instituted; because they are not anything at all in the worship of God. The man that prays in such a particular place may do it without doing anything more in God's worship than he has expressly commanded, although his praying in such a particular place is not expressly commanded of God; because his being in such a place is nothing in the worship or belonging to it.

77. CONVERSION. What is held by some,[6] that none can be in a state of salvation before they have particularly acted a reception of the Lord

---

5. MS: "And that tis the same thing."
6. See above, No. 27b, p. 214, n. 7.

Jesus Christ for a Savior, and that there cannot be sanctification one moment before the exercise of faith, as they have described it, cannot be true, as they explain this reception of Christ. There must be the principle before there can be the action, in all cases; there must be an alteration made in the heart of the sinner before there can be action consequent upon this alteration; yea, there must be a principle of holiness before holiness is in exercise. Yea, this alteration must not only be before this act of faith in nature (as the cause before the effect) but also in time, if this embracing of Christ as a Savior be a successive action, that is, an action where one thought and act of the mind in any wise follows another, as it certainly is.

For first, there must be an idea of Jesus Christ in the mind, that is an agreeable and truly lovely idea to him;[7] but this cannot be before the soul is sanctified. There must also be the acts of true belief, of his willingness to receive, etc.; neither can this be before sanctification. There must also be a hatred of sin before Christ can be received as a Savior from sin; neither can this be without sanctification. And after this, there must be the act of embracing; neither is there properly an act of faith, as they explain [it], before this is done. Now these thoughts must succeed one another, whether in this order or not, although it be as quick as one thought can follow another; but sanctification must be in the soul before one of them is in the mind.

78. REGENERATION.[8] When we say that all men by nature are altogether depraved and corrupted, and without the least grain of true holiness, children of wrath, nothing else can truly be intended but that every man is so of himself, as he is of nature. Nothing else is belonging to us but sin and misery, as we are in Adam; nothing but misery belongs to us according to the first covenant, that we are all under in

---

7. I.e. the sinner.

8. This entry is preceded by another, also bearing the numeral 78, entitled "Excellency." It was obviously left unfinished and was deleted with a large X mark (for an exact transcription, see *Works, 6,* 332). The opening lines of "The Mind" no. 1 (ibid.) are practically identical with the abandoned entry:

78. EXCELLENCY. There has nothing been more without a definition than excellency, though it be what we are more concerned with than anything else; yea, we are concerned with nothing else. But what is this excellency? Wherein is one thing excellent and another evil, one beautiful and another deformed? Some have said that all excellency consists in harmony, symmetry and proportion, but they have not yet explained it. They have told us of a thing that is excellent, viz. proportion; but we would know why proportion is more excellent than disproportion, that is, why proportion is pleasing to the mind and disproportion unpleasing. Proportion is a thing that may be explained yet further: 'tis an equality or likeness of ratios.

our first state; and when we are born, nothing else is in us according to the first constitution of things.

Not but that saving grace may be infused, not only indefinitely near to the first moment of creation, but may as well be infused in the very moment that the man begins to [be]; and yet he may be said to be as much a child of wrath by nature, or wholly depraved by nature, as one that is regenerated twenty years after. 'Tis properly a conversion and regeneration, because although he never was in one sense otherwise, so that there is no alteration properly since the time of his birth, yet there is an alteration from his first state in Adam; and if he has grace infused, it is as much new grace and mere grace as [in] one that is converted when twenty years old. Both justification and sanctification are as much a deliverance and as merciful a change, and his righteousness is the righteousness of God, according to No. 66; 'tis what entirely is communicated from God anew, none of it appertaining to his nature according to his old nature, that is, according to the old state and constitution in which he was concerned. What he has given him now is according to a new and extraordinary way; 'tis being born again, although done at the same time of his first birth.

79. LAW. The natural reason why it is as Rom. 7:8 ff. [says], "But sin, taking occasion by the commandment, wrought in me all manner of concupiscence," etc. [The][9] reason why man has the more strong inclination to moral evil when forbidden, is because obedience is submission and subjection, and the commandment is obligation. But natural corruption is against submission and obligation, but loves the lowest kind of liberty as one of those apparent goods that it seeks; and when he disobeys, he looks upon it that he has broke the obligation. When he thinks of the perpetration of such a lust, and thinks how he is strictly upon pain of damnation forbidden, tied by such strict bonds from it, it makes him exceeding uneasy, the consideration is so against corrupt nature; which uneasiness takes away all liberty of thought, and makes the mind dwell upon nothing but the contrary and supposed good, the liberty, causes [him] to meditate upon the pleasantness of the act, and makes it appear much greater than otherwise it would do.

But now we are delivered from the law, that being dead wherein we were held, that we should serve in newness of spirit and not in the oldness of the letter. The motives to believers to perform the com-

---

9. The word is broken off at the margin; no early copy is extant.

mands of God, are [not][1] because salvation is [upon] the condition of doing them, and damnation what we are obliged to for disobedience; but the amiableness of God, to whom sin is contrary, the loveliness of virtue, and its natural tendency to happiness, which has no such tendency as the other.[2] Wherefore now in gospel times, 'tis requisite that all ceremonial commands should be abolished, which have no intrinsic direct loveliness, nor agreeableness to the lovely God, or tendency to happiness.

80. MORALITY. See No. 4. Only there is this difference: the morality of some duties is more immediate and direct than others, and even of those duties which are commonly called moral there is a difference; so there are gradual steps from the most immediate to the most indirect.

81. COMMUNION. 'Tis probable that the faculties of the man Christ Jesus, now in his glorified state, are so enlarged that he can, with a full view and clear apprehension of mind, at the same time think on all the saints in the world, and be in the exercise of an actual and even of a passionate love (such as we experience) to all of them in particular. 'Tis certain that human souls can have two ideas and more at the same moment in the mind; otherwise, how could the mind compare ideas and judge between them? 'Twill not suffice, that they are very speedily one after another in the mind, for comparing; for let the second idea be in the mind never so quick after the first, yet the mind cannot at that moment compare the second idea with the first, if the first be entirely gone out of the mind: for how can the mind compare an idea that is in the mind with another, at the same time that 'tis not in the mind? And I don't see why a mind can't be of such powers, as to be exercised about millions of millions of ideas, with as great intenseness and clearness of apprehension as we about two only.

No doubt but that the man Christ Jesus loves believers, not only the church in general without particularly viewing one person, but that he loves believers in particular. No doubt but that the man Christ Jesus loves the church in general, because it is made up of those particular persons that he loves. He loves the church because of the loveliness he

1. Ibid.
2. It is not clear what the precise antecedent of "which" is or to what "the other" refers. JE apparently means that the just mentioned set of motives to believers "has no such tendency" to incite natural corruption "as the other," i.e. the obligation to obey the commandments of the law.

sees in the church, but he sees loveliness nowhere else but in particular persons. Nor can we suppose that the man Jesus only loves the persons that are most eminent with a particuar love, but that every true saint may have the comfort of this consideration; and being that he loves them, no doubt but that he, with a proper desire, desires communion with them. And even the man Christ has communion with them. He being the same person with the divine Logos, has communion with them by the communion of this person, as much as if his human soul were present and suggested, and answered by suggestions, those sweet meditations; and there is the same delight in the man Christ as if he were bodily present with them, talking and conversing with them. And this seems to be one glorious end of the union of the human to the divine nature, to bring God near to us; that even our God, the infinite Being, might be made as one of us; that his terrible majesty might not make us afraid; that Jehovah, who is infinitely distant from us, might become familiar to us.

This capacity of the man Jesus is so large, by reason of the personal union with the divine nature. By this means he knew the thoughts of men while on earth, and knew things acted at a distance. No doubt but if the man Christ Jesus were, with his glorified powers, now on earth, and should meet here and there with holy men, he would be perfectly acquainted with them at first sight. What kind of powers are they, besides his own incommunicable attributes, that God cannot create a finite being with? And what kind of powers may we justly conclude his are, who is the firstborn of every creature and is personally united to the Deity! This seems to have been the universally received belief of the primitive church, which nobody ever thought of questioning.

82. DECREE. They say, to what purpose are praying and striving and attending on means, if all was irreversibly determined by God before? But to say that all was determined *before* these prayers and striving is a very wrong way of speaking, and begets those ideas in the mind which correspond with no realities with respect to God. His decrees of our everlasting state were not before our prayers and strivings, for these are as much present with God from all eternity as they are the moment they are present with us. They are present as part of his decree, or rather as the same, and they did as really exist in eternity with respect to God as much at one time as another. Therefore we can no more fairly argue that these will be in vain because God has foredetermined,

than we can that they would be in vain if they existed as soon as the decree; for so they do, inasmuch as they are a part of it.

83. THEOLOGY. The things of Christianity are so spiritual, so refined, so high and abstracted, and so much above the things we ordinarily converse with and our common affairs, to which we adapt our words; and language not supplying of us with words completely adapted to those high and abstracted ideas, we are forced to use words which do no otherwise exhibit what we would than analogically. Which words in their ordinary use do not in everything, but only in some part, exhibit what we intend they should when used in divinity; and therefore [does] religion [abound] with so many paradoxes and seeming contradictions. And it is for want of distinguishing thus in the meaning of words in divinity, from what is intended by them in their ordinary use, that arise most of the jangles about religion in the world. And to one who is not much [used] to elevated thought, many things, that are in themselves as easy and natural as the things we every day converse with, seem like impossibility and confusion. 'Tis so in every case: the more abstracted the science is, and by how much the higher nature those things are of which that science treats, by so much the more [will] our way of thinking and speaking of the things of that science be beside our way of thinking and speaking of ordinary things, and by so much the more will that science abound with paradoxes and seeming contradictions.

84. PERSEVERANCE. There is just the same reason for those commands of earnest care, and laborious endeavors for perseverance, and threatenings of defection that are in the Word of God, notwithstanding its being certain that all that have true grace shall persevere; as there is for earnest endeavors after godliness, and to make our calling and election sure, notwithstanding that all that are elected shall undoubtedly be saved. For as the case with reference to this is the same, decree or no decree, it's so, that everyone that believes shall be saved, and he that believes not shall be damned; they that will not live godly lives do find out for themselves that they are not elected; they that will live it have found out for themselves that they are. So it is here: he that to his utmost endeavors to persevere in ways of obedience finds out that his obedience and righteousness is true, and he that does not discovers that 'tis false. In this respect it is all one, whether he that is

once righteous must be so always or no; there is not at all the less diligence is necessary for that, yea, necessary in order to salvation.

85. DECREE. That we should say, that God has decreed every action of men, yea, every action that they do that is sinful, and every circumstance of those actions; [that] he determines that they shall be in every respect as they afterwards are; [that] he determines that there shall be such actions, and so obtains that they shall be so sinful as they are; and yet that God does not decree the actions that are sinful *as sinful*,[3] but decrees [them] as good,[4] is really consistent. We do not mean by decreeing an action as sinful, the same as decreeing an action so that it shall be sinful; but by decreeing an action as sinful, I mean decreeing [it] for the sake of the sinfulness of the action. God decrees that it[5] shall be sinful for the sake of the good that he causes to arise from the sinfulness thereof, whereas man decrees it for the sake of the evil that is in it.

86. KINGDOM OF CHRIST.[6] The meaning of that portion of Scripture in I Cor. 15:24, "Then cometh the end, when he shall have delivered up the kingdom to God, even the Father; when he shall have put down all rule, and all authority and power," will be perceived if we consider that Christ, God-man, Mediator, is now made head over all things to the church. That is, as Mediator he rules all events, every change, and every part of the universe so as to conduce to the good of his church, and to bring to pass the ends of his mediation, and to suit the purposes of his kingdom of grace. And thus the motion of every atom is under his mediatorial government, that he guides so as shall be best for his church; all so as to conduce to the great end of his mediation, the conquering of all his church's enemies, the bringing of his own to their fullness, and to the marriage of the Lamb.

But when the end shall be entirely accomplished and the church is brought to the consummation of glory, there will be no more need of this governing and ordering of all things to this end; there will be no more need of a mediatorial government of the universe, inasmuch [as]

3. MS: "as sin." The rest of the discussion assumes that the word here is "sinful," but JE wrote "as sin" twice. Perhaps it was in his draft as the result of an uncompleted revision.

4. The clause, "but decrees as good" occurs in the MS after "consistent." It was evidently an afterthought that JE failed to transfer to its proper place.

5. MS: "they."

6. This entry appears in the Table only under "End of the world, or consummation"; see note to No. 68.

all will be accomplished, all enemies will be put under his feet. Then Christ Jesus shall govern the universe no more as Mediator, but shall deliver up the kingdom to the Father, having accomplished fully all the ends of his government, and nothing else will remain to be done that is proper to a Mediator. Christ then shall present the church before his Father, having redeemed those whom his Father gave him to be redeemed by him. Not but that Christ will still remain as highly exalted as ever, yea in some respects as Mediator more glorious; being now complete, being married to her who is the fullness of him who filleth all in all, being yet sovereign King in their souls, reigning with them for ever and ever, being the eternal object of the joyful praises of all the hosts of heaven. See Nos. 609 and 434.

87. HAPPINESS.[7] 'Tis evident that the end of man's creation must needs be happiness, from the motive of God's creating the world, which could be nothing else but his goodness. If it be said that the end of man's creation might be that He might manifest his power, wisdom, holiness or justice, so I say too. But the question is, *why* God would make known his power, wisdom, etc. What could move him to will, that there should be some beings that might know his power and wisdom? It could be nothing else but his goodness.

This is the question: what moved God to exercise and make known

---

7. An earlier draft of this entry was written on the back of the sermon on Rom. 12:18. It consists of three paragraphs with large spaces between them. The third paragraph is really a question raised by the first two, a question to which JE does not address himself in No. 87 but which may have inspired No. 92. This is the longer of the only two extant drafts containing portions of early miscellanies (see also below, p. 275, n. 3). Except for one short illegible deletion, it is printed below as JE wrote it:

> Tis Evident that the End of mans Creation must needs be happiness from the motive of Gods Creating the World, which Can be nothing but his Goodness. if it be said that the end of it ["the end of it" in shorthand] might be to manifest the wisdom of [?] or the Power of God, the power of God must the wisdom and Power of God are exercised for some End God Power is shewn by his br Powerfull bringing about his End not in Exerting much Power for nothing. Wisdom is wisely Contriving to bringing about some End and Whatever is Done for no other End is not Wisdom, Wherefore if God made the world to meerly out of [?] from Goodness this Goodness Every Whit of it must Ultimately terminate in the Consciousness of the Creation
>
> 2 it appears from the Nature of happiness Which is the perception of Excellency and Excellency Consists in Correspondency & Proportion Now tis most Evident that man was Created for the Perception of to be the Consciousness of the world intelligent beings are Created to be the Consciousness of the Creation that is to Percieve what God is and what he Does &c—, to percieve the Excellency thereof
>
> In What sense the highest End of all things is the Glory of God

these attributes? We are not speaking of subordinate ends but of the ultimate end, of that motive into which all others may be resolved. 'Tis a very proper question, to ask what attribute moved God to exert his power, but 'tis not proper to ask what moved God to exert his goodness; for this is the notion of goodness, an *inclination* to show goodness. Therefore such a question would be no more proper than this, viz. what inclines God to exert his inclination to exert goodness—which is nonsense, for it is an asking and answering a question in the same words. God's power is shown no otherwise than by his powerfully bringing about some end. The very notion of wisdom is, wisely contriving for an end; and if there be no end proposed, whatever is done is not wisdom. Wherefore, if God created the world merely from goodness, every whit of this goodness must necessarily ultimately terminate in the consciousness of the creation; for the world is no other way capable of receiving goodness in any measure. But intelligent beings are the consciousness of the world; the end, therefore, of their creation must necessarily be that they may receive the goodness of God, that is, that they may be happy.

It appears also from the nature of happiness, which is the perception of excellency;[8] for intelligent beings are created to be the consciousness of the universe, they they may perceive what God is and does. This can be nothing else but to perceive the excellency of what he is and does. Yea, he is nothing but excellency; and all that he does, nothing but excellent.[9]

88. NAME [OF THE LORD]. The children of Israel used to speak of the name of the Lord, to us very unintelligibly; used to attribute those things to it that merely a name is not capable of, but only persons or distinct beings. Thus, they spake of it as what they trusted in, what delivered them and defended them (Ps. 20:1–4), what was as a strong tower, what dwelt and inhabited in the temple. They seemed to have meant by it, frequently, the sensible manifestation of his presence: God put his "name" to his house; that is, he there put the special manifestations of himself and tokens of his being, as the shechinah

8. At this point in the draft occur the words "and excellency consists in correspondency and proportion." JE probably deleted them because they introduce an idea not needed for his argument in No. 87. He also omitted the last sentence of the draft, which raises a question he later addressed in No. 92.

9. This paragraph comes close to "Excellency" (especially the fifth paragraph and the first addition) in content, though not precisely in terminology. See *Works, 6,* 335–37.

responses, the means of the immediate communications of himself. They were sensible that God was omnipresent, and hence that he did not in a proper sense inhabit a house or tabernacle; therefore, they called it his name. I Kgs. 8:27, "But will God indeed dwell on earth? behold the heaven and the heaven of heavens cannot contain thee; how much less this house that I have builded!" He[1] therefore prays (29th verse) that God's eyes might be open toward that house night and day, even toward the place of which He had said His name should be there. So that, though they spake of the name of God as if it had been God himself, they yet also spake of it as if it were another person, and made a distinction between "the Lord" and "the Name of the Lord." The Name of the Lord was he that most immediately appeared in the temple, and is the only Redeemer of God's Israel, and that manifested and declared God the Father all along from the beginning, who was the Shechinah, in whom they trusted, and for whose sake they desired that their requests might be answered.

89. JUSTICE. It appears plain enough, that an omnipotent and omniscient being can have no desire of being unjust for his own interest, because he can as easily bring about all his ends without it. But this appears beyond all objection if we consider the nature of excellency, which is being's consent to entity. And we have shown[2] that this must necessarily be consentaneous or agreeable to perceiving being, and the contrary, contradiction or dissent to entity, must necessarily be disagreeable to it; from hence it follows that all excellency, when perceived, will be agreeable to perceiving being, and all evil disagreeable. But God, being omniscient, must necessarily perfectly perceive all excellency, and fully know what is contrary to it; and therefore, that all excellency is perfectly agreeable to his will, and all evil perfectly disagreeable; and therefore, that he cannot will to do anything but what is excellent. But justice is an excellency.

90. NATIONAL CHURCH. We have shown, that they that live together, or near one another, ought to worship God together, [and] we have shown what is intended by living near (see No. 69). We have also shown, that for those that live [near] to them to reject them from their communion is a punishment, and such a punishment as they have power to

---

1. I.e. Solomon.
2. This is JE's first reference to "Excellency," the main entry under no. 1 of "The Mind" (*Works, 6,* 335–36).

inflict [see Nos. q, qq]. And I add this, that 'tis further evident, that they that are together ecclesiastically are bound to concern themselves in cases of scandalous sins because they have great occasion to do with them, lest they should countenance wickedness and the cause of the devil. And in case a particular congregation is scandalous, the congregations (or the power of [the] congregations) near ought to concern themselves in that matter, for the same full reason as a particular congregation ought to concern themselves with particular persons; inasmuch as different congregations have communion one with another, as well as the members of particular congregations.

But if they ought to concern themselves, they ought to take cognizance; which cannot be done without a convention of churches, that is, of the power of them. And as 'tis the duty of members of particular congregations to be silent, though the power of that church have carried otherwise than he would have done, except in extraordinary cases; so ought the power of particular congregations to be silent, when the power of the other congregations of the same church carry the matter. 'Tis also further evident, if this be granted, that the neighboring churches have power to find fault with a particular congregation, in matters of their rejecting [from] their communion particular persons, and may think it their duty to receive the same person which they rejected; yea, may see their mismanagement so gross as to be obliged to reject that congregation. Wherefore, a particular congregation, in such cases, [ought][3] to yield to the judgment of neighboring churches; which is the same thing as to say, they ought to allow of appeals. So [also], a congregation may appeal to a higher synod yet.[4]

91. BEING OF GOD. 'Tis acknowledged by all to be self-evident, that nothing can begin to be without a cause. Neither can we prove it, any other way than by explaining of it: when understood, 'tis a truth that irresistibly will have place in the assent. Thus, if we suppose a time wherein there was nothing at all, it is [self-evident that][5] a body could

3. Except for the first letter, the word is broken off at a lower corner of the page and was probably missing when Dwight's copy was made. The scribe first wrote "would," then replaced it with "are." The amount of space available and the occurrence of "ought" in the latter part of the sentence make it likely that JE wrote "ought" here also.
4. MS: "yet and ɫ [ɟ?]."
5. JE must have inadvertently omitted these words while copying from his draft; note the first words of the next paragraph. He seems to have been working from a relatively complete draft; this and his returning more than once to make slight revisions would suggest that he considered the entry a statement of more than usual importance.

not of its own accord begin to be: 'tis what the understanding abhors, that it should be, when there was no manner of reason why it was.

So 'tis equally self-evident, that a being cannot begin to be as to the manner of its being, without a cause. Thus, when a body has been perfectly at rest, that it should begin to move without any reason, either within itself or without: to say, because it so happened, will not satisfy the mind at all; the mind asks, what was the reason? So it is equally self-evident, if equally understood, that there must be a cause[6] why a body should be after this manner and not after another. Thus if a body is a moving body, there must be some reason or cause why it is a moving body and not a resting body; it must be because of something; otherwise, there is something without a cause, as much as when a body starts into being of itself.[7]

Supposing there are two globes, the one is a moving globe, the other a resting. The mind asks why the one moves and the other rests; it is natural to the mind to say, something is the reason why this body moves and not the other. And if it should be said, no, there is not, nor ever was any cause or reason why this body should move more than why the other should, the mind immediately returns: if there be no reason why one should move more than the other, why then does one move and the other rest? It abhors the supposition that there is none. So if two bodies are of different figures, there is some reason why this is of this shape, and that of the other. So when one body moves with one degree of velocity and another with another, when one body is of one bigness and another of another, when one body moves with one direction and another with another, one possesses this place [and] another another; 'tis exceeding evident, that there must be some cause or other for these things. Wherefore now I ask the question: of the different bodies in the world, why is this body in this place and not in that or some other; why is this body of such dimensions and not of others; why is this body of this figure and that of that; why doth this move and that rest; why doth this body move with just such a degree of velocity; why do the planets move west to east and not from east to west? Something must be the reason of it.

If it be said, it is so because it was so from all eternity, or because there were such successions of alterations from eternity as to cause it to be so now; how came it to be so from eternity? If there can be abso-

6. JE inserted the words "that there must be a cause" shortly after writing No. 94, to judge from the ink.
7. The words "otherwise . . . of itself" were also inserted later by JE.

lutely no reason or cause why it should be so, any more than why it should be infinite other ways, then I say, it was not so from eternity. And why was there not another succession of alterations from eternity, so as to cause such an alteration; why was there not [yet] another succession of alterations, so as to cause another sort of alteration now?

92. END OF THE CREATION. How then can it be said that God has made all things for himself, if it is certain that the highest end of the creation was the communication of happiness?[8] I answer, that which is done for the gratifying of a natural inclination of God, may very properly be said to be done for God. God takes complacence in communicating felicity, and he made all things for this complacence. His complacence in this,[9] in making happy, was the end of the creation. Rev. 4:11, "For thy pleasure they are and were created." See No. 581.

93. I AM THAT I AM. The essence of God, and his nature, is most wonderfully expressed in this, I AM; his excellency, in this, THAT I AM.

94. TRINITY.[1] There has been much cry of late against saying one word, particularly about the Trinity, but what the Scripture has said; judging it impossible but that if we did, we should err in a thing so much above us.[2] But if they call that which necessarily results from the

8. See above, No. 87 and earlier entries on this theme. No. 92 may be considered a partial answer to the question with which the draft of No. 87 ends: "In what sense the highest end of all things is the glory of God."

9. Or "in this, that is"; MS: "in this this." The second "this" may be the result of an abridgment.

1. This is JE's first attempt to deal with the Trinity in his extant MSS and is fundamental to all his later thinking on the subject; see above, pp. 14, 47, 57–58. JE's account of the Trinity goes back to Augustine's fundamental human analogy: the self, its knowledge, and its love (*De trinitate*, Bks. IX–X (esp. chs. 15–18, XV (chs. 27–37), probably as developed by Melanchthon and Keckermann (see Heinrich Heppe, *Reformed Dogmatics* (rev. ed. transl. G. T. Thomson [London, George Allen & Unwin, 1950], pp. 106–08). JE's proximate source may have been a passage in Cotton Mather's *Blessed Unions* (Boston, 1692, pp. 46–48), which is remarkably similar to JE's argument.

2. Samuel Clarke's *Scripture-Doctrine of the Trinity* (London, 1712) initiated a bitter controversy over Arianism which had raged for a decade, with Dissenters hotly engaged on both sides. Hubert Stogdon sought to moderate the violence of the debate in his anonymous *Seasonable Advice Relating to the Present Disputes about the Holy Trinity, Address'd to Both Contending Parties* (London, 1719). More recently Isaac Watts had written *The Christian Doctrine of the Trinity . . . Asserted and Prov'd,* [and] . . . *Vindicated by Plain Evidence of Scripture, without the Aid or Incumbrance of Human Schemes* (London, 1722). Both authors condemned giving the status of fundamental doctrines to "*Unscriptural Terms and Phrases*" justified as "Scripture consequences," arguing that only what is "plainly reveal'd" in "express Scripture" is necessary to salvation (Stogdon, *Seasonable Advice,* pp. 23–24).

In No. 94 JE is not directly concerned with that controversy, for he assumes the truth of

putting [together] of reason and Scripture, though it has not been said in Scripture in express words—I say, if they call this what is not said in the Scripture, I am not afraid to say twenty things about the Trinity which the Scripture never said. There may be deductions of reason from what has been said of the most mysterious matters, besides what has been said, and safe and certain deductions too, as well as about the most obvious and easy matters.

I think that it is within the reach of naked reason to perceive certainly that there are three distinct in God, each of which is the same [God], three that must be distinct; and that there are not nor can be any more distinct,[3] really and truly distinct, but three, either distinct persons or properties or anything else; and that of these three, one is (more properly than anything else) begotten of the other, and that the third[4] proceeds alike from both, and that the first neither is begotten nor proceeds.

'Tis often said[5] that God is infinitely happy from all eternity in the view and enjoyment of himself, in the reflection and converse love of his own essence, that is, in the perfect idea he has of himself, infinitely perfect. The Almighty's knowledge is not so different from ours, but that ours is the image of [it]. It is by an idea, as ours is, only his [is] infinitely perfect. If it were not by idea, it is in no respect like ours; 'tis not what we call knowledge, nor anything whereof knowledge is the resemblance; for the whole of human knowledge, both in the beginning and end of it, consists in ideas. 'Tis also said that God's knowledge of himself includes the knowledge of all things; and that he knows, and from eternity knew, all things by the looking on himself and by the idea of himself, because he is virtually all things; so that all God's knowledge is the idea of himself. But yet it would suppose imperfection in God, to suppose that God's idea of himself is anything different from himself. None will suppose that God has any such ideas as we [have], that are only as it were the shadow of things and not the very things. We cannot suppose that God reflects on himself after the imperfect manner we

---

the orthodox doctrine and only seeks to make it more intellectually satisfying. But he was well aware of the debate over "Scripture consequences," e.g. as it affected the licensing of ordinands (see above, No. 17).

3. MS: "that there ~~is~~ ⟨are not nor⟩ ~~and~~ can be ~~no~~ ⟨any⟩ more distinct." JE made these changes in 1730 while writing the "Essay on the Trinity." All other alterations of the text of No. 94 seem to have been made at the time of composition or shortly afterwards, perhaps while JE was writing Nos. 96 and 98.

4. MS: "the other."

5. Here and later in the paragraph, JE is referring not so much to Scripture as to commonly accepted notions in the tradition of rational theology. There are other such expressions throughout the essay.

reflect on things, for we can view nothing immediately. The immediate object of the mind's intuition is the idea always, and the soul receives nothing but ideas; but God's intuition on himself, without doubt, is immediate. But 'tis certain it cannot be, except his idea be his essence; for his idea is the immediate object of his intuition. An absolutely perfect idea of a thing is the very thing, for it wants nothing that is in the thing, substance nor nothing else. That is the notion of the perfection of an idea, to want nothing that is in the thing.[6] Whatsoever is perfectly and absolutely like a thing, is that thing: but God's idea is absolutely perfect.

I will form my reasoning thus: if nothing has any existence any way at all but in some consciousness or idea or other, and therefore those things that are in no created consciousness have no existence but in the divine idea—as supposing the things in this room were in the idea of none but of God, they would have existence no other way, as we have shown in our Natural Philosophy;[7] and if the things in this room would nevertheless be real things—then God's idea, being a perfect idea, is really the thing itself. And if so, and all God's ideas are only the one idea of himself, as has been shown, [then God's idea of himself] must be his essence itself. It must be a substantial idea, having all the perfections of the substance perfectly; so that by God's reflecting on himself the Deity is begotten, there is a substantial image of God begotten. I am satisfied that though this word "begotten" had never been used in Scripture, it would have been used in this case: there is no other word that so properly expresses it. 'Tis this perfection of God's idea that makes all things truly and properly present to him from all eternity, and is the reason why God has no succession. For everything that is, has been, or shall be, having been perfectly in God's idea from all eternity, and a perfect idea (which yet no finite being can have of anything) being the very thing; therefore, all things from eternity were equally present with God, and there is no alteration made in [his] idea by presence and absence as there is in us.

Again, that which is the express and perfect image of God, is God's idea of his own essence. There is nothing else can be an express and fully perfect image of God but God's idea. Ideas are images of things;

6. This sentence is an interlined insertion; JE wrote the last two words in shorthand in order to get them on the same line with the rest. The insert occurs in the first part of the entry (the ink of which is gray) but is written in the same shade of brown ink used in the latter part; this and other (but slighter) revisions were probably made while JE was completing the essay.

7. JE has in mind the same part of "Being" to which he refers in No. 44 (Works, 6, 203–06).

and there are no other images of things, in the most proper sense, but ideas, because other things are only called images as they beget an idea in us of the thing of which they are the image; so that all other images of things are but images in a secondary sense. But we know that the Son of God is the express and perfect image of God, and his image in the primary and most proper sense. II Cor. 4:4, "Lest the light of the glorious gospel of Christ, who is the image of God, should shine unto them." Phil. 2:6, "Who, being in the form of God." Col. 1:15, "Who is the image of the invisible God." Heb. 1:3, "Who being the brightness of his glory, and the express image of his person."

Again, that image of God which God infinitely loves and has his chief delight in, is the perfect idea of God. It has always been said, that God's infinite delight consists in reflecting on himself and viewing his own perfections, or which is the same thing, in his own perfect idea of himself; so that 'tis acknowledged, that God's infinite love is to, and his infinite delight in, the perfect image of himself. But the Scriptures tell us that the Son of God is that image of God which he infinitely loves. Nobody will deny this, that God infinitely loves his Son; "The Father loveth the Son" (John 3:35, 5:20). So it was declared from heaven by the Father at his baptism and transfiguration, "This is my beloved Son, in whom I am well pleased" [Matt. 3:17]. So the Father calls him his Elect, in whom his soul delighteth, Is. 42:1; he is called the Beloved, Eph. 1:6. The Son also declares that the Father's infinite happiness consisted in the enjoyment of him, Prov. 8:30, "I was daily his delight, rejoicing always before him." Now none, I suppose, will say that God enjoys infinite happiness in two manners, one in the infinite delight he has in enjoying his Son, his image, and another in the view of himself different from this. If not, then these ways wherein God enjoys infinite happiness are both the same; that is, his infinite delight in the idea of himself is the same with the infinite delight he has in his Son; and if so, his Son and the idea he has of himself are the same.

Again, that which is the express image of God, in which God enjoys infinite happiness, and is also the Word of God, is God's perfect idea of God. The Word of God, in its most proper meaning, is a transcript of the divine perfections. This Word is either the declared Word of God[8] or the essential: the one is the copy of the divine perfections given to us, the other is the perfect transcript thereof in God's own mind. But the perfect transcript of the perfections of God in the divine [mind] is

8. MS: "his declared word ⟨of God⟩."

the same with God's perfect idea of his own perfections. But I need tell none, how the Son of God is called the Word of God.

Nextly, that which is the express image of God, in which he infinitely delights and which is his Word, and which is the reason or wisdom of God, is God's perfect idea of God. That God's knowledge, or reason or wisdom, is the same with God's idea, none will deny; and that all God's knowledge or wisdom consists in the knowledge or perfect idea of himself, is shown before and granted by all. But none needs to be told, that the Son of God is often called in Scripture by the names of the Wisdom and Logos of God. Wherefore God himself has put the matter beyond all debate, whether or no his Son is not the same with his idea of himself; for it is most certain, that his wisdom and knowledge is the very same with his idea of himself—how much does the Son of God speak in Proverbs under that name of Wisdom!

There is very much of [an] image of this in ourselves. Man is as if he were two, as some of the great wits of this age have observed. A sort of genius is with man, that accompanies him and attends wherever he goes; so that a man has a conversation with himself, that is, he has a conversation with his own idea. So that if his idea be excellent, he will take great delight and happiness in conferring and communing with it; he takes complacency in himself, he applauds himself; and wicked men accuse themselves and fight with themselves, as if they were two. And man is truly happy then, and only then, when these two agree, and they delight in themselves, and in their own idea and image, as God delights in his.

The Holy Spirit is the act of God between the Father and the Son infinitely loving and delighting in each other. Sure I am, that if the Father and the Son do infinitely delight in each other, there must be an infinitely pure and perfect act between them, an infinitely sweet energy which we call delight. This is certainly distinct from the other two; the delight and energy that is begotten in us by an idea is distinct from the idea. So it cannot be confounded in God, either with God begetting or [with] his idea and image, or Son. It is distinct from each of the other two, and yet it is God; for the pure and perfect act of God is God, because God is a pure act. It appears that this is God, because that which acts perfectly is all act, and nothing but act.

There is an image of this in created beings that approach to perfect action: how frequently do we say that the saints of heaven are all transformed into love, dissolved into joy, become activity itself, changed into mere ecstasy.[9] I acknowledge, these are metaphorical in this case; but yet it is true that the more perfect the act is, the more it resembles the infinitely perfect act of God in this respect. And I believe it will be plain to one that thinks intensely, that the perfect act of God must be a substantial act. We say that the perfect delights of reasonable creatures are substantial delights; but the delight of God is properly a substance, yea an infinitely perfect substance, even the essence of God.

It appears by the holy Scriptures, that the Holy Spirit is the perfect act of God. (1) The name declares it: "the Spirit of God" denotes to us the activity, vivacity and energy of God. And (2) it appears that the Holy Spirit is the pure act of God and energy of the Deity, by his office, which is to actuate and quicken all things, and to beget energy and vivacity in the creature. And it also appears that the Holy Spirit is this act of the Deity, even love and delight, because from eternity there was no other act in God but thus acting with respect to himself, and delighting perfectly and infinitely in himself, or that infinite delight there is between the Father and the Son; for the object of God's perfect act must necessarily be himself, because there is no other. But we have shown that the object of the divine mind is God's Son and idea: and what other act can be thought of in God from eternity, but delighting in himself? The act of love, which God is—I John 4:8, "He that loveth not, knoweth not God; for God is love," and v. 16, "God is love; and he that dwelleth in love dwelleth in God, and God in him"—doubtless this intends principally the infinite love God has to himself; so that the Scripture has implicitly told us, that that love which is between the Father and the Son is God. The Holy Spirit's name is the Comforter; but no doubt but 'tis the infinite delight God has in himself, in the Comforter, that is the fountain of all delight and comfort.

It may be objected, that at this rate one may prove an infinite number of persons in the Godhead, for each person has an idea of the other persons. Thus, the Father may have an idea of his Son; but you will argue that his idea must be substantial. I answer, that the Son himself is the Father's idea, himself; and if he[1] has an idea of this Idea, 'tis yet the same Idea: a perfect idea of an idea is the same idea still, to all intents and purposes. Thus, when I have a perfect idea of my idea of an equilateral triangle, it is an idea of the same equilateral triangle,

9. JE had used this kind of language himself in his New York sermon on Ps. 89:6 (first use) (*Works, 10,* 429–30).
1. I.e. the Father.

to all intents and purposes. So if you say, that God the Father or Son may have an idea of their own delight in each other; but I say, a perfect idea or perception of one's own perfect delight cannot be different, at least in God, from the delight itself. You'll say, the Son has an idea of the Father; I answer, the Son himself is the idea of the Father. And if you say, he[2] has an idea of the Father; his idea is still an idea of the Father, and therefore the same with the Son. And if you say, the Holy Spirit has an idea of the Father; I answer, the Holy Ghost is himself the delight and joyfulness of the Father in that idea, and of the idea in the Father: 'tis still the idea of the Father. So that, if we turn it all the ways in the world, we shall never be able to make more than these three: God, the idea of God, and delight in God.

I think it really evident from the light of reason that there are these three distinct in God. If God has an idea of himself, there is really a duplicity; because [if] there is no duplicity, it will follow that Jehovah thinks of himself no more than a stone. And if God loves himself and delights in himself, there is really a triplicity, three that cannot be confounded, each of which are the Deity substantially.

And this is the only distinction that can be found or thought of in God. If it shall be said that there are power, wisdom, goodness and holiness in God, and that these may as well be proved to be distinct persons because everything that is in God is God; [I answer,] as to the power of God, power always consists in something—the power of the mind consists in its wisdom, the power of the body in plenty of animal spirits and toughness of limbs, etc.—and as it is distinct from those other things, 'tis only a relation of adequateness and sufficiency of the essence to everything. But if we distinguish it from relation, 'tis nothing else but the essence of God. And if we take it for that by which God exerts himself, 'tis no other than the Father; for the perfect energy of God with respect to himself is the most perfect exertion of himself, of which the creation of the world is but a shadow. As to the wisdom of God, we have already observed that this wholly consists in God's idea of himself, and is the same with the Son of God. And as to goodness, the eternal exertion of the essence of that attribute, it is nothing but infinite love, which the apostle John says is God. And as we have observed that all divine love may be resolved

2. I.e. the idea of the Father? Unless there is some confusion in the text, JE seems to be representing the objector as countering with the observation that even if the Son be defined as the idea of the Father, that idea can still be said to have an idea of the Father. JE's answer, again, is to convert an objective into a subjective or possessive genitive.

into God's infinite love to himself, therefore this attribute, as it was exerted from eternity, is nothing but the Holy Spirit; which is exactly agreeable to the notions some have had of the Trinity.[3] And as to holiness, 'tis delight in excellency, 'tis God's sweet consent to himself, or in other words, his perfect delight in himself; which we have shown to be the Holy Spirit.

95. HAPPINESS OF HEAVEN. When the body enjoys the perfections of health and strength, the motion of the animal spirits are not only brisk and free, but also harmonious; there is a regular proportion in the motion from all parts of the body, that begets delight in the soul and makes the body feel pleasantly all over—God has so excellently contrived the nerves and parts of the human body. But few men since the fall, especially since the flood, have health to so great a perfection as to have much of this harmonious motion. When it is enjoyed, one whose nature is not very much vitiated and depraved is very much assisted thereby in every exercise of body or mind; and it fits one for the contemplation of more exalted and spiritual excellencies and harmonies, as music does.[4]

But we need not doubt, but this harmony will be in its perfection in the bodies of the saints after the resurrection; and that, as every part of the bodies of the wicked shall be excruciated with intolerable pain, so every part of the saints' refined bodies shall be as full of pleasure as they can hold; and that this will not take the mind off from, but prompt and help it in spiritual delights, to which even the delight of their spiritual bodies shall be but a shadow. See Nos. 721, 182, 263.[5]

96. TRINITY. It appears that there must be more than a unity in infinite and eternal essence, otherwise the goodness of God can have no perfect exercise. To be perfectly good is to incline to and delight in making another happy in the same proportion as it is happy itself, that is, to delight as much in communicating happiness to another as in enjoying of it himself, and an inclination to communicate all his happiness; it appears that this is perfect goodness, because goodness is delight in communicating happiness. Wherefore, if this goodness be perfect this delight must be perfect, because goodness and this delight

3. See above, p. 256, n. 1.
4. See *Works, 6,* 335–36.
5. At the time he wrote No. 721, JE added these citations and added a similar set to each of the other entries listed here.

are the same. But this delight is not perfect, except it be equal to the highest delight of that being, that is, except his inclination to communicate happiness be equal to his inclination to be happy himself. Goodness in the exercise is communication of happiness; but if that communication be imperfect, that is, if it be not of all the happiness enjoyed by the being himself, the exercise of the goodness is imperfect, inasmuch as the communication of happiness and the exercise of goodness is the same.

But to no finite being can God either incline to communicate goodness so much as he inclines to be happy himself, for he cannot love a creature so much as he loves himself; neither can he communicate all his goodness to a finite being. But no absolutely perfect being can be without absolutely perfect goodness, and no being can be perfectly happy which has not the exercise of that which he perfectly inclines to exercise; wherefore, God must have a perfect exercise of his goodness, and therefore must have the fellowship of a person equal with himself. No reasonable creature can be happy, we find, without society and communion, not only because he[6] finds something in others that is not in himself, but because he delights to communicate himself to another. This cannot be because of our imperfection, but because we are made in the image of God; for the more perfect any creature is, the more strong this inclination. So that we may conclude, that Jehovah's happiness consists in communion, as well as the creature's.

97. HAPPINESS. As [to what] was said in No. 96, that no being could be happy without the exercise of this inclination of communicating his happiness. Now the happiness of society consists in this, in the mutual communications of each other's happiness; neither does it satisfy in society only to receive the other's happiness without also communicating his own. Now it is necessary that to those whom we love most, we should have the strongest desire of communicating happiness—to any but one that has infinite, and cannot receive additions of happiness. And although God is the object of the creature's love (of a creature not depraved), yet God being infinitely happy, he cannot desire to communicate his happiness to Him, which is nothing to the happiness God enjoys. But in the gospel God is come down to us, and the person of God may receive communications of happiness from us. The man Christ Jesus loves us so much, that he is really the happier for our delight and happiness in him.

6. MS: "it."

98. TRINITY.[7] It further appears that the Holy Spirit is nothing but the infinite love and delight of God, by his symbol, a dove; which is the symbol of love, and which is a bird beyond all other irrational animals in the world is remarkable and wonderful for its love to its mate, both in expressions of it by billing together and the like while together, and for its mourning for the loss of its correlate.

And 'tis evident that the dove is used as a symbol of love in the Scriptures: Cant. 1:15, "Behold, thou art fair, my love; behold, thou art fair; thou hast doves' eyes"; and 4:1, "Thou hast doves' eyes within thy locks"; and 2:14, "O my dove, who art in the clefts of the rock"; and 5:2, "Open to me, my sister, my love, my dove, my undefiled"; and 6:9, "My dove, my undefiled is but one"; Ps. 74:19, "Deliver not the soul of thy turtledove [unto the multitude of the wicked]." And this I believe to be the reason that a dove, of all birds alone (except only the sparrow in the singular case of the leprosy), was appointed to be offered in sacrifice, because of its innocence and because it is the symbol of love, love being the most acceptable sacrifice to God.

It was under this representation that the Holy [Spirit] descended on Christ at his baptism, signifying the infinite love of the Father to the Son, and that thereby is signified that infinite love that is between the Father and the Son; which is further illustrated by the voice which came with the dove, "This is my beloved Son, in whom I am well pleased" [Matt. 3:17]. When Christ says to his Father (John 17:26) that he would declare his name to his disciples, "that the love wherewith thou hast loved me may be in them," I can understand nothing else by [it] but that the Holy Spirit might be in them and dwell in them, which is the love of the Father to the Son.

99. FUTURE STATE. 'Tis evident, that man was made to behold and be delighted with the excellency of God in his works, or in short, to be made happy by beholding God's excellency; as it has been shown that intelligent beings, the consciousness of the creation, must be.[8] But if man was made to delight in God's excellency, he was made to love God; and God being infinitely excellent, he ought to love [Him] incompara-

---

7. Immediately preceding this entry, JE began another with the same numeral but deleted it after writing two lines: "98. END OF CREATION. 'Tis certain that 'tis utterly impossible, but that God should be always infinitely happy, or happy as he can be, and that all this happiness is in the enjoyment of himself, and it is impossible his happiness should be added to; yet this does not contradict, but that."
8. See especially Nos. gg, 1, and 20.

bly more than any man is capable of loving a fellow creature; and every power, and all that is in man, ought to be exercised as attendants on this love.[9]

But if man ought so ardently to love God, so vehemently and wholly to delight in God, he ought also with his whole [soul] to love the enjoyment of God, and to desire the continuance of his delight in God; and so with his whole soul to abhor the being deprived of the enjoyment of God, and the discontinuance and end of his delight in God; that is, he ought with his whole soul to abhor annihilation, wherein it must be discontinued. So he ought with his whole soul to desire a future state. This God has made his duty; and if he does love God with his whole soul, [he] will necessarily so desire a future state, and so abhor annihilation, yea, will necessarily dread it, according as he loves God. So [if there be no future state], the pain and torment of the apprehension would be increased in proportion to his love; according as the man was more or less perfect, so would he the less answer the end of his creation, in enjoying delight from the sight of God's excellency. For by how much the more he loves and sees of God's excellency, so much the more pain would he feel; so, by so much the more perfect his reason and knowledge is, by so much would the time he should live in the world appear the less, and as nothing.

Again, if there be no future state, then God has so constituted things, that in some cases 'tis prudence for a person to go contrary to his duty; as supposing a man should suddenly clap a loaded pistol to his breast, and bid him forthwith commit some great sin. Now 'tis his prudence to do that which, all things considered, is best for himself (that I mean by prudence, when I say 'twould be prudence in a man to go contrary to his duty): now it would no way be good for himself to refuse to do the sin, because in an instant he might be annihilated. If he could enjoy the pleasures of religion thereby[1] for a full minute, either from the manifestation of the glory of God or in consideration of the good of men; yet[2] the pain of the consideration of his being forthwith eternally, certainly deprived of so good a happiness, would fully counterbalance it: but he might have on the other hand, if he

9. Arguments to support this statement are given in Nos. kk and tt. This paragraph furnishes the main premises on which No. 99 is built.
  1. I.e. by refusing to commit the sin.
  2. The words "from the manifestation . . . yet" occur on a badly tattered lower margin; they are preserved in the Andover copy, and most of them can be verified from the fragments of text which remain.

lived, a probability of something better than annihilation. But certainly, 'tis prudence for a man to choose a probability of good before the certainty of no good.

Again, it has been proved, that God made intelligent beings for the taking delight in his works. But if intelligent beings are to be annihilated, there are some of God's works which it is impossible for the intelligent being to take delight in, yea, which 'tis necessary that he should have pain in the view of: even His constituting the creation so that the intelligent being, in so short a time, must be annihilated. Neither doth this necessity arise at all from the imperfection of man's nature; but the more perfect and intelligent he is, the more pain will the consideration give him.

Again, I cannot doubt but that if there be no future life, God would have so ordered it, that we should have some pretty certain and obvious means of discovering that there is none. For eternal happiness and eternal misery are things so great, that the bare possibleness of the thing, and there being no certain reasons against it, they in duty and prudence oblige every man to make it the whole care and concern of his [life]. This is evident according to certain rules of proportion; for whatever is wanting in the probability must certainly be more than made up in the greatness of the happiness or misery, for they are infinite. But I cannot think that God has so ordered matters with man, whom he has created to serve and enjoy him (as has been already proved), as to make his duty, and the whole business of his life, in providing for that which shall never be. There is the same disproportion between the good of seventy years and eternal good and evil, as there is between the worth of a minute's good and [that of] an eternal. But who will deny, but that it would be prudence and duty for a man to forego the good of a farthing, for the sake of escaping a very possible eternal misery, and the obtaining a possibility of enjoying an eternal blessedness, which is believed by most and he has no certain reasons to disbelieve.

It has been proved that 'tis necessary, that man must be made [in order] to behold the excellency of God and his works, and to delight and be made happy therein. But the sight of the excellency of God and his works here, in the best [of men], is so obscure, and the love of God and admiration [of him] is so small and so unworthy of the excellency of the object, and their delight in God and spiritual happiness is so exceeding imperfect and inconsiderable; that when [I] let reason have exercise, I cannot think that this is all that man was made for, and that the ends of his creation are to perfection obtained only by these. I cannot think but that, if man was made to love God and delight in him, he was made to do it worthily and proportionately, in a due proportion to the excellency of the object and the capacity of the agent; seeing God doth all things according to the exactest harmony.

Furthermore, all that the best can enjoy of the end of their creation, even a sight of God's excellency and delighting therein, does nothing but enrage his appetite and cause a hunger for more, because he finds nothing near adequate to his capacity here. But we cannot rationally think [but] that, if God created man for happiness, he created him with an appetite and capacity proportionated to the happiness intended for him. If he intended [him] for happiness, we may very justly conclude he intended to satisfy him, and did not order the matter so, that the more happiness he enjoyed the more he should be dissatisfied.

Also, when good men do experience their greatest spiritual delights in this world, they cause pain also, a great restraint and struggle with nature; they find the delight too big and strong for the present state; they find a weakness and feebleness in them very inadequate to such pleasures. But doubtless, if God created us only for happiness, he intended us for a state wherein we might enjoy them freely and without oppression to nature. They also find a great restraint and inward struggle, for want of being able to express and to give vent to their internal motions and the energy of their hearts.

Again, in this world the godly live here and there interspersed among the wicked, and meet with great obstruction in the pursuing of the end of their creation, from them. We may very reasonably conclude, that [if] God intended them only for this happiness, that he intends to place them in such a state where they shall be pure from others, where they may freely and without obstruction assist each other in this happiness. 'Tis evident that men were intended for society, that is, to assist each other in their interests, and chiefly to assist each other in their chief interest; and if in subservient interests, surely most of all in the great happiness for which he was created, and to which all other interests were only intended to subserve. And if so, doubtless God intended that they should be under advantages to obtain this only end of society without obstruction.

100. ISRAEL. See No. 49. "The proselytes were looked upon as born anew, so that they that were born of Gentile parents, were not

looked upon as their children, when become Jews."—*Dictionarium Sacrum.*[3]

101. BODILY WORSHIP. I don't suppose that any understanding men, of whatsoever sect or opinion, will say that God is really pleased with bodily worship as such, that is, that merely such and such gestures and motions of body are what delights him as a part of virtue; but only as they are helps to the exercise of real virtue and the worship of the mind. Now there is an indissoluble, unavoidable association, in the minds of the most rational and spiritual, between things spiritual and things bodily. Thus when we are joyful and express our joy, 'tis natural to do it with a lively voice; and when we express sorrow, to do it with what we call a mournful voice. This is natural to us, and the association becomes much stronger by use in other matters.

Therefore if, when we come to praise God or confess our sins, we resolved not in any measure to alter our manner of expression for sorrow or joy, we must restrain that which is strongly associated with the joy and sorrow; and thereby shall unavoidably, in some measure, forever restrain the spiritual affections themselves, till we quite dissolve the association: which cannot be, in the most rational, while in the body. So we are necessitated to join some gestures to some habitudes of mind in common affairs, as uncovering the head, and some other gestures besides fitting with reverence. Thereby there grows a strong association, so that if one be restrained the other will unavoidably be restrained too. So that some bodily worship is necessary to give liberty to our own devotion; yea though in secret, so more when with others. For we having associated the idea of reverence and other habitudes of mind to such and such gestures of body, it would restrain our notion or apprehension of another's reverence, etc., if we should see those gestures which we have associated to contrary dispositions; so that our own devotion would not be so much assisted by theirs but restrained, and the communion in the duty in some measure destroyed, and so the end of social devotion. 'Tis necessary that there should be something bodily and visible in the worship of a congregation; otherwise, there can be no communion at all.

3. [Daniel Defoe], *Dictionarium Sacrum seu Religiosum. A Dictionary of All Religions, Ancient and Modern* (London, 1704), art. "Proselites." It is not clear whether JE used this or the 2nd ed. (London, 1723), in which this article was reprinted practically without changes and without any at all in the sentence quoted.

I acknowledge, that the more rational a person, the less doth his disposition of mind depend on anything in his body; and that if he practises gestures of body in worship, where there is no necessary and unavoidable association, it tends to make him, or to keep him less rational and spiritual. But yet there are some associations of this nature that [are] equally unavoidable, and coeval with the association of soul and body. So many as are thus necessary, we are allowed in gospel worship, and more [than that] are contrary to its nature; for the gospel supposes the church to be no longer an infant, but as come to the stature of a man. Wherefore the weak and beggarly elements are rejected, and the childish bodily ceremonies cashiered, as being fit only for children, and unworthy of those who are come to riper years; and the worship that is now required of [us] is only that which is manly, rational and spiritual.

102. PROVIDENCE. A more special providence of God may be discerned in those things that do most highly concern us. By special providence I mean remarkable and palpable, things being more apparently and evidently guided by an invisible direction. Thus, in the preservation of our lives. I believe that there is but few persons that would live till they are thirty years old, if it were not for this; it might be said of him, that he has run hundreds of chances for his life, wherein it was as likely he should lose his life as not, and many times more likely. How often do men say in their lifetime, it is a wonder I had not been killed; 'tis a wonder I had not fallen, or, a wonder we were not lost; 'tis a wonder such and such a fatal thing did not befall me; and, 'tis a wonder that such a thing did not happen—which, although it would not have been fatal immediately, yet would probably have brought other things that would (or at least would have, it's likely as not) have brought death at the end of the chain of events that have brought death.[4] And we pass through innumerable more of these that are to us invisible, and that we take no manner of notice of. There are thousands of ways that death can have access to us, many of which 'tis as like will befall us as not; we pass through many changes that are as likely to bring them as not. There are thousands of times, wherein the least thing in the world would bring death—the least wrong turn of the foot, a slip of the hand, a little mistake—'tis a thousand to one, that such things don't happen innumerable other ways that persons may think of.

4. I.e. in other cases? The last four words of the sentence may well be an unintentional repetition.

Now 'tis evident, that if events were not under a direction and government, that taking one time with another, death would happen as often as not at such times wherein 'tis as likely that it should happen as not; but to me it appears that it does not so often, by hundreds to one. So there is a special providence in other things of great concern, preserving of houses from burning, etc.

103. INCARNATION. It seems to me very proper and suitable, that the human nature should be advanced far above the angelical nature by[5] the incarnation of Christ. For men are a more ultimate end of the creation than the angels; for everything, even the highest heaven and the angels themselves, are created for men more than men for the angels. In the gradation of ends among the creatures, man is the highest step; the next immediate step is to God. Man was not created for any other creature, but it cannot be said so of the angels; for they are created for this end, to minister to the creatures. It is proper, therefore, that if the divine nature is united to the creatures, that it should be to that nature which, in the order of ends, is next immediately unto [the divine nature], and not to those who are created to be ministers to other creatures.

It will be objected, that then it would be improper that the angels should have more excellent natures than men, for it is suitable that the highest end should be the highest nature. I answer, that the angels will indeed evermore excel the saints in strength and wisdom, for their office requires [them] to be the universal ministers of God in the universe, but not in grace and sweet holiness and love to God; which excellencies are the highest, and the end of the order of power and wisdom: and only for the exercise of these it is that man is made, and these are the highest end of creatures in general.

Therefore the children of God and the spouse of Christ, is more nearly related and more closely united to God than the angels; for whom God has done more than ever [he has] for the angels, and who in many respects shall be advanced above them in glory, and shall be objects of the dearer love of God. This spouse of the Son of God, the bride, the Lamb's wife, the completeness of him who filleth all in all, is that for which all the universe was made. Heaven and earth were created that the Son of God might be complete in a spouse, on whom

5. MS: "as in by"; JE apparently started to give an example but after changing his mind failed to delete "as."

the barons and nobles of the court of heaven shall esteem it their honor to attend. See No. 702, corol. 2.

104. END OF THE CREATION. We have proved that the end of the creation must needs be happiness and the communication of the goodness of God; and that nothing but the Almighty's inclination to communicate of his own happiness, could be the motive to him to create the world; and that man, or intelligent being, is the immediate object of this goodness, and subject of this communicated happiness [Nos. 3, 87, 92]. And we have shown also, that the Father's begetting of the Son is a complete communication of all his happiness, and so an eternal, adequate and infinite exercise of perfect goodness, that is completely equal to such an inclination in perfection [No. 96].

Why, then, did God incline further to communicate himself, seeing he had done [so] infinitely and completely? Can there be an inclination to communicate goodness more than adequately to the inclination? To say so is to say, that to communicate goodness adequate to the inclination is not yet adequate, inasmuch as he inclines to communicate further, as in the creation of the world. To this I say, that the Son is the adequate communication of the Father's goodness, is an express and complete image of him. But yet the Son has also an inclination to communicate himself, in an image of his person that may partake of his happiness: and this was the end of the creation, even the communication of the happiness of the Son of God; and this was the only motive hereto, even the son's inclination to this (see No. 115).[6] And man, the consciousness or perception of the creation, is the immediate subject of this.

Therefore the church is said to be the completeness of Christ (Eph. 1:23), as if Christ were not complete without the church, as having a natural inclination thereto. We are incomplete without that which we have a natural inclination to. Thus, man is incomplete without the woman, she is himself; so Christ is not complete without his spouse. The soul is not complete without the body, because human souls have a natural inclination to dwell in a body. So Eph. 1, the two last verses, "And given him to be head over all things to the church, which is his body, the fullness of him who filleth all in all." So the church is everywhere spoken of, as being so nearly united to Christ that she is one with

---

6. JE placed an asterisk here to indicate where he wished to insert No. 115.

him; and Christ, as having an inclination that believers should be partakers of his glory: "Father, I will that they whom thou hast given me be with me where I am, that they may behold my glory, which thou hast given me; for thou lovedst me before the foundation of the world" [John 17:24]. So his delights are said to be with the sons of men, Prov. 8:30–31. First we are told where the Father's delight was, and also the mutual delight of the Son, and then where the Son's delight is, in the objects of his communication of his goodness: "Then I was by him, as one brought up with him; and I was daily his delight, rejoicing always before him, rejoicing in the habitable part of his earth; and my delights were with the sons of men." The Son is the fullness of God, and the church is the fullness of the Son of God.

Corol. 1. Then doubtless, he is the only proper and fit Person to be the redeemer of men.

Corol. 2. Therefore they are so nearly united to Christ, and shall have such intimate communion with him; shall sit down with him in his throne, even as he is set down in his Father's throne, and sit with him in the judgment of the world; and their glory and honor and happiness shall be so astonishing great as is spoken in the Scripture.

Corol. 3. Therefore the Son created and doth govern the world; seeing that the world was a communication of him, and seeing the communicating of his happiness is the end of the world.

Corol. 4. We may learn in what sense Christ says, John 15:9, "As my Father hath loved me, so I have loved you." As the Father loveth the Son as a communication of himself, as begotten in pursuance of his eternal inclination to communicate himself; so the Son of God loveth the church, or the saints, as the effect of his love and goodness, and natural inclination to communicate himself.

Corol. 5. Hence the meaning of Col. 1:16–17, ["For by him were all things created . . . and for him; and he is before all things, and by him all things consist"].

In this[7] also there is a trinity, an image of the eternal Trinity; wherein Christ is the everlasting father, and believers are his seed, and the Holy Spirit, or Comforter, is the third person in Christ, being his delight and love flowing out towards the church. In believers the Spirit and

7. I.e. the self-communication of the Son as described in the first paragraphs of the entry. What follows is not an explication of Col. 1:16–17 but a continuation of the main part of the entry.

delight of God, being communicated unto them, flows out toward the Lord Jesus Christ. See note on Dan. 9:25 and Mark 14:3 and Gen. 28:11–12 ff. (second part).[8]

Corol. 1[a][9] Hence we may easily perceive how these expressions of the Lord Jesus are to be understood: John 17:21–24,

> That they all may be one; as thou, Father, art in me, and I in thee, that [they] also may be one in us: that the world may believe that thou hast sent me. And the glory which thou gavest me I have given them, that they may be one, even as we are one; I in them, and thou in me, that they may be made perfect in one; and that the world may know that thou hast sent me, and hast loved them as thou hast loved me. Father, I will that they also, that thou hast given me, be with me where I am, that they may behold my glory, which thou hast given me; for thou lovedst me before the foundation of the world.

And John 14:20, "At that day ye shall know that I am in my Father, and you in me, and I in you." These sayings at first seem like nothing but words carelessly cast together, very abstruse and dark; but yet we may see that Christ knew what he meant. Many other of Christ's speeches may receive light from hence, the meaning of the Apostle John's Gospel and Epistles particularly, and many passages throughout the whole Bible.

Corol. 2[a]. How glorious is the gospel, that reveals to us such things![1]

Corol. 3[a]. Hence we see why it is most suitable and proper, that the Son of God should have the immediate management of the affairs of the church; and that it should be this person of the Trinity that has all along manifested himself by the visible tokens of his presence to the antediluvians, the patriarchs, and Israelites.

---

8. These citations are an interlined insertion made all at the same time, probably in the latter 1730s. The notes occur in the "Blank Bible" and are linked together by cross-references. Their common theme (as it is expressed in the note on Dan. 9:25) is that Christ is the Messiah or anointed one, "as he is anointed by the church or by every believing soul, by the exercise of the grace of the Holy Spirit towards him, and as it were pouring out his soul in divine love upon him."

9. Letters are here added to the numerals of JE's second series of corollaries in order to distinguish them from the former.

1. JE originally wrote this as corol. 4 in the preceding series but transferred it when he reached this point in his composition.

105. HEAVEN.[2] That the glorified spirits shall grow in holiness and happiness to eternity, I argue from this foundation, that their number of ideas shall increase to eternity. How great a number of ideas soever when they are first glorified, it is but finite. And 'tis evident the time will come wherein they shall have lived in glory so long, that the parts of duration (each equal a million million ages) that they have lived will be more in number [than] their ideas were at first. Now we cannot suppose, that they will ever entirely forget everything that has passed in heaven and in the universe, for a whole million million of ages. 'Tis undoubted, that they never will have forgot what passed in their life upon earth: the sins they have been saved from, their regeneration, the circumstances which did heighten their mercies, their good works which follow them, their death, etc. They must without doubt retain innumerable multitudes of ideas, of what passed in the first seventy years. So also, they shall retain to eternity their ideas of what was done in the ages of the world with relation to the church of God, and God's wondrous providences with respect to the world of men. And can we then think, that a whole million million ages of those great and most glorious things that pass in heaven, shall ever be erased out of their minds? But if they retain but one idea for one such vast space, their ideas shall be millions of times more in number than when they first entered into heaven; as is evident because, by supposition, the number of such ages will be millions of times more in number.

Therefore, their knowledge will increase to eternity; and if their knowledge, doubtless their holiness. For as they increase in the knowledge of God and of the works of God, the more they will see of his excellency;[3] and the more they see of his excellency, *cæteris paribus*, the more will they love him; and the more they love God, the more delight

2. JE began this number on another topic, but stopped in the middle of a sentence and deleted the whole with a large X mark: "105. SUCCESSION. If one infinite succession can't exceed another infinite succession, 'tis evident that eternity is inconsistent with the nature of succession; because then, the successions that have been to this time would be no more than the successions that have been the last year. That the successions of this year being . . ."

JE may have decided that he could not make his case, for he proceeded instead with a meditation on heaven which very much requires the idea of succession, in all future eternity at least.

3. From this point onward the draft of No. 105 is extant on the last leaf of the sermon on Prov. 24:13–14. Since JE copied the draft with very slight revision, only portions relating to textual problems will be printed here.

and happiness, *cæteris paribus*, will they have in him. See note on Ps. 89:1–2, in Harmony of the Old and New Testaments.[4]

It will be objected, that at this rate we might prove that the damned increase in perfection. I answer, no, for though it is true that they shall increase in knowledge, [they shall] increase[5] in odiousness in the same proportion. For the more knowing good is, *cæteris paribus*, the more good; so the more knowing evil is,[6] *cæteris paribus*, the more evil; the more ignorant, capable of less wickedness; the more knowing, *cæteris paribus*, capable of more. All in hell shall be as full of wickedness as they can hold, but the more knowing, in their kind of knowledge, the larger is the vessel; as in heaven the more knowing the blessed are, *cæteris paribus*, they are capable of greater holiness and happiness.

106. HAPPINESS. We argue very justly, that seeing God has created the whole world for his own glory, that therefore he will glorify himself exceeding transcendently; but we have showed that is, he will give his creatures occasion to glorify him exceedingly: but glorifying of God, as we have remarked in No. 3, is nothing but rejoicing in the manifestations of him. Wherefore it may with equal evidence be argued that man's happiness, i.e. the happiness of the saints, will be very transcendent, as transcendent as the glory of God, seeing it is the same. Again, seeing that God has created man as the intelligence of the creation, to behold the manifestation of God's excellency—and we have proved that God created all things only for the happiness of the intelligence of the creation [No. gg], and we have showed that happiness is the perception and possession of excellency[7]—therefore, in proportion as

4. This reference is a later addition; JE probably did not begin the MS notebook that it cites before the late 1730s. From his exegesis of these verses, JE concludes that "God will be always carrying on the design of his mercy and love towards his church to greater and greater perfection . . . So that God's love shall more and more appear, and the effects of it be carried to a greater height, like a building that rises higher and higher."

5. MS: "but increase." The draft reads: "I answer, it is true they shall increase in knowledge, but increase." In copying, JE started to change the construction by adding "though," but he did not delete "but."

6. MS: "so the more ~~knowing~~ great knowing ~~and powerfull~~ evil is." The draft reads: "the more knowing and great ~~and powerfull~~ evil is." JE at first followed the draft, then, as the rest of the sentence shows, abandoned the contrast of greatness and power; he failed, however, to delete the word "great."

7. It is possible that JE is thinking of a previous entry, such as No. 89 or No. 99, but it is more likely that he is referring to one or more of the addenda to the essay "Excellency" in "The Mind" no. 1 (*Works*, 6, 336–338). The writing to which JE refers may not be extant, for it is possible that a leaf containing further addenda to "Excellency" was missing when the MS came into Dwight's hands; see ibid., 6, 317, n. 8.

God has manifested his excellency, will the intelligence or perception of the world be happy. We therefore may be without doubt, that man shall be exceeding happy beyond conception.

Again, that the saints will be full of happiness, will have as much happiness as they can contain (that is, they will have happiness completely adequate to their capacity), is evident, because happiness is nothing, as we have showed, but the perception and the possession of excellency. Therefore if they are not full, it must be for want of excellency or the possession of it. But they can't want excellency to behold in God, he being infinite in it; neither will they want the means of beholding or perceiving it, as far as their capacity allows; nor will they want possession.

107[a]. FALL. Corollary from No. 104. Seeing that this will [be] all the end for which the Son of God created the world, to communicate his own excellency and happiness—as we have shown in No. 104, and as 'tis evident it must be, if God created the world only from goodness, as we have elsewhere proved[8]—and seeing that men only, intelligent being, are the only capable subjects of this intended excellency and happiness; we therefore learn that man is undoubtedly in a fallen state, because, as men are naturally, there is hardly anything of this excellency to be seen in him. They have indeed power and intellect; but we have shown (No. 105) that these are not excellencies without holiness and grace, but only a capacity of more odiousness.

107[b]. GRACE. Corollaries from No. 104. Seeing that Christ created the world only to communicate his excellency and happiness, hence we learn,

Corol. 1. That all the excellency, virtue and happiness of the godly is wrought in them by Jesus Christ.

Corol. 2. That Christ loves nothing in man any otherwise, or any further than it is a communication from himself; that is, he loves no pretended excellencies but what are merely and wholly communicated by him; for only they are the end of the creation, and for which only he inclined to create them. And it is thus and thus only that God delights in their prayers, takes pleasure in their good works, and smells a sweet savor in their sacrifices, even as he delights really and not metaphorically in communications of himself; for it is his essence to incline

8. See above, Nos. 3, 87, and 92.

to communicate himself. So that he delights as properly in the devotions, graces and good works of the saints.

108. EXCELLENCY OF CHRIST.[9] When we behold a beautiful body, a lovely proportion, a beautiful harmony of features of face, delightful airs of countenance and voice, and sweet motion and gesture, we are charmed with it; not under the notion of a corporeal, but a mental beauty. For if there could be a statue that should have exactly the same, could be made to have the same sound, and have the same motions precisely, we should not be so delighted with it; we should not fall entirely in love with the image, if we knew certainly that it had no perception or understanding. The reason is, we are apt to look upon this agreeableness, these airs, to be emanations of perfections of the mind, and immediate effects of internal purity and sweetness. Especially it is so, when we love the person for the airs of voice, countenance and gesture; which have much greater power upon us, than barely colors and proportion of dimensions. And 'tis certainly because there is an analogy between such a countenance and such airs, and these and those excellencies of the mind—a sort of I know not what in them, that is agreeable and does consent with such mental perfections—so that we cannot think of such habitudes of mind without having an idea of them at the same time. Nor can it be only from custom, for the same dispositions and actings of mind naturally beget such kind of airs of countenance and gesture; otherwise, they never would have come into custom. (I speak not here of the ceremonies of behavior, but of those simple and natural motions and airs.) So it appears, because the same habitudes and actings of mind do beget airs in general the same amongst all nations in all ages.

And there is really likewise an analogy, or consent, between the beauty of the skies, trees, fields, flowers, etc. and spiritual excellencies; though the agreement be more hid and requires a more discerning, feeling mind to perceive it than the other. These have their airs too, as well as the body or countenance of man, which have a strange kind of agreement with such and such mental beauties. This makes it natural in such frames of mind to think of them, and fancy ourselves in the midst of them. Thus there seems to be love and complacency in flowers

9. This essay, with No. 112 attached, has become well known through the reprint in *Jonathan Edwards: Representative Selections*, ed. Clarence H. Faust and Thomas H. Johnson (New York, American Book Co., 1935), pp. 372–74. Its first paragraph may contain personal references, especially when taken together with JE's tribute to Sarah Pierpont (ibid., p. 56).

and bespangled meadows; this makes lovers delight so much in them. So there is a rejoicing in the green trees and fields, [and] majesty in thunder, beyond all other noises whatever.

Now we have shown [No. 104], that the Son of God created the world for this very end, to communicate himself in an image of his own excellency. He communicates himself properly only to spirits; and they only are capable of being proper images of his excellency, for they only are properly beings, as we have shown. Yet he communicates a sort of a shadow or glimpse of his excellencies to bodies, which, as we have shown, are but the shadows of being, and not real beings.[1] He who by his immediate influence gives being every moment and by his Spirit actuates the world, because he inclines to communicate himself and his excellencies, doth doubtless communicate his excellency to bodies, as far as there is any consent or analogy. And though beauty of face and sweet airs in man are not always the effect of the corresponding excellencies of mind, yet the beauties of nature are really emanations, or shadows, of the excellencies of the Son of God.

So that when we are delighted with flowery meadows and gentle breezes of wind, we may consider that we only see the emanations of the sweet benevolence of Jesus Christ; when we behold the fragrant rose and lily, we see his love and purity. So the green trees and fields, and singing of birds, are the emanations of his infinite joy and benignity; the easiness and naturalness of trees and vines [are] shadows of his infinite beauty and loveliness; the crystal rivers and murmuring streams have the footsteps of his sweet grace and bounty. When we behold the light and brightness of the sun, the golden edges of an evening cloud, or the beauteous bow, we behold the adumbrations of his glory and goodness; and the blue skies, of his mildness and gentleness. There are also many things wherein we may behold his awful majesty: in the sun in his strength, in comets, in thunder, in the towering thunder clouds, in ragged rocks and the brows of mountains. That beauteous light with which the world is filled in a clear day is a lively shadow of his spotless holiness and happiness, and delight in communicating himself.

And doubtless this is a reason that Christ is compared so often to those things and called by their names; as, the sun of righteousness, the morning star, the rose of Sharon and lily of the valleys, the apple

1. The background of this and the preceding sentence is of course "Being," and "Excellency," particularly the third addendum in the latter essay (*Works*, 6, 337).

tree amongst the trees of the wood, a bundle of myrrh, a roe, or a young hart. By this we may discover the beauty of many of those metaphors and similes, which to an unphilosophical person do seem so uncouth.

In like manner, when we behold the beauty of man's body in its perfection, we still see like emanations of Christ's divine perfections, although they do not always flow from the mental excellencies of the person that has them. But we see far the most proper image of the beauty of Christ, when we see beauty in the human soul.

Corol. 1. From hence 'tis evident that man is in a fallen state, that he has naturally scarcely anything of those sweet graces, which are an image of those which are in Christ; for no doubt, seeing that other creatures have an image of them according to their capacity, so all the rational and intelligent part of the world once had according to theirs.

Corol. 2. There will be a future state, wherein man will have [those graces] according to his capacity. How great a happiness will it be in heaven, for the saints to enjoy the society of each other! For if one may see so much of the loveliness of Christ in those things which are only shadows of being—with what joy are philosophers filled in beholding the aspectable world!—how sweet will it be to behold the proper images and communications of Christ's excellencies in intelligent beings, having so much of the beauty of Christ upon them as Christians shall have in heaven. See No. 112.

109. END OF THE CREATION. See. No. 104.[2] So neither are we complete without Jesus Christ, as the woman is not complete without the man. Col. 2:10, "And ye are complete in him, who is the head of all principality and power."

110. DISCIPLINE. Relating to what has been said of this before [No. 69]. What is easier and more evident to reason, than that the children of the same heavenly Father and members of the same body, as many as cohabit and live in a convenient nearness, should often meet together, to join in the same worship, and with mutual consent worship God in Christ, in prayer, praise, word, sacraments, etc.?

111. FALL. As reason tells us that man is in a fallen state, so it also telleth us that God is willing to be reconciled to him again; the contin-

2. See especially the third paragraph of No. 104.

ual bounty of God to him evidences it. There is manifestly much contrivance for man's good, subsistence and comfort in the world; yea, 'tis evident that infinite wisdom and power are continually exercised for us. Now what in the world could be meant by all this, if God had irrevocably set himself against man, and had finally withdrawn all his favor from him, and had irreversibly sentenced him to eternal misery? Why then so much wisdom and power continually exercised for his good, and why has it been so, for thousands of years? God hath not left himself without witness in natural reason, in that he does us good, and gives us rain from heaven and fruitful seasons, filling our hearts with food and gladness.

112. HEAVEN. Addition to No. 108, corol. 2. What beauteous and fragrant flowers will these be, reflecting all the sweetnesses of the Son of God! How will Christ delight to walk in this garden, among these beds of spices, to feed in the gardens and to gather lilies!

113. MEDIATOR. But supposing, if God might have pardoned sin and yet be just, yet 'tis a thing really incredible that God should let sin go, without any manner of public manifestation of his abhorrence of it. That sin should come into the world and God make no opposition to it, is really incongruous.

Again, if there was no satisfaction for sin, nor any promises of forgiveness; seeing the best are daily renewing their sins, they would [be] in a dreadful case, not knowing whether there be any hope for pardon again, seeing God had pardoned them so often after they had renewed their[3] disobedience.

114. FUTURE STATE. I cannot believe that, seeing God created man to communicate his excellency and happiness to him, and that he might behold his excellency and rejoice in the sight; but that there will [be] a state wherein he shall do this, and enjoy this sight of God and communion with him, without continually sinning against and disobeying him, and doing that which he above all things abhors. I cannot think that, seeing that rational beings' communion with God is the very highest end and only end of the whole universe, that God created man for such communion with him for forty or fifty years, which is so exceedingly defective, poor and miserable, and wherein man is con-

3. MS: "after he had renewed his."

tinually mixing sin with his communion. See my sermon on Rev. 21:18.[4]

And 'tis [as much] a sort of ocular demonstration to me that man's excellency, happiness, sight of God's excellency, rejoicing in it, and communion with God in this world, are vastly disproportionate to so great a work as the creation of the world, and [sufficient] to be the highest end of God's communicating himself neither as to degree nor duration; as I have when I see a mountain and a pea together, that there is a great inequality.

115. END OF THE CREATION. Appendix to No. 104.[5] But God the Father is not the object of this (for the Father is not a communication of the Son, and therefore not the object of the Son's goodness), but men, that is, those of them that are holy; as the Son says, Ps. 16:2–3, "O my soul, thou hast said unto the Lord, Thou are my Lord; my goodness extendeth not to thee, but to the saints that are in the earth and to the excellent, in whom is all my delight." 'Tis Christ here speaks, as is evident by the following passage.

116a. FREE WILL. Although it be said that 'tis most absurd that there [should] be liberty and yet necessity, that these are most inconsistent; that is, that there should be liberty, when yet 'tis impossible in nature but that the thing will be: yet 'tis not worth the while to dispute it, as if liberty and necessity were contraries, for they are not; and 'tis most certain, that that which in any proper sense is called liberty is certainly consistent with absolute necessity. Thus the glorified [saints], or at least the glorified man Jesus, has as much liberty as any man; but yet 'tis absolutely impossible that he should sin.

116b. PREPARATORY WORK. This with me is established, that grace and the exercise of grace is given entirely by the Spirit of God, by his free and most arbitrary motions; but that his ordinary method, notwithstanding, is to give grace to those that are much concerned about it, and earnestly and for a considerable time seek it, or continue to do

---

4. This reference appears to be an integral part of the entry and, if so, was the only sermon reference before 1729 that was not a later addition. The sermon on Rev. 21:8 was written at Bolton (see above, pp. 81–82) and probably contemporaneously with Nos. 105–106. Its doctrine is, "There is nothing upon earth that will suffice to represent to us the glories of heaven." In the second main doctrinal division JE argues that since God's end in creation was the happiness of man, "there will be a time" when this end will be fully attained.

5. See above, No. 104, p. 272, n. 6.

things in order to it. That is, 'tis the Spirit's ordinary method, first to make them concerned about it, so as to convince them that 'tis best to seek it, so far as to make them seek it much, and then to bestow it. Wherefore 'tis established, that in those that are brought up under the gospel, God's ordinary way is thus first to convince them; so that there is doubtless, ordinarily, a preparatory work of conviction.

This conviction, that causes men to think it worth the while to seek salvation, is hardly ever a conviction of the worth of the reward, but of the dreadfulness of the punishment. So that there is doubtless in God's ordinary way a preparatory conviction of sin, that is, [of] the danger of it, before conversion. In the more unthinking people, such as husbandmen and the common sort of people, who are less used to reasoning, God commonly works this conviction by begetting in their minds a dreadful idea and notion of the punishment. In the more knowing and thinking men, the Holy Spirit makes more use of rational deductions, to convince them that 'tis worth their while to seek earnestly for salvation. For God makes use of these things, viz. good nature, a good understanding, a rational brain, moral prudence, etc. as far as they hold.

117. TRINITY. Love is certainly the perfection as well as happiness of a spirit. God, doubtless, as he is infinitely perfect and happy, has infinite love. I cannot doubt but that God loves infinitely, properly speaking, and not only with that which some call self-love, whereby even the devils desire pleasure and are averse to pain; which is exceeding improperly called love, and is nothing at all akin to that affection or delight which is called love.

Then there must have been an object from all eternity which God infinitely loves. But we have showed that all love arises from the perception, either of consent to being in general, or consent to that being that perceives. Infinite loveliness, to God, therefore, must consist either in infinite consent to entity in general, or infinite consent to God. But we have shown that consent to entity and consent to God are the same, because God is the general and only proper entity of all things.[6] So that 'tis necessary that that object which God infinitely loves must be infinitely and perfectly consenting and agreeable to him; but that which infinitely and perfectly agrees is the very same essence, for if it be different it don't infinitely consent.

6. Here and in the preceding sentences of this paragraph JE is obviously building on the first addendum to "Excellency." See *Works, 6,* 336–37.

Again, we have shown that one alone cannot be excellent, inasmuch as, in such case, there can be no consent. Therefore, if God is excellent, there must be a plurality in God; otherwise, there can be no consent in him.[7]

118. RIGHTEOUSNESS OF CHRIST. By the law, the covenant made with man, that immutable covenant or eternal reason, Christ was obliged to suffer; and by the same law he was obliged to obey; and by the same law he, after he had taken man's guilt on him, could not be acquitted till he had suffered, nor rewarded till he had obeyed. But he was not acquitted as a private person, but as a head, and in his acquittance we are acquitted. And why then, should [he] be rewarded as a private person for his active obedience? Are not we accepted in his acceptance?

119. TYPES. The things of the ceremonial law are not the only things whereby God designedly shadowed forth spiritual things, but with an eye to such a representation were all the transactions of the life of Christ ordered. And very much of the wisdom of God in the creation appears in his so ordering things natural, that they livelily represent things divine and spiritual, [such as] sun, fountain, vine; as also, much of the wisdom of God in his providence, in that the state of mankind is so ordered, that there are innumerable things in human affairs that are lively pictures of the things of the gospel, such as shield, tower, and marriage, family.[8]

120. ANGELS. Doubtless the happiness of man before the fall, and of angels, consists most immediately in the enjoyment of the Son of God. The Father, it seems, communicates himself to them by the Son, as well as to fallen man; hence the manna, as it typified Christ, is called angels' food (Ps. 78:25). And the angels enjoy very glorious benefits by Christ's incarnation; 'tis a glorious benefit to all creatures that love God, that God is become a creature, in innumerable regards, as might be shown. The angels and saints make up but one family, though members of a different character; as in one royal house there is the queen, the children, the barons, etc. He is the head of all the rational creation; saints and angels are united in Christ, and have communion in him. Eph. 1:10, "That in the dispensation of the fullness of times, he might

7. JE here cites the third addendum to "Excellency" (ibid., 337).
8. MS: "such as shield tower / marriage family." This phrase and "sun, fountain, vine" above are later inserts.

gather together in one all things in Christ, both which are in heaven, and which are on earth."

Therefore, when the angels rejoiced so much at the birth of Christ, they did not merely rejoice in the happiness of another that they were no wise partakers in, but doubtless saw glorious things that accrued to them by it. They desire to look into those things, admiring at the bounty of God to them as well as to us, in coming so near to them as to become a rational creature like themselves. Yea, there is a kind of reconciliation, that is procured thereby for the angels by Christ's incarnation: for though there never was an alienation, yet there is a great distance between a God of infinite majesty and them; which would in some measure forbid that intimate enjoyment, and familiar fellowship, which so great love desires. But by God's thus coming down to the creature, everything is entirely reconciled to the natural propensity of most dear love. Col. 1:15–22,

> Who is the image of the invisible God, the firstborn of every creature. For by him were all things created, that are in heaven and that are in earth, visible and invisible, whether they be thrones, or dominions, or principalities, or powers; all things were created by him, and for him; and he is before all things, and by him all things consist. And he is the head of the body, the church, who is the beginning, the firstborn from the dead, that in all things he might have the preeminence. For it pleased the Father that in him should all fullness dwell; and, having made peace through the blood of his cross (that is, *between one creature and another,*[9] Eph. 2:14–16), by him to reconcile all things; by him, I say, whether they be things in earth or things in heaven. And you, that were sometime alienated and enemies in your mind by wicked works, yet now hath he reconciled.[1]

I Tim. 3:16, Christ "manifested in the flesh, seen of angels."

121. INCARNATION. Christ took the nature of a creature, not only because the creature's great love to him desired familiar communion with him, more familiar than his infinite distance would allow, but also because his great love to us caused him to desire familiar communion with us. So he came down to us, and united himself to our nature.

9. JE's italics.
1. JE did not quote the last verse of the passage (v. 22) but began a quotation of Eph. 4:10, which he immediately deleted. The fragmentary quotation of I Tim. 3:16 which follows is a later addition.

122. AFFLICTION. This is one way whereby the future happiness of saints is increased: happiness receives all its relish from a sense of the contrary; if it were not for this, joy would be dull and flat. Now this sense is obtained by a reflection on the miseries of this life, and looking on the torments of the damned. Wherefore, the greater the afflictions of this life were, the more sweet, *cæteris paribus,* will the heavenly happiness be.

123. SPIRITUAL SIGHT. When we explain spiritual things, that consist in mental motions energies and operations, though we give the most accurate descriptions possible we do not fully explain them, no, not so much as to give any manner of notion of them to one that never felt them; any more than we can fully explain the rainbow to one that never saw [it], though a rainbow is a very easy thing to give a definition of.

Thus, for instance, there is a certain sweet motion of the mind that I call benevolence. It's easily explained by general terms, circumstances, effects and objects, etc.; but yet the complex idea I have of benevolence consists chiefly of some simple ones, that are got only by the internal feeling and sense of the mind. Yea, these spiritual ideas are of such a nature, that a person that has once had them in the mind, having obtained them by actual sense, yet it may be impossible for him to bring the idea into his mind again distinctly, or indeed at all. We can't renew them when we please, as we can our ideas of colors and figures, but [only] at some times; and at no time,[2] except when [the] mind is particularly adapted to the reception of that idea. I can't have in my mind the idea of benevolence, except the disposition of my mind is something benevolent, or agreeable to that idea. At other times, I have only a general idea of it by the effects of it, to wit, that 'tis an inclination to another's happiness etc.; but those simple spiritual ideas, that are most essential and considerable in it, my mind is destitute of; and I have no more an idea of benevolence than a man has of a rainbow, that has lost the idea of the colors. So it is in the more complex spiritual ideas, as holiness, humility, charity; which include many of those simple spiritual ideas,[3] that are to the mind as color to the eye, not to be obtained by description.

2. MS: "at all times."

3. MS: "simple spirituals," doubtless an extreme case of abridgment. Locke's discussion of simple and complex ideas in the *Human Understanding,* Bk. II, chs. 1–12 (ed. Nidditch, pp. 104–66) underlies JE's argument. Cf. *Religious Affections,* where he calls spiritual perception "a new simple idea" (*Works,* 2, 205).

'Tis thus in all virtues. So that 'tis no wonder the wicked man sees not the amiableness of holiness, for he has not that idea that is expressed by the name of holiness. 'Tis not because their minds are not as apt to be delighted with harmony and proportion as others', but because they have not those ideas in which the sweet harmony consists; and it's impossible they should, because they never obtained them by internal sense and experience. The godly man's idea of God consists very much of these spiritual ideas, that are complicated of those simple ones which the natural man is destitute [of]. But as soon as ever he[4] comes to have the disposition of his mind changed, and to feel some of those operations of mind by means of which he gets those simple ideas, [then it is] that he sees the beauty of them; so he gets the sight of the excellency of holiness and of God. Though after this, when his mind is again indisposed, he will not be able to repeat those ideas; and [only] at some times, according as God makes the internal disposition of his mind more or less agreeable thereto, will he have ideas more or less clear.

Corol. 1. Hence we learn the reason, why regeneration is so often in Scripture compared to opening the eyes of the mind, to calling out of darkness into marvelous light, enlightening the dark understanding, etc.

Corol. 2. Why the things of the gospel seem all so tasteless and insipid to the natural man. They are a parcel of words to which they in their own minds have no correspondent ideas; 'tis like a strange language or a dead letter, that is, sounds and letters without any signification. This is the reason they commonly account religion such a foolish thing, and the saints fools. This is the reason the Scripture is no more sweet to them, and why the godly are called by the name of fanatics, and the like.

Corol. 3. Why spiritual knowledge is increased only by the practice of virtue and holiness. For we cannot have the idea without the adapted disposition of mind, and the more suitable the disposition the more clear and intense the idea; but the more we practice, the more is the disposition increased.

Corol. 4. From hence it necessarily follows, that the best and most able men in the world, with their greatest diligence and laboriousness, most eloquent speaking, clearest illustrations and convincing arguments, can do nothing towards the causing the knowledge of the things of the gospel; for the disposition, as we have shown, must necessarily be changed first.

4. I.e. the natural man.

124.[5] EXISTENCE OF GOD. There is just the same sort of knowledge of the existence of an universal mind in the world from the actions of the world, and what is done that is objected to our senses or that is effected by this mind, as there is of the existence of a particular mind in an human body from the observation of the actions of that, in gesture, look and voice. And there wants nothing but a comprehensive view, to take in the various actions in the world and look on them at one glance, and to see them in their mutual respects and relations, and these would as naturally, as quick, and with as little ratiocination, and more assuredly, intimate to us an universal mind, than human actions do a particular.

125[a]. GOD'S EXISTENCE. 'Tis certain with me that the world exists anew every moment, that the existence of things every moment ceases and is every moment renewed. For instance, in the existence of bodies, for there to be resistance, or tendency to some place; 'tis not numerically the same resistance that exists the next moment, 'tis evident, because this existence may be in different places. But yet this existence is continued so far, that there is respect had to it in all the future existences; 'tis evident in all things continually. Now past existence can't be continued so that respect should be had to it, otherwise than mentally. If the world this moment should be annihilated, so that nothing should really and actually exist any more; the existence of the world could not be continued so that, if another world after a time should be created, that world should exist after this or that manner from respect to the manner of the existence of this, or should be so only because this had been thus or thus. Indeed, we every moment see the same proof of a God as we should have seen, if we had seen [him] create the world at first. Rev. 4:11, "For thy pleasure they are and were created."[6]

'Tis only this way that respect can be had to existence distant as to place as well as time, but as much respect is had to distant existence in one sense, as in another.

125[b]. CHRISTIAN RELIGION. It seems exceeding proper and reasonable, that if God takes any care of human affairs (as I cannot doubt of, when I behold the nature he has given him, and the state that he has

---

5. Nos. 124, 125a, and 125b were probably written between Nos. 191 and 192.

6. The verse from Revelation was added by JE on a subsequent reading, probably some years afterwards.

placed him in), and seeing the whole world of mankind was so miserable blind and sottish, as 'tis certain they were before the appearance of Jesus—I say, it seems exceeding proper, that God should send some person to be a common instructor, savior and redeemer of mankind from that misery with which they had been overwhelmed for so many ages, and yet without prospect of remedy; 'twas so proper that some of the wise heathen expected it. Seeing the misery of mankind was so great, so universal, so settled and long continued, and without prospect of remedy; 'tis but exceeding reasonable to think that God would, some time or other, take some extraordinary method to help the world. But if this is not the method that God has taken, what is? What other method has ever attained the effect, to bring the world out of darkness into light? If this is not the person that was sent by God for the relief and instruction of mankind, who is? Or what indication have we, that there will ever any other extraordinary method be taken?

126. SPIRITUAL UNDERSTANDING OF THE SCRIPTURES. 'Tis what is remarkable, that the same persons reading the same portion of Scripture, at one time shall be greatly affected with it, and see what is astonishingly glorious in it, [what] shall seem wonderful with respect to the things expressed, the pertinency and pithiness of the expression, admirable majesty, coherence, and harmony; and at another time shall seem insipid, mean, impertinent, and inconsistent.

The reason is the same mentioned in No. 123, that the mind has those ideas at one time, with which the Bible harmonizes, which cannot be called into the mind at another. At one time, the mind has those ideas of things spiritual, and therefore perceives what agrees and harmonizes with it; and if anything be mentioned that is congruous and harmonious to it, the mind feels it immediately and echoes to it: it sees wherein the agreement is, and how it naturally falls in with it. And at such a time the soul, as soon as it looks into God's Word and sees a thing spiritual of which it has an idea, there mentioned, and reads the dependent passages, it sees that there is an exact correspondency, and that things consent in the same manner. But at another, when he has not the ideas themselves in his mind, 'tis no wonder that he can see no agreement. Supposing he is reading of Christian charity; if he has no idea in his mind of it, 'tis no wonder if he don't feel the correspondency, consent and naturalness of the expressions used about it. When the mind is affected with a thing much, it is led into such schemes of thought about [it] as, if they were written down, would seem very

impertinent to one that was not affected—'tis so in all matters; the
Scripture falls in with the natural stream of one's thoughts, when one[7]
is affected with the things of which it speaks, but is very wide of their
series of thoughts who are not affected.

For instance, the text that says, "One generation passeth away, and
another cometh; but the earth abideth forever" [Eccles. 1:14]. This, to
one in a common frame of mind, seems insipid; the latter part of the
verse seems impertinently to be brought in, as what very little tends to
illustrate the former. The thought of the earth being the same does
not seem very naturally and affectingly to fall in after the thought of
one generation passing and another coming. What is it to the purpose,
whether the earth remains the same or no? This makes not the change
of the inhabitants either more or less affecting. But yet, when upon an
occasion I was more than ordinarily affectd with the passingness of
one generation after another, how that all those who made such a
noise and bluster now, and were so much concerned about their life,
would be clean gone off from the face of the earth in sixty or seventy
years' time, and that the world would be left desolate with respect to
them, and that another generation would come on that would be very
little concerned about them, and so one after another; it was particularly affecting to me, to think that the earth still remained the same
through all those changes upon the surface, the same spots of ground,
the same mountains and valleys where those things were done remaining just as they were, though the actions were ceased and the actors
quite gone—and then this text came into my mind.

Corol. 1. Hence we learn, in what sense the Word of God is said to be
written in the hearts of believers. There is that disposition of the mind,
that when it comes to be put forth into action, raises such a series and
succession of thoughts, as sweetly corresponds and harmonizes with
the expressions of God's Word.

Corol. 2. Hence we learn, how places of Scripture are often suddenly
brought into the mind, which were almost forgotten perhaps, before;
the motions that are then in the mind being so exactly agreeable
thereto, that if there be any footsteps of it in the memory, it will bring
them before the mind. So that the Spirit of God don't immediately
suggest the places to us, as though by inspiration, but by stirring up
correspondent affections of mind, whereby the mind is naturally put
in mind of the text that is so agreeable to it; as much as one speech or

7. MS: "it."

sentence puts us in mind of another that is like it, or as one instrument of music answers of itself to another in harmony and concord.

127. CHRISTIAN RELIGION. I suppose 'twill be acknowledged by the deists, that the Christian religion is the most rational, pure and congruous religion that is or ever was established in any society of men whatsoever—and will except only themselves, that serve God more according to his will! But can any believe, that God has so wholly thrown away mankind, that he has not so ordered it, that there [should] ever yet be any service or obedience paid to him in society but what is odious to him, and very dissonant to his will? that there [should] never yet be a society of men, that have rightly paid respect to their Creator and the Supreme Being? yea, so that there should not be (if any) not above twenty or thirty from the beginning of the world, that ever gave the true sort of service to God? For I believe it will not be pretended, that there were ever more deists in the world [than that], that lived pure and moral lives according to the dictates of reason.

'Tis easily provable, that the highest end and happiness of men is to view God's excellency, to love him and receive expressions of his love; and that therefore their[8] greatest business is to meditate [on] and use means to understand God's bounty, and to express suitably their love; this love including all those other affections which depend upon it and are necessarily connected with it, which we call worship. The highest end of society, therefore, must be to assist and join with each other in this. But how comes it to pass, that this end of society was never yet obtained? When was any social worship performed by deists? And if there should be a society of deists that were disposed socially to express their love to God, and honor of him, which way would they go to work? They have nothing from God to direct them. Doubtless there would be innumerable jangles about [it] and eternal dissensions, except they were all resolved to fall in with the Christian model. We may be therefore convinced, that revelation is necessary in order to right social worship.

128. CHRISTIAN RELIGION. There never was any religion but that which we profess, and those that have formed from it, that ever pretended to let us into the nature of God; or told us that there was but one God; or gave an account of God's works, how the world came into

8. MS: "his."

being, and how God governs it; or tells us anything of God's great designs; or tells us what is God's will and how he will be served; and declares the reward of obedience and punishment of disobedience, the nature of man's happiness, his end, and what he was made for; that gives us good moral rules; or tells us what will become of the world hereafter; that explains to us how we came to be sinful and miserable, and how we may escape sin and misery and be redeemed; that gives an account of the great revolutions of the world, and the successions of God's works in the universe, and where his true worshipers have been all along, and what has befallen them; [or] told how the world came to apostatize from the true worship of God; the only religion that ever pretended that there should a time come, wherein it would be the religion of the world in general.

129. CHRISTIAN RELIGION. The Jewish religion as at present professed, 'tis most certain, differs from what reason evidently declares to be the essence of religion; does not state the highest end and happiness [of man], his chief business, and his greatest misery, and the pure worship of God, right. Undoubtedly the Messiah was to come, to advance the best interest and true happiness of mankind; which certainly consists in what the gospel declares our Jesus advanced, and not in what the Jews expect their Messiah will do. The Messiah undoubtedly was to be our king in our highest and most important concerns, was to be our deliverer from our greatest evils and enemies; which all must confess to be such concerns as the gospel says Christ was exercised in. And it is also certain, if this is the chief business of the Messiah, he does not carry it on by an external earthly government; the saving us from sin, the making us holy and spiritually happy, and bringing of us into the favor of God, is not advanced by such means. And I will say further, 'tis evident it could be done no otherwise than by satisfying God and interceding with him; by giving precepts, promises and threatenings; by immediately changing the heart; by restraining and conquering the invisible spirits that are hurtful to our spirits.

Revelation may be argued, not only from the necessity we have of it, by reason of the darkness we have contracted by the fall, [but also from the end of our creation]; for seeing man is created for that end [for] which he certainly is, it is a strange thing that there should be no mutual communication between him and God.

130. PELAGIANISM. That there should be an immediate operation of God's Spirit upon the hearts of the godly, to beget and exercise grace,

seems much the most reasonable to me. For seeing man is made for such an end that his business is wholly with God, seeing he is made for nothing but to pay respects to and receive from God, it seems very incongruous to me, that the world should be left altogether without immediate communications from God.

131. CHRISTIAN RELIGION. I think it certain that, seeing the miracles of Christ were done for three years and an half so publicly all over Judea, and seeing there was such dreadful opposition in Judea so soon after against the Christians; if the matters of fact had been false, they would have been denied by the Jews generally. And if they had been, we should have known of it. The Jews afterwards would much more have denied them,[9] which 'tis evident they did not. If they had,[1] they would have been denied by the heathens that writ against the Christians; but they were not.

'Tis impossible that the whole world should turn Christian in three hundred years after the facts were so publicly done, if they had been generally false, and it should never once be suspected or objected. If the Jews had denied [the] matters of fact at first, they would undoubtedly have denied them at this day,[2] seeing they are so tenacious of the traditions of their fathers. Christ was made the most public that possibly could be, within a few days after his death, on the day of Pentecost. 'Tis undoubted that the number of Christians increased everywhere exceedingly from that time, so that within a little while there was a considerable alteration made in the face of the world by it; whether the matters of fact were written or no, 'tis undoubted they were universally talked of. The conversion of the Roman Empire to the Christian religion was the most remarkable thing that ever happened amongst the nations of the world, and 'tis strange it should be done upon the story of a few obscure men, without inquiring into matters related.

And 'twould be a very strange thing, if the Old Testament religion was true, that there should be no prophecies of it there; especially when almost [all] the other great and general changes of the nations thereabouts, though far less remarkable, were foretold. And it is no wonder that there should be prophecies of so great a change amongst the heathen, as in the Sibylline books,[3] etc.

9. MS: "it." JE is referring to "the matters of fact," not to the Jews' denial of them.
1. I.e. if the Jews afterwards had denied them.
2. I.e. 300 years later.
3. The words "as in the Sibylline books" were heavily canceled, indeed almost obliterated, by JE, Jr., so that the reading of the first two words is not entirely certain.

132 (*147*).[4] CHRISTIAN RELIGION. I am convinced that God is willing to be reconciled to man, and has a design to advance him to the happiness he was created for, by the tokens of his good will in the creation and common providence; and that he therefore would give us those advantages, which are necessary to a holy life and salvation. And I am convinced of the necessity of a revelation, by considering how negligent, dull and careless I should be, if there were no revelation about a future happiness but I was left to work it out by unassisted reason; especially if there were no revelation at all about what is pleasing to God, how he accepts it, after what manner he loves his servants, how he will pardon sin, etc.

133 (*148*). NEW HEAVEN AND NEW EARTH. With relation to what was said upon the two last chapters of Revelation.[5] Another confirmation that this will be without the visible world, or in the highest heavens (which is the same thing), is that it is reasonable to conclude that seeing the sun and moon shall not be seen, that neither the stars will; for certainly they will have no need of stars, either for ornament, to give light, or measure time, if not of sun or moon. And besides, there are many places of Scripture that really do imply a final departure of the stars, as well as sun and moon; so that the heavens shall be new in all regards. Doubtless those heavens here spoken of, that flee away, include the stars, or principal part of them, and what are chiefly observable in them. And there is the same reason for not particularly speaking of this new heaven and new earth being in a new place, as there is why this earth in Scripture is not spoken of as in a different place in summer from what it is in winter; for it is in the same regard in a different place, wherein this may be said so to be. And there is no more reason for the representing Christ and his church moving, and the visible world standing, than for representing the visible heavens standing, and the earth moving.

Corol. We learn from hence how the heavens will be rolled together

4. While the text runs continuously from No. 132 to No. 156, JE numbered the entries 147–156, 132–146 and never corrected the error. These entries are here printed in the order of composition, and the first numeral before each entry indicates its place in that order. JE's numeral follows within parentheses and in italics. The numbering of these entries has been corrected in JE's Table and cross-references, and the corrected numbering is used in the Introduction and notes.

5. The note to which JE refers is "Apocalypse" no. 41 (*Works*, 5, 140–42). There is also another brief note on chs. 21 and 22 in "Apocalypse" to which JE appended a reference to "Miscellanies" No. 133 (ibid., 5, 124).

as a scroll; for according to this explication, the fixed stars and all the stars will be rolled together on one side in an heap, before they are out of sight.

134 (*149*). BEING OF GOD. 'Tis evident that none of the creatures, none of the beings that we behold, are the first principle of their own action; but all alterations follow, in a chain, other alterations. Now therefore, there must necessarily be something in itself active, so as that it is the very first beginning of its own action; or some necessary being, that has been the cause of all the rest: which cannot be matter, as is evident from the nature of matter.

135 (*150*). DEITY. Many have[6] wrong conceptions of the difference between the nature of the Deity and created spirits. The difference is no contrariety, but what naturally results from his greatness and nothing else, such as created spirits come nearer to, or more imitate, the greater they are in their powers and faculties. So that if we should suppose the faculties of a created spirit to be enlarged infinitely, there would be the Deity to all intents and purposes, the same simplicity, immutability, etc.

136 (*151*). IMMORTALITY. The souls of beasts (as we are forced to call 'em, whatever they are), there is no manner of need of a miracle to annihilate them when the body of beasts is destroyed, any more than everything in nature is done by a miracle; for they are all done by the immediate exertion of divine power, with only this difference, that some are done according to a constant law, and others not. So that if it be the constant law of God, according to harmony, that that principle in beasts should cease with their bodies, what need this be accounted a miracle? If we can (as we do in many cases), and as we may with respect to man's soul, show that this[7] does not harmonize with other things in the nature of beasts' bodies and spirits, and laws in other things; we may conclude, it is not according to the established law that they should cease.

137 (*152*). HEAVEN. The saints in heaven will doubtless eternally exercise themselves in contemplation; they will not want employ this

---

6. MS: "~~We are apt to~~ ⟨many⟩ have"; the change was made later, in ink like that of Nos. 152 ff.

7. I.e. that man's soul should cease with his body.

way. Not in exercising[8] their thoughts and study upon intricacies and seeming repugnancies, to unfold them and discover truth further and further that way, as it is here; but by viewing in their minds one thing after another, as they will naturally be led and sweetly drawn by love and delight, and with such intenseness as the natural bent of their heart will cause. Their sight shall reach further and further, and new things shall [be] plainly present to their minds without the mixture of any error. 'Tis error always from whence intricacy proceeds, and seeming repugnance; and not from ignorance.

The object of their thought shall be the glory of God; which they shall contemplate in the creation in general, in the wonderful make of it, particularly of the highest heavens, and in the wonders of God's providence. It shall most clearly and delightfully be manifested in the church of saints and angels; which they shall discover more and more by their conversation, assisting one another to discoveries in other things; and, most of all mediate ways, in the man Christ Jesus. They shall employ themselves in singing God's praise, or expressing their thoughts to God and Christ, and also to one another; and in going from one part of heaven to another, to behold the glories of God shining in the various parts of it.

138 (*153*). SPIRIT. I, for my part, am convinced of an immediate communication between the Spirit of God and the soul of a saint; because when a person is in the most excellent frame, most lively exercise of virtue, love to God and delight in him, he naturally and unavoidably thinks of God as kindly communicating himself to him, and holding such a manner of communion with [him], as much as if he saw God smiling on him, giving to him, and conversing with him. Yea, if he did not so think of God, 'twould greatly quell his holy motions of soul. But I cannot think that the greatest exercise of virtue naturally leads into such an error, or that the life of virtue depends so much on an error; and [I cannot think but] that virtue would not incline a man so much to such ideas, were it not that they are most congruous and harmonious. For when a man has the liveliest sense of the spiritual world, he sees best what is congruous to the spiritual world.

139 (*154*). DIFFICULTIES IN RELIGION. I am convinced that there are many things in religion and the Scriptures that are made difficult on

---

8. I.e. "They will not exercise," as JE first wrote before deciding to recast his sentence.

purpose to try men, and to exercise their faith and scrutiny, and to hinder the proud and self-sufficient; by many of Christ's speeches upon earth, which gave great offense and were very much of a stumbling block, which yet he could easily have explained. Yea, he himself gives this account of the matter.

140 (*155*). CHRISTIAN RELIGION. 'Tis certain that Jesus Christ had none of the advantages of education, to get learning and knowledge; and 'tis also certain that everywhere in his speeches he showed an uncommon insight into things, a great knowledge of the true nature of virtue and morality, and what was most acceptable to God, vastly beyond common men, vastly beyond the rest of the nation, take scribes and Pharisees and all. And how came he by it? How did he get it at Nazareth? Those who have not an education in these days may get much by books, which are so common, but books of learning were not to be had then. Yea 'tis evident, that he knew vastly more than any of the philosophers and wise men in the whole world, by those rational descriptions of God and his attributes, and of his government and providence, and of man's nature, business, end and happiness. How came he to be able to tell so exactly about the immortality of the soul and a future state (what is now demonstrable by reason but was never found out before), and also what was truly pleasing to God? How came all his doctrines to be so very rational, such as the resurrection, the day of judgment, God's absolute decrees and predestination, original sin, reconciliation by the death of the Son of God, [justification] by faith of mere grace, regeneration, etc.?

141 (*156*). SPIRITUAL UNDERSTANDING. 'Tis doubtless true that holiness of heart doth of its own nature and tendency, considered abstractedly from any immediate guidance of the Holy Spirit, keep men from errors in judgment about religion and directs them to truth; and that holiness is as a touchstone whereby they try doctrines; and that they have a distinguishing taste and relish, more and more perfect as they have more holiness. The reason is, that as the sanctified mind is let into the spiritual world, or has those ideas (not only those judgments) as we have shown [No. 123], which an unsanctified mind is not capable of, or is easily receptive of those ideas, and has them the more clear the more holy [it is]; it easily perceives what ideas are harmonious and what not. For nothing else is requisite in order to seeing the proportion of ideas but clearness, or having the ideas themselves clear; but the holy mind

does, and safely may, reject for false everything in divinity that is not harmonious. The soul distinguishes as a musical ear; and besides, holiness itself consists in spiritual harmony; and whatever don't agree with that, as a base to a treble, the soul rejects.

Corol. As harmony in the mind will keep it from embracing unharmonious spiritual things, so will an embracing things generally and notably unharmonious, so as to lead the mind in the general into an unharmonious scheme, effectually keep harmony or holiness out of the mind, for it keeps the run and series of thought unharmonious; and as long as the action of the mind is kept so, the disposition will not be harmonious. Then, therefore, the man errs fundamentally.

142 (*132*).[9] DIVINITY OF CHRIST. The expression of "Son of God," only that, as it is used κατ' 'εξοκήν (in the highest and most eminent sense) as his most distinguishing character, fully implies Christ's divinity; for what can be the Son of God, but God of God? What is the "son of man," in the proper sense, but man of man? Can we believe that this Son of God is of a nature infinitely inferior to the Father? Would he then be so properly called the Son of God? for the difference is infinitely greater than between an earthly father and the newborn infant. We don't call an effect produced of vastly another nature from the efficient, a son, and apply sonship to it as its[1] perpetual and distinguishing character.

143 (*133*). TRINITY. Corollary to a former meditation of the Trinity.[2] [*1.*] Hence we see how generation by the Father and yet coeternity with the Father, or being begotten and yet being eternal, are consistent. For it is easy to conceive how this image, this thought, reason or wisdom of God, should be eternally begotten by him, and begotten by him from eternity and continually through eternity; and so how the Holy Spirit, that personal energy, the divine love and delight, eternally and continually proceeds from both.

Corol. 2. Hence we see how and in what sense the Father is the fountain of the Godhead, and how naturally and properly God the Father is spoken of in Scripture as of the Deity without distinction, as

9. See above, No. 132, p. 294, n. 4.
1. MS: "his."
2. JE left space for the number but never filled it. There are four previous entries on the Trinity; JE is thinking of the first and fundamental essay, No. 94.

being the only true God; and why God the Son should commonly [be] spoken of with a distinction, and be called the Son of God; and so the Holy Spirit, the Spirit of God.

Remember to look, the next time I have the opportunity of [doing so], to see if "spirit" in Scripture phrase is not commonly put for affections and never for understanding; and to show that there is no other affection in God but love to himself.[3]

144 (*134*). TRINITY. The Son, we know, in Scripture is often represented as being the light and refulgency of the Father, as if he were the luminary and the Son, his light or brightness, proceeding from him; so he is said to be "the brightness of his glory" [Heb. 1:3]. So in Rev. 21:23 and 22:5, the Father is spoken of as being him from whom the light of the new Jerusalem proceeded, or he that gives the light; the Son, the light itself that proceeded from him. Now what else is the light of a mind than its wisdom, its reason, its logos, thought, or idea? Now this is much more properly spoken of as light proceeding from the infinite mind, than the thought or understanding [as] the light proceeding from a finite mind; for this is as a light let into a finite mind, but the light or understanding of the divine mind originally proceeds from this mind itself and is derived from no other.

145 (*135*). DIVINITY OF CHRIST. See No. 142. And no doubt but that Christ is called the Son of God in the same sense wherein he so frequently calls himself the Son of man; by which, it is evident, he principally intended to denote his being one of mankind, as partaking [of] the nature of man. This the manner of his speaking of it, and the like manner of expressions in the Hebrew tongue, make manifest.

146 (*136*). TRINITY.[4] The word "spirit," most commonly in Scripture, is put for affections of the mind; but there is no other affection in God essentially, properly and primarily, but love and delight—and that in himself, for into this is his love and delight in his creatures resolvable.

I don't remember that any other attributes are said to be God, and

---

3. JE set about the task soon afterwards, for No. 146 was written in partial fulfillment of the memorandum and No. 157 continued the investigation.

4. See the preceding note.

God to be them, but λόγος and ἀγάπη, or reason and love; I conclude, because no other are in that (a personal) sense.

I think that in the 4th chapter of I John, in which we are twice told that God is love, it is intimated to us that this love is the Holy Spirit, in the 12th and 13th verses; they are these: "No man hath seen God at any time. If we love one another, God dwelleth in us, and his love is perfected in us. Hereby know we that we dwell in him, and he in us, because he hath given us of his Spirit." We are often told in Scripture, in what sense it is that God dwells in believers, even by his Spirit; they are the temples of God, in that they are the temples of the Holy Ghost. So here also we are told in what sense God dwells in us, in the first of these verses, viz. in that love dwells in us; which is explained in the next verse (which is evidently exegetical of the foregoing), that God dwells in us because the Holy Spirit dwells in us. And again, in the 16th verse, we are told that God dwells in us because love dwells in us, which is God; it runs thus, "And we have known and believed the love that God hath to us. God is love; and he that dwelleth in love dwelleth in God, and God in him." We may compare these with the 23rd and 24th verses of the 3rd chapter, "And this is his commandment, that we should believe on the name of his Son Jesus Christ, and love one another, as he gave us commandment. And he that keepeth his commandments dwelleth in him, and he in him. And hereby we know that he abideth in us, by the Spirit which he hath given us." Certainly this refers to the love whereby we keep his commandments.

147 (*137*). INFUSED GRACE. I suppose it will not be denied by any party of Christians, that the happiness of the saints in the other world consists chiefly in perfect holiness and the exalted exercises of it; and that the souls of saints shall enter upon this happinesss at once at death, or (if any deny that) at least at the resurrection, that the saint is made perfectly holy as soon as ever he enters into heaven. And I suppose none will say this perfection is obtained by repeated acts of holiness, but [will grant that it] is wrought in the saints immediately by the power of God, and yet that it is virtue notwithstanding.

And why are not the beginnings of holiness wrought in the same manner? Why should not the beginnings of a holy nature be wrought immediately by God in a soul that is wholly of a contrary nature, as well as holiness be perfected in a soul that has already a prevailing holiness? And if it be so, why is not the beginning, thus wrought, as much virtue as the perfection thus wrought?

148 (*138*). CREATION. Relating to a former.[5] The Father also created the world, as well as the Son, as we know; and he did it for his Son. The Scripture is plain in that, that the world and the church are a gift of the Father to the Son.

149 (*139*). NEW EARTH. The beauty of the bodies of saints in the new earth, the new Jerusalem, shall not only consist in the most charming proportion of features and parts of their bodies, and their light and proportion of colors, but much in the manifestation of the excellencies of their mind; which exceeding readily will appear in their bodies, the bodies being more easily and naturally susceptive and manifestative of the affections and dispositions of the mind, than here. 'Twill consist very much in the air of their actions and speech, and cast of their countenance, denoting the greatest wisdom and prudence and purity of mind; and such as will naturally result from an inexpressible sweetness, the greatest benevolence and complacence, and the highest joy. The manner and air of that bright and yet not dazzling light, which shall flow from their faces, shall also denote those dispositions of mind.

150 (*140*). DIVINITY OF CHRIST. How can Christ be said to be such an "express image" [of God (Heb. 1:3)], as long as he is in many respects infinitely otherwise than God is? May we not believe reasonably, that inasmuch [as] he is said to be his Son and image, that he is his Son and image in the same regard, as the son that Adam [begot] in his own image was his son and image; that is, one proceeding from him, of the same kind with himself? See . . .[6]

151 (*141*). TRINITY. See . . .[7] I believe that Jesus Christ not only is exactly in the image of [God], but in the most proper sense *is* the image of God. Now however exactly one being, suppose of one human body, [is] like another; yet, I think, one is not in the most proper sense the

5. As in No. 143, JE failed to fill in the space he had left for the numeral. His reference is to No. 104, particularly corol. 3. No. 108 also expresses the idea that the Son created the world.

6. JE wrote "vid." and left space on the line but never completed the reference. There is a relatively long passage in No. 94 (above, pp. 259–60) treating the Son as the "express image" of the Father; JE is probably thinking of this, and possibly also of No. 142 or No. 145, where divine and human sonship are compared with respect to community of nature.

7. Again, there is a short unfilled space for the number. The content of the first paragraph suggests that No. 94 contains the discussion JE has in mind (see the preceding footnote). It is unlikely that Nos. 150 and 151 were meant to cite each other, for if so JE would almost certainly have written "vid. the next" and "vid. the last" instead of leaving spaces for numbers.

image of the other, but more properly *in* the image of the other. Adam did not beget a son that was his image properly, but in his image: but the idea of a thing is, in the most proper sense of all, its image; and God's idea, the most perfect image.

From an obscure notion of the truth, got from the Jews or by tradition from the antediluvians, I believe that opinion of the heathens to be, who asserted that all things owed their beginning and production to love; [which is] a shadow of the truth, that the Spirit of God moved upon the face of the waters. And further they say, God was moved to create the world, by the love of his own principle. God's love to himself, that is, to his Son, I suppose to be the Holy Spirit.

152 (*142*). CHRISTIAN RELIGION. That Christ was really dead appears, inasmuch as 'tis not to be imagined that in such a death as is caused merely by pain, all the exercise of life and vital action should be gone before life itself (as it may be in convulsions and some stupifying diseases), especially considering how leisurely his death was. And if he was not dead when they came to him, doubtless he was almost dead; and the piercing of his side would undoubtedly quite have dispatched him. And it is very unreasonable to imagine that he feigned himself dead. For what reason had he to think he should have success if he did, or to expect they would take him down before he was quite dead? Or if he had had such a design, such an intolerable condition would have banished all intrigues out of his thoughts; or if he had them still in his thoughts, 'twas not possible that he shall have the power of himself so well, when he was so weakened by pain and the loss of blood, and every nerve in his body was so wracked with torment, and he almost dead, life struggling with death—I say, 'twas impossible he should act his part so accurately as not to be discovered or suspected. Besides, if he was not dead when they took him from the cross, he was very near it; and no doubt but his grievous wounds, and the loss of most of his blood, and fasting so long, he would have died before the third day.

And if then he only rose out of a swoon, how came he perfectly sound at once? Where did he get his blood again so suddenly, as to be as strong and hearty as ever? How came [the] wounds in his hands, feet and side to heal up at once? Surely one would have thought that his feet were so lame that he could not walk on them. Doubtless his hands and feet were much torn, by bearing his weight so long upon iron spikes drove through them. And if he rose from the dead in no supernatural sense, where did he go when he rose? What became of him? We have no account of his dying again; nor was he yet to be found after a few weeks.

153 (*143*). HEAVEN. In the future world, the saints' love one to another will be such, that it will be a very delightful consideration to them that Christ Jesus dearly loves the other saints; and it will fill them with joy to see him manifesting his love to them. They, again, shall see the other saints rejoicing that Christ loves and delights in them.[8]

Singing is amiable, because of the proportion that is perceived in it; singing in divine worship is beautiful and useful, because it expresses and promotes the harmonious exercise of the mind. There will doubtless, in the future world, be that which, as it will be an expression of an immensely greater and more excellent harmony of the mind, so will be a far more lively expression of this harmony; and shall itself be vastly more harmonious, yea, than our air or ears, by any modulation, is capable of. Which expressions, and the harmony thereof, shall be sensible, and shall far more lively strike our perception than sound.

154 (*144*). DIVINITY OF CHRIST. 'Tis a good argument for Christ's divinity, that he is to be the author of the resurrection. The atoms and particles in one little finger are capable of so many removes and such dispersions, that I believe it would surpass any finite understanding, at two or three thousand years' end, to tell what distinct particles of the universe belonged to it. It would require a vast strength and subtlety of mind, to trace but one atom so nicely as to know the individual atom in the universe after so long a time; after it had been a particle of air, water, oil or animal spirit, or an effluvium, etc., and had been transported with prodigious swiftness from place to place, backwards and forwards, millions of times in a third minute,[9] amongst innumerable others of the same kind. Especially would it be exceeding difficult, so narrowly to watch two of such at once. If so, what would it be, to follow every atom in a man's body, yea, of all the bodies that ever have died or shall die; [and] at the same time to have the mind exercised with full vigor upon innumerable other matters that require an equal strength of understanding—and all this with such ease, that it shall be no labor to the mind!

8. I.e. the saints first mentioned.
9. At this point JE wrote, then deleted, the following words: "as those particles which cause heat, 'tis probable, are."

155 (*145*). Resurrection. For the same reason why it is said, that it was impossible that Christ's body should be held by death, being a part of Christ; it is also impossible that the bodies of his saints should be held by death, because they are parts of believers, and have such a relation to the souls of the saints, who are members of Christ. It clearly appears that the bodies of believers are taken into union with Christ and have to do in gospel benefits, inasmuch as they are called the temples of the Holy Ghost, as well as the persons; and this is given as a reason why we should not defile them. We are not to think that the temple of the Holy Ghost will always lie in ruins.

156. (*146*).[1] Satan Defeated. See in Natural Philosophy:[2]

'Twas the dignity of our nature that was greatly envied by Satan; and that which particularly galled him [was] that man, who was of an earthly original, should be advanced to such honors when he, who was of [an] heavenly, and of so great strength and knowledge, should be cast down to such dishonor. His haughtiness and pride, which made [him] aspire to divine honor, could not bear that, that this new, meanly born race should be made so much of and come in their room! And oh, how may we conclude Satan triumphed when he had brought 'em down! How did he as it were laugh, to think how sorrowfully they found themselves disappointed in their expectations of coming to higher honor and being like gods. But their fall has been the occasion of their being advanced to much greater dignity than before, brought much nearer to God, far more nearly united to him, [and] are become his members, his spouse, and in many respects more honored than the angels. This very thing which Satan triumphed about, of their becoming like gods, is come to pass, and Satan's temptation is turned into a prophecy. This very act of Satan has been the occasion of bringing about the very thing, the destruction of which he therein aimed at, and that in higher degrees.

God's strange dealings with mankind after the fall, especially relating to the Israelites, made him suspect God intended some such thing; but he was more confirmed in it when he saw such a wonderful person as Jesus Christ appear in the world; when he perceived many proph-

1. This is the last in the series of entries (Nos. 132–156) misnumbered by JE; see above, No. 132, p. 294, n. 4.

2. See *Works*, 6, 265, n. 2. JE wrote an essay on Satan in the philosophy notebook and did not discover the mistake until afterwards. His note at the beginning of No. 156 means in effect to incorporate the essay into the "Miscellanies." The essay is printed here as the first part of No. 156.

ecies aimed at, he suspected that some great thing would certainly now be done. All hell was in fear that all that he had done would now be brought to naught, and mankind would some way or other by this man be restored. And now, how did all hell set their wits to work to destroy this man; and when it was brought to pass, how did all those spirits triumph again! But how soon did they see that they had again brought about the very thing they feared, when they began to see mankind advanced to a far higher pitch of glory than he[3] by his means had fallen from; when he begins to see them made like gods, and that he himself had been the occasion of it, first in tempting them to fall, and again in bringing about the death of Christ.

And what a consternation were all the devils in when they saw the gospel, this new doctrine, begin to spread so fast in the world; against which they had made no preparations, it being what they never in the least suspected, that the preaching of this death of Christ should be a means of saving the world. With what regret did the devil see it go on spreading and conquering irresistibly, notwithstanding all that he could do, with more regret than the inhabitants see their city and substance consuming by raging flames which they cannot quench. How suddenly had Satan the grief to see the world wrenched out of his hands, and in spite of all his persecutions, in three hundred years become Christian.[4]

Satan doubtless knew of the Messiah's coming into the world, and could by the prophecies guess pretty near at the time of it. And though he did not know what to make of him, being much confounded by the strange descriptions of him in the Old Testament, yet he expected he would be a person of wondrous wisdom and superlative excellency, and that he was to do wonderful things, and by some means overthrow his kingdom in the world. And 'tis probable, he thought that he was to conquer all the heathen world and to reign over them in great glory here on earth, as well as to bring them off from heathenism to the true religion and holiness, one in order to the other; this appears to be his expectation, by his temptation on the high mountain.

And against this he made great preparation; in this, he thought, he would be beforehand with him, knowing nearly the time of his coming. His contrivance was, to be a means of setting up some other monarch of the heathen world, and making of him exceeding potent

3. I.e. mankind; the next "his" refers to Satan.
4. The text of No. 156 begins with the next paragraph.

and strong, and to get the world into his possession; so that he might be able, with his great power, wealth and immense numbers, having all the world on his side, to resist the Messiah when he came: which he thought he had effectually brought to pass in the Roman monarchy, the kingdom of iron, by far the most potent that ever was. Hereby he thought to disappoint the Messiah in his design of conquering the world. For what could he, and his little handful of Jews, do against Caesar, with the strength of the whole world? Yea, Satan succeeded so well that he got the Roman monarchy thoroughly settled, against the time that he thought Christ was to come. The world began to be easy under the Roman government, insomuch that there was an universal peace at the time; and the power and strength of the empire was at its highest pitch under Augustus. Thus Satan contrived it, to prevent the kingdom of the Messiah.

But thus God contrived [it] on purpose, to make way for Christ's kingdom and the spreading of the gospel through the world. This very thing, chiefly, rendered the time the fittest for Christ's appearing of any that ever had been; this was the fullness of time. Hereby the world became one body; which was a vast advantage to the quick propagating of the gospel through the whole. How much would the preaching of the gospel by the apostles [have] been disadvantaged, if the Roman Empire had been divided into so many kingdoms as it was a thousand years before, that had so little knowledge of or commerce with one another. The world being one body, what was done in one part was quickly known in another, there being a continual communication between all the parts; what is remarkable in one part is easily and quickly known in another; what is received in one part, by reason of the continual intercourse, is soon communicated. The knowledge of the Jewish nation, their Scriptures, their customs and religion, was the more universal, they being a part of the empire; the Jews themselves, and the Scriptures in the Septuagint, by this means were scattered all over the world. By this means the miracles, resurrection, and matters of fact of Christ and of the apostles were abundantly the more public, those things being public to all nations which otherwise would have been but to one; as appears by those numbers that were at Jerusalem on the day of Pentecost. Hereby the apostles' traveling from one country to another was facilitated. They were still under the same government, wherever they went; were not put to those difficulties nor subject to those dangers, as they would have been [had] they traveled through strange kingdoms. They could more easily write from one part of the world to another, there being continually persons passing and repassing. They had the more frequent opportunities to go by water from place to place. Different nations came to an understanding of each other's languages, and many in all nations understood the same languages. Arts and sciences and thoughtfulness, which before were chiefly confined to Greece, were made universal. To all these, the peace the empire enjoyed very much contributed.

How miserably therefore was Satan disappointed, when he saw the kingdom was not of such a nature as to be propagated or resisted by force of arms, but by preaching the word of God and the declaration of the gospel; which all that he had been doing promoted instead of preventing.

157. TRINITY. The name of the Holy Ghost denotes this another way.[5] The Spirit of God is the same with the breath of God, or what God breathes. Now what are so properly said to be the breathings of the soul, as its affections? It's evident, that it's most natural to call those its breathings, inasmuch as nature has led men to agree upon the similitude, whereby to represent the exercise of (especially, holy) affections.

158. KINGDOM OF CHRIST.[6] It seems probable there will be a time wherein the gospel will prevail so far, as to be a very great defeat and glorious disappointment of Satan in his design of making man miserable. His ends in tempting mankind were, to deprive of holiness and happiness, and to bring into sin and misery. 'Tis probable he will [be] disappointed this way, by the fall's being an occasion of more happiness to mankind in general, than he[7] otherwise would have had.

Now in order to know whether there be less misery and more happiness considered jointly, we must not only consider whether there be more happiness to man than otherwise there would have been; for may be, and yet Satan may in some measure obtain this design of

5. See No. 146, of which this entry is apparently a continuation, and also the memorandum at the end of No. 143.

6. This entry is entered in the Table only under "Millennium"; see above, No. 68, p. 236, n. 3. Its content links it with No. 156 and the "Satan Defeated" essay in "Natural Philosophy"; the three pieces were written about the same time and were all carefully revised and punctuated by JE. Since the main ideas in No. 158 continued to be part of JE's thinking, the vertical line through the middle of the entry probably indicates no more than dissatisfaction with the form of its argument, which is negative and incomplete; it may mean that the material was copied into another place for further development.

7. I.e. mankind.

making mankind miserable, for there may be more happiness and yet as much more misery, so as to counterbalance it. For though there were but few saved, yet their happiness might be so great that, jointly considering the degree of happiness and number of the happy, there may be more happiness than there would have been if man had not fallen; and at the same time, the misery of the damned might be so great, that though there were not so many, yet numbers and degree of misery considered together, the misery might be greater than if Christ had never appeared.

We must therefore lay the happiness, considered jointly according to numbers and degrees, in one scale, and the misery so considered in the other. And if the misery of mankind thus considered be as great as it was before that, if the excess of the misery above the happiness be as much as all the misery would have been if Christ had not come, Satan in this respect obtains his end. If there be an excess of the scale of misery above that of blessedness, but not so much, Satan is frustrated but in part. And if the scales are equal, yet Satan is but in part frustrated; for that makes the happiness and misery equal, and mankind is to be looked upon as if he were in a perfect medium between happiness and misery. So that Satan obtains his end so far, that he sees mankind deprived of all his happiness though not made miserable. But if the excess of the scale of blessedness above that of misery, be so great as to be just equal to the happiness that mankind would have enjoyed if he had not fallen, then Satan is wholly disappointed of all his aim; he has labored for nothing. And if the excess of the scale of blessedness above that of misery, be much greater than the happiness mankind would have enjoyed if he had not fallen, then Satan is so overthrown by Christ, that his works are the occasion of his own confusion; he is taken in his own snare and fallen into his own pit; and what he intended for man's misery has proved an occasion of his greater blessedness. Now I think 'tis evident by the Scripture, that Satan is thus overthrown. Not but that he may be as effectually overthrown another [way] indirectly, that is, in disappointing of him in his higher end, which was injury to God, and making of him miserable in obtaining his lower, viz. injury to man.[8]

8. MS: "in making of him miserable even in the obtaining his end and disappointing of him in his higher end which was injury to God and making him miserable in obtaining his lower viz. injury to man." JE reversed the order of his two points by restating the first after writing the second, but he failed to delete its first form. This sentence is an insert in space at the end of the paragraph.

Now in order to judge whether this has yet been obtained, we must consider several things: (1) That if Christ had not died, the sins of the world would have been nothing to what they have been; inasmuch as they would be punished only for Adam's transgression and original sin, and would have had no time of probation. And if you suppose they would be punished for their actual transgressions, yet those sins would not be committed in a time of probation; for certainly there would have been no offers of mercy if there had been no redemption. Their sins therefore would [not] have been aggravated by any mercy; how far less therefore would the sins, and so the misery, of the sinful part of the world have been, yea, of the heathens, for the heathen sin against mercy as well as others. Cast this, therefore, into the scale of misery. (2) Consider how small a part of the world the visible church of God has been since the fall of man in comparison of the rest of the world, taking one time with another. (3) Consider how small a part of the visible church have been truly godly, taking one time with another. (4) How much more the sins, and so the misery, of those that have been in the visible church and under means of grace, are aggravated above the sins of others. (5) How much the sins of those that are out of the visible church but have been neighboring to it, and have had the light offered them, have been aggravated above what they otherwise would have been; and how many sins this light has been the occasion of, as persecution, contempt, mockery, and the like. (6) Consider particularly, how long and how universal has been the reign of Antichrist, and that the sins of that church have been far greater than if it had been heathen, and greater than of any heathen church whatever.

On the other hand, consider that those who are saved by the gospel are doubtless advanced to far greater happiness than Adam would have enjoyed.

Now weighing all these things together, can we think that the gospel has yet obtained such a complete and direct overthrow of Satan? Or will the excess of the happiness of mankind (considered jointly, according to the numbers of the blessed and the degree of their blessedness) above the misery (considered the same way) be far greater than the happiness of mankind would have been if they had never fallen? But may we not hope, that this will be accomplished before the world is at an end? Yea, have we not reason for such a hope from Scripture?

159. CHRISTIAN RELIGION. Either God was the author of that body of civil laws by which the Israelites were governed, or they themselves

were the authors of them and afterwards attributed the making of them to God. But if God was not the author of them, 'tis certain that the Jews were anciently a very ignorant thoughtless people, to be so dreadfully imposed upon in the whole of their constitution, civil and religious: to be made to believe that God brought [them] after such a manner out of Egypt, and that their nation beheld such miracles for forty years together; that he gave all their laws, and that every family could trace their genealogy up to the persons that saw those things; and that God now daily manifested himself to them in a wonderful manner by shechinah, urim, thummim, miracles, prophecy, and the like. But if they and not God were the authors of those laws, 'tis certain they were anciently a very wise and thoughtful people; for 'tis certain, whosoever was the author of those laws was[9] very wise, and therefore could never be thus imposed on.

160. LORD's DAY. See sermon on I Cor. 16:1–2.[1] If the Scripture says so much as is sufficient for us plainly to perceive by the eyes of our mind or the exercise of our reason, that it is the will of God and of Christ that the Lord's day should be celebrated, this is enough; then the Lord's day is plainly instituted by the Scripture, which is the only rule of our faith and practice. And,

1. I need nothing to convince me that 'tis evident to the light of reason, that there ought to be a time set apart to be spent wholly in the service and worship of God and the more immediate duties of religion amongst all nations, yea, in gospel times.

2. I am confirmed in it that reason, experience, and the knowledge of human nature and affairs teach that these times ought not to be far distant, not much to exceed the distance of seven days, nor yet to be much less.

3. That the intimations of God's mind in this matter in the Old Testament, supposing them to refer only to the times of the Old Testament, are sufficient argument that the distance of seven days is the fittest and best, and therefore most agreeable to the mind and will of God.

9. MS: "were."

1. This sermon was written in the spring of 1731; it is printed in Worcester Rev. ed., *4,* 615–37. While writing the sermon JE added a reference to it in a narrow blank space at the bottom of the page, clearly meaning it to apply to the whole entry. No. 160 is incorporated, almost without remainder, into the doctrinal part of the sermon and provides most of its content. Small additions and changes were made in the entry on three different occasions; the most important of these will be noted.

4. I do think that God's working six days and resting the seventh was to be of general use, and was designed some way or other to regulate the practice of mankind in general: else I don't know what should be the meaning of God's resting the seventh day, and hallowing and blessing of it (which he did before the giving of the fourth commandment), except it was with respect to mankind; for God did not bless it nor sanctify the day with respect to himself. And I believe he did not do this only to give an example to the Jewish nation, nor that this blessing and sanctifying was only with an eye to them; I believe God meant that the week of mankind, that is, the space between rest and rest, should be seven days.

5. But I think God's will is clearly revealed by the fourth commandment: which I believe is everlasting as to the substance of [it], as well as the rest of the decalogue; that 'tis founded on the same eternal reason as the other commands, and that the writing of it in tables of stone was at least partly designed to intimate its perpetuity; and that Christ never abolished any command of the ten, but that there are the complete number ten yet; and that this command stands good with respect to us in another than a mysterious sense, otherwise 'tis only a summary of the other commands and not distinct therefrom.

6. That the fourth command affords no objection against keeping that day of the seven which according to our reckoning is the first of the week, and doing of it because Jesus Christ rose on that day, instead of keeping that which according to the Jewish reckoning of time is the last day of the week. For every word of the fourth commandment may stand good nevertheless. These [words], "Six days thou shalt labor and do all thy work; but the seventh day is the sabbath of the Lord thy God" [Ex. 20:9–10]—I don't see that these words in themselves mean more than this, that six days we must work, but the next after the sixth is the sabbath. It's no matter at all by what names the days are called. If Monday were called the first day and the sabbath was on Sunday, the sabbath would not be kept on the seventh day in the sense of the fourth commandment more than it is now; nor if Sunday is called the first day and the sabbath is on Saturday.[2] Or if Wednesday were called the first day and the sabbath were kept on Tuesday, the words of the fourth command no more contradict it than if Sunday were the first.

The Jewish reckoning of time is elsewhere determined: doubtless

2. JE may have copied this clause prematurely from a position later in his draft. His writing "Saturday" instead of "Tuesday" in the next sentence may also have been a scribal error.

'twas determined before now,[3] and the week was reckoned from the day after they came out of Egypt, as it seems by Deut. 5:15. 'Tis unreasonable to suppose, that God by the fourth command ordered all nations in all ages to conform to the Jewish reckoning of time, taken from the times of events that were only shadows of things that are since come to pass and of universal concern. These words did not determine the particular day in which this rest should be; that was determined before, as the first words of the fourth command intimate, "Thou shalt remember the sabbath day" [Ex. 20:8]. There were sabbaths kept before this. We find the sabbath a new thing, Ex. 16:22–36. Then the particular day was determined for the Jews, and not [for] now. There is nothing in the fourth command that determines the particular day for all nations in gospel times, but it supposes the day determined by other means.

These words also yet remain in full force: "For in six days the Lord made heaven and earth, the sea, and all that in them is, and rested the seventh day: wherefore the Lord blessed the sabbath day, and hallowed it" [Ex. 20:11]. For, for what reason is it that Christians, after they have labored six days, rest the seventh? Why is it every seventh day, and not every sixth, ninth, or tenth? 'Tis because God was six days creating the world, because God has taught us by his example to work six days and rest the seventh. He has told us what proportion of time he thinks best for us to celebrate, in that he has sanctified the seventh day; thereby intimating to us thus much, that we should keep every seventh day holy, as those do who sanctify the Lord's day every seventh day. Yet I do believe that these words import, that the sabbath was to be kept in commemoration of the creation. Wherefore,

7. I am confirmed in it, that every seventh day ought to be kept in commemoration of the gospel redemption, because it was to be kept by the Jews in commemoration of the creation. I think those expressions in the fourth command which speak of the creation, are an intimation of the mind of God to us, that it ought to be kept in remembrance of redemption; and that they are of the same force to us under the gospel with respect to the latter, as they were to the Jews under the old testament with respect to the former. For when God creates a new heaven and a new earth, then by the fourth command, those that belong to this new heaven and new earth, and have nothing

3. I.e. the time at which the decalogue was given. The theory of the reckoning of the Mosaic sabbath which JE here accepts is mentioned in No. 28 and developed later in a long study of the subject (No. 691).

to do with the old, are commanded to keep every seventh day in commemoration of the creation of *their* heaven and earth; the words are as binding to the one as to the other.

But now the old creation is destroyed, and more than annihilated, by sin; we come into the world far worse than nothing. And God has taught us to call gospel restoration and redemption a creation of new heavens and a new earth. Is. 65:17, "For behold, I create new heavens and a new earth," etc.; Is. 51:16, "And I have put my words in thy mouth, and have covered thee in the shadow of mine hand, that I may plant the heavens, and lay the foundations of the earth, and say unto Zion, Thou art my people"; and 66:22, "For as the new heavens and the new earth, which I will make, shall remain before me," etc. The coming of Christ is often in the Old Testament spoken of as the end of the world. The world by sin is turned again into a chaos, without form and void, as Jer. 4:23. The gospel state is everywhere in the New Testament spoken of as a renewed state of things, wherein all old things are done away and all things become new. We are said to be created anew in Christ Jesus. All things are restored and reconciled, whether in heaven or in earth, and a more glorious light has shone out of greater darkness than shone at the first creation.

8. The latter part of Is. 65:17 confirms and establishes it, that the old creation is not any longer to be commemorated in this manner. The whole verse is thus, "For behold, I create new heavens and a new earth; and the former shall not be remembered, nor come into mind." So 'tis the new creation we belong to, and have not to do with the old in that manner as the Israelites had: if in the gospel state the former shall not be remembered nor come into mind, then I don't believe that in the gospel they shall keep one day in seven on purpose to remember them and call them to mind. The words import, that the new creation shall be so much more excellent than the old that the glory of this shall quite put out the glory of the other, so that it shall not be taken notice of. This, therefore, we are to commemorate with joy (v. 18), "But be you glad and rejoice forever in that which I create: for behold, I create Jerusalem a rejoicing, and her people a joy." See Ps. 118:22 ff.; No. 710 corol. 9.[4]

I am yet more confirmed in it, that the fourth command will reach God's rest from the new creation as well as the old, because I find one

---

4. MS: "No. 702, corol. 9." This corollary occurs in an appendix to No. 710, which is designated as a continuation of No. 702.

compared with the other in the New Testament: Heb. 4:10, "For he that [is] entered into his rest, he also hath ceased from his own works, as God did from [his]." See No. 464.[5]

But if it be an objection with any, that the same words should be of different force with respect to different ages, I answer, that those words, "Honor thy father and thy mother," have different force with respect to all of different fathers and mothers. But if that don't satisfy, I say, there were other words which were written in those tables of stone, which, as they respect us, are not of the same import which they were of as they respected the Israelites, viz. these: "I am the Lord thy God, which hath brought [thee] out of the land of Egypt, out of the house of bondage" [Ex. 20:2]. As these words are directed to us, and are used as an argument to persuade us to keep the following commands, they must respect the redemption by Christ, of which the redemption out of Egypt was a type. And those words in the commandments, Deut. 5:15, "And remember [that] thou wast a servant in the land of Egypt, and that the Lord thy God brought thee out thence through a mighty hand and by a stretched out arm: therefore the Lord thy God commanded thee to keep the sabbath day," which words, if we have anything to do with them, must also chiefly regard what this was a type of.

But if any would be yet more satisfied if the words stood in force forever in their most literal signification, I say, so let them, for our creation ought not wholly to be excluded from the Lord's day; but as 'tis a day for the exercise of religion in general and a day of praise, so 'tis for the commemoration of all God's works of goodness towards us, which may be referred to the heads of creation and redemption. Yea, it may all be reduced to redemption, and the creation ought to be commemorated in subserviency to our meditation on redemption; for the creation is not goodness any otherwise than in Christ, yea, nothing is any way profitable to us but through redemption, and God is to be praised only in Christ Jesus.

9. I am satisfied that the Jewish sabbath was not to be perpetual, because they were commanded to keep it in remembrance of their

5. In the spring of 1730 JE added at the end of § 8 the words, "Christ's resting from the work of redemption is in Scripture paralleled with God's resting from the work of creation, Heb. 4:10." This sentence he then deleted, wrote a much fuller interpretation of Heb. 4:10 in No. 464, and added a citation of No. 464 at this point. He did not, however, use No. 464 in the original version of the sermon; see below, No. 464, p. 506, n. 2.

deliverance out of Egypt; and the reason why it was instituted was because God thus delivered them, as we are expressly told in the decalogue itself, Deut. 5:15. I do not think that God would have all nations under the gospel, and to the end of the world, keep a day every week that was instituted in remembrance of the Jews' deliverance out of Egypt. But,

10. I am persuaded that God did intend to intimate to us, and has intimated, that Christians ought to keep the sabbath in remembrance of Christ's redemption, in that he has declared that it was instituted among the Jews in remembrance of their deliverance out of Egypt, this being a most notable type of that. If we must thus commemorate the type, why not the substance? If we must thus solemnize the remembrance of a petty redemption, why not of the grand redemption, of infinitely more glory and concern? The Egypt that we are redeemed from is the spiritual Egypt; our house of bondage is our thralldom to sin. The meaning of those words therefore to us must be this: "And remember thou wast a servant to sin and Satan, and the Lord thy God delivered thee from this bondage with a mighty hand and outstretched arm; therefore the Lord thy God commanded thee to keep the sabbath day." How particularly is the observing that insisted on; and why not this day, of which that was intended only for a shadow?[6]

11. 'Tis certain, that our redemption by Christ is vastly more glorious [and] of more importance to us than the old creation; it was even as nothing in those regards, in comparison of it. Yea, I believe the old creation was a type and shadow of the new. 'Tis certain also, that all the reasons we can find out by Scripture and reason to be why we should so solemnly commemorate the old creation, appear by Scripture and reason to be the same, and vastly stronger, why we should in like manner celebrate the remembrance of our redemption.

12. I think that the Holy Ghost has told us implicitly, that that sabbath that was instituted in remembrance of the deliverance from Egypt shall no longer be kept, in that place of Scripture, Jer. 16:14–15 and 23:7–8, "Therefore behold, the days come, saith the Lord, that it shall no more be said, The Lord liveth, that brought up the children of Israel out of the land of Egypt, but The Lord liveth, that brought up the children of Israel from the land of the north," etc. And because

6. This sentence was added during the writing of the sermon on I Cor. 16:1–2.

that reason tells us there must be [a] day kept holy, I believe, therefore, it shall be in remembrance of that which is spoken of in the latter verse, viz. the redemption by Christ; whereby the elect are redeemed not only in Judea, but from all parts of the world. See Is. 43:18.

13. Again, I believe that the sabbath is to be perpetual, because 'tis evident by the Old Testament that God set much more by this than any of the other sabbaths of the Jews or any of their ceremonies. 'Tis mentioned in the prophets amongst moral duties, [and] more weight laid upon it abundantly than other things, in many places. Neh. 9:14.

14. I doubt not but that the weekly sabbath is [not] included in those sabbaths that are mentioned as abolished, Col. 2:16.

15. If all this is not a satisfying revelation of the will of God that the first day of the week is to be kept holy, yet reason telling of us that there must be some day or other kept holy; and God sufficiently having told [us] that this must be one in seven; and we being assured from the reason of the thing, and the prophecies of the Old Testament, and the testimonies of the New, that the Jewish sabbath is abolished; and reason, and the tenor of God's commands, and of the Old Testament, and the reason of institutions of this nature (so far as God has revealed them to us), as also types and prophecies, giving us undoubted reason to believe that this sabbath is to be kept in remembrance of redemption, and so on the day that God rested from this work; and Christ having evidently from time to time, upon choice and design, appeared unto the apostles upon this day, and also sent down the Holy Ghost upon them, and extraordinarily revealed himself to John on that day; and it being evident by Scripture, that this was the day of the primitive Christians' public worship: it is full evidence to me, taken with the other, that this was the will of God.

16. The day in the New Testament is called the Lord's day. What day is meant by this expression we know, just the same way as we know the meaning of other expressions in any ancient language—Hebrew or Greek in the originals. And I think its name of "Lord's day" includes in it all that we plead should be in the Christian sabbath.

17. I am confirmed in all, inasmuch as we have all evidence by tradition and history, that this was the universal custom of the church throughout the whole world from the apostles' times, and that none can be found anywhere, either orthodox or heretics, that did not practise it.

18. That there is nothing more plainly said about it before the apos-

tle John wrote his revelations, is not an obstacle to my believing that this is the will of the Holy Ghost, that this day should be set apart and kept to the end of the world. It seems reasonable to me to think, that this was purposely avoided by the Holy Spirit in the first settling of churches in the world, both amongst [Jews] and heathen, but most especially for the sake of the Jews. For 'tis evident they[7] declared one thing after another, as they could bear it. The sabbath was dear to them, doubtless, above anything else in the law of Moses; and there was that in the Old Testament which tended to uphold them in the observance of this, much more strongly than of anything else that was Jewish. Nothing would have been so shocking to them, than to tell them plainly that their sabbath was abolished, and that another was set up—that sabbath which God had made so much of, so solemnly frequently and carefully commanded, and so often dreadfully punished the breach of. They therefore dealt very tenderly in this point.

Other things of this nature, we find very gradually revealed. Christ had many things to say which he said not, because the disciples could not bear them yet; Christ revealed his gospel to them by little and little as they could bear [it]. 'Twas a long time before he told them plainly the principal doctrines of the kingdom of heaven; he took such opportunities to tell them of his death and sufferings, when they were full of admiration of some signal miracle, and were confirmed in it that he was the Messiah. He told them much more after the resurrection than before, for being confirmed by his resurrection they could bear much more than before; but yet he told them not all, but left more to be revealed by the Holy Ghost; they were therefore much more enlightened after this than before, but yet all was not revealed.

The apostles were in the same manner careful and tender of those they preached and wrote to. 'Twas a long time before they plainly taught them of the abolishing of the ceremonies of the law, of circumcision, distinction of meats, purifications, feasts, etc. They conformed themselves a great while, yea, commanded others by the direction of the Holy Ghost to conform in some things. How tender the Apostle is with them that scrupled eating unclean meats; he would have other

---

7. The sermon here reads "Christ and the apostles" instead of "they." The next "they" and the following two sentences refer to Jewish Christians. The word "they" in the last sentence of the paragraph is changed to "Christ" in the sermon.

Christians forbear for their sakes.[8] But I need say[9] no more to evince this.

But I will say, that 'tis very possible that the apostles themselves might not have this fully revealed to them; for though the Holy Ghost at his descent at Pentecost revealed much to them, yet there was much of the gospel doctrine they were very ignorant in yet, yea, a great while after they did the part of apostles by preaching, baptizing, and governing the church. Peter was surprised when he was commanded to eat unclean meats; so were the apostles in general, when Peter was commanded to go to the gentiles and preach to them. Thus tender was the Holy Ghost of the church while an infant. Nor did the Holy Ghost yet feed them with the strong meat, but was careful to bring in the observation of the Lord's day by degrees, and therefore took all occasions to honor it: Christ, of choice, from time to time appearing on this day, sending his Spirit on this day, ordering Christians to meet on this day, and come together to break bread upon it, and to have their contributions upon it, thus working of it in by degrees; and the Holy Ghost did not speak very plainly about it. Yet God took special care to do so much, that there might be sufficient marks left of God's will in this matter to be found out by the Christian church, when it should be more established and settled and come to the strength of a man. See note on John 3:30.[1]

19. I believe the abrogation of the Jewish sabbath is intimated by Christ lying buried on that day, who was the Lord of the sabbath. The Creator of the world, that rested from all his works and was refreshed on that day, is now held in the chains of death on this day. The God that created the world, now in his second work did not follow his own example. The sabbath was a day of rejoicing; but Christ says, when the Bridegroom is taken from them they shall fast and

8. JE added this sentence in space available at the bottom of the MS page, probably while writing the sermon, without giving directions for its placement. It has been inserted at this point because it occurs at the same place, slightly altered, in the parallel sermon passage.

9. MS: "need not say." The "not" is probably a slip caused by a change of intention; it is omitted at the corresponding point in the sermon.

1. The note on John 3:30 is an entry in the "Blank Bible" in which JE states that "the New Testament dispensation increased before and after Christ's resurrection and the Old Testament decreased, much after the same manner as the ministry of Christ increased and the ministry of John the Baptist decreased." His point is the gradualness with which the new dispensation superseded the old, as in this paragraph of No. 160. JE added this reference, and probably wrote the note, when he repreached the sermon on I Cor. 16:1–2 in the late 1730s.

mourn [Matt. 9:15]. See Mastricht, pp. 932, 1141.[2] See note on Gen. 2:3.[3]

20. Christ says he is Lord of the sabbath, and argues that he may therefore dispense with the sanctification [of it]. If so, he may change it.[4]

161. RIGHTEOUSNESS OF CHRIST. God insisted upon Adam's active obedience before he would fix him in blessedness, doubtless that Adam might honor his law. God gave a law, that he might have an opportunity to honor God by obeying of it; and God now insists upon satisfaction, that this law may not go without its honor. And it's certain, that Christ by his obedience has done much more honor to God's law than Adam by his obedience could have done, and doubtless God hereby is satisfied; so that we are no doubt justified by what Christ did, as it is obedience, as well as by his enduring punishment.

162. ANGELS OF THE APOCALYPSE.[5] In these visions everything almost was represented as living, acting, speaking, mourning or rejoic-

2. Petrus van Mastricht, *Theoretico-practica theologia*, ed. nova (Utrecht, 1699). There were several reprints, but JE owned a copy of the 1699 edition, which is now in the Library of Princeton University. In his copy p. 424 was succeeded by p. 325, with the result that pp. 325–424 were repeated and all pages after the first p. 424 must be increased by 100 to fit the corrected pagination of the 1724 edition. JE's references to the pagination of the 1699 edition will be given in the text but the pagination of the 1724 edition, if different, will be supplied in the notes.

Mastricht, who had studied under Vœtius at Utrecht, became professor of theology there in 1677 and died in 1706. He is one of the major influences on JE's theology from his graduate days onward. On p. 932 (i.e. 1032) Mastricht states that though the "decalogic" hallowing of a seventh day is still in force, the Jewish sabbath, which prefigured Christ's rest in the grave, has been abrogated. In the second reference (pp. 1141–43; i.e. 1241–43) Mastricht insists that God has prescribed to each their own seventh day: to the Jews their seventh day, counting from God's rest after the work of creation, "& nos etiam Christiani obligemur ad *nostrum* diem septimum, numerandum à resurrectione Christi."

3. This reference occurs in the MS at the end of § 20, for lack of space at the end of § 19, to which it belongs; both note and reference were written in 1738–39. The note is printed in Grosart, *Selections*, p. 59.

4. This section is a later insert which JE squeezed into space between §§ 18 and 19 about the time he wrote the sermon on I Cor. 16:1–2. It is clearly not all he wanted to say on the point, for he continued the discussion in No. 495. Neither the added section nor No. 495 appears in the sermon (though an addition to § 19 in the same ink as § 20 was included), so it is likely that § 20 was an additional reflection shortly after JE had finished the sermon. See note to No. 495.

5. This whole entry is deleted with a large X mark and is not entered in the Table. In spite of the difficulties which the view expressed here might make for JE's usual historical literalism in dealing with the Apocalypse, he probably eliminated the entry because it properly

ing; those things that were without life, and other things to which personal acts cannot properly be attributed.

163. COVENANT. The new covenant itself evidences that it is made with Christ, and not with believers considered as distinct from him. Heb. 8:10 ff., "For this is the covenant that I will make with the house of Israel after those days, saith the Lord; I will put my laws into their mind, and write them in their hearts; and I will be to them a God, and they shall be to me a people," etc. This promise is not made to the elect immediately, though it be made of them, inasmuch as none know they are the elect till the promise is performed; neither can they do anything whereby they can know before the performance of the promise. 'Tis not what any can lay hold of as a promise, before the law be written in their hearts. Jer. 32:40, "And I will make an everlasting covenant with them, that I will not turn away from them, to do them good; but I will put my fear in their hearts, that they shall not depart from me."

164. In what sense may THE UNREGENERATE be said to desire grace? For it is certain they cannot desire it properly and absolutely. A desire is an inclination; but 'tis certain, their inclination is not to grace simply; grace considered alone has no share in the inclination. But grace has[6] a necessary, universal connection with other things that have a share in the inclination; and if they have a greater share of inclination than grace [has] of disinclination,[7] so that, taking grace collectively with those things that it's universally and necessarily tied to, the[8] inclination to it be greater than the inclination to a state of destitution of grace, taken also with its appendages, the man may be said to choose grace. N.B. that into those necessary appendages to grace and sin, we in each take in the bad as well as the good. But thus, the unregenerate don't choose grace: for the forsaking of every sin, and the doing of every duty, is one part of grace; and it's evident by his actions that he don't choose this.

When therefore they say they desire grace, they say so because they

---

belonged in the notebook on Revelation. "Apocalypse" no. 44 (written about three years later) expresses a view similar to that of No. 162, for it denies that the angels of the seven churches, the four horsemen, or the four angels at the Euphrates "represent real particular persons."

6. MS: "having."

7. I.e. if a man's inclination to the things that go with grace is greater than his disinclination to grace itself.

8. MS: "if the."

don't know what it is. Grace is to turn from every wicked way to every good one; this they don't desire, except to turn thus were easier than it is. Their real desire, therefore, is that this may be made easier and less contrary to their inclination; and that, they mean when they pray for grace. There are two things in the scale, grace with its appendages and sin with its appendages. They desire [them] as they are now in the scale; the man prefers sin, but he wishes the scale were otherwise, that sin was made heavier, and grace lighter. This is what they hope for; they hope that God by his Spirit will make it easier. Thus, if a man has a wound that he thinks will kill him if he don't lance it: he has the lance in his hand, but has such an aversion to the putting himself to so much pain, that he neglects to lance it; though he thinks 'tis best for him, yet of choice he neglects to lance his wound. In the same sense as this man chooses rather to die than himself to lance his wound, in that sense does every unregenerate man choose sin before grace. The man wishes that he had more courage, and it were easier for him to lance his wound.

165. COVENANT. See . . . [9] The new covenant as a mutual agreement, or as a conditional promise, is only with Christ: but as "covenant" sometimes signifies an absolute promise, so it is with believers, and with none other of mankind than those that actually believe. This is called "new" in contradistinction to the old, which promised Canaan.[1]

166. FATHERS. 'Tis most certain and undeniable, that so far as the history of the primitive church is probably true, so far it is to be looked upon as probable; and so [far] as the state and general belief of those times, according to the exercise of reason, makes any other matters of fact relating to the apostles' times, or their doctrine, or anything else relating to the Christian religion [probable]; so far we are to look upon these or those things as more probable for it. So that we may be confirmed hereby, with a rational and right confirmation, with respect to the apostles' doctrines or facts; for this is but exercising our reason about the Scripture, and not the making another thing the standard of our faith. No man is to blame for making use of the fathers or primi-

9. The space was never filled. No. 163 is the last preceding entry devoted to this topic and is probably the place meant. Earlier entries on the covenant (including the very first, No. 2) also discuss the question as to who are the parties to the covenants of grace and redemption.

1. The sentence as originally written contained the following additional words, which JE deleted: "and in contradistinction to that with Adam, in that it was upon a new foot; that was conditional, this free and absolute."

tive histories, but the fault is in depending too much upon them for more than they are to be depended upon; to which men are exceeding apt.

167. CHRISTIAN RELIGION. I am firm in it, that if Christianity was not true it would never afford so much matter for rational, understanding, penetrating brains to be exercised upon. If it were false, such heads would find it empty; and it would [be] a force upon the intellect, to set upon[2] meditating upon that which has no other order, foundation and mutual dependence to be discovered than what is accidental: I am sure, a strong and piercing mind would feel itself exceedingly bound and hindered. But I am sure, there is the like liberty in it, and as much improvement of the mind, as in natural philosophy or any study whatsoever; yea, I am convinced, a great deal more. And whatever may be said about Mahometan divines, I cannot be convinced but that a mind that has the faculty and habit of clear and distinct reasoning, would find nothing but chains, fetters and confusion if he should pretend to fix his reason upon it.[3]

168. REWARD. How is it said that our happiness is the reward of holiness and good works, and yet that we are made happy wholly and solely for the sake of Christ? I answer, 'tis not solely by Christ that we have holiness and good works given us, but 'tis only by him that our holiness and good works are capable of a reward. He purchased holiness for us, which is indeed not different from happiness; and he purchased that they should be capable of a reward, and should be rewarded, yea that their good works should be worthy of a reward. So that properly, now, the good works of saints are worthy of being rewarded; the saints are worthy to walk in white [Rev. 3:4].

169. FUTURE STATE. 'Tis certainly natural and regular in its own nature, that at last there should be a separation of good and bad; that the good and excellent may be together, and the wicked together. And the present mingled state, considered without regard to a future separate state to which things tend, is certainly confusion, and contrary to general beauty and regularity.

2. Or "set [it] upon"; it is not altogether clear what JE intends to be the initiators of the actions implied in "force," "set," and "meditating."
3. I.e. Mahometan theology.

170. WILL OF GOD. When a distinction is made between God's revealed will and his secret will, or his will of command and decree, "will" is certainly in that distinction taken in two senses: his will of decree is not his will in the same sense as his will of command is. Therefore 'tis no difficulty at all to suppose that one may be otherwise than the other. His will in both senses is his inclination; but when we say he wills virtue or loves virtue, or the happiness of his creatures, thereby is intended that virtue, or the creature's happiness, is what, absolutely and simply considered, alone is agreeable to the inclination of his nature. His will of decree is his inclination to a thing, not as to that thing absolutely and simply, but with respect to the universality of things that have been, are, or shall be. So God, though he hates a thing as it is simply, may incline to it with reference to the universality of things. Though he hates sin in itself, yet he may will to permit it for the greater promotion of holiness in this universality, including all things and at all times. So, though he has no inclination to a creature's misery, consider it absolutely, yet he may will it for the greater promotion of happiness in this universality. God inclines to excellency, which is harmony; but yet he may incline to suffer that which is unharmonious in itself, for the promotion of universal harmony or for the beautifying of the harmony that there is in the universality, and making of it shine the brighter.

And thus it must needs be; and no hypothesis whatsoever will relieve a man, but that he must own these two wills of God. For 'tis [what] all must own, that God wills sometimes not to hinder the breach of his own commands, because he does not hinder [it]; he wills to permit sin, it is evident, because he does permit it. None will say that God himself does what he don't will to do.

But, you will say, God wills to permit sin, as he wills the creature should be left to his freedom; and if he should hinder it, he would offer violence to the nature of his own creature. I answer, this comes nevertheless to the same thing that I say. You say, God don't will sin absolutely, but rather than alter the laws of nature he wills it; he wills what is contrary to excellency in some particulars for the sake of a more general excellency and order. So that this scheme of Arminians don't help the matter at all.

171. NEW BIRTH AND NEW COVENANT. As, if Adam had stood and got the victory, all his posterity would have had a right to the reward without another trial, so, seeing Christ has done the work in which

Adam failed and has gotten the victory, all his children have a right to the reward. In Adam's posterity there would nothing else have been required but their being born; so in Christ's posterity nothing else is required but their being born again, in order to their being entitled to happiness. The first Adam was to have performed the condition of life; his posterity were not properly to perform any condition. Their being born was only their existing; merely by existing they could not be said properly to perform a condition. So the new birth is but existing, for by our fall we are as it were reduced to our first nothing; by the new creation, or new birth, we reexist.

172. TREE OF KNOWLEDGE OF GOOD AND EVIL. 'Tis the tree of knowledge of good and evil, not only because thereby we came to know the difference between good and evil—for that properly is only the knowledge of evil to Adam, seeing he knew good before—but without doubt it was a tree of the knowledge of good properly, as much as evil. And the lively perception of good so much depends on the knowledge of its contrary, evil, that there was as much attained of new knowledge of good, as there was knowledge of evil; and this was the end of it principally, the knowledge of good. And by this means is our happiness advanced highly above what it was before the fall, and the promise of the devil, "Ye shall be as gods, knowing good and evil" [Gen. 3:5], is fulfilled in another sense and manner than he intended it should.

173. FALL OF MAN. Doubtless Adam made use of the beasts for his pleasure, and they were matter of pleasure to him as well as plants, trees and flowers, etc.; and perhaps more, being more perfect creatures and having an image of reason; and particularly the serpent, as having most of this image of reason. And being of a beautiful make and pretty to be handled, as he was more subtle than any beast of the field, so 'tis probable they were more familiar with him than with any other; and therefore [he] was cunningly chosen by the devil to be the instrument of the temptation. The Bible tells us that Satan chose him because of his subtlety.

Now his subtlety could advantage the temptation no other way than this. The serpent doubtless used much to delight man with his pretty subtle actions but yet wanted speech; but, 'tis like, pretended he had gotten it by eating the fruit of the forbidden tree. The woman was doubtless surprised and pleased to hear the pretty serpent, with whom she was so well acquainted, speak; and was easily persuaded that if it had such an effect on the beast, as to change him to a rational [being], that it would by a like advancement make gods of them. God says, he will put enmity between the seed of the serpent and the woman; which may be the rather mentioned as part of the serpent's curse, because the woman especially had been so familiar with him, more than other beasts, in time past. It seems the man and his wife knew the name of the tree by the serpent's using this argument, that they shall be as gods, knowing good and evil. Hereby he was wonderfully advantaged in his temptation: he might pretend that he was concerned for their welfare, and desirous that they might be advanced, from their acquaintance with him and pleasedness with him; and telling them the effect that the fruit had on him, together with the name that God had given to the tree, easily gained Eve's belief.

There is an agreeableness, in this affair, with spiritual things, and a plain shadow and resemblance of them. So we may be warned of dallying with earthly lusts, the serpents of our hearts, that are of a beastly nature and afford only an inferior pleasure, that work in a blind serpentine manner;[4] and many such like things we may be taught hereby.

174. FALL. Whether man's body before the fall shone or no, I believe his flesh looked glorious, and appeared with a beautiful cast and a sort of splendor, which was immediately lost upon the transgression; and that their bodies looked filthily and nastily in comparison of what they did before, so that they could no longer bear to see themselves, or be seen by God or each other. And this was probably the natural effect of the fruit two ways: one, by its baneful nature altering the sweet constitution of the body; and the other, by the influence which the falling of his mind had on his body. For the sweet disposition and joy of the heart will sometimes almost make the face to shine without a miracle. And how differently doth the face appear, in the different extremes of the dispositions and affections! And probably before the fall, when our bodies were not such dull sluggish things, the affections of the mind had a more quick, easy and notable influence upon the whole body, as it has on the face now.

175. FUTURE STATE. God, if he made the world, he undoubtedly ordered all things wisely in it. But he has made man and placed him in

4. MS: "man"; note similar sounds in the next two words.

such circumstances, that he has made [it] his prudence[5] with all his might and with all possible vigor to be providing for a future state. For he has made him so, and placed him in such circumstances that, let him exercise his reason never so much, he cannot be sure that there is no future state; but the more rational and most virtuous men are most apt to believe it—we find that by experience. God has given us no proofs that there is no future state, and he has placed man in such circumstances that, let him exercise his reason never so well, he will see many arguments for a future state which he cannot get over; and it can be proved by mathematical demonstration, that a probability or possibility of eternal happiness on one hand and misery on the other, is more to be regarded than the certainty of anything that has an end. But if God has made it our prudence to spend our lives in providing for a future state when there is none,[6] he has not ordered things wisely.

176. ANGELS. I can't see why it should be thought more disagreeable to reason to suppose that angels may have influence on matter, so as to cause those alterations in it which are beyond the established laws of matter, more than to suppose that our spirits should have such an influence. And I don't see why other spirits should not have influence on matter according to other laws, or why, if we suppose spirits have an influence on matter, that it must necessarily be according to the same established rules as our spirits. We find that from such motions of mind there follows such alteration in such and such matter, according to established rules; and those rules are entirely at the pleasure of him that establishes them: and why we should not think that God establishes[7] other rules for other spirits, I cannot imagine. And if we should suppose, that according to established laws angels do make alterations in the secret springs of bodies, and so of minds, that otherwise would not be, I can't see why it should be accounted more of a miracle [than] that our souls can make alterations in the matter of our hands and feet, which otherwise would not be.

177. PROVIDENCE. Seeing that all creatures and all the operations of the universe are only the immediate influence of God, and seeing there is nothing else is the rule of this influence but only harmony and

5. MS: "that he is made his prudence"; cf. the clause that begins the last sentence of the entry.
6. MS: "not": note the proximity of the next "not."
7. Or "established"; the word was left incomplete at the end of a line.

general proportion; I can't imagine why men's minds are so apt to find fault with this way of God's exerting himself amongst the creatures and with that way, as if it were not credible that God should so exert himself: whereas they are not capable to judge, till they can tell whether this or that way be disagreeable to general harmony. But how much too narrow a comprehension have we, to tell that!

178. SPIRIT OF GOD. 'Tis exceeding evident in natural philosophy,[8] that all the operations of the creatures are the immediate influence of the divine being; and that the method of influence is most simple and constant and unvaried in the meanest and simplest beings, and more evident, compounded and various, and according to less simple rules, in beings that are more perfect and compounded, and that in proportion as they are more or less perfect. 'Tis most simple in inanimate beings, less so in plants, more compounded still in the more perfect plants, more evident in animals than in them, and most so in the most perfect animals, and most compounded and least of all bound to constant laws in man. And 'tis certainly beautiful that it should be so, that in the various ranks of beings, those that are nearest to the first being should most evidently and variously partake of his influence; and 'twill be no more than just to make out the proportion, if the soul of man be influenced by the operation of the Spirit of God, as the Scripture represents.

179. LOGOS. It the more confirms me in it, that the perfect idea God has of himself is truly and properly God, that the existence of all corporeal things is only ideas.

180. CHRIST'S LOVE. Such thoughts as these are ready to run into our minds, when we think on the death of Christ and would inflame our hearts with a sense of his love therefrom, that we cannot certainly argue so great love of the eternal Logos from it; for the Logos felt nothing, no pain, and suffered no disgrace, but 'twas the human nature [that suffered]. But I answer, the love the human nature had to mankind, and by which he was prompted to undergo so much, it had only by virtue of its union with the Logos; 'twas all derived from the love of the Logos, or else they would not be one person. Many other things also might be said together with this.

8. See above, No. 64, p. 235, n. 9. No. 178 restates the theme of No. 64, a theme to which JE seems to have returned by way of the ideas expressed in Nos. 176–177.

181. TRINITY AND DECREES. I used to think sometimes with myself, if such doctrines as those of the Trinity and decrees are true, yet what need was there of revealing of them in the gospel? what good do they do towards the advancing [of] holiness? But now I don't wonder at all at their being revealed, for such doctrines as these are glorious inlets into the knowledge and view of the spiritual world, and the contemplation of supreme things; the knowledge of which I have experienced how much it contributes to the betterment of the heart. If such doctrines as these had not been revealed, the church would never have been let half so far into the view of the spiritual world, as God intends it shall be before the world is at an end. I know by experience, how useful these doctrines be to lead to this knowledge.[9] God doubtless knew what was needful to be revealed.

182. HEAVEN. See Nos. 95, 721, 263.[1] How ravishing are the proportions of the reflections of rays of light, and the proportions of the vibrations of the air![2] And without doubt, God can contrive matter so that there shall be other sort of proportions, that may be quite of a different kind, and may raise another sort of pleasure in the sense, and in a manner to us inconceivable, that shall be vastly more ravishing and exquisite. And in all probability, the abode of the saints after the resurrection will be so contrived by God, that there shall be external beauties and harmonies altogether of another kind from what we perceive here, and probably those beauties will appear chiefly on the bodies of the man Christ Jesus and of the saints. Our animal spirits will also be capable of immensely more, fine and exquisite proportions in their motions than now they are, being so gross. But how much more ravishing will the exquisite spiritual proportions be that shall be seen in minds, in their acts: between one spiritual act and another, between one disposition and another, and betweeen one mind and another,

9. See the "Personal Narrative" (Hopkins, *Life and Character,* pp. 24 ff.), where JE describes his intellectual acceptance of the doctrine of the decrees and his later "experience" of God's sovereignty as expressed in that doctrine.
1. These references were added later, probably when No. 721 was written or soon afterwards. The main themes of No. 182 (the nature of spiritual harmony and the analogy between corporeal and spiritual proportion) link it directly with Nos. 42 and 108. No. 182 and the entries immediately following (esp. Nos. 185–187) are also very close in subject matter and even wording to the first part of "Beauty of the World" (*Works,* 6, 305–06), which seems from its appearance to have been written contemporaneously with these entries.
2. This entry is a meditation probably inspired by JE's writing of "Natural Philosophy" US no. 23, "Colors," which must have taken place shortly before, since the two pieces have identical ink and hand (*Works,* 6, 283–85).

and between all their minds and Christ Jesus and the supreme mind, and particularly between the man Christ Jesus and the Deity, and among the persons of the Trinity, the supreme harmony of all.

And it is out of doubt with me, that there will [be] immediate intellectual views of minds, one of another and of the supreme mind, more immediate, clear and sensible than our views of bodily things with bodily eyes. In this world we behold spiritual beauties only mediately by the intervention of our senses, in perceiving those external actions which are the effects of spiritual proportion; hereby the ravishingness of the beauty is much obscured, and our sense of it flattened and deadened. But when we behold the beauties of minds more immediately than now we do the colors of the rainbow, how ravishing will it be! All that there wants in order to such an intellectual view, is that a clear and sensible apprehension of what is in [another] mind should be raised in our own minds constantly, according to such and such laws; for 'tis no other way that we perceive with our bodily eyes, or perceive by any of our senses.

Then, also, our capacities will be exceedingly enlarged, and we shall be able to apprehend, and to take in, more extended and compounded proportions. We see that the narrower the capacity, the more simple must the beauty be to please. Thus in the proportion of sounds, the birds and brute creatures are most delighted with simple music, and in the proportion confined to a few notes. So little children are not able to perceive the sweetness of very complex tunes, where respect is to be had to the proportion of a great many notes together in order to perceive the sweetness of the tune. Then perhaps we shall be able fully and easily to apprehend the beauty, where respect is to be had to thousands of different ratios at once to make up the harmony. Such kind of beauties, when fully perceived, are far the sweetest.

183. CHRIST'S LOVE. Such was the love of the Son of God to the human nature, that he desired a most near and close union with it, something like the union in the persons of the Trinity, nearer than there can be between any two distinct [beings].[3] This moved him to make the human become one with him, and himself to be one of mankind that should represent all the rest, for Christ calls us brethren and is one of us. How should [we] be encouraged, when we have such a

3. Or "any two [that are] distinct." See No. 184, which develops the thought contained in the last clause of this sentence.

Mediator! 'Tis one of us that is to plead for us, one that God from love to us has received into his own person from among us. And 'tis so congruous that it should be so, and is also so agreeable to the Scripture, that it much confirms in me the truth of the Christian religion.

184. UNION, SPIRITUAL. What insight I have of the nature of minds, I am convinced that there is no guessing what kind of union and mixtion, by consciousness or otherwise, there may be between them. So that all difficulty is removed in believing what the Scripture declares about spiritual unions—of the persons of the Trinity, of the two natures of Christ, of Christ and the minds of saints.

185. EXCELLENCE OF CHRIST. When we see beautiful airs of look and gesture, we naturally think the mind that resides within is beautiful. We have all the same, and more, reason to conclude the spiritual beauty of Christ from the beauty of the world; for all the beauties of the universe do as immediately result from the efficiency of Christ, as a cast of an eye or a smile of the countenance depends on the efficiency of the human soul.

186. FALL. Seeing the beauty of the corporeal world consists chiefly in its imaging forth spiritual beauties, and the beauties of minds are infinitely the greatest, we therefore undoubtedly may conclude that God, when he created the world, showed his own perfections and beauties far the most charmingly and clearly in the spiritual part of the world. But seeing spiritual beauty consists principally in virtue and holiness, and there is so little of this beauty to be seen now in that part of the spiritual world that is here on earth; hence we may certainly conclude, and it fully convinces me, that there has been a great fall and defection in this part of the spiritual world from their primitive beauty and charms.

Corol. Seeing it is so, and this is so agreeable to the account that the Christian religion gives of the matter; and seeing it is evident by many arguments that God don't intend to give over man as lost, but has a merciful intention of restoring of him to his primitive beauty; and seeing we are told of this and of the manner of it alone in the Christian religion; and seeing the account is so rational; it is a great confirmation of the truth of the Christian religion.

'Tis also evident to me that the lower corporeal world has not its primitive beauty, but that only the ruins are to be seen; and seeing this is so exactly agreeable to the account the Christian religion gives of the matter, and the account of the marring of the beauty of the world by the fall and flood being so rational, this also confirms the Christian religion.

187. SPIRIT. Seeing the beauty of minds is so much the greatest, and corporeal beauties but the shadows of them; and the beauties of the corporeal world being so immediately derived from God that they are but emanations of his beauty, and much more the primitive beauty of spirits, wherein the beauty of God's works chiefly consisted; and seeing this beauty is lost and is to be restored again, as we have just now shown [No. 186]: when it's restored again it will undoubtedly be by way of immediate emanation from his beauty, and not of our own or another's operation—except the original of the beauty of the world is to be looked upon as almost wholly alien to the perfection and efficiency of God. I therefore certainly conclude, that virtue and holiness are given by way of immediate emanation from God. This is exceeding congruous to nature and philosophy, and the contrary would be exceeding incongruous. How easy then is it, to believe what the gospel teaches of this matter; yea, the congruity and reasonableness of this doctrine is a confirmation of the gospel.

188. HEAVEN. The best, most beautiful, and most perfect way that we have of expressing a sweet concord of mind to each other, is by music. When I would form in my mind an idea of a society in the highest degree happy, I think of them as expressing their love, their joy, and the inward concord and harmony and spiritual beauty of their souls by sweetly singing to each other. But if in heaven minds will have an immediate view of one another's dispositions without any such intermediate expression, how much sweeter will it [be]. But to me 'tis probable that the glorified saints, after they have again received their bodies, will have ways of expressing the concord of their minds by some other emanations than sounds, of which we cannot conceive, that will be vastly more proportionate, harmonious and delightful than the nature of sounds is capable of; and the music they will make will be in a medium capable of modulations in an infinitely more nice, exact and fine proportion than our gross air, and with organs as much more adapted to such proportions.

189. LOVE OF CHRIST. We see how great love the human nature is

capable of, not only to God but fellow creatures. How greatly are we inclined to the other sex! Nor doth an exalted and fervent love to God hinder this, but only refines and purifies it. God has created the human nature to love fellow creatures, which he wisely has principally turned to the other sex; and the more exalted the nature is, the greater love of that kind that is laudable is it susceptive of; and the purer and better natured, the more is it inclined to it.

Christ has an human nature as well as we, and has an inclination to love those that partake of the human [nature] as well as we. That inclination which in us is turned to the other sex, in him is turned to the church, which is his spouse. He is as much of a purer and better and more benevolent nature than we, whereby he is inclined to a higher degree of love, as he is of a greater capacity, whereby he is capable of a more exalted, ardent and sweet love. Nor is his love to God, in him more than in us (nor half so much), an hindrance or diversion to this love; because his love to God and his love to the saints are an hundred times nearer akin than our love to God and our love to the other sex. Therefore when we feel love to anyone of the other sex, 'tis a good way to think of the love of Christ to an holy and beautiful soul.

190. CHRISTIAN RELIGION. 'Tis a convincing argument for the truth of [the Christian] religion and that it stands upon a most sure bottom, that none have ever yet been able to prove it false; though there have been many of all sorts, many [of] fine wits and great learning, that have spent themselves, and ransacked the world for arguments against it, and this for many ages.

191. FREE GRACE. We plead for freedom of grace as being that whereby the abundance of the benevolence of the giver is expressed, and gratitude in the receiver is obliged; and nothing else that can be called freedom is worth pleading for that does neither of these. But if anything that is called freedom that doth these, be not acknowledged to pertain to God's gifts which doth[4] indeed belong to them, thereby God's beneficence is abused. Now without doubt, all that contributes to the freedom of a gift, that is, that exalts God's beneficence and obliges our gratitude, does concur in gospel benefits. This being granted, what we have to do is to see wherein freedom does or can consist; and then we may venture to say that they meet in gospel grace.

4. JE wrote "do" by attraction to "gifts," but its subject is "anything."

Now I think these three things do constitute the freedom of grace, or that at least they do certainly appertain to that freedom which expresses the abundance of benevolence and increases gratitude. (1) When the gift is to an offender, without satisfaction paid by him. This will be acknowledged. (2) When 'tis given without retribution by way of condition, or without the receiver's profiting or pleasuring the giver. This will not be denied.[5] (3) When 'tis given without our worthiness; I mean, without that excellency in our persons or actions that should move the giver to love and beneficence. For it certainly shows the more abundant and overflowing goodness, or inclination to communicate good, by how much the less loveliness or worthiness there is to entice beneficence; for one with but little goodness may be drawn by abundant beauty to incline to do good, when he whose goodness is more abundant will be inclined to do good to the less deserving. And certainly 'tis agreeable to the common sense of mankind, that the less worthy and excellent the receiver is, the more is he obliged and the greater gratitude is due; as appears in all nations. How much more is a prisoner, pardoned, affected when he considers his unworthiness, than if he thought he were worthy. And further, 'tis certain by the Word of God, that in this partly does consist freedom of grace; because God often uses this very argument with men, to move them to love him and acknowledge his goodness, even their unworthiness: but nobody that has any manner of acquaintances with the Scripture will deny, that this is there spoken of as what enhances the goodness of God.

The question about free grace with respect to the first of these is, whether or no pardon and salvation be not given to us without our satisfying for our sins, or at least in some measure satisfying for them, or doing something towards it. [With respect to the] second [the question is], whether God gives men salvation without their previous profiting or in some way pleasuring God, or upon condition of their so doing, as a retribution of what he bestows. The question with respect to the third is, whether or no God be not at least in some measure moved and inclined, by the excellency and beauty of our persons or actions, to bestow salvation upon us.[6]

---

5. As originally written, the paragraph contained four specifications, of which the third was, "(3) When 'tis given without our labor and pains; because so much trouble as there is in the prerequisite pains and labor to counterbalance the good of the gift, so much is to be subtracted from the gift, and beneficence is so much the less. This is mathematically certain." JE deleted it and changed the numerals while writing the last paragraph of the entry.
   6. Entry Nos. 124–125b were probably composed between Nos. 191 and 192.

192. WISDOM OF THE CREATION. The contrivance of the organs of speech is peculiarly wonderful. In the first place, no other way in the world can be thought of so convenient for the communicating our minds, as by sounds. But one would think that it would be impossible that it should be done by sounds, or that organs should be contrived that should quickly and easily give so many clearly distinguishable sounds, and yet short ones, as there are innumerable different sentiments of mind to be expressed; for we see nothing else in the world by which such a distinction can be made, or anything like. We can make but few distinct sounds by anything else we can find or make; but with the organs of speech an infinite number, by the various ordering of the throat and tongue. And these distinctions are very clear and plain, and yet all reducible to a very few simple ones; so that almost every sound may be by rule easily reduced to four and twenty letters, and at the same time these organs shall be excellently adapted to innumerable other uses.

193. SABBATHS. 'Tis strange to see what a wonderful influence it has upon one's mind, only to think that this or that time, in itself not differing from other times, is appropriated or set apart for this or that. Thus our elections are times of pleasure and rejoicing; and what an influence has it on the mind of the youth all over the Colony,[7] to think this time is by general agreement made a time of mirth. How uneasy are they if they are alone and not in company, and han't opportunity to be merry as well as others; how extraordinarily unnatural and unpleasant does serious business and solitude seem at such a time, which would seem pleasant at another time; and how does it promote mirth, to think that the whole country are then merry. This abundantly convinces me of the rational foundation of sabbaths, and holy days of fasts and thanksgivings. For why should not a time's being set apart for holy exercises, promote a holy disposition; a time's being set apart for holy joy, promote that; and a time's being set apart for sorrow and humiliation, promote that; and the consideration that the whole country is at devotion, joyful, or sorrowful, beget like dispositions in men?[8]

194. GOD. That is a gross and an unprofitable idea we have of God, as being something large and great as bodies are, and infinitely ex-

----

7. At this time Connecticut Colony still retained the right to elect its own governor, while Massachusetts had become a royal province with a governor appointed by the crown.

8. Entry No. 27a was written very close in time to Nos. 193 and 194, indeed probably between them.

tended throughout the immense space. For God is neither little nor great with that sort of greatness, even as the soul of man; it is not at all extended, no more than an idea, and is not present anywhere as bodies are present, as we have shown elsewhere.[9] So 'tis with respect to the increated Spirit. The greatness of a soul consists not in any extension, but [in] its comprehensiveness of idea and extendedness of operation. So the infiniteness of God consists in his perfect comprehension of all things and the extendedness of his operation equally to all places. God is present nowhere any otherwise than the soul is in the body or brain, and he is present everywhere as the soul is in the body. We ought to conceive of God as being omnipotence, perfect knowledge and perfect love; and not extended any otherwise than as power, knowledge and love are extended; and not as if it was a sort of unknown thing that we call substance, that is extended.

195. CHRISTIAN RELIGION. There are a great many expressions in the Scripture that the penmen of them did not know enough of nature to say of themselves; for instance, where the apostle John in his Revelation represents the noise that he heard, caused by the exalted praises of the hundred forty and four thousand upon Mount Zion. Rev. 14:2, "And I heard a voice from heaven, as the voice of many waters, and as the voice of a great thunder; and I heard the voice of harpers harping with their harps." How exceeding natural and beautiful is this, to represent the loud and exalted praises and singing of the heavenly multitude heard at a great distance by a noise that partly represented loud thunder at a distance, and of many waters roaring, and yet the music could be distinguished. How exceeding natural and beautiful is this! Now what should move an ignorant man, that pretended he had heard the voice of the armies of heaven in their singing, to say that it seemed like loud thunder or the roaring of many waters, and yet like the sound of harps? For if the learnedest man in the world should study his whole lifetime, he could not represent it more naturally. And again, in the 19th chapter at the 6th verse. And indeed this book of the Revelation is full of such strokes, that for their naturalness exceed all human invention or imitation, and denote a knowledge of nature beyond what ever I saw anywhere in human writings.

9. Behind this entry lies "Being," which JE had been perusing when he wrote No. 27a (see previous note) and possibly "Atoms," prop. 2, corol. 11 (*Works, 6,* 215); it is also likely that he had reread "The Mind" no. 2 (ibid., pp. 338–39) and had written no. 31 and possibly No. 32 (ibid., pp. 352–53) shortly before writing No. 194.

196. CHRISTIAN RELIGION. 'Tis exceeding improbable that it should ever enter into the head of any mortal, to go to invent such a strange system of visions as that of the Revelation, that he himself could give no manner of account of their meaning or design, nor did not pretend to it. What design could he have in it? But if he had a design, the frame and make of the visions is not a whit like a random invention, without any view or design as to interpretation.

197. CHRISTIAN RELIGION. It seems to me exceeding congruous and [in] the highest manner consentaneous, that God, a being of infinite goodness and love, who, it's evident from mere reason, created the world for this very end, to make the creature happy in his love—I say, it seems exceeding congruous, that he should give to the creature the highest sort of evidence or expression of love. For why should not that love which is infinitely higher than any others, and the love of a being infinitely more excellent, of which other love is but the emanation and shadow, why should not that love have the highest and most noble manifestations, and the surest evidences?

Now we know that the highest sort of manifestation and evidence of love is expense for the beloved. How much soever the lover gives or communicates to the beloved, yet if he is at no expense himself, there is not that high and noble expression of love, as if otherwise. Now I can clearly and distinctly conceive, how the giving of Christ should have all that in it, that renders it every way an equal and like and perfectly equivalent expression of love, as the greatest expense in a lover, as I have shown elsewhere.[1] And this is a way that is exceeding noble and excellent, and agreeable to the glorious perfections of God. But no other way can be conceived of, and they that deny the Christian religion can pretend no other; and if they do, 'tis impossible they should think of any in any measure so exalted, noble and excellent.

198. HAPPINESS. How soon do earthly lovers come to an end of their discoveries of each other's beauty; how soon do they see all that is to be seen! Are they united as near as 'tis possible, and have communion as intimate as possible? how soon do they come to the most endearing expressions of love that 'tis possible to give, so that no new ways can be

1. This notion of equivalence may be found in No. b, in association with Christ's love (though not with the Father's giving of Christ), but not in other entries prior to No. 197. "Elsewhere" here probably means elsewhere than in the "Miscellanies," but the writing to which he refers does not seem to be extant.

invented, given or received. And how happy is that love, in which there is an eternal progress in all these things; wherein new beauties are continually discovered, and more and more loveliness, and in which we shall forever increase in beauty outselves; where we shall be made capable of finding out and giving, and shall receive, more and more endearing expressions of love forever: our union will become more close, and communion more intimate.

199. GOD'S EXISTENCE. The existence of our own souls, which we know more immediately than anything, is an argument of exceeding glaring evidence for the existence of a God. Our souls were not always, but they are wonderful beings, certainly exceeding in contrivance everything that is seen or can be seen with eyes. They are pieces of workmanship so curious, and of such amazing contrivance, that their operations infinitely exceed those of any machines that are seen.

Let us consider what has been done, and what is daily done, by human souls. What strange contrivance is this, to take in the sun moon and stars, and the whole universe, and bring all distant things together; and to make past and future things present; and to move the body after such a manner, to produce such strange effects on other souls and in the corporeal world! If our souls are material machines, certainly they are so curious, that none will deny that they are the effect of contrivance. Let them be created immediately, or let them be by propagation, the contrivance is wonderful; for what contrivance is necessary to make such machines, that will produce and propagate other such machines in an infinite succession! And if they be not material, whence are they, if not from a superior immaterial being? And if we say our souls existed from eternity, who is it orders it so, that upon every generation a soul shall be brought and united to such a parcel of matter? Or if we say our souls existed in the bodies from eternity, existing one within another *in infinitum*, who contrived this matter so?

200. GOD'S EXISTENCE. If the atheist will not acknowledge any great order and regularity in the corporeal world, he must acknowledge that there is in spirits, in minds; which will be as much an argument for a contriver, as if the contrivance was in bodies. He must acknowledge that reason, wisdom and contrivance are regular actions; but they are the actions of spirits. Many of the works of men are wonderfully regular, but certainly no more regular than the contrivance that was the author of them. And who made these beings, that [they] should act as

regularly as the nicest machines of men? Did such nice beings come by chance, or were they not the effect of a superior contrivance?

Corol. Hence we see that all men's works, and human inventions and artifices, are arguments for the existence of God, as well as those that are more immediately the works of God; for they are only the regular actings of God's works. When we walk in stately cities or admire curious machines and inventions, let us argue the wisdom of God, as well as of the immediate contrivers; for those spirits who were the contrivers are the most wonderful contrivances.

201. FAITH. There is such a thing as an appearing real, that is, a conviction of the reality of a thing, that is incommunicable, that cannot be drawn out into formal arguments or be expressed in words, which is yet the strongest and most certain conviction. We know how things appear that are real, with what an air; we know how those things appear which we behold with waking eyes. They appear real, because we have a clear idea of them in all their various mutual relations, concurring circumstances, order[2] and dispositions—the consent of the simple ideas among themselves, and with the compages of beings, and the whole train of ideas in our minds, and with the nature and constitution of our minds themselves: which consents and harmony consists in ten thousand little relations and mutual agreements that are ineffable.

Such is the idea of religion, which is so exceedingly complex, in the minds of those who are taught by the Spirit of God. The idea appears so real to them, and brings so many strong yet ineffable marks of truth, that 'tis a sort of intuitive evidence, and an evidence that the nature of the soul will not allow it to reject. This is the testimony of the Spirit, and is a sort of seeing rather than reasoning the truth of religion; which the unlearned are as capable of as the learned, and which all the learning in the world can never overthrow.

202. CHRISTIAN RELIGION. 'Tis proof that Scripture history [is true], that the geography[3] is consistent. Were it a mere fiction, the geography must be feigned too, at least in great measure, and there would unavoidably be innumerable blunders and inconsistencies. Take the Acts of the Apostles for instance: if that history be not in the main true, there would doubtless be many blunders in accounts of so many travel-

2. Or "orders."
3. MS: "proof of the truth that Scripture history that that the geography."

ing through so many parts of the world, inconsistencies about the position or distance of places, inconsistencies in one part with another of the account, or great inconsistencies with the truth of geography.

203. CHRISTIAN RELIGION. It don't seem to me at all likely, that anybody amongst the Jews so long ago should have so perfect a knowledge of nature and the secret springs of human affections, as to feign anything so perfectly and exquisitely agreeable to nature as the incidents in Joseph's history and the other histories of the Bible, particularly the history of Genesis.

204. CHRISTIAN RELIGION. If man's natural reason were never so perfect, and however little need we had of revelation for the enlightening our darkness and correcting our errors, yet it would be most unreasonable to suppose that there never should be any revelation made to man; that there should [be] no intercourse between the Supreme Being and the order of beings next to him, even rational beings; that communication should be cut off between God and the highest order of his creatures, though it is continued through all other steps and degrees; that God should make a perceiving, conscious and understanding creature to think that he may perceive and understand Him and His works, and yet forever entirely shut Himself out from him, and have nothing to say to him or to do with him by way of communion. God has communication with or influence upon all other creatures according to their nature, upon bodies according to the nature and capacity of body; and how unreasonable is it to suppose that he holds no communication with spirits according to their nature and capacity.

Now we know that the proper way of spirits' communicating one with another is by communion or conversation. This is as much the proper way of spirits' communication one with another, as bodies' mutual attraction, motion and impulsion is the proper way of bodies' communication. And 'tis evident, God made spirits to have communion; and will he not have any communion with them himself, although they are made for this very end, to meditate on him and to love [him]? How unreasonable is it then to suppose, that God will so abscond himself from these his understanding creatures, that were made to be conversant about him!

And the way of God's holding communion with men that the Christian religion supposes, is the most congruous that can possibly be

thought of towards men in a fallen estate and in a wicked world, viz. to
have his word written in a volume: where the matter is so various, so
exceeding comprehensive and diversified, and suited to every circumstance; the texts having so many different aspects, respects, aptitudes
and senses, as beheld in different lights and compared with God's
providences or other parts of his Word. And there are such influences
and teachings of the Spirit of God accompanying it to exhibit this Word
thus in its various lights, continually bringing forth something new
suited to the present stream of our thoughts, affections, and our case;
that is just as if God held up a continual conversation by word of
mouth to those that read, understand and believe. And God doth
indeed hold communion with [them]; and yet this is done in a secret
way hidden from the wicked world, who it is not proper should see and
intermeddle, nor is it exposed to their abuse and mockery—pearls are
not cast before swine—for though they can read the Bible, there is
nothing of this communion with God enjoyed by them, but all is to
them as a déad letter. What other way can be thought of, so congruous
as this?

205. ΘΕΆΝΘΡΟΠΟΣ. The man Christ Jesus, being the same person with
the eternal Son of God, has a reminiscence or consciousness of what
appertained to the eternal Logos, and so of his happiness with the
Father. Therefore we often find Christ speaking as being very well
acquainted with the Father before he came into the world, and speaking of transactions betwixt him and the Father before he came, as if
there were an agreement about the work of redemption, what he
should teach, what he should do and who should be his. Thus Christ
frequently tells us, what he doth he don't do of himself, but as he was
ordered of the Father; and that he did not teach of himself, but that he
had received of his Father what he should teach, before he came down
from heaven, etc. So he speaks of his coming down from heaven, as if
he remembered how he was once there and how he came down.

Now when he remembered those things, he could not remember
[them] as they were in the infinite mind, for the idea of the Creator
cannot be communicated to the creature as it is in God; but the remembrance, as it was in his mind, was the same after a different manner: the things which he remembered were from all eternity in the
Logos after the manner of God; and the man Christ Jesus was conscious to himself of them as if they had been after the manner of a
creature. Those transactions which Christ speaks of in the covenant of

redemption was [in] the Deity no other than the eternal and immutable gracious design, both of the Father and Son, of what was to be done by the Son and what was to be the fruit of it. 'Twas impossible that the man Christ Jesus should remember this as it was in the Deity, for then an idea of the eternal mind could be communicated to a finite mind even as it is in the infinite mind; but he remembered it as if it had been really such a transaction, before the world was, between him and the Father. Not that he was deceived, for he knew how it was; but as the consciousness of it was communicated to him, it must of necessity seem thus. So he prays in the forementioned place [John 17:5] that God would glorify him with the glory he had with him before the world was. 'Tis very manifest that he speaks as remembering, but 'twas impossible that he should remember infinite glory and happiness; but he remembered and was conscious [of it] to himself. His idea was finite, otherwise he could not pray that he might have the same glory again; for the man did not desire infinite glory, but he desired such glory as he remembered, that was the same as God the Son had, as near as the same could be communicated, either in conception or enjoyment, to Christ the creature.

That in the general it was thus is no bold conjecture, but so it must of necessity be; though the particular manner of this consciousness, and how far the ideas of a creature can be after the manner of the divine, and how a creature may be said to remember what is in God, is uncertain.

Corol. And this may satisfy, with respect to all that can be said about a glorious created spirit, which was the Son of God, being created before the world was created. Christ Jesus did indeed remember, as if he had existed a creature before the foundation of the world; because 'twas impossible that the idea of the Logos should be communicated to a creature, otherwise than as the idea of a creature, nor cause a creature to remember it, otherwise than as if it had been the idea of a creature.

206. HEAVEN. In heaven 'tis the directly reverse of what 'tis on earth; for there, by length of time things become more and more youthful, that is, more vigorous, active, tender and beautiful.

207. CONFIRMATION is undoubtedly a gospel institution, and sacrament too; and 'tis the sacrament of the Lord's Supper: that is the confirmation that Christ has instituted. Children, as soon as ever they are capable of it, should come and publicly make what was done in

their baptism their own act by partaking of the Lord's Supper; and he is confirmed by him who has the care of his soul when he admits him to that ordinance and administers it to him. Christ Jesus likewise hereby confirms him, and seals over again the same covenant, and to a worthy partaker gives the seal of the Spirit. Christ appointed it for that very end, to confirm and renew the covenant sealed in baptism, his covenant with them and theirs with him, and to confirm their union with the church (signified in baptism) by this holy communion with them in the bonds of love and peace. And what is there that is pretended to be done in episcopal confirmation that Christ did not design the Lord's Supper for? and what need of any new invented confirmation? Is Christ's institution less conducing to the end of it than theirs?

208. GLORY OF [GOD]. God loves his creatures, so that he really loves the being honored by them, as all love to be well thought of by those they love. Therefore we are to seek the glory of God as that which is a thing really pleasing to him.

209. HOLY GHOST. For this reason, very probably, is the Holy Ghost called "the oil of gladness" [Ps. 45:7; Heb. 1:9], being the infinite joy and delight of God.

210. SPIRIT OF GOD. Man's reason and conscience seem to be a participation of the divine essence. The giving of the Holy Spirit, therefore, in sanctification, is a sort of adding a new soul to this that is come to nothing, or is making a new soul of this: whence we may explain the manner of the Spirit's operation.

211. COMMUNION OF THE HOLY GHOST. In this Scripture phrase [II Cor. 13:14], [by] the word "communion" seems to be meant our communion or common partaking of the Holy Ghost with other saints; for this the apostles frequently insisted on in their epistles.

212. FAITH, SAVING. As in other things 'tis the dictate of the understanding, in conjunction with the clearness and liveliness of the idea, that determines the will, so it is in heavenly things: 'tis the determination of the understanding that the offer of the gospel is true, in conjunction with a clear and sensible idea of the excellence of it, that is true faith. A man may in a sort believe that good people shall be happy

forever, but have no notion of the excellence of such an happiness; and therefore it influences not his[4] actions.

213. LOVE OF GOD. God's love to the saints may be said to be infinite. For the more holy the saints are, the more they love the saints: for the same reason, Christ, who is infinitely holy, loves the same saints infinitely.

214. ASCENSION OF CHRIST. 'Tis most reasonable to suppose that the settled place of the Messiah's reign should not be anywhere but in heaven. If he be God, he must be immensely exalted above earthly princes; but the place of his exaltation is where God gloriously manifests himself, which is the highest part of the creation; we can't suppose that the Messiah should all this while be kept from heavenly glory. Though he is in heaven, he is not out of sight. And 'tis proper and congruous to the constitution of the heavenly kingdom, that he should be viewed with a spiritual eye; and inconsistent with it, that he in this world should be the object of sight and not of faith. The Old Testament, when speaking of gospel times, speaks of God's being in the heavens, whereas then God was between the cherubims: partly for this reason is the gospel kingdom the heavenly, and the church of the Israelites the earthly, kingdom.

215. JUDGMENT DAY. We need no more than the knowledge of the nature of things, to know that this world must come to an end: mutual attraction, stoppage by attrition, and *vis inertiæ* of matter, and the gradual evening of the face of the earth, will either of them in time unavoidably bring its ruin. But who can imagine that this earth, which God has made for one of the dwelling places of his reasonable creatures, who God doubtless placed here for some business—I say, who can imagine that it should be utterly destroyed, without God's taking any notice of or saying anything about what has been done upon it, but let all the transactions of mankind go off in public silence, without his sentence about 'em?

216. FAITH, JUSTIFYING. The soul's believing Jesus Christ to be its own Savior may very commonly be joined with the first act of saving

4. MS: "their."

faith. For having constantly been instructed that Christ is willing to receive and save all that come to him (that is, that are disposed to him with entire inclination), and having habitually that notion of Christ by hearing and reading it so often, the idea of readiness to save is joined with that of Christ, though not by faith yet by the association of ideas. So that the first time the sinner, while thinking of Christ, feels the exertion of a willing disposition and loving desire to submit and resign (it seeming an excellent and desirable thing to be saved by Christ), and having habitually the notion that Christ sees his heart, he in the same moment by habit conceives of him as accepting him to be one of his; which habitual conception the alteration of the nature of his soul turns into belief.

These things, for aught I see, may be as much in the mind at once as the parts of a complex idea. If we consider our own minds, we shall find we do very often upon occasion, by virtue of habit and prepossession of our understandings, think of many things at once, so as to act upon those thoughts. We see persons do things with regularity and exactness, and at the same time have their thoughts fixed, and words and actions too, on something else. But it's no matter, I don't insist upon it, whether it be at the same moment or no: it's equivalent, if these acts are as naturally drawn one by another as the links of a chain, as quick as one thought can follow another.

The habitual notion we spake of, that Christ is ready to save all, is begotten by the outward call. But when the sinner feels such a submissive disposition towards [Christ that] this belief is[5] as if he heard the voice of Christ calling him, and he finds that motion in his mind that can be represented by nothing but coming, then is he effectually called.

217. TRINITY. The infinite delight of the Father in the Son may be denoted by the name of David, which signifies "beloved," by which name Christ himself is sometimes called in the Old Testament; and by the name of "beloved" in the New, or, by a word that [is] the same in Greek as David in the Hebrew.

218. FAITH, JUSTIFYING. 'Tis the same agreeing or consenting disposition that according to the divers objects, different state or manner of exerting, is called by different names. When 'tis exerted towards a Savior, [it is called] faith or trust; when towards one that governs us

---

5. Or "towards this belief [that it] is."

and orders our affairs for us, faith or trust; when towards one that tells and teaches us, faith or belief; when towards a Savior, a governor and instructor (or a king, priest and prophet) in one, by no other name than faith; when towards doctrines, whether of things past, present or to come, faith or belief; when towards unseen good things promised, faith and also hope; when towards a gospel or good news, faith; when towards persons excellent, love; when towards commands, obedience; when towards God with respect to changes, 'tis properly called resignation; when with respect to calamities, submission.

Believing must be to the degree of trust before it is saving. Though unregenerate men may in some measure believe the gospel, yet they don't believe it so that they dare to trust to it; they are not willing to perform its prescriptions, trusting to its offers, which is true believing in Christ. And surely good works are supported by such a faith.

219. FAITH, JUSTIFYING. 'Tis more properly called faith than acceptance, because the things received are spiritual and unseen, and because they are received as future.

220. GRACE. HOLY SPIRIT. All gospel righteousness, virtue and holiness is called grace, not only because 'tis entirely the free gift of God, but because 'tis the Holy Spirit in man; which, as we have said, is grace or love.

N. B. Rightly are "grace," "favor" and "beauty" one word in the Hebrew language and some others. This grace is the Holy Spirit; because it is said, we receive of Christ's fullness, and grace for his grace [John 1:16].[6]

221. MEDIATION OF CHRIST. When we say, "for the sake of" such or such a person, it implies that the thing we speak of will be for the advantage of that person, and that he will get by it. Wherefore, when we pray for grace for the sake of Christ, we should intend thereby to desire God to remember that 'twill be to his Son's joy and happiness; for the bestowment of God's grace upon us was the joy that was set before him, the reward he expected, that made him cheerfully subject himself to such torments. Our happiness was a thing he really desired, and made an agreement with God about, by which he was to undertake great labors, such as never were undertaken by another, and this was

6. This sentence is an interlined addition, in a kind of ink that does not appear before No. 330.

the prize and crown that he did it for; and the more of us obtain grace, and the more grace and happiness we obtain, the more pleasure and glory doth he enjoy. And therefore 'tis for his sake we may ask of God, for our grace is his joy.

222. COVENANT, NEW. See what has been said of the new covenant.[7] To be the mediator of a covenant is to stand in the stead of the rest as their representative, in making the covenant at least, and it may be in performing it: and so he will be mediator both ways, of the other party covenanting to them he represents, and of them to him. So Christ is called the Mediator of the new covenant, the new covenant being made with him before the foundation of the world, as the first covenant was made with Adam, our first representative.

223. HOLY SPIRIT. TRINITY. The Apostle's blessing, wherein he wishes "the grace of the Lord Jesus Christ, the love of God the Father, and communion of the Holy Ghost" [II Cor. 13:14], contains not different things but is simple: 'tis the same blessing, even the Spirit of God, which is the comprehension of all happiness. Therefore the Apostle in his blessing to the Corinthians [I Cor. 16:23–24] says, "The grace of our Lord Jesus Christ be with you. My love be with you in Christ Jesus. Amen"—Christian love being the communication of God's love, and the Holy Ghost dwelling in us.

224. HOLY SPIRIT. The Holy Spirit is given[8] much in the resemblance of its being given to Christ from the Father, as appears from John 1:32–33.

225. HOLY SPIRIT. The name of the Son of God is Messiah and Christ, not only because there was an extraordinary pouring out of the Holy Ghost upon the man Christ Jesus, and giving the Spirit without measure unto him, as separating him to and preparing him for his work; nor are these names proper to Christ only as man, or as Mediator: but God the Son from all eternity was Christ, or anointed with the Holy Spirit without measure, strictly speaking, or with the infinite love of the Father towards him.

As the sons of men are begotten of earthly love, so the sons of God are begotten of divine love, or born of the Spirit.

7. JE is probably referring to Nos. 163, 165, and 171; he may also have in mind an earlier series, Nos. 2, 30, and 35.
8. I.e. to believers.

226. Holy Spirit. Oil well represented excellence and love because of its flowing smoothness, and because it was used by them for the sake of beauty; as the Psalmist says (Ps. 104:15), it was to make the face to shine; which is the proper effect of an extraordinary effusion of the Holy Spirit and exercise of divine grace, as in Moses and Stephen. The shining of man's face, we know, is put for beauty, excellence and joy; and of God's countenance, [for] his love and favor. Especially did the holy anointing oil resemble love and excellence by its great preciousness and fragrance. Love is compared to this anointing oil by the Psalmist; "Like the precious ointment," says he, etc. (Ps. 133). 'Tis again compared to ointment (Cant. 4:10) and to the spices with which the holy oil was perfumed, all over that song.

227. Holy Spirit. See the foregoing. By these reflections we may perhaps gain light into many things in Scripture: as the meaning of burning lamps before God in the tabernacle and temple that were fed with oil; why the Holy Ghost is represented by lamps burning before the throne; and understand the parable of the ten virgins, with their lamps and oil in their vessels; why Christ is called the true olive tree, and the ministers of grace olive trees; how we are made partakers of the divine nature; and another reason why the dove, the emblem of the Holy Ghost, brought an olive leaf in his mouth, a leaf of the tree from whence their oil was taken, by which love and peace was signified.

228. Communion of Saints. What the primitive Christians meant by the communion of saints seems to be this, that believers or Christians (which at first were most commonly called saints) of the gentiles and all nations, were equally partakers of the peculiar benefits and blessings of God's people. This was a great article of faith among them, and strongly opposed by the unbelieving Jews and by many of those that believed; which 'tis probable was the occasion of making it an article of the Creed. This seems to be the first meaning of the phrase, as with respect to this it is commonly used in the New Testament; which is by the apostles spoken of in an exalted manner as a very glorious discovery, doctrine, and blessing of the gospel, and is much insisted on by them.

229. Scripture. God had a design and meaning which the penmen never thought of, which he makes appear these ways: by his own interpretation, and by his directing the penmen to such a phrase and manner of speaking, that has a much more exact agreement and con-

sonancy with the thing remotely pointed to, than with the thing meant by the penmen. And this very frequently[9] (which is a very reasonable way of arguing), both where their meaning was not agreeable to strict philosophical verity, and he condescended to their manner of speaking and thinking, and likewise where the more immediate and remote meanings were properly true—very frequently in the Old Testament, and sometimes in the New.

230. HEAVEN. The saints whom we shall so ardently love loving others as well as ourselves, will be so far from raising jealousy in us, that it would raise jealousy if they did not. For their love of other saints is so much for the same things, and is so much the same principle, that 'tis equivalent to love to ourselves; it will be only the love to us multiplied.

We shall not be jealous of those that are higher in glory, not only because we shall love them most, and because they will be most humble, but because they will love us most; because the highest will be the holiest, and the most holy will love holiness best, and they that love holiness best will love the saints best.

231. INSPIRATION. See The Mind, p. 7, no. 7.[1]

232. MISERY OF THE DAMNED. When wicked men are solitary, without any exercise or objects to amuse or divert their minds, then a horror and doleful sense is wont to seize their mind from the apprehension of their state; everything begins to grow dark and dismal to them. So they say 'tis sometimes with the pirates early in the morning, before their spirits are heated and raised by the talk and actions of the day. The souls of the wicked departed will therefore naturally fall into horror and amazement, when they shall have no employment, no company, no diversion or exercise besides thinking of their own wickedness and misery, shall see none of those pleasant objects that used to lull their consciences asleep; they shall see nothing but darkness and damned ghosts; [they] then shall not see a pleasant adorned and smiling world as now, but everything about them shall appear with the footsteps of God's wrath and hatred.

Again, the ill will and hatred of any being, though the meanest—

9. MS: "frequent."
1. MS: "p. 7. 7," i.e. the seventh entry on p. 7 according to the pagination used in JE's earlier (and now lost) index to "The Mind"; the item is the one numbered 20 by Dwight (*Works, 6,* 346). On the pagination of "The Mind," see ibid., pp. 321–22.

absolutely and in itself considered—is ungrateful and contrary to the disposition of nature, whether we in the least fear any injury as the effect of it or no. (And this will appear by what has been said under the head of excellency and love in our Discourse on the Mind.)[2] However, there may be considerations that may lift one quite above [it], as one may disregard a small bodily pain in the midst of abundance of pleasure and prosperity, and when we know that we shall not be really the worse for it; yea, we may rejoice in it as the case may be, if we are sure of gaining by it, etc. As pleasure supports against pain, so the good will of those we apprehend great and excellent, or of many, may cause us to despise the ill will of few, and those that are inconsiderable.

There are these things that render the displeasure of any being [painful], considered abstractedly from the evil that he [may] do us from that displeasure: (1) 'Tis according as a being is great, whether this greatness be in one single being or be made up in a multitude, for many small are equal to one great. (2) According to the excellency of any being. If a being be of great power and knowledge, and so are great, yet if they are odious and hateful it don't affect us so much to be the object of their anger. (3) According as what cause there be for their displeasure. If their displeasure be just, we are more exposed to uneasiness from an apprehension of it; but if we know that however angry anyone [is] with us we are innocent, this supports us—though this perhaps arises from a secret apprehension of being vindicated by some invisible superior being. (4) According as our minds are nearly concerned with a person, that is, according as there are frequent occasions of receiving very lively and strong ideas of his displeasure. Thus if some man in China were very angry with me, I should not regard it so much as the displeasure of one that lived near me, who I often saw and had frequent occasion to observe the expressions of his anger. (5) Such sort of circumstances as these do exceedingly aggravate our uneasy sense of a superior being's displeasure if we formerly had his favor, or might easily have had it, to a great degree.

Now with respect to the displeasure of God, the wicked in the other world will clearly see, and be in the strongest manner impressed with, the greatness of God. And there [will] be the regard of no other being as considerable to support against the apprehension of his wrath; for he shall then appear as immensely the greatest being, yea he shall appear as the comprehension of all being. Nor indeed shall they have

2. It is evidently no. 45 to which JE refers, and in particular § 14 *(Works, 6, 365–66).*

the good will of any being whatever. The devil and other damned will hate them with perfect hatred—there will be the perfection of hatred in hell, as well as the perfection of love in heaven. They shall likewise know that God is immensely excellent, and they shall be hated by all other excellent beings whatever. And then their consciences shall tell them that this displeasure and wrath is most just. And the angry God will appear as most intimately present with [them]: he with his wrath will be in them and before them and everywhere round about them, expressing his furious displeasure; and they shall see and feel and be as sensible of God's presence, as we are of a man's that stands before our eyes. And everything that is seen will have an impression of God's anger upon it; all things round about will look grim and dreadful with the appearances of God's anger in them. So that there will be that aggravation of ever being concerned immediately with God, and having continual occasion to see the expressions of God's displeasure. I say, there will be that in the highest degree.

The[3] appearances of the presence of [an] angry God in them and everywhere round about them, can be represented by nothing better than by their being in the midst of an exceeding hot and furious fire, that with its heat so pierces all their inward parts and so entirely possesses them, that their whole bodies without and within, their heart and their brains and all, are more than red with the glowing heat, and yet alive. Doubtless God is able to make us as miserable as any such comparisons can represent, and yet fully sustain being and life. I have sometimes thought of it when a worm or spider have been thrown into the fire, when they have retained their shape after burned to a coal, and looked white with the fierceness of the heat: how great pain would that insect endure, if every part were now as sensible as when first thrown into the fire!

And all this will be aggravated by the remembrance, that God once loved us so as to give his Son to bring us to the happiness of his love, and tried all manner of means to persuade us to accept of his favor, which was obstinately refused.

233. HAPPINESS OF HEAVEN. We know not what sort of bodies the saints shall have after the resurrection. But it seems to me probable,

---

3. JE wrote this paragraph after completing the entry and marked it for insertion at this point. As a purely physical description of hell torment, it interrupts the continuity between the preceding ontological-psychological treatment of divine displeasure and what is now the last sentence of the entry.

that as the bodies of the wicked shall be tormented as well as their souls (in that Christ says both soul and body shall be cast into hell), so the glorified spiritual bodies of the saints shall be filled with pleasures of the most exquisite kind that such refined bodies are capable of; not with any pleasures that in the least tend to clog the mind, and divert from mental and spiritual pleasure and the pure joys of holiness. They shall in no measure be equal to them,[4] but as an additament to them; the mind shall not be so naturally and strongly affected by them as by spiritual satisfactions, and so there will be no danger of being diverted from them. The pleasures of the body shall rather assist those of the mind, and shall put the mind into a sprightly frame, and shall be the effects of a holy exercise of mind, and shall be in proportion to the divine joy of the soul. The sweetness and pleasure that shall be in the mind, shall put the spirits of the body into such a motion as shall cause a sweet sensation throughout the body, infinitely excelling any sensual pleasure here.

There are none of the arguments made use of to prove that the bodies of sinners must be punished as well as their souls (having been companions in sin, etc.),[5] but what are of equal force to evince that the bodies of the saints shall be rewarded. And certainly 'tis represented in Scripture that the bodies of saints shall be gainers by the resurrection, which they can be in no other sense.

234. CHRISTIAN RELIGION. AFFLICTION OF THE GODLY. It was requisite that those that are redeemed by Christ should experience affliction, and death itself, upon this account as well as others, that they may experimentally be sensible of the evils they are saved from, that their hearts may be more filled with joy, love and praise for their redemption.

235. COVENANT OF GRACE. DEATH. Christ has redeemed his people from all the curse of the law, from the whole guilt of sin. How then shall we reconcile the death, and those afflictions previous to it that are as so many deaths, and the covenant of grace? for it seems part of the curse of the law still remains taken away for none, but is unavoidable by believers as well as others. I answer, the same death that was the curse of the law remains, but the curse of the law remains not. God has taken

4. I.e. the pleasures the saints receive from their glorified bodies will not equal their mental and spiritual joys.
5. JE had already given some of these arguments in No. cc.

as many of the threatenings of the law as he pleased into his own new covenant; and those adversities and death, that were so many degrees of that curse, are, according to the new covenant, so many steps that are necessary in order to deliverance from that curse. So they are delivered from the curse of the law by death.

Such is the state of man already before his redemption, that he can't be completely redeemed without he passes through death in order to it. The sinner, before the new covenant, is got a great way into darkness; and he must be led back through darkness awhile, before he can get out of it into the light. He is already gotten into the land of iniquity, that land of pits and drought and the shadow of death; and if he is delivered out of it, he must pass through that valley that encompasses it. 'Tis true, Christ has paid down a price, whereby he has bought him from all the horrors of that land; but not so that he shall be instantly free from them, but so that he shall be led out of them, through the midst of them that already lie between him and heaven. The body is already infected, and the great Physician has bound himself by his covenant perfectly to heal; but the nature of the disease requires some irksome medicine, which medicine is taken into the covenant.[6]

236. CHRISTIAN RELIGION. Such kind of miracles as healing the sick, the blind, the deaf, dumb, lame, etc. and creating bread [and] flesh, and turning water into wine, are greater miracles than those that are so much more pompous, of causing universal darkness, dividing the sea, the shaking and burning of Mount Sinai, etc. 'Tis a greater work to give exactly that disposition of parts to air or earth that shall cause bread or fish, than to cause such great motions that are merely the exercise of strength.

And the healing of the sick and distracted do more especially manifest divine power for this reason, because we may conclude that mankind are especially subject to God's providence, and that their health and the exercises of their reason, etc. are alone in his hand; and that it is not in the power of any evil spirit to give 'em and take 'em at their pleasure, however great power they may be supposed to have over the inanimate creatures.

When a person appears that has evidently the whole course of na-

6. JE began a new sheet and made four entries, which he numbered 236–239. At that point he left New Haven for Northampton, laid the sheet aside, and did not completely fill it for nearly two years, at which time he renumbered the entries Nos. 261–264. See above, pp. 83–84.

ture at all times subject to his command, so that he can alter it how and when he pleases, we have the greatest reason to think that that person has divine authority, and that the author and upholder of nature favors him and gives approbation to what he pretends thereby. For we know that the course of nature is God's established course of acting upon creatures, and we can't think that he would give power to any evil spirit, to alter it when he pleases for evil purposes; but Christ manifestly had the course of nature so subject to his will and command.

237. ETERNAL PUNISHMENT. It seems to me certain that the wicked that are punished by God will continue to hate God all the while they are punished, and that their punishment, instead of humbling them, will stir up their hatred to God and make them blaspheme him. Now it is not probable that their punishment will be either taken off or mitigated whilst they do so, nor that they will cease so to do while their punishment is upon them. Those minds that are so destitute of principles of virtue, will unavoidably dreadfully hate that being that brings so much misery upon them. Therefore, the punishment of the damned will be eternal.

238. TRINITY. Those ideas which we call ideas of reflection—all ideas of the acts of the mind, such as the ideas of thought, of choice, love, fear, etc.—if we diligently attend to our own minds, we shall find they are not properly representations, but are indeed repetitions of those very things, either more fully or more faintly; they therefore are not properly ideas. Thus 'tis impossible to have an idea of [a] thought or of an idea but it will [be] that same idea repeated.

So if we think of love, either of [our] own past love that is now vanished or of the love of others which we have not, we either so frame things in our imagination that we have for a moment a love to that thing or to something we make represent it, or we excite for a moment that love which we have and suppose it in another place, or we have only an idea of the antecedents concomitants and effects of love, and suppose something unseen, and govern our thoughts about [it] as we have learned how by experience and habit. Let anyone try himself in a particular instance and diligently observe. So if we have an idea of a judgment not our own, we have the same ideas that are the terms of the proposition repeated in our own minds, and recur to something in our own minds that is really our judgment, and suppose it there (that is, we govern our thoughts about it as if it were there), if we have a distinct idea of that judgment; or else we have only an idea of the attendants and effects of the judgment, and supply the name and [our] own actions about it as we have habituated ourselves.

And so certainly it is, in all our spiritual ideas. They are the very same things repeated, perhaps very faintly and obscurely, and very quick and momentaneously, and with many new references, suppositions and translations. But if the idea be perfect, it is only the same thing absolutely over again.

Now if this be certain, as it seems to me to be, then it's quite clear that if God doth think of himself and understand himself with perfect clearness fullness and distinctness, that that idea he hath of himself is absolutely himself again, and is God perfectly to all intents and purposes. That [idea] which God hath of the divine nature and essence is really and fully the divine nature and essence again; so that by God's thinking of himself the Deity must certainly be generated. This seems exceeding clear to me.[7] God doubtless understands himself in the most proper sense, for therein his infinite understanding chiefly consists; and he understands himself at all times perfectly, without intermission or succession in his thoughts.[8]

When we have the idea of another's love to a thing, if it be the love of a man to a woman that we are unconcerned about, in such cases we han't generally any proper idea at all of his love; we only have an idea of his actions that are the effects of love (as we have found by experience), and of those external things which belong to love, and which appear in case of love. Or if we have any idea of it, it is either by framing our ideas so, of persons and things as we suppose they appear to them, that we have a faint vanishing motion of that affection. Or if the thing be a thing that we so hate that this can't be, we have our love to something else faintly and least excited, and so in the mind as it were referred to this place; we think this is like that.

239. SPIRITUAL KNOWLEDGE. From what has been said under the foregoing head, we learn wherein spiritual knowledge consists. For seeing [that] in order to the knowledge of spiritual things there must be those things in the mind, at least in order to a knowledge anything clear and adequate, sinners must be destitute even of the ideas of

7. At this point JE began the next entry; but after writing the first three words he deleted them, completed the paragraph, and left an inch of additional space before No. 239.

8. The following paragraph was added later, in the space JE had left at the end of the entry, but probably before he wrote No. 240, judging by the ink.

many spiritual and heavenly things and of divine excellencies, because they don't experience them. It's impossible for them so much as to have the idea of faith, trust in God, holy resignation, divine love, Christian charity; because their mind is not possessed of those things, and therefore can't have an idea of the excellencies and beauties of God and Christ, of which those things are the image—he "knows not the things of the Spirit of God" [I Cor. 2:14].

240. URIM AND THUMMIM. There has been great inquiry, what was that urim and thummim that was in the breastplate of the high priest, whereas I think we have it plainly described in Ex. 28:17–21.[9] And I don't see that, from anything said in Scripture about it, we have reason to think it any other than those twelve precious stones with the names of the twelve tribes on them. And when it is said in v. 30, "And thou shalt put in the breastplate of judgment the urim and thummim," it is as if he had said thus, thou [shalt] put in the breastplate the urim and thummim which has been described. The drift of this verse does not seem to be to order anything new, but only to give a name to that which had been before described and to tell the use of it, viz. that Aaron might bear the judgment of the children of Israel upon his heart before the Lord continually; the which seems to me to intend, that the high priest might bear that upon his breast which in God's account and judgment should represent the children of Israel, and should stand for 'em before him upon the heart of the high priest their mediator. Every jewel stood for a tribe, and had the name of that tribe written on it that it stood for. God's people are called his jewels. So Christ bears our judgment; that is, he is our representative in judgment and, as to God's dealings with respect to his law, he stands for us.

The name "urim and thummim" signifies light and perfection; and it being 'tis the plural number, may more properly be rendered "glisterings" (or "brightnesses") and "beauties," because of the charming appearances that the jewels made by their different kinds of glister-

9. Matthew Poole summarized the inquiry up to his time in *Synopsis criticorum* (5 vols. London, 1669–76), *1*, Pars I, cols. 463–65; he more briefly sketched the chief answers to the riddle in his *Annotations* (Ex. 28:30, in loc.). John Spencer's epoch-making *Dissertatio de urim et thummim* (Cambridge, 1669) appeared in the same year as the first volume of Poole's *Synopsis*, but Poole ignored it in the *Annotations* (1683). Prideaux (see n. 2 below) mentioned Spencer but dismissed his ideas as "absurd and impious." Spencer had identified the urim and thummim with the teraphim and had cited parallels from Egyptian priestly divination. Poole considered the urim and thummim a "singular piece of Divine Workmansip," now indescribable, required as a condition for obtaining answers from God, and for Prideaux they meant simply the "divine vertue and power" which the breastplate possessed when properly used.

ings, and the beautiful proportion of their different colors. (The church that those jewels represented is in Ps. 50:2 called by a name that is much like to this, viz. "the perfection of beauty.") Some say there was an extraordinary brightness given those jewels beyond what was natural to them. That the urim and thummim were not two distinct things in the breastplate appears, because sometimes when they are spoken of, but one of the names are mentioned; it's called urim only, as Num 27:21 and I Sam. 28:6.

The use of it seems to be much the same with the plate of gold on the miter mentioned in Ex. 28:36, whereon was engraved "holiness to the Lord"; which the high priest was to have on his forehead, that he might bear the iniquity of the children of Israel, and that he might be accepted when he came in before the Lord (as v. 38). By the urim and thummim he was to bear the judgment of the children of Israel on his heart; by this plate of gold he was to bear the iniquity of the children of Israel on his head. We find them both mentioned after the same manner, where we have an account of Moses putting the holy garments upon Aaron, as in Lev. 8:8–9, "And he put the breastplate upon him; and he put in the breastplate the urim and the thummim. And he put the miter upon his head; also upon the miter, even upon his forefront, did he put the golden plate, the holy crown, as the Lord commanded Moses." That which was properly called the breastplate, was a cloth curiously wrought, doubled (as Ex. 28:15–16), and the urim and thummim was[1] the four rows of stones set in it [vv. 17–18].

The manner of inquiring of God by it was the priest's appearing with it on before the most holy place, waiting for an answer from off the mercy seat; and when they inquired in the camp there was a tabernacle that the ephod was kept in, made in the resemblance of the tabernacle of the congregation (of which see Prideaux's *Connection*, Part I, p. 222).[2] The urim and thummim, by the beauty and excellency of its

---

1. Here occur the words, "that plate of gold that was fastened on it with"; JE deleted them at the same time he changed the page reference to Prideaux (see next note).

2. MS: "p. ~~156~~ ⟨222⟩." Humphrey Prideaux, *The Old and New Testament Connected in the History of the Jews and Neighboring Nations, from the Declension of the Kingdoms of Israel and Judah to the Time of Christ* (2 pts. in 2 vols. fol. London, 1716–18). JE's original page number shows that when he wrote No. 240 he owned or had access to the 2nd (1716–18), 4th (1718), 6th (1719), or 8th (1720) edition. The 9th edition (London, 1725) was a genuinely new edition in 4 vols. 8vo. Sometime before writing No. 597 JE acquired the 9th edition (which he cites in *Humble Inquiry* [*Works, 12*, 281, n. 2]), and then or later went back and changed the page reference in No. 240 to fit that edition. In the passage to which JE refers, Prideaux contends that the ark which the Israelites carried into battle was not the ark of the covenant but a chest containing the ephod and breastplate.

appearance, was as proper to obtain acceptance and counsel of God, as incense by the sweetness of its smell was to render their prayers and sacrifices acceptable.

It will [be] objected, that if the urim and thummim were nothing but that plate of gold with the jewels in it, why is it said in Ezra and Nehemiah, that those priests that could not prove their genealogy should not eat of the most holy things till there stood up a priest with urim and thummim (as Ezra 2:63)? for if it had been only gold and jewels, they could have gotten them before now. I answer, so if it had been any other material thing they could have gotten them as well as those jewels. But it seems that being lately returned from captivity they had not yet gotten them; and it's no wonder they should not, in the circumstances they were in. But it seems by this, that they expected to get them in a short time; which if it had been something that must be immediately given by God, they had not so much reason to expect it, for it seems that God had denied them hitherto. But if the objection be allowed, all that it can argue is that the urim and thummim was not any material thing, but a power given to the breastplate of foretelling or of obtaining divine responses. For we can't imagine in reason, that any material thing was expected to be sent down from heaven, to be put into the breastplate; but Lev. 8:8 proves it was [a] material thing. Therefore, if they had those jewels in the breastplate at that time, the reason of their speaking in this manner must be, because they did not think them worthy the name of urim and thummim till they had such a power given them as[3] the former urim and thummim had.

241. REGENERATION. It may be in the new birth as it is in the first birth. The vivification of the fetus in the womb is exceeding gradual; the vital operations of it arise from the most imperfect to the more perfect by an insensible increase, so that there is no determining at what time it first begins to be [a] living creature and to have a rational soul. Yet there is a certain moment that an immortal spirit begins to exist in it by God's appointment; so that if the fetus should be destroyed before that moment, there would be an end to its existence; but if at any time after, there would remain an immortal spirit, that would be translated into another world. I don't see why it may not be sometimes so,[4] though at other times there is doubtless a remarkable and very sensible change made at once when the soul is newborn.

3. MS: "and."
4. I.e. in the new birth also.

In the new birth there is certainly a very great change made in the soul: so in the first birth there is a very great change when the rational soul is first infused, for the fetus immediately upon it becomes a living creature and a man, that before had no life; yet the sensible change is very gradual. It likewise seems reasonable to me to suppose that the habit of grace in adults is always begun with an act of grace that shall imply faith in it, because a habit can be of no manner of use till there is occasion to exert it; and all habits being only a law that God has fixed, that such actions upon such occasions should be exerted, the first new thing that there can be in the creature must be some actual alteration. So in the first birth it seems to me probable that the beginning of the existence of the soul, whose essence consists in powers and habits, is with some kind of new alteration there, either in motion or sensation.

242. CHRISTIAN RELIGION, the reasonableness of it. It would not have done for Christ constantly to dwell among men after his resurrection. Men would be exceeding apt to fall into idolatry, and because they saw the man Christ Jesus with their eyes, would be apt to worship him as directing their worship to the human nature. Therefore we are not to see the man Christ Jesus till we are perfected, and ben't liable to temptation on such occasions. For this reason likewise, it would not be convenient for Christ to appear in great majesty and glory when on earth, but the contrary: for this reason Christ used to endeavor to hide his transfiguration till after he was risen, and many other miracles, and for this reason he did not converse constantly with his disciples after his resurrection as before. All these things were done the most wisely and fitly that can be imagined.

243. GLORY OF GOD.[5] John 17 (first part) and 12:28, Is. 42:8 and 48:11, and many other such passages of Scripture make me think that God's glory is a good independent of the happiness of the creature; that it is a good absolutely and in itself, and not only as subordinate to the creature's real good, not only because 'tis the creature's highest good; [that it is] a good that God seeks (if I may so speak) not only as he seeks the creature's happiness but for itself, seeks absolutely as an independent, ultimate good[6]—and many passages in the Old Testa-

5. There is a vertical line in the left margin of this entry indicating its use in the *End of Creation* (cf. *Works, 8,* 475–502).

6. At this point JE deleted with a large X mark about five lines of writing. This may have happened during the composition of No. 243, but it was more likely while he was writing No.

ment that seem to speak as if the end of his doing this or that was his honor's sake or his name's sake. Though it still appears to me exceeding plain that to communicate goodness is likewise an absolute good, and what God seeks for itself, and that the very being of God's goodness necessarily supposes it; for to make happy is not goodness if it be done purely for another superior end.

244. FAITH, SAVING. It don't seem congruous, and in itself it is not condecent, for God quite to pass over sin rebellion and treachery, and receive the offender into his entire favor, either without a repentance and sorrow and detestation of his fault adequate to the aggravation of it (which can never be); or, if there be another that appears in his stead, and has done and suffered so much as fully to satisfy and pay the debt, it will not be condecent to forgive him, whatever is done for him by his representative for his expiation, except there be an accepting of it by the offender for that end, a sense of its being adequate to the offense, and an applying of the mind to him, and a recumbence upon him for satisfaction. This now seems to me evident to the very light of nature.

245. FAITH, SAVING, AND SATISFACTION OF CHRIST. The satisfaction of Christ by his death is certainly a very rational thing. If any person that was greatly obliged to me, that was dependent on me and that I loved, should exceedingly abuse me, and should go on in an obstinate course of it from one year to another, notwithstanding all I could say to him, and all new obligations continually repeated; though at length he should leave it off, I should not forgive him (except upon gospel considerations).[7] But if any person that was a much dearer friend to me, and one that had always been true to me and constant to the utmost, and that was a very near friend of him that offended me,

---

247, which implies a rejection of the solution to the problem of the relation of goodness and glory in God proposed in the deleted passage. JE had written: "Though his goodness, or inclination to communicate happiness, be the prime motive of his creating the world (which seems to me to be true), yet the world being created, he is inclined absolutely to glorify himself in the existing [world]; that is, it is not any superior inclination that is the original of it, but his infinitely excellent nature necessarily inclines him to it, inasmuch as he cannot act according to that nature if he does it not, much after the same manner as to act justly is an absolute good and that which God seeks absolutely. He did not create the world that he might act justly; but the world being created, his excellent nature necessarily inclines him to act justly in it."

7. This phrase was added later above the line, apparently in connection with the writing of the next entry.

should intercede for him, and out of the entire love he had to him should put himself to very hard labors and difficulties, and undergo great pains and miseries to procure him satisfaction; and the person that had offended should with a changed mind fly to this mediator and should seek favor in his name, with a sense in his own mind how much his meditor had done and suffered for him; I should be satisfied, and feel myself inclined without any difficulty to receive him into my entire friendship again. But not without the last mentioned condition, that he should have a sense how much his mediator had done and suffered. For if he was ignorant of most of it, and thought he had done only some small matter, I should not be easy nor satisfied. So a sense of Christ's sufficiency seems necessary in faith.

246. GOSPEL. That there [are] some moral duties required by the gospel that before were not duties, I believe thus: that Christ being made known to them, with what he did and suffered for [them], those things that pertain to the redemption of the world become condecent and reasonable to be done, that if Christ had not come into the world [would] not have been reasonable. For instance, fully forgiving a great injury without satisfaction, considering what things have been done for us and the world, and what things are made known to us in the gospel, is very reasonable, that otherwise would be impossible. Such precepts as these are gospel precepts; they become duty under gospel circumstances by the same moral unalterable reason as the ten commandments do; but such gospel circumstances are the foundation of those unalterable reasons taking place here. If the instance I have given here ben't true, yet certainly it may be so; it is not unreasonable to suppose there may be such instances.

247. GLORY OF GOD.[8] For God to glorify himself is to discover himself in his works, or to communicate himself in his works, which is all one; for we are to remember that the world exists only mentally, so that the very being of the world implies its being perceived or discovered. Or otherwise for God to glorify himself, is in his acts *ad extra* to act worthy of himself, or to act excellently. Therefore God don't seek his own glory because it makes him the happier to be honored and highly thought of, but because he loves to see himself, his own excellencies and glories, appearing in his works, loves to see himself communica-

---

8. This entry continues the line of thought initiated by No. 243. The vertical line through it near the left margin seems to indicate its use in the *End of Creation* (cf. *Works, 8,* 512–36).

ted. And it was his inclination to communicate himself that was a prime motive of his creating the world.[9] His own glory was the ultimate [end], himself was his end; that is, himself communicated.

The very phrase "the glory" seems naturally to signify [this]. Glory is a shining forth, an effulgence; so the glory of God is the shining forth or effulgence of his perfections, or the communication of his perfections, for effulgence is the communication of light. For this reason, that brightness whereby God was wont to manifest himself in the wilderness, and in the tabernacle and temple, was called God's glory. So the brightness of the sun moon and stars is called their glory (I Cor. 15:41). John 1:14, "We beheld his glory," that is, his brightness, in his transfiguration. II Pet. 1:17, "For he received from God the Father honor and glory, when there came such a voice to him from the excellent glory." Heb. 1:3, "Who is the brightness of his glory." Rev. 18:1, "The earth was lightened with his glory," that is, brightness. Rev. 21:10–11, "The holy Jerusalem . . . having the glory of God," and v. 23, "For the glory of God did lighten it." So that the glory of God is the shining forth of his perfections; and the world was created that they might shine forth, that is, that they might be communicated.

248. SPIRITUAL KNOWLEDGE. It need not be at all strange that sin should so blind the mind, seeing that our particular natural temper oftentimes very much blinds us in secular affairs; as when our natural temper is melancholy or jealous, cowardly, and the like.

249. CHRISTIAN RELIGION. If human reason, by anything that has happened since the creation, be really very much corrupted, [and] if God[1] is still propitious and is willing that we should attain the good for which we are created, and don't throw us [off] but reserves us still for that end for which he made us—if so I say, it can't be imagined that God would leave [us] to our reason as the only rule to guide us in that knowledge and business which is the highest end of life, for it is not to be depended upon. We exceedingly need something that may be depended upon, in that which our everlasting welfare depends on; and if God be still inclined to mercy to us, and don't cast us off, he doubtless

9. At this point JE deleted the words, "as well as his inclination to make happy."
1. MS: "corrupted; then it can't be imagined, if God." Having added more material to the condition, JE failed to delete the abortive introduction to the conclusion. JE, Jr. canceled the words "then it can't be imagined" and inserted "&," a solution which requires the least change in the text.

will be very merciful, and will consider our great need of a better rule. It don't seem to me reasonable to suppose, that if God be merciful after we have forfeited his favor, that he will manifest his mercy only in some mitigations of that misery that we have plunged ourselves into, leaving of us inevitably to endure the rest, but will quite restore us, in case of our acceptance.

250. COVENANT.[2] I think really that the covenant that God made with the children of Israel was the covenant of works. He still held them under that covenant; that is, what is required in that covenant is to them particularly deciphered, and many additional positive commands which answer to the precept concerning the forbidden fruit; and God proposes this covenant to them as the condition of his favor, and gives them to understand that none of those promises he had made could be challenged without perfect obedience: but yet gives them to understand so much of his merciful nature and his inclination to pity them and to accept of a propitiation for them, that they, finding that they could not challenge anything from those promises [on the ground] of obedience, trusted only to the mere undeserved mercy of God and were saved by grace, and expected life only of mere mercy.

We are indeed now under the covenant of works so, that if we are perfectly righteous we can challenge salvation. But herein is the difference betwixt us and them: to us God has plainly declared the impossibility of obtaining life by that covenant, and lets us know that no mortal can be saved but only of mere grace, and lets us know clearly how we are made partakers of that grace. All ever since the fall were equally under the covenant of grace so far, that they were saved by it all alike, but the difference is in the revelation: the covenant of works was most clearly revealed to the Israelites, to us the covenant of grace. The church, which was then in its infant [state], could not bear a revelation of the covenant of grace in plain terms; and so with them the best way to bring them off from their own righteousness was to propose the covenant of works to them, and to renew the promise of life upon those conditions. God did with them as Christ did with the young man that asked what he should do for eternal life: Christ bids him keep the

2. The vertical line through this entry (down the right half of the MS page), made almost certainly by JE, may indicate its use elsewhere or it may only record some dissatisfaction with its content, for No. 250 is entered twice in the Table. JE returned again and again to the problem of the degree of continuity and difference between the Mosaic and Christian dispensations, the old and new covenants, and the Jewish and Christian churches.

commandments. And in that sense they were under the covenant of works, that it was proposed to them as the condition of life, that they might try. To us it is not so.

The covenant of grace was indeed insinuated to them and proposed under covert, but 'twas to that they were all forced to fly. The promises seem to be so contrived as to give them to see that they can't challenge anything except they perform a perfect obedience, if God will be strict, but yet that he will of his mere mercy accept them into his favor if they perform a sincere obedience proceeding from the true love and fear of him; so that the fruits of faith are proposed instead of faith itself. But by this, none but such as had faith could hope for life; and by God's contrivance of that dispensation they were led not to depend on these as works, but as a disposition to receive, as so many manifestations of repentance and submission; and they depended on them as such only, for life.

251. Prophecy of the Old Testament. There are many of the Psalms, and some other parts of Scripture, wherein the penmen immediately intended the affairs of the church of Israel. But these things being represented poetically, in those beautiful and exalted images, which a poetical genius and fire, excited and invigorated by an extraordinary exercise of grace and a holy and evangelical disposition, in which excitations there was the afflatus of God's Spirit—their minds naturally conceived such poetical images of the Jewish church, as very exactly described the affairs of the gospel and the Christian church. They agreed much more properly with the latter than the former: for with [respect to] these[3] they were tropical representations; but the fire of grace, together with a true poetical genius, naturally guided them to make use of such images as almost literally described the affairs of the gospel; of which all in the Jewish church was a shadow and representation, the most natural that could be, and representations so natural that a poetical genius, so exalted and animated by lively and vigorous grace, would by them be naturally led to the ideas of gospel things.

For there is a most wonderful analogy and natural correspondence between one and the other; which one will see the more, the more they have of a poetical and gracious disposition, and clear and comprehensive understanding of these matters. The affairs of the Jewish church are so much of a shadow, that a mind so prepared and exercised would

3. I.e. the affairs of the gospel and the Christian church.

naturally be led to the substance, for a poetical and hyperbolical representation. The Spirit of God excited those extraordinary flames in their minds, and they were likewise (it is probable) subject to his special direction; for he intended that gospel things should be represented by them, and that they should hereafter be used in the church for such representations.

252. COVENANT. The covenant that God made with the children of Israel with respect to outward blessings was entirely legal, a covenant of works.

253. CHRISTIAN RELIGION. Strife and contention, malice, and mutual ill will have bore a great and universal dominion amongst mankind, and are some of the greatest miseries of this apostate world. How do men that are made of the same blood, and are come of the same first father and mother, devour, malign and persecute one another, and with heart and hand work out one another's misery! Now it seems to me a thing most worthy and becoming a merciful and beneficent God, to send down some extraordinary messenger from heaven to the earth, to be a peacemaker among men and to reconcile them one to another, and bring [them] to love [one] another and seek each other's good. And how congruous it seems, that it should be his own Son.

254. FAITH. Even the being of God can be made most rationally and demonstratively evident by divine revelation and by gracious spiritual illlumination, after the same manner as we have shown the Christian religion, the superstructure built upon that foundation, is evident.[4] Suppose all the world had otherwise been ignorant of the being of God before, yet now they might know it; because God has revealed himself, he has shown himself, he has said a great deal to us and conversed much with us. And this is every whit as rational a way of being convinced of the being of God, as it is of being convinced of the being of a man who comes from an unknown region, and shows himself to us, and converses with us for a long time: we have no other reason to be convinced of his being, than only that we see a long series of external concordant signs of an understanding, will and design, and various affections—the same way God makes known himself to us in his word. And if we have a full and comprehensive knowledge of the revelation made, of the things revealed, and so [of] the various relations and

4. Here JE has particular reference to the series of miscellanies entitled "Christian Religion."

respects of the various parts, their harmonies, congruities, and mutual concordances; there appear most indubitable signs and expressions of a very high and transcendent understanding, together with a great and mighty design, an exceeding wisdom, a most magnificent power and authority, a marvelous purity, holiness and goodness. So that if we never knew there was any such being before, yet we might be certain that this must be such an one.

255. CONVERSION. That argument to prove that God's usual method is to make sinners very sensible of their misery, and bring them to a despair of help from themselves or any other creature before he converts them, viz. that 'tis agreeable to his wisdom to bestow his blessings and grace in that way as makes it most seen and admired, and received with the greatest thankfulness, has certainly some force in it. For it seems by the Scripture, that he does regard a disposition of the heart whereby it is prepared thus to receive his benefits before he bestows them. Therefore it is, that he insists upon being inquired of for his mercy before he bestows it (Ezek. 36:37). Just as Israel were brought into the greatest strait and to utter despair of helping themselves at the Red Sea, God appeared. So he appeared for the three children after they were cast into the furnace, for Daniel after he was in the lions' den, Christ for the woman of Canaan after repulses, to Lazarus after he was dead, and many such instances. See the *Commonplace Book to Holy Scripture*, pp. 264 ff., 400.[5]

256. FAITH.[6] One that is well acquainted with the gospel and sees the beauties, the harmonies, the majesty, the power and the glorious wisdom of it, and the like, may only by viewing of it be as certain that it [is]

5. [John Locke], *A Common-Place Book to the Holy Bible* (London, 1686); JE used the 3d ed. enl. (London, 1725). The first reference is to a section entitled "That the greater the Afflictions and Distresses of the Righteous have been, the more astonishing have their Deliverances been," which Locke illustrates by stories such as Israel at the Red Sea and Daniel in the lion's den. The second reference contains "Encouragements to Hope in and Cry to God, when our Case seems desperate," such as the story of the valley of dry bones and Jonah in the fish.

JE concluded a sheet with No. 255 and began a new one with the entry now numbered 279. Of the intervening entries, Nos. 261–264 and 267–274 had been written previously; Nos. 256–260, 265–266, and 275–278 were written later. See above, Fig. 5, pp. 156–57, for their order of composition.

6. MS: "C̶H̶R̶I̶S̶T̶I̶A̶N̶ FAITH." JE evidently started to entitle this entry "Christian Religion"; it is entered in the Table under that heading as well as under "Faith" and "Spiritual knowledge."

Nos. 256–260 were preceded by Nos. 306–310 and followed by No. 266 in the spring of 1728; see above, Fig. 5, p. 157.

no human work, as a man that is well acquainted with mankind and their works, by contemplating the sun may know it is not a human work; or when he goes upon an island and sees the various trees, and sees the manner of their growing and blossoming and bearing fruit, may know that they are not the work of man. See No. 410.

257. RESURRECTION. Surely if it was proper that the serpent should be cursed because it was an instrument the devil made use of to tempt mankind, it is proper that the body, that the soul makes use of as an instrument of sin or of holiness, should be either cursed or blessed with the soul.

258. HELL. I don't think we have good ground to be assured, that the sins of damned spirits that they commit after their damnation are no way liable to punishment because they ben't in a state of trial but in a state of punishment; however, I believe this in one sense is true, and in another not. I believe all the misery that ever they endure or shall endure to all eternity is a punishment of their sin while in a state of trial, and every part of that misery a part of that punishment, and all the deserved and justly due punishment of that sin; so that those that have sinned most in a state of trial shall be punished most to all eternity, and in an exact proportion: and yet it shall be so ordered by the wisdom of God, that various parts of their punishment shall be so timed and placed and circumstanced as to be punishment also of their several acts of pride, or malice and spite against God and against his creatures that are not in a state of punishment.

Thus God brings the punishment of the devils upon 'em for their proud rebellion in heaven in this way, by making them the cause of their own torment and vexation to all eternity by their continually renewed acts of pride and spite. He gives them over forever to that same disposition which they exercised when they fell, and by that means makes them forever a procuring their own misery; and this is a misery they are plunged into as a punishment of their first rebellion. 'Tis certain by the word of God that the devils are thus punished. They are punished for their procuring the fall of mankind: God curses the serpent for it, and without doubt God in that curse had a principal reference to the devil, who is the old serpent; the seed of the woman's breaking his head is in punishment for that act of his. By means of Christ the Redeemer, God renders all Satan's incessant labors and endeavors for the overthrow of mankind, and for defeating God's design of glorifying himself in them, a means of his own confusion and vexation, and of abundantly more brightly manifesting the glory of God and advancing the happiness of the elect. He is a means of one of mankind being his judge. And so the event of his own great endeavors will prove every way [an] exceeding contradiction and mortification of his own restless, ｜ ᵢud, malicious and revengeful spirit.

259. TRINITY. 'Tis evident that there are no more than these three really distinct in God: God, and his idea, and his love or delight. We can't conceive of any further real distinctions. If you say there is the power of God, I answer, the power of a being, even in creatures, is nothing distinct from the being itself, besides a mere relation to an effect. If you say there is the infiniteness, eternity, and immutability of God, they are mere modes or manners of existence. If you say there is the wisdom of God, that is the idea of God. If you say there is the holiness of God, that is not different from his love (as we have shown),[7] and is the Holy Spirit. If you say there is the goodness and mercy of God, they are included in his love; they are his love with a relation. We can find no more in God that even in creatures are distinct from the very being; or, there is no more than these three in God, but what even in creatures are nothing[8] but the same with the very being, or only some mere modes or relations. Duration, extension, changeableness or unchangeableness, so far as attributed to creatures, are only mere modes and relations of existence. There are no more than these three that are distinct in God, even in our way of conceiving.

There is in resemblance to this threefold distinction in God a three-fold distinction in a created spirit, namely, the spirit itself, and its understanding, and its will or inclination or love; and this indeed is all the real distinction there is in created spirits.

7. JE probably has reference to the last paragraph of No. 94, which closely parallels the present entry and ends with the statement that God's holiness is "delight in excellency, 'tis God's sweet consent to himself, or in other words, his perfect delight in himself; which we have shown to be the Holy Spirit." Later miscellanies on the Trinity discuss the Holy Spirit as divine love, and the following have special reference to holiness: Nos. 146, 157, and 220. Cf. also "The Mind," no. 45, especially § 9 (*Works, 6,* 364), where the Holy Spirit is called the holiness of God and this in turn is equated with his love.

8. MS: "are only ~~the either~~ thing." Apparently, JE first intended to write "only the same," etc.; then, thinking of the alternative phrase, he wrote "either"; then, after deleting that, he looked back at "only," which he had failed to delete because it was at the end of the previous line, and read it as "any" (it looks like "any"!). Here JE illustrates the grammatical problems he created for himself by employing involved negative modes of expression, as well as the fact that even he sometimes had difficulty reading his handwriting.

260. TRINITY. There is no other properly spiritual image but [an] idea; although there may be another spiritual thing that is exactly like, yet one thing's being exactly like another don't make it the proper image of that thing. If there be one distinct spiritual substance exactly like another, yet [it] is not the proper image of the other; though one be made after the other, yet it is not any more an image of the first than the first is of the last.

That Christ is the spiritual image and idea of God: John 12:45, "He that seeth me seeth him that sent me." John 14:7–9, "If ye had known me, ye should have known my father also; and from henceforth ye know him and have seen him. Philip saith unto him, Lord, show us the Father and it sufficeth us. Jesus saith unto him, Have I been so long time with you, and yet hast thou not known me, Philip? He that hath seen me hath seen the Father; and how sayest thou then, Show us the Father?"

Seeing the perfect idea of a thing is to all intents and purposes the same as seeing the thing; it is not only equivalent to seeing of it, but it *is* seeing of it, for there is no other seeing but having an idea. Now by seeing a perfect idea, so far as we see it we have it; but it can't be said of anything else that in seeing of it we see another, speaking strictly, except it be the very idea of the other.[9]

The oil that signifies the Holy Ghost, with which Christ is anointed, is called "the oil of gladness." The Holy Ghost is God's delight and joy (Ps. 45:7). Is. 61:3, "the oil of joy for mourning"; they anointed themselves to express joy.

Another name of the Son of God that shows that he is God's perfect idea, is "the AMEN" [Rev. 3:14], which is a Hebrew word that signifies truth. Divine truth, or the eternal truth of God, is God's perfect understanding of himself, which is his perfect understanding of all things.

261.[1] CHRIST'S RIGHTEOUSNESS. We are justified by Christ's active obedience thus: his active obedience was one thing that God saw to be needful in order to retrieve the honor of his law, as well as his suffering for the breach of it. That the eternal Son of God should subject himself to that law which man had broken, and become obedient to it, was what greatly honored the law and the authority that established it. So that we are saved by that, as well as his death.

9. The two last paragraphs were added a few months later, in the fall of 1728.
1. Nos. 261–264 were originally numbered 235–239 and were JE's last entries before leaving New Haven in 1726. See above, Fig. 5, p. 156.

262. MILLENNIUM. 'Tis probable that this world shall be more like heaven in the millennium in this respect, that contemplative and spiritual employments, and those things that more directly concern the mind and religion, will be more the saints' ordinary business than now. There will be so many contrivances and inventions to facilitate and expedite their necessary secular business, that they shall have more time for more noble exercises, and that they will have better contrivances for assisting one another through the whole earth, by a more expedite and easy and safe communication between distant regions than now. The invention of the mariner's compass is one thing by God discovered to the world for that end; and how exceedingly has that one thing enlarged and facilitated communication! And who can tell but that God will yet make it more perfect; so that there need not be such a tedious voyage in order to hear from the other hemisphere, and so the countries about the poles need no longer to lie hid to us, but the whole earth may be as one community, one body in Christ.

263. HEAVEN. If the saints after the resurrection shall see by light, and speak and hear by sounds, 'tis probable that the medium will be infinitely finer and more adapted to a distant and exact representation. So that a small vibration in sound, though the undulations may proportionably decrease according to the distance from their rise or fountain, yet may be conveyed infinitely farther with exactness, before they begin to be confused and lost through the sluggishness of the medium or through the bulk, the roughness or tenaciousness of the particles; and the conveyance may likewise be with far greater swiftness. The organ also will be immensely more exquisitely perceptive, so that perhaps a vibration a thousand times less than can now be perceived by the ear may be distinctly and easily perceived by them; and yet [they] be far more able to bear a very strong vibration than we in this state, and through the niceness of the organ shall be able to distinguish in the greatest multitude of sounds according to their distance and direction more exactly by the ear than we do visible objects by the eye; and we know not how far they may clearly hear one another's discourses. So the eye may be so much more sensible, and the medium (the rays) so much more exquisite, that for aught we know they may distinctly see the beauty of one another's countenances and smiles, and hold a delightful and most intimate conversation, at a thousand miles' distance.

The light of the heavenly regions shall be the brightness of glorified bodies, and especially their countenances, but chiefly of the man Christ Jesus, and the glory of God, if there shall be any visible appearance representing the presence of the Deity. The light of the face of Christ will (for the abovementioned cause) be an infinitely more excellent and delightful sort of refulgence than the light of this world. The brightness of the saints shall far excell that, but the splendor of the Sun of Righteousness shall be immensely more sweet and glorious: except that the light of the bodies of the saints shall be some way or other a communication of the light of Christ; and then the difference will be rather in degree of brightness than kind, as the light which is reflected from a lily is the same light but less bright than the sun. This world is pleasant to us because the light is sweet and the sensation is pleasant to the mind. How delightful a place then is heaven, with its [light] so much more fine, more harmonious, more bright, but yet easy and pleasant to behold! See note on Rev. 21:11; see Nos. 721, 95, 182.[2]

264. SPIRITS, SEPARATE.[3] Though we don't certainly know that separate spirits can properly be said to be in any place, seeing that a spirit can't be said to be in place at all [but] only with respect to the immediate mutual operation there is between that and body—now we know not whether there be any such mutual operation with regard to separate spirits, whether or no there be any immediate excitation of any corporeal ideas, or any other way than as they see them in minds that are united to bodies or remember them formerly excited in themselves—I say, though we don't certainly know this, yet it don't seem probable that their manner of existence and receiving ideas shall be so exceeding different from what it is here and from the church on earth, with whom they are of the same family, and so exceeding alien [from] what it will be after the resurrection, so exceeding different from the existence of the man Christ Jesus their head and husband, so exceeding alien from Enoch and Elijah, some of their number and who are now

2. These citations are later additions made in two (possibly three) installments at about the time JE wrote No. 721. In the note on Rev. 21:11, JE comments that the "visible brightness and glory that will be seen in heaven," though a light "immensely exceeding the corruscation of the sun," will "not be at all painful to the eyes of the saints . . . but shall be perfectly easy . . . sweet and pleasant." The note was probably not written before the mid-1730s.

3. No. 264 extends the line of thought explored in the preceding entry, which in turn was probably suggested by No. 262 with its discussion of communication in the millennium; see also No. 182. JE's speculations in "The Mind" nos. 2 and 3 (*Works*, 6, 338–39) also provided background for such speculations as these.

of the same glorified society. Doubtless they are not more so than the angels, who never were united to bodies; but it seems very improbable to me that there should be no corporeal world with respect to the angels, who have so much to do with the church on earth, and that shall be conversant with the saints after the resurrection, and with whom they shall be conversant. I therefore cannot think that as soon as a spirit leaves a body the corporeal world is annihilated with regard to it, but that corporeal ideas are excited in them by some law. Why is Christ's body made glorious now in heaven if there are none in heaven to behold his glory, or if separate spirits don't perceive the beauty of bodies?[4]

265.[5] CHRIST'S DEATH. If it be said, there was no despair in Christ, and how then could his punishment be of the same kind with what we had deserved, seeing despair is a principal part of it; I answer, that as the infinite dignity of Christ's person answered the eternity of punishment, so his dying with a sense of this his dignity, and the infinite happiness he had before the world was, answered the sense of the eternity of punishment in the damned.[6] He had for the present lost infinitely more than the damned lose, because his blessedness in the love and communion with God was infinitely greater. When a man has lost much, his grief is greater than his[7] that has lost but little, though they are both become equally poor. (Observe how much greater trial Job's sufferings were to him for his former prosperity.) See Nos. 516, 664b [§ 5], 1005 (§ II, par. 2).[8]

4. For his next entries after Nos. 261–264 JE began on a new sheet of paper and wrote four entries which were later numbered 311–314.

5. Ink, hand, and subject matter make it likely that while writing on the inside pages of the Fleur de lis/EYD sheet (which contain Nos. 317–323) JE laid inside it the uncompleted second London/GR sheet (which had Nos. 267–274 on its recto and Nos. 261–264 on its verso), finished its recto with No. 275, and wrote No. 265 on its verso opposite No. 321b. No. 265 discusses a possible objection to the position JE had taken in No. 321b concerning the sufferings of Christ. Since the texture of the ink changes decisively at No. 323, it is possible that No. 265 was composed just before or (more likely) after No. 322.

6. The next two sentences were added shortly afterwards, probably about the same time as Nos. 324–325b. The last sentence was inserted in the mid-1740s or later.

7. MS: "he."

8. MS: "1005, p. 4 of that number near bottom." No. 265 and these three miscellanies are listed in the Table under "Sufferings of Christ, how equivalent to the misery of hell," and in each of the four the other three are cited. The Table entries and cross-references were apparently made at the time No. 1005 was written.

After writing No. 265 on the second London/GR sheet (above, n. 5), JE laid that sheet aside and finished filling the Fleur sheet with Nos. 323–328.

266.[9] CHRISTIAN RELIGION. It seems much the most rational to suppose that that universal law by which mankind are to be governed should be a written law. For if that rule by which God intends the world shall be regulated, and kept in decent and happy order, be not expressed in words that can be resorted to, and be supposed to be no other way expressed than by nature, men's prejudices will render it in innumerable circumstances a most uncertain thing. For

> though it must be granted, that men who are willing to transgress may abuse written as well as unwritten laws, and expound them so as may best serve their turn upon occasion; yet it must be allowed, that in the nature of the thing revelation is a better guard than a bare scheme [of] principles without it.
>
> For men must take more pains to conquer the sense of a standing written law, which is ready to confront them upon all occasions; they must more industriously tamper with their passions and bribe their understandings, before they can bring themselves to believe what they have a mind to believe, in contradiction to the words of an express and formal declaration of God Almighty's will; than there can be any pretense or occasion for, when they have no more than their own thoughts and ideas to manage. These are flexible things, and a man may much more easily turn and wind 'em as he pleases, than he can evade a plain and positive law, which determines the kinds and measures of his duty, and threatens disobedience in such terms as require long practice and experience, to make handsome salvos and distinctions to get over.—Ditton on the Resurrection.[1]

And upon this account also, because it is fit in every law, when the law is made known, that the sanctions should also be made known at the same time, the rewards and punishments; but nature never would with any certainty have determined this.

9. No. 266 was written next after No. 260 in order of composition and was followed by Nos. 276–278; see above, Fig. 5, p. 157.
1. Humphrey Ditton, *A Discourse Concerning the Resurrection of Jesus Christ,* 3rd ed. (London, 1722), p. 47. The *Discourse* was first published at London in 1712, but JE's orthography and punctuation agree more nearly with the third than with the two previous editions. The quotation is taken from Pt. I, § 23, the thesis of which is that believers in the Christian revelation are more firmly bound to the precepts of the law of nature than are those who reject that revelation.

267.[2] GOD'S EXISTENCE. The mere exertion of a new thought is a certain proof of a God. For certainly there is something that immediately produces and upholds that thought; here is a new thing, and there is a necessity of a cause. It is not antecedent thoughts, for they are vanished and gone; they are past, and what is past is not. But if we say 'tis the substance of the soul (if we mean that there is some substance besides that thought, that brings that thought forth), if it be God, I acknowledge; but if there be meant something else that has no properties, it seems to me absurd. If the removal of all properties, such as extendedness, solidity, thought, etc. leaves nothing, it seems to me that no substance is anything but them; for if there be anything besides, there might remain something when these are removed.

268. GOD'S EXISTENCE. INNATE IDEAS. That secret intimation and sort of inward testimony that men have upon occasion of the being of a God, and is in the minds of all men, however they may endeavor to root it out, is this. In the first place, the arguing for the being of a God according to the natural powers, from everything we are conversant with, is short and easy and what we naturally fall into. And in the next place, it appears decorous and orderly that it should be so; and that natural inclination that persons have to excellence and order does as it were prejudice in favor of it. When we suffer great injustice, we seek to some superior being to set things to rights; because there is a great renitence of the soul against that sort of indecorum, and we don't know how to believe that injustice should be done without ever being mended, 'tis so abhorrent to nature. So when we have done good or evil, we naturally expect from some superior being reward or punishment. Thirdly, there is a habit of the mind in reasoning: we are wont every day from our very infancy to argue causes from effects, after the same manner in the general; and we have such a habit that we believe this or that without standing to argue about it. Thus we do in many other cases; and as long [as] we are thus forced to judge in other things continually, it will return upon us unavoidably when we think anything about the being of a God.

269. GOD'S EXISTENCE. If we allow generation to be purely mechanically performed, yet that the bodies of men and of all animals and

---

2. Nos. 267–274 were probably the first entries to be written after JE moved to Northampton; see above, pp. 83–84.

plants should be so contrived, that there should spring endless successions of the same kind of like curious frame from them, is an exceeding bright argument of a Deity.

270. GLORY OF GOD. That no actions are good but what have the
honor of God as their chief end proposed, is not necessary. 'Tis very
true that no actions are good any further than they have God for their
end, either the glorifying him or pleasing him or enjoying him; and
love to God, or inclination towards him, must be its spring and motive.
Even glorifying God is not a good end any further than our seeking his
glory springs from love; and if a desire of enjoying God springs more
from love than [does] a desire [of] honoring him, it is a better principle.

271. END OF THE CREATION. It is indeed a condecent thing that God
should be the ultimate end of the creation as well as the cause, that in
creating he should make himself his end, that he should in this respect
be Omega as well as Alpha. (And the Scripture saith [Rev. 4:11], God
hath made all things for himself.) And this may be, and yet the reason
of his creating the world be his propensity to goodness, and the communication of happiness to the creatures be the end.

It perhaps was thus: God created the world for his Son, that he
might prepare a spouse or bride for him to bestow his love upon; so
that the mutual joys between this bride and bridegroom are the end of
the creation. God is really happy in loving his creatures, because in so
doing he as it were gratifies a natural propensity in the divine nature,
viz. goodness. Yea, and he is really delighted in the love of his creatures
and in their glorifying him, because he loves them, not because he
needs. For he could not be happy therein, were it not for his love and
goodness. Col. 1:16, "All things were made by him and for him," that
is, for the Son.

272. HAPPINESS OF HEAVEN. 'Tis only for want of sufficient accurate-
ness, strength and comprehension of mind, that from the motion of
any one particular atom we can't tell all that ever has been, [all] that
now is in the whole extent of the creation (as to quantity of matter,
figure, bulk and motion, distance), and everything that ever shall be.[3]
Corol. What room for improvement of reason is there, for angels and
glorified minds!

3. Cf. "The Mind" no. 34 (*Works, 6,* 353–55).

273. ELECTION. God's loving some and not others, antecedent to any manner of difference in them why he should love one more than the other, may appear reasonable thus: God of his own natural disposition really loves his reasonable creatures. Therefore his love to us before the foundation of the world is not merely an act of his wisdom choosing to make some happy and not others, as some have seemed to suppose, but real love; such as ours but only infinitely more sweet and pure, and void of all imperfection. Now God in his wisdom sees it best that all should not be his, which is the same thing to God[4] as an absolute impossibility. Now we find by experience, that however our natural disposition would lead us to love these or those, as to any qualification in them; yet if circumstances are such that we never in the least conceived that there could be any possibility of their being ours, we find no disposition to love them. Though divine things ben't like human, yet comparison from one to the other may in some cases help us to conceive.

274. GOD'S EXISTENCE. The being of God may be argued from the desirableness and need of it thus: we see in all nature everywhere that great necessities are supplied. We should be miserably off without some light in the night, and we have the moon and stars; in Egypt and India they are very much without rain, and they have the floods of Ganges and Nilus and great dews; in Greenland the sun's rays are exceeding oblique, and he is above the horizon so much the longer to make it up. Moles have poor eyes, and they have little occasion for them. Beasts are without reason, and they are guided by instinct, that supplies its place as well. Men are without natural weapons to fight, and they have reason, and hands to make weapons. The young of insects, they are not able to provide for themselves nor do their dams take care of them, but they by instinct are laid where they have their food round about them. Camels are forced, being in dry countries, to go long without water, and they have a large vessel within them, which being filled supplies them a long time. And so it is in everything.

Therefore we can't think there should be so great, and essential, and universal, and eternal a defect, that there should be no wise, just and good being to govern the world; that the miseries amongst reasonable creatures, both through the defect of nature and through wickedness

4. MS: "thing as to God"; this "as" is probably a doublet caused by a false start on the next phrase.

and injustice (who are infinitely more than all the rest of the creation), can never be relieved.

275.[5] HELL TORMENTS. Hell is represented by fire and brimstone; and if by that is meant such fire as lightning, then without doubt the torments of hell are inconceivably great. For the fire of lightning is many degrees hotter than the fire of the hottest furnace; as appears by the effects of it, that it will in a moment, by only touching, in the twinkling of an eye dissolve the solidest and hardest metals. What then would it do if it were continued, and in a body, and not a transient stream? Lightning is a stream of brimstone; and if that stream of brimstone which we are told kindles hell be as hot as streams of lightning, it will be vehement beyond conception.

'Tis probable that this earth, after the conflagration, shall be the place of the damned. We read that the heat of the conflagration will be so violent as to melt the very ground (II Pet. 3:10, 12); and if the heat continues to the same degree, the heat will be inexpressibly great. If the heat of hell is like the heat of the sun or the comets, it will [be] many thousand times hotter than ordinary fire.

276.[6] CHRISTIAN RELIGION. 'Tis evident that the gospels were written by some persons that lived in Judea and very near the very time of Jesus Christ, by an evident familiar acquaintance with the state and circumstances, manners and customs of that people at that time. It must be some persons that lived before the destruction of Jerusalem. If their history had been written by them that did not dwell in the land, errors and inconsistencies in geography would evidence it. And indeed, that there are not very gross and innumerable inconsistencies in geography is an evidence of the truth of the whole history of the Bible.

277. FEAR OF GOD. Herein is the difference between a godly fear, or the fear of a godly man, and the fear of a sinner: the one fears the effects of God's displeasure, the other fears his displeasure itself.

---

5. Having inserted the unfinished second London/GR sheet inside the Fleur de lis/EYD sheet (above, p. 371, n. 5), JE completed No. 317 and then wrote No. 275 at the bottom of the facing London/GR recto, probably before continuing with Nos. 318 ff. on the second recto of the Fleur sheet.

6. Nos. 276–278 were preceded by No. 266 and followed by Nos. 329 ff.; see above, Fig. 5, p. 157.

278. Righteousness of Christ.

Righteousness, in the general conception of it, is a relative thing, and has always relation to a law. The formal nature of righteousness, properly understood, lies in a conformity of actions to that which is the rule and measure of them. This is the general notion of it, and runs through every kind and species of it. And according to the different kind of the measure or rule, the conformity and agreeableness to it is also different. Now righteousness here may be understood [to respect] either righteousness as it is in him, or righteousness as it is in us, suitably to the double exigence of a fallen creature. And because I conceive both may be fitly included here, I shall briefly state and open the nature of each.

1. We are to consider righteousness as it is in him. And here we are to understand that the Messiah has an essential righteousness as he is God, which is nothing else but the perfect rectitude of his nature; or the conformity of all his actions to his own nature, which is the highest measure of right: and he had an human righteousness as he was man, which is a conformity to the divine law given to the reasonable creature, and which is the rule of all his actions. But now the righteousness here spoken of must be understood, as I apprehend, neither of the one or the other of these precisely; but of his righteousness as Mediator, or Immanuel. And as he is a mixed person in this consideration of him, so is his righteousness of a mixed nature; for though this differs from both the former in its measure and formal nature, and is not exactly the same with the one or the other of them; yet it partakes of the common nature of both, and must be estimated by the same principles; that is, as it is a conformity to that which is the proper rule of it.

To understand this we must consider, that the Messiah entered into a covenant of redemption for the recovery of the fallen world, and came under the obligation of the mediatorial law. The whole matter was wisely agreed and adjusted between the Father and the Son; he was to become incarnate, to reveal the will of God to men, to work miracles, and lay down his life a sacrifice. He *"received a command"* of the Father, to *"lay down his life"*; and finished the work which *"he gave him to do."*[7] And then he was to "see his seed" and to

7. These words, being slightly altered biblical quotations, are italicized in the text JE was copying, but so were several others which immediately follow. JE underlined only these, perhaps in order to emphasize the main provisions of the "mediatorial law" which Christ fulfilled. For that reason these italics are retained, and Harris' quotations are represented by quotation marks.

"prolong his days," and the "pleasure of the Lord was to prosper in" his hands; he was to be "satisfied with the travail of his soul," and by "his knowledge to justify many"; he was to have "all power given him in heaven and earth," and to be "highly exalted, and to have a name above every name." He consented to the terms which were fixed, and obliged himself to do whatsoever was necessary to the end proposed. Now his conformity to this rule, or whatsoever he did or suffered by virtue of his consent to the covenant of redemption, and the obligation of the mediatorial law; his whole active and passive obedience, was properly his righteousness. 'Tis true he obeyed the law of nature as he was man and a reasonable creature, and he observed the law of Moses as he was a Jew and of the seed of Abraham; but that was by virtue of the mediatorial law, and as a part and branch of it: so that all he did in this world, and what he is now doing in heaven, in obedience to his Father's will and for the salvation of men, is properly his righteousness.

This was personal and inherent in himself, and incommunicable to any other; the acts of righteousness were performed by him, and not by us; and in this sense 'tis his righteousness, and not ours; though the saving influence of it descends upon us, as did the malignant influence of Adam's sin. And 'tis absolutely perfect; there was no defect in the matter of his obedience, or in the manner of it; he observed every instance of the divine law, and came up to the utmost height. His whole obedience was bright and clear as a sunbeam, without any spot or shadow of darkness; he "fulfilled all righteousness" and "knew no sin." And it was of the highest value, for everything he did was under the influence of his divinity, and derived its value from thence. It was the action of one who was God as well as man; hence it was of the highest value in God's account, and infinitely pleasing to him; capable of making an atonement to God, and being a propitiation for sin. Nothing was so displeasing and injurious to God, as the righteousness of the Mediator was pleasing and honorable to him.—Harris' *Messiah*, pp. 418 ff.[8]

8. William Harris, *Practical Discourses on the Principal Representations of the Messiah throughout the Old Testament* (London, 1724), pp. 418–21. This work comprises a series of twenty sermons, the fifteenth of which is entitled "Messiah *Our Righteousness*." JE copied out the entire first section with its introductory paragraph, which suggests that he valued and probably agreed with Harris' contributions on two topics of special interest to him, the "mediatorial" righteousness of Christ and the covenant of redemption.

279.[9] ETERNITY OF HELL TORMENTS. I am convinced that hell torments will be eternal from one great good the wisdom of God proposes by them, which is, by the sight of them to exalt the happiness, the love, and joyful thanksgivings of the angels and men that are saved; which it tends exceedingly to do. I am ready to think that the beholding the sight of the great miseries of those of their species that are damned will double the ardor of their love, and the fullness of the joy of the elect angels and men. It will do it many ways. The sight of the wonderful power, the great and dreadful majesty and authority, and the awful justice and holiness of God manifested in their punishment, will make them prize his favor and love exceedingly the more; and will excite a most exquisite love and thankfulness to him, that he chose them out from the rest to make them thus happy, that God did not make them such vessels of wrath, according to Rom. 9:22–23, "What if God, willing to show his wrath," etc. "and that he might make known the riches of his glory on the vessels of mercy." And then, only a lively sense of the opposite misery makes any happiness and pleasure double what it would be. Seeing therefore that this happiness of the blessed is to be eternal, the misery of the damned will be eternal also.

280. TORMENTS OF HELL. I am convinced that the torments of hell are literally as great as they are represented by fire and brimstone, a lake of fire, and the like—and that without any hyperbole—by the greatness of the agonies of Christ in the garden. I am ready [to] think that such agonies of mind as are sufficient to put nature into such a violent commotion and ferment, so as to cause the blood to strain through the pores of the skin, are as great affliction as one would endure, if they were all over in a fiery furnace. I think the souls of the wicked must endure greater agonies than Christ in the garden, because they have despair and many other dreadful sensations of mind, that it's impossible an innocent person should have.[1]

281. CHRIST'S SATISFACTION. The threatening, "Thou shalt surely die," is properly fulfilled in the death of Christ, not only fulfilled in its equivalent but in the same, as it is fairly to be understood. [By] this

9. Nos. 279–305 followed No. 255 in order of composition and probably occupied the summer and early fall of 1727; see above, Fig. 5, p. 156.
1. Immediately after this entry, JE began another with the same title, but wrote only "The consideration of the eternity of hell torments will be more insupportable" before deleting it.

threatening, according to the proper and true sense of it, is to be understood that mankind, or the human nature, should die; so that death should belong to all the persons. Now if any way can be found out, whereby an actual death should as much belong to all the persons as if every person died, so that it may properly be called their death and yet they saved alive, the threatening is fulfilled. But this is done by the union of their persons with Christ's person: they are made so much one that his death belongs to them; they own it, it is their death, in as proper a sense as Adam's sin is their sin—they sin in Adam and they die in Christ. See Nos. 357, 506, and 1083.[2]

282. TORMENTS OF HELL. The principal objection I can think of against the extremity of hell torments is this, viz. we have no reason to conclude that the torments of separate souls are greater than those of the devils; but if they were in such extremity they never would so diligently attend to their schemes and crafty designs here on earth amongst men. I answer, that although the strength of their pain is very great, which tends to take off their minds from all attendance on such things, yet the strength of their malice is proportionably great; which puts them forward industriously to pursue their works of malice, even in the midst of extreme pain.

283. CHRISTIAN RELIGION, the reasonableness and congruity of it. It is most reasonable and gloriously wise, that seeing God created this earth for so great happiness to the creature in the enjoyment of himself, to suppose that there should be one that should be the head of the rest, that hath the nature of that sort of beings that is the end of the creation, in an ineffable manner most united to the Godhead; and that he should be proportionably more happy than the rest; and therefore that he should have a trial and endure greater sufferings: for these contraries, pains and happiness, exceedingly advance one another, as we have shown.[3]

284. CONVERSION. Since that the will universally and most strictly follows the proportion of the soul's sense of good, therefore the change of the disposition of the soul, in any case, is the very same as the

2. All three citations were apparently added at the same time and hence no earlier than the writing of No. 1083. These four entries are linked together by a similar set of citations attached to each one. See also below, No. 357, p. 429.

3. No. 279 is the most recent example of this favorite theme.

causing that for the future the mind shall have more lively ideas of such a sort of good. Therefore conversion is nothing but God's causing such an alteration with respect to the mind's ideas of spiritual good. But that this alteration should be begun with an idea more than ordinarily strong and lively, that is, more than is ordinary afterwards, or always with an idea of such a particular sort of gospel good and introduced just in the same method and by the same antecedent ideas, I see no reason to determine.

285. THE FALL OF OUR FIRST PARENTS. This to me looks as a plausible reason, why such a sort of curse was denounced to the serpent as going on his belly. The serpent, in the exercise of his subtlety and craft, used to hide his head and clap down upon his belly. In this temptation he had remarkably exercised that sort of craft and hid himself; therefore he should go after this manner forever after.

286. CONVERSION. 'Tis much according to God's way of dealing, that the sinner should first be terrified with a sense of his danger before God manifests his favor, and that way learn to be thankful for his mercy and to know how to prize [it]. Christ learned by suffering himself how to pity those that suffer or are in danger of suffering; though God could easily have given it to him without that, yet that was a way most agreeable to nature.

287. CHRISTIAN RELIGION, its reasonableness. One end of Christ's passion, his suffering the substance of hell torments, [was] that he might learn how [to][4] pity those that were in danger of hell. His knowing what it is by his own experience has made him exceeding compassionate, as it becomes the character of a Savior and Mediator to be.

288. ETERNITY OF HELL TORMENTS. As God's favor is infinitely desirable, so 'tis a part of his infinite awful majesty that his displeasure is infinitely dreadful; which it would not be, if it were contrary to the perfection of his nature to punish eternally. If God's majesty were not infinite, and his displeasure were not infinitely dreadful, he would be less glorious.

289. CONVERSION. It's evident that the habit of grace is always begun by an act of grace in adult persons, in that the Scripture so fully teaches

4. The word is broken off at the margin.

us that we are to be judged by our works. For if some should die having the habit of grace without any act, as it might be if there were ever the habit before the act, they either would be condemned with the habit of grace or would not be judged according to their works. But this don't conclude with respect to infants; for when the Scripture tells us we are to be judged according to our works, it says it for our warning but don't say it of those that ben't capable of being warned by it.

290. FALL. It has been a matter attended with much difficulty and perplexity, how sin came into the world, which way came it into a creation that God created very good. If any spirit had at first been created sinful, the world would not have been created very good. And if the world had been created so, things placed in such order, the wheels so contrived and so set in motion, that in the process of things sin would unavoidably come out, how can the world be said to be created good?

If it be inquired how man came to sin, seeing he had no sinful inclinations in him, except God took away his grace from him that he had been wont to give him and so let him fall, I answer, there was no need of that; there was no need of taking away any that had been given him, but he sinned under that temptation because God did not give him more. He did not take away that grace from him while he was perfectly innocent, which grace was his original righteousness; but he only witheld his confirming grace, that grace which is given now in heaven, such grace as shall fit the soul to surmount[5] every temptation. This was the grace Adam was to have had if he had stood, when he came to receive his reward. This grace God was not obliged to grant him (see Mastricht, "De violatione fœderis naturæ"),[6] and so the sin certainly followed the temptation of the devil. So that, as to the sin of mankind, it came from the devil.

Then the question is, how came the devil by it, seeing he had no

---

5. For the words "that grace which . . . to surmount" the text is mainly dependent on the Andover copy. The margin at the bottom of the page is now badly tattered and faded; more of it seems to have been available to Dwight and his scribe, both of whom worked at deciphering the words.

6. The passage cited is Lib. IV, cap. 1 of the *Theoretico-practica theologia* (see above, No. 160, p. 319, n. 2). Throughout the chapter, the point is made that God is not the cause of the fall by withdrawing any necessary grace or aid from Adam, since this could not have been done without injustice prior to Adam's sin. The citation is an integral part of JE's text, which shows that he now possesses a copy of the work; indeed, the paragraph in which it occurs seems to be indebted to Mastricht's discussion.

tempter? I answer, 'tis probable some extraordinary manifestation of God's sovereignty was his temptation, the occasion of his sin and rebellion.

291. FALL AND FREE WILL. See No. 436. Man has not so much freedom now as he had before the fall, in this respect: now he has a will against a will, an inclination contrary to his reason and judgment, which begets a contrary inclination; and this latter inclination[7] is often overcome and suppressed by the former. But before the fall, the inclination that arose from reason and judgment never was held down by the inferior inclination; so that in that sense he was more free, or, as they speak, had more freedom of will.

292. SUPRALAPSARIANS. The dispute is, whether or no creation and the fall of some was not appointed that they might be saved, and of others that they might be damned; whether salvation and damnation was not the end of their creation and fall, and whether their creation and fall were not appointed as means to that end.

'Tis said that that which is last in execution is first in intention; which is true with respect to the end and all the proper means, but not with respect to every prerequisite condition. Thus we ben't to conceive that God first intended a man's conversion before he intended his creation, though his conversion be last in execution, for creation is not the proper means of his conversion; nor it can't properly be said that God created him that he might be converted. 'Tis true that man's creation and fall were intended last with respect to his last end, but not with respect to his subordinate ends; because they[8] are proper means of the last end, but not [of][9] his third or fourth or fifth end—for at this rate, man was created for this end, that he might repent! But we are to conceive of things in this order: that that is first in execution is last in intention with respect to the ultimate end; that that is second in execution is last in intention with respect to the next[1] end, etc.

So man was created for the glory of God, because his creation was a proper means of it; and everything else that is decreed concerning

---

7. I.e. the "contrary inclination" of reason and judgment. JE's double use of "contrary" and his use of the singular "begets" are confusing and make the antecedent of "which" less than obvious, at least on first reading.

8. I.e. man's creation and fall.

9. MS: "with respect to." JE inadvertently repeated the phrase from the first part of the sentence, but his meaning requires "of."

1. I.e. next-to-last, penultimate.

man is in intention after this end, because they are all a means of it. So man's fall was intended that God might glorify himself this way, by manifestating his mercy and his just wrath, for that is[2] properly the end of God's determining the fall; and all that is after the fall is later in intention to that end. The coming of Christ and the preaching of the gospel and believing therein, is later in intention than salvation and eternal blessedness;[3] effectual calling is later in intention than justification.[4] See Turretinus, "De prædestinatione," q. 9,[5] and Mastricht, "De prædestinatione," § 12.[6]

293. SPIRIT. CREATION. It was more especially the Holy Spirit's work to bring the world to its beauty and perfection out of the chaos, for the beauty of the world is a communication of God's beauty. The Holy Spirit is the harmony and excellency and beauty of the Deity, as we have shown;[7] therefore 'twas his work to communicate beauty and harmony to the world, and so we read that it was he that moved upon the face of the waters [Gen. 1:2].

2. At this point are the deleted words, "the proper means of it. So the sending of Christ into the world and believing on him are." The cancellation was done within the next several months.

3. The words, "and obstinacy and unbelief is later in intention than persons' eternal misery," were deleted at this point, probably at the same time as the preceding cancellation (see n. 5 above).

4. Here JE deleted the following words: "and justification is later in intention than glorification." He may also have done this later than the writing of the entry, but the ink of this cancellation is not so obviously different as in the two preceding cases.

5. Franciscus Turretinus (François Turrettini) was professor of theology at Geneva from 1653 until his death in 1687. The three volumes of his *Institutio theologiæ elencticæ* were published at Geneva in 1679, 1682, and 1685 respectively, and the whole was reprinted there in three volumes in 1680–86 and finally in 1688–89. In the last Geneva reprint, Vol. 1 was a revised edition with new pagination. In two places where JE cites Vol. 1 by page, his pagination agrees with the revised edition; he therefore probably owned a 1688–89, 1696, or 1701 set.

In Loc. IV ("De prædestinatione"), quæstio 9 (*1*, 376–86) Turretine asks: is the object of predestination "homo creabilis, aut labilis" (supralapsarianism), or is it "homo conditus, & lapsus" (infralapsarianism)? Turretine affirms the latter view.

6. The Mastricht citation was probably added after No. 293 was written, but not long afterward, judging by hand and ink. Mastricht writes on predestination in Lib. III, cap. 2 of his *Theoretico-practica theologia,* of which § 12 (pp. 284–85) concerns the object of predestination. (See above, No. 160, p. 319, n. 2.) Mastricht attempts to reconcile supra and infralapsarians; he places predestination before creation and fall but makes its object merely the two classes of elect and reprobate, whereas election and reprobation proper are of individuals and presuppose man as fallen.

7. This conception of the Holy Spirit is implicit in Nos. 94, 117, and other miscellanies on the Trinity; but JE may well be thinking of "The Mind," no. 45 (*Works, 6,* 362–66); see especially §§ 4, 8–9, and 12.

294. SPIRIT. INCARNATION.[8] So it was the Spirit's work to impregnate the blessed Virgin, for it is the office of love to beget; generation is the work of love. It is probable that by this divine love her mind was filled with a divine and holy pleasure instead of sensual pleasure.

295. CONVERSION. Deut. 8:2–3, "And thou shalt remember all the way which the Lord thy God led thee these forty years in the wilderness, to humble thee and to prove thee, to know what was in thine heart, whether thou wouldst keep his commandments or no. And he humbled thee, and suffered thee to hunger . . . that he might make thee know that man doth not live by bread only, but by every word that proceedeth out of the mouth of the Lord." This doctrine is taught us in the words, that 'tis God's manner, before the bestowment of some signal blessing and a remarkable manifestation of his favor, to humble men by showing them the evil of their own hearts and how little they deserve his favor, and to teach them their dependence upon him.

296. DEVILS. 'Tis probable, one reason why man has the offer of a Savior and the devils never had, was because their sin was attended with that malice and spite and haughty scornfulness, that was equivalent to the sin against the Holy Ghost. Their sin was a downright spiteful rebellion and a direct malicious war against God, a scorn of subjection and a proud seeking of his throne.

297. SIN AGAINST THE HOLY GHOST. One reason why this sin is called the sin against the Holy Ghost is that spite and malice and scorn, the ingredients of it, are so directly contrary to the nature of the Holy Ghost, who is love.

298. SATAN DEFEATED. The devil envied man, whom he esteemed so much inferior to himself, his happiness in God's protection; and thought to have made a slave and captive of him, to have held him in his chain, to have had him under his feet, and forever to have plagued him and triumphed over him. But how remarkably will he be mortified

8. This entry has been deleted by a horizontal stroke through each line (the title is only partially canceled). Yet JE did not re-use the numeral; he also indexed the entry under two heads in the Table and did not delete them. The ink of the cancellation resembles that sometimes used by JE, Jr. and also one of the inks with which Dwight left marks on some of the MSS. Both Dwight and JE, Jr. would have found the content of No. 294 somewhat offensive. It was probably Dwight who deleted the entry while checking the scribe's copy, but JE, Jr. or some other custodian of the MSS may have been the culprit.

at the last day, when he shall be judged by a man, by one of the race, yea one that is as it were all the redeemed. They[9] must be brought in chains to have their judgment and condemnation before his throne, [he] (being united personally to the Deity) then sitting on the throne of God and clothed with his glory, together with all his assessors with him in his throne, judging of those fallen angels that thought to have had such good sport in their destruction.

299. COVENANT. FAITH. In every covenant there is required the consent of both parties. Consent on man's part to God's covenant is only an acceptance of the covenant proposed by God. In the first covenant, after man had consented he was yet to do that work which was the condition of the covenant; and therefore that is a covenant of works. In the second covenant, there is nothing to do but only to consent: there is no work to be done afterwards; the work is done by Christ. This therefore is not a covenant of works; for although faith be a good work, yet in such a case 'tis no more properly called a work than Adam's consenting to the first covenant was part of the work of that covenant. As Adam consented to the first covenant, so Christ consented to the second, for he was to do the work of it; and believers consent with him, and all that consent with Christ are looked upon as sharers in the covenant, and perform the work of the covenant in him.

This consent of theirs, whereby with their souls they accept of the second covenant to be performed by Christ, is justifying faith. Consenting to a covenant is consenting to the terms of it; therefore consenting to the second covenant is with the heart consenting to Christ's working out a perfect righteousness by his obedience and suffering for them, for this is the terms of the second covenant. The reason is very plain why it is faith that is required, because consent to a covenant is necessary to the very being in that covenant; a man can't be in any covenant till he consents to it. There is nothing else to do but [consent to the terms of the new covenant, which Christ has fulfilled.][1]

300. ORIGINAL SIN.[2] One reason why God under the old testament used to punish the posterity for the sins of their ancestors, and in-

9. I.e. the devils.

1. Conjecture for the last dozen-odd words of the entry, which were illegible when the Andover copy was made, based on the context and the tops of such letters as are visible along the bottom margin of the page.

2. Between Nos. 299 and 300 is the following unnumbered entry, deleted with a large X mark: "HAPPINESS. FALL. The forbidden tree was called the tree of knowledge of good

structed and trained up the children of Israel in that way, was to prepare the church for a [Savior][3] and an acknowledgment of the doctrine of the imputation of the sin of our first parents.

301. SIN AND ORIGINAL SIN. The best philosophy that I have met with of original sin and all sinful inclinations, habits and principles, is undoubtedly that of Mr. Stoddard's, of this town of Northampton:[4] that is, that it is self-love in conjunction with the absence of the image and love of God, that natural and necessary inclination that man has to his own benefit together with the absence of original righteousness; or in other words, the absence of that influence of God's Spirit, whereby love to God and to holiness is kept up to that degree that this other inclination is always kept in its due subordination. But this being gone, his self-love governs alone; and having not this superior principle to regulate it, breaks out into all manner of exorbitancies, and becomes in innumerable cases a vile and odious disposition, and causes thousands of unlovely and hateful actions. There is nothing new put into the nature that we call sin, but only the same self-love that necessarily belongs to the nature working and influencing, without regulation from that superior principle that primitively belongs to our nature and that is necessary in order to the harmonious existing of it. This natural and necessary inclination to ourselves, without that governor and guide, will certainly without anything else produce, or rather will become, all those sinful inclinations which are in the corrupted nature of man.

'Tis by God's continual and immediate influence every moment, as

---

and evil. By the experience of evil we not only know what that is, but the perception of good is exceedingly heightened in creatures; and also the enjoyment of good heightens the sense of evil succeeding. These contraries double one another: good is abundantly better and evil abundantly worse. So that this tree is the occasion of the experimental knowledge of good as well as evil; it has exceedingly quickened and exalted the sense of happiness in those that are happy."

The deletion was made after the ink on the entry was thoroughly dry but probably within a few months. It was surely not disagreement with the contents of the entry that caused JE to abandon it. He may simply have discovered that he had already written almost exactly the same thing, and more fully, in No. 172.

3. Or "[sense]"; only traces of the word remain at the right margin. Dwight's scribe read "a" as an *o* and wrote "others." Dwight solved the problem by deleting "and" as well as "others." The first letter of the word looks like an *s* or an *f*.

4. Stoddard's "philosophy" of original sin may be found in his *Three Sermons Lately Preach'd at Boston* (Boston, 1717), pp. 34–64, and *Treatise Concerning Conversion* (Boston, 1719), pp. 27–28. In the sermon on Rom. 7:14, written a year or so after Stoddard's death, JE explicitly acknowledges his dependence on Stoddard at this point; see below, No. 459b.

we have elsewhere shown,[5] that all the exercises and actings of the powers or inclinations of our souls are performed. Now he withdrawing that influence from the soul whereby it exercised itself about spiritual things, it comes to pass that the soul is blind and dead and unconcerned about such things, and is destitute of holy inclinations that are necessary in order to the regular[6] existence of the soul. An inclination is nothing but God's influencing the soul according to a certain law of nature; therefore the influence that upholds one inclination being withdrawn, and God continuing the same influence to the upholding of the other inclination according to the former rule and method, according to that law which we call the law of nature, it naturally and of itself breaks out into all those exorbitances. It might easily be shown how this will unavoidably, without any new infusion, produce all those inclinations that we call pride, covetousness, lasciviousness, malice, envy, etc.[7]

There is probably this also: the temperament of the body being very much vitiated (which indeed may be the natural fruit of ungoverned [self-love]),[8] the sensual appetites are very much increased, and the mind much clogged and hindered in its more exalted exercises. A sinful inclination is increased by practice, increasing the sensual appetite and vitiating the body more and more; and also by contracting of habits whereby the [ideas and] exercises[9] of the mind are led into a path wherein the soul is led to the acts of sin, and the contrary ideas that would restrain [the][1] exercises of sin are habitually kept out. The ideas of such false goods as draw most contrary to God's commands

5. Nos. 267 and 284, taken together, seem at least to imply the position stated here. Since "elsewhere" usually means elsewhere than in the "Miscellanies," JE may have been thinking of something he had written in "The Mind," perhaps nos. 2–3 (*Works, 6*, 238–39), 13 or 15 (ibid., pp. 344–45). It is also possible that the reference is to a writing no longer extant.

6. I.e. according to rule; note "the harmonious existing of it" in the previous paragraph. Cf. No. 34, where the original order or hierarchy of man's faculties and inclinations is described.

7. Cf. JE's comment in *Original Sin*, "It were easy to show, how every lust and depraved disposition of man's heart would naturally arise from this *privative* original, if here were room for it" (*Works, 3*, 383). The argument of No. 301 is used in that treatise (Pt. IV, ch. 2) against the charge that the doctrine makes God the author of sin.

8. Possibly "[sinful inclinations]"; MS: "of ~~the others~~ ungoverned."

9. Dwight's copy: "just exercises." Of the first word there now remain at the margin only the first letter (*I* or *J*) and part of a second. "Just" does not seem long enough to account for the space available on the original margin, and the references to "contrary ideas" and ideas of good and evil in this and the next sentence suggest the reading adopted.

1. While not absolutely required by the context, this word probably occurred on the missing margin.

hang much on, the mind being habituated to them; and the ideas of that good or that evil, or that[2] that would carry the soul another way, are kept out.

Corol. Therefore original sin comes thus into every man. When Adam had transgressed the covenant, God withdrew that grace which was dwelling in him, which we call original righteousness. And there is the same reason why it's denied to all his posterity, because they also transgressed the covenant. For it was made with both Adam and his posterity, equally with both; and therefore upon the breach of the covenant the holy image of God was equally denied to both: and so [both][3] Adam and his posterity are become corrupt.

302. CONVERSION. If there ever are any that are regenerated in their infancy that live till they are adult, then doubtless there are some whose first exercise of grace is not such a particular manner of closing with Christ[4] as some think necessary, and as perhaps is commonly the first gracious act in those that have for some time lived in an allowed way of sinning. For such infants without doubt exercise grace gradually as they exercise their reason.

303. SCRIPTURE. SOLOMON'S SONG. CHRISTIAN RELIGION. I imagine that Solomon, when he wrote this song, being a very philosophical, musing man, and a pious man, and of a very loving temper, set himself in his own musings to imagine[5] and to point forth to himself a pure, virtuous, pious and entire love; and represented the musings and feelings[6] of his mind, that in a philosophical and religious frame was carried away in a sort of transport: and in that [frame][7] his musings and the train of his imaginations were guided and led on by the Spirit of God. Solomon, in his wisdom and great experience, had learned the

2. MS: "tha[ ]" or "tho[ ]." Dwight's scribe read (or conjectured) "that," though possibly because he incorrectly read the preceding word as "as." Nevertheless, the reading of the copy has been accepted, since there may not have been enough space on the margin for "thoughts," the only likely alternative.

3. Given JE's repeated emphasis on "both," it is likely that the word occurred on the right margin, which must have been missing when Dwight's copy was made. The scribe conjectured "that," but to make it work he also omitted "and" before "so."

4. JE has deleted, at this point, "and coming unto him, as our old divines [. . . (illegible word)]."

5. Or "image"; the right margin is defective. Dwight probably had no copy of this entry made, and no other copies are extant.

6. Or "feeling"; only the first three letters are legible.

7. This or some such word is probably broken off at the margin.

vanity of all other love than of such a sort of one. God's Spirit made use of his loving inclination, joined with his musing philosophical disposition, and so directed and conducted it in this train of imagination as to represent the love that there is between Christ and his spouse. God saw it very needful and exceeding useful that there should be some such representation of it. The relation that there is between Christ and the church, we know, is very often compared to that that there is between a man [and]8 his wife—yea, this similitude is abundantly insisted on almost everywhere in the Scripture—and a virtuous and pious and pure love between a man and his spouse is very much of an image of the love between Christ and the church. So that it is not at all strange that the Spirit of God, which is love, should direct a holy amorous disposition after such a manner as to make such a representation, and 'tis very agreeable to other the like representations.

304. CRUCIFIXION. When Christ hung dying upon the cross, he was doing that that was the most wonderful act of love that ever was; and the posture that he died in was very suitable to signify his free and great [love]:9 he died with his arms spread open, as being ready to embrace all that would come to him. He was lift up [upon the] cross above the earth with his arms thus open, and there he made an offer of his love to the world; he was presented in open [view to] the world as their Savior. By this love he drew men to him, as he says, "If I be lift up from the earth, I will draw [all men] unto me" [John 12:32]. See Is. 25:11, "And he shall spread forth his hands in the midst of them, as he that swimmeth spreadeth forth his hands to swim."

305. HOLY GHOST. That the Holy Ghost is love. II Cor. 6:6, "By kindness, by the Holy Ghost, by love unfeigned." Rom. 15:30, "Now I beseech you, brethren, for the Lord Jesus Christ's sake, and for the love of the Spirit." Phil. 2:1–2, "If there be therefore any consolation in Christ, [if] any comfort of love, if any fellowship of the Spirit, if any bowels and mercies, fulfill ye my joy, that ye be likeminded, having the same love, being of one accord, of one mind."1 Rom. 5:5, "Having the

8. This word must have been on the missing margin.
9. All the insertions in this entry are required by broken margins. Dwight's copy of this entry is not extant.
1. The preceding text of No. 305 was originally written as an entry between Nos. 302 and 303. After writing No. 304 JE transferred the entry to the top of the next page and added more texts. When he wrote No. 306 he left about two inches of space for additions.

love of God shed abroad in our hearts by the Holy Ghost which is given to us." Gal 5:22–23, "But the fruit of the Spirit is love, joy, peace, longsuffering, gentleness, goodness, faith, meekness, temperance." Eph. 5:9, "For the fruit of the Spirit is in all goodness and righteousness and truth." Col. 1:8, "Who declared unto us your love in the Spirit." I Thess. 1:6, "Having received the word in much affliction, with joy of the Holy Ghost." Rom. 14:17, "The kingdom of God is righteousness, and peace, and joy in the Holy Ghost."[2]

306.[3] SATISFACTION. It hardly carries a right idea with it, to say that God is obliged in justice to punish sin. 'Tis a mere act of justice to punish sin; yet if he did not punish it nobody could charge God with any wrong. It seems to me to exhibit the thing more properly to say that God is obliged in holiness and in wisdom to punish sin. It would not be a prudent, decent and beautiful thing for a being of infinite glory and majesty, and the sovereign of the world, to let an infinite evil go unpunished. And as God's nature inclines him [to][4] order all things beautifully, properly and decently, so it was necessary that sin should be punished; God in his infinite wisdom saw that there was such a necessity as this. There is this necessity, besides what arises from the [verac]ity[5] of God.

307. SATAN DEFEATED. God prepared the Jewish world to receive[6] the doctrine of satisfactory sacrifice by appointing the sacrifices of beasts; and the devil prepared the Gentile world for receiving the same by mimicking God in this thing of sacrificing, intending thereby the more effectually to promote his own interest. And they were the more prepared by the devil's going such lengths as to require human

2. At this point JE's studies were interrupted, almost certainly because of the awakening that occurred while he was Stoddard's colleague. When he returned to writing in the "Miscellanies" he left the rest of the page blank after No. 305 (possibly thinking to add more texts on the Holy Spirit) and continued on another sheet after Nos. 311–314, which he had written about the time he went to Northampton. His next entries, Nos. 315 ff., concentrate on issues related to evangelistic preaching, counseling of sinners, and the experience of conversion.

3. Nos. 306–310 were probably written between Nos. 328 and 256 in the spring of 1728; see above, p. 85, and Fig. 5, pp. 156–57.

4. Broken off at margin.

5. The first part of the word is lost at the left margin; of the visible letters the last three are clear and the reading of the other two is probable.

6. MS: "the ~~Jews to receive~~ world to receive."

sacrifices, which were common among the heathen, and sacrificing of children (and sometimes only sons), [to][7] receive this human sacrifice, Jesus Christ. Their minds were hereby possessed with such sort of notions [as] the satisfaction and propitiation of slain sacrifices, that it was a great preparation. And so indeed was [the] heathenish doctrines of deities' being united to images, and the heathenish fables of heroes' being begotten [by] gods, a preparation for their receiving the doctrine of the incarnation, of the Deity's dwelling in a human [body],[8] and the Son of God's being conceived in the womb of a virgin by the power and Spirit of [God].

308. TRINITY. With respect to that objection against this explication of the Trinity,[9] that according to this [sort][1] of reasoning there would not only be three persons but an infinite number—for we must suppose that the Son understands the Father, as well as the Father the Son; and consequently the Son has an idea of the Father, and so that idea will be another person; and so may be said of the Holy Ghost. This objection is but a color without substance, and arises [from][2] a confusion of thought and a misunderstanding of what we say.

In the first place, we don't suppose that the Father, the Son, and the Holy Ghost are three distinct beings that have three distinct understandings. It is the divine essence understands, and it is the divine essence is understood; 'tis the divine being that loves, and it is the divine being that is loved. The Father understands, the Son understands, and the Holy Ghost understands, because every one is the same understanding divine essence; and not that each of them have a distinct understanding of their own.

Secondly, we never suppose the Father generated the Son by understanding the Son, but that God generated the Son by understanding his own essence, and that the Son is that idea itself, or understanding of the essence. The Father understands the Son no otherwise than as

7. This and the other bracketed insertions in this entry represent text now missing at the broken left margin.

8. Or "[form]."

9. I.e. the line of argument begun in No. 94 and continued (or assumed) in subsequent entries on the Trinity. JE's earliest answer to the objection in this particular form may be seen in No. 94; cf. No. 259.

1. Only a portion of the last letter of this word now remains at the left margin. Dwight's scribe read the word as "truth," perhaps influenced by his misreading "this" as "the." Dwight accepted both readings and editorially inserted "this" after "of."

2. The word is now broken from the left margin. The Andover copy reads "arises in," but "in" is not JE's usual idiom with "arises."

he understands that essence, that is, the essence of the Son. The Father understands the idea he has merely in his having that idea, without any other act; thus a man understands his own perfect idea merely by his having that idea in his mind. So the Son understands the Father in that the essence of the Son understands the essence of the Father, as in himself being the understanding of that essence; and so of the Holy Ghost.

After you have in your imagination multiplied understandings and loves never so often, it will be the understanding and loving of the very same essence, and you can never make more than these three: God, and the idea of God, and the love of God. But I would not be understood to pretend to give a full explication of the Trinity, for I think it still remains an incomprehensible mystery, the greatest and the most glorious of all mysteries.

309. TRINITY. The name of the second person in the Trinity, Λόγος, evidences that he is God's idea, whether we translate the word the "reason" of God or the "word" of God. If the "reason" or the "understanding" of God, the matter is past dispute; for everyone will own, that the reason or understanding of God is his idea. And if we translate it the "word" of God, he is either the outward word of God or his inward. None will say he is his outward. Now the outward word is speech, but the inward word, which is the original of it, is thought— the Scripture being its own interpreter; for how often is thinking in the Scripture called speaking, when applied to God and men. So that 'tis the idea, if we take the Scripture for our guide, that is the inward word.

310. TRINITY. Concerning the Holy Ghost. What the Holy Ghost is, is confirmed from that sin which is called the sin against the Holy Ghost, which consists in a knowing, direct, professed scorn, spite and malice against God; which is diametrically contrary to the Holy Ghost, who is God's love and the love of God.[2]

311.[3] CHRISTIAN RELIGION. The rite of circumcision is an argument with me that the Jewish religion was of divine authority. It is a ceremony the most unlikely to [be] of human institution, of any in the world. Those nations that contrive religions for themselves will not think of nor effect any such thing, that seemed so much to discounte-

3. Nos. 311–314 were written between Nos. 261–264 and 267–274 during JE's move to Northampton in the fall of 1726; see above, pp. 83–84, and Fig. 5, p. 156.

nance the pleasure of lasciviousness. False religions are always favorable enough to those strong appetites of human nature. Besides, it would contradict men's pride, and they could not but know [it] would expose them to the ridicule and scorn of other nations. But 'tis evident the Jews were of a temper that could not easily bear that. False religions always spare those two lusts of lasciviousness and pride.

312. BEING OF GOD. If we should suppose that the world is eternal, yet the beauty, contrivance and useful disposition of the world would not less strongly conclude for the being of an intelligent author. It will appear by this question: whether or no, if we should see such a poem as Virgil's *Æneid,* it would be any more satisfying to us if we were told that it was from eternity transcribed from copy to copy, though we supposed that a succession of men had actually existed from eternity—I say, would it be at all more satisfying, than if we were told that it was made by the casual falling of ink on paper?

313. CHRISTIAN RELIGION. The union of a soul or spirit with matter so as to produce a vital communication between them being an arbitrary institution of divine wisdom, and the laws of this connection being performed by voluntary and immediate divine efficacy (there being no reason or foundation in the separate nature of either substance why any motion in the body should produce any sensation at all in the soul, or any one more than another, or why any action in the soul should produce any motion in the body) it follows that when once that union is dissolved none but God himself can restore it, seeing that the union depends on his arbitrary efficacy alone, and the laws of it are such as he has established and he only upholds—except we say that some creature has the management of the divine will and efficacy in their power.

And if we deny the immortality of the soul and say that the soul is annihilated upon the death of the body, 'tis equally manifest that a resurrection must be God's own work and his only. For the soul is certainly [a] distinct substance from the body, and it will be confessed that no creature can bring that substance from nothing again. Therefore whatever may be supposed of other miracles, of the possibility of their being performed by creatures, we know of this that it cannot. I can think of no other miracle whatever that would be so full an evidence and manifestation of the finger of God; it must therefore be a certain evidence of the truth of that that it is done in confirmation of.

And especially the resurrection of the person himself in proof of his own authority, foretold by the person that he would rise and thereby give a demonstration of it. For seeing it must be done by God, as we have shown, it is as incredible that he should show so extraordinary a favor to an impostor, as that he should interpose his power to confirm a falsehood. Besides, when the person is dead there is an utter impossibility of cheating and juggling; if Christ deceived persons' senses when he was alive, he surely did not when he was dead. Witches' juggling is at an end when they are dead.

314. FREE GRACE. This appears to me to be a rational account of God's free grace, and also a certain one. God has in his own nature a propensity to communicate goodness and to make happy; and having created creatures for that end, he has a propensity to communicate happiness to those of them that he in his wisdom chooses, without any consideration of anything that is good of one kind or other to incline him. For he would have an inclination to it though they were considered as nonentities; for he has an absolute inclination to goodness in his own nature, which is the reason even of their being, so that he loves them with a love of benevolence for nothing at all in them, and without being inclined thereto by any of their perfections natural or moral. Now a love free in this sense is a perfection of God, and what rationally obliges our love to him more than any love for anything good in us can do, because 'tis a greater manifestation of a loving and good nature. He therefore wills absolutely, and freely in this sense, all the happiness that he ever confers on the elect; and his wisdom determines the degree of happiness antecedent to any consideration of the degree of goodness in them.

But because God does everything beautifully, he brings about this their happiness which he determined, in an excellent manner; but it would be a grating, dissonant and deformed thing for a sinful creature to be happy in God's love. He therefore gives them holiness, which holiness he really delights in—he has really complacence in them after he has given them beauty, and not before—and so the beauty that he gives, when given, induces God in a certain secondary manner to give them happiness. That is, he wills their happiness antecedently, of himself, and he gives them holiness that he may be induced to confer it; and when it[4] is given by him, then he is induced by another consider-

4. I.e. holiness.

ation besides his mere propensity to goodness. For there are these two propensities in the divine nature: to communicate goodness absolutely to that which now is nothing, and to communicate goodness to that which is beautiful and holy, and which he has complacence in. He has a propensity to reward holiness, but he gives it on purpose that he may reward it; because he loves the creature, and loves to reward, and therefore gives it something that he may reward.[5]

315.[6] JUSTIFICATION. To be justified is to be approved of by God as a subject of pardon and a right to eternal life. And when we say he is justified by faith only, we mean that it's only his having faith that renders him approvable, or renders it a fit thing that he should be approved, in God's esteem. 'Tis not so properly making that the only condition of salvation, if by a condition we mean that that[7] is proposed as that without which it shall not be, and that with which it shall be; for so are many things that accompany and follow faith. So are the love of God and good works in a multitude of places proposed as the condition of salvation; that is, they are proposed as that without which salvation can't be, and with which it will be. But good works in fallen man, let there be never so many of them—if they could be without faith—don't render it [at] all a more fit and proper thing in God's esteem that he should be saved. But his believing does render it a fit and a worthy thing in God's esteem that he should be saved. See No. 412.

316. TORMENTS OF HELL. One thing that convinces me that the torments of hell will be exceeding great, is that it is called "hell" and "hell-fire" from the valley of the son of Hinnom, where they used to burn their children to death in brick kilns, and to put them into hollow brazen vessels over the fire, and so by heating the vessels red hot to burn and scald them to death, crying out in a very lamentable manner. Christ teaches us that by saying "Thou fool" [we] should be in danger

5. There follows a sentence which originally concluded the entry but which JE (probably later) bracketed and deleted with a large X mark: "I conclude that there is a propensity in the divine nature to communicate happiness to that which is holy, because it is in itself absolutely a beautiful thing that that which is holy should be happy." For his next entries JE went back to the sheet containing Nos. 261–264 and, on the outside recto, wrote Nos. 267–274.

6. Nos. 315–328 were written next after No. 305 and represent the period of the earthquake awakening in the fall and winter of 1727–28; see above, pp. 84–86.

7. I.e. which. The first "that" is demonstrative and refers to "condition"; the second "that" introduces a relative clause modifying the first "that."

of hell-fire [Matt. 5:22]. Being angry without a cause exposed to death, to the being slain with the sword, which was the death the judgment had power to inflict;[8] saying "Raca" exposed to stoning, the death the council condemned to; but saying "Thou fool" exposed to hell-fire, that is, to this sort of death in the valley of the son of Hinnom. But if only saying "Fool" exposes to so great a punishment in another world, how great torment will all the sins of a man's life expose him to!

The similitude of a furnace of fire, to which hell is compared, is not unlike this of a brick kiln, or those brazen vessels, [i.e.] a hollow place filled with glowing heat.

317. THE WORK OF HUMILIATION, as I understand it according to Mr. Stoddard,[9] is in the first place an utter despair of help from ourselves. The man tries a great while to be a means of his own salvation, by his own strength to change and sanctify his own heart, and by his righteousness to engage God to show mercy to him: but now he is quite discouraged; the heart gives out and gives up such endeavors; he finds by experience after all his trials, that his heart is as hard as ever. This is very possible to be while the heart has no grace, and seems very agreeable to God's wisdom and his methods of dealing.

Secondly, by setting before his conscience the heinousness and aggravation of his sins, either sinful actions or dispositions, he is convinced that he deserves God's wrath and eternal misery; he is convinced of it against his inclination. This can't be denied to be possible while the heart is at enmity with God, for doubtless it will be so with wicked men at the day of judgment: their consciences will be thus convinced, though their hearts are as full of enmity against God as they can hold. This seems also to be possible, that the soul, having been a great while terrified and weakened and wearied out, and being now discouraged of helping itself, and being thus convinced of its deserts, there may be a sort of submission, as a stubborn man that has been quite worn out with vexations, troubles and labors, at length becomes tame and pliant, though his heart be yet full of a principle of enmity. And this method also seems very consonant to God's wisdom and his manner of ordering things.

8. MS: "which was the death the judgment has power to inflict death."

9. This entry is in part a dialogue with Stoddard, as are several ensuing ones on conviction, conversion, and humiliation. Stoddard insisted on the necessity of a consciously experienced "work of humiliation" before conversion but denied that there was any grace in such an experience.

As to the necessity of it, this is certain, that it is necessary for the soul to suppose that he can't be his own savior and that he deserves ruin, when he actually receives Christ and his salvation as a free gift. 'Tis impossible to receive him as a free gift without supposing so at the same time.[1]

As to being convinced by trial and experience that he is not able to make his heart any better, 'tis certain it is not always so, as in those many conversions that were wrought in a few hours that we have an account of in the Scripture.

And though it be necessary that it should be supposed indeed true that he deserves ruin at the time that he actually receives Christ's salvation as a free gift, yet it don't follow that it is absolutely necessary that the soul should think of it and be explicitly convinced of it before-hand. There are many other things that must necessarily be supposed as really true by the soul at the time that it actually receives [salvation], that yet there is no need of being explicitly convinced of beforehand; as the being of God, that Jesus Christ suffered and died in this world, that there is a future state, that we are in a fallen state. These things sinners ben't really convinced of, according to them,[2] before a closing with Christ, and yet must be supposed to be convinced of 'em then.

Indeed if he has denied the being of a God till then and believed the contrary, he must be expressly convinced in the first place. So if he has explicitly disbelieved his deserving ruin or insisted upon scruples and doubts of it, it is necessary that he should expressly be convinced of it before he explicitly receives Christ; and indeed persons very often, under great convictions and fears of hell, do much insist upon objections against the justice of damning them.

'Tis acknowledged that a self-righteous disposition is not at all mortified before actual conversion, but God convinces men against their nature and inclination that their own righteousness is vain. Nor are they always brought to a conviction of the insufficiency of their own strength and righteousness by their own experience of its ineffectualness, as in the multitudes that were in a few hours converted by the preaching of the apostles. But then it must be by God's more immediately convincing them by his suppressing such a spirit of self-confidence when it rises, not mortifying [it]—and how do we know but that God may as well sometimes keep it from working from the first?

1. JE added the next four paragraphs later in space he had left blank before the Scripture passages.
2. JE is probably referring to the testimony of converts.

Scriptures concerning conviction and humiliation.[3] Acts 2:37–38, "Now when they heard this, they were pricked in their heart, and said unto Peter and to the rest of the apostles, Men and brethren, what shall we do?" Acts 9:6, 9, "And he (Paul) trembling and astonished said, Lord, what wilt thou have me to do? . . . And he was three days without sight, and neither did eat nor drink." Acts 16:29–30, "Then he called for a light, and sprang in, and came trembling and fell down before Paul and Silas, and brought them out and said, Sirs, what must I do to be saved?" Matt. 11:28, "Come unto me, ye that labor and are heavy laden, and I will give you rest." Rom. 3:19–20, "Now we know that what things soever the law saith, it saith to them who are under the law; that every mouth may be stopped, and all the world may become guilty before God" (compared with Hos. 5:15, margin).[4] Rom. 7:9, "For I was alive without the law once; but when the commandment came, sin revived and I died." Gal. 2:19, "I through the law am dead to the law." II Cor. 10:4, "The weapons of our warfare are mighty through God for the pulling down of strongholds." Luke 15:16–18, "And he would fain have filled his belly with the husks that the swine did eat, and no man gave unto him. And when he came to himself he said, How many hired servants of my father's have bread enough and to spare, and I perish with hunger! I will arise," etc.

Is. 50:4, "The Lord God hath given [me] the tongue of the learned, that I should know how to speak a word in season to him that is weary." I Kgs. 19:11–12, "And behold, the Lord passed by, and a great and strong wind rent the mountains, and brake in pieces the rocks before the Lord, but the Lord was not in the wind; and after the wind an earthquake, but the Lord was not in the earthquake; and after the earthquake a fire, but the Lord was not in the fire: and after the fire a still small voice." II Cor. 1:9, "But we had the sentence of death in ourselves, that we should not trust in ourselves, but in God that raiseth the dead"; that is, I see that the case was past all human help, and that except God especially interposed I should certainly die.

We have an instance in Adam and Eve: they had doubtless a season of great fears and terrors before Christ was revealed to them, and probably most of all just before. Is. 61:1 and Luke 4:18, "The Spirit of

---

3. JE wrote this paragraph in the middle of the entry and left space for more material, adding the next two paragraphs shortly afterwards. This set of texts interrupts his main discussion, which resumes at "There is this to be said," etc.

4. Hos. 5:15 begins, "I will go and return to my place, till they acknowledge their offense." An alternate reading for the latter clause is given in the margin: "till they be guilty."

the Lord is upon me, because the Lord hath anointed me to preach glad tidings to the meek; he hath sent me to bind up the broken-hearted, to proclaim liberty to the captives, and the opening of the prison to them who are bound, to proclaim the acceptable year of the Lord, to comfort all that mourn." See I Sam. 22:2; John 16:8.

There is this to be said, that wicked men, till they have had particular convictions, are insensible of the heinousness of sin and so can't be sensible of its desert, can't see the agreeableness between so great a punishment and their sin. To this I say two things: (1) There must be allowed to be a great difference in the degree of this conviction; some see more of the heinousness of sin, some less. There are none in this world that see all its heinousness, and I believe none but what, if they had a true idea of the misery of the damned or a very much enlarged idea of the duration of their punishment, without[5] further conviction would see the agreeableness between their sin and so great misery. (2) The sight of God's glory is sufficient to convince of the heinousness and desert of sin. The man may have a notional belief of it before, as [he] has of other things that it is necessary for him to believe in order to his coming to Christ, viz. that God is true, that he is merciful, that he is holy, etc., that yet don't take hold of 'em; they don't see till they have their eyes open to see the glory of God. So at the same moment they may have a sense given them of the heinousness of sin, and indeed never have a right sense till then.

'Tis very congruous and agreeable to God's wise methods, to make men see what bad hearts they have before he gives them good hearts, that he should make them see how wicked they be before he gives them holiness, to make them see that they are in bondage to sin before he gives them liberty.

There are these three things necessary: (1) to see our danger of eternal misery, (2) to see the absolute necessity of a savior, and (3) to see the sufficiency and excellency of the Savior that is offered. The first is given in conviction, the second in humiliation, the third in conversion.

It seems very congruous, that God should prepare the heart [of the sinner] for the receiving of Christ by a sense of his sin and misery, and a despair of help in himself and in all others.[6]

5. MS: "that without."
6. No. 275 was probably composed between Nos. 317 and 318; see above, p. 376, n. 5.

318. HELL TORMENTS. Another thing[7] that convinces me that the miseries of the damned are exceeding great, are those two places of Scripture: Luke 23:31, "If they do these things in the green tree, what shall be done in the dry?" For how exceeding great were the miseries that Christ endured; and yet I think this expression [intimates] that the misery of wicked men shall be much greater. And the other place is I Pet. 4:17–18, "For the time is come that judgment must begin at the house of God; and if it first begin at us, what shall the end be of them that obey not the gospel of God? And if the righteous are scarcely saved, where shall the ungodly and sinner appear?" How great have the torments of some of the martyrs been; and yet this intimates that the torments of the wicked shall be vastly greater.

319. CHRIST'S SATISFACTION. Though God's infinite holiness and justice obliges him to exert his hatred and wrath against that that is infinitely odious, and an affront to an infinite majesty and authority; yet if a person infinitely great and lovely loves them so well as to intercede for them, a respect to him may justly take off this hatred and anger from the sinner. And if you say, it is not just that this infinitely excellent person should love this infinite offender so much, I answer: yes, if he offers to bear it himself and to suffer in his stead, he acknowledges the infinite odiousness and demerit of the sin, and manifests his sense of that, and gives a sufficient testimony of his hatred of that, though he loves the person.

320. DEVILS. See No. 702 (corol. 3). It seems to me probable that the temptation of the angels that occasioned their rebellion was that when God was about to create man, or had first created him, God declared his decree to the angels that one of that human nature should be his Son, his best beloved, his greatest favorite, and should be united to his eternal Son, and that he should be their head and king; that they should be given to him and should worship him and be his servants, attendants and ministers. And God, having thus declared his great love to the race of mankind, gave the angels the charge of them as ministering spirits to men.

Satan, or Lucifer, or Beelzebub, being the archangel, one of the highest of the angels, could not bear it, thought it below him and a

7. "One thing" is discussed in No. 316.

great debasing of him; so he conceived rebellion against the Almighty, and drew away a vast company of the heavenly hosts with him. But he was cast down from the highest pitch of glory to the lowest hell for it, and himself was made an occasion of bringing that to pass which his spirit so rose against. Yea, his spite and malice was made an occasion of it, and that same act of his by which he thought he had entirely overthrown the design; and that same person in human nature, which they could not bear should rule over them in glory and should be their king and head to communicate happiness to them, by this means proves their king in spite of them and becomes their judge; and though they would not be his willing subjects, they shall be his unwilling captives; he shall [be] their sovereign to make them miserable and pour out his wrath upon them. And mankind, whom they so envied and scorned, are by occasion of them advanced to higher glory and honor and greater happiness, and more nearly united to God; and though they disdained to be ministering spirits to them, yet now they shall be judged by them as assessors with Jesus Christ.

321a. CHRISTIAN RELIGION. Raising the dead to life is given in the Old Testament as a certain [proof] of the authority and mission of a prophet, and that what he says is the word of God and the truth. I Kgs. 17:24, "And the woman said to Elijah, By this I know that thou art a man of God, and that the word of the Lord in thy mouth is truth." So that if the Old Testament is the word of God, Jesus was a true prophet.

321b. CHRIST'S SATISFACTION. Christ suffered the very same misery that sinners are condemned to, so far as a person of his nature was capable of it. The green tree and the dry tree are cast into the same fire, but there is a great deal of difference in the power that the fire has upon one and the other, arising only from their different nature and not from the difference of the fire.[8] So it was impossible that Christ should have this sense, that God was really angry with him and that he was the object of his hatred, and it was impossible that he should utterly despair of ever being delivered from that doleful state. God sees meet that that misery, which is the same as far as Christ's nature allows of it, should be accepted in him as satisfying.

322. RIGHTEOUSNESS, CHRIST'S ACTIVE. Christ came into the world to render the honor of God's authority and his law consistent with the

8. Cf. JE's recent use of the same figure in No. 318.

salvation and eternal life of sinners. He came to save them, and yet to assert and vindicate the honor of God's authority and holy law. Now if the sinner, after his sin was satisfied for, had eternal life bestowed upon [him] without active righteousness, the honor of His law would not be sufficiently vindicated. Supposing this were possible, that the sinner himself could suffer and so pay the debt, and afterwards be in the same state that he was in before his probation; if he now at last should have eternal life bestowed upon him without performing that condition of obedience, then God would recede from his law and would give the promised reward, and his law never have respect and honor shown to it in that way, in being obeyed. But Christ, by subjecting himself to the law and by obeying of it, has done a great honor to the law, a great honor to the authority of God who gave it; that so glorious a person should become subject to the law, has done much more honor to it than if man had obeyed.

That Christ might the more fully honor God's authority, he was made under and obeyed the cermonial law also. Christ's obedience to positive laws of God, [such] as the ceremonial laws, was equivalent to Adam's obedience to that positive precept of not eating the forbidden fruit. As that precept was given for the trial of Adam's obedience, so the ceremonial law was given for the trial of the second Adam's obedience.

323. OLD TESTAMENT DISPENSATION, as it was the covenant of works that was proposed to the children of Israel. That is, it was proposed to them that they might be convinced that they were all sinners and condemned by that covenant, that they might be brought to trust in the mere saving grace of God which was also revealed to them. So that the covenant might be in all things like that proposed to Adam, God proposed to them not only the moral law but positive precepts also: the ceremonial law answered to the precept about the forbidden fruit. Therefore also[9] it became Christ as our Mediator and the second Adam also to obey the ceremonial law.

324. SATAN DEFEATED. The devil in heaven thought to have overcome God by strength; but he was convinced by experience, by his being cast out down to hell, that it was in vain to oppose his strength to God's. Therefore in the next place, though he saw God was stronger than he, yet he thought to get the better of him by craft and subtlety.

9. I.e. in addition to the reason given in No. 322.

Therefore God shows by the wonderful wisdom of the gospel that he can as easily overcome him by wisdom as power.

325. THE WORK OF HUMILIATION. If you say there is no need of any other sense of our own misery as we are by nature, and of the dreadfulness and heinousness of our sin, than what grace gives; I answer, that no doubt there may be grace and the exercise of it without any other sense, but yet this may be needful in order to the proper exercise of grace in a more suitable manner. There are many things that are useful in order to the proportionable and harmonious exercise of grace which are not grace, as knowledge, experience, [etc.] Why is the preaching of the gospel necessary? God could, if he pleased, give a principle of grace the same nature and disposition, if we never had heard of Christ. But God sees this necessary in order to the proper and harmonious exercise of grace.[1]

As thus: it might, for aught I know, be possible for the principle of grace to be put into a man that does not know that there is a hell, and this might carry him forth to love God and Christ. But there could not be the proper and congruous exercise of grace, which is to desire Christ, to love him, to give himself to him, humbly and thankfully to rejoice in him, and trust in him as a savior from destruction and great misery: this is the exercise of grace becoming such sinful and miserable creatures as we are; this is proper for us. And in many other things also, both in duties of heart and life, and indeed in everything, this is necessary in order to a suitable exercise of grace. So from a suitable preparation, as there arises a more proper exercise of grace, so there will naturally flow more of the exercises of grace from the same degree of the principle. So a man that has a great deal of knowledge has the opportunity of more of the exercise of grace, than he that has but little knowledge but the same degree of the principle of grace. So if grace were infused into a very ignorant heathen, there would be hardly any opportunity for the exercises of grace. So [in] a man that did not know there was a hell,[2] there would be but little opportunity.

I don't know but that in more rational, understanding and considering men, such a sense of their own misery and danger and helplessness as they are in a natural condition, as God may give them by means of

---

1. The original entry ended here, space being left before the beginning of No. 326. The three paragraphs which follow were added together not long afterwards. The short last paragraph and the concluding citation are still later additions.
2. MS: "no hell."

their own rational consideration, together with that sense of the vileness of sin and its great demerit which arises from a sight of God's glory given in conversion itself, may be as sufficient, if not more useful, for the proper, congruous and suitable exercises of grace, than those lively strong imaginations of misery and danger that are generally given to the more unlearned and less rational. In such persons, I believe, God don't make so much use of the imagination as he does in others; they ben't so disposed to it, neither is there that need of it.

God took great care in the work of redemption to assert the honor of his authority, holiness and jealousy, as well as to manifest the glory of his mercy and grace. So that it is reasonable to suppose, in order to persons' being partakers of this redemption, that they should acknowledge as well the glory of his authority and hatred of sin as the glory of his mercy. This acknowledgment can be by nothing else than an inward sense of his authority and hatred of sin, and the deserved manifestations of it on himself; which humiliation therefore is necessary in all saints.

When it is found that none other can open the book, then Christ opens it (Rev. 5); so when it is seen and found that none other can save, then Christ saves. See Is. 40:6, notes.[3]

326. OLD TESTAMENT DISPENSATION. The sacrifices were necessary under the Old Testament dispensation for the maintaining the honor of God's law and authority. If they had only been taught that upon their repentance and flying to God's mercy they should be pardoned by mercy, without giving any hints wherefore, it would lead them into this thought, that howsoever wicked men were and how much soever they had provoked and affronted God, yet he was ready at any time to forgive them; which would tend to their despising and making little of God's commanding authority, and to lessen their thoughts of his holy majesty. Therefore God was very careful to instruct them that he was a jealous God and would in no wise clear the guilty; and by requiring these sacrifices intimated to them that he would not pardon without satisfaction, and by the sufferings of the slain beast intimated that sin must be suffered for, hereby showing his holy hatred and discountenancing of sin and trespasses against his authority. So that they were

---

3. The note is a brief comment: "John the Baptist was sent to prepare the way for Christ to follow, by preaching the law and thereby convincing men of their own utter insufficiency and helplessness; and thus showed that all flesh, all the strength and worthiness of man, is as grass that withers and fades away."

led by this contrivance to trust in the mere mercy of God, with this sense of the heinousness of sin, and a humble sense and fear and respect to the glory of the holiness, sovereign authority, and jealousy of God; which is the exercise of the same disposition of mind as is exercised in actually believing on Christ crucified, and is the same sort of act.

This was not the only means to give them a sense of God's authority and jealousy; but there were also the frequent signal temporal punishments of sinners, of sinful men and cities and nations, [and] punishing the iniquity of the fathers upon the children, which was an intimation that punishment did not cease when a man was dead.

327[a]. END OF THE INCARNATION AND DEATH OF CHRIST. The infinite love which there is from everlasting between the Father and the Son is the highest excellency and peculiar glory of the Deity. God saw it therefore meet that there should be some bright and glorious manifestation made of [it] to the creatures, which is done in the incarnation and death of the Son of God. Hereby was most clearly manifested to men and angels the distinction of the persons of the Trinity. The infinite love of the Father to the Son is thereby manifested, in that for his sake he would forgive an infinite debt, would be reconciled with and receive into his favor and to his enjoyment those that had rebelled against him and injured his infinite majesty, and in exalting of him to that high mediatorial glory; and Christ showed his infinite love to the Father in his infinitely abasing himself for the vindicating of his authority and the honor of his majesty. When God had a mind to save men, Christ infinitely laid out himself that the honor of God's majesty might be safe and that God's glory might be advanced.

[327b]. PERSEVERANCE.[4] If grace being once in the heart ben't a certain and infallible sign that a man shall have eternal life, how is the Spirit of God an earnest of glory, when a man may have the Spirit and it be no assurance that he is to be glorified?

328. HUMILIATION, CONVICTION, ETC. *Scriptures.* I Kgs. 8:38—whether by "the plague of his own heart" is meant the sin of his own heart or the affliction of his own heart, it don't much alter.[5] Joseph's

---

4. This entry was made in space left between Nos. 327 and 328, probably within a month or two, and was missed when JE numbered his entries a year or so later.

5. JE's original entry ended here. He wrote the rest in successive additions during the next few months.

brethren in great distress, and brought to resign up themselves to be his slaves, before he revealed himself to them [Gen. 42–45]. Deut. 32:10, "He found him in a desert land; he led him about, he instructed him." Ex. 13:17. Gal. 3:22–24.

John the Baptist, Christ's forerunner, in order to prepare men for Christ, discovers to 'em the vanity of their false confidences: "And think not to say within yourselves, We have Abraham to our father" (Matt. 3:9). That place of Scripture, John 16:20–21 ("Ye shall be sorrowful, but your sorrow shall be turned into joy. A woman when she is in travail hath sorrow, because her hour is come; but as soon as she is delivered of the child, she remembreth no more the anguish, for joy," etc.) is an argument that 'tis God's usual way to prepare the heart by concern and uneasiness when he is about to bestow remarkable comfort.[6]

329.[7] FAITH. 'Tis called believing rather than choosing or loving, because those words seem to hold forth something more of the nature of a work, something that is morally excellent; there is moral excellency in those acts of the will, but none in believing or the acts of the understanding any further than they depend upon the will or disposition. Therefore, that we mayn't take it that we are saved at all upon the account of any moral goodness or excellency, 'tis called by the name of believing rather than choosing.

Faith is very often in the Scripture called trusting, especially in the Old Testament. Now trusting is something more than mere believing. Believing is the assent to any truth testified; trusting always respects truth that nearly concerns ourselves, in regard of some benefit of our own that it reveals to us, and some benefit that the revealer is the author of; it is the acquiescence of the mind in a belief of any person that by his word reveals or represents himself to us as the author of some good that concerns us. If the benefit be a deliverance or preservation from misery, 'tis a being easy in a belief that he will do it; so if we say a man trusts in [a] castle to save him from his enemies, we mean his mind is easy and rests in such a persuasion, that it will keep him safe. If the benefit be the bestowment of happiness, 'tis the mind's acquiescing

6. No. 328 was the last entry on the sheet. JE then returned to the space he had left at the end of a sheet after No. 305 and filled it with Nos. 306–310.

7. No. 329 was the next entry written after No. 278 and represents JE's abandonment of his intention to fold his sheets in quires. With one major exception (No. 370), Nos. 329–386 seem to have been written, for the most part, consecutively.

in it that he will accomplish it; that is, he is persuaded he will do it; he
has such a persuasion, that he rejoices in confidence of it. Thus if a
man has promised a child to make him his heir: if we say he trusts in
him to make him his heir, we mean he has such a belief of what he
promises that his mind acquiesces and rejoices in it, so as not to be
disturbed by doubts and questions whether he will perform it. These
things all the world means by trust.

The first fruit of trust is being willing to do and undergo in the
expectation. He that don't expect the benefit so much as to make him
ready to do or undergo, then we say he durst not trust it, he dare not
run the venture of it. Therefore they may be said to trust in Christ, and
they only, that are ready to do and undergo all that he requires, in
expectation of his redemption; and them that durst not, their faith is
rotten. Therefore when a man is brought to such trials, they are called
the trials of faith.

But this is to be considered, that Christ don't promise that he will be
the author of our redemption but upon condition, and we han't performed that condition till we have believed; and therefore we have no
grounds, till we have once believed, to acquiesce in it that Christ will
save us. Therefore the first act of faith is no more than this, the acquiescence of the mind in him, in what he does declare himself to them
absolutely. 'Tis the soul's resting in him and adhering to him so far as
his word does reveal him to all as a Savior for sinners, as one that has
wrought out redemption, as a sufficient Savior, as a Savior suited to
their case, as a willing Savior, as the author of an excellent salvation,
etc.; so as to be encouraged heartily to seek salvation of him, to come to
him, to love, desire and thirst after him as a Savior, and fly for refuge to
him. This is the very same thing in substance as that trust we spake of
before,[8] and is the very essence of it. This is all the difference, that that
was attended with this additional belief, viz. that he[9] had performed
the condition, which don't belong to the essence of faith. That definition which we gave of trust before holds, viz. the acquiescence of the
mind in the word of any person who reveals himself to us as the author
of some good that nearly concerns us.

Trusting is not only believing that a person will accomplish the good
he promises. The thing that he promises may be very good, and the
person promising or offering may be believed, and yet not properly
trusted in. For it may [be], the person to whom the offer is made is not

8. See the second paragraph of this entry.
9. I.e. the believer.

sensible that the thing is good; he don't desire it. If he offers to deliver him from something that is his misery, perhaps he is not sensible that it is his misery; or it may be, he offers to bestow that which is his happiness, but he is not sensible that it is his happiness. If so, though he believes him, he don't properly trust in him for it; for he don't seek or desire what he offers, and there can be no adherence or acquiescence of mind. If a man offers another to rescue him from captivity and carry him to his own country, if he believes he will do it, and don't desire it, he can't be said to trust in him for it; and if the thing be accounted good and be believed, yet if the person to whom it is offered don't like the person that does it, or the way of accomplishment of it, there can't be an entire trust, because there is not a full adherence and acquiescence of mind.

330. HOLY GHOST. It appears that the Holy Spirit is the holiness, or excellency and delight of God, because our communion with God and with Christ consists in our partaking of the Holy Ghost (II Cor. 13:14; I Cor. 6:17; I John 3:24, and 4:13). The oil that was upon Aaron's head ran down to the skirts of his garments [Ps. 133]; the Spirit which Christ our head has without measure is communicated to his church and people. The sweet perfumed oil signified Christ's excellency and sweet delight. Phil. 2:1.[1]

Communion, we know, is nothing else but the common partaking with others of good: communion with God is nothing else but a partaking with him of his excellency, his holiness and happiness.

331. TRINITY. God is said to be light and love. Light is his understanding or idea, which is his Son; love is the Holy Spirit. We are expressly told that Christ is the light (John 1:9, 8:12, and many other places).

This supposition of the Logos being God's perfect understanding of himself highly agrees with his office, his being the revealer of God to creatures (Matt. 11:27, "No man knoweth the Father save the Son, and he to whomsoever the Son will reveal him"; John 1:18, "No man hath seen God at any time; the only begotten Son, which is in the bosom of the Father, he hath declared him"; and John 8:12, "I am the light of the world"), his being the great prophet of God to reveal him to the world. Who can be more properly the revealer of God, than he who is

---

1. Rom. 14:17 was also listed but then deleted. JE left blank a little space before the next paragraph, apparently for additional Scripture citations.

the perfect understanding of God itself? Who can more properly be God's great prophet, than God's truth himself?—as the supposition of the Holy Ghost's being the love, the joy, the excellence, the holiness of God highly agrees with his office. He is therefore the light of the world, because he is the image of the Father (John 12:45–46); the Scripture seems to point forth this as the reason (Col. 1:15).

332. END OF THE CREATION.[2] The great and universal end of God's creating the world was to communicate himself. God is a communicative being. This communication is really only to intelligent beings: the communication of himself to their understandings is his glory, and the communication of himself with respect to their wills, the enjoying faculty, is their happiness. God created the world for the shining forth of his excellency and for the flowing forth of his happiness. It don't make God the happier to be praised, but it is a becoming and condecent and worthy thing for infinite and supreme excellency to shine forth: 'tis not his happiness but his excellency so to do.

333. SCRIPTURES. BEING OF GOD. CHRISTIAN RELIGION. The being of God is evident by the Scriptures, and the Scriptures themselves are an evidence of their own divine authority, after the same manner as the existence of a human thinking being is evident by the motions, behavior and speech of a body of a human form and contexture, or that that body is animated by a rational mind. For we know this no otherwise than by the consistency, harmony and concurrence of the train of actions and sounds, and their agreement to all that we can suppose to be in a rational mind. These are a clear evidence of an understanding and design that is the original of those actions.

So there is that wondrous universal harmony and consent and concurrence in the aim and drift, such an universal appearance of a wonderful glorious design, such stamps everywhere of exalted and divine wisdom, majesty and holiness in matter, manner, contexture and aim; that the evidence is the same that the Scriptures are the word and work of a divine mind, to one that is thoroughly acquainted with them, as 'tis that the words and actions of an understanding man are from a rational mind, to one that has of a long time been his familiar acquaintance.

An infant, when it first comes into the world and sees persons act and hears their voice, before it is so much acquainted with their actions

2. The vertical line in the left margin beside this entry doubtless indicates its use in the *End of Creation;* see especially ch. 2, § 7 of that work (*Works, 8,* 526–36).

and voice, before it has so much comprehension of them as to see something of their consistence, harmony and concurrence, makes no distinction between their bodies and other things, their motion and sounds and the motion and sounds of inanimate things; but as its comprehension increases, the understanding and design begins to appear. So 'tis with men that are so little acquainted with the Scriptures as infants with the actions of human bodies: [they] can't see any evidence of a divine mind as the original of it, because they have not comprehension enough to apprehend the harmony, wisdom, etc.

334. TRINITY. 'Tis a confirmation of it,[3] that the river of water of life spoken of in the 22nd of Revelation, which proceeds from the throne of the Father and the Son, is called the river of God's pleasures (Ps. 36:8): 'tis a confirmation that the Holy Ghost is the infinite delight and pleasure of God. That river is the Holy Ghost; for the rivers of living water, or water of life, is the Holy Ghost, by Christ's own interpretation, John 7:38–39. (This to come after the next but one.)[4]

335. VISIBLE CHRISTIANS. In order to men's being regularly outwardly members of the Christian church, they should be visible Christians, or visibly Christians. Now by being "visibly Christians" nothing else can be understood but being in appearance Christians, appearing really Christians, true Christians. When we say "true Christians in appearance," it can't be understood that it is meant that he should appear so to a prejudiced and weak and unfair, uncharitable judgment, but that he should appear so in the eye of a Christian judgment. Nor yet can it be understood that we mean that he should appear so in the eye of every particular man. One man may have some particular reason to think him not a Christian from some secret thing that he knows that no mortal else knows, either some secret wickedness that he has seen or from a man's privately declaring his thoughts and experiences to a particular person; but yet he may have a right to be looked upon as a real Christian by the public. Therefore, to be a visible Christian is to appear to be a real Christian in the eye of a public Christian judgment, and to have a right in Christian reason and according to Christian rules to be received and treated as such. See Nos. 338, 345.

3. I.e. "that the Holy Ghost is the infinite delight and pleasure of God." The intervening clause is the confirmation.

4. It is not certain whether this memorandum was later added to No. 334 or whether the whole entry was written after the composition of No. 336 in space left at the end of No. 333.

336. TRINITY. All the metaphorical representations of the Holy
Ghost in the Scripture, such as water, fire, breath, wind, oil, wine, a
spring, a river of living water as proceeding from God, do abundantly
the most naturally represent the perfectly active flowing affection,
holy love and pleasure of God. So the Holy Ghost is said to be poured
out and shed forth (Acts 2:32–33; Tit. 3:5–6), as love is said to be shed
abroad in our hearts [Rom. 5:5].

337. WISDOM OF GOD IN THE WORK OF REDEMPTION. God's wisdom
appears in his timing his first revelation of his redeeming grace towards man soon after the dreadful destruction of such multitudes of
the angels, and the execution of vengeance upon them without mercy,
which had filled the hearts of the spectators with a deep, strong and
awful sense of the infinite majesty, holiness, authority, sovereignty and
justice of God; whereby their hearts were prepared for such a wonderful revelation of God's grace. His marvelous mercy, condescension and
love to another fallen creature, coming so soon after the other, the one
exceedingly set off the glory of the other. The glory of the dreadful
majesty and sovereign authority of God appeared much the more
glorious, for being joined with such transcendent mercy; and this
marvelous grace appeared exceedingly the more honorable, precious
and amiable for its being his grace, that was a Being of such dreadful
majesty and justice, with which their minds had lately been so strongly
impressed.

Corol. This being the method God takes with the world, first to make
a revelation of his dreadful majesty and justice before he reveals his
grace, as in this instance—and so he first revealed the law with thun-
ders and lightnings from Mount Sinai before the full revelation of his
grace by Jesus Christ, to prepare the more for the reception of that
grace, and so in the destruction of Jerusalem before the preaching the
gospel to the Gentile world, and the dreadful destruction of Antichrist
before the full revealing his grace to the whole world; many instances
the Scripture history is full of—so 'tis but reasonable to suppose that
this is his common method with particular persons, first to awaken
them to a sense of the dreadful justice of God and his displeasure
against sin, and then to give them a sense of his grace.

And as there are generally these legal awakenings before grace is
bestowed, so very commonly after a principle of grace is infused, repentance is generally first in exercise (or at least this is first in a very

sensible exercise) before the plain exercise of faith in Jesus Christ; as John the Baptist was sent to preach repentance to prepare the way for Christ. There generally precedes the sinner's humble sense of his exceeding sinfulness, of his unworthiness of God's mercy and desert of his wrath; if not precedes, yet always accompanies.

338. VISIBLE CHRISTIANS. See No. 335. This is to be considered, that persons must either be treated as Christians or as no Christians, they must either be let in or shut out; there is no medium. And there are a great many that we have no particular reason positively to determine in our private judgment that they are Christians, that at the same time we have no particular reason to determine that they are not Christians, and to treat them accordingly; there may therefore be reason for our treating some persons as true Christians, that we have no particular reason to determine that they are so. The Christian church should indeed use all proper means to discriminate true Christians from others, that is, the strictest trials that would not be likely to shut out multitudes that are true Christians. Gospel rules in this case are to determine what is agreeable to Christian reason: Christ is better able to judge than we how strict trials and conditions must be, not to expose to an exclusion of many that are true Christians.

The gospel rule seems to be, to receive those that make a profession of a hearty believing the truth of the gospel, and a walking in all the ordinances and according to the moral rules of the gospel. We ben't directed to try them by an examination of their particular experiences, of their discoveries, illuminations, and affections; because such trials in multitudes of cases would leave us very uncertain, and multitudes would be shut out that are real Christians; Matt. 13:29, "Lest while ye gather up the tares, ye root up the wheat with them"—Christ is very careful that wheat is not excluded. There is no man that is persuaded of the truth of the gospel, and truly resolves and endeavors to walk in all the ordinances and according [to] the moral rules of God's Word, and allows himself in no sin, that can certainly know himself not to be regenerated; much less can the public community of Christians know. If we mean by "believing the truth of the gospel," believing the reality of the gospel salvation and believing the necessity and sufficiency of Christ as a Savior, and other doctrines upon which these directly depend, 'tis saving faith truly to believe these. See No. 345.

339. CHURCH.[5] There is abundance of talk in the world about a "true church," but it is a very difficult thing to me to know what they mean by it. By the church in Scripture is certainly meant nothing else but God's or Christ's people, either really or at least externally and in appearance; and by a particular church is meant a company of God's people joined together for God's worship and service. I can therefore think of no other sensible meaning of the phrase "true church," or "truly God's church," than either those that are truly and really God's people, and Christ's people, or saints; or else those that are God's people outwardly, or that truly have those outward appearances of being God's people, that they are so in the eye of a Christian judgment, and according to gospel rules are to be looked upon, respected and behaved towards as such. And by a particular true church must be meant a society of men that are visibly God's people, or so really in the eye of Christian judgment, and that are indeed joined together in the Christian holy public worship.

340. ANTICHRIST. There is a very great resemblance in many things between the devil and the devilish apostasy, and Antichrist and the antichristian apostasy. The former, of angels became devils: so the pope and his clergy were gospel ministers, who are called angels—the angels are called stars; Satan is called Lucifer; so ministers are called stars. The apostasy of the angels was in heaven and from heaven: so the apostasy of Antichrist is in and from the Christian church, the heavenly Jerusalem; Antichrist sits in the temple of God; the king of Babylon sits upon the mount of the congregation (Is. 14:13). The sin of the devil was his pride and his attempting to get into God's throne and to be obeyed and worshiped as God: so Antichrist through his great pride opposeth and exalteth himself above all that is called God or is worshiped, so that he as God sitteth in the temple of God showing himself that he is God. So the king of Babylon says (Is. 14:14), "I will ascend above the height of the clouds, and I will be like the most High." Satan attempted to make himself king and sovereign over the other angels: so the pope arrogates to himself to be the king and sovereign over all Christ's ministers and over the universal church. The king of Babylon said (Is. 14:13), "I will ascend into heaven, I will exalt my

5. This entry is very deliberately written, with deletions amounting to over half the text. The changes, however, seem to reflect a concern for precise expression rather than a struggle to choose between different ideas.

throne above the stars of God: I will sit upon the mount of the congregation."

'Tis probable, as we have said elsewhere,[6] that the particular occasion of Lucifer's fall was God declaring his decree when he was about to create man, or had created him, that his Son in that nature should be the head of the angels, and that they should not only be Christ's servants but ministering spirits to his beloved race. Satan could not bear this and upon it rose in rebellion; and so the devil was antichrist, or against Christ, scorned to submit to him, and set up himself in opposition to him; and what he aimed at was to make himself that king of the angels which God declared his Son should be. So Antichrist, his name,[7] signifies his crime to be of the same nature: the pope is too proud to be Christ's servant, and sets up himself as universal king of the church in his room, and usurps his throne; and he is too proud to [be] a minister and servant unto Christ's people, as God commands gospel ministers to be, but makes him[self] an absolute monarch over God's heritage—besides many other things wherein he very much resembles the devil, and especially in his cruelty. The similitude is such that they seem to be spoken of under one, Is. 14:12 ff.; it appears to [me] undoubted, that the king of old Babylon and new[8] and Satan were all meant in that place.

341. TRINITY. I can think of no other good account that can be given of the apostle Paul's wishing grace and peace, or grace, mercy and peace, from God the Father and the Lord Jesus Christ in the beginnings of his epistles without ever mentioning the Holy Ghost, but that the Holy Ghost *is* the grace, the love and peace of God the Father and [the] Lord Jesus Christ. We find it so fourteen times in all his salutations in the beginnings of his epistles; and in his blessing at the end of his second epistle to the Corinthians, where all three persons are mentioned, he wishes grace and love from the Son and the Father, but the *communion* of the Holy Ghost, that is, the partaking of him. The blessing from the Father and the Son is the Holy Ghost; but the blessing from the Holy Ghost is himself, a communication of himself.

6. See above, No. 320. In this case at least, "elsewhere" seems clearly to include other miscellanies, unless JE had prepared a paper on this subject which is now lost.

7. I.e. "Antichrist's name"; the reference is to the pope.

8. I.e. the king of new Babylon, Antichrist.

342. AXIOM. Let this be laid down first as a postulate before treating of those doctrines about free will: that whatever is, there is some cause or reason why it is—and prove it.

343. MORAL LAW. GOSPEL. The precepts of the gospel are moral rules and are virtually implied in the moral law, that is, there is the same sort of moral reason to enforce these duties as those that were expressed in the moral law; but yet there are some of these precepts may in a sense be said to be new. They are in a manner newly revealed and commanded, not only because the duty is more fully revealed and more expressly commanded, but because that which is the greatest obligation in reason to it, is in a manner new and newly revealed.

For instance, the duty of heartily loving of enemies and wishing and praying for their good. 'Tis not only as it were newly commanded, but great part of the foundation and obligation, and that which renders it most reasonable and the contrary unreasonable, is also in a manner new; that is, Jesus Christ the eternal Son of God, his so greatly loving of us enemies, and even to that degree as to lay down his life for us. It was a duty before, but 'tis a much greater duty now, much more expected, and the contrary much more resented than before. So the revelation of the love of Christ, the wonderful condescencion of Christ, the humiliation and sufferings of Christ for us, etc.—they make the duties of charity, humility, meekness and patience, as they are commanded in the gospel, new duties as it were; they are gospel duties. Not but that they were duties always; but great part of their foundation is in these gospel revelations, these new things that were kept secret from the foundation of the world: that is, though they should be done upon other accounts, yet they are reasonable to be done, and appear beautiful and amiable, more upon the account of these things than anything that was known before; and those things that were known before, they are known abundantly more now.

Duties are founded on doctrines; and the revelation we now have of the Trinity, of the love of God, of the love of Christ to sinners, of his humiliation, of the infinite evil and desert of sin, of an eternal world, of blessedness and misery, of life and immortality, and the like; they make a vast alteration with respect to the reason and obligations to many amiable and exalted duties, so that they are as it were new. Though indeed neither the doctrines themselves nor the duties are really new, yet some of the duties are in the same sense new as the doctrines. There were many duties that were not much insisted on in the Old

Testament, for the same reason as many doctrines were not revealed, because of their infant blindness and prejudice, and the hardness of their hearts; such as a man's having but one wife, and not putting away a wife upon any other account but adultery. And so it was with other duties, which therefore were as it were new when Christ appeared.

As it became the wisdom of God in a great measure to conceal many glorious doctrines from preceding ages, to be revealed at Christ's appearing in the world, though men's salvation in all those ages depended upon the truth of these doctrines; so he from the same wisdom in a great measure concealed, or suffered to be unknown, some of the most amiable and exalted duties of life from preceding ages (that yet they were obliged to do), to be revealed by Christ, to add to the glory of his appearance, as the great prophet of God and light of the world: such duties as not looking at things seen, having our conversation in heaven, the denying of ourselves, the loving of our enemies with a sincere love, desiring and rejoicing in their good, an universal love to all mankind, rejoicing in persecution, loving one another as Christ has loved us, serving one another as Christ came not to be ministered to but to minister, submitting one to another, in honor preferring one another, etc. Not but that these duties were commanded either expressly or implicitly, yet it was sparingly and not so expressly and fully.

344. Satan Defeated. Satan is wholly disappointed every way of his end in tempting mankind. He principally designed to frustrate God of his end in creating this lower world, to rob [God] of his glory he intended by it to himself and especially to his Son; but what he has done has been the very occasion of the accomplishment of that exceeding great glory which God designed, and which was probably foretold in heaven before the angels fell.

His inferior end was to gratify his envy in the misery of mankind; but this is disappointed, in that what he has done has been an occasion of a far more exalted degree of happiness to the elect of mankind, to all that God intended happiness to in the creation. And though some are made miserable, yet in the long run he won't obtain his end, nor any part of his end, by it. In the first place, because [though] they are miserable, yet no more of them are miserable, and they are no more miserable, than will best disappoint Satan's main end against the glory of God, for it will exceedingly contribute to God's glory; and he is wholly frustrated in an action, if his main design is more crossed and contradicted than his inferior answered. But then secondly, his inferior end is not obtained, because the misery of those that are damned contributes exceedingly to the happiness of elect men and angels and to the glory of heaven; so that part of the world which God loved and designed happiness to when he made the world, are abundantly the more happy for it. And lastly, it will be an occasion of abundance of misery to the devil; he revenges upon himself: it will occasion the bringing on the consummation of his punishment at the day of judgment; he does as it were pull it down on his own head.

That punishment which the devils will receive at the day of judgment, which they tremble at the thought of, will be the completing of their punishment for their rebellion in heaven; for when they were cast out of heaven, they were put in prison in chains of darkness till the judgment. And it is also a punishment of what they do against God in the world of mankind. They ben't punished for these works as subjects are punished by a lord, but as unjust and cruel enemies are punished by a victor.

345. [By] VISIBLE CHRISTIANS must be meant being Christians in what is visible, or in what appears, or in what is outward. To be a Christian really, is to have faith and holiness and obedience of heart. To be outwardly a Christian is to have outward faith, that is, the profession of faith, and outward holiness in the visible life and conversation.

Christ would have the disciples treat strangers as good honest men, and not to treat them otherwise till they proved otherwise. Luke 10:5, "Into whatsoever house ye enter, first say, Peace be to this house. And if the son of peace be there, let your peace remain; if not, let your peace return to you again." The grounds upon which they were directed at first to say, "Peace be to this house," were two, viz. their hearing a good report of them as to their conversation, and secondly their giving them entertainment in their houses (Matt. 10:11–12).

346. CREATION. PROVIDENCE. It [is] most agreeable to the Scripture, to suppose creation to be performed new every moment. The Scripture speaks of it not only as past but as a present, remaining, continual act. Job 9:9; Ps. 65:6, 104:4; Is. 40:22, 44:24; Amos 5:8; and very commonly in the Scripture.

347. SATAN DEFEATED. It is accounted one of the most glorious characters that any man can sustain, to be a conqueror; it was so accounted

in all ages and amongst all nations. God suffered Satan to do what he has done in the world, on purpose that his Son might have his glory, to obtain a complete victory over the devil and his armies. It was a glorious sight in Israel to see David carrying the head of Goliath, the proud champion of the Philistines, in triumph to Jerusalem; it appeared glorious to the daughters of Israel who came out to meet King Saul with timbrels and with dances, and sang, "Saul hath slain his thousands, and David his ten thousands" [I Sam. 18:7]. But it's a far more glorious sight to see the meek, the patient, lovely and loving Lamb of God, our dear Savior that was dead and is alive, triumphing over the proud monarch of hell, and leading captive that mighty foe, treading under foot that haughty and malicious enemy, the god of this world, while he himself sits in sweet glory in the throne of God. This is a glorious sight in heaven, and to the virgin souls that follow the Lamb; who were typified by the daughters of Israel that met King David, and that joined with Moses in his song at the Red Sea: these virgins sing again the song of Moses (Rev. 15:3).

It is not glorious to see a proud and haughty or cruel prince conquering and triumphing; but it is exceeding glorious to see one so meek, so infinitely loving and charitable, who is of such infinite condescension, who has been afflicted, persecuted, despised and slain, and a person so amiable and glorious, thus triumphing over his and our mighty, proud and cruel enemy.

348. DECREES. We have shown,[9] 'tis a proper and excellent thing for infinite glory to shine forth; and for the same reason, it is proper that the shining forth of God's glory should be complete; that is, that all parts of his glory should shine forth, that every beauty should be proportionably effulgent, that the beholder might have a proper notion of God. It was not proper that one glory should be exceedingly manifested and another not at all, for then the effulgence would not answer the reality. For the same reason, it is not proper that one should be manifested exceedingly and another but very little. It is highly proper that the effulgent glory of God should answer his real excellency, that the splendor should be answerable to the real and essential glory, for the same reason that it is proper and excellent for God to glorify himself at all. Thus 'tis necessary that God's awful majesty, his authority and dreadful greatness, and justice and holiness [should be

9. See previous entries on "End of Creation" and "Glory of God," especially Nos. 247 and 332.

manifested]; and this could not be except sin and punishment were decreed, or at least might be decreed. So that the glory shining forth would be very imperfect,[1] both because these parts of divine glory[2] would not shine forth as the others do, and [because] then the glory of his goodness and love and holiness would be faint without them; nay, they could scarcely shine forth at all.

If it were not right that God should decree and permit and punish sin, there could no such thing as justice be conceived of by men or angels, neither in rewarding nor punishing, in conferring good or inflicting evil. There could be no such thing as justice in punishing, because there could be no such thing as punishing. There could be no justice in rewarding, because he that did a great deal would deserve no more than he that did little, or than he that did nothing, by the same way of arguing; because whatever anyone does is decreed, and brought about by providence. There could be no such thing as the justice of God by the justice of his law, by the same sort of reasoning still: what would a law signify, when it was impossible for men to do any evil? There could be no manifestation of God's authority; for what authority can there be without a law or without commandments? There could be no such thing as any manifestation of God's holiness in hatred of sin, or in showing any preference in his providence to godliness before it.

It would be no manifestation of God's grace or true goodness to be free from all sorts of evil, for it would be absolutely impossible that any should be any otherwise; and how much happiness soever he bestowed, his goodness would be nothing near so much prized and admired, and the sense of it not near so great, as we have shown elsewhere.[3] We little consider how much the sense of good is heightened by the sense of evil, both moral and natural.

And as it [is] necessary that there should be evil, because the glory of God could not but be imperfect and incomplete without it, so it is necessary in order to the happiness of the creature, in order to the completeness of that communication of God for which he made the world; because the creature's happiness consists in the knowledge of

1. I.e. if sin and punishment had not been decreed.
2. I.e. God's awful majesty, etc.
3. No extensive essay on this subject has been encountered prior to No. 348, especially outside the "Miscellanies," but the principle stated here can be found in several earlier miscellanies; see especially Nos. 122, 172, 279, and 283. Also, several of the entries on conviction and humiliation stress the idea that the sinner's present sense of misery and danger will increase the happiness of his subsequent conversion.

God and the sense of his love, and if the knowledge of him be imperfect, the happiness must be proportionably imperfect. And the happiness would also be imperfect upon another account; for as we have said, the sense of good is comparatively dull and flat without the knowledge of evil.

349. CHURCH GOVERNMENT. Ex. 18:21–22, "Moreover thou shalt provide out of all the people able men, such as fear God," etc. "and place them to be rulers over thousands, and rulers over hundreds," etc. "and let them judge the people," etc. "and it shall be, that every great matter they shall bring unto thee." Deut. 1:17, "And the cause that is too hard for thee, bring it unto me." Deut. 17:8–9, "And if there arise a matter too hard for thee in judgment," etc. "then thou shalt arise, and get thee up into the place which the Lord thy God shall choose; and thou shalt come unto the priests the Levites, and unto the judge that shall be in those days, and shalt inquire; and they shall show thee the sentence of judgment"—they were to go to the sanhedrim. It is unreasonable to suppose, that there is no cause can arise in the church too hard for a particular minister or a particular congregation, and that there should be no need in no case of any resort, or appeal, or referring of the cause to a higher judgment.

350. CHRISTIAN RELIGION. See notes on Rom. 13:1–2.[4] Were it not for divine revelation, I am persuaded that there is no one doctrine of that which we call natural religion [but] would, notwithstanding all philosophy and learning, forever[5] be involved in darkness, doubts, endless disputes and dreadful confusion. There are many things, now they are revealed, seem very plain, and as if we could easily arrive at a certainty of them if we never had had a revelation of them. It is one thing to see that a truth is exceeding agreeable to reason, after we have been told it and have had it explained to us, and have been told the reasons of it; and another to find it out, and clearly and certainly to explain it, by mere reason. 'Tis one thing to prove a thing after we are showed how, and another to find it out and prove it of ourselves.

If there never had been any revelation, I believe the world would be

4. This note, one of the earliest in the "Blank Bible," contains a reference to No. 350; the citation in No. 350 was probably added at the time the note was written. JE interprets Rom. 13:1–2 to mean "that in the beginning of things God appointed civil government; he taught men to form themselves into civil societies and to appoint judges and rulers, and that all nations derived the custom from thence."

5. MS: "would forever."

full of endless disputes about the very being of a God, whether the world was from eternity or not, and whether the form and order of the world don't result from the mere nature of matter: ten thousand schemes there would be about it. And if it was allowed that there was a first cause of all things, there would be endless disputes and abundance of uncertainty, to determine what sort of a thing that first cause was. Some, it may be, would think that it was properly an intelligent mind and a voluntary agent; others might say that it was some principle of things that we could have no sort of ideas [of]; some would have called it a voluntary agent; some would call it a principle exerting itself by natural necessity: there might be a great many schemes contrived about this, and some would like one best and some another. And amongst those that held that the original of all things was superior intelligence and will, there probably would have been everlasting doubts and disputes, whether there was one only or more. Some, it may be, would say there was but one; some would say there was two, the one the principle of good, the other the principle of evil; others, it may be, would say that there was a society of 'em, or a world of 'em.

And amongst them that held there was but one mind, there would be abundance of uncertainty what sort of being he is: whether he is wholly good or evil, whether he was just or unjust, holy or wicked, gracious or cruel; or whether he was partly good and partly evil; and how far he concerned himself with the world since he had made it; and how far things were owing to his providence, or whether at all; how far he concerned himself with mankind; what was pleasing to him in them and what was displeasing, or whether he cared anything about it; whether he delighted in justice and order or no; and whether he would reward one and punish the other; and how, and when, and where, and to what degree.

There would be abundance of doubt and dispute, what this mind expected from mankind and how we should behave towards him, or whether he expected we should any way concern ourselves with him; whether we ever ought to apply ourselves to him any way; whether we ought to speak to him as expecting he would take any notice of us; how we should show our respect to him; whether we ought to praise and commend him to him; whether we ought to ask that of him that we need; whether or no he would forgive any after they had offended him, and when they had reason to think they were forgiven, and what they should do that they might be forgiven; and whether it is ever worth the while for them that are so often offending, to try for it;

whether there ben't some sins were so great, that God never would upon [any] terms forgive 'em, and how great they must be in order to that. Men would be exceedingly at a loss to know when they were in favor with [him], and upon what terms they could be in his favor.

They would [be] in a dreadful uncertainty about a future state, whether there be any; and if there be, whether 'tis a state of rewards and punishments; and if it was, what kind of state it was, and how men were to be rewarded and punished, to what degree, and how long; whether man's soul be eternal or not; and if it was, whether it was to remain in another world in one fixed state or to change often.

And it would be so also with respect to abundance of moral duties that respect ourselves and one another. Every man would plead for the lawfulness of this or that practice, just as suited his fancy and agreed with his interest and appetites; and there would be room for a great deal of uncertainty and difference of opinion amongst those that were most speculative and impartial. There would be uncertainty, in a multitude of instances, what was just and what unjust: 'twould be very uncertain how far self-interest should govern men, and how far love to our neighbor; how far revenge would be right, and whether or no a man might hate his neighbors, and for what causes; what degree of passion and high-spiritedness and ambition was justifiable and laudable; what acts of venery were lawful and what not; how far we ought to honor and respect and submit to our parents and other superiors; how far it would be lawful to dissemble and deceive. It seems to me there would be infinite confusion in these and such like things, and that there hardly would be any such thing as conscience in the world.

The world has had a great deal of experience of the necessity of a revelation. We may see it in all parts of mankind, in all ages, that have been without a revelation: what gross darkness and brutal stupidity have such places in these matters always been overwhelmed in! and how many, and how great and foolish mistakes, and what endless uncertainties and differences of opinion, have there been amongst the most learned and philosophical! Yet there never was a real trial how it would be with mankind in this respect, without having anything any way from revelation. I believe that most of those parts of natural religion that were held by the heathens before Christ came into the world, were owing to tradition from those of their forefathers that had the light of revelation; and many of these, being exceeding evidently agreeable to reason, were more easily upheld and propagated: and especially because many of their wise men, and men that had influence and rule over them, who saw their rectitude and agreeableness to reason better than others, did as it were renew them from time to time, and used to travel into other countries and gather up remains of truth which they found scattered about in other parts of the world, preserved in the same manner by tradition; and some of them traveled to that part of the world that had divine revelation in their possession, and those things amongst them which appeared most agreeable to their reason, they transplanted to their own country.

Judea was a sort of a light amongst the nations, though they did not know it. The practice and principles of that country had this influence, that it kept the neighboring nations in remembrance of their traditions which they had from their forefathers, that professed the same truths, and so kept them from degenerating so much as otherwise they would have done. The philosophers had the foundation of most of their truth from the ancients or from the Phoenicians, and what they picked up here and there of the relics of revelation.

How came all the heathen nations to agree in that custom of sacrificing? the light of nature did not teach it [to] 'em. Without doubt they had it by tradition; and therefore it need not seem strange, that what of natural religion they had amongst them came the same way. And I suppose, most of the principles of justice and right rules they had of behavior towards themselves and their neighbors, was also by tradition. They were the more easily obtained, partly because they were agreeable to reason, and partly because their rulers saw the necessity of 'em in order to their quiet, strength and prosperity.

I am of the mind that mankind would have been like a parcel of beasts with respect to their knowledge in all important truths, if there never had been any such thing as revelation in the world, and that they never would have rose out of their brutality. We see that those that live at the greatest distance from revelation, as to time and place, are far the most brutish. The heathens in America and in some [of] the utmost parts of Asia and Africa, are far more barbarous than those [that] lived at Rome, Greece, Egypt, Syria and Chaldea formerly; their traditions are more worn out, and they are more distant from places enlightened with revelation. China probably, being from the people that Noah, that holy man, immediately ruled over for many hundred years, and being much separated from other nations, have held more by tradition from Noah than other nations, and so were a more civilized people.

The increase of learning and philosophy in the Christian world is owing to revelation: the doctrines of the Word of God are the foundation of all useful and excellent knowledge. The Word of God leads barbarous nations into the way of using their understandings, and brings their minds off from being confined to mere sensitive objects, and leads them into a way of reflecting and abstracted reasoning and consideration, and delivers from uncertainty in first principles; such as the being of God, and the dependence of all things upon him, and being subject to his influence and providence, and being ordered by his wisdom. Such principles as these are the basis of all true philosophy, as appears more and more as philosophy improves. Revelation delivers mankind from that distraction and confusion which discourages all attempts to improve in knowledge. Revelation is that light in the world from whence has beamed forth not only the knowledge of religion, but all valuable truth; 'tis the fountain of that light which has lightened the understandings of men with all sorts of knowledge. Revelation actually gives men a most rational account of religion and morality, and the highest philosophy, and all the greatest things that belong to learning concerning God, the world, human nature, spirits, providence, time, eternity.

Revelation brings nations to rational studious consideration, and there is nothing else will do it; for nothing else will convince them that it's worth the while to be at the pains of it. Revelation does not only give us the foundation and first principles of all learning, but it gives us the end for which [it should be sought], and the only end that would be sufficient to move men to the pursuit. If it were not for revelation, nations and public communities would see no reason to encourage such speculations, and to uphold an order of men who should make speculation the business of their lives. Revelation redeems nations from a vicious, sensual, brutish way of living, which will effectually keep out learning. 'Tis therefore unreasonable to suppose that philosophy might supply the defect of revelation; for without revelation there would be no such thing as any good philosophy, that is, except now and then in some rare instances, and then[6] attended with abundance of darkness and imperfection.

We hardly can have a conception how it would be, if there never had been any revelation, for we are bred up in the light of revelation from our very infancy. If there was a nation of philosophers, where all were

---

6. Possibly "that" or "there"; JE, Jr., wrote "those" on top of the word, obliterating its original ending.

taught philosophy as soon as they came to be capable of understanding anything, and so were bred up in [it], they would admire at the ignorance and the thoughtlessness of a people that did not meddle with it; they would wonder that they could have so little reflection, and that they should be so ignorant of these and those things that were so plain and easy to them. Knowledge is easy to us that understand by revelation; but we don't know what brutes we should have been, if there never had been any. See No. 492.

351.[7] END OF THE WORLD. MILLENNIUM. SCRIPTURE. 'Tis an argument with me that the world is not yet very near its end, that the church has made no greater progress in understanding the Scriptures. The Scripture and all parts of it were made for the use of the church here on earth, and it seems reasonable to suppose that God will by degrees unveil the meaning of it to his church. It was made obscure and mysterious, and in many places having great difficulties, that his people might have exercise for their pious wisdom and study, and that his church might make progress in the understanding of it; as the philosophical world makes progress in the understanding of the book of nature, and unfolding the mysteries of it. And there is a divine wisdom appears in ordering of it thus: how much better is it to have divine truth and light break forth in this way, than it would have been, to have had it shine at once to everyone without any labor or industry of the understanding. It would be less delightful, and less prized and valued and admired, and would have vastly less influence on men's hearts, and would be less to the glory of God.

It seems to be evident, that the church is not as yet arrived to that perfection in understanding the Scriptures, as we can imagine is the highest that God ever intended the church should come to. There are a multitude of things in the Old Testament which the church then did not understand, but were reserved to be unfolded to the Christian church, such as the most of their types and shadows and prophecies, which make up the greatest part of the Old Testament; so I believe

7. No. 351 certainly and No. 352 probably were written before No. 350; for when, during the composition of No. 350, JE came to the bottom of the first verso of the sheet, he concluded the entry in the middle of the second (opposite) recto between Nos. 351 and 352. It is even possible that he wrote the contents of the second leaf (Nos. 351–358) before those of the first (Nos. 346–350), and then reversed the leaves in order to be able to conclude No. 350 on the same sheet. The ink is too nearly uniform to determine the order of composition with certainty.

there are many now thus veiled, that remain to [be] discovered by the church in the coming glorious times.

Another thing that argues it, is that 'tis the manner of God to keep his church on earth in hope of a still more glorious state; and so their prayers are enlivened, when they pray that the interest of religion might be promoted and God's kingdom may come; and therefore that the most glorious state of the church will be in the latter age of the world. God kept the church under the old testament in hope of the times of the Messiah; the disciples of Christ were kept in hope of the conversion of the Roman empire, which was done about three hundred years after. But it seems to me not likely, that the church from that time should have no more to hope for from God's word, no higher advancement till the consummation of all things. Indeed there will be a great but short apostasy a little before the end of the world: but then, 'tis probable, the thing that the church will hope and long for will be Christ's last coming, to advance his church to its highest and its everlasting glory, for that will then appear to be the only remedy; for the church will expect no more from the clear light and truth, which will have been so gloriously displayed already under the millennium.

Another end of thus keeping his church in hope, is to quicken and enliven their endeavors to propagate religion and to advance the kingdom of Jesus. It is a great encouragement to such endeavors, to think that such times are coming wherein Christianity shall prevail over all enemies; and it would be a great discouragement to the labors of nations or pious magistrates and divines, to endeavor to advancing of Christ's kingdom, if they understood that it was not to be advanced. And indeed, the keeping alive such hopes in the church has a tendency to enliven all piety and religion in the general amongst God's people, that it should be carried on with greater earnestness and cheerfulness and faith.

352. INSPIRATION OF THE SCRIPTURE. Moses then was so intimately conversant with God and so continually under the divine conduct, it can't be thought that when he wrote the history of the creation and fall of man, and the history of the church from the creation, that he should not be under the divine direction in such an affair. Doubtless he wrote by God's direction, as we are informed that he wrote the law and the history of the Israelitish church. And the other histories of the Old

Testament, they were written by their prophets; for they used to be their writers of the history of the church, I Chron. 29:29.

353. ANGELS. The fall and misery of the rebel angels contributes exceedingly to the happiness of the faithful angels. It greatly exalts and gives life to their joy, their love and admiration and praise, to see the miserable state of those of the same kind from whom they are distinguished by God's electing love, to think what great evil they have escaped by withstanding the temptation of the chiefs of the rebellious angels.

354. CONVICTION, HUMILIATION. Christ himself endured great trouble and a sense of God's wrath before his exaltation and the enjoyment of God's love. The people of Israel endured cruel bondage and were forty years in a desolate wilderness before they came to the pleasant land.

As men are in two exceeding different states, first a state of condemnation and then a state of justification, so it seems reasonable and wise that they should be so sensibly; first that they should be sensibly in a state of condemnation, before they are sensibly in a state of justification: that so the sense of the mind should be in the same order as the state of the soul. For as the glory of the thing is in its being in this order—tis the glory of redemption that it is after so exceeding miserable, extreme, necessitous [a] condition—so it tends much to the sensibleness of the glory, that the man should be first sensible of his misery and extreme necessity, and afterwards of Christ's sufficiency and salvation. It tends much to the perception of the glory, for there is no glory without perception; and the perception God intended is surely as much in the person that is the subject of the work, as any. It may in some measure answer the end to look back and see past misery and danger, and so only to be sensible of [them] after they are past, but ordinarily not so well. And if this order ben't observed and they are not made sensible so, I believe God often, by one means or other, keeps them or brings them into doubts about their condition after they are converted, and so makes them sensible, or some other way makes it up.

Flying for refuge denotes fear preceding safety, or at least a sense of danger and necessity attending the application of the soul to Christ. He that comes to Christ does as it were resort to him as an hiding place from the wind and as a covert from the tempest, and as he that resorts to a cool shadow in a weary land after he has been scorched and made faint by the heat, and as he that comes at length to a river of refreshing water in a dry place after he has been sore distressed with thirst; and Christ is so much the sweeter to him. Prov. 18:10, "The name of the Lord is a strong tower; the righteous runneth into it, and is safe."

355. THE UNPARDONABLE SIN is called the sin against the Holy Ghost (1) because it is sin against great light and convictions of the Holy Ghost; (2) because it consists in malice and spite, which [are] the direct contrary to love, which the Holy Ghost is; (3) because it is malice against the Holy Ghost, which is the very loveliness of God, and so a scornful hatred of it [as] represented[8] in the Word and appearing in the hearts and lives of men.

356. MILLENNIUM. As the cold increases a considerable time after the sun begins to return from the southern tropic, so it's probable that vice and wickedness may increase, or at least continue, for some time after knowledge and light begin to increase, and truth to be gloriously displayed and vindicated.

357. SATISFACTION. The threatening, "Thou shalt surely die" [Gen. 2:17], is properly fulfilled in the death of Christ, according to the fair meaning of the words. It is said, "When thou eatest thou shalt die." Why should the word "thou" in the latter part of the sentence, "thou shalt die," be understood more personally than in the former part, "When thou eatest"? In the former part it is not to be understood, "When thou eatest personally"; else we had not been sinners, and Adam would have been a sinner alone: why then should we understand it, "Thou shalt die personally?" They are looked upon as eating, according to the tenor of the former part of the sentence, that eat in a surety; therefore, why is it not fair to look upon him as dying that dies in a surety, according to the tenor of the latter part of the sentence? See Nos. 506, 281, 1083.[9] See sermons on Is. 32:2 (sermon 1, the third particular).[1]

---

8. Possibly "presented"; the first two and perhaps the third letters are canceled. This is very likely a slip, since the five words preceding are also canceled and "represented" is JE's usual word in a phrase of this kind.

9. See above, No. 281, p. 380, n. 2.

1. Though the sermon citation is a much later addition, the sermon itself was written on London/PD paper within a few weeks or months of No. 357. It was first printed in the Dwight ed., *8*, 355–78. The third particular (ibid., p. 359) states that "the threatening, 'thou shalt surely die,' is properly fulfilled in the death of Christ, as it is fairly to be understood" (ibid.).

358. Inspiration of the Scriptures. 'Tis certainly necessary that in the Word of God we should have a history of the life of Christ, of his incarnation, of his death, resurrection and ascension, and of his actions in the world, and of the instructions he gave the world. If there be any history that is divine, without doubt we have some divine history of this, because we can't be Christians without it. And it's reasonable to suppose that we have some further revelation of the doctrines of the gospel, besides what we have in this history of the life of Christ; because we are there informed that the disciples were not fully instructed, because they could not bear many Christian doctrines at that time. John 16:12–13, Jesus said, "I have yet many things to say unto you, but ye cannot bear them now. Howbeit when the Spirit of truth is come, he will guide you into all [truth]." 'Tis reasonable to suppose that the Christian church should have delivered unto them that more full discovery of truth that the Holy Ghost gave the apostles when he descended, for those more full and clear revelations were given them for the Christian church, and not only for themselves; but we have not this at all, if we have it not in the epistles of the apostles.

It also is exceeding agreeable to reason and necessary, that we should have some divine account of the first beginning and establishment of the Christian church, and the success of the gospel after Christ's resurrection so much spoken of by Christ and in the Old Testament, and of the calling of the gentiles and the acts of the apostles; but we have this nowhere but in Luke's Acts of the Apostles. 'Tis also exceeding reasonable to expect, that the Christian church should have some prophecy of the future changes that it has to pass through to the end of the world; for it has, we know, been God's method from the beginning of the world, to inform his church beforehand something of their future fate. We can't therefore think that the Christian church from Christ to the end of the world should have nothing of this nature; 'tis upon many accounts very unreasonable: [but] we have such a prophecy nowhere but in the book of the Revelation.

We may certainly conclude, that God expects, that those books of the New Testament which are and have been received by the Christian church as apostolical writings, should be received by us as parts of the New Testament; except there be some distinguishing mark, some apparent difference in 'em or in something relating to 'em that we can come at, that shall be of direction to us which to choose and which to refuse. If God expects we should receive any New Testament at all, we must suppose that God's providence would be concerned in this matter. If he has ordered it so in his providence, that such and such books should be put into the New Testament received by his church, and from age to age delivered down as such without any distinguishing properties or circumstances, 'tis his plain voice to us that we must receive it as his word.

God took this care with respect to the books of the Old Testament, that no books should be received by the Jewish church and delivered down in the canon of the Old Testament, but what was his word and owned by Christ. We may therefore conclude, that he would still take the same care of his church with respect to the New Testament.

359. INSPIRATION OF THE SCRIPTURES. It seems to me evident, that there are none of the parts of the Old Testament but what are necessary in order to its being complete, and all that are necessary.

It seems necessary that we should have some account of the creation of the world and of our first parents, their primitive state, the fall, and a brief account of the old world and of the degeneracy of it, and of the universal deluge, and some account of the original of nations after this destruction of mankind.

It seems necessary that there should be some account of the succession of the church of God from the beginning. And seeing that God suffered all the world to degenerate, and only took one nation to be his people, to preserve the true worship and religion until the Savior of the world should come; that in them the church might gradually be prepared for that great light and those wonderful things, that they might be a typical nation, and that in them God [might] shadow forth and teach as under a veil all future glorious things of the gospel: it was therefore necessary that we should have some account of this thing, how it was first done by the calling of Abraham, by their being bond slaves in Egypt, and how they were brought to Canaan. It is necessary we should have an account of that revelation which God made of himself to that people, and of giving the law, and the appointment of those things wherein the gospel is veiled as[2] their typical worship, and of the forming of that people, both as to their civil and ecclesiastical state; and it seems exceeding needful that we should have some account of their being actually brought into Canaan, in the country that was their promised land and where they always dwelt.

It seems very necessary that we should have [a] history of the succes-

2. Or "veiled, or."

sion of the church of Israel, and of those providences of God towards [them] that were most considerable and fullest of gospel mystery: as I could show particularly, how it is necessary that we should have some account of them from the time they came to Canaan; and that we should have an account of the highest promised glory of that nation under David and Solomon; and that we should have a particular account of David, whose history is so full of the gospel and so necessary in order to introduce the gospel into the world, and in whom began the race of their kings; and that we should have some account of the building of the temple, that was also so full of gospel. And 'tis a matter of great consequence that we should have some account of Israel's dividing from Judah, and of the ten tribes' captivity and utter rejection, and a brief account why, and therefore a brief history of them till that time. 'Tis necessary that we should have an account of the succession of the kings of Judah and of the church till their captivity into Babylon, and that we should have some account of the acts of the great prophets that were among them, and that we should have some account of the return from the captivity and their resettlement, and of the original of that last state that the church was in before the coming of Christ. A little consideration will convince anyone, that every one of these things were necessary and that we could not do without them.

And in the general, it was necessary that we should have a history of God's church till such times as come within our view and reach, that we might have some tolerable account of it without revelation. And it was of utmost[3] importance that we should have the history of those times of the Jewish church, wherein there was kept up a more immediate and extraordinary intercourse between God and them, and [God] used to dwell amongst them as it were visibly, revealing himself by shechinah, by urim and thummim, and by prophecy, and so more immediately to order their affairs.

It was exceeding suitable that there should be a number of prophets raised up successively, one after another, who should foretell the coming of the Son of God, and the nature and glory of his kingdom, to be as so many harbingers to make way for him, and that their prophecies should be continued to the church. It was necessary that the church should have continued to them the most considerable of those prophecies whereby God revealed himself to his people, and foretold the things relating to the great Savior and the things of the gospel, which

3. MS: "most."

are so necessary in order to introduce the gospel, and that foretell many things relating to the church and the world that were of the most considerable consequence; and particularly that, seeing we have no divine history of the church after its resettlement in Canaan till Christ, that we should have the most remarkable things relating to it represented in prophecy, and also a prophecy of those great changes of the world and shakings of the nations, that were preparatory to the introducing of the kingdom of heaven, as in Daniel.

It was also a matter of great consequence that the church should have a book of divine songs, given by inspiration from God for the use of his church, wherein there should be a lively representation of the true spirit of devotion, of faith, of hope, of divine love, joy, resignation, humility, obedience, repentance, etc.; and that we should have from God a book of moral instructions relating to the affairs and state of mankind, and the concerns of human life, containing rules of true wisdom and prudence for our conduct in all circumstances; and that we should have particularly a song representing the great love between Christ and his spouse the church, particularly adapted to the dispositions and holy affections of a true Christian's soul towards Christ, and representing his grace and marvelous love to and delight in his people. And how excellently has infinite wisdom contrived to give us that sort of instruction, relating to God's perfections, his sovereignty, his wisdom and his providence, and our duty relating thereto, so exceeding useful and needful, in the book of Job. See more concerning the book of Job, No. 810.

360. CONVICTION. The very nature and design of the gospel seems to argue it to be necessary, that a sense of God's jealousy, his hatred of sin, and his just wrath against it should either go before or with a trusting in his grace. For the very end of Christ's dying for sin, was that the glory of God's jealousy, holiness and justice might be consistent with this grace; that while God thus manifested his mercy, we might not conceive any unworthy thoughts of God with respect to his majesty and authority and justice, as we should be in danger to do if grace was offered absolutely: we should not know what a great evil sin was, and how dreadful a thing it is to offend an infinite majesty, and how holy and jealous God is. Seeing therefore that this is the end of Christ's coming, that we might be sensible of this, though we are saved and all sin forgiven; it seems therefore necessary that we should be made sensible of it, in order to our being brought into a state of salvation.

God is exceeding careful, that we should not have such an apprehension that our sins are forgiven, and we brought into a state of favor with him, by an act of absolute and immediate mercy.

361. SOUL OF MAN. MATTER. THOUGHT. See The Mind, p. 8.[4]

362. TRINITY.[5] We have a lively image of this Trinity in the sun. The Father is as the substance of the sun; the Son is as the brightness and glory of the disk of the sun; the Holy Ghost is as the heat and continually emitted influence, the emanation by which the world is enlightened, warmed, enlivened and comforted. The various sorts of rays and their beautiful colors do well represent the various beautiful graces and virtues of the Spirit, and I believe were designed on purpose. And therefore the rainbow is a sign of the covenant: and St. John saw a rainbow round about the throne of God (Rev. 4:3) and a rainbow upon the head of Christ (Rev. 10:1); Ezekiel saw a rainbow about the throne (Ezek. 1:28).

For indeed the whole outward creation, which is but the shadows of beings, is so made as to represent spiritual things. It might be demonstrated by the wonderful agreement in thousands of things, much of the same kind as is between the types of the Old Testament and their antitypes, and by spiritual things being[6] so often and continually compared with them in the Word of God. And it's agreeable to God's wisdom that it should be so, that the inferior and shadowy parts of his works should be made to represent those things that are more real and excellent, spiritual and divine, to represent the things that immediately concern himself and the highest parts of his work. Spiritual things are the crown and glory, the head and soul, the very end and

---

4. See *Works, 6,* 346–48.

5. JE's note in the lower margin near the beginning of the entry: "See this paragraph written fairer on the next leaf, No. 370" (numeral added later). This note refers to the first paragraph as printed here, plus a sentence that JE had made the last paragraph of the entry by inserting the rest of the text in front of it.

About March or April 1729, in connection with the composition of No. 396, JE attempted to revise the paragraph, mainly by extensive interlineation; then, the text having become nearly illegible, he copied it, with further revision, after No. 369 in space he had left for Scripture references. Numerals were not attached to these entries until he had reached No. 411.

6. MS: "and by their being spiritual things being." JE apparently started to write "their [i.e. things of the outward creation] being compared with spiritual things," which would have yielded a straight parallelism with "types" and "antitypes." Instead, he reversed the order and produced a chiasmus—but forgot to cancel "their being."

alpha and omega of all other works: what therefore can be more agreeable to wisdom, than that they should be so made as to shadow them forth?

And we know that this is according to God's method which his wisdom has chosen in other matters. Thus, the inferior dispensation of the gospel was all to shadow forth the highest and most excellent, which was its end; thus almost everything that was said or done that we have recorded in Scripture from Adam to Christ, was typical of gospel things: persons were typical persons, their actions were typical actions, the cities were typical cities, the nation of the Jews and other nations were typical nations, the land was a typical land, God's providences towards them were typical providences, their worship was typical worship, their houses were typical houses, their magistrates typical magistrates, their clothes typical clothes, and indeed the world was a typical world. And this is God's manner, to make inferior things shadows of the superior and most excellent, outward things shadows of spiritual, and all other things shadows of those things that are the end of all things and the crown of all things. Thus God glorifies himself and instructs the minds that he has made.

There is also an image of it[7] in every created mind: there is the mind, and its understanding or idea, and the will or affection or love.

363. FREE WILL. 'Tis not against men's natural sense that they have of just and right, that men should be punished for voluntary ill actions, though it be necessary that the will should be determined to those actions. *'Tis* against men's natural notions of justice, that men should be punished for actions that they are forced to, or are under a necessity to do against their wills, or for those things in which they are not active or voluntary but passive; this strongly contradicts men's natural sense of right. And 'tis from the confusion of terms, of "necessary" and "impossible," and some other terms and phrases generally used by nations in reference to human actions in quite another sense, and the confusion of ideas that is hence made, that makes it seem to anybody not right, that men should be punished for those voluntary actions that there is a prior certainty and determination of, that a man should be punished for an act of will that there is a certain infallible causedness of from anything foregoing.

---

7. I.e. the Trinity. This sentence occurs at the end of the first paragraph but was displaced when JE marked the next two paragraphs for insertion at that point.

Almost all the phrases that are used by them that dispute against this sort of necessity do exhibit wrong ideas and confound the subject. They say, how unreasonable is it that men should be punished for what they can't help. Such a way of expression as this carries this notion or idea with it: that it may be sorely against his inclination and endeavors, but the man has a hard fate; there is *dura necessitas;* he must do it, and when he has done it he must be punished for it! The minds of readers and hearers are confounded by the strength of such phrases, and the natural sense of justice is stirred up to a great degree against what these phrases seem to signify.[8]

But 'tis evident by the practice of all nations in all ages, that it was agreeable to the natural notions of justice that men should be punished for ill actions, without inquiring whether the act of their will were infallibly determined by something else besides the will; if the action were voluntary and were an ill action, that was enough. If you say, 'twas because the light of nature taught them the will determines itself—if it did, they would have as much reason to inquire still, how the will came to determine itself thus; what was it that determined the will to determine itself this way?

365. TRINITY. That the Spirit of God is spiritual joy and delight, is confirmed by those places where we are told that the Holy Spirit is the "earnest" of our future inheritance [Eph. 1:14] and the "first-fruits" (Rom. 8:23). The earnest is a part of the inheritance; which shows that our future inheritance, that happiness spoken of that God will give his saints, is nothing but a fullness of his Spirit. This is that "river of water of life" which comes from the throne of God and the Lamb [Rev. 22:1].

365. BEING OF GOD. The only reason why we are ready to object against the absolute, universally unconditional necessity of God's being, is that we are ready to conceive as if there were some second. We are ready to say, why could not there have been nothing? as if this were a second. But 'tis because of the miserableness of our conceptions, that we are ready to imagine there is any such supposition. We can't tell whether there be any such supposition or no, except we knew what Nothing was; but we can't know what it is, because there is no such thing.

8. There is a vertical line in the left margin beside the latter half of this paragraph, indicating its use elsewhere. It contains the germ of Pt. I, § 3, of the *Freedom of the Will* (see especially *Works, 1,* 149–51).

366. CHRIST'S DEATH AND SATISFACTION. Christ's suffering was far less than the sufferings of the damned, upon several other accounts besides his not having despair. He had at the same time a sense of the glory of God and . . . [9]

367. DEGREES OF GLORY.[1] Christ by his righteousness purchased for everyone perfect happiness; that is, he merited that their capacity should be filled with happiness. But this don't hinder but that the saints, being of various capacities, may have various degrees of happiness, and yet all their happiness be the fruit of Christ's purchase. Indeed, it can't be properly said that Christ purchased any particular degree of happiness; but in the general he purchased eternal life, that is, perfect happiness, or which is the same thing,[2] that everyone's capacity should be filled. The saints are like so many vessels of different sizes cast into a sea of happiness, where every vessel is full: this is eternal life, for a man forever to have his capacity filled. But after all, 'tis left to God's sovereign pleasure, 'tis his prerogative, to determine the largeness of the vessel; and he may determine how he pleases (Eph. 4:7). Christ's death and righteousness meddled not with this, but left in God's prerogative to determine according to his pleasure; and therefore he may dispense in this matter according to what rule he pleases: nevertheless for what Christ has done, he may either dispense without condition or upon condition, and upon what condition he pleases to fix.

The covenant of works did not meddle with this matter. If Adam had perfectly obeyed the law, he and his posterity would have had eternal life; that is, they would have been completely blessed, or so as to fill their capacity; but God would have been at liberty to have made some of one capacity and others of another, as he pleased. The angels had eternal life by a covenant of works, upon condition of perfect obedience. They all of them performed the same condition, and they

---

9. JE canceled the unfinished second sentence of No. 366 with a horizontal line before starting the next entry. He deleted the rest with a large X mark, probably after numbering it (which was several months later) but before indexing adjacent entries, since it does not appear in the Table.

1. No. 367 was copied, with only minor editorial changes, into the sermon on Titus 3:5 ("There are none saved by their own righteousness"), in which JE raises and answers this objection: if the good works of the saints are rewarded (as Scripture says), there must be differences of reward and thus of happiness in heaven; whereas if the saints' happiness is solely the fruit of Christ's righteousness, all ought to be equally happy in heaven.

2. JE supplied this word while copying the passage into the sermon; it had been accidentally dropped at the beginning of a new line.

all thereby obtained complete blessedness, that every one should be filled. But yet we are made acquainted, that there are degrees amongst the angels, because God gave them their capacities as he pleased; their perfect obedience did no way meddle with that matter. And if the covenant of works don't meddle with this matter, then if follows that Christ's righteousness don't meddle with it. If Adam's perfect obedience would not have been concerned in it, then Christ's perfect obedience is not; for Christ only fulfilled the covenant of works for us, and performed that obedience which Adam should have performed. And if so, God is still at liberty to dispense as to that matter, upon what terms he pleases or without any terms; but he has been pleased to fix the degrees of capacity, and so of glory, to the proportionable degrees of grace and fruitfulness. 'Tis his free and sovereign act that he doth so; he gives higher degrees of glory as a reward to the higher degrees of good works, not because it deserves it but because it pleases him.

Thus it appears that all the happiness of everyone is purchased by Christ, in the same sense as the angels have all their happiness in reward of their perfect obedience, although they have different degrees of happiness, and all performed but the same condition, the same perfect obedience. If it had been but one man that Christ died for, and it had pleased God to make him of a very large capacity, Christ's perfect obedience would have purchased that his capacity should be filled; and then all his happiness might properly be said to be the fruit of Christ's perfect obedience. Although if he had been of a less capacity, he would not have had so much happiness by the same obedience; and yet he would have had as much as Christ merited. And yet Christ's righteousness don't properly meddle with the degrees of happiness, any otherwise than that he only merits that it should be perfect; and so it may be said to be concerned in degrees, as perfect is a degree with respect to imperfect, but it meddles not with degrees of perfect happiness.[3]

Remember, where I have here used such expressions as that Christ purchased "that everyone's capacity should be filled," to put instead

---

3. At this point, JE skipped a short space, began another paragraph with "Their capacity is nothing else but the degree of knowledge," and then canceled it. He later inserted the memorandum in the unused space probably, to judge by ink and pen, after the original parts of the next three entries, at least, had been written. The corresponding passage in the sermon shows no awareness of the suggestion in the memorandum, which must therefore have been written after No. 367 was used in the sermon.

thereof this: that Christ purchased "complete and perfect happiness for everyone according to his capacity." Because 'tis uncertain, in what sense glorified saints' capacity may be said to be filled.

368. ANTICHRIST. One end of that great apostasy and long time of darkness, was that the church might be brought off from all dependence upon tradition, and from pinning our faith upon the faith of the[4] generality of Christians, and making their customs our rule (which the primitive church was much given to), that they might depend to the end of the [world] only upon God's revelation of his will, which he has given for our rule.

369. HUMILIATION. CONVICTION. As to what may be said from the devils' and damned ones' seeing that their punishment is just, to evidence that a natural man may have such a sense. I answer, that the devils also believe; they know assuredly that the gospel is true; but the devils' and damned's conviction [arises] not from a sense of God's excellency but only of his greatness. The wickedest may have a sense of God's greatness—greatness, as we have shown already,[5] is not excellent in itself. This sense of God's greatness gives them a conviction of the justice of the punishment [of] sin which is committed against him, as a man may be convinced of justice that hates justice, but yet not a sense of the harmony and beautiful congruity of punishment. Natural men may have the same sense of their deserving punishment, from the sense of God's greatness, power, etc. See No. 393 (pars. 4 and 7).[6]

CONVICTION.[7] The very word "gospel," "glad tidings," seems to be to signify a discovery of salvation after fear and distress, and sense of misery and despair of helping ourselves. Matt. 18:24 ff., the servant that owed ten thousand talents. First his master held him to his debt, and pronounced sentence of condemnation against him, and ordered him to be sold, and his wife and children, and so humbled him. He fell down and worshiped him, and acknowledged the justice of the debt:

---

4. MS: "the ~~church~~."

5. This demonstration cannot be identified with certainty. Possible references include nos. 1 and 14 of "The Mind" (*Works*, 6, 332–38, 344) and "Miscellanies" Nos. 42, 194 and 232.

6. JE uses symbols to designate specific passages in No. 393; see below, pp. 457, n. 5 and 458, n. 7.

7. This paragraph and the next are probably later additions in space left below the original entry.

"Have patience with me, and I will pay thee all." And then his lord forgave and comforted him.

CONVICTION. Another thing in Scripture that seems to favor the need of such conviction before conversion, is the frequent comparisons made between the church's spiritually bringing forth Christ and a woman in travail, in pain to be delivered. John 16:21, "A woman when she is in travail hath sorrow, because her hour is come: but as soon as she is delivered of the child, she remembreth no more the anguish, for joy that a man is born into the world"; and to the same purpose, Rev. 12:2. Now the conversion of a sinner is also represented by the same thing: 'tis a bringing forth Christ in the heart. Therefore Christ says, everyone that believes in him is his mother.[8]

Scriptures.[9] Christ casting out a devil [from one] that had been possessed from a child, that we read of in the ninth of Mark, is, I believe, a type of the dispossessing Satan of our hearts in conversion, who possesses them from [the time we were] children. When Christ commanded the unclean spirit to come out of him, the spirit "rent him sore and came out of him: and he was as one dead; insomuch that many said, He is dead. And Jesus took him by the hand, and lifted him up; and he arose." So I believe that ordinarily, when Satan is about to be cast out of the heart, he rends it and leaves them as it were dead in self-desperation; sin and guilt revives and grievously wounds them, and they die, before Christ takes them by the hand and lifts them, and gives them peace, and revives the heart with true comfort. I Sam. 22:2, "And everyone that was in distress, and everyone that was in debt, and everyone that was bitter of soul" (as 'tis in the original), "gathered themselves unto him; and he became a captain over them." Herein David was a type of Christ.

8. The later sermon on Hos. 5:15, which incorporates this paragraph (cf. in Dwight ed., *8,* 53) identifies Matt. 12:49–50 as the form of the saying JE has in mind.

This paragraph is followed by another, which is deleted with a large X mark: "Those that are brought to true repentance are often represented as being of broken hearts and contrite spirits. The heart before repentance is hard like the rock of flint; but when a man is brought to repentance, then his heart is broken and made soft; and ordinarily God takes this method."

9. This and the following paragraph comprise several still later additions. Both handwriting and orthography suggest that they were written in the first two or three months after Stoddard's death. The last paragraph of No. 369, however, was probably written at the time of the original entry and was intended as the first of a series of Scripture texts. The later "Scriptures" additions precede it because JE had in the meantime used the rest of the page for No. 370.

Scriptures. See Ezek. 20:33–37. See note on Judg. 6:8–10, 11 ff.[1] It was a thing agreeable to the wisdom of God, to suffer the world for a long time to try by their own wisdom to know God; and after there had been sufficient trial, and it was seen that they could not, then it pleased God to reveal himself by the gospel (I Cor. 1:21). So 'tis agreeable to the same wisdom, to suffer men first to try to obtain holiness and God's favor of themselves, by their own strength and righteousness, till it be sufficiently proved that they cannot, and they are convinced of it; then to bestow it. 'Tis agreeable to God's method that men should sow in tears and then reap in joy (Ps. 126:5), that is, that tears should make way for joy. The woman, after she had spent all her living upon physicians and could not be healed, came to Christ (Luke 8:43).

Scriptures. Christ, after he had humbled the woman of Canaan, had told her that it was not meet to give children's bread to dogs, then gives her comfort and tells [her], great is her faith, and that it shall be as she will [Matt. 15:22–28]. God suffered the bondage of the children of Israel in Egypt to come to be very extreme, before he delivered them.

370. TRINITY. (Note that this is only a paragraph in the foregoing leaf, No. 362, written over again.)[2] There are two more eminent and remarkable images of this Trinity amongst the creatures. We have a lively image of this Trinity in the sun. The Father is as the substance of the sun; the Son is as the brightness and glory of the disk of the sun, or that bright and glorious form under which it appears to our eyes; the Holy Ghost is as the heat and powerful influence which acts upon the sun itself and, being diffusive, enlightens, warms, enlivens and comforts the world. The Spirit, as it is God's infinite love and happiness, is as the internal heat of the sun; but as it is that by which God communicates himself, is as the emitted beams of God's glory. II Cor. 3:18, "We are changed into the same image from glory to glory, even as by the Spirit of the Lord." That is, we are changed to glory (or to a shining

1. In his brief comment, JE gives a typological interpretation of the scolding prophet and the angel that appeared to Gideon: "Here was a prophet raised up to convince the people of sin, before Christ comes giving comfort and with the glad tidings of salvation, which we have an account of in the 11th and following verses—very much as it was when Christ came into the world by his incarnation: John the Baptist, a prophet, comes first as his forerunner, to convince of sin and to preach repentance, to prepare the way before him."

2. After a false start ("Though we have a lively image and shadow of this"), JE wrote, "We have a lively image of this Trinity," etc. and copied the first paragraph of No. 362 with his revisions, including what was originally its last sentence on the human soul (see No. 362, p. 434, n. 5). Finally, he interlined a sentence at the beginning of the entry to introduce both images and added the explanatory notes to both entries.

brightness) as Moses was, from or by God's glory or shining, even as by the Spirit of the Lord, i.e. which glory or shining is the Spirit of the Lord. This word that is translated "from" with respect to glory, and "by" with respect to the Spirit, is the same in the original—'tis 'από in both—and therefore would have been more intelligibly translated, "We are changed *by* glory into glory, even as *by* the Spirit of the Lord." Moses was changed by God's glory shining upon him, even as we are changed by God's Spirit shed as bright beams on us. The Spirit of God is called the Spirit of glory (I Pet. 4:14, "the Spirit of glory resteth upon you") upon two accounts: because 'tis the glory of God and [is] as it were his emitted beams, and as it is the believer's glory and causes him also to shine.

The various sorts of rays of the sun and their beautiful colors do well represent the Spirit, or the amiable excellency of God, and the various beautiful graces and virtues of the Spirit. The same we find in Scripture are made use [of] by God for that purpose, even to signify and represent the graces and virtues of the Spirit. Therefore, I suppose, the rainbow was chosen to be a sign of the covenant: and St. John saw a rainbow round about the throne of God (Rev. 4:3) and a rainbow upon the head of Christ (Rev. 10:1); so Ezekiel saw a rainbow round about the throne (Ezek. 1:28). And I believe the variety that there is in the rays of the sun, and their various beautiful colors, were designed in the creation for this very purpose. See Shadows of Divine Things, no. 58.[3]

There is yet more of an image of the Trinity in the soul of man: there is the mind,[4] and its understanding or idea, and the will or affection or love—the heart, comprising inclination, affection, etc.—answering to God, the idea of God, and the love of God.

371. RESURRECTION. See No. 664 (§ 9). The addition of happiness and glory made to the saints at the resurrection, it seems to me evident by the current of the Bible when it tells of these things, will be exceeding great: it is the marriage of the Lamb and the church. The state of things then is the state of perfection; all the state of the church before,

3. This citation does not occur in No. 362 and is a later addition to No. 370. "Shadows of Divine Things" was JE's earlier title for "Images of Divine Things." Image no. 58, an essay on the typological significance of colors, carries an instruction to "join this to Miscell. nos. 362 and 370"; see *Works, 11*, 67–69.

4. MS: "~~spiritual substance~~ (mind)." Since JE quoted the first two words in the first (deleted) beginning of No. 396 but omitted them in the rewritten version, he must have canceled "spiritual substance" and inserted "mind" in No. 370 while revising the first part of the later entry; see below, No. 396, p. 461, n. 1.

both in earth and in heaven, is a growing state. Indeed, the spirits of just men made perfect will be perfectly free from sin and sorrow, will have inexpressible, inconceivable happiness and perfect contentment; but yet part of their happiness will consist in hope of what is to come. They will have as much happiness as they will desire in their present state, because they will choose to have the addition at that time and in that order which God has designed; it will be every way most pleasing and satisfying and contenting to them that it should be so. Their having of perfect happiness don't exclude all increase, nor does it exclude all hope; for we don't know but they will increase in happiness forever. The souls of the saints may now have as much happiness as they while separate desire, and such happiness as so answers their nature in its present state, as to exclude all sort of uneasiness and disquietude; and yet part of that happiness, part of that sweet rest and contenting joy, consists in the sight of what is future. They don't desire that addition should be now; they know that it will [be] exceedingly most beautiful, most for God's glory, most for their own happiness, and most for the glory of the church, and every way most desirable, that it should be in God's order.

But the more properly perfect and consummate state of God's people, of the church, will be after the resurrection; and the whole is now only a growing and preparing for that state. All things that are now done in the world are but preparations for it. The accession of happiness will consist partly in these things:

1. Then the saints will be in the natural state of union with bodies, glorious bodies, bodies perfectly fitted for the uses of a holy glorified soul.

2. Then the body of Christ will be perfect, the church will be complete; all the parts of it in being, no parts of it under sin or affliction, all the parts of it in a perfect [state], all the parts of it together, no longer mixed with ungodly men: then the church will be as a bride adorned for her husband; therefore the church will exceedingly rejoice.

3. Then the Mediator will have fully accomplished his work, will have destroyed and will triumph over all his enemies; then Christ will fully have obtained his reward; then shall be perfected the full design that was upon his heart from all eternity: and then Jesus Christ will rejoice, and his members must needs rejoice with him.

4. Then God will have obtained the end of all his great works that he had been doing from the beginning; then all the deep designs of God will be unfolded in their events; then the wisdom of his marvelous

contrivances in his hidden, intricate and inexplicable works will appear, the ends being obtained; then God's glory will more abundantly appear in his works, his works being perfect: this will cause a great accession of happiness to the saints who behold it. Then God will fully have glorified himself, and glorified his Son and his elect; then he will see that all is very good, and will rejoice in his own works, which will be the joy of all heaven. God will rest and be refreshed; and thenceforward will the inhabitants keep an eternal sabbath, such an one as all foregoing sabbaths were but shadows of.

5. Then God will make more abundant manifestations of his glory and of the glory of his Son, and will pour forth more plentifully of his Spirit, and will make answerable additions to the glory of the saints; as will be becoming the commencement of the ultimate and most perfect state of things, and as will become such a joyful occasion, as the finishing of all things and the marriage of the Lamb. Then also the glory of the angels will receive proportionable additions; for as the evil angels are then to have the consummation of their reward, so then the good angels will have the consummation of their reward. This will be the day of Christ's triumph, and this day will last forever. This will be the wedding day between Christ and the church, and this wedding day will last forever; the feast, and pomp, and entertainments, and holy mirth and joys of the wedding will be continued to all eternity.

372. HEAVEN. It seems to be quite a wrong notion of the happiness of heaven, that it is in that manner unchangeable, that it admits not of new joys upon new occasions. The Scripture tells us that there is joy in heaven and amongst [the angels] upon the conversion of one sinner; and why not among the saints? And if there be new joy upon such an occasion, how great joy have they upon the conversion of nations, and the spiritual prosperity of the whole church on earth! It seems to me evident, that the church in heaven have received new joys from time to time upon new occasions, ever since the first saint went to heaven. Their joy is continually increased, as they see the purposes of God's grace unfolded in his wondrous providences towards his church. Their happiness is increased as their number increases; as it will be greatly for the happiness of the body of Christ to be completed, as it will be at the resurrection, so it is increasing as the body grows towards perfection.

The coming of Christ, I believe, made an exceeding great addition to the happiness of the saints of the old testament who were in heaven, and especially was the day of his ascension a joyful day amongst them. Then Abraham, and David, and holy men that lived under the old testament, "received the promise" which was matter of such joyful expectation to them when on earth [Heb. 11:13, 39]. When Christ arose, many bodies of saints of the old testament that slept arose and went to heaven with Christ [Matt. 27:50–53]; for 'tis unreasonable to suppose they only arose for a few days to die again. The saints must needs have new discoveries of God's glory upon this occasion, as the angels had (Luke 2:14; Eph. 3:10; I Pet. 1:12): it is evident by these scriptures, that the angels saw much more of the glory of God by these things; and if they, undoubtedly the saints also. It was a great addition to the glory of heaven, to have Jesus Christ, God-man, made their head: they had a far more near admittance unto God, and more familiar communion with him, and many other ways did this increase their happiness; and their happiness has been exceedingly greater ever since. Thus the Old Testament prophecies of the glories and blessedness that should attend the coming of the Messiah, I believe, not only aimed at the glory that should be brought to the church on earth by it, but also to that part of the church that was in heaven; that the church of Israel, those same saints to whom those promises were given, do receive them in heaven.

I believe also that it greatly contributed to the happiness of the saints in heaven, to see the success of the gospel after Christ's ascension, and its conquering the Roman empire; and that they greatly rejoiced at the reformation from popery, and will exceedingly rejoice at the fall of Antichrist and the conversion of the world to Christianity (these things seem clear to me by many passages in the Revelation); and that their joy is increasing and will be increasing, as God gradually in his providence unveils his glory till the last day.

373. TRINITY. SPIRIT. See . . .[5] The graces of the church are compared to those beautiful colors of the sunbeams. Ps. 68:13, "Though ye have lain among the pots, yet shall ye be as the wings of a dove covered with silver, and her feathers with yellow gold"—the wings of a dove, the bird that is the emblem of the Holy Ghost. The same is signified by the beautiful colors reflected from the precious stones of the breastplate, and in the gates and foundation of the new Jerusalem. Is. 54:11 ff., "O thou afflicted, tossed with tempest, and not comforted, behold,

5. JE left space for the number but never supplied it. No. 362 is undoubtedly the entry he had in mind, for the reference is integral to the entry and No. 370 had not yet been written.

I will lay thy stones with fair colors," etc. And the stones of the temple, I Chron. 29:2.

374. ORIGINAL SIN. It was of necessity, when once man had sinned, that original righteousness should be taken away; for it would have been not proper, after man was accursed of God and God was become his enemy, for him to have continued to him his Holy Spirit, his own divine love, dwelling in his heart. How improper would it have been for God to have continued a holy, gracious love to himself and a sweet humble delight in him, in the heart of him that had by his rebellion made God his enemy, and incurred that eternal displeasure which by God's law and covenant belonged to him. It was impossible therefore, but that original righteousness must be taken away upon man's sinning.

IMPUTED. Adam's eating the forbidden [fruit] might have some peculiar aggravations, as he did it, that are imputed only to him. We don't know what thoughts [he had] at the time that he did the fact—a fact is greatly aggravated in the sight of God by the particular disposition, frame, and thoughts and workings of heart that it was done with. We don't know how greatly the sin was aggravated in these respects as Adam did [it], nor does it concern us to know. And for the same reason, it does not concern us with what views Adam did it; whether it was to gratify his wife, or out of pity to her, or whether it was because he thought the tree exceeding pleasant to the taste and so did it to gratify his appetite, or whether it was because he thought he should have his eyes enlightened, or whether it was because he had a mind to be like God, or whether it was because he thought if he did not eat it he should be miserable, being parted from his wife. Adam's personal guilt might be greatly aggravated, according to the views he had. And then it might be done under some peculiarly aggravating circumstances that we are not concerned with. We don't know what aggravating circumstances there might be; it might be done perhaps presently after some appearance of God to 'em, or presently after some converse with angels, etc.

Nor is that aggravation of Adam's sin imputed to any but himself, that he thereby undid all his posterity, that his sin was to be imputed to all mankind. For if we are guilty upon that account in the same manner as Adam was, then aggravations in that manner would be multiplied *in infinitum:* for in the first place, Adam's sin is aggravated in eating the forbidden fruit, in that that eating was to be imputed to his posterity; and secondly, his posterity's sin is aggravated upon the same account; and thirdly, Adam's sin is aggravated again in that his sin was so imputed to his posterity, and not only so but was to be imputed with that aggravation; and fourthly, therefore his posterity's sin is aggravated with this additional aggravation; and fifthly, Adam's sin is yet further aggravated, in that his sin was to be imputed to his posterity with the aggravation of his committing what was to be imputed to them, and with this additional aggravation, that he by committing it transferred it to his posterity with these additional aggravations; and so *in infinitum.*

Therefore, the peculiar personal aggravations of the act are not imputed to us; and his sin concerns his posterity only as it was a direct breach of God's covenant, and an act of rebellion against God's express law. And only those aggravations are imputed to us, that arise from circumstances that would have been common to all mankind, if they had been then living in an unfallen state and under the same law. See this more particularly explained and reasons given in [my] sermon on Gen. 3:11.[6]

375. Spirit's Witness that we are God's children. See No. 374 at the beginning; see No. 686. If God held sinners in a state of condemnation, and as the objects of his hatred and wrath, it would be utterly incongruous that they should have his Spirit. It is utterly unbeautiful and inharmonious that a person have anything of those holy, sweet, humble dispositions and motions of heart, which are a participation of the divine nature, given him while he is held as the object of God's utter displeasure and loathing. Therefore, when a person feels the Spirit of God in those divine dispositions and exercises, it assures him that God does not hold him as an enemy, but that he is in a state of favor with God. For when he feels those motions he knows what they be, and he sees that it would be utterly incongruous for him to have them, that God should give them to him, if he did not accept of him. This is that seal and that earnest of the Spirit that we read of; this is that white stone and new name, which no man knows but he that receives it [Rev. 2:17]. Thus the Spirit of God bears witness together with our spirits,

6. This citation is a later interlined insertion and refers to a sermon of Feb. 1738, on Adam's sin. The first main doctrinal division deals with the heinousness of Adam's sin as it concerned him personally, under three subheads that closely parallel the positions stated in the final three paragraphs of No. 374.

that we are the children of God, Rom. 8:16. (Place this under the head of Signs of Grace.)[7]

376. TRINITY. It can no other way be accounted for, that in I John 1:3 our fellowship is said to be "with the Father, and with his Son Jesus Christ," and that it is not said also, "with the Holy Ghost," but because our communion with them *consists* in our communion of the Holy Ghost with them. 'Tis in our partaking of the Holy Ghost that we have communion with the Father and Son and with Christians: this is the common excellency and delight in which they all [are] united; this is the bond of perfectness, by which they are one in the Father and the Son, as the Father is in the Son and the Son in the Father.

377. VISIBLE CHRISTIANS. Explicitly professing Christianity and the covenant of grace is the duty of everyone: for it seems evident by many places of Scripture, that publicly vowing and swearing by God's name is part of instituted religion; which seems to be nothing but publicly giving themselves up to God in covenant. Phil. 2:11, "Every tongue shall confess"; in the place of the Old Testament here quoted, it is, "Every tongue shall swear."

378. CHRISTIAN RELIGION. It seems to me an unaccountable dullness, that when intelligent men read David's psalms and other prayers and songs of the Old Testament, that they ben't at once convinced, that the Jews had the true worship and communion of the one great and holy God, and that no other nation upon earth had—it is as clear as the sun at noonday. And so indeed from all the histories and prophecies of the Old Testament.

379. CHRISTIAN RELIGION. We need not wonder at all, that God should so often and continually reveal himself by prophets and miracles, and by external signs and tokens of his presence and will, to the Israelitish nation; and that now we should see nothing of this nature, no immediate open revelations or communications, any more than if

7. This memorandum, a later addition to No. 375, refers to the notebook "Signs of Godliness," which was originally entitled "Signs of Grace" and which was probably begun in the fall of 1728, about the same time JE was writing miscellanies in the 340s. The first entry on the third page of that notebook, entitled "Having the Spirit of Christ," ends thus: "We know that we have the Spirit immediately by feeling that divine, holy, humble, amiable disposition and motion in us, whereby we are assured that we must be God's children. Vid. Miscell. Ref[lections], No. 375." This must have been written not long after No. 375.

there was no God. We need not wonder at it, for this way of revealing himself, as God used to do to that nation, is not at all suitable to the present state of the church. The church was then confined to one particular nation, that God chose out on purpose to make them the receptacle of his revelation and the conveyancer of it to the rest of the world. And I can think of no other way that it could be done with any tolerable convenience, but by a chosen peculiar nation that should alone be God's people and have the true religion among them. Therefore this was highly convenient and necessary, that there should be such a manner of communication with such a nation.

It was also necessary in the first *transitus* of this revelation from the Jews to the world, as it was in the apostles' times; that the world might receive this revelation from them, seeing God still revealing himself, and so might receive [it] at first from God in the same manner as they received it. And upon many other accounts, it was necessary that inspiration and miracles should be continued, while divine revelation was *in transitu* from [the] Jews to the world. It was necessary for the establishing of the truth of the gospel, which was now revealed and brought out from under its types and shadows and dark prophecies; it was necessary for the introducing of this new and most perfect and everlasting dispensation; it was necessary till the completing of the canon of Scripture, etc.

But that God should now from time to time reveal himself after that manner to his church, is no way necessary, nor at all suitable to the gospel state of the church, which is not any particular enclosure but is dispersed through the whole world. The church is made up of the true worshipers of God through the world, without any walls or dividing bounds; and how is it practicable, that God should treat with [the] church now in such a way as he did with that peculiar nation? Besides, if it were practicable, it would be very impertinent; for what need of there being new revelations to the end of the world? Is it not better that God should give the world a book that should be the summary of his will, to which all nations in all ages may resort, to know the mind of God?

It would be impertinent [also] because that extraordinary and miraculous way was made use of once, only for the introducing of the more perfect way, in which the catholic church of all nations was forever to be instructed. God now communicates himself to his church in a much more excellent and glorious way than that by miracles, etc., by the communications of his Spirit of holiness to the hearts of his people, and his teaching and spiritually instructing of us out of the Word. This is infinitely a more excellent way, as the Apostle says (I Cor. 12:31), "Covet earnestly the best gifts: and yet I show you a more excellent way. Though I speak with the tongues of men and angels, and have not charity," etc. This is the end of the other way; it is excellent in itself; but inspiration and miracles are good for nothing without it, as the Apostle plainly tells us in the thirteenth chapter of I Corinthians. He tells us, prophecy and miracles are nothing without charity, like a sounding brass, etc., or the shell without the substance; and seeing the substance is come, what need the shadow be continued? Seeing the end is come, it would be impertinent still to continue the means. The church now enjoys that glory, in comparison of which all the glory of prophecy and miracles, even those of that extraordinary prophet Moses, is no glory at all, as the Apostle tells us, II Cor. 3:10.

380. UNPARDONABLE SIN.[8] It seems to me by the Scripture, that the sin against the Holy Spirit is this: for a man, when convinced in conscience, to set himself with a free and full will to reproach, or otherwise openly and contumaciously to malign the Holy Ghost in his office, or with respect to his gracious operations. I say, with a free and full will; that is, the man must be perfectly free from any disorder, and he must do it without restraint. (Sometimes men commit sin when there is one will against another, so that he[9] may be said in some respect to do what he would not; there is something in him that resists it.) It is free and deliberate choice, and not from any violent push of satanic suggestion, or from being under the power of great distress, or violent fears of damnation, and the like. 'Tis from [a] full will, from a settled malice, with a rational, deliberate, full design.

381. CHRIST'S RIGHTEOUSNESS. There is no need that it should be exactly the very same law that Christ should obey, that Adam was to have obeyed, so that there should be no precepts wanting nor none added; for there was wanting the precept about the forbidden fruit, and there was added the ceremonial law: the thing required was perfect obedience. It is no matter whether the positive precepts of the law

8. JE drew a single diagonal line through the middle of this entry, probably sometime during the writing of the next few entries. Since the entry is indexed in the Table, the line may indicate the use of the material elsewhere. Possibly JE started to delete the entry but changed his mind before completing the X mark.
9. MS: "it."

were the same, if they were equivalent. The positive commands that Christ was to obey were some of them infinitely more difficult, as particularly the command that he had received as Mediator, to lay down his life; which was the principal act of his obedience, and which above all others is concerned in our justification. See after No. 384, and No. 794.

As[1] that act of disobedience by which we fell was disobedience of a positive precept that Christ never was under, viz. that of abstaining from the tree of knowledge of good and evil; so that act of obedience by which principally we are redeemed is obedience to a positive precept that we never were under, viz. the precept of laying down his life. It was most suitable that it should [be] a positive precept that should try both Adam's and Christ's obedience, for positive precepts are the greatest and most proper trial of obedience: because a spirit of obedience is respect to God's will or command; but in them the mere will or command of the legislator is the sole ground of the obligation, and therefore is the greatest trial of persons' respect to that will or command. See. No. 399.

382. CHRISTIAN RELIGION. If there be any such thing needful, or any ways proper and suitable, that God should reveal himself to mankind; it is impossible that he should do it in any other way, or with any other kind of evidence, than he has done it. There are no other possible ways but these: either inspiration, or God's appearing (causing some visible appearance and audible voice), or sending his angels, or his own assuming a body and becoming incarnate. And there are all the kinds of evidence of this revelation that it is possible a revelation should have: there are all kinds of internal evidences from the majesty, holiness, sublimity, harmony, etc.; and there are all kinds of external evidences, prophecy and miracles. And as to the miracles that it has been confirmed with, there are all kinds that can be conceived of: there is no kind of miracle can be thought of that would be more evidential, than those that Christianity has been confirmed by.

383. BEING OF GOD. That [the] first supreme and universal principle of things, from whence results the being, the nature, the powers and

---

1. This paragraph is a later insert between Nos. 384 and 385, and is designated as an addition to No. 381. Within the body of the paragraph is a canceled reference to No. 399 written during composition; hence it must postdate that entry.

motions, and sweet order of the world, is properly an intelligent willing agent, such as our souls only without our imperfections, and not
some inconceivable, unintelligent, necessary agent, seems most rational; because, of all the beings that we see or know anything of, man's
soul only seems to be the image of that supreme universal principle.

These reasons may be given why we should suppose man's soul to be
the image of that first principle. In the first place, it is evidently the
most perfect and excellent of all the beings in the lower world. It's very
plain that the other creatures are put in subjection to him and made to
be subservient to him. 'Tis rational to conclude, that the most perfect
of things that proceed from this principle should bear most of the
image of itself. Secondly, 'tis only the soul of man that does as that
supreme principle does; that is,[2] is a principle of action, has a power of
action in itself as that first principle has, and which no unperceiving
being in this lower world has. Man's soul determines things in themselves indifferent (as motion and rest, the direction of motion, etc.), as
the supreme cause does. Man's soul has an end in what it does, pursues
some good that is the issue of its actions, as the first universal principle
doth. Man's soul makes, forms, preserves, disposes and governs things
within its sphere, as the first principle does the world. Man's soul
influences the body, continues its nature and powers and constant
regular motions and productions, and actuates it, as the supreme
principle does the universe.

So that if there be anything amongst all the beings that flow from
this first principle of all things, that bears any sort of resemblance to it
or has anything of a shadow of likeness to it, spirits or minds bid
abundantly the fairest for it.

384. ORIGINAL SIN. The guilt a man has upon his soul when he
comes into the world, is one and simple. The guilt of the sin whereby
mankind rebelled and apostatized and the guilt of the corruption of
nature, are not to be looked upon as two distinct and independent
imputations; as when a man commits murder at one time and adultery
at another, where the imputed guilt of each is perfectly distinct and
independent of the guilt of the other. But a man is guilty before God as
soon as he is born, upon the account of the corruption of his nature, as
it is the *continuation* of the first apostasy. 'Tis the remaining of the filth

2. MS: "this," almost certainly an abridgment by attraction to the next word. "This" as the
beginning of the new sentence would not distort JE's meaning, but it is uncharacteristic of his
style.

of that sin—as the guilt of that foul apostasy remains, so doth the filth of it—and this filth is imputed as being the filth of that sin remaining; and as by it the soul of the infant does consent to it, and as it were act and commit it, 'tis imputed as being the same poison then in act, and now remaining in habit.[3] This seems to be evident, by considering how it must be supposed to be with Adam himself: the corruption of Adam's nature began with the act of sin; the corruption of nature began in exercise. (See a loose paper in one of the shelves of the scrutore upon this subject.)[4]

385. CHRIST'S RIGHTEOUSNESS. Seeing Christ took upon him our nature, that he might as it were appropriate human nature in general to himself, that he might become the head of those that had the human nature, that he might represent the whole, that he might be as they, to be for them, to appear in their stead and to answer for them; how can it be otherwise, than that what is acceptable and amiable unto God in his human nature, which is the head of the whole, should be imputed to the whole? so that as God accepts him, and delights in him, and favors him for it, so he should upon the account of it favor, and accept of, and delight in those that are in him, that he represents and that are his members. Surely if God loves and accepts the head for its holiness and amiableness, he won't separate head and members; but he will accept of and delight in the members for the sake of the excellency of the head. That is our great encouragement, that God has declared from heaven that Christ is his beloved Son, in whom he is well pleased; and we have confidence that seeing it is so, and we are in him, that he will be well pleased with us for his excellency's and righteousness' sake. I think we are plainly taught this doctrine, Eph. 1:6, "He hath made us accepted in the Beloved," where we are plainly taught this, that we are accepted and beloved because we are in him who is beloved. Christ is

3. At this point in the MS JE wrote: "And that rebellion also is imputed to the infant, as it does now as it were make it its own act by original corruption. Original corruption and the guilt of man's apostasy are mutually dependent; they have the ratio of causes and foundations of one another: Adam's sin is imputed, because by corruption of nature the child consents to it and commits it; and the corruption of nature comes upon the soul, because it has apostatized from God by the first rebellion." These sentences are marked off from the rest of the entry and canceled with a single vertical line. JE may not have totally rejected this speculation about a "mutually dependent" causality between habit and act, for he later carried it further in *Original Sin* (*Works, 3,* 389–94).

4. The "loose paper" cannot now be identified. It was probably absorbed into a later entry, a sermon, or the *Original Sin* itself. The "scrutore" (cf. *escritoire*) was JE's desk; a photograph of the scrutore appears as the frontispiece of this volume.

more than our head, he is as the whole body; and we are not only joined to him as the members to the head, but he covers us all over; he is as clothing to us; we are commanded to put him on, so that our deformity don't appear. Seeing we are clothed with him who is so beautiful, and for his beauty with which we are clothed, are we accepted and loved.

386. INCARNATION. Christ, although he was conceived in the womb of one of fallen mankind, yet he was conceived without sin; because he was conceived by the Holy Ghost, which is divine love and holiness itself. That which infinite holiness and love immediately forms, it is impossible that it should have any sin.

387.[5] CHRIST'S RIGHTEOUSNESS. See sermon on John 16:8.[6]

388. SATISFACTION OF CHRIST. See sermon on John 16:8, on that part, the conviction of righteousness.[7]

389. FAITH. See sermon on John 16:8, on the second part of the verse.[8]

5. JE's next entry after No. 386 was No. 393, to which he devoted a fresh page. The space that he left blank after No. 386 was later filled by Nos. 387–392. Nos. 387–390, all references to his sermons on John 16:8, were probably written between Nos. 409 and 410 in the spring of 1729 (above, Fig. 5, pp. 156–57).

6. The sermon on John 16:8 has the doctrine, "The work of the Holy Ghost as Christ's messenger, is to convince men of sin, of righteousness and of judgment." It is developed in three main propositions, to which are devoted 2, 3, and 2 preaching units respectively, making seven "sermons" in all.

The reference in this entry is to the first of the three sermons under "righteousness," in which JE argues that Christ's mediatorial righteousness is of two kinds, negative and positive. Christ's negative righteousness consists in the fact that "he fully removed the guilt of all that believe in him, by his sufferings," whereas his positive righteousness refers to his "perfect obedience to God's law."

7. In the same sermon (see n. 6 above) JE discusses Christ's righteousness as satisfaction by proposing "to show how his righteousness can be properly looked upon to be the believer's": First, it is "consistent with the reason of things" because of Christ's infinite worthiness and the love uniting him both to God and to man; second, it is "consistent with the law," for if the law allows the imputation of Adam's guilt, it must also allow the imputation of Christ's righteousness.

8. See above, n. 6. In the second sermon under "righteousness" JE discusses faith as a conviction of truth wrought by the Spirit; in the third he treats faith as the response of the soul to that truth.

390. SPIRIT'S OPERATION, the difference of the manner of his operation upon unbelievers and believers. See sermon upon John 16:8, first part, about convincing of sin.[9]

391.[1] TRINITY. Gal. 5:16, "This I say then, Walk in the Spirit, and ye shall not fulfill the lusts of the flesh." This seems only to be an insisting upon and further urging of the same advice the Apostle had given in the three foregoing verses: "For, brethren, ye have been called unto liberty; only use not liberty for an occasion to the flesh, but by love serve one another. For all the law is fulfilled in one word, even in this, Thou shalt love they neighbor as theyself. But if ye bite and devour one another, take heed that ye be not consumed one of another." The Apostle had plainly argued in the 13th verse, that Christian liberty did not make way for walking after the flesh, because the principle of love which believers had would prevent it. And in this verse he again asserts the same thing in other words: "This I say then, Walk in the Spirit, and ye shall not fulfill the lusts of the flesh." So that walking in the Spirit and walking in love, with the Apostle, are the same thing.[2]

392. WISDOM OF GOD IN REDEMPTION. It was wisely contrived, that he that is the most glorious of all the creatures, the firstborn of every creature, the head of all, should perform the most eminent obedience, as Christ did by his sufferings and death. He became obedient even unto death; and though he was a Son, yet learned he obedience by the things that he suffered.

It was wise in God, that the head of all the creatures should be in some peculiar and glorious manner united unto God; that so the creatures, who are as his body, should be united [to God] by him.

393.[3] HUMILIATION. That humiliation is grace it appears, because

9. See No. 387, p. 454, n. 6. In this portion of the sermon JE argues that the "Holy Ghost influences the souls of believers as an indwelling principle"; with unbelievers, however, the Spirit acts only as "an external occasional agent."

1. Nos. 391 and 392 were probably written (in reverse order) between Nos. 405 and 406, as JE was concluding studies associated with the sermons on John 16:8 (above, Fig. 5, pp. 156–57).

2. This entry consists of an unacknowledged quotation and paraphrase from John Howe's comments on Gal. 5:16 in his *Prosperous State of the Christian Interest before the End of Time* (London, 1726, p. 185). JE thought highly of Howe's argument and mentioned it in both *Treatise on Grace* and *Essay on the Trinity* (*Treatise on Grace*, pp. 59, 112).

3. No. 386 was almost certainly JE's last entry before Stoddard's death and No. 393 was probably begun shortly afterwards (see above, pp. 86–87).

Christ says, "Blessed are the poor in spirit, for theirs is the kingdom of heaven" [Matt. 5:3]. Now we can understand nothing by the poor in spirit, but those that see their own poverty; that are emptied of themselves; that see they are wretched, and miserable, and poor, and blind and naked; that see that in themselves they are nothing; that are not trusting in any of our own riches, either inward, in any endowments of mind that we have of ourselves, or outward, in temporal wealth and honor, etc.; and that is sensible of its great wants.[4] This is meant by the poor spoken of, Is. 66:2, "But to this man will I look, even to him that is poor," and in Luke 6:20, "Blessed are ye poor" (a parallel place with this in that evangelist [Matt. 5:3]), and in abundance of other places in the Scripture; as appears, because by the rich, which in Scripture are spoken of as opposite to these, are meant those that trust in their own riches, either bodily or mental possessions. Matt. 19:24, ["It is easier for a camel to go through the eye of a needle, than for a rich man to enter into the kingdom of God"]. There, by the context, by a rich man Christ seems to mean he that trusts in both outward and mental riches, as the rich young man did that was the occasion of Christ's saying thus. Christ explains himself to mean them that trust in riches, Mark 10:24. In I Cor. 4:8, 'tis evidently meant of trusting in mental riches. This rich man is set in opposition to this poor man in spirit spoken of in Christ's Sermon on the Mount, as appears by Luke's account of this sermon. Luke 6:24, "But woe unto you that are rich!"

That calm of mind, and hope, and removing of the burden from their hearts they speak of, is an evidence that it is grace, and even of the exercise of faith; it is a rest of soul in submission and resignation to God, in a complacential acknowledgment of his sovereignty and mercy.

'Tis God's manner to give special discoveries of his glory and grace after brokenness of spirit, not only at first conversion but through the whole Christian course. And many have been wont to call their first remarkable discovery of God's grace their conversion, and they perceive that it is generally after such a humiliation; so they make that a distinct work of the Spirit of God, that must necessarily precede conversion.

4. The clauses "and not trusting in any of our own riches . . . in temporal wealth and honor, etc.," and "and that is sensible of its great wants," are additions, in two installments, to what was originally the end of a paragraph, which accounts for the changes in person and number.

It[5] seems to me to be very evident,[6] that there is an exercise of faith in that humiliation. For as they are then brought to see that God may damn them if he pleases, so they see that God may show them mercy if he pleases. A natural man is not convinced of either of them; he is not convinced that God may justly damn, neither is he convinced that God may save him: but when he has the sense of guilt upon his mind, and considers how he has contemned God's authority, violated his law, and cast contempt upon his majesty, it seems to him that God's honor and greatness and jealousy as it were obliges him to punish them; he don't see which way such a sin-hating and jealous God can be willing ever to forgive his sins; this is a great burthen upon his heart. But when he is humbled, he sees that God may save him if he pleases; he sees the way so clear, that he sees nothing that hinders, if it be God's pleasure; and this takes off a weight from the mind, and raises hope, and makes the mind calm. Now it is impossible that that weight which was upon the mind, through its thought of God's obligation to punish him, should be removed any other way but by a discovery of a sufficiency of mercy, the secret revelation of a way that God may save if he pleases, consistent with his own honor and majesty: which is faith. It is impossible a man should see that God is at liberty, that there is nothing stands in the way of his showing him mercy if he pleases, except he has a discovery of some way how it may be done consistent with his majesty and honor; for it was the thought of pardon's being inconsistent with those things that was his burden, that gave guilt its weight. And if he sees a way how God may show mercy consistent with those attributes, that must be by a secret discovery of the sufficiency of the way of salvation by Christ.

A principal thing that made Mr. Stoddard think that there was no grace in humiliation, was because he looked upon an explicit act of faith in Jesus Christ as evermore the first gracious act that ever was exerted. And what seems to have made him think that, seems to be his sense of faith's being the only condition of salvation, and for want of a sufficient explaining of what was meant by our being justified by faith alone, as being that grace which alone God has respect to, as being what he accounts renders it a suitable thing, that we should be justified for the sake of Christ. The graces of the Spirit, especially those that

5. This paragraph is cited above, No. 369, p. 439, n. 6; it and the rest of No. 393 were added in two or more later sittings.
6. MS: "There seems to me to be a very evident."

more directly respect God and another world, are so nearly allied that they include one another; and where there is the exercise of one, there is something of the other exercised with it: like strings in consort, if one is struck, others sound with it; or like links in a chain, if one is drawn, others follow. So that humiliation that there is in repentance implies a principle of faith, and not only so, but something of the exercise too; so that a person according to the gospel may be in a state of salvation, before a distinct and express act of faith in the sufficiency and suitableness of Christ as a Savior. Persons are justified upon the first appearance of a principle of faith in the soul by any of the soul's acts: but a principle of faith appears and shows itself by the exercise of true repentance and evangelical humiliation; for the graces are all the same in principle, especially those that more immediately respect God and Christ and another world.

I believe that the case is generally thus, because it is so very congruous to God's manner of dealing with the children of men learned by Scripture history; viz. that the soul, while in a natural condition, is brought to such a conviction of danger, that he sees he can't deliver himself by any strength or contrivance, and that except God helps him he shall not be helped, and that God will do with him as he pleases: thus far a natural [man] may go. And then they are brought to an acknowledgment of the sovereignty of God, and that he may do with them what he pleases, and quietly to own that it would be just with God so to do; and *then* there is a discovery of the mercy of God in Christ, whereby he becomes justified in his conscience, and acquires a sense of his own justification.

The[7] conviction that the damned have of the justice of their punishment, is the same in a more perfect degree that persons under awakenings of conscience have all along: natural justice seems to be against [them], and that presses the conscience (of which see above).[8] But for all such a conviction as the damned have, they feel never the less disposition to quarrel, wrangle and blaspheme, nor less in the exercise of that disposition. 'Tis far from such a submission as Mr. Stoddard used to speak of.[9]

The first comfort is generally given after the exercise of true repentance; Is. 61:1 and Luke 4:18, "The Spirit of the Lord God is upon me; because the Lord hath anointed me to preach glad tidings to the meek,

---

7. This paragraph is cited above, No. 369, p. 439, n. 6.
8. JE's reference is to the fourth paragraph of this entry.
9. This and the preceding references to Stoddard in this entry imply that he is now dead.

to bind up the broken-hearted . . . to comfort those that mourn." By [those] that mourn is doubtless partly meant those that mourn for sin, the same sort of mourners mentioned in the fifth chapter of Matthew, "Blessed are they that mourn," etc. Christ don't bind up or comfort souls till they have been broken-hearted, as appears by the same text; but the broken-hearted are they that truly repent of their sins, as appears by Ps. 51:17 (with context and occasion) and Is. 57:15 (with context).

When[1] God has manifested himself by extraordinary visions, it has frequently been in that way first by that which was terrible, then by that which was comfortable; so to Moses in the mount. So it was to Elijah in Mt. Sinai, first appearing in the wind and earthquake and fire, and then in the still small voice; so it was to Daniel (Dan. 10), and so [to] John (Rev. 1). So Christ, when coming to his disciples to deliver 'em from being swallowed up in the waters of the Lake of Gennesareth in a great storm, first terrified 'em, and then revealed himself to 'em and comforted 'em [Matt. 14:24–27]; and [so] Abraham (Gen. 15:12 ff.); so Ezekiel (Ezek. 3:12 ff.).

Mark 9:26–27, "And the spirit cried, and rent him sore, and came out of him: and he was as one dead; insomuch that many said, He is dead. But Jesus took him by the hand, and lifted him up; and he arose." Which seems to be an emblem of what often is in conversion. The devil often, when he is about to be cast out of a soul, rends it sore—or at least the soul is sorely rent with sin, its old ghost, before it is fully disposed and ready finally to part with it, before there is a separation made between the soul and sin—and the man is left as it were dead; as the Apostle says, "Sin revived and I died" [Rom. 7:9]. 'Tis sensibly helpless and undone, all that which used to be its life being taken away, [the man] being stripped of his former dependences and all his former happiness, that used to support him and keep comfort alive, and as yet not sensibly receiving spiritual comfort; so that he is left as it were dead.[2] See notes on Matt. 14:24–27.[3]

1. This paragraph and the next occur in the MS after No. 394. Though they are not there accompanied by an explicit instruction to "add" them to No. 393, it is clear that this was JE's intention from his reference to them at the end of No. 393 as "after No. 394," from the heavy double line by which they are separated from the rest of No. 394, and from the fact that they deal with humiliation, the subject of No. 393. They were probably written in the middle or late 1730s.

2. The same passage (Mark 9:26–27) is cited, with similar commentary, in No. 369.

3. In this note (printed in Grosart, *Selections*, pp. 137–38), Christ's walking on the water to his disciples is elaborated as an image of the experience of sinners in process of conversion

394. CONVERSION. The imagination of a natural man is much easier wrought upon so as to imitate spiritual discoveries than the heart to imitate holy charity, and gracious inclinations, and a Christian spirit; and either of them may be much easier imitated for a few minutes, by advantage of the emotion the soul is in under great fears and strong natural affections, than they can in a course of life.

Persons[4] may much easier be deceived by the power of imagination in such things as these: seeing themselves[5] in the hands of God, seeing that they are blind, seeing that they are nothing,[6] seeing of Christ in some place of Scripture, hearing of him speak to them, seeing a light, seeing Christ shedding his blood.[7] The devil may much easier deceive persons in those things, by working on the imagination and so imitating spiritual discoveries, than he can imitate an habitual persuasion of the truth of the gospel, and sense of its excellency, and a holy, humble, charitable, meek, patient, heavenly disposition, and an universal and persevering obedience to Christ's commands, and following of him. Therefore the Spirit of Christ, who knows what we are least liable to be deceived in, everywhere in the gospel lays the most weight upon these things, and gives us these things to try ourselves by. 'Tis abundantly safer therefore, to follow the light of Scripture, than to draw up rules from our own experiences.

The common people, when they are under great convictions and fears of hell, are commonly very evidently greatly under the power of imagination; they imagine they see lights, and hear voices, and see and hear many things.

'Tis doubtless possible for the devil, if God give him leave, to make strong impressions on our imagination, about ourselves and about Christ, etc. and in such order that, if the main stress be laid upon such things, may deceive persons; and God has not told us that he will not give Satan liberty. But 'tis not possible for Satan to make any such impressions on the mind, as to imitate a Christian spirit and a Christian life; the Scripture is very careful to lay the main stress upon such things as Satan cannot imitate.

(cf. the penultimate paragraph of No. 393). The note mentions "the late extraordinary pouring out of the Spirit here in Northampton"; hence this citation cannot have been added earlier than 1735.

4. MS: "a person."

5. MS: "himself."

6. After "blind," JE left space for a line or two of further examples; one only was later added.

7. Space was left here also for further examples.

It[8] is argued, that a particular distinct act of faith in the Lord Jesus Christ is the first gracious act, because it is said [Mark 16:16], "He that believeth not shall be damned," and John 3:18, "He that believeth not is condemned already, because he hath not believed on the only begotten Son of God": whence they say it is plain, that he that hath not actually believed is in a state of condemnation, and consequently never hath put forth one act of grace. But 'tis not fairly argued from hence, that the first act of grace is always faith (though ordinarily I believe it is), any otherwise than as faith is implied in the acts of other graces. We often say (and it is properly enough said), when a man falls into some very grievous sin under warnings, etc., that God never will forgive him till he repents of it, and unless he repents of it he cannot be saved; but yet this don't infer, that the first act of grace shall be an explicit act of repentance of that sin.

395. CHRISTIAN RELIGION. It is no argument against the reality of the incarnation of Jesus Christ, whereby God became the same person with a man, that it is such a strange thing, that there is nothing else like it or that bears any shadow of it, anywhere to be seen; because it was evidently God's design, to show his wisdom by doing a thing that was, and forever would have been, far beyond the thoughts of any creatures. Man's fall was God's opportunity, to show how far his device and contrivance was beyond that of all creatures.

396. TRINITY.[9] The word "spirit," or πνεῦμα, in Scripture is used in these two senses, either for a spiritual substance or mind, or for the temper of the mind; when it is not put for a spiritual substance itself (angel, or human soul, or divine essence), it is put for the disposition, temper, inclination or will of that spiritual substance. Eph. 4:23, "Be renewed in the spirit of your mind." So it is doubtless to be understood, I Thess. 5:23, "I pray God your whole spirit, soul and body be preserved blameless,"[1] [and Luke 9:55], "Ye know not what spirit ye

8. This paragraph is a still later addition (by two or three years) to JE's debate with Stoddard over the nature of the first saving act of the soul in conversion. JE wrote it after No. 394 above his earlier continuations of No. 393. It is not labeled as part of No. 393, probably because not technically on "humiliation" but "conversion." Its real affinities, however, are with No. 393, to which it constitutes a kind of postscript.

9. The first part of this entry is deleted with a large X mark; except for one passage which will be noted, all the material is incorporated (largely recast) in what follows and is therefore not printed.

1. At this point in the first draft, JE wrote: "Heb. 4:12, 'dividing asunder soul and spirit,' where doubtless by the spirit is meant the disposition or will of the mind; which confirms

are of." So we read of a meek and quiet spirit, that is, of a meek and quiet temper. I need not go to reckon up instances; 'tis plain that very often the word "spirit" is so used in Scripture, and from thence it is commonly so used amongst us nowadays.

So the word "spirit," when it [is] used concerning God: when it is not used to signify the divine essence (as sometimes it is, as when we read that God is a Spirit) it signifies the holy temper, or disposition or affection of God, as when we read of the Spirit of God. If we read of the meek spirit, of the peaceable spirit, of the pure spirit or holy spirit of a man, we understand it of the meek, peaceable, pure or holy temper: so when we read of the good Spirit or holy Spirit of God, we should likewise understand it of the divine temper and affection. When we read of having the Spirit of Christ, we can understand nothing else by it than having the temper and disposition [of Christ]; and when Christ told his disciples (Luke 9:55) that they knew not what spirit they were of, he had plainly a respect to their temper and disposition. And whenever the Scripture speaks of the Spirit of God's dwelling in us, or our being filled with the Spirit, it will signify much the same thing if it be said, a divine temper or disposition dwells in us or fills us. Now the temper and disposition or affection of God is no other than infinite love. This Holy Spirit of God, the divine temper, is that divine nature spoken of, II Pet. 1:4, that we are made partakers of through the gospel. As God's understanding is all comprehended in that, that he perfectly understands [himself], so his temper or disposition is perfectly expressed by that, that he infinitely loves himself. Num. 14:24, "another spirit."

397. CONVERSION. SPIRITUAL KNOWLEDGE. See No. 411. *Corol.* [to No. 396]. Hence we learn that the prime alteration that is made in conversion, that which is first and the foundation of all, is the alteration of the temper and disposition and spirit of the mind; for what is done in conversion is nothing but conferring the Spirit of God, which dwells in the soul and becomes there a principle of life and action. 'Tis this is the new nature and the divine nature; and the nature of the soul being thus changed, it admits divine light. Divine things now appear

------

what we before said [No. 370], that the soul of man was an image of the Trinity: the spiritual substance the Father, the understanding the Son, the inclination or will the Spirit of God." While revising, JE decided to omit this passage, and he also deleted from No. 370 the reference to the Father as the "spiritual substance"; see above, No. 370, p. 442, n. 4.

excellent, beautiful, glorious, which did not when the soul was of another spirit.

Indeed the first act of the Spirit of God, or the first that this divine temper exerts itself in, is in spiritual understanding, or in the sense of the mind, its perception of glory and excellency, etc. in the ideas it has of divine things; and this is before any proper acts of the will. Indeed, the inclination of the soul is as immediately exercised in that sense of the mind which is called spiritual understanding, as the intellect. For it is not only the mere presence of ideas in the mind, but it is the mind's sense of their excellency, glory and delightfulness. By this sense or taste of the mind, especially if it be lively, the mind in many things distinguishes truth from falsehood.

398. SATISFACTION AND SURETYSHIP OF CHRIST. *Query.* What are those qualifications and circumstances of the person of Christ that renders it a just, proper and suitable thing, that he should be looked upon by God as representing those he undertook for in suffering, so that his suffering shall be looked upon as equivalent to theirs, and answering to it, or so that his suffering should be really equivalent, and properly answering to their suffering?

Ans. 1. One thing is, that he was so united to them, so much one with them, that he may be justly looked upon as the same. Now there is no other way of different spirits' being thus united, but by love. Now how shall he determine how much love is sufficient for that? I answer: if Christ so loves men that when they are to be destroyed, he out of mere love is willing to take their destruction upon himself, or what is equivalent to their destruction, so that they may be saved; then he loves them so, that he may be looked upon as being the same; for this reason, because then his love is such, that of itself it puts him thoroughly in the beloved's stead, even to the utmost, in the most extreme case. Such love as this makes a thorough union. If the lover's love is such as makes him willing to put himself in the other's stead in many cases where the other's interest is much concerned, but yet not in a case where all is concerned, then he is but partially and not thoroughly united. But if his love is such as to go through, and makes him willing to put himself in the other's case even in the last extremity, and where the beloved is to be utterly and perfectly destroyed, then he is as to love sufficiently united to be taken for the person beloved: he has this one needful qualification. See No. 1352 (obs. 4).

Ans. 2. That the person should be infinitely worthy of God's love, so that it may be proper for God to receive into favor those whom the Son thus loves, for his sake. The union must hold with God, as well as with the person beloved by the mediator; the person must be worthy of infinite love, be worthy not only to be loved himself, but that all should be loved that he loves. If a person had loved the offender never so well, yet there would have been no propriety in his suffering being accepted for the other's, if he himself was [not] also perfectly worthy of God's love and infinitely near to him: for how can another person's suffering appease God's anger, unless his[2] love to that person be heavy enough to counterpoise his anger? And if his love to the suffering person be heavy enough to counterpoise his anger to the offending, yet it will not counterpoise it unless it be laid in the balance with it to counterpoise it, unless it be put in the opposite scale; which it is not, unless the suffering person suffers for the sake of the offending and out of mere love to him, or unless his love be great enough to put him in the place of the offender. See sermon upon John 16:8, concerning the Holy Ghost's convincing of righteousness.[3]

399. RIGHTEOUSNESS OF CHRIST. See No. 381. The law that Christ was subject to and obeyed was the same that Adam was subject to and was to have obeyed, notwithstanding that the positive precepts, which they both by virtue of that law were subject to, were not the same. There are many and even most particular duties that are required by the law only conditionally, and are comprehended in it by virtue of some general rule of that law. For instance, innumerable particular acts of obedience to parents are not required of us by the law considered absolutely, but only upon condition that parents command them, and as they are included in the rule of subjection to parents and obedience to their commands. So in like wise, many acts of obedience to God are not included in the moral law considered absolutely; as for instance Abraham's going about to sacrifice his son, and the Jews circumcising their children at eight days old, [and] Adam's not eating of the tree of knowledge of good and evil. They [are] included in the law only conditionally (that is, in case God required them) and by virtue of that general rule of the moral law, that we should obey God and be subject to him in whatsoever he commands us; and thus all that Adam, and all that Christ was commanded, even his observing the rites and

2. I.e. God's.
3. The reference here is to the same portion of the sermon cited in No. 388. See above, No. 388, p. 454, n. 7.

ceremonies of the Jewish worship, and his laying down his life (Phil. 2:8; Heb. 5:8).

'Tis no objection against the last thing mentioned, Christ's laying down his life being included in the law, that the law itself, when given to Adam, allowed of no occasions for such a thing: because the only possible occasion for it was the breach of the law. For the moral law will include all right acts, not only upon all occasions consistent with the law, but upon all possible occasions. Thus we are required to mortify our lusts and repent of our sins by the moral law, though the law don't allow of sin and lust; but yet it will follow directly, that if the moral law requires any duty at all of those that have lust and sin, it requires the mortification of lust and turning from sin.

Every [act] that Christ performed in obedience to the Father, after he once put himself into a state of subjection, was part of his righteousness imputed to us, and performed in obedience to the same law that Adam was made under. See No. 794.

We[4] are obliged to keep all positive precepts by the covenant of works. The Jews were obliged to observe the ceremonial law by the covenant of works; and therefore if they broke the ceremonial law, that breach exposed 'em to the penalty of the law, or covenant of works, viz. eternal death: and nothing exposes to death or damnation judicially but by the law which threatened, "Thou shalt surely die." The law is the eternal, unalterable rule of righteousness between God and man, and therefore is the rule of judgment by which all that a man does shall either be justified or condemned; and no sin exposes to damnation, but by the law. So now, he that refuses to obey the precepts that require an attendance on the sacraments of the New Testament, is exposed to damnation by virtue of the law, or covenant of works. It may be argued, that all sins whatsoever are breaches of the law, or covenant of works: because all sins, even breaches of positive precepts as well as others, have atonement by the death of Christ; but Christ died only to satisfy the law, or to bear the curse of the law for us (Gal. 3:10–13; Rom. 8:3–4).

400. COVENANT. *Corol.* 'Tis therefore a distinction that is apt to mis-

4. Between the end of the preceding paragraph and the later reference to No. 794 is the note, "Vid after No. 462." A paragraph which occurs in the MS after No. 462 (but was written some time later) is there designated as an addition to No. 399; it is therefore printed here as the last paragraph of this entry.

lead the mind, that is made [first,] of the law given to our first parents, into the moral law, and the positive precept of not eating of the tree of knowledge of good and evil; and [secondly,] of the condition of the covenant made with Adam, into abstaining from the tree of knowledge of good and evil, and perfect obedience to the law of nature.

401. COVENANT. The reason why there was no express threatening for any other breach of the covenant of works but only disobedience to that positive precept which God gave Adam, was this, that as God required other duties but by the voice of nature and reason, so he threatened the breach of 'em only by the same voice of nature, well understood by Adam. There was no more need of an express threatening than of an express precept. So well as Adam knew that such and such things were his duty, so well he knew that if he did the contrary, he should deserve punishment; so well as he knew that such and such things were pleasing to God, so well he knew that the contrary would incur his displeasure. We have not, that I know of, any reason to conclude that the angels had an express threatening of destruction in case of rebellion; but the dictates of nature, which taught them that they ought not to rebel, gave them also to expect God's enmity and wrath if they did rebel. God's threatening Adam that he should die if he [should] eat of that tree, no way implied that he could incur God's displeasure and vengeance, and his own destruction, no other way.

402. WORK OF REDEMPTION. WISDOM OF GOD IN REDEMPTION. SPIRIT OF GOD. The sum of all that Christ purchased is the Holy Ghost. God is he of whom the purchase is made, God is the purchase and the price, and God is the thing purchased: God is the Alpha and the Omega in this work. The great thing purchased by Jesus Christ for us is communion with God, which is only in having the Spirit; 'tis participation of Christ's fullness, and having grace for grace, which is only in having of that Spirit which he has without measure; this is the promise of the Father, Luke 24:49. He purchased God's love, favor and delight, which is still the Holy Ghost, for us. Gal 3:2, "This only would I learn of you, Received you the Spirit by the works of the law, or by the hearing of faith?" and 3:13–14, "He was made a curse for us . . . that we might receive the promise of the Spirit through faith." "Good things" and "the Holy Spirit" are synonymous. Matt. 7:11, "How much more shall your heavenly Father give good things to them that ask him?" Luke 11:13, "How much more shall your heavenly Father give the Holy

Spirit to them that ask him?" Therefore 'tis called the "Spirit of promise" (Eph. 1:13), because it is the great subject of the promises, the sum of the gospel promises.

Christ purchased for us grace and many spiritual blessings in this world, but they are all comprised in that, in having the indwelling of the Holy Ghost. Christ purchased glory for us in another world, that we should be like God, that we should be perfect in holiness and happiness; which still is comprised in that, in having the indwelling of the Holy Ghost. (The Spirit is that river of water of life, which in heaven proceeds from the throne of God and the Lamb [Rev. 22:1].)[5] Therefore the Holy Ghost that believers have, here is said to be the earnest of the inheritance, or purchased possession [Eph. 1:14]. The earnest is some of the same given beforehand; the purchased possession is only a fullness of that Spirit.

As the persons of the Trinity are equal among themselves, so there seems to [be] an exact equality in each person's concern in the work of redemption, and in our concern with them in that great affair; and the glory of it equally belongs to each of them. The benefits and blessedness of redemption are wholly and entirely from each of them: it is wholly originally from the Father; the Son is the medium of it all; the Holy Ghost immediately possesses us of it all, or rather is the sum of it all—he possesses us of it by coming and dwelling in us himself. Thus "of him, and through him, and to him" (or in him) "are all things," Rom. 11:36.

If it be said that more glory belongs to the Father and the Son because they manifested a more wonderful love, the Father in giving his Son infinitely dear to him, the Son in laying down his life; yet let it be considered, that the Holy Ghost *is* that wonderful love. Just so much as the two first persons glorify themselves, by showing the astonishing greatness of their love and grace, just so much they glorify that love and grace, who is the Holy Ghost. God's giving his dear Son, and the Son's suffering so much, glorifies the Holy Ghost, as it shows the worth of the Holy Ghost, that the Father should give his Son, and the Son pay so great a price that the Holy Spirit might be purchased.

403. REWARDS. DEGREES OF GLORY. CHRIST'S RIGHTEOUSNESS. How we should be saved only upon the account of Christ's righteousness, and yet have greater degrees of glory in reward of our good works,

---

5. This sentence is a later insertion that interrupts the flow of JE's thought.

may be yet better understood, if we consider that Christ and the whole church of saints are one body, of which he is the head, and they members of different place and capacity.

Now the whole body, head and members, have communion in Christ's righteousness; they are all partakers of the benefit of it; Christ himself, the head, is rewarded for it, and every member is partaker of the benefit and reward. But it does by no means follow, that every part should equally partake of the benefit, but every part in proportion to its place and capacity: the head partakes of far more than the other parts, because 'tis of a far greater capacity, and the more noble members partake of more than the inferior. As it is in a natural body that enjoys perfect health, the head and the heart and lungs have a greater share of it, they have it more seated in them, than the hands and feet, because they are parts of greater capacity; so in the mystical body of Christ, all the members are partakers of the benefit, of the righteousness of the head, but 'tis according to their different capacity and place they have in the body.

And God determines that place and capacity he pleases: he makes whom he pleases the feet, and whom he pleases the hand, and whom he pleases the lungs, etc.; I Cor. 12:18, "But now hath God set the members [every one of them in the body, as it hath pleased him]." And God efficaciously determines the place and capacity of every member here in this world, by giving different degrees of his Spirit: them that he intends for the highest place in the body, he gives them, while in this world, most of his Spirit, the greatest share of the divine nature of the Spirit, and nature of Christ Jesus the Head, whereby they perform the most excellent works.

404. COMMUNION is a common partaking of benefits, or of good, in union or society.

405. TRINITY. It may be thus expressed: the Son is the Deity generated by God's understanding, or having an idea of himself; the Holy Ghost is the divine essence flowing out, or breathed forth, in infinite love and delight. Or, which is the same, the Son is God's idea of himself, and the Spirit is God's love to and delight in himself.

406. UNPARDONABLE SIN. Those that are willing to use the means of grace have not committed the unpardonable sin. This may convince us of it: if there were any such, then there would be some that

are willing to attend God's appointments, unto whom the Word of God would be a just restraint from it; but it seems to me that the Word of God can be a just restraint to none from the duties of religion, that would be willing to attend them. If we suppose that those that have committed the unpardonable sin are those that have wilfully and maliciously rejected and renounced the Christian religion, then it can be no restraint to them, because it never meets with any disposition or willingness to restrain. The calls of the gospel are universal to whosoever will, both to the external and spiritual duties and privileges of the gospel.

407. HELL TORMENTS. The terribleness of God is part of his glory; and that a sense of it should be kept up in the minds of creatures is needful in order to their right and just apprehensions of his greatness and gloriousness, and that perfect and becoming and answerable joy and happiness, in the spiritual sight and knowledge of him. That awful and reverential dread of God's majesty that arises from such a sense, is needful in order to the proper respect of the creature to God, and the more complete happiness in a sense of his love.

God made his terribleness to appear, when he descended on Mount Sinai; and so he gives us an idea of it in thunder, not in any real works of terribleness executed upon any, but he only by the appearances and sounds gives a shadow of it: he by those shadows signifies how terrible his displeasure would be in reality. This might be sufficient for a present occasion, to impress the minds of beholders; but we can't think that God will think it sufficient, to manifest this part of his glory to the immortal spirits he has made, to all eternity, only in such shadows or noises and appearances. But doubtless it will be seen by realities, by some real effects of his terribleness, or effects really terrible. Shadows would not be sufficient forever to continue the impression; if we heard thunder perpetually, and never saw any hurt by it, it would lose all its impression upon our mind. So if the children of Israel had perpetually heard and seen what they did at Mount Sinai, and saw no real effects, the noises and sights would have ceased to have made the impression. We may therefore conclude, that there will forever be some exceeding dreadful realities forever to show forth God's exceeding terribleness, some realities that will far more than answer those shadows at Mount Sinai, or those of thunder, lightning, earthquakes, etc.

408. SPIRITUAL KNOWLEDGE. When the ideas themselves appear

more lively, and with greater strength and impression, as the ideas of spiritual things do [to] one that is spiritually enlightened, their circumstances and various relations and connections between themselves and with other ideas appear more; there are more of these habitudes and respects taken notice of, and they also are more clearly discerned: and therefore hereby a man sees the harmony between spiritual things, and so [comes] to be convinced of their truth. Ratiocination, without this spiritual light, never will give one such an advantage to see things in their true relations and respects to other things and to things in general.

A mind not spiritually enlightened beholds spiritual things faintly, like fainting, fading shadows that make no lively impression on his mind, like a man that beholds the trees and things abroad in the night: the ideas ben't strong and lively, and [are] very faint; and therefore he has but a little notion of the beauty of the face of the earth. But when the light comes to shine upon them, then the ideas appear with strength and distinctness; and he has that sense of the beauty of the trees and fields given him in a moment, which he would not have obtained by going about amongst them in the dark in a long time. A man that sets himself to reason without divine light is like a man that goes in the dark into a garden full of the most beautiful plants, and most artfully ordered, and compares things together by going from one thing to another, to feel of them and to measure the distances; but he that sees by divine light is like a man that views the garden when the sun shines upon it. There is as it were a light cast upon the ideas of spiritual things in the mind of the believer, which makes them appear clear and real, which before were but faint, obscure representations.

409. Resurrection of Christ. See sermon on I Pet. 1:3.[6]

410. Faith.[7] II Pet. 1:16, "For we have not followed cunningly devised fables, when we made known unto you the power and coming of our Lord Jesus Christ, but were eyewitnesses of his majesty." The apostle Peter was convinced (and had good reason so to be) of the truth of the gospel from the sight he had of Christ's majesty and glory at his transfiguration. It was such as removed all doubt; he saw such divine

6. This sermon is not extant; for its location among JE's sermons see above, p. 103, n. 3.
7. The writing of this entry or its perusal soon afterwards probably inspired the sermon on II Pet. 1:16. The sermon was written before No. 419 (which cites it) and incorporates No. 410 into two of its introductory paragraphs.

glory, it was so admirably excellent, and had such a bright and evident appearance of divinity, that it perfectly assured him that Christ was the Son of God, as he professed to be. And doubtless, if he might rationally be assured from that, then a person may be rationally assured from the spiritual discoveries of the divine majesty, holiness and grace, and admirable harmony and excellency of the gospel, that it is divine and true. Doubtless there is such an admirable excellency, beauty and glory in the gospel; and if there be, why mayn't some men see it? And if they do see it, why may it not be a certain evidence to those men[8] of the divine authority and truth [of the gospel], as much and much more than Peter's seeing the outward glory of Christ at his transfiguration? Peter, when he saw this, his mind was strongly carried to believe, and he was sure that Christ was a divine and holy person without sitting down to reason about it; he was convinced and assured at once irresistibly, and was as it were intuitively certain.

411. FAITH. That even faith, or a steadfastly believing the truth, arises from a principle of love; as appears by Deut. 13:1–3, "If there arise a prophet . . . and giveth thee a sign or a wonder, and the sign or wonder come to pass . . . saying, Let us go and serve other gods, . . . thou shalt not hearken unto the words of that prophet, . . . for the Lord your God proveth you, to know whether you love the Lord your God with all your heart and all your soul." See No. 397.

412. JUSTIFICATION. See No. 315. Nor[9] if we mean by condition, that which is directly proposed to be pursued or performed by us in order to eternal life; or that which if done or obtained, we shall have eternal life, and if not done or not obtained, we shall surely perish. There is a great deal of ambiguity in such expressions as those which are commonly used, viz. the condition of salvation, what is required in order to salvation or justification, the terms of the covenant, and the like; and I believe they are understood in very different senses by different persons.[1]

In one sense of the word, Christ alone performs the condition of salvation; he has performed those things which God looks upon as

---

8. MS: "that man."

9. Cf. No. 315, "if by a condition we mean . . . that without which it shall not be, and that with which it shall be." JE wove together material from Nos. 315 and 412 when revising his 1734 lectures on justification by faith for publication (see Worcester rev. ed., *4*, 67–68).

1. At this point occur two paragraphs that JE omitted from No. 412; see below, n. 3.

necessary to belong to the fallen creature, in order to its being a meet thing that he should be freed from an obligation to punishment and have a right to eternal life. In another sense, faith, or the heart's giving entertainment to Christ and the gospel, is the only condition of salvation, viz. as it is that in men, which as He accounts renders it a meet thing (as the case now stands, there being a Savior), that they rather than others should be received to salvation; that is, that they should be looked upon as being in Christ, and so that what Christ has performed should be looked upon as belonging to them.

And[2] in another sense, an universal and persevering obedience, and bringing forth the fruits of love to God and our neighbor, are conditions of salvation; as they may be put into a conditional proposition, and often are so in Scripture (if we have them, we shall have eternal life; and if we have them not, we shall not have eternal life), by reason of their necessary and immutable connection with faith, as immediately flowing from the nature of it. And they are as much and as immediately proposed to be sought for by us, as we would obtain and make sure to ourselves eternal life, as faith itself is; because they are in their nature so related to faith and so connected with it, that in seeking them we seek faith, in obtaining them we obtain faith, and in obtaining faith we obtain them. And they are also conditions of salvation, as they are included in that salvation and eternal life itself: the salvation is, to be made holy, to have the image of God, to have God's Spirit, and the love of God, etc.; God offers to us no other salvation. And therefore being holy is as necessary a condition of salvation as receiving money, or taking possession of goods or lands, is to becoming rich.

But 'tis not obedience and good works, which is that which God has any primary respect to in any man, that makes it appear to him a suitable thing so to look upon him as in Christ, and so to impute to him Christ's righteousness. Indeed it would not be a meet thing, that he which is not holy should be reputed as being in Christ and entitled to his salvation. But 'tis for no other reason but only because God don't see it meet that there should be any other than a holy Savior, a holy gospel, and a holy way of salvation; and therefore a receiving the gospel, which is nothing else but the suitableness and agreement of the soul to the gospel Savior and salvation in actual exercise, in entirely according and consenting to it, can't be without holiness. See No. 416.

2. A cue mark at the beginning of this paragraph matches one at the beginning of No. 488, thus indicating the place in No. 412 to which No. 488 refers.

But[3] there is something in some persons, that God has respect to as being that in them, which as he accounts renders it a meet thing, that they should be reputed as being in Christ and adjudged rather than others, for Christ's sake, to that freedom from punishment and to that eternal life which Christ purchased; and this is not their obedience or good works, but their souls' giving entertainment to the gospel, and their receiving Christ and his salvation. Indeed it would not be a meet thing, for one that don't sincerely obey to be pardoned and have a title to eternal life, but only because that would be an immediate evidence that the gospel was not received. For such is God and such is Christ, such is the gospel and such is the eternal life offered, that giving entertainment to the gospel, to Christ and his salvation, implies holiness, or a disposition to obedience and good works, in the very nature of it; and upon that account it would be a contradiction to say, that 'twould not be a meet thing to justify without faith and yet would be a meet thing to justify without good works. So that it would not be meet to look upon a man as in Christ, and to give a man a right to the gospel salvation without obedience, only by reason of the necessary relation that obedience stands in to faith, a principle of obedience being implied in the nature of it. So that obedience can't be set upon a level with faith in this matter, nor can it be fairly said that God has respect to obedience, as well as to his receiving the gospel salvation, as being that in him which renders it a meet thing, that God should accept him to the gospel salvation.

But, you'll say, let the nature of faith be what it would, it would in itself be an unmeet thing that a person that is unholy should be received to gospel salvation. But, [I answer] 'tis for no other reason than only because God don't see it meet that there should be any other than a holy gospel and a holy way of salvation; and therefore it is impossible that this gospel, or way of salvation, should be heartily entertained without holiness being implied in the nature of that reception. The only reason why it is not meet that an unholy person should be received to gospel salvation, is because unholiness and gospel salvation don't suit and agree together. But faith, or receiving the gospel salva-

---

3. See above, n. 1. After writing this and the following paragraph, JE marked his text of No. 412 to continue without them. Then, after writing two more paragraphs, he supplied cue marks to insert the omitted paragraphs at what would have been the end of the entry, but instead canceled them with a vertical line near the left margin and summarized their main argument in a new final paragraph of the entry. Since he later drew on but did not exhaust the canceled passage while writing No. 316, it has been placed at the end of No. 412.

tion, is nothing else but the suitableness of the heart to the gospel salvation, exercised in an actually according and consenting of the soul to it.

413. HEAVEN. SEPARATE SPIRITS. One reason why the apostles so much insisted upon the resurrection of the dead, rather than the blessedness of a separate state, as an encouragement to Christians, was because they in those days looked upon Christ's coming, and so the resurrection, as just at hand.

414. SOVEREIGNTY OF GOD. AFFLICTIONS OF THE GODLY. 'Tis part of God's sovereignty, that he may if he pleases bring afflictions upon an innocent creature if he compensates it with equal good; for affliction with equal good to balance it is just equivalent to an indifference. And if God is not obliged to bestow good upon the creature, but may leave it in the state of indifference, why mayn't he order that for the creature that is perfectly equivalent to it? God may therefore bring many and great afflictions upon the godly, as he intends to bestow upon them an infinitely greater good, and designs them[4] as a means of a far greater good, though all their sins are satsified for.

415. PERSEVERANCE. ASSURANCE. As persons are commanded and counseled to use all possible endeavors to be converted, though it is already determined whether they shall be converted or no; after the same manner and with like propriety persons are commanded and counseled to persevere, although by their being already converted 'tis certain they shall persevere. For as by endeavoring to be converted, persons are in the way to obtain a certain evidence of their election, and by their continued neglecting of it they procure to themselves a certain evidence of their not being elected; so by their resolutely and steadfastly persevering through all difficulties and opposition and trials they obtain an evidence of the truth and soundness of their conversion, and by their unstableness and backsliding they procure an evidence of their unsoundness and hypocrisy. And evermore those persons that have most need of being cautioned and counseled against falling and apostasy, by reason of the weakness of their grace, have most need of an evidence of the truth of their grace; and those that have the least need of any evidence, by reason of the strength and

4. I.e. the afflictions.

lively exercise of grace, they have least need of being warned against falling; they are least in danger of it. And so the same persons, when they are most in danger of falling, by reason of the languishing of their graces, their ill frames, and workings of corruption, they have most need of evidence; and have least need of evidence, when they are in least need of care and watchfulness not to fall, by reason of the strength and vigorous actings of grace.

So that there is as much need of persons' care and diligence to persevere, in order to their salvation, as there is of their care and diligence, etc., to be converted. For our own care and diligence is as much the proper and decreed means of perseverance, as of conversion; and the want of perseverance is as much an evidence of the want of true conversion, as the want of conversion is a sign of the want of election; and labor and diligence to persevere is as rational a way to make sure of the truth of grace, as labor and diligence to be converted is, to make sure of the truth of election.

God's wrath and future punishment are proposed as motives to all sorts, to an universal and constant obedience, not only to the wicked, but also to the godly. Indeed those that have obtained full assurance of their safe estate ben't capable of this motive, and they have no need of it; but when persons are most capable of the fear of hell, by reason of their want of assurance, and their uncertainty whether or no they are not exposed to damnation, by reason of the weakness of their grace, then they have most need of it. See No. 428.

Corol. Here we may observe, that 'tis not the Scripture way of judging of the truth of grace, to be determined principally by the method and steps of the first work, but by [the] exercise and fruits of grace in a holy life.

416. JUSTIFICATION. When it is said that we are not justified by works, nothing else can be intended but this, viz. that nothing that we do procures reconciliation with God for us and an admittance into his favor by virtue of the loveliness of it, or by reason of any influence the loveliness of it has to move God's love or favorable respect, or any attracting or uniting influence the excellency and amiableness of it has with him, that should incline him so to abate of his anger or to receive into favor. God don't justify us in this manner, upon the account of any act of ours, whether it be the act of faith or any other act whatsoever, but only upon the account of what the Savior did.

But *'tis* something that we do, that renders it in God's account (as the case now stands, there being a Savior) a meet thing, that God should let go his anger and admit us into his favor, as it may render it a meet thing in the sight of God that we in particular should be looked upon as united to the Savior, and [as] having the merit of what he did and suffered (upon the account of which we are so justified) belonging to us; by reason of its being the primary and most simple and direct exercise of an uniting, harmony and agreement in the soul with that Savior and his salvation, and the way of it, and the proper act of reception of him, or closing and uniting with him as a Savior. This is quite a different thing from the former.

And thus it is that we are said to be justified by faith alone: that is, we are justified only because our souls close and join with Christ the Savior, his salvation, and the way of it, and not because of the excellency or loveliness of any of our dispositions or actions that moves God to it. And we are justified by obedience or good works only as a principle of obedience or a holy disposition is implied in such a harmonizing or joining, and is a secondary expression of the agreement and union between the nature of the soul and the gospel, or as an exercise and fruit and evidence of faith. See Nos. 412,[5] 507.

417. FREE GRACE. Let us inquire how many ways a gift may be bestowed, and yet be bestowed perfectly freely in the most absolute sense. (1) If it [be] bestowed without any prerequisite qualification or condition whatsoever. (2) If it be bestowed only for such a suitableness in the nature and inclination of the subject to the benefit, that there may be a harmony and not a war [between the] benefit and the subject, and an openness or preparedness for the entertainment of it. (3) If it be given only for the actual exercise of such an agreeableness and suitableness of nature and inclination, in accepting and closing with the offer. (See, for the evidence of this,[6] No. 191.) In the first way, election, Christ's sufferings and obedience, and effectual calling are given; in the two last, justification and salvation [are] given, in that we are justified and saved by faith.

5. The reference to No. 412 was made at the same time as the rest of the entry; see No. 412, p. 473, n. 3.

6. "This" apparently refers to all three conditions. The first of these is the subject of No. 191; but in that entry the second and third are only implied, in that an inclination to accept the gift by faith is the subject's acknowledgment of the freedom of grace and thus a "suitableness" in him to the gift.

418. HELL TORMENTS. Without doubt the misery of the least of sinners that are damned is as terrible or more terrible than no existence, and such that those that endure it would choose rather to cease to be, and be in a state of eternal nonexistence. Or otherwise, it would not deserve the name of eternal death, nor the promise of eternal life made in the gospel be so considerable and desirable as the sound of it, which at least suggests thus much, that by Christ we may have our existence or life continued forever; whereas otherwise we should eternally lose our existence some way or other, it must be either by not existing or by a state of existence as terrible to think of, and that which men would not prefer before it. But the affliction of a state of existence must be very great,[7] as we see by experience to be thus.

We are taught by the Scriptures that one sin, however small, deserves eternal death; that is, at least, an afflicted state that is as terrible to nature as a ceasing to be forever: and [even] if it be no more [than that], how terrible will this argue the case of most of those to be that are damned, that have been guilty of so many, so great and aggravated sins! how many thousand times less terrible will eternal nonexistence be than their state! For we are taught that wicked men shall be punished in hell fully up to their deserts; they shall be made to pay the whole ten thousand talents, the uttermost farthing.

419. FAITH, or a true believing the gospel. See sermon on II Pet. 1:16.[8]

420. PROMISES. ENCOURAGEMENTS. Why should we suppose that God would make any promises of spiritual and eternal blessings to that which has no goodness in it? Why should he promise his grace to a seeking of it that is not right, or to those that don't truly seek it? Why should he promise that they shall obtain conversion that don't do any right thing, or use any proper means in order to obtain it? For the proper means of obtaining grace is seeking of it truly, with a love and

7. I.e. for men to prefer nonexistence to such a state of existence; cf. JE's comment in "The Mind," no. 62, corol. 3 (*Works, 6,* 382).
8. This sermon, which is based on the story of the transfiguration, has the doctrine, "Seeing the glory of Christ is what tends to assure the heart of the truth of the gospel." The phrasing of No. 419 may have been suggested to JE by the "use of self-examination," the first section of which begins, "Hereby you may distinguish true faith from a common assent to the truth of religion. A true believing the gospel is what arises from a discovery of the gloriousness and excellency of spiritual things."

appetite to it, and desire of it, and sense of its excellency and worthiness, and a seeking of it of God through Christ; and to such as seek it thus, God has faithfully promised that he will bestow it.

421. HEAVEN. It seems to me probable that that part of the church that is in heaven have been, from the beginning of the world, progressive in their light and in their happiness, as the church on earth has; and that much of their happiness has consisted in seeing the progressive wonderful doings of God with respect to his church here in this world. Thus Moses with great joy saw the promises of God fulfilled in bringing the children of Israel into Canaan, with far greater satisfaction than he would have seen it on earth; because he much better could see the glorious ends God proposed by it, and his wonderful wisdom in that work. So will those saints that die now, before the accomplishment of those glorious things to the church that God has foretold, that are not yet fulfilled, and that they have prayed and waited for, see the fulfillment of them with greater satisfaction than if they lived upon earth till they were accomplished. The church in heaven and the church on earth are more one people, one city, and one family than generally is imagined.

422. PROVIDENCE. DECREE. There is a more special providence appears in ordering and determining matters of greater concern and importance, as in determining the limits of men's life; that is, there is less of a connection of the effect with any second causes, within the reach of our power or knowledge.

423. ELECTION. 'Tis owned,[9] that God did choose men to eternal life upon a foresight of their faith. But then here is the question: whether God decreed that faith, chose them that they should believe.

424. UNIVERSAL REDEMPTION. Christ did die for all in this sense, that all by his death have an opportunity of being [saved]; and he had that design in dying, that they should have that opportunity by it. For it was certainly a thing that God designed, that all men should have such an opportunity, or else they would not have it; and they have it by the death of Christ.

---

9. I.e. by JE, or Calvinists, as a concession to the Arminians—but with a different meaning, as the next sentence shows.

425. HELL. ETERNAL DEATH. When God threatens eternal death for sin, we may reasonably conclude that he means some sensible sort of death and not a mere nonexistence; that is, that the wicked shall die eternally some such way that they shall know of it, they shall be sensible of their own calamity under that death. For God will repay the wicked to his face; they[1] shall know and be sensible of it, when God's threatenings are executed upon them. Hence this expression, "Ye shall know that I am the Lord," so commonly annexed to threatenings; and what is designed by that expression may be well understood by Ezek. 22:22, "And ye shall know that I the Lord have poured out my fury upon you." They shall be sensible at the same time, they shall be sensible all the time through that whole eternity, that their eternal death is to continue. See Job 21:19–20, which is much to the purpose; see Jer. 10:18 and 23:20. Eternal death without doubt is some evil that [the] subject of [it] may be sensible of.

Corol. (see No. 418). Therefore it seems to [me], that the threatening of eternal death carries in it an eternal state of doleful darkness, and gloomy, horrible, and desperate misery and dolors, answerable to those awful and horrid aspects and appearances which attend death, that the body is insensible of, such as that ghastly countenance, being laid in the dark and silent grave forever, and rotting and putrifying there, etc.

426. SCRIPTURE. When we inquire whether or no we have Scripture grounds for any doctrine, the question is, whether or no the Scripture exhibits it any way to the eye of the mind, or to the eye of reason. We have no grounds to assert that it was God's intent by the Scripture, in so many terms to declare every doctrine that he would have us believe; there are many things the Scripture may suppose that we know already. And if what the Scripture says, together with what is plain to reason, leads [us] to believe any doctrine, we are to look upon ourselves as taught that doctrine by the Scripture. God may reveal things in Scripture which way he pleases: if by what he there reveals, the thing is any way clearly discovered to the understanding, or eye of the mind, 'tis our duty to receive it as his revelation.

427. HELL. The least that can be supposed to be intended by eternal death is a being deprived forever of all good, which will imply an

---

1. MS: "he," doubtless influenced by the preceding clause, which is a partial quotation of Deut. 7:10.

exceeding degree of misery. The soul of man and all other created minds, are exceeding necessitous things; they stand in great necessity of good. The mere absence of good don't leave the soul in a state of indifferency without either good or evil; but it is to a thinking, reasonable thing, in itself an exceeding great evil; it's an evil necessarily accompanied with dismal, doleful, horrible darkness—it's death. And that makes death appear so doleful; that is the reason that the sight [of a] corpse with pale face, and eyes set, and limbs motionless, etc. strikes such a horror upon our hearts: we look upon those appearances as holding forth thus much, that the object we behold is deprived of all good. And then the damned have, necessarily attending this loss of all good, a sense that it is from God's anger, a being utterly destitute of all manner of favorable respect from him, and being finally and totally, and to all intents and purposes cast off by him; which will also necessarily cause extreme horror in the soul. And besides these, there is despair of its ever being any otherwise to all eternity.

This is the least that can be supposed to be intended by eternal death, and this the least sinner deserves. How much, then, do the generality of the wicked deserve, and how much must they endure!

428. See No. 415. PERSEVERANCE IN FAITH in one sense is the condition of justification; that is, the promise of acceptance is made only to a persevering sort of faith, and the proper evidence of its being of that sort is actual perseverance. Not but that one may have good evidences of his faith being of that sort before he has finished a perseverance, yea, the first time that he exercises such a faith, if the exercises of it are lively and vigorous. But when the believer has those vigorous exercises of faith, by which he has clear evidences of its being of a persevering kind, he evermore feels most of a disposition and resolution to persevere, and most of a spirit of dependence upon God and Christ to enable him so to do.

429. ASCENSION. See No. 421. We need not wonder that the Messiah, the promised glorious King of the church, that the church so earnestly expected and waited so long for, when he came, should make such a short stay here upon earth, that after his resurrection he should ascend into heaven and there be detained out of our sight. For the greatest part of the church is in heaven; there is the proper place of the church; that is their own country; that is the proper land of Israel; it is

their home, their resting place: it is proper that when the Messiah, the promised King, comes, that the place of his abode should be there, where is the proper abiding place of the church. Those that are here upon earth are in a strange land; they are pilgrims and strangers, and are all going hence, and heaven is their center where they all tend. When the Messiah comes, it is proper that the place of his abode should be in the land of Israel, where is his people's proper dwelling place, and not with traveling companions that were strangers, in other countries. There in heaven are those of the church unto whom the Messiah was so much promised, and by whom he was so much expected; there they receive and enjoy him, and there he reigns over them.

Corol. From what has been said, we may draw an argument for the souls of the saints living and acting in a separate state.

Before man fell, this world was designed as the place of man's habitation, it was fitted for the rest of God's people; but when man had fallen, this world was given up or lost; 'tis condemned to the fire; and though God is pleased to choose out some of mankind still to be his people, yet he has appointed their place of abode elsewhere. Therefore it is said of the saints, that they are "redeemed from the earth" and to be "redeemed from among men" (Rev. 14:3, 4).

430. HEAVEN. As there will be various members of different degrees in the body of Christ in heaven, so it seems to me probable, that there will be members of various kinds and different offices, as it is in the church on earth (I Cor. 12). That is, there will be some especially distinguished for one grace, others for another; some of one manner of the exercise of grace, others of another; some more fitted for this work, others for that. Everyone will have their distinguishing gift, one after this manner and another after that, the perfection of the saints in glory nothing hindering; for that perfection will not be of such a kind, that one saint may not be more eminent than another in grace, or that they shall not be capable of increasing, and so attaining to higher degrees, nor that one grace in the same saint shall not have a more remarkable and eminent exercise than others. And 'tis most probable, if it be so, that they shall excell most in the same graces, and the same kind of works, by which they were most distinguished on earth, God rewarding their graces and works by giving of them grace more abundantly of the same kind; as Christ has promised, that to him that hath shall be given. This difference will be for the beauty and the profit of

the whole: they will profit one another by their distinguishing graces; with respect to those graces, they will not be beyond being profited by one another, as well as delighted; they will still be employing and improving themselves.

431. HEAVEN. DEGREES OF GLORY. The exaltation of some in glory above others, will be so far from diminishing anything of the perfect happiness and joy of the rest that are inferior, that they will be the happier for it. Such will be the union of all of them, that they will be partakers of each other's glory and happiness. I Cor. 12:26, "If one of the members be honored, all the members rejoice with it."

432. HEAVEN. Though the saints in heaven will see their exceeding folly and vileness in much of their behavior here in this world, will see a thousand times as much of the evil and folly of sin as they do now; yet they will not experience no proper sorrow or grief for it, for this reason: because they will so perfectly see at the same time, how that 'tis turned to the best, to the glory of God, or at least will so perfectly know that it is so; and particularly, they will have so much the more admiring and joyful sense of God's grace in pardoning them, that the remembrance of their sins will rather be an indirect occasion of joy. Sorrow and grief for sin is a duty, because we are not capable of having so perfect views of these things, but that a right sense of the odiousness and folly of sin will necessarily cause grief. A sense of the great evil of sin is good, absolutely considered; but grief for sin is so, only in a certain presupposed state and circumstances.

433. DEVIL'S CORRUPTION AND MEN'S COMPARED. See sermon on John 8:44.[2]

434. CHRIST, AT THE END OF THE WORLD, SHALL DELIVER UP THE KINGDOM TO THE FATHER. See explication of I Cor. 15:28.[3]

2. The doctrine of this sermon, probably preached in the summer of 1729, is that "wicked men are children of the devil." In its second main division, JE argues that like the devil wicked men "are absolutely destitute of any manner of principle of real goodness." But JE sees three differences: (1) the devil, being of much greater capacity, is proportionately more wicked; (2) the devil "has habitually a greater exercise of sin"; and (3) "man has restraining grace, the devil has none."

3. This "explication" is contained in "Scripture" Bk. 1; it is no. 158 in the Dwight ed. (9, 511–12). The note was probably written in the summer of 1729.

435. HEAVEN. The church now in heaven is not in its[4] fixed and ultimate, but in a progressive, subordinate and preparatory state; the state which they are in is in order to another. In the employments they are now exercised in, they look to that which is still future, to their consummate state, which they have not yet arrived at; and their present happiness is in many respects subordinate to a future, and God in his dealings with them has a constant and perpetual respect to the great consummation of all things. So it is, both with respect to the saints and angels. All things in heaven and earth and throughout the universe are in a state of preparation for the state of consummation; all the wheels are going, none of them stop, and all are moving in a direction to the last and most perfect state.

As the church on earth is in a state of preparation for the resurrection state, so is that part of the church which is in heaven. 'Tis God's manner to keep things always progressive, in a preparatory state, as long as there is another change to a more perfect state yet behind.[5] The saints in this world are progressive, and all things relating to 'em are subordinate and preparatory for the more perfect state of heaven, which is a perfect state; that [is], it is a state of freedom from sinful and uneasy imperfections. But when the saints are got to heaven, there is yet another great change yet behind; there is yet another state, which is that fixed and ultimate and most perfect state, which the whole general assembly both in heaven and earth are designed for; and therefore they are still progressive. Not but that I believe the saints will be progressive in knowledge and happiness to all eternity. But when I say the church is progressive before the resurrection, I mean that they are progressive with a progression of preparation for another and more perfect state; their state is itinerary, viatory; their state, their employments, their glory and happiness, is subordinate and preparatory to a future more glorious state.

As the state of the devils and damned spirits is thus, only in order to a future state of more perfect misery—as a criminal in a prison or a dungeon suffers misery—but 'tis only a subordinate misery, being in order to his approaching execution, so they are spirits in prison; they are bound in chains of darkness to the judgment of the great day. Much of the misery of the devils and damned souls consists in fear. The devil is dreadfully afraid of his approaching punishment, as ap-

4. MS: "The ~~saints~~ ⟨church⟩ now in heaven ~~are~~ ⟨is⟩ not in ~~their~~ ⟨its⟩"; JE did not continue the revision beyond this point.
5. I.e. beyond.

pears by his so crying out when he was afraid that Christ was going to execute it upon him; he beseeches him not to torment him, and says, "Art thou come to torment me before the time?" So, much of the happiness of the saints and angels in heaven consists in hope.

The happiness the church in heaven now has in Christ, compared with their ultimate happiness, is like that of lovers in mutual conversation and manifestation of love, after they are betrothed, and that are in hope and expectation of nearer union and more full enjoyment. And introducing of the glorious state that succeeds the resurrection is like the marriage of the Lamb. The glorification of the separate soul is a marriage, compared with its state in this world. The coming of Christ into the world, and introducing of the gospel state of the church, is a marriage with respect to the state of the church under the old testament; and the appearing of Christ incarnate in heaven upon his ascension, together with the great access of glory to the church, was like a marriage with respect to the state of the glorified church before; and the glorious times of the church on earth after the destruction of Antichrist will be like the marriage of the Lamb. But these are but lower steps; and in comparison of the final consummation, are but as betrothings in order to that everlasting marriage of the church with the Lamb, which shall be in the end of the world. Much of the happiness of the saints now consists in beholding and contemplating the wonderful works of God that are in order to the consummation, the works of God in his church, in this world and in heaven.

436. ADAM'S FALL. ORIGINAL SIN. FREE WILL. See Nos. 291, 501. Adam's will was free in a respect that ours since the fall is not. Now, man has as it were two wills; he has a will against a will. He has one will arising merely from a rational judgment of what is best for him; this may be called the rational will: and he has another will or inclination, arising from the liveliness and intenseness of the idea, or sensibleness of the good of the object presented to the mind, which we may call appetite; which is against the other, rational, will, and in fallen man in his natural state overcomes it, and keeps it in subjection. So that although man with respect to his whole will, compounded of these two (either arising from the addition of them together when they concur, or the excess of one above the other when they are opposite), is always a free agent; yet with respect to his rational will, or that part of his inclination which arises from a mere rational judgment of what is best for himself, he is not a free agent, but is enslaved; he is a servant of sin.

Thus our first parents were not, but were perfectly free agents with respect to their rational will; the inclinations which we call appetites were not above, did not keep it in subjection.

And this must be what is meant when we say, that God gave our first parents sufficient grace, though he witheld an efficacious grace, or a grace that should certainly uphold him in all temptations he could meet with. I say, this must be meant by his having sufficient grace, viz. that he had grace sufficient to render him a free agent, not only with respect to [his] whole will, but with respect to his rational, or the will that arose from a rational judgment of what was indeed best for himself.

When I say, his judgment of what is best for himself, I don't mean his judgment of what is best absolutely, and most lovely in itself; for the minds's sense of the absolute loveliness of a thing directly influences only the will of appetite: if the soul wills it merely because it appears lovely in itself, it will be because the loveliness draws the appetite of the soul. It may indirectly influence what I call the rational will, as the judgment may be convinced that what is most lovely in itself will be best for him and most for his happiness. Merely the rationally judging that a thing is lovely in itself, without a sensibleness of the beauty and pleasantness of it, signifies nothing towards influencing the will, except it be this indirect way, that he thinks it will therefore be best some way or other for himself, most for his good. Therefore, if a man has only a rational judgment that a thing is beautiful and lovely, without any sensibleness of the beauty, and at the same time don't think it best for himself, he will never choose it; though if he be sensible of the beauty of it to a strong degree, he may will it, though he thinks 'tis not best for himself; as persons from a sensibleness of the good and pleasantness of sensual enjoyments, will them, though they are convinced they are not best for themselves. Hence it follows that a person, with respect to his rational will, may be perfectly free, and yet may refuse that which he at the same time rationally judges to be in itself most lovely and becoming, and will that which he rationally knows to be hateful.

Therefore man, having that sufficient grace as to render him quite free with respect to his rational will (or his will arising from mere judgment of what was best for himself), could not fall without having that judgment deceived, and being made to think that to be best for himself which was not so, and so having his rational will perverted: though he might sin without being deceived in his rational judgment of what was most lovely in itself, or (which is the same thing) without having his conscience deceived and blinded, might rationally know at the same time, that what he was about to do was hateful, unworthy, etc.; or in other words, though he[6] might know that it was what he ought not to do. See the next.

437. PERFECTION OF HOLINESS, or how much grace a person must have in order to be sinless. See the last. In order to our first parents' having grace sufficient to their being free with respect to their rational will, and in order to their being without habitual sin, they must have so much sense of spiritual excellencies and beauties, and so much inclination or appetite to them, as that that should be of itself above any of the inferior kind of appetites, so as to keep the same in subjection without the help of the rational will. If the gracious appetite ben't above other appetites, although those appetites may constantly be kept under and ruled with the help of the rational will, yet 'tis with difficulty, and there is a war and struggle; 'tis labor for the rational will to maintain its ground, so that that will is not entirely free. The excess of the inferior appetite above the gracious is lust, is a principle of sin; 'tis an enemy in the soul, and makes a great deal of disturbance there. (To have a sinful inclination is sin, but the inclination of the man is to be found by composition of inclinations; the excess of one above the other is the inclination of the man: if the excess of inclination be to inferior objects in many cases, the prevailing inclination will be [away] from God.)[7] And though the man might do his duty in such a case constantly with the help of the rational will, yet 'twould be grievous to him; which would be a sinful and abominable defect in the manner of doing of it.

The case must be thus, therefore, with our first parents, when tempted: their sense of their duty to God and their love to it must be above their inferior appetite, so that that inferior appetite of itself was not sufficient to master the holy principle; yet the rational will, being perverted by a deceived judgment and setting in with the inferior appetite, overcame and overthrew the gracious inclination. Besides, the holy inclination to obedience, as to its exercise at least, must be greatly diminished by their error of judgment concerning God, or their doubting whether he was true in what he threatened, and their

6. MS: "the"; this is surely an abridged "tho he," as JE had written it earlier in the sentence.
7. This sentence is an interlined insertion and, though relevant, somewhat breaks the sequence of JE's thought.

error as though he were not good in forbidding [them].[8] So Satan's suggestion, "Yea, hath God said," etc. Satan suggested that He had forbid them, because He was unwilling that they should be so much like Himself in honor and happiness. See the next.

438. FALL OF ANGELS. See the last. So it was also with the angels: their judgment was likewise deceived. They probably thought it would be a degrading and misery, to be ministers to such a creature of an inferior nature as God was about to create, and subjects and servants to one in that nature, not knowing particularly how it was to be, God having only in general revealed it to 'em. They thought it would be best for themselves to resist, and endeavor to be independent on God's government and ordering; and having an appetite to their own honor, it overcame holy dispositions, which, when once overcome, immediately wholly left 'em to the full and unrestrained rage of the principles that overcame. And their holy inclination to subjection was greatly damped by their opinion of God, as though he intended to deal unbecomingly by 'em in subjecting them to one of such a nature, and so it was the more easily overcome.

439. COVENANTS. TESTAMENTS. The covenant that God made of old with the children of Israel is spoken of in Scripture as different from that which he makes with his people in these gospel times. We will consider what difference there was. And here,

1. God proposed a covenant to them that was essentially and entirely different, which was the covenant of works: he promulgated the moral law to them, together with many positive precepts of the ceremonial and judicial law, that answered to the prohibition of eating the forbidden fruit; which God proposed to them with the threatening of death, and the curse affixed to the least defect in obedience. If it be inquired, in what sense God gave this covenant to them more than to us, I answer, that although it was as much impossible for them to be saved by it as it is for us, yet it was really proposed to them as a covenant for them, for their trial (Ex. 20:20), that they might this way be brought to despair of obtaining life by this covenant, and might see their necessity of free grace and a Mediator. God chose this way to convince them, by proposing the covenant of works to them, as though he expected they

8. Possibly "[of it]," but cf. the last sentence of the entry. Only a few specks of ink remain of the word or words at the lower right corner of the MS page.

should seek and obtain life in this way, that everyone, when he came to apply it to himself, might see its impracticableness; as being a way of conviction to that ignorant and infantile state of the church. God did with them as Christ did with the young man, when he came and inquired what he should do to inherit eternal life: Christ bid him keep the commandments. There was this difference also: the law, or covenant of works, was more fully and plainly revealed to them than the gospel, or covenant of grace, was.

2. The covenant which God made with them, and by which they indeed obtained blessings of God, though in some respects it was the same, yet in other respects it was different. Covenants that God makes with men can be different but these two ways, by having different conditions, and different things promised upon those conditions. Now the conditions were the same with respect to the general nature of them, that is, the exercise of the same spirit of true holiness, and gracious respect to God in faith, and a sincere and universal obedience; but yet the particular matter of that faith [and] obedience was in considerable part different. Such explicit acts of faith with respect to the Mediator and the gospel doctrines, was in no wise necessary then. And the obedience was not the same, because the commands were different. There were innumerable laws that they of old must obey in order to their salvation, that now are abolished; all those laws came into the terms of the covenant, Jer. 34:13–14.[9] And [there are] some duties we are now obliged to do in order to our salvation, that they could be saved without; some moral duties that though they were obliged to, yet they could then be saved in great neglect of them, that we cannot now, by reason of our being under so much stronger obligations to perform them now, and by reason of the much clearer revelations of them and the foundation of them. And so there are duties that respect the Messias and his salvation and another world that are necessary now to salvation, that were not then, by reason of the different state of the church and of revelation. Though they could not be saved without the same principle and spirit, of old, yet they might be saved without such exercises and explicit acts thereof. So that the covenant is a new covenant, because the conditions of it are in some respect new.

3. There were also things promised that were different. The cove-

9. Jeremiah here urges as part of the Sinaitic covenant the law that a slave who is a fellow Hebrew must be freed in the seventh year. JE cites the passage as an example.

nant, as it was made with the nation as a nation, had the promises of Canaan, and of prosperity, and many public tokens of God's favor in it.

4. And as to particular persons, the promises of eternal life and immortality, which are the great and main things promised in the gospel, they are in a respect new. For, though they of old had general promises of God's grace and favor, that did indeed infer a future state, yet there were no express promises in the law of Moses, of any discoveries or fruits of that grace and favor after this life; the other were very much kept out of sight: all that was expressly promised, either of outward or spiritual blessings, extended not beyond this present state of mankind in this world.

5. That which is more primarily the condition of the covenant of grace (see explication of Jer. 31:33),[1] viz. faith, was not so fully revealed. Herein the church now has the advantage of the Old Testament church as to comfort, in the advantages they are under of being assured of their justification. Then, the secondary conditions, the fruits of faith, were more fully revealed and insisted on than the primary.

440. OLD TESTAMENT. The people of God under the old testament were kept vastly more at a distance, than now under the gospel. When the law was given, bounds must be set about the mount, and whosoever touched the mount was to be put to death, and if man or beast touched it he must be surely stoned or shot through; the holy of holies must never be entered, but only by the high[2] priest once a year; many thousands of the people were smitten and died, because they looked into the ark, and many other such things. And there was need of it then, in order to the maintaining the honor of the divine greatness and majesty, and the dread of his spotless holiness.

But there is no need of it now. Now the honor and dread of God's majesty and holiness is consistent with the most free access and familiar communications, since the Mediator and eternal punishment are so plainly revealed. The sacredness of God's majesty and holiness are abundantly more effectually secured another way, and that is, by the humiliation of Christ and the eternal damnation of sinners. Now the coming most freely and intimately conversing with God, with a dependence on those sufferings and the righteousness of Christ, and also a

1. The note is found in "Scripture," Bk. 1; it is no. 179 in the Dwight ed.(9, 399–400). No. 439 and the note were probably written about the same time.
2. MS: "holy," surely an echo of the preceding "holy of holies."

view of the punishment of the damned, don't at all take off the sense of the awfulness of God's greatness and holiness, but only causes an admiration of his free and sovereign grace.

441. HELL TORMENTS. I don't think that, from anything the Scripture says about the state of the damned, it can be inferred that the torment of the damned is so always alike, that it admits of no sort of difference in different moments—such a supposition is hardly consistent with the nature of a finite mind, that is perpetually roving and altering as [to] the objects of its thoughts—though I don't suppose they ever have anything that can properly be called any rest. Yet I believe the devil has sometimes a kind of a pleasedness when he accomplishes a design, and a torment when disappointed (he was pleased when Adam fell, and when Christ was crucified, and when the Antichrist rose, etc.), i.e. there is some present gratification of malice and pride; though he never has any such pleasure as to be rest from torment, and never any pleasedness but what works torment, and is continually turning into torment. His pleasedness is but in order to his greater torment.

442. ANGELS CONFIRMED. The angels that stood are doubtless confirmed in holiness and their allegiance to God, so that they never will sin, and they are out of any danger of it. But yet I believe God makes use of means to confirm them. They were confirmed by the sight of the terrible destruction that God brought upon the angels that fell; they see what a dreadful thing it is to rebel. They were further confirmed by the manifestation God had made of his displeasure against sin, by the eternal damnation of reprobates amongst men and by the amazing discovery of his holy jealousy and justice in the sufferings of Christ. They are confirmed by finding by experience their own happiness in standing, and finding the mistake of the angels that fell with respect to that which was their temptation, and by new and greater manifestations of the glory of God which have been successively made in heaven, and by his dispensations towards the church, and above all by the work of redemption by Jesus Christ (Eph. 3:10; I Tim. 3:16; I Pet. 1:12). See No. 515.

Corol. Hence we learn that the angels were not unconcerned in the work of redemption by Jesus Christ.

So I believe the saints in heaven are made perfectly holy and impeccable by means, viz. by the beatific vision of God in Christ in glory, by experiencing so much the happiness of holiness, its happy nature and issue, by seeing the wrath of God on wicked men, etc.

443. CHRISTIAN RELIGION. It was often prophesied of old amongst the children of Israel, that other gods, the gods of the nations round about, should perish from off the earth, and that they should cease to be acknowledged and worshiped as gods; but that the worship and acknowledgment of their God should remain forever, and should in due time take [the] place of those other gods; and that the nations abroad in the world, which then worshiped other gods, should be brought to an acknowledgment of him as the only true God (Jer. 10:11).[3] And so it is come to pass: all those deities are exploded, and the acknowledgment of the God of Israel as the only true God takes [their] place in all the then known part of the world, and four times as much; and it holds still. And this came to pass by means of the Christian religion; 'tis Christ's appearing and the preaching of his doctrine in the world, that has been the means of it all. 'Tis by means of that, the Mahometan parts of the world came to acknowledge the true[4] God, and 'tis by this means that even the deists come by it.

Again, it has been only by means of Jesus Christ's appearing and teaching, that the world ever came to have any clear and distinct rational notions about a future [state]; notions most agreeable to the obscurer intimations in the Old Testament, that were evidently only those things set in plain and open view, that were then seen but through a veil; notions most agreeable to the divine nature and dispensations, and every way agreeable to reason.

This is a confirmation that [God] designed that the Christian religion should succeed the Jewish, that speedily after the bringing in of the Christian religion into the world, God in his providence made the Jewish religion impracticable by the destruction of the temple and dispersion of the nation of the Jews; and so has continued it[5] for a longer time than ever it has been practicable, for a longer time than from the first institution of it till that time. It was prophesied of old, that God should be acknowledged and worshiped by other nations,

3. JE apparently intended to gather other texts, for he left space for two or three lines after this sentence.
4. This word was canceled, probably by JE, who may have intended to write "only" or "only true" as earlier in the paragraph. But the deletion may have been by JE, Jr., who wrote "one" above it.
5. I.e. the Jewish religion in its impracticable condition.

and that other nations were to be God's people. Therefore there was a religion to succeed the Jewish, very different from it as to external worship: because the Jewish religion was not fitted for more than a single nation, nor is it practicable by the world in general; but the Christian religion is exceedingly fitted for universal practice.

444. CHRISTIAN RELIGION. CHRIST'S MIRACLES. There are[6] these things remarkable in Christ's raising Lazarus from the dead (John 11), viz. that he called upon God before he did it, to do it for him, and thanked him that he had heard him, and told him that he knew that he heard him always; and when he spake to him, he called him Father, and told him that he spake for that end, that others that stood by, when they [should] see that what he asked of him, he granted, in such an extraordinary thing, might believe that he sent him.

Now can it be imagined that God would hear an impostor? or so order or suffer it, that so extraordinary a thing should be done immediately in consequence of the word and act of an impostor, upon his asking it of him; that was so impudent, when he asked it, [as] to call him Father, and tell him that he always heard him, and tell him that he spake thus for this end, that others might see that he did indeed give a testimony to his mission and authority, by doing of it so, at his request, in such a manner?

445. END OF THE CREATION.[7] There is a necessity of supposing that the exercise of God's goodness, or the communication of his happiness, is not merely a subordinate end but stands in the place of an ultimate end, though there is no necessity of supposing it the only ultimate end. But if God's making his glory to appear be an ultimate end, this must stand not in subordination to it but fellow to it, and in the same rank with it. For to suppose that God's communication of goodness is wholly subordinate to some other end, is to suppose that it is not from God's goodness. That which is done by any being entirely in subordination to some other end, or that is not done at all for the sake of itself, but wholly and only for some other thing that is more ultimately in view; the attribute or disposition that excites to that action, is wholly that which seeks that more ultimate end. Thus if God

6. MS: "is."

7. There is a vertical line in the left margin along the entire length of this entry. The distinction of ends which JE makes here is refined and elaborated in the introduction to the *End of Creation* (*Works, 8,* 405–15).

makes the creature happy only for a further [end], viz. that he may manifest his own perfections by it, then his making the creature happy is not indeed from his goodness, or his disposition to communicate good, but wholly from that attribute or disposition of the divine nature whereby he is disposed to show forth his own excellency. It is not consistent with the nature of goodness to be wholly moved and excited by something else that is not goodness.

If it be said that God communicates good to the creature only to manifest that part of his essential glory, viz. his goodness, this implies a great absurdity; for it supposes that God is good only to manifest his own goodness, which goodness is only an inclination to manifest his glory this way. So that now it comes to this, that God is good to manifest his inclination that he has to manifest his inclination to communicate good: he communicates good for this end, that he may glorify his goodness; which goodness itself is nothing else but an inclination to communicate good for this end, viz. to glorify his inclination to communicate good to this end—and so we may run on to endless nonsense.

If God is good only to manifest the glory of his goodness, then this would be that glory which was manifested, even his inclination to manifest his own glory; God has an inclination to manifest his own glory, and the glory which he manifests is this, viz. his disposition to manifest his own glory. For his goodness is nothing else, if the sole ultimate end of communicating good be to glorify himself, or to show forth the glory of his goodness.

Surely God's glory that is to be manifested must be considered as something prior to his disposition or design to manifest it. God's inclining or designing or exerting himself to show his glory, surely is not that very glory which he shows; the glory must be something else beside the manifestation of it.

You'll say, why mayn't the same be said of God's justice? why can't the exercise of that be argued to be an ultimate end of the creation? I answer, that when the world is already created, merely the glorifying his justice cannot be the only motive to his acting justly, though the glorifying that attribute might be the motive for his giving himself occasion for the exercise of that attribute by making the creatures. See No. 461.[8]

But the attribute of justice, or a just disposition of the divine nature,

---

8. JE's cue mark indicates the last paragraph of No. 461.

can't be directly the motive to God's creating the world, as his goodness may. For a just disposition has for its object only being *existing*, either in act or design. 'Tis absurd to suppose, that an inclination to do justice upon all occasions should properly be the motive to give creatures being, that there may be occasions; for that is not any part of the notion we have of justice, a disposition to make occasions for the exercise of justice; it must be some other disposition that does that. And in God, it is his disposition to cause his attributes to shine forth, or to glorify himself.

But now goodness, or an inclination to communicate good, has merely possible being as much [for] its proper object as actual or designed being. A disposition to communicate good will move a being to make the occasion for the communication; and indeed, giving being is one part of the communication. If God be in himself disposed to communicate himself, he is therein disposed to make the creatures to communicate himself to; because he can't do what he is in himself disposed to, without it. God's goodness is not an inclination to communicate himself as occasion shall offer, or a disposition conditionally to communicate himself, but absolutely. But God's just and righteous disposition is only his disposition to act justly upon every occasion. If God be in himself just, that supposes no more than that he will certainly act justly, whenever there is occasion for his being concerned with the rights or deserts of any; it don't imply in its nature a disposition to make occasions for it. If God be disposed to make occasions for the exercise of that attribute, that must be only because he is disposed to cause his excellencies to shine forth, or to glorify himself. See No. 461; see note on Ps. 136.[9]

446. TRINITY. Christ is called the "face" of God (Ex. 33:14) and the "angel of God's face" [Is. 63:9]; the word in the original signifies face or looks, form or appearance, of a thing. Now what can be so fitly called so, as God's own perfect idea of himself, whereby he has every moment a view of his own essence? This is that face, aspect, form or appearance whereby God eternally appears to himself, and more perfectly than man appears to himself by his form or appearance in a looking glass. The root that the word comes from signifies to "look upon" or "behold." Now what is that which God looks upon or beholds in so emi-

---

9. This brief note is printed in Grosart, *Selections*, p. 117. The citation was written after the reference to No. 461, and its special appropriateness is to a paragraph of No. 461 that JE may have considered a part of No. 445; see below, No. 461, p. 502, n. 4.

nent a manner, as he doth on his own idea, or the perfect image of himself, which he has in view? This is that which is eminently in his presence; this is the "angel of his presence."

447. RIGHTEOUSNESS OF CHRIST. The positive righteousness of Christ, or that price by which he merited, was of equal value with that price by which he satisfied; and indeed it was the same price. He spilled his blood to satisfy, and by reason of the infinite dignity of his person, his sufferings were looked upon [as] of infinite value, and equivalent to the eternal sufferings of a finite creature. And he spilled his blood from respect to the glory of God's majesty that we had injured, and from respect to God's will commanding him: his obedience was of infinite value, because he was at infinite expense to obey. So much the greater is the obedience, by how much the greater the cost of it is to him that obeys; because it testifies so much the greater respect to God's authority.

448. END OF THE CREATION.[1] God is glorified within himself these two ways: (1) by appearing or being manifested to himself in his own perfect idea, or, in his Son, who is the brightness of his glory; (2) by enjoying and delighting in himself, by flowing forth in infinite love and delight towards himself, or, in his Holy Spirit.

So God glorifies himself towards the creatures also two ways: (1) by appearing to them, being manifested to their understandings; (2) in communicating himself to their hearts, and in their rejoicing and delighting in, and enjoying the manifestations which he makes of himself. They both of them may be called his glory in the more extensive sense of the word, viz. his shining forth, or the going forth of his excellency, beauty and essential glory *ad extra*. By one way it goes forth towards their understandings; by the other it goes forth towards their wills or hearts. God is glorified not only by his glory's being seen, but by its being rejoiced in, when those that see it delight in it: God is more glorified than if they only see it; his glory is then received by the whole soul, both by the understanding and by the heart. God made the world that he might communicate, and the creature receive, his glory, but that it might [be] received both by the mind and heart. He that testifies his having an idea of God's glory don't glorify God so much as he that testifies also his approbation of it and his delight in it. Both these ways

---

1. This entry has a vertical line in the left margin along its entire length; see *End of Creation*, especially ch. 2, § 7 (*Works, 8,* 526–36).

of God's glorifying himself come from the same cause, viz. the over-flowing of God's internal glory, or an inclination in God to cause his internal glory to flow out *ad extra*. What God has in view in neither of them, neither in his manifesting his glory to the understanding nor communication to the heart, is not that he may receive, but that he [may] go forth: the main end of his shining forth is not that he may have his rays reflected back to himself, but that the rays may go forth.

And this [is] very consistent with what we are taught of God's being the Alpha and Omega, the first and the last. God made all things; and the end for which all things are made, and for which they are disposed, and for which they work continually, is that God's glory may shine forth and be received. From him all creatures come, and in him their well-being consists; God is all their beginning, and God received is all their end. From him and to him are all things; they are all from him and they are all to be brought to him: but 'tis not that they may add to him, but that God might be received by them. The damned indeed are not immediately to God, but they are ultimately; they are to the glorified saints and angels, and they to God, that God's glory may be manifested in them unto the vessels of mercy.

It is said that God hath made all things for himself [Prov. 16:4], and in the Revelation [4:11] it is said, they are created for God's pleasure; that is, they are made that God may in them have occasion to fulfill his good pleasure, in manifesting and communicating himself. In this God takes delight, and for the sake of this delight God creates the world. But this delight is not properly from the creature's communication to God, but in his to the creature; it is a delight in his own act. Let us explain the matter how we will, there is no way that the world can be "for" God more than [this]; for it can't be so for him, as that he can receive anything from the creature.

449. BLOOD OF CHRIST WASHES AWAY SIN. CHRIST'S RIGHTEOUS-NESS. So it is represented in the Scripture, that we are washed from our filthiness in Christ's blood; whereas, although the blood of Christ washes us from our guilt, yet 'tis the Spirit of Christ that washes from the pollution and stain of sin. But however, the blood of Christ washes also from the filth of sin, as it purchases sanctification; it makes way for it by satisfying, and purchases it by merit. As the sacrifices under the law typified Christ's sacrifice, not only as a satisfaction but as meritorious obedience, they are called a sweet savor upon both those ac-

counts; and therefore we find obedience compared with sacrifice, Ps. 40:6 ff.

The sacrifice of Christ is a sweet savor, [first], because as such it was a great honor done to God's majesty, holiness and law, and a glorious expression and testimony of Christ's respect to that majesty etc.; that when he loved man and so greatly desired his salvation, he had yet so great respect to that majesty and holiness of God, that he had rather die than that salvation should be any injury or dishonor unto those attributes. And then secondly, it was a sweet savor, as it was a marvelous act of obedience, and so an expression of a wonderful respect to God's authority. The value of Christ's sacrifice was infinite, both as a propitiation and as an act of obedience; because he showed an infinite regard to the majesty, holiness, etc. of God, in being at infinite expense from regard to it. See Nos. 451, 452.

450. God's Mercy to His People, in Scripture, Is Often Called His Truth and His Righteousness. It is called his truth, as it is in fulfillment of his covenant. 'Tis called his righteousness, as it is what he determines for them as he is judge of the world. He distinguishes them from wicked men as he sits in judgment; he judges between the righteous and the wicked, and makes a great distinction between them in his sentence he passes: which is the part of a righteous judge. Not that God is obliged in justice to bestow those mercies upon the godly; but nevertheless, it is [a] manifestation of God's righteousness as a judge between the righteous and the wicked, that he makes such a distinction: the whole goodness of a judging, with respect to judging, is called his righteousness in Scripture. But this is part of God's excellency as a judge, that he makes so great a distinction between [them], and especially in causes where the righteous and the wicked are parties, are concerned one with another, as when the wicked oppress and persecute the righteous; then it is the part of a righteous judge between them to plead the cause of the righteous and innocent, and to deliver him from his oppressors. Thus God is said to plead their cause; his mercies to his people are called his righteous judgments (see Pss. 35:24, 72:2, 4); thus David, when he is praising God for his delivering him from his enemies, says, Ps. 9:4, "For thou hast maintained my right and my cause; thou sittest in the throne judging right."

And again, 'tis part of God's righteousness, in strictness, to make a proportionable distinction between the righteous and the wicked, though he is not obliged to bestow any positive rewards upon the righteous. 'Tis indeed part of God's righteousness as a judge, to make a distinction between the righteous and the wicked, in what he adjudges to them according to their deserts; and as God's people now stand in Christ, 'tis really a part of his judicial justice to make such a distinction as he doth, in so destroying the wicked and so gloriously rewarding the righteous. See No. 453.

451. CHRIST'S SACRIFICE. See No. 449. The sacrifices under the law are said to be most holy; but the sacrifice of [Christ] may properly be said to be infinitely holy, as it was an expression of an infinite regard to the holiness, majesty, etc. of God; as we showed, Nos. 449, 452.[2]

452. CHRIST'S RIGHTEOUSNESS. The death of Christ as positive righteousness, or what merits positive blessings, is to be considered not only as an act of obedience, but all ways wherein it was an expression of infinite respect to God; which it was two ways: one was, in that he was willing to be at infinite expense, rather than the salvation of men should be any injury to the glory of God's majesty, etc.; and another was, as he was at infinite expense to obey God's commands to him.[3]

The death of Christ merited positive blessings by virtue of the holiness, or which is the same thing, the righteousness of that act. Now the holiness of it consisted in its being an expression of infinite love or regard to God, these two ways: [1] his being so concerned for the glory of God's majesty and justice, as that he would die rather than the salvation of men should be any injury to it; and (2) as an act of obedience.

453. FREE GRACE. See No. 450. The righteousness of a judge consists in his judging according to law, or to that rule of judgment which has been fixed by rightful legislators, especially if the law and rule of judgment fixed be good, whatever good principles influenced the legislators in making such laws, whether justice, or goodness and mercy.

2. The original reference was to No. 449; JE added "452" later, perhaps when he made that entry.

3. The following sentences at the end of this paragraph are marked off and canceled with a vertical line: "But in order to the sufferings of Christ being looked upon as negative righteousness, that is, satisfaction for sin, they need to be considered only as his sufferings laid upon him by God for our sins, and his motive, his love to us. This seems sufficient to render his sufferings satisfactory but not meritorious, and must be considered as prior to either."

But God in the blessings he adjudges to his people, judges according to the fixed rule of judgment which is his covenant. God shows his holiness by fulfilling his promises to his people—God's faithfulness is part of his holiness—and this is what is meant by righteousness; see Ps. 22:3.

454. RIGHTEOUSNESS OF CHRIST.[4] Jesus Christ, if we look upon him as being actually become man, does not purely by virtue of that become God's servant. He would not merely by that become so proper a subject to God's authority, that it would have been fitting that a law should have been given him; he would not merely by that have become a proper subject of divine laws and commands upon penalty, for he was the same person with the eternal Logos, that was equal with God. He became properly God's servant, therefore, only by virtue of agreement or covenant; he voluntarily put himself in subjection and into the state of a servant, as the servant that had his ear bored, and therefore his obedience was properly meritorious.

Indeed, it would have been fitting and excellent in him, that his will and his actions should be conformed to the Father's will and be subject to him, as it is in itself fit and excellent that the Logos itself should love the Father, and that the Father should love the Son. But it don't follow hence that Christ, merely because he had human nature, was the proper subject of God's commanding and legislative authority.[5]

455. JUSTIFICATION BY FAITH. See sermon on Rom. 4:16.[6] Justification is God's judging or determining of a person, that he has righteousness belonging to him, and adjudging to him an answerable treatment.

When it is said we are not justified by works, the meaning of it is, that it is [not] any amiableness of anything we do that God has respect to, upon the account of which he looks upon it meet that we should in any

4. This entry is indexed in the Table, but it has a vertical line through it near the left margin.

5. The final sentence of the paragraph, which is deleted by a horizontal line, reads: "If we make a supposition that it was possible for the Son not to do the Father's will (though it be impossible), yet it would not be fit that he should be punished."

6. The doctrine of the Rom. 4:16 sermon is, "The grace of God in the new covenant eminently appears in that, that it proposes justification only by faith." It must have been written shortly before No. 455 near the end of 1729. It contains the 1734 lecture series *in nuce*, even to the attacks (in the application) on Socinians, Arminians, and all whose doctrines "derogate from the glory of the new covenant, that maintain justification in any other way than this of faith."

wise be accepted, or have any favor adjudged to us. It is not upon the account of the amiableness of faith that God judges it meet that he that believes should be accepted, or looked upon as in Christ; for if a man could have as much amiableness without closing with Christ, it would not be fit that [he should be accepted] for the sake of that amiableness. Believers ben't received for that reason, because they are so lovely, having the lovely qualification of faith, but because 'tis a receiving of Christ and a uniting the heart to him as Savior; God upon the account of it judges it proper that the believer should be looked upon as being in Christ, and so having Christ's righteousness belonging to him. In the first covenant, respect was had to the excellency and loveliness of what we do, in proposing justification by it.

456. HELL TORMENTS. "As is thy fear, so is thy wrath" [Ps. 90:11]. Whence we may infer, that God's wrath is indeed answerable to those manifestations of the majesty of God in thunder, earthquakes, etc.[7]

457. SIN. CORRUPTION OF NATURE. (See how man's nature came to be corrupt, Dr. Williams' *Discourses*, 5, 249–52.)[8] *Question*. Whether or no upon the fall, and the departure of a spirit of love to God, every other natural inclination that man was made with, by that means became a lust, because they became exorbitant, being no longer in subordination to that superior principle of love to God.

I answer, no, for this reason, because some of them are of that kind that they cannot be exorbitant, as the love of our happiness in general, or love of our eternal welfare. So that when a natural man seeks salvation from a fear of hell, he can't be said properly to serve a lust in it; because there is no excess in a fear of hell. As to many of the particular appetites and inclinations, they brake bounds as soon as a spirit of love to God, that was wont to restrain and govern them, left the soul; as, a love to his outward pleasure and profit and honor. These appetites, not being governed by the superior, of love to God, moved them to

7. See No. 491.

8. Daniel Williams' *Discourses* were published at London in 5 vols. as follows: Vols. 1–2 as *Practical Discourses on Several Important Subjects* (1738), and Vols. 3–5 as *Discourses on Several Important Subjects* (1750). This citation of Vol. 5 is of course a much later insert. The passage to which JE refers is entitled, "How our nature became corrupt." Williams' account of how corruption took over human nature was similar to JE's: "The soul being clothed with flesh, doth for want of holy principles become subject to sensible inclinations . . . and its intercourse with unseen things is cut off, for want of that light which should perceive them, and that holy love which might relish and desire them" (*ibid.*, 251–52).

many actions that were unlawful; but the love of eternal life cannot be out of its bounds, nor can it become irregular or clash with his duty. A man's love to sensual pleasure, if love to God be gone, will very often be contrary to love to God, or excite to those things that love to God, if it were present, would restrain from.

458. FAITH. See sermon on Hab. 2:4.[9]

459[a]. LIFE OF THE SOUL SPIRITUAL, ETERNAL. See sermon on Hab. 2:4.[1]

459[b]. ORIGINAL SIN AND ITS PROPAGATION. See sermon on Rom. 7:14.[2]

460. INCARNATION. WISDOM OF GOD IN THE WORK OF REDEMPTION. This end is obtained by Christ's incarnation, viz. that the saints may see God with their bodily eyes as well as by an intellectual view. They may see him in both ways of seeing which their natures, being body and spirit, are capable of; they may see him as they see one another, which shall not only be spiritually but outwardly. The saints in heaven will have two sorts of sight, intellectual and corporeal; it is the will of God that he himself, or a divine person, should be the principal entertainment of both those kinds of sight. Thus God saw it meet that it should be, and therefore assumed a body that appears with that transcendent visible majesty, glory and beauty, that is exceeding expressive of the divine greatness, holiness and grace. This is a much more perfect and real way of seeing God with bodily eyes, than to behold some glorious preternatural representation, as God sometimes appeared under [un-

9. Hand, ink, paper, and its citation here combine to date this sermon in the winter or early spring of 1730. Under the doctrine, "The saints do live by faith," JE develops a distinction between faith (1) "as it respects God in the whole of our concern with him, either in the affairs of our souls or bodies," and (2) "as it respects Jesus Christ in the particular concern of the salvation of our souls." The latter is justifying faith.

1. MS: "vid. ibid." In the second inquiry of the sermon JE states: "Herein consists what we call spiritual life, viz. in the soul's being endowed with that holiness and image of God, and those spiritual principles of action, wherein consists the proper perfection and excellency of the soul of man . . . And herein also consists eternal life, only brought to perfection."

2. For the date of this sermon see above, n. 9. Its doctrine is, "Men as they are by nature are perfect slaves to corruption, or, they are entirely under the dominion of sin." In its second inquiry JE is especially interested in proving that since the corruption of human nature is not a positive but a negative, i.e. the lack of original righteousness, it cannot be derived by necessity of nature through either the souls or the bodies of the parents. How then is it transmitted? His answer is the federal doctrine of divine judicial imputation.

der] the old testament. Job comforted himself, that he should see God
with his bodily eyes.

461. END OF THE CREATION.[3] See Nos. 445, 702 (corol. 1). If God
delights in the creatures' participation of his happiness for its own
sake, then it is evident that the communication of good is not merely a
subordinate end, but must be allowed the place of an ultimate end; for
if it be for its own sake, then it is not wholly for the sake of something
else as its end. But 'tis evident that God delights in goodness for its own
sake, by such places: Micah 7:18, "He delighteth in mercy." Ezek.
18:23, "Have I any pleasure at all that the wicked should die? saith the
Lord: and not that he should return from his ways, and live?" and v.
32, "For I have no pleasure in the death of him that dieth." And again,
Ezek. 33:11, "Say unto them, As I live, saith the Lord God, I have no
pleasure in the death of the wicked; but that the wicked turn from his
way and live: turn ye, turn ye from your evil ways; for why will ye die, O
house of Israel?" Lam. 3:33, "For he doth not afflict willingly, nor
grieve the children of men."

Such passages of Scripture show, that God delighteth in the creatures' happiness in a sense that he doth not in their misery. 'Tis true
that God delights in justice for its own sake, as well as in goodness; but
it will by no means follow from thence, that he delights in the creatures'
misery for its own sake as well as [in their] happiness. For goodness
implies that in its nature, that the good of its object be delighted in for
its own sake; but justice don't carry that in its nature, that the misery of
those it's exercised about is delighted in for its own sake: as is evident,
because justice procures happiness as well as misery, according as the
qualification of the object is; but it carries the contrary in its nature,
viz. that misery be not delighted in for itself, but only for further ends.

(See No. 445.)[4] Indeed, the glory of God cannot be considered as the
proper end of God's acts of justice. For if it be, 'tis the glory of his
justice is the end; which will imply those absurdities mentioned, concerning God's goodness being altogether for the glory of his goodness.
A view to the glorifying of God's justice is not the sole motive to God's
acting justly when there is occasion, for he acts justly because 'tis agreeable to his nature, and he delights so to do; though God's glorifying

---

3. This entry has a vertical line down the left margin; a development of the material in it
will be found in JE's introduction to the *End of Creation* (*Works, 8,* 405–15).

4. JE's reference is to No. 445 at the end of its fifth paragraph (above, No. 445, p. 494,
n. 9).

himself might be his end, in giving himself occasion for the exercise of his justice. So that although God's glorifying and communicating himself were the sole ends for which he created the world, yet they cannot be properly considered as the sole ends of all that God does in the world. Thus God, when he speaks the truth to his creatures, [does not have the glorifying of his truth as][5] the sole motive to his speaking the truth when he does speak, for 'tis impossible he should speak anything else; he speaks the truth, because he delights in truth for its own sake.

462. CHURCH ORDER. The method in all congregations[6] of Christians ought to be this: none should be admitted to any church privilege, to have their children baptized, or to be looked upon as of the visible church of Christ, but those that come to the Lord's Supper. And therefore all of the congregation should be pressed and urged to come; and effectual care should be taken by parents, and by the elders (or pastors) of the church,[7] that all the children of the church do come, as they would be willing that their children should be in the church of Christ and be Christians, as well as they.

But yet they ought all to be sufficiently instructed, that they must be Christians really, in order to come—for only the righteous have any right to the privileges of the church; the wicked[8] are sojourners, Ezek. 20:38 and Ps. 50:16[9]—and therefore must examine and prove themselves, whether or no they believe the gospel with all their hearts, or are heartily convinced of the truth of it; and whether or no they are brought thoroughly to forsake all ways of sin, to deny every lust, and live in the performance of all Christ's commands universally; and whether they are fully and seriously determined so to do to the end, through all opposition; and whether they live in charity with all Christians, without entertaining any malicious or revengeful spirit towards any, but on the contrary loving them and seeking their good. For in really believing the truth of the gospel, and in universally forsaking sin and performing God's commands with full and fixed determination of mind, and perseveringly through opposition and temptation, and in

5. JE apparently lost his place in the draft from which he was copying; this or something similar is needed to complete the thought as well as the sentence.

6. MS: "all ~~our churches~~ congregations."

7. MS: "by ~~mi~~[nisters] the elders ⟨or pastors⟩ of the church." In the congregational churches of JE's day, the minister usually was "the elder"; see JE's usage in the 5th paragraph of this entry.

8. MS: "they." For "the wicked" see Ps. 50:16; for "sojourners" see Ezek. 20:38.

9. The two preceding clauses are an interlined insertion.

forgiving, and in deeds, loving the brethren, consists the Scripture evidence or visibility of Christianity to ourselves; and in the outward appearances of them, the visibility of Christianity to others. And therefore this is what they should make a profession of, when they come to the Lord's table.

There are other things that are evidential of sincerity besides those, such as the sensible exercises of grace in the breathings and flowings of love and joy, and lively actings of trust and dependence. But these sensible exercises are not constant; there are many times that we cannot see them, and when they are gone, sometimes it can't be perfectly remembered how it was; the ideas can't be repeated at will. The principles of these are universal, but the lively actings are not so universal as those other signs: if these be what we must be positive that we have before we come to the Lord's Supper, a great number of truly upright ones would be excluded. But if persons are godly, and don't at that time experience a willingness to forsake all sin and to live universally in obedience to God's commands, 'tis not best they should know it, or treat themselves as if they were godly, till they are come again to an actual willingness universally to obey.

And this is what thorough care should be taken to bring all the children of the church [to] by parents and ministers, viz. to a believing the truth of the gospel, and to a thorough willingness to forsake all ways of sin and obey all God's commands, and to forgive injuries and do good to their brethren. All that are without [it] should be pressed and urged to it, as directly in order to their salvation and as the condition of it, as well as the condition of their enjoying the privileges of the church. But [they] should at the same time be taught, that they must conclude and come to a preparedness of mind, to do it through all opposition and temptations; because if they fail, they will miss of salvation. They should therefore be put in mind of the cost, and be put upon counting of it.

And when the children of the church are become adult, they should be put upon it to come and join with the church; but it should be understood as with those conditions, for 'tis presumed that they know how dreadful 'tis to come without them. If they don't come when they are become adult, it should be seen to what the cause is; and if they object their want of any of these conditions, as particularly of a believing the truth of the gospel, thorough care should be immediately taken to convince them: the elder should come and argue with them, books suitable for the purpose should be read, and he should never be left till he is convinced. If he objects that he is not willing to forsake all his sins and do all duties through all difficulties, then he will be condemned out of his own mouth; his own fault and inexcusableness will stare him in the face, and it will be easy to come at him with arguments, for he himself will open the way. And those that enjoy gospel light will be ashamed to offer that as an excuse, that they ben't willing to forgive injuries and to do good to their neighbors.

After they are admitted, they ought often to be put in mind of the danger of hypocrisy, and to have the signs of hypocrites laid before them; and before every sacrament, examination should in a more solemn manner be renewed; and upon their discovery of their hypocrisy, they still lie as open to conviction of its being their own fault, and to arguments and persuasives to an immediate turning to God with more full determination, and without reserve, and without suffering any competitor in their hearts with God and religion.

Men's hearts may not be fully determined in a way of universal and persevering obedience; they may not be so disposed as fixedly to embrace religion and obedience, considered as attended with all its difficulties; they may have some reserve, may indulge some competitor and not be sensible of it. But they are strictly to examine themselves; and if they cannot perceive it, they are to come, though they are not certain; but if they question it, 'tis their business immediately to devote themselves more fully to Christ and his commandments.

If this way were taken, wicked men (those that are sensible they are such) could much more easily be come at in the preaching of the Word; they would lie abundantly more open to conviction, and to the force of the calls and motives of the gospel. They would visibly be separate from Christ, in that they are separate from the church, and don't come and join themselves. In keeping away from the church, they would implicitly own that they were not willing to forsake their sins and come to Christ, and to embrace their duty with its difficulties. It would be an owning that it was merely from their unwillingness and obstinacy; and they could not avoid the conviction of it themselves, because they are taught from their childhood that that is all that is required of 'em, to be willing to break off their sins and obey Christ's commands. If they therefore did not come to the Lord's Supper, it would be a visible and shameful obstinacy in their sin; and they would be mightily exposed to the force of arguments [and] expostulations, which would put them upon thoughts. And their being denied all privileges while keeping away from the Supper, of having their children baptized, etc., and upon their proving obstinate being publicly reproved and rebuked, it would put them upon it to come; and being well instructed, that if they do come without forsaking their sins, they will eat and drink judgment to themselves, it would put them upon turning from all their sins and complying with the rules of Christianity, and seeking sincerity therein.

If these things are to be insisted on as the terms of going to heaven, and also the terms of being in the church, such instructions are easy and natural to the understandings of children. See No. 873.[1]

463. WISDOM OF GOD IN THE WORK OF REDEMPTION. The sufferings of Christ have this advantage of the eternal sufferings of the wicked, for impressing upon the minds of the spectators a sense of the dreadful majesty and justice of God and his infinite hatred of sin, viz. that the eternal sufferings of the wicked are what never will be seen actually accomplished; whereas they have seen that which is equivalent to those eternal sufferings actually fulfilled in the sufferings of Christ.

464. LORD'S DAY.[2] See No. 160. "There remaineth therefore a rest" (or as it is in the original, a "sabbatism," or the keeping a sabbath) "to the people of God. For he that is entered into his rest, he also hath ceased from his own works, as God did from his" (Heb. 4:9–10). This much at least we are taught by these words: (1) We are taught by 'em to look upon Christ's rest from his work of redemption as parallel with God's rest from the work of creation. (2) They are spoken of as parallel, particularly with respect to the relation that they bear to the keeping a sabbath amongst God's people, or with respect to the influence these two rests have as to sabbatizing in the church of God. The word in the original, here in the 9th verse translated "rest," is *sabbatismós;* the word translated "rest" in the 10th and 11th verses and other places of the context, is not the same, but is *katápausis.* So that here is an evident reference to God's blessing and hallowing the day of his rest from the creation [to] be a sabbath, and appointing a sabbath in imitation of him; for the Apostle is speaking of this, 4th verse. Thus far is evident, whatsoever the Apostle has respect to by this sabbatism that remains to

1. JE left most of a page blank for further consideration of the subject. The space was later filled with an addition to No. 399 (above, p. 465, n. 4) and one to No. 536 (to be printed with that entry).

2. In connection with a repreaching of the sermon on I Cor. 16:1–2 (see above, No. 160), probably in the latter 1730s, JE incorporated No. 464, along with No. 536, into new material which he inserted into the sermon on four additional leaves; cf. No. 464 with the sermon in the Worcester rev. ed., *4,* 625.

the people of God, whether a weekly sabbatizing on earth or a sabbatizing in heaven. (3) The preference is given to the latter rest, viz. the rest of our Savior from his works, with respect to this influence it has upon, or the relation it bears to the sabbatizing of God's people now under the gospel, evidently implied in the expression, "There remaineth therefore a sabbatism to the people of God. For he that is entered into his rest," etc., intimating that the old sabbatism, in remembrance of the former of those rests, ceases and remains not; but that another sabbatism, following from this rest of Christ from his works, remains instead of it.

465. CHRISTIAN RELIGION. 'Tis an evidence that the apostles had their doctrine from the inspiration of some invisible guide and instructor, that there was such a vast and apparent difference made in them at once after Pentecost. They were illiterate, simple, undesigning, ignorant men before; but afterward, how do they talk in their speeches and epistles! They don't speak as being anything at a loss about the scheme of salvation and divine gospel mysteries. With what positiveness and authority do they teach, in how learned, understanding a manner! How came Paul by his schemes and by all his knowledge of the Christian doctrines and mysteries, immediately upon his conversion? He was evidently under the guidance and influence of some Spirit in his teaching.

466. LORD'S DAY.[3] God blessed the sabbath day, or determined to confer his blessings on men especially on that day, as it were as an expression of his own joyful remembrance of that day, and of the rest and refreshment he had in it (Ex. 31:17). God takes delight to honor the day and to give his blessing on this day upon that account, as princes will give gifts on their birthdays, marriage days, etc. But how much more reason has Christ to bless the day of his resurrection, and to delight to honor it, and be conferring his graces and blessed gifts on men on this day, in a joyful remembrance of his rest and refreshment from his extreme labors and sufferings on this day! It was a day of refreshment to Christ Jesus in a literal sense, a day of great joy; being the day of his deliverance from the chains of death, the day of his completing that great and arduous work of redemption which he had

---

3. There is a close relation between this entry and a portion of the sermon on I Cor. 16:1–2 (cf. Worcester rev. ed., *4*, 634). Comparison of the two MSS suggests that the original sermon incorporated No. 466 with few revisions.

upon his heart from eternity, the day of his justification, the beginning of his exaltation, and the fulfillment of the promises of the Father to him, and when he had eternal life that he purchased given into his hand.

467. PERSEVERANCE. As to passages of Scripture like that, Ezek. 18:24, wherein is declared the fatal consequence of turning or falling away from righteousness, they don't at all argue, but that there is an essential difference in the very nature of the righteousness of those that persevere, and the righteousness of those that fall away. The one is of a lasting sort, the other not; and so falling away or holding out are in those places respected as natural fruits or discoveries of the nature of the righteousness. If a man that had a prospect of being ere long in calamitous circumstances, of being poor and the object of general contempt, etc., should make this declaration concerning his friend— him that now appeared as such—that if his friend would cleave to him through all circumstances, he would receive him and treat him ever after as his true friend, but otherwise he would utterly desert him as a false friend: this would not argue, that he thought there was no difference between the love or friendship that was persevering, and that that failed before this trial; but only that those difficulties discover the difference, and show whose love is of a lasting sort and whose not. The promises in Scripture are commonly made to the signs, though God knows whether men be sincere or not without the signs whereby man knows.

468. WORK OF HUMILIATION. As we have shown,[4] there[5] are these two things that influence and govern the soul in its acts: (1) the judgment that is made by the understanding, (2) the impression that is made upon the apprehension, [i.e.] the liveliness, strength, or impression of the ideas. Now it seems that the Holy Ghost, when he works upon a soul in those convictions that are given before conversion, he works immediately by the latter. By only increasing the liveliness and impression of those ideas which a natural man is capable of, a man that before was senseless may be made sensible of his great guilt and dreadful, dangerous condition.

God, by giving a man a more lively and deep and fixed impression of

4. This distinction is made at the beginning of No. 436.
5. MS: "that there."

the misery of hell, and by giving him a sensibleness of his greatness, power, knowledge, and authority and terribleness, which a natural man is capable of, may make him sensible of the miserable condition he is in; it will make him sensible of the heinousness of his sins (for [by] this means wicked men will be made sensible, at the day of judgment, of the heinousness of their sins), and by this means he will see the connection between his sin[6] and that dreadful punishment. Men's natural conscience naturally makes 'em expect punishment after crimes, because it suggests a relation between their crimes and punishment. But by this sense of the greatness and authority of God, they are made sensible how angry he must be for their manifold disobedience; and this helps natural conscience, makes 'em see more plainly the connection between their sins and punishment. And this is all the conviction that natural men have, of the justice of their being cast into hell: they have strong impressions of the greatness of God, and so of that kind of heinousness of sin which consists in its being disobedience [to] so great a being; and so the conscience is made much more sensible of the connection between their sin and punishment, or their desert of punishment.

And then God giving them a sense withal of the greatness of that misery which the Scripture threatens, this must needs make 'em sensible that they are in a very doleful condition by reason of their guilt; and a sense of God's greatness will make 'em sensible of the terribleness of his wrath; as also, a sense of the dreadfulness of the punishment tends to beget a sense of the majesty and greatness of God. This lively impression of the ideas tends to make the things appear more real; it the more inclines them to think they are true. Mark 9:25–27, "I charge thee, come out of him, and enter no more into him. And the spirit cried, and rent him sore, and came out of him: and he was as one dead; insomuch that many said, He is dead. But Jesus took him by the hand, and lifted him up; and he arose." The account we have (I Kgs. 19:11–12) of the strong wind that rent the rocks, and earthquake, and fire, and still small voice, is to the present purpose. The awful and terrible manifestations of God's majesty were to prepare Elijah for that more familiar converse with God that followed. So the awakenings, the sense of danger and of God's terribleness that a sinner has, are to prepare a sinner for that near approach to God, and those manifesta-

6. MS: "they will see the connection between their sin." Since the parentheses are JE's, he apparently meant these words to apply to the subject of the earlier part of the sentence.

tions of him, and his love and friendship, which a sinner has in his first true comfort.

One [of] the principal things (see two other reasons in sermon on Hos. 5:15;[7] see sermon on Ps. 2:11, the second reason of the doctrine)[8] that make it needful in God's account, that men should have a sense of their sins and danger before God first reveals his redeeming love to their souls, is that when his mercy and love is revealed they may not have undue apprehensions of God; lest their sense of his love and grace, and their apprehension of his majesty and justice, should not be in a due balance agreeable to the true glory of the divine nature. God would discover his true glory to the soul at the same time that he discovers his love; he would discover his love and grace as part of his glory and beauty. But now if there was this love and grace without infinite majesty, sacred divine authority, infinitely dreadful hatred and wrath against sin, this love would be no part of God's glory: the manifestations of his love would be derogatory to his glory. So he that sees God's love, and don't see his hatred of sin and his wrath against [it], don't see God's glory. A discovery of the love of God, without an answerable discovery of the awful and terrible majesty and holiness of God, has a tendency to dispose the soul in some respects unsuitably towards God: there will not be a due reverence with love and delight; the soul will be attracted to God, but will come with an undue boldness. 'Tis the will of God that when we rejoice it should be with trembling; and so [he] won't discover his love without showing his terrible majesty.[9] See the next.

469. WISDOM OF GOD IN THE WORK OF REDEMPTION.[1] And even the man Christ Jesus was made sensible of the terrible wrath of God, before his exaltation to that exceeding height of enjoyment of his

7. The reference is interlined here; a reference to the sermon as a whole appears in the middle of the upper margin. The sermon on Hos. 5:15 is printed in the Dwight ed., *8*, 44–69. The first "reason" in the sermon is based on this paragraph of No. 468 and also incorporates No. 469. The second reason is, that by means of conviction men are prepared to be sensible of God's sovereign freedom in bestowing mercy; and the third, that conviction prepares them to see the glory of Christ as Mediator. Its composition probably parallels that of Nos. 470–475, i.e. in the fall of 1730.

8. The sermon on Ps. 2:11 is not extant. The hand and ink of the citation belong to the latter 1730s, and it is likely that the sermon was written during that time.

9. This sentence is an interlined insertion. JE's caret places it after "delight," where it would obviously be an interruption.

1. See above, n. 7.

Father's love; his sense of wrath was something in proportion to his after exaltation.

470. WORK OF HUMILIATION, a sense of the awful and terrible greatness of God. It assists conscience the more strongly and fully to suggest the relation that there is between their sins and punishment, and assists it to intimate a relation or proportion between their sins and a very great punishment. That is the proper work of conscience, to suggest a relation between sin and punishment, or sin's desert of punishment. If there be anything at all of conscience in a natural man, there is something of this; and the more sense a man's conscience has of the heinousness of sin, the more strong sense will he have of its desert of punishment, and he will have a sense of its desert of the greater punishment.

But merely this, unless a man has a discovery of the glory and excellency and loveliness of God as well as his terrible greatness, will not in this world make a man leave off quarreling and objecting. They will neither be freed from a disposition to quarrel, nor indeed will it convince 'em that they are every way justly dealt with. (The damned in hell will not be freed from a disposition to quarrel, and doubtless they will spend their eternity in blaspheming.) Such a discovery as this won't convince a man that he is justly dealt with, it won't free a man from such objections as these: Why did God give me a being, when he knew I must perish forever? Why did he decree my damnation, and decree my sin in order [to] it? Why was I born with a corrupt nature, and under a necessity of sinning? How could I help my own corrupt nature? I had not the making of myself! Why am I born in such a miserable condition for Adam's transgression, that I had no hand in? Why did God withold from me his assistance and let me fall into sin, when it was impossible that it should be otherwise, and then punish me for it? I can't convert myself! The sight of the awful greatness of God, gives [a man] a sense of the proportion between his sins and a very great punishment, provided he were but convinced that the blame was altogether from and in himself.

There are but these two ways of the soul's being convinced and silenced and stilled with respect to such things as these, either (1) by explaining of them to his understanding, untying the knots and unfolding the mysteries, so as to make the reason and justice of the things comprehensible by his reason: as probably the wicked will be con-

vinced when they come to be judged; they will have their understandings so enlarged that they will be able to comprehend these things, and
their Judge will set clear light before them, to convince them of the
justice of their condemnation. And (2) the other way is by giving of the
soul a sense of the glorious, holy and excellent nature of God. That
gives it true humility and assures it that God must be right and just in
all things, and even in those things that it[2] cannot comprehend. Surely
none will say, that it is necessary that the soul be convinced and quieted
the first of these ways in order to conversion.[3]

It may be as well demonstrated, that a man will never receive Christ
till his pride is really mortified and he has[4] gracious humility, as that he
won't till brought off from any dependence on his own righteousness
(as, see sermon on Job 11:12, under the first inference);[5] but yet this
won't prove, that pride must first be mortified and humility infused in
a distinct work before conversion.

471. SPIRIT'S OPERATION. CONVICTION. CONVERSION. Difference
between [the] Spirit's operation in converted and unconverted men.
The Spirit of God influences and operates upon the minds of both
natural and regenerate men; but doubtless there is a great difference,
not only in the works he does or the effects he produces, but also in the
manner of his operation: for wicked men are sensual and have not the
Spirit; those that are none of Christ's have not the Spirit of Christ. And
the difference seems to be this: the Holy Ghost influences the godly as
dwelling in them as a vital principle, or as a new supernatural principle
of life and action. But in unregenerate men, he operates only by
assisting natural principles to do the same work which they do of

2. MS: "he."
3. No. 470 originally ended here, a small amount of space separating it from the next
entry. Shortly afterwards JE added this sentence: "We read of God's leading the children of
Israel through the terrible wilderness to prove 'em and to humble 'em and to know what was
in their heart." This is canceled with two slanted lines, possibly due to its use in the sermon on
Hos. 5:15 (cf. Dwight ed., *8*, 46). What is now the final paragraph of the entry is still later (see
n. 5 below).
4. MS: "till their pride is really mortified and they have."
5. This sermon has the doctrine, "Man is naturally a proud creature." JE's main interest is
the sermon's discussion of "a reason why God doth sometimes keep men long under terrors
of wrath before he comforts them: . . . God doth subdue their proud hearts. . . . till men
shall become desperate in themselves . . . and they [are] brought to yield themselves to God
as captives, and shall fall down before him as submitting to him." The paragraph in which
this citation occurs is a later addition, probably made while JE was writing No. 524, which
cites the same inference. Since No. 524 was probably written during the writing of the
sermon, both compositions can be roughly dated around the end of 1731.

themselves, to a greater degree. As for instance, the Spirit assists natural conscience. The work of natural conscience that it doth of itself, is
to give an apprehension of right and wrong, and to suggest to the
mind the relation that there is between right or wrong and a retribution. (See No. 472.)[6] Sin and sensuality, by its stupifying nature, greatly
hinders conscience in doing this work; it clogs and lames it, but don't
destroy its power so that it shall not be able to do it; but though sin has
the dominion in the heart, yet conscience continues to do this work
still. But the Spirit of God, when It convinces and awakens a sinner,
assists it to do it[7] to a greater degree by Its assistance, frees it in a
measure from its clog and hindrance by sin.

But in the sanctifying work of the Holy Ghost, not only remaining
principles are assisted to do their work to a greater degree, but those
principles are restored that were utterly destroyed by the fall; [so that]
the mind habitually exerts those acts that the dominion of sin had
made the soul wholly destitute of, as much as a dead body is destitute
of vital acts.

And then there is this other difference: the Spirit of God in the souls
of his saints exerts its own proper nature; that is to say, it communicates and exerts itself in the soul in those acts which are its proper,
natural and essential acts in itself *ad intra,* or within the Deity from all
eternity. The proper nature of the Spirit of God, the act which is its
nature and wherein its being consists, is (as we have shown)[8] divine
love. Therefore the Holy Ghost influences the minds of the godly by
living in the godly. The Spirit of God may operate upon a mind and
produce effects in it, and yet not communicate itself in its nature in the
soul. The Spirit of God operates in the minds of the godly by only
being in them, uniting itself to their souls, and living in 'em and acting
itself.

But the Spirit of God influences the minds of the ungodly otherwise.
Indeed he acts according to his nature in what he does upon them, for
he never acts any otherwise. He acts according to his nature in awakening a sinner, in assisting natural conscience, as he opposes that which is
so contrary to his nature, viz. sin, by assisting the natural principles of
reason and conscience which do oppose it, by making the soul uneasy
with it; but he don't exert his proper nature in them and in union with
their souls, so that there shall be a communication of his own natural,

6. By his cue mark JE indicates that it is this sentence to which No. 472 is related.
7. I.e. assists conscience to "do this work."
8. In No. 94 (latter part), No. 98, and subsequent entries on the Trinity.

essential and eternal act. The Spirit of God may act and not, in acting, communicate itself. The Spirit of God, as well as any other person in the Trinity, may act upon inanimate creatures, as we read that the Spirit of God moved upon the face of the waters. So the Holy Ghost may act upon the mind of [a] man many ways, and communicate himself no more than when he acts upon [an] inanimate creature; for instance, he [can] excite thoughts in him, or he can assist his reason and natural understanding, or he can assist other natural principles. He in these things acts as any agent acts upon an external object; but as he acts in holy influences in men's souls, he acts by way of peculiar communication of himself. See No. 626.

472. CONSCIENCE. NATURAL MEN.[9] See No. 471.[1] And indeed, the whole work of natural conscience seems to consist in the latter; it gives no other notion to natural men of right and wrong, but only as it suggests the relation or adaptedness there is between such and such things and a being hated by others and having evil brought upon them. The notion that natural conscience gives of wrong is not of something deformed and loathsome: natural men in strictness see nothing of the proper deformity of wrong, but only they see an agreeableness between such certain things and being hated, or being the object of displeasure, or suffering ill. They see an equality, proportion and likeness of nature. If a man injures another, his understanding suggests to him an agreeableness between his causing his neighbor to suffer and suffering himself, not from a sense of the deformity of causing his neighbor to suffer. See Nos. 623 and 489.

473. NATURAL MEN. CONVERSION. COMMON WORK OF THE SPIRIT. SELF-LOVE.[2] From a principle of self-love, that is to say, from a love of pleasure and a love of being loved, and a hatred of pain and an aversion to the being hated, many things may arise.

1. There may arise the affection of gratitude. For as the soul necessarily loves pleasure or respect, so [it may love] that which the soul sees to be the cause of that pleasure or good, or to be the person that

---

9. There is a vertical line beside this entry in the left margin; its ideas, though not its precise language, reappear in *True Virtue*, ch. 5 (*Works, 8,* 589–99).

1. See above, No. 471, p. 513, n. 6, where JE identifies the sentence of which No. 472 is an elaboration.

2. This entry also has a vertical line to the left of it; see *True Virtue*, ch. 4, into which No. 473 is incorporated (ibid., pp. 575–88).

exercises that love and respect. A person may have a kind of benevolence and complacence in an inanimate thing that has been the occasion of much delight and pleasure to him, by a certain kind of association of ideas, inclinations and acts of the mind: ideas that are habitually associated together do partake of one another's love and complacence and benevolence, i.e. of the benevolence and delight the soul exercises towards them. But especially is it natural to the soul to exercise gratitude to persons that it conceives of as not only causes of pleasure, but also therein exercising respect, and that both as it loves the pleasure and the respect. As 'tis natural to the soul to exercise anger or malevolence to a person that it conceives of as hating him and doing him ill, so is there also a natural gratitude in the soul. Matt. 5:46, "If ye love them that love you, what reward have ye? do not even the publicans the same?"

2. From self-love a person may come to love another person for good qualifications of mind, if a person conceives of another as having those qualifications of mind that would enable him to do him good and minister to his profit or pleasure; and [as] disposed to respect and benevolence, which he will look upon as more or less valuable as he conceives of the person as greater or less, more or less considerable and honorable. This may beget in his mind strong desires of a person's friendship and of having a propriety in him and union with him; and may for the present cause a kind of benevolence from the person's imagination, whereby he imagines himself as being in friendship and union and enjoyment of him; and a complacence from that love of virtue which there may be from self-love, which we now are about to speak of.

3. There may be a love to many virtues that arises from self-love. So there may be a love of justice and a love of generosity, because a person[3] conceives of such virtues as tending directly to men's good, and finds and knows that they tend to his own good whenever exercised towards him. And when the contrary vices are exercised, they are for his ill, and excite his anger; and so a person may habitually hate it[4] (our dislike is habitually associated with it), for the person is restrained from such acts himself, and therefore he is not an actor but only a sufferer by such vices, and so he has no benefit but only injury by 'em.[5]

3. MS: "because it." JE's subject in both this and the preceding paragraph is "a person."
4. I.e. such behavior.
5. Here is written, then canceled, "and as we have shown already." There are two previous attempts in the paragraph similarly deleted, to introduce what was probably the same

A man may come to scorn some vices from pride: he greatly affects his honor, and his natural conscience suggests to him the relation between some vices, and shame and contempt. A man may hate other vices from the things that usually attend them; as he may hate drunkards for their other vicious dispositions that attend it, as their boisterousness and ungoverned spite and passions, which he may hate for the reason aforesaid. A man may dislike men for some vices, from envy; for he is restrained, and he has not the pleasure of 'em; and his envy in such a case is without restraint, for he looks upon his zeal as good, and gives it the reins.

474. SINCERE OBEDIENCE. ARMINIANS.[6] [Sincere obedience] is what we are not justified by. There are these two opinions that are contrary to the gospel doctrine of justification by faith: viz. first, that which makes our obedience the matter of our justification, or to be the righteousness for which we are justified, and so [they] place it in the room of Christ's righteousness; and the other is that which supposes it to be the qualification that God has respect to, in looking upon us as having a propriety in Christ's righteousness and satisfaction, and so they place it in the room of faith. And indeed [they] come to the same,[7] nearly; for if it be supposed to be the qualification that God has respect to, in giving us a propriety in Christ's satisfaction—not merely as it is a reception of Christ and the gospel, as those that maintain this doctrine do not intend—it is the same in effect as to suppose that God partly at least justifies men upon the account of our obedience as a righteousness, or moral loveliness. For it supposes that God receives men into favor, or at least abates of his anger and is more propitious to them, that he is willing upon the account of it to give 'em an interest in Christ; so that the abatement of God's anger, or his favorable inclination to them, is partly at least upon the account of their obedience.

If men have a mind to say that we [are] justified partly by obedience,

thought; the longer of these is: "For as we have shown elsewhere, we conceive of spiritual actions or passions in others only . . . ," sc. as we observe the effects of these in their physical behavior? If so, JE is most likely thinking of No. 333, where he uses as a premise the notion that we know of the existence and character of a human rational mind only through "the motions, behavior and speech of a body of a human form and contexture."

6. JE inserted this word in the heading after he had begun the entry, thus breaking into the first sentence. Cf. the first paragraph of the entry with *Justification by Faith Alone*, where JE seems to be attributing both of "these two opinions" to the Arminians (Worcester rev. ed., *4*, 101–02). On the Arminians, see above, pp. 12–13.

7. I.e. as those who hold the former opinion.

and explain themselves, that it is as obedience is a part of the reception of Christ and the gospel, as acts of evangelical obedience are acts of reception; why, it does not alter the case at all as to the doctrine of justification and free grace: there is nothing that it is worth the while in the least to controvert about.

475. SIN AGAINST THE HOLY GHOST. There seem to be three things essential to this sin, viz. conviction, malice and presumption (presumption in expressing that malice). Christ says (Matt. 12:31–32), "Blasphemy against the Holy Ghost shall not be forgiven unto men. And whosoever speaketh a word against the Son of man, it shall be forgiven him: but whosoever speaketh against the Holy Ghost, [it shall not be forgiven him], neither in this world, neither in the world to come." Here I would observe,

1. In order to a man's speaking against or reviling the Holy Ghost in the sense of this text, he must have some knowledge of him. If a man only hears the name "Holy Ghost," having no notion what is meant by it, and reviles he knows not what, he don't blaspheme the Holy Ghost in the sense of the text; or if he has only such a notion, that he is one of the persons in the Godhead, and speaks against him as he does against the other persons, having no notion in his mind of anything that is a distinction of nature or work. One man would not be said to blaspheme or revile another, if he spake against him having only heard his name, having no notion at the same time in his mind, of anything belonging to him that distinguished him from the rest of mankind; or to revile his person in particular, if he had no other notion of him than only of his being of such a company, if he has no notion in his mind, of anything that distinguishes his particular person that he expresses spite against. Therefore when men blaspheme the Holy Ghost, they express spite against something that they have an idea or notion of in their minds, that is particularly pertaining to and distinguishing of this divine Person.

Therefore I determine thus, that those that blaspheme the Holy Ghost unpardonably, they express their contumely and spite against the Holy Ghost with respect to those acts of his wherein consists his nature and office, viz. divine love, either expressing the love of God, or breathing love to God, or (which is the same thing) with respect to his gracious and holy acts. It is no matter whether they have a distinct notion of a person of the Holy Ghost, if they out of malice revile those things wherein his nature and work consists. The Pharisees out of malice reviled the Holy Ghost in his expressing the love and mercy of God to men, in casting out devils and delivering men from captivity to that cruel enemy—a gracious and glorious work, something of the same nature with his casting Satan out of men's souls, and an image of it. And we are not to understand it, as though Christ charged them with this sin merely because they reviled the Holy Ghost in this work, but in all his doctrine and works; they against conviction laid all those things in Christ that were the fruits of the Spirit, to the devil; they charged him with acting and being acted by an unclean spirit (Mark 3:30).

Christ, in mentioning the blasphemy against the Holy Ghost, has respect to their laying all that he did as acting by the Holy Ghost, to an unclean spirit; he has not only a respect to this particular instance of casting out devils, for they did not only mean that this, but that all was from the devil. He rather takes occasion to mention it now, because such a miracle was a powerful argument to convince them ("the people were all amazed, and said, Is not this the Son of David?" Matt. 12:23), and they were now convinced by the strength of it, as he saw who knew their thoughts (as it is said, v. 25); and they showed their conviction by what they said, as we observed before. The Pharisees did but repeat what they used to say, upon this occasion; they used to say, "He hath an unclean spirit," and that he had Beelzebub (Matt. 10:25), and 'tis this that Christ has respect to (as Mark 3:30). They repeat that now, with this addition, that the unclean spirit he had was the prince of 'em, to take off the objection [that anyone] did or might raise against them, "You say that he acts by the spirit of the devil; if so, how does he cast out devils out of others?" They answer, that the devil that he has is the chief of 'em, and by that he is able to cast out the rest.

2. In order to a man's blaspheming the Holy Ghost in the sense in which Christ speaks, his so doing must be attended with conviction; he must be sensible that he does it; he must be sensible that the thing he reviles is God's Spirit, or at least that it is from God. He must have conviction that God is God, and must have a malice against him, and must from malice against him express his contempt or despite of some gracious or holy spiritual operation of his; or, in a word, he must revile the grace of God that he has light to know is His. A man is not said to blaspheme or revile another in the sense that the expression is used in this text, if he don't know who he is: if a man meets another that is his father, and reviles him, he don't revile his father if he don't know that it is his father.

A man may have light sufficient to know a thing, and may inwardly and secretly be convinced, and yet his spite and malice may keep him from owning [of it], and keep him as it were from owning of it to himself. A man may have abundant evidence of some worthy qualification in another that he mortally hates, and may as it were keep from owning of it to himself, and yet indeed be inwardly sensible of it; but he does as it were willfully stop the mouth of his understanding, won't suffer it to speak out: so, I believe, it was with those Pharisees. That miserable, unreasonable shift of theirs, to take off the evidence of his miracles, seems to show that they were convinced, but were willfully resolved to object and not to own, viz. that he had one of the strongest of the devils in him, and so by him cast out the rest. See No. 707.[8]

3. By speaking against the Holy Ghost, I understand any way outwardly and presumptuously declaring malice by reproaching and blaspheming. A having malice inwardly is not sufficient, though it be against convictions of conscience. But when a person has with his malice also the presumption as to appear in it, [when] he has that spirit of contempt that he is not restrained by any fear or awe, but is so horribly daring as outwardly to express his malice by reproaching; then he commits the unpardonable sin against the Holy Ghost. Generally words and actions go together. See No. 703.[9]

4. The spite and malice that they do this from may be against God, or against the Son of God, or against the people of God. But it is not [just] any spite or malice against God, or the Son of God, or the people [of God], that, being declared, is the sin against the Holy Ghost; but their spite must be because of the Holy Ghost. If their spite is declared against God, it must be because of the gracious or holy breathings and operations of the Spirit that he is the author of; if it be against the Son of God, it must be because of what of the Holy Ghost appears in him, his holy doctrine, holy precepts, holy life, or what of the gracious or holy influences of the Holy Ghost come from him; or if it be against the people of God, it must be because of the Holy Ghost in them, their holy religion, [or] holy graces. Their spite and malice is evermore terminated upon the Holy Ghost, or the Holy Ghost is the foundation of their malice, and their spite and contumely: when it is declared, it must be declared against that or for that. They need not declare that their spite is for the Holy Ghost, but they must declare that it is for that

8. JE's cue mark indicates that No. 707 is to be added to No. 475 as a continuation of § 2.
9. JE's cue mark indicates that a block of text following No. 703 is to be added to No. 475 as a continuation of § 3.

which is indeed (and which they are convinced is) divine, the Holy Ghost.

For instance, if a man, when convinced, appears in avowed enmity against another for his holiness, his love to God, or his humility, [or] faith in Christ alone; if he openly appears in avowed hatred and contumely against him for those things, either by reproaching him for them or maliciously persecuting of him declaredly for those things: whether he will call them the Holy Ghost or no, yet if he is convinced that they are, or that they are divine things in him, he commits the unpardonable sin. The Pharisees, though they were inwardly convinced, yet had a mortal spite against Christ for his holy doctrine, and manner of life, and precepts and miracles, because they were so contrary to them; and therefore reproached them as though they were hellish and from the devil.

We have reason to think that conviction is one thing essential to this sin; for this is everywhere in Scripture spoken of, as a sin the more difficulty pardoned. Num. 15:29–30. Speaking there of the sacrifices that were to be offered for sins of ignorance, God says, "But the soul that doth aught presumptuously, whether born in the land or a stranger, the same reproacheth the Lord; and that soul shall be cut off from among his people." Luke 23:34, "Father, forgive them; for they know not what they do." I Tim. 1:13, "But I obtained mercy, because I did it ignorantly and in unbelief." So in the beginning of the 6th chapter to the Hebrews, speaking probably there of this unpardonable sin, and [in the] 10th chapter, the 26th verse.

Mr.[1] Baxter says, that it don't appear that the Pharisees were convinced.[2] But we have reason to think that many of them were convinced, by their behavior at other times as well as now. Particularly, by their behavior when the watch came and showed them of Christ's rising from the dead: their actions plainly showed that they believed

---

1. This paragraph is a later addition marked for insertion here; for its approximate date, see next footnote.

2. Richard Baxter expressed this opinion in *For Prevention of the Unpardonable Sin against the Holy Ghost* (London, 1655), which was published both separately and as one of four discourses issued under the title, *The Unreasonableness of Infidelity* (London, 1655). These discourses were printed in the second volume of Baxter's *Practical Works* (4 vols. London, 1707), which JE was reading in 1733 or 1734. The passage to which JE refers (pp. 324–25) falls in the middle of the tract on the unpardonable sin. Baxter's main effort in this piece was to refute what he called the common notion that the unpardonable sin of Matt. 12 is the malicious rejection of the "inward Illumination" of the Spirit; rather, it is the rejection of the "objective Testimony of the Spirit" to Christ and his teaching; this was the Pharisees' sin (*Practical Works*, 2, 307).

them; for they did not blame the watch at all, that they had not been faithful in watching and keeping the body of Jesus, but gave them large money to hire them to keep it secret, and invented a lie for 'em to tell, and told 'em they would plead their cause with the governor, and would persuade him and secure them (Matt. 28:11–14). By the 6th [chapter] of Hebrews it appears that 'tis against a great degree of light; and Heb. 10, 'tis said, if they sin willfully after they have received the knowledge of the truth.[3]

Here a question may arise, viz. why is this more unpardonable than to have a spite against and to blaspheme the divine Being in general, or either of the other persons of the Trinity? [I answer], if a man that was convinced of the being of a God, should blaspheme and reproach him, and charge him with folly, or with injustice and cruelty; or wickedness, that is not unpardonable. But he that blasphemes against the Holy Ghost willfully and maliciously reproaches that [which] should attract our love and win our hearts, viz. the beauty and grace of God; they are malicious against God for his love and loveliness; they are malicious against God's saving grace and presumptuously blaspheme it: wherefore God never will bestow it upon them. (See Nos. 703, 706.) When men blaspheme the Father or the Son and may be pardoned, they blaspheme him by denying that of him wherein the Holy Ghost consists, by denying goodness or holiness and attributing contrary qualities to him, or else by denying wisdom of them.

The Apostle says, "If we sin willfully after we have received the knowledge of the truth," etc. (Heb. 10:26). Now persons may be said to sin willfully in three senses: (1) As all sins are willful, even sins of ignorance; the actions are voluntary actions, and they spring from a depraved disposition or inclination. (2) When men know that acts are sins at the same time that their wills determine them, as a man may do when he is overpowered by a temptation, by fear, or some appetite. (3) When his will is determined to wickedness for opposition's sake, without any cause for it but a mere spite against, and contumacy towards that to which sin is the opposite, against true religion and its principles and exercises, or against the Holy Ghost in his actings and fruits; for the Holy Ghost is the opposite to sin. Verse 29, "He hath done despite to the Spirit of grace." This is to sin *sponte*, ἑκουσίως, or willingly in the sense of this text. They rebel for the sake of rebelling, oppose for the

---

3. JE added these texts from Hebrews about 1739 or 1740, apparently not noticing that he had already done so in what is now the preceding paragraph and had discussed Heb. 10:26 in the last paragraph of the entry.

sake of opposition, or (which is the same thing) out of spite to that which is opposed. See No. 703. See my description of this sin in my sermon on Cant. 4:8, in the application.[4]

476. CONVERSION. FAITH. As we do really depend upon Christ for salvation and all spiritual blessings; so, if ever we truly believe, we must *sensibly.*[5] We do really depend upon Christ; it would not be condecent and agreeable with God's excellency and glory to bestow them, but only for his sake. True faith is but a sensibleness of what is real in this matter of our redemption: we must see that it would not be condecent, not suiting with God's excellency, to bestow mercy upon us without Christ's mediation. This is seeing our necessity of a Savior, and being sensible that it will be consistent with condecency and excellency, to show mercy through his mediation; this is seeing the sufficiency of Christ.

I argue that this is necessary in true faith, because it is necessary in prayer. Christ has told us that whatsoever we ask the Father in his name shall be given us. Now by asking in Christ's name, nobody will suppose is meant our saying of it in words, that we ask in Christ's name or for his sake, but that it is something in [the] mind; that we really in our minds are sensible that it must be bestowed through him if at all, that we ben't fit for it any other way, and that through him it may be bestowed. That which is necessary in prayer is necessary in faith; for prayer is only the particular exercise and expression of our faith before God.

477. HAPPINESS OF HEAVEN. See notes on John 4:14.[6]

478. HELL TORMENTS may increase this way, viz. as the damned may

4. This sermon (dated Jan. 1737) has the doctrine, "Christ calls and invites souls that are under the most dark and dismal circumstances to look to him." After listing the reasons sinners may have for considering their case hopeless, JE comforts them with the thought that if they have never blasphemed against the Holy Ghost, they are still invited to look to Christ. His discussion of the characteristics of the unpardonable sin in the sermon closely parallels No. 475.

5. I.e. depend on Christ for salvation.

6. Commenting on the words "shall never thirst," JE proposes in this note several senses in which "spiritual joys and delights . . . are satisfying." This is the first "Miscellanies" reference to the "Blank Bible" that is not a later addition. The note seems to have been written at one sitting, except for two brief additions at the end, one from the latter 1730s and the other from the early 1750s. The ink and hand of the original note make it likely that it was written, at most, within a few months before No. 477.

have more and more of a sense of eternity. After they have endured misery a thousand years, they may have a more dreadful sense of an eternity of misery than they had at first.

479. WORK OF REDEMPTION. TYPES. Things even before the fall were types of things pertaining to the gospel redemption. The old creation, I believe, was a type of the new. God's causing light to shine out of darkness, is a type of his causing such spiritual light and glory by Jesus Christ to succeed, and to arise out of, the dreadful darkness of sin and misery. His bringing the world into such beautiful form out of a chaos without form and void, typifies his bringing the spiritual world to such divine excellency and beauty after the confusion, deformity and ruin of sin.[7]

480. HELL TORMENTS. See sermon on Is. 33:14;[8] see notes on Deut. 32:22.[9]

481. SPIRIT'S OPERATION. In grace not only consists the highest perfection and excellency, but the happiness of the creature: and therefore, although other things are bestowed on men by ordinary providence, that is, according to the fixed laws of the succession of events from preceding events or preceding human voluntary acts; yet this has God reserved to be bestowed by himself, according to his arbitrary will and pleasure, without any stated connection, according to fixed laws, with previous voluntary acts of men, or events in the series of natural things. Common benefits are as much immediately from God as men's highest perfection and happiness; i.e. one is as much by the direct present exercise of the power of God as the other. But there is this difference: common benefits are statedly connected with preceding things in the creature, so that they are in a sense depen-

7. JE began another sentence with "The tree of life in the midst of paradise typified Christ Jesus," then canceled it. The tree of life is not called a type of Christ in "Types of the Messiah" (No. 1069), "Images of Divine Things," or any of the relevant Scripture notes. Perhaps it is not a mere type, since it remains in the consummation of the new creation.

8. The doctrine of this sermon is, "Wicked men cannot bear the misery of damnation." In explaining this doctrine, JE states that "the misery will be so great that the soul shall perfectly sink under it. . . .God's mighty wrath will so weaken the soul that all the strength of it shall be utterly abolished, all power to act for himself or seek his own good." This sermon is not to be confused with another on the same text which JE wrote ten years later, in Dec. 1740, and which was published in 1788 (see Worcester rev. ed., *4*, 488–501).

9. From his exegesis of this verse, JE concludes that the "dolors and agonies" of death and the "horrors of the grave" are images of the misery and horrible darkness of hell.

dent on the creature; but this excellency and blessedness of the soul is connected only with the will of God, and is dependent on nothing else. As to the exercise of power, they are both alike immediately from God; the exercise of God's power does as immediately reach one effect as the other: but as to prerequisites, the one is not so immediate as the other; the creature after a certain manner is statedly prerequisite in one case, and not in the other. Other gifts are dependent in a sort on the creature, and are bestowed by the creature, because the perfection and happiness of the creature do not consist in them.

482. CONCERNING THE ECONOMY OF THE PERSONS OF THE TRINITY AND THE CHURCH'S COMMUNION WITH GOD. See Mastricht, Lib. II, cap. 24, § 11.[1]

483. RIGHTEOUSNESS AND SATISFACTION OF CHRIST. The divine excellency of Christ and the love of the Father to him, is the life and soul of all that Christ did and suffered in the work of redemption. Indeed, men have their sins pardoned for the sake of the divine excellency of Jesus Christ, and we are accepted into God's favor and have a title to eternal life for the sake of Christ, and because the Father infinitely loves him. Because of the infinite worthiness and excellency of Christ and his dearness to the Father, the Father is willing for his sake to accept of those that have deserved infinite ill at his hands. The excellency of the Son is so great that he is worthy of this, and God's love to his Son is great enough.

And the next thing that comes in consideration as the foundation of our acceptance, is Christ's love to us. If God accepts them for the sake of the worthiness and amiableness of Christ, and the infinite love that God has to him, it must be because of some friendship that Christ has for them and some love he has to them. Why should God be favorable to others for his sake, that he has no love to? And then again, it is not [just] any degree of love, but doubtless it must be a very great love of Christ to them that causes the Father to accept of them that have been infinitely odious and ill-deserving. If it be inquired how great a love it

1. In this chapter of the *Theoretico-practica theologia*, § 11, the Trinitarian "œconomia" is described after the analogy of a household: there is a "Pater-familias," a begetting and being begotten, and a common "emissarius"; there is the Father's love of and delight in the Son, the Son's honoring of the Father, and the Spirit's searching of the deep things of both and glorifying of both. Of particular interest to JE was Mastricht's representation of God as having taken up the church into the "communion" and "society" of this family (p. 238).

ought to be, in order to their being accepted for his sake, I answer: the love should be so great as to be justly looked upon [as] a thorough union with them, so great that Christ may justly be looked upon as making himself one with them, such a love as is thoroughly assuming them into union with himself.

If it be asked, how it shall be judged when love is sufficient for that, I answer: such a love as is sufficient to cause the lover to place himself in the beloved's stead for his sake in the most extreme case, and even in the case of [the] beloved's loss of his all, and his utter destruction. That love that is sufficient thus to unite the lover with the beloved in such a case, where the beloved's all is concerned, and in his utter destruction, ought to be looked upon as thoroughly uniting, or uniting to the utmost; for this is the utmost trial that there can be. That love that unites the lover with the beloved, or that is sufficient to put the lover in the beloved's stead, only in cases of loss of part of his welfare, or of partial destruction, is but a partial union of the lover with the beloved; but that love that is sufficient to put the lover in the beloved's stead even in the total loss of himself, and in his perfect destruction, that may be looked upon as perfectly or thoroughly uniting.

Again, when the lover's love is such that he sets a value upon the beloved's welfare or life equal to what he himself[2] doth, then the lover[3] by his love is thoroughly united to the beloved, and becomes as himself. But that lover that from love is not averse to bear the beloved's destruction for him (that is, his own suffering equivalent to it), that he may be free and may enjoy his welfare, he sets a value upon the beloved's welfare equal to what he doth himself. For the value that a person sets upon his own life or welfare is just exactly equal to the dread he has of his own destruction, and indeed they are the same thing. So that if it were possible, he would not be averse to suffer his own destruction, to purchase that welfare or life of which it is the destruction, if he had a perfect conception of both.

But here another question will arise, viz. how can it be a fit and becoming thing in Christ, thus to love and unite himself to those that are infinitely ill-deserving, and when justice requires that they be the objects of eternal hatred and indignation? Is not the thus taking their

2. Taking "himself" in this paragraph to refer to "the beloved."

3. MS: "beloved." If instead the next "beloved" is changed to "lover," we must take "himself" as referring to "the lover"; but in that case, "equal to what he himself doth" and its variant will mean, equal to the value the lover sets on his own life, which is less likely. JE's precise meaning is obscured by the shifting reference of "he" and "his," as well as by the error just noted.

part and uniting himself to them a making himself guilty of their sin? I answer, Christ does as it were hereby bring their guilt upon himself, but not in any blameable sense. It was not esteemed a fit thing for Christ thus by love to unite himself to such guilty ones, unless he had manifested a readiness to bear their guilt himself and suffer their punishment. It would have been a greatly countenancing of their wickedness; it would be a kind of taking their part against God. But now he shows that he does not countenance it; he acknowledges its infinite evil and ill desert, by his appearing ready to suffer the punishment deserved, himself. It was but fair, and what justice required, that seeing Christ would so unite himself by love to sinners that had deserved wrath, that they might be partakers of the Father's love to him and so they be screened and sheltered, that he himself should receive the Father's wrath to them. That love of Christ which united him to sinners, assumed their guilt upon himself. So that Christ's death and sufferings were absolutely necessary, in order [to] our being delivered from destruction for the sake of Christ's worthiness and excellency, and through the love of God to him that loved us.

And seeing that when Christ, in uniting himself to sinners, or assuming them by love into union with himself, he did not only seek that they might be restored to a state of indifference and probation, such a state as they were in before they fell, but that they should be brought to a sure title to the eternal life, such as they would have had [had they] acquitted themselves well in their probation, and had honored God's authority by a perfect obedience; therefore, it was judged meet that Christ himself should do that honor to God's authority, which God at first required of man as the condition of his having a title to eternal life. For this was the reason why God saw meet to place man at first in a state of trial, and not to give him a title to eternal life as soon as he had made him, because it was his will that man should first give honor to his authority by perfectly obeying his law; and therefore still it is God's will, that man should not have eternal life without this honor to his authority being done. It became Christ therefore, seeing he in assuming man to himself he bought a title to eternal life for him, that he himself should become subject to God's authority, should be in the form of a servant, that he might do that honor to God's authority by his obedience, the principal instance of which was his laying down his life in obedience to his Father. Christ having obeyed and given this honor and respect to God's authority, it is given for us.

Therefore the death of Christ was needful for our salvation upon three accounts, and influences in that affair three ways: (1) as it was a manifestation of the sufficient love to us, and his thorough uniting himself with us, which was necessary in order to our being accepted as in him, and upon his account, and for the sake of his excellency and dearness to the Father; (2) as it was necessary in order to the making expiation for sin; and (3) as it was the main instance of Christ's obedience.

484. WISDOM OF GOD IN THE WORK OF REDEMPTION. How a living a wicked life is inconsistent with the nature of justifying faith, or trusting in Christ for salvation. See sermon on Micah 3:11, together with note on Gal. 2:18.[4]

485. EXCOMMUNICATION. They that are regularly and justly excommunicated, they are bound in heaven; the wrath of God abides upon them. While they justly stand excommunicated, they ordinarily stand bound to damnation. I say ordinarily, because it is possible that the case may be so, that they may desire to do what is proper to be restored, and may not have opportunity. For we may take that, Matt. 16:19, "Whatsoever ye shall bind on earth shall be bound in heaven," etc. as an implicit declaration of Christ, that he never will suffer a truly godly man by his obstinacy justly to bring such a censure upon him, and that he never will give an excommunicate person repentance, except it be in that way of his using proper means to be restored. So that excommunication does as much mark out men as being in a damnable condition, as if it made them so.[5]

---

4. The doctrine of the sermon is, "A pretense of trusting in Christ is a vain pretense as long as men live wicked lives." JE's defense of this doctrine primarily consists in arguing that "a wicked life is inconsistent with the nature of true trusting in Christ." In commenting on the words, "the things which I destroyed" (Gal. 2:18), JE states, "He that truly believes in Christ . . . sees the evil of sin . . . but he that sees the evil of sin and its desert of hell, he destroys it, his heart is divorced from it." Both citations appear to have been written at the same time. The sermon must have been written shortly before No. 484 (judging by the ink) and therefore in late 1730; the note may have been also.

5. This is followed by a paragraph, probably incomplete, which is canceled by a vertical line near the left margin: "They are bound in heaven also in this, that 'tis God's manner to withhold all kindly influences of his Spirit in any other way, excepting only as setting in with the censure, and the judgments and frowns of heaven that accompany it, and those terrors and threatenings of the Word that belong to his case, to humble him and bring him to repentance. But God refuses to assist and bless him, or afford any kindly influences of his Spirit, in his prayers or any of his exercises of religion." The form of cancellation may indicate some reservation or desire for further consideration.

486. WISDOM OF GOD IN THE WORK OF REDEMPTION appearing in God's so ordering of it, that man should in everything be so absolutely, immediately and apparently dependent on God, so that God alone should be exalted. See sermon on I Cor. 1:29–31.[6]

487. INCARNATION OF THE SON OF GOD AND UNION OF THE TWO NATURES OF CHRIST. As the union of believers with Christ be by the indwelling of the Spirit of Christ in them, so it may be worthy to be considered, whether or no the union of the divine with the human nature of Christ ben't by the Spirit of the Logos dwelling in him after a peculiar manner and without measure. Perhaps there is no other way of God's dwelling in a creature but by his Spirit. The Spirit of Christ's dwelling in men causes an union, so that in many respects [they may be] looked upon as one: perhaps the Spirit of the Logos may dwell in a creature after such a manner, that that creature may become one person [with the Logos],[7] and may be looked upon as such and accepted as such.

There is a likeness between the union of the Logos with the man Christ Jesus and the union of Christ with the church, though there be in the former great peculiarities. Christ dwells in believers as his temple (I Cor. 3:16–17; II Cor. 6:16); the Logos dwells in the human nature of Christ as his tabernacle: therefore Christ is said to tabernacle among us, and this human nature is typified by the temple and tabernacle of old. Christ dwells in his church as in his body (Eph. 1:23); so the Logos dwelt in the human nature as in his body. Heb. 10:5, "A body hast thou prepared me." There is a likeness in the manner of God's dwelling in the man Christ, and in believers: God dwells in the man Christ, and in the rest of men of which he is the head, as in one body, one Christ, and one church. I Cor. 12:12, "For as the body is one, and has many members, and all the members of that one body, being many, are one body: so also is Christ." Only there is this difference, that God dwells in the man Christ as the head, and in us as the members, as the head is the seat of the soul after a peculiar manner; 'tis the proper seat of the soul; though the soul also dwells in the members, but 'tis by derivation from and participation with the head. So in Christ dwells all

6. This sermon was JE's first publication. He wrote it for his Northampton congregation probably during the winter or spring of 1731 and preached it in revised form to the Boston clergy on July 8, 1731; it was published as *God Glorified in the Work of Redemption* (Boston, 1731). As published, its doctrine is, "God is glorified in the work of redemption in this, that there appears in it so absolute and universal a dependence of the redeemed on him."

7. This or a similar expression appears again in the entry. The context shows that JE had in mind something like the phrase here inserted.

the fullness of the Godhead bodily, Col. 2:9 (the Holy Ghost is the fullness and riches of the Godhead); where I suppose the apostle Paul means the same thing as the apostle John, John 3:34, "For God giveth not the Spirit by measure unto him." And that fullness of the Godhead which the apostle Paul speaks of, I suppose to be the same with that fullness which John speaks of (John 1:16), as being that of which we receive; for God also dwells in us, as we are often told by the same apostle, and we are partakers of the divine nature (II Pet. 1:4); and believers also are filled with the fullness of God (Eph. 3:19), though it don't dwell in them bodily. And the way that we partake is no otherwise than by partaking of the Spirit of God; God dwells in us by his Spirit. See note on Eph. 1:22–23, no. 235 in book of notes.[8]

The man Christ is united to the Logos these two ways: first, by the respect which God hath to this human nature. God hath respect to this man and loveth him as his own Son; this man hath communion with the Logos, in the love which the Father hath to him as his only begotten Son. Now the love of God is the Holy Ghost. And secondly, by what is inherent in this man, whereby he becomes one person;[9] which is only by the communion of understanding and communion of will, inclination, spirit or temper.

'Tis not [just] any communion of understanding and will that makes the same person, but the communion of understanding is such that there is the same consciousness. Thus [1] the man Christ Jesus was conscious of the glory and blessedness the Logos had in the knowledge and enjoyment of the Father before the world was, as remembering of it (John 17:5). (2) He has the same spirit or disposition towards the Father; not as believers have a filial spirit, or spirit of children, but he has the Spirit of the only begotten of the Father. He is disposed towards the Father as being his own Father in the manner that he is the Father of the Logos, and is conscious of a respect in the Father to him as the only begotten Son; he hath the Spirit therefore in a peculiar and inconceivable manner, and not by measure. The Spirit therefore dwells in Jesus not as the Spirit of the Father, but as the Spirit of the Son. All divine communion, or communion of the creatures with God or with one another in God, seems to be by the Holy Ghost. 'Tis by this that believers have communion with Christ, and I suppose 'tis by this that the man Christ Jesus has communion with the eternal Logos. The

8. This citation is a later insert; it is written in the ink of the latter 1730s, as is the note itself. The note is in "Scripture" Bk. 1, and is printed in Dwight ed., 9, 527–28.

9. See above, n. 7.

Spirit of God is the bond of perfectness by which God, Jesus Christ, and the church are united together.

The man Jesus becomes one person[1] by a communion of knowledge and will; but as in believers all divine knowledge is by the Spirit—'tis by the Spirit that the knowledge of inspiration and prophecy is given, and 'tis by the Holy Ghost that the spiritual knowledge of all believers is given: "The Spirit searcheth all things, even the deep things of God" [I Cor. 2:10]—so, I suppose, 'tis by the Spirit that divine knowledge and consciousness is given to the man Jesus. And so, as 'tis by the Spirit of God that a divine temper is given to men and angels, so I suppose 'tis by the Spirit of the Logos that the man Jesus hath the spirit and temper of the only begotten Son of God.

Therefore I suppose the name of our Mediator, "Messiah," or "Christ," or "Anointed," signifies the union of the divine nature to the human. When Jesus is called Christ, or Anointed, it imports that he is a divine person and signifies the manner how he becomes so, viz. by the communication of the Spirit of God, the true oil which was poured upon him without measure. And I suppose that the union of the human with the divine nature was signified by the miraculous vision there was at Christ's baptism; and the Holy Ghost that descended on Christ from heaven as a dove, was the bond of union that in descending from the divine nature of Christ which was in heaven, on the human which was on earth, united earth with heaven. By this Holy Ghost's descending on Christ, was signified the same as by the voice, viz. that this was God's beloved Son. The Holy Ghost did not first descend on Christ at his baptism; Jesus was united to the divine nature before this. No, it first descended on him at his conception. Jesus was conceived by the power of the Holy [Ghost], so that he was anointed as united to the divine nature when he first began to be; by this the Logos was made flesh in the womb of the Virgin Mary.

Christ's anointing don't only mark out Christ as being our mediator, but 'tis his anointing that qualifies and fits him for the work of mediator; hence arises the value and efficacy of his sufferings and obedience. If he had not been anointed, they would not have availed; because if it had not been for this anointing with the Holy Ghost, he would not have been united to the divine nature.[2] 'Tis by the Holy Spirit that Christ is

1. Ibid.
2. MS adds: "and 'tis by the union of the human nature with the divine ~~from whence arises the value of Christ's sacrifice~~." JE transferred the canceled clause to the next sentence but one; he must have meant to delete the other clause also, but it is at the end of the preceding line on the MS and was probably passed by inadvertently.

the Son of God. Rom. 1:3–4, "Concerning his Son Jesus Christ, which was made of the seed of David according to the flesh; and declared to be the Son of God with power, according to the Spirit of holiness." Hence arises the value of Christ's sacrifice. Heb. 9:14, "How much more shall the blood of Christ, who through the eternal Spirit offered himself without spot to God, purge your consciences from dead works." It was by virtue of this anointing, his thus having the Spirit, that he was accepted and justified as our mediator. I Tim. 3:16, "Justified in the Spirit." And therefore, the same Holy Ghost by which he was begotten in the womb of the Virgin Mary, was that by which he was begotten again from the dead in the womb of the earth. I Pet. 3:18, "Put to death in the flesh, quickened by the Spirit."

The[3] same Spirit begat Christ in the grave, that begat him in his mother's womb. (The mother's womb is compared to the lower parts of the earth in Ps. [139:15], and Christ's resurrection is called his being begotten [Rev. 1:5]).[4] And without doubt, both these begettings were by the same Spirit. And therefore that Spirit that is spoken of, by which Christ was raised, was without doubt the Holy Ghost, and not the divine Logos as is generally supposed. 'Tis given as a reason in Rom. 8:11, why believers should be raised from the dead, that the Spirit of him that raised up Christ from the dead dwells in them; they have an immortal, vivifying Spirit dwelling in them. 'Tis said, that God will quicken their mortal bodies by his Spirit that dwelleth in them; and without doubt God raised up Christ by the same Spirit. And this also was the reason why Christ was raised, and why it was impossible he should be detained in the grave: because that Spirit of God did in such a manner dwell in his human nature, viz. so as to cause a personal union between him and the Godhead.

This was that Spirit by which not only Christ offered up himself in sacrifice, but it was the Spirit by which he did all he did when on earth: it was by the Spirit that he taught, it was by this Spirit that he cast out devils, it was by this Spirit that he wrought all his miracles; this Spirit they called Beelzebub.

If 'tis by the Spirit of God that the human nature of Christ was conceived, and had life and being, why should we not suppose that 'tis also by the Spirit that he has union with the divine nature? The principal objection that I can think of against it, is that thus the union of the

---

3. This paragraph occurs between Nos. 492 and 493; it was probably written in the latter 1730s.

4. JE may also have had in mind Col. 1:18. Here and in the previous reference, he left space but never completed the citation.

human nature with the Holy Ghost will be nearer than with the Son of God, because 'tis more immediate, and so he should rather be the same person with the Holy Ghost than with the Son. But this objection is without substance, for the union we speak of is not an union of contact or influence, but a personal union. Christ may be by the indwelling and influence of the Holy Ghost personally united[5] to the Son of God, and yet not be personally united to the Holy Ghost, through whose indwelling and influence it[6] is. Believers are united to the person of Christ as their head by the indwelling of the Spirit; but it don't therefore follow, that they are more nearly united to the person of the Holy Ghost as their head. As it can't be argued that the Holy Ghost is rather the father of the man Jesus than God the Father because 'twas most immediately by the Holy Ghost that he was begotten in the womb of the Virgin; so neither can it be argued that Jesus is rather the same person with the Holy Ghost than with the Son because 'tis by the Holy Ghost that he is united to God.

In Jesus who dwelt here upon earth, there was immediately only these two things: there was the flesh, or the human nature; and there was the Spirit of holiness, or the eternal Spirit, by which he was united to the Logos. Jesus who dwelt among us, was as it were compounded of these two; the one from the earth, which he received of the Virgin Mary, the other from heaven, which descended on the Virgin at his conception. See Nos. 513 and 624.

488. CONDITION OF SALVATION, UNIVERSAL AND PERSEVERING OBEDIENCE. See No. 412.[7] Universal and persevering obedience is as directly proposed to be sought and endeavored by us, in Scripture, as necessary to salvation [and] as the condition of our salvation, as faith in Jesus Christ; and a wicked man may properly be exhorted directly to strive to break off his sins and resist his temptations, and to bring himself to a thorough willingness, and fixed resolution and disposition of mind, utterly to have done with gratifying his lusts, or allowing himself in any way of sin; with that to enforce it, that if he doth, he shall have eternal life. And he would do prudently, and according to the direction of God's Word, in directly attempting of it and immediately

5. While composing No. 487 JE wrote Nos. 488, 489, and probably 490 on a fresh sheet. At this point the space he had reserved proved insufficient, and he concluded the entry in spaces still available after Nos. 488 and 489.
6. I.e. the union.
7. Above, No. 412, p. 472, n. 2.

setting about [it], in beginning to deny himself, and resolutely resisting the temptations as they come. For although he never will come to such a fixed sincere resolution and real disposition of mind, utterly and finally to forsake sin, without regeneration and faith in Jesus Christ and a true principle of love to him; yet if a man from fear and conscience sets himself to strive against sin, and restrains his sin in times of notable temptations, and goes on in such a way, that is the way to obtain regeneration. 'Tis God's manner to give his Spirit in a way of earnest striving, and upon acts of notable self-denial, especially if repeated and continued in. God is wont in this way to give men such a knowledge and sense of divine things, as enables men to come to a thorough disposition utterly to forsake sin. See No. 415.

489. FAITH, OR SPIRITUAL KNOWLEDGE. Preamble to the Discourse on Faith, or Spiritual Knowledge.[8] There are these two ways, in which the mind may be said to be sensible that anything is good or excellent: (1) When the mind judges that anything is good or excellent, as by the agreement of mankind is called good or excellent, viz. that which is most to general advantage, and that between which and reward there is a suitableness, or that which is agreeable to the law of the country or law of God. 'Tis a being merely convinced in judgment that a thing is, according to the meaning of the word, "good," as the word is generally applied. (2) The mind is sensible of good in another sense, when it is so sensible of the beauty and amiableness of the thing, that 'tis sensible of pleasure and delight in the presence of the idea of it. This kind of sensibleness of good carries in it an act of the will, or inclination, or spirit of the mind, as well as the understanding.

490. SOVEREIGNTY OF GOD. If God has not a right of sovereign and arbitrary determining in such cases as these, viz. whether man shall fall or no, what sins a man shall and what he shall not commit, who shall be

8. JE originally wrote this title as "FAITH. Preamble to the Discourse on Faith," meaning the treatise for which he was gathering material in the notebook on faith. His sermon on Matt. 16:17, dated Aug. 1733, was published as *A Divine and Supernatural Light* (Boston, 1734). When he revised the sermon for publication, JE incorporated No. 489 into the first main division of the doctrine (cf. Worcester rev. ed., *4*, 442). The sermon MS has a large *E* to indicate the place where the new material was to be inserted, but the MS of the insert is missing. However, a scrap leaf inserted into the May 1734 sermon on Prov. 24:13–14 contains the canceled right-hand portion of two paragraphs; the second of these is a slightly revised version of No. 489. These two paragraphs are woven together in the printed sermon. The words, "or spiritual knowledge" were added to No. 489 sometime between its composition and JE's decision to use the entry in the sermon.

converted and saved and who shall be left to perish, it can be for no reason but this, that an absolute determination on one part would be injurious to the creature; and so God can't be left at liberty to determine either way, because he is bound, in justice to the creature, not to determine one of the ways. As for instance, that an absolute determining that man should fall, or a determining that a man shall be left to perish, would be injurious to the creature; and therefore that God is obliged either not to intermeddle in the affair, but leave the thing to fall out as shall happen; or if he does intermeddle and determine at all, he is obliged to determine the other way, viz. that man shall not fall, and that man if he be fallen shall be saved, and that such and such sins shall not be committed.

But[9] this seems to me to be reasonable, viz. that in all those things in which God is not obliged, in justice to the creature, to intermeddle in determining, but might for matter of obligation to the creature leave to fall out as they would, and which if God did not intermeddle in determining them, the determination of them would be left to mere chance (by being left to mere chance, I mean being left to be determined by those causes that are blind, undesigning and involuntary, supposing that such a thing were possible); in all such things God has a right to determine, and is sovereign and arbitrary in determining, for this reason: because 'tis much better that the determination should be left to the good pleasure of an infinitely wise being, than to blind causes (which, though blind, are as certain and necessary in obtaining a particular effect, as seeing and designing causes). Because in all events there is a better and a worse, one event an infinite wisdom may see to be better, and to suit better in the universality of things, and to be of better consequences, viewing those consequences universally, that is, beholding all things together that it ever will be the occasion of: but chance judges not of better or worse.

Thus for instance, God is arbitrary in determining whether man shall fall or no. Because, first, God is not obliged in justice to man, to determine that man surely shall not fall. Because if he [is] obliged to determine that, that no creature shall sin, then there can be no such thing as a trial: for there can reasonably be no such thing as any threatening of punishment; for [since] there is no possibility of punishment, there can be no such thing as fear of God's anger. Indeed,

9. This paragraph originally stood at the beginning of the entry; JE moved it by copying it almost verbatim, rather than by supplying cue symbols, probably because it was badly marked up during composition.

there can reasonably be no such thing as any law or commands, with enforcements of promises and threatenings. And [secondly], it will be left to mere chance, if God don't determine. For though man's will has to do in determining man's act, yet 'tis chance that determines man's will; if one motion of the will determines another, yet 'tis chance that determines the first motion. But 'tis not fit that such a matter[1] should be left to be determined by chance, because the determination is doubtless of great consequence in the universality of things. Therefore, God has a right to determine either way as he will. And so it might easily be shown, that God has a sovereign right of determining in those other things that were mentioned.

491. MISERY OF THE DAMNED. Moses says (Ps. 90:11), "According to thy fear, so is thy wrath"; that is, God's wrath is dreadful according as God's majesty is great and awful. Whence we may gather two things: first, that the wrath of God is dreadful according to the greatness and highness of God as he is in himself, that is, that it is infinitely dreadful, as it[2] is, in that it is eternal; second, that the present misery of those that bear the wrath of God is so great, or their misery is intensively so great, as to be in a proportion to the discoveries and manifestations that are made of his majesty; so that they that behold both may see a proportion. 'Tis fit there should be a visible proportion, for therein consists much of the majesty of God, viz. in his terribleness. 'Tis fit that those in heaven, that see the awfulness of God's majesty, as it is manifested immediately to their minds or when they consider it in his works, should see answerable proportionable discoveries of it in the misery of those that bear his wrath; and this they can't do unless their present misery is in proportion.

If you [ask], why not? why can't they have such a conception of the dreadfulness of a future eternity of sufferings that the discovery of God's dreadfulness in his wrath to their conception shall be in proportion, though the present misery be not? I answer, that the conceptions of the damned themselves, of the dreadfulness of future misery, are doubtless as strong as the spectators'; and their present misery will be proportionably great to what conception they have of that: the appearance of the dreadfulness of God's wrath to them is doubtless as great as to spectators; but their present misery is great in proportion to that appearance. And therefore, if the appearance of the dreadfulness of

1. I.e. as the fall of man.
2. I.e. the greatness and highness of God.

God's wrath to the spectators be in proportion to the appearance of divine majesty other ways, then also is the present misery of the damned in that proportion.

As the majesty of God is in itself infinite, so the calamity of being the object of his wrath is in itself infinite; and as the majesty of God in its manifestations, or the visible majesty of God, [is] exceeding great, so the calamity of being subject to the wrath of God is visibly great, or, the visible calamity of it is great in proportion. But so great as the visible calamity is, so great is their present calamity; for what is visible to others is visible to them, and proportionably as their own case now appears dreadful to them is their present suffering. Indeed the present misery of the damned is not in proportion to what they conclude in reason of the dreadfulness of their case, but in proportion to the mind's sense of it. So neither do I mean, that the discoveries of the majesty of God are proportionable to what may be argued from those things in which it appears, but proportionable to what they tend immediately to suggest to the mind, according to the awful sense and dread it tends to impress upon the mind; so that as Moses says, "According to thy fear, so is thy wrath."

When the majesty of God is beheld, the appearances of it naturally suggest to the mind, that it would be a dreadful thing to offend him. God's majesty is the same with his terribleness, or is the language of his great and glorious attributes, whereby they declare how terrible his displeasure is, and is deserved [to be], against those that offend him. Those, therefore, that see this majesty and hear this language, when they turn their eyes to those that do suffer his wrath they will see a misery proportionable.[3] And if we consider how great the manifestations of God's majesty are in his various works of creation and providence, and what we may reasonably conclude they will be in heaven, how dreadful doth this argue that the misery of the damned is.(See No. 493.)[4] See No. 866.

Some may be ready to think, that it's incredible that God should bring miseries upon a creature that are so extreme and amazing, and also eternal and desperate. But the dreadfulness and extremity of it is no argument against it; for those that are damned are entirely lost and utterly thrown away by God as to any sort of regard that he has to their

3. The following sentence occurs in the MS at the end of the second paragraph. JE skipped it when indicating the order of the paragraphs and forgot to mark its new position. This seems to be the most appropriate place for it.

4. JE's cue mark identifies the place in No. 491 to which No. 493 is related.

welfare. Their very existence is for nothing else but to suffer; the wicked are "made . . . for the day of evil" [Prov. 16:4]; they are, on purpose that God may show the dreadfulness of his wrath upon them. So that for matter of any pity in God towards [them], or any regard that he has to their welfare, a misery of a million degrees is as credible as one of ten degrees. Indeed, God will have a strict regard to justice in the degree of their punishment; but who can tell how great a punishment the sins of men do deserve?

492. CHRISTIAN RELIGION. This in addition to No. 350. If there were no revelation, we should be miserably in the dark after what manner to pray to God (if that was determined, that we should pray to him), whether or no it was acceptable to him, to commend and praise him in our prayers. We should be at a loss about the punishment that is due for sin; there would be no end to doubts about the degree of punishment, and who are liable to punishment, whether children, whether heathen.

493. MISERY OF THE DAMNED. See No. 491.[5] The discoveries of God's majesty are two ways. (1) Immediately by intuition. The manifestations of God's majesty in heaven, and at the day of judgment, and in many of his works, as thunder and earthquakes, etc., tend immediately to impress the mind with a sense of majesty, without any reasoning or reflection. And (2) by reflection. The saints in heaven will have a sense of exceeding majesty immediately impressed, but they will have more[6] by reflecting and reasoning from God's works; and the more they consider, the more sensible they will be of the infinite majesty of God.

So likewise, the sense they will have of the calamity of the damned will be either by intuition, the impression they will have by mere beholding their present misery, and that sense of eternity that immediately occurs and goes along with it, without reflection; or that which they will have by reflection, or by dwelling upon the consideration of the eternity of their punishment. I suppose their intuitive view of the torment of the damned, or what they will immediately have by only seeing that misery without reflection, will give a sense of dreadfulness proportionable to the immediate discoveries of the majesty of God in other ways. See Nos. 505 and 545.

5. Above, No. 491, p. 536, n. 4.
6. I.e. in addition, not by comparison.

494. FREE GRACE. The freedom of gospel grace is ordinarily explained thus, that the blessing is bestowed only for accepting. But 'tis sometimes in the Word of God expressed by its being bestowed only for seeking or asking: "Seek, and ye shall find; ask, and [ye shall] receive; knock, and it shall be opened unto you" [Matt. 7:7]. There is both a seeking and accepting implied in the nature of faith. The thing, in short, that God has respect to, is the disposition of a receiver; which consists in the receiver's being so disposed, that the gift should be acceptable to him, that he should be disposed to receive it of the giver and to acknowledge his dependence on him and his bounty for it; that there should be a suitableness between the gift, or thing given, and the subject, which appears in the acceptableness of the thing given; and suitableness between the grace of the gift, or the quality of the action of giving as in the giver, and the subject, which appears in a disposition to acknowledge freeness and absolute dependence: which is shown by seeking, asking, trusting, etc. Herein, therefore, lies the difference between the first and the second covenant. According to the first covenant, the blessing would have been bestowed as a manifestation of God's love of the excellency of the subject; now, it is given to this rather than that, because the subject hath the disposition and spirit of a receiver with respect to such a gift of God. See Treatise of Faith, p. 13.[7]

495. LORD'S DAY. It was most meet that the day should be changed, to show that the cause that was now given for the keeping a sabbath, viz. the resurrection of Christ and the accomplishment of the work of redemption, far outweighed all events that had preceded, in commemoration of which the sabbath had been kept. By this change it is testified, this was sufficient to supersede all the rest; this was so much more worthy that a weekly sabbath should be kept from respect to it, that all that had gone before was not accounted worthy to be had in consideration with [it]. This therefore determines the time, without any respect to the times that had been determined by former events.

496. CHRIST'S RIGHTEOUSNESS. All the obedience which Christ performed as standing in man's stead and representing man, is accepted

7. On pp. 13–14 of the notebook "Faith" is a short essay in proof of the proposition, "Faith is that inward sense and act, of which prayer is the expression" (printed as § 43 in Worcester rev. ed., 2, 613–14). It was probably written in the mid-1730s.

for man. But all the obedience that Christ performed as mediator, his coming into the world when sent, his delivering those doctrines and doing those miracles which the Father commanded him, and his laying down his life, and whatever else he performed as mediator, he performed as representing man; for it was by this means that he came to be subject to the Father's command, that he took on him the office of mediator, and thereby put himself in man's stead. Though he was in himself equal with God, yet placing himself as the representative of a creature, he became subject to the Father as a creature; and God commanded him and exercised authority over him as if he had been that creature: and therefore, whatever he did in obedience and subjection to that authority, which he was under as representing that creature, was properly accepted for that creature.

After[8] Christ had once placed himself in man's stead, or stood forth as man's representative, all which he did by taking upon himself the character of mediator, all the excellency that was seen in him in that character, or all his mediatorial excellency, was properly and fitly accepted for man; or rather, was fitly accepted for Christ mystical, that is, for Christ himself and for all his: whatever he did as mediator, he did as representing the whole body, head and members. Christ's excellency as mediator was his excellency as head of this body, and was rewarded in both head and members. When Christ took upon him to be mediator, or man's representative, he then was as it were out of God's favor; because he represented man who was so, and he made the offer of doing whatever God would have him do, and suffering whatever he would have him suffer. It was as if it had been possible for man himself to have made such an offer for himself; and then whatever excellency had been seen in man worthy to be accepted in anything that he did or suffered, it would doubtless have been fit to [be] accepted for himself. And therefore, why is not any excellency that is seen in man's representative, in anything that he does or suffers, accepted for him?

497. CHRIST'S RIGHTEOUSNESS. We are saved by Christ's death as much as it was an act of obedience, as it was a propitiation. For as it was not the only act of obedience that merited, so neither was it the only suffering that was propitiatory: all his sufferings from the beginning

8. JE wrote this paragraph as an addition to No. 496 immediately after No. 497, probably at a new sitting but before the writing of No. 498; see the next footnote.

were propitiatory, as every act of obedience was meritorious. Indeed this was his principal suffering, and it was as much his principal act of obedience. Heb. 5:8, "Yet learned he obedience by the things that he suffered." John 18:11, "The cup which my Father hath given me, shall I not drink?"

Worthiness of Christ's obedience: see sermon on John 15:10, last use.[9]

498. COVENANT OF GRACE. FREE GRACE. CONDITION OF SALVATION. Christ now stands instead of that tree of life that grew in the garden of Eden. Man, if he had finished his obedience, was upon that to be called and invited by God to eat of the tree of life, that he might live forever. He was not immediately invited to that when he was first created, but he was first to obey; he was to perform the term of obedience, and after that was to be invited freely, without any remaining terms yet to be fulfilled, but only to come, and take and eat. Christ now stands as the tree of life did in paradise, and we stand as man would after he should have finished his righteousness: we are immediately invited and called to Christ, to come to him, to take and eat, without any other terms, because the condition of righteousness is fulfilled already by our surety.

499. HADES. SEPARATE SPIRITS. HEAVEN. HELL. Our first parents enjoyed great happiness; they dwelt in a paradise, and there had a confluence of spiritual and outward blessings and delights, before they had so much as performed the condition of eternal happiness, or had had a trial for it. It need not therefore be wondered at, that the separate spirits of saints should be in a very happy state before they are judged at the last judgment, and that the wicked should be very miserable.

500. LORD'S DAY. The sabbath of rest is typical of the great sabbath of the world after the sixth thousand years, when the spiritual, or first, resurrection of the church shall begin, and of the eternal sabbath or rest of the church after the second resurrection, of bodies. But how

9. The doctrine of the sermon on John 15:10 is, "Jesus Christ kept all his Father's commandments." The original entry of No. 496 has material in common with both main doctrinal divisions of the sermon, and the first paragraph of No. 497 also parallels a portion of the sermon. These entries seem to be based on the sermon rather than vice versa, but the entries and the sermon are nearly contemporaneous and can probably be placed in the late spring of 1731 (above, p. 88).

fitly is this kept on the day of Christ's rest and resurrection, who is the head of the church, who shall then rise and rest, and is in rising and resting the earnest of the whole church's both first and second resurrection: "Christ the firstfruits, and afterwards those that are Christ's at his coming" [I Cor. 15:23].

APPENDIXES

APPENDIX A

PREVIOUS PUBLICATION OF THE "MISCELLANIES"

By his will, probated on May 13, 1758, Edwards bequeathed his manuscripts to his wife, Sarah, whom he also appointed his executrix. The inventory of his estate listed, of his manuscripts, only 1074 sermons and the larger notebooks: fifteen volumes of folios and fifteen of quartos; of these, eight folios (if the Table is included) and two quartos probably belonged to the "Miscellanies."[1]

Sarah immediately placed the manuscripts in Samuel Hopkins' hands with the request that he publish some of them and write a biography of Edwards. In the biography that he published in 1765, Hopkins described how Edwards had organized his "miscellaneous writings," obviously meaning the "Miscellanies," then added, "There might be a number of volumes published from his manuscripts, which would afford a great deal of new light and entertainment to the church of Christ: tho' they would be more imperfect, than if he himself had prepar'd them for publick view."[2]

Sarah Edwards died on October 2, 1758. In 1767, following the provisions of Sarah's will, the Edwards children formally committed the manuscripts to the custody of Jonathan Edwards, Jr., the only one of the three sons to pursue a ministerial career, along with responsibility for seeing to their publication.[3] From both sides of the Atlantic the new literary executor received encouragement to publish not only sermons but also extracts from the "Miscellanies."[4] He began with the

1. "Jonathan Edwards' Last Will, and the Inventory of His Estate," *Bibliotheca Sacra, 33* (1876), 441, 446.

2. Hopkins, *Life and Character,* p. 83.

3. Her will stipulated that the manuscripts were to be "put into the hands of some one of my family; which one shall be agreed upon by my children," but—in a far-seeing provision—that ownership should continue to reside in all the children and their heirs ("Copyright of President Edwards' Works," *New England Puritan, 4* [Nov. 4, 1843], p. [2]). The document itself, dated Mar. 27, 1767, is in the Beinecke Library.

4. One English correspondent offered, should he die without heir, to leave everything to be used for publishing JE's MSS. "Surely," he added, "there is an increasing taste for his

sermons, but the project was cut short by the Revolutionary War and the economic distress that followed it.

In 1788 a volume of Edwards' *Practical Sermons* appeared at Edinburgh. In its prefatory "Advertisement" Jonathan, Jr., wrote,

> As to the manuscripts of my father, his Miscellanies are the most complete and important. They contain his Thoughts on the various doctrines of Theology; and what is written on any doctrine is kept distinct, though written at different times, and interspersed through one thousand pages. These distinct essays may be collected under their proper heads, and would afford great pleasure and improvement to all who have a taste for his writings. Perhaps enough out of these Miscellanies may be collected to fill three such volumes as that on the "Freedom of the Will." Nor is any thing wanting to the publication of them, but a prospect of their sale.

The response to this overture was evidently encouraging, for during the next decade he and John Erskine, his editor in Scotland, produced two volumes of extracts, chiefly from the "Miscellanies." *Miscellaneous Observations on Important Theological Subjects* appeared at Edinburgh in 1793 and *Remarks on Important Theological Controversies* in 1796.[5]

In a severely abbreviated and rearranged form, these two collections were included in the first edition of *The Works of President Edwards*, which was published in eight volumes at Leeds, England, between 1806 and 1811.[6] The first American edition of the *Works*, also in eight volumes, appeared at Worcester, Massachusetts, in 1808–1809;

---

writings and I cannot but hope his Miscellanies might be printed with a great prospect of a good sale" (letter of John Ryland of Northampton, England, June 29, 1787 [Beinecke Library]). I am indebted to Kenneth Minkema for this reference.

5. JE, Jr. was fairly accurate in his transcriptions and faithful to his father's text except for a few alterations in grammar and style, rearrangements, and omissions within entries. He also collected the materials under various doctrinal heads (though generally in chronological order), removed the original entry numbers from miscellanies and other sources, and numbered them as sections in each chapter. Only essays that directly addressed the controversies of the day were selected, with the result that JE was presented only as an orthodox rationalist, with scarcely a hint of other aspects of his thought that are to be found in the "Miscellanies."

6. Ed. Edward Williams and Edward Parsons. Both collections were printed in Vol. 8; the excisions were mainly of JE's extracts from other authors, but the remaining text was often extensively rearranged. In 1817 this set was reissued at London with some new matter in Vols. 4 and 5; the type for the selections in Vol. 8 was reset but only accidentals were changed. This edition (sometimes called the London ed.) was photographically reprinted with two extra volumes of material taken from the Dwight ed. in 1968 (10 vols. New York, Burt Franklin).

it contained parts 2 and 3 of *Miscellaneous Observations* and three chapters of *Remarks*.[7] The Worcester edition was reprinted in four volumes at New York in 1843. The editors retained Austin's selections and added the other four chapters of *Remarks* from the 1796 edition without further omissions.[8] With the exception of *Miscellaneous Observations*, part 1 (which it did not reprint), and the omissions in the three chapters of *Remarks* taken from the former printing, the Worcester revised edition is the most accurate and most complete reproduction available today of the two 1790s volumes.

The next collected edition of Edwards' works was prepared by his great-grandson, Sereno E. Dwight.[9] Dwight had come into possession of the manuscripts through his father, President Timothy Dwight of Yale, who had received them after the death of Jonathan Edwards, Jr., with the intention (never fulfilled) of writing a new biography of Edwards. In his seventh volume Dwight used the 1817 Leeds edition of *Miscellaneous Observations* but for the *Remarks* drew on not only the Leeds and Worcester editions but the 1796 edition as well.[1] Dwight intended to publish all the "Miscellanies" that had not been included in the Edinburgh volumes. To this end he organized the entries under the traditional doctrinal heads and commissioned a scribe to copy the texts according to that arrangement. However, the only new "Miscellanies" text he succeeded in publishing was the long essay on "Types of the Messiah" (No. 1069) and a set of 93 entries on angels, devils, heaven, and related topics.[2]

7. The editor, Samuel Austin, used the original editions of both volumes but slightly abridged the text of the chapters from *Remarks*. He also scattered the selections in three volumes.

8. This 4-vol. "reprint," really a new edition, was reissued several times in the 19th century. It is cited here as the Worcester rev. ed.

9. 10 vols. New York, 1829. Dwight's biography of JE occupied the first volume.

1. In 1829 Dwight was content to reprint the Leeds rev. ed. of both Edinburgh volumes. Subsequently, however, he became dissatisfied with the Leeds edition of *Remarks* and reissued Vol. 7 in a variant form, in which the reprint of Leeds stops at the end of the second chapter. The new chapters 3, 4, and 7 he reprinted from the Worcester edition. Chapters 5 and 6 were not at that time in that edition; Dwight omitted chapter 5 but reprinted chapter 6—oddly enough, from the 1796 edition.

2. The main series of transcriptions from the "Miscellanies," amounting to 1646 pages, are in the Trask Library, along with other sets of copies prepared for Dwight or for JE, Jr. No. 1069 will be found in Vol. 9 and the collection of shorter entries in Vol. 8 of his edition. Unlike JE, Jr., Dwight did all his correcting and editing on the transcriptions rather than on the autographs. All too often he substituted editorial emendation for careful study of difficult passages, and sometimes he dealt with a particularly difficult passage by the simple expedient of deleting it, of course without annotation. Dwight was also a mild bowdlerizer, making emendations for the purpose of "improving" JE's style. Nevertheless, he produced

The last collected edition in the nineteenth century was in two large quarto volumes and was published at London in 1834.[3] All the materials from the "Miscellanies" are contained in its second volume and were apparently all taken from the Leeds and Dwight editions.[4]

In 1847 Sereno Dwight, at the behest of the surviving grandchildren, turned over most of the manuscripts to Tryon Edwards, grandson of Jonathan Edwards, Jr., and minister at New London, Connecticut. In the early 1850s a Scottish publisher became interested in a new edition of Edwards' works, in the preparation of which Tryon Edwards, William T. Dwight (Sereno's brother), and Edwards A. Park, professor at Andover Seminary, were to collaborate. The publishing firm failed, however, and the project came to nothing. Probably in the late 1860s Tryon Edwards turned over the manuscript collection to Park, with whom it remained until Park's death at the end of the century, when the surviving great-grandchildren agreed to deposit it at Yale. Meanwhile, Sereno Dwight had died in 1850, and his papers, which included not only the copies he had made but also some of Edwards' autographs, came to his brother William. Dwight's daughter married Egbert C. Smyth, also a professor at Andover, with the result that by the 1870s both collections were at Andover, though in different hands.

The next publication from the "Miscellanies" came about as the result of aspersions cast on Edwards' orthodoxy with respect to the doctrine of the Trinity. In 1851 Horace Bushnell (himself under suspicion of heresy on the same subject) announced that he had recently learned of the existence of an Edwards manuscript containing an "*a priori* argument for the Trinity," the publication of which "would excite a good deal of surprise." He had been denied access to it, he said,

---

text that was on the whole as good as that of JE, Jr., and he did it without spoiling the autograph for subsequent readers.

3. *The Works . . . with an Essay . . . by Henry Rogers and a Memoir by Sereno E. Dwight.* It was reprinted at least nine times in London during the 19th century, with a New York issue in 1835 (which, however, omitted *Remarks* and the MS material first edited by Dwight). It has more recently been photographically reprinted by Banner of Truth Trust (2 vols. Edinburgh and Carlisle, Pa., 1974–75).

4. *Miscellaneous Observations* and the first two chapters of *Remarks* were reprinted directly from the Leeds ed., not from Dwight's reprint. Beginning at ch. 3 of *Remarks*, Dwight's *variant* text was used; but for ch. 5, which Dwight had omitted in his later version, the editor returned to the Leeds ed. and placed the chapter at the end of *Remarks*. Hence the chapter numbers are confused in the 1834 edition: the original chs. 5–7 are numbered 4–6 and the original ch. 5 is numbered 7.

on the ground of "the nature of the contents."[5] Rumors began to fly that Edwards had lapsed into Arianism, Sabellianism, even Pelagianism. Finally, in 1880, Oliver Wendell Holmes and several other prominent writers publicly challenged Edwards' literary executors to clear his name by publishing the suspected document.[6]

In response, Egbert Smyth published "Miscellanies" No. 1062 from the transcript in his possession, under the title *Observations Concerning the Scripture Œconomy of the Trinity and Covenant of Redemption.*[7] Smyth believed this to be the treatise under discussion since Jonathan Edwards, Jr., had withheld it from publication, but he could think of no theological reason for this hesitation, there being no noticeable heterodoxy in it. In an appendix to the volume Smyth published fifteen other miscellanies (some only partially), including Nos. 108 and 112 on "The Excellency of Christ."

Meanwhile Park was preparing an answer, which appeared early in 1881 as a long two-part article.[8] Park admitted the existence of an essay on the Trinity other than that published by Smyth but confessed that he had mislaid it. He did, however, include three miscellanies in which Edwards had made excerpts from statements by A. M. Ramsay on the Trinity, arguing that since these were orthodox and Edwards did not register any objection, he must have agreed with them.[9] The missing treatise eventually turned up, and after Park's death it was published by George P. Fisher, who could find no grounds for disputing its orthodoxy.[1]

On three other occasions Smyth published excerpts from the Dwight copies of the "Miscellanies." In 1890, in a review of Allen's *Jonathan Edwards*, Smyth took the opportunity to print portions (many

---

5. *Christ in Theology* (Hartford, 1851), p. vi. The last phrase was quoted by Bushnell from a letter of W. T. Dwight to his nephew Timothy Dwight of New Haven, through whom Bushnell had applied for permission to examine the MS (see W. T. Dwight to Edward W. Hooker, Apr. 21, 1851 [Trask Library]).

6. A summary of the discussion through the 1880s will be found in A. V. G. Allen's *Jonathan Edwards* (Boston, 1889), pp. 338–45. The story is told in more detail, with several excerpts from the correspondence in the Trask Library, by Richard D. Pierce in "A Suppressed Edwards Manuscript on the Trinity," *Crane Review, 1* (1959), 66–80.

7. New York, 1880.

8. "Remarks of Jonathan Edwards on the Trinity," *Bibliotheca Sacra, 38* (1881), 147–87, 333–69.

9. Nos. 1180, 1252, and 1253 (ibid., pp. 179–86). The work was Ramsay's *Philosophical Principles of Natural and Revealed Religion* (2 vols. Glasgow, 1748–49).

1. *An Unpublished Essay of Edwards on the Trinity with Remarks on Edwards and His Theology* (New York, Scribners, 1903).

of them very brief) of over twenty entries.[2] Sixteen of these again appeared (most of them now complete) in Smyth's appendix to the Edwards bicentenary *Exercises*.[3] There Smyth printed a total of 25 entries on the Trinity and twenty on the end of creation. He had also, in 1897, published an article on "Jonathan Edwards' Idealism," in which he quoted extensively from nineteen different entries.[4]

For over forty years after the bicentenary volume, nothing was published from the "Miscellanies." Then in 1948 Perry Miller printed No. 782 with an introduction as "Jonathan Edwards on the Sense of the Heart."[5] In the same year, Miller brought out a first edition of Edwards' *Images or Shadows of Divine Things*, in which seven miscellanies to which Edwards referred were printed more or less completely.[6] In 1955 appeared *The Philosophy of Jonathan Edwards from His Private Notebooks*, edited by Harvey G. Townsend.[7] Along with "The Mind" and the first three essays in "Natural Philosophy," Townsend printed 159 entries from the "Miscellanies" which contain some of Edwards' more strictly philosophical writing. Unfortunately, Townsend's transcriptions, especially in the earlier entries, are often very faulty.

The following table contains all the significant efforts to publish "Miscellanies" text through the publication of the Townsend volume. With the exception of the Worcester revised edition (see title "Remarks," below), each is a first edition, though a few individual entries have been printed two or three times. Most of the printed entries are complete or reasonably so. Those in which a significant amount of text has been omitted are marked with an asterisk. Fragmentary quotations are not listed.

Edwards marked some entries to be added to or inserted in others, and Jonathan Edwards, Jr., often combined short entries or embedded them in longer essays. This and the lack of entry numbers in several of the editions made identification difficult; it is probably too much to hope that this table is complete and perfectly accurate. No

2. "Professor Allen's "Jonathan Edwards,' with Extracts from Copies of Unpublished Manuscripts," *Andover Review, 13* (1890), 285–304.

3. *Exercises Commemorating the Two-Hundredth Anniversary of the Birth of Jonathan Edwards* (Andover, Mass., Andover Press, 1904), app. 1, pp. 3–60.

4. *American Journal of Theology, 1* (1897), 950–64.

5. *Harvard Theological Review, 41* (1948), 123–45.

6. New Haven, Yale Univ. Press, 1948. Miller quoted portions of a few others in his introduction.

7. Eugene, Univ. of Oregon Press, 1955. The work was published posthumously, Townsend having died in 1948.

effort has been made to indicate precisely the point on the page at which the item occurs, but a few entries broken by inserted matter have been rendered easier to follow by employing a five-fold page division (*a–e*), e.g. pp. 498–99*d*, 502*e*–06.

SHORT TITLES

Dwight   Dwight ed., Vol. 8 (1830). N.B. Vol. 9 contains only one entry (No. 1069), for which both volume and page are given.

Exercises *Exercises Commemorating the Two-Hundredth Anniversary of the Birth of Jonathan Edwards* (1904), "Appendix I" (ed. E.C. Smyth), 3–60.

Idealism   E.C. Smyth, "Jonathan Edwards' Idealism," *American Journal of Theology, 1* (1897), 950–64.

Images   *Images or Shadows of Divine Things*, ed. Perry Miller (1948).

Miscell. Obss. *Miscellaneous Observations on Important Theological Subjects*, ed. Jonathan Edwards, Jr. (1793).

Œconomy   *Observations Concerning the Scripture Œconomy of the Trinity and Covenant of Redemption*, ed. E.C. Smyth (1880).

Park   E.A. Park, "Remarks of Jonathan Edwards on the Trinity," *Bibliotheca Sacra, 38* (1881), 147–87, 333–69.

Remarks   *Remarks on Important Theological Controversies*, ed. Jonathan Edwards, Jr. (1796). The volume and page numbers in parentheses following most citations of the Remarks refer to the Worcester rev. ed., where the text is more readily available.

Sense   Perry Miller, "Jonathan Edwards on the Sense of the Heart," *Harvard Theological Review, 41* (1948), 123–45.

Smyth   E.C. Smyth, "Professor Allen's 'Jonathan Edwards,' with Extracts from Copies of Unpublished Manuscripts," *Andover Review, 13* (1890), 285–304.

Townsend   *The Philosophy of Jonathan Edwards from His Private Notebooks*, ed. H.G. Townsend (1955).

* * *

Entry	*Publication*	*Entry*	*Publication*
f	Idealism, 953	*h*	Dwight, 526
	Townsend, 193	*o*	Remarks, 217–18 (2, 566)

Entry	Publication	Entry	Publication
p	Remarks, 218–19 (2, 566–67)	75	Remarks, 100 (2, 515)
u	Remarks, 96 (2, 513)		Townsend, 516
w	Townsend, 235–36	80	Townsend, 209
x	Townsend, 236	81	Œconomy, 76–78
aa	Townsend, 244–45	82	Remarks, 100–01 (2, 515)
dd	Miscell. Obss., 181–82		Townsend, 157
ff	Dwight, 526–27	83	Townsend, 210
gg	Exercises, 34–35	84	Remarks, 288 (3, 509)
	Townsend, 236–37	85	Remarks, 101 (2, 515)
ii	Dwight, 527		Townsend, 157
kk	Exercises, 35	87	Smyth, 295*
	Townsend, 237		Exercises, 35–36
ll,	Exercises, 35		Townsend, 128–29
	Townsend, 237	88	Smyth, 295–96*
pp	Idealism, 953	89	Smyth, 296
	Townsend, 74		Townsend, 183
tt	Townsend, 126–28	91	Townsend, 74–75
1	Townsend, 195–96	92	Exercises, 36
2	Œconomy, 64–67*		Townsend, 129
3	Townsend, 193	94	Smyth, 296–98*
4	Townsend, 208–09		Exercises, 8–16
5	Dwight, 527–29		Townsend, 252–58
6	Miscell. Obss., 182–83	95	Dwight, 532
7	Remarks, 96–97 (2, 513)		Townsend, 193–94
8	Townsend, 197	96	Smyth, 299*
10	Townsend, 197–98		Exercises, 16–17*
11	Townsend, 198		Townsend, 194–95
14	Townsend, 198–99	97	Townsend, 195
16	Remarks, 97–98 (2, 513–14)	104	Smyth, 299*
	Townsend, 153		Exercises, 37–39
17	Townsend, 199–200	105	Dwight, 529–30*
19	Remarks, 149 (2, 534)	108	Œconomy, 92–97[8]
20	Townsend, 196	112	Dwight, 530
26	Townsend, 207		Œconomy, 97
27a	Idealism, 953–54	115	Exercises, 37
	Townsend, 74	116b	Townsend, 109–10
29	Remarks, 98–99 (2, 514)	117	Exercises, 17–18*
	Townsend, 153–54		Townsend, 258
31	Townsend, 154	121	Œconomy, 73
34	Townsend, 241	123	Townsend, 245–46
40	Townsend, 200	124	Townsend. 75–76
42	Townsend, 238	125a	Townsend, 76
44	Townsend, 241–42	127	Miscell. Obss., 1–2
48	Dwight, 509–10	128	Miscell. Obss., 2–3
51	Remarks, 99 (2, 514–15)	129	Miscell. Obss., 3
63	Remarks, 149–51 (2, 534–35)	131	Miscell. Obss., 3–4
		132[9]	Miscell. Obss., 4–5*
69	Townsend, 200–01	(147)	
70	Townsend, 201–02	134	Townsend, 76
71	Townsend, 155–56	(149)	
74	Remarks, 99–100 (2, 515)	135	Exercises, 19

8. Smyth's ed. of Nos. 108 and 112 was reprinted in *Jonathan Edwards: Representative Selections*, pp. 372–74. See above, p. 278, n. 9.

9 Nos. 132–140 are incorrectly numbered 147–155 in the "Miscellanies" MS and in all previous publications; see above, p. 155.

Entry	Publication	Entry	Publication
(150)		206	Dwight, 533
	Townsend, 183	208	Townsend, 129
137	Dwight, 530	219	Remarks, 452 (2, 627)
(152)		236	Miscell. Obss., 8–9
140	Miscell. Obss., 5	238	Exercises, 20–22
(155)			Townsend, 247–48
143[1]	Exercises, 18	239	Townsend, 248
(133)		242	Miscell. Obss., 9
146	Exercises, 18–19*	243	Exercises, 40–41
(136)			Townsend, 129
147	Remarks 273, (2, 590–91)	244	Remarks, 452 (2, 626–27)
(137)		245	Remarks, 355–56
150	Miscell. Obss., 466–67	247	Smyth, 300*
(140)			Exercises, 41
151	Exercises, 19*		Townsend, 129–30
(141)		248	Townsend, 248
152	Miscell. Obss., 5–6	249	Miscell. Obss., 9–10
(142)		254	Remarks, 452–53 (2, 627)
153	Dwight, 530-31		Townsend, 77–78
(143)		256	Remarks, 453 (2, 627)
154	Miscell. Obss., 467		Townsend, 249
(144)		259	Exercises, 22–23
167	Miscell. Obss., 6–7		Townsend, 259–60
170	Remarks, 101–02 (2, 516)	260	Exercises, 23–24
176	Dwight, 485	262	Townsend, 207–08
178	Townsend, 259	263	Dwight, 533–34
179	Idealism, 961	264	Dwight, 534
	Exercises, 19	266	Miscell. Obss., 10–11
	Townsend, 259	267	Idealism, 957
180	Smyth, 303		Townsend, 78
182	Dwight, 531–32	268	Townsend, 78–79
183	Œconomy, 72	269	Townsend, 79
184	Smyth, 299–300	270	Townsend, 202
	Exercises, 20	271	Smyth, 300–01
	Idealism, 962		Exercises, 42
	Townsend, 210	272	Dwight, 534
186	Miscell. Obss., 7	274	Townsend, 79
188	Dwight, 532	293	Townsend, 260
190	Miscell. Obss., 7–8	296	Dwight, 510
192	Townsend, 263	301	Townsend, 242–43*
194	Smyth, 300*	308	Smyth, 301*
	Exercises, 20*		Exercises, 24–25
	Townsend, 183–84		Townsend, 260
196	Miscell. Obss., 8	309	Exercises, 25
197	Smyth, 300		Townsend, 261
	Exercises, 39–40	312	Townsend, 79–80
198	Dwight, 532–33	320	Dwight, 496–97
	Townsend, 195	321a	Miscell. Obss., 11
199	Townsend, 76–77	327a	Smyth, 301
200	Townsend, 77	327b	Remarks, 335 (3, 532)
201	Townsend, 246–47	329	Remarks, 453–55* (2, 627–28*)
203	Miscell. Obss., 8	330	Smyth, 301*
205	Œconomy, 74–76*		Exercises, 26

1. Nos. 143–154 are incorrectly numbered 133–144 in the "Miscellanies" MS and in all previous publications; see above, p. 155.

Entry	Publication	Entry	Publication
332	Exercises, 42	448	Smyth, 301–02*
	Townsend, 130		Exercises, 46–48
333	Miscell. Obss., 11–12		Townsend, 133–34
	Townsend, 80	449	Remarks, 389–90 (*1*, 610)
336	Exercises, 26	451	Remarks, 390 (*1*, 610)
341	Exercises, 26–27	453	Townsend, 184
342	Townsend, 157	461	Townsend, 134, 131–32
346	Townsend, 130*	465	Miscell. Obss., 25
348	Remarks, 102–04, (2, 516–17)	467	Remarks, 290–91 (*3*, 510)
350	Miscell. Obss., 12–18	473	Townsend, 238–39
351	Miscell. Obss., 183–84	477	Dwight, 540
352	Miscell. Obss., 18	487	Œconomy, 73–74*
353	Dwight, 510	489	Remarks, 455–56 (2, 628)
358	Miscell. Obss., 18–20		Townsend, 250
361	Townsend, 252	499	Dwight, 540
362	Exercises, 28–29	504	Remarks, 456 (2, 628–29)
	Images, 63–64	512	Miscell. Obss., 25–26*
365	Idealism, 954–55	515	Dwight, 510–13, 516
	Townsend, 80	518	Miscell. Obss., 26–27
370	Exercises, 27–28	519	Miscell. Obss., 27–28
	Images, 64*	529	Dwight, 540–42
371	Dwight, 534–36	530	Townsend, 202–05
372	Dwight, 536–37	533[2]	Townsend, 110–11
376	Exercises, 29	538	Remarks, 286–87
378	Miscell. Obss., 20	540	Townsend, 250
379	Miscell. Obss., 20–22	541	Townsend, 250–51
382	Miscell. Obss., 22–23	546	Dwight, 542–43
383	Idealism, 958*	547	Miscell. Obss., 28–29*
	Townsend, 81		Townsend, 134–36
395	Miscell. Obss., 23	552	Miscell. Obss.,29
397	Townsend, 249	553	Smyth, 302
405	Exercises, 29–30		Exercises, 48–49
408	Townsend, 249–50		Townsend, 136–37
413	Dwight, 537	555	Dwight, 543–44
415	Remarks, 289–90 (*3*, 509–10)	565	Dwight, 544–45
420	Remarks, 286	566	Townsend, 243–44
421	Dwight, 537–38	567	Townsend, 205
423	Remarks, 104 (2, 517)	570	Dwight, 513–14
426	Miscell. Obss., 184–85	571	Dwight, 545–50
428	Remarks, 290 (*3*, 510)	573	Townsend, 160–61
430	Dwight, 538	576	Dwight, 550
431	Dwight, 538	581	Townsend, 137
432	Dwight, 538–39	582	Miscell. Obss., 29–30
435	Dwight, 539–40	583	Miscell. Obss., 30–32
436	Townsend, 157–59		Townsend, 210–12
437	Townsend, 159–60	584	Miscell. Obss., 32–33
438	Dwight, 496	585	Dwight, 550–51
442	Dwight, 485–86	586	Townsend, 137*
443	Miscell. Obss., 23–24	587	Idealism, 955
444	Miscell. Obss., 24–25		Townsend, 81–82
445	Exercises, 42–46	590	Miscell. Obss., 34–35
	Townsend, 130–32	591	Dwight, 514–15
446	Exercises, 30	598	Miscell. Obss., 35–36

2. In Townsend's edition this entry is misnumbered 353.

Entry	*Publication*	*Entry*	*Publication*
972	Miscell. Obss., 61–87	1119	Dwight, 598
976	Townsend, 103–09	1120	Remarks, 458–59 (2, 630)
977	Miscell. Obss., 161–62	1121	Dwight, 598
979	Miscell. Obss., 162–68	1122	Dwight, 581
980	Dwight, 499–502	1123	Townsend, 209–210
981	Miscell. Obss., 99–102	1126	Dwight, 581–82
983	Miscell. Obss., 102–04	1130a	Remarks, 459–60 (2, 630–31)
984	Miscell. Obss., 112–19	1130b	Remarks, 460–62 (2, 631)
986	Miscell. Obss., 168–70	1134	Dwight, 598–99
	Townsend, 212–13	1137	Dwight, 599
990	Townsend, 265	1145	Remarks, 385–86 (1, 608)
991	Images, 117–19*	1151	Smyth, 303*
994	Dwight, 526		Exercises, 51–52
1000	Images, 108–09	1153	Townsend, 165–80
1002	Miscell. Obss., 119–20	1154	Townsend, 180–82
1005	Remarks, 375–82 (1, 603–06)	1155	Townsend, 182–83
1006	Remarks, 19 (1, 574)	1156	Miscell. Obss., 129–42
	Townsend, 196–97	1158	Miscell. Obss. 147
1007	Miscell. Obss., 120–28	1160	Remarks, 20–32 (1, 574–81)
1015	Miscell. Obss. 107–08	1162	Exercises, 31–33
1020	Miscell. Obss., 108–12	1167	Remarks, 32 (1, 581)
1026	Miscell. Obss., 375	1168	Townsend, 252
1035	Remarks, 384–85 (1, 607–08)	1169	Miscell. Obss., 391
1038	Townsend, 265–66	1170	Miscell. Obss., 147
1041	Townsend, 267–68		Townsend, 213
1044	Miscell. Obss., 88–95	1171	Miscell. Obss., 391
1057	Dwight, 507		Townsend, 213
1059	Dwight, 590	1173	Remarks, 386 (1, 608)
1060	Miscell. Obss., 185–223	1174	Miscell. Obss., 469–73
1061	Dwight, 590–92	1180	Park, 179–80
1062	Œconomy, 21–57	1182	Townsend, 140
1065	Exercises, 30–31	1188	Remarks, 299–300, (3, 514–15)
1066	Townsend, 139	1190	Miscell. Obss., 147–52
1069	Dwight, 9, 9–111	1192	Miscell. Obss., 152–53
1072	Dwight, 592	1193	Miscell. Obss., 95–97
1075b	Townsend, 165	1194	Miscell. Obss., 97–99
1076	Remarks, 385 (1, 608)	1196	Townsend, 184
1077	Townsend, 184	1197	Miscell. Obss., 475
1082	Smyth, 302–03*	1198	Miscell. Obss., 52–53
	Exercises, 49–50	1199	Miscell. Obss., 53–57
1087	Miscell. Obss., 128	1206	Miscell. Obss., 154–60
1089	Dwight, 592–97	1208	Remarks, 386–88* (1, 608–09*)
1090	Remarks, 458 (2, 629–30)		Townsend, 140–49*
	Townsend, 251–52	1212	Remarks, 374 (1, 602)
1091	Œconomy, 69–71*	1214	Remarks, 373–74 (1, 601–02)
1095	Dwight, 597	1217	Remarks, 372* (1, 601*)
1098	Dwight, 494–95	1218	Exercises, 52–56
1100	Miscell. Obss., 390–91		Townsend, 149–52*
	Townsend, 213	1225	Townsend, 152–53
1102	Miscell. Obss., 474	1226	Miscell. Obss., 170–72
1103	Remarks, 284–85 (2, 596)	1228	Miscell. Obss., 172–73
1105	Miscell. Obss., 474	1229	Miscell. Obss., 174–76
1109	Miscell. Obss., 45	1230	Miscell. Obss., 176–81
1111	Miscell. Obss., 128–29	1231	Miscell. Obss., 173–74
1114	Miscell. Obss., 475	1232	Remarks, 372 (1, 601)

Entry	Publication	Entry	Publication
1233	Miscell. Obss., 391–92	1300	Miscell. Obss., 142–45
	Townsend, 213–14	1303	Townsend, 219
1234	Miscell. Obss., 392–94*	1304	Miscell. Obss., 316–31
1239	Miscell. Obss., 181	1306	Miscell. Obss., 145–47
1241	Miscell. Obss., 475–76	1309	Miscell. Obss., 331–36
1243	Miscell. Obss., 476	1312	Miscell. Obss., 377–78
1246	Dwight, 600	1316	Miscell. Obss., 336–39
1247	Dwight, 495	1317	Miscell. Obss., 378–82
1249	Miscell. Obss., 476	1318	Miscell. Obss., 382–83
1252	Park, 180–81	1321	Miscell. Obss., 383–86
1253	Park, 181–86	1324	Miscell. Obss., 386–87
1258	Remarks, 34–35 (*1*, 582)	1327	Miscell. Obss., 339–49*
1261	Dwight, 507–09	1329	Dwight, 526
1263	Townsend, 184–93	1332b	Miscell. Obss., 87*c*–88*b*
1266a	Exercises, 57–58	1333	Miscell. Obss., 349–50
1266b	Dwight, 509	1334	Miscell. Obss., 350–58
1275	Exercises, 58–60	1335	Miscell. Obss., 358–66
1276	Dwight, 495–96	1336	Miscell. Obss., 336–68
1281	Dwight, 600–03	1337	Miscell. Obss., 279–83
1284	Remarks, 94 (*1*, 641–42)	1338	Miscell. Obss., 283–98
1285	Miscell. Obss., 377	1340	Miscell. Obss., 257–79
1286	Miscell. Obss., 375		Townsend, 219–35
1288	Miscell. Obss., 376–77	1341	Miscell. Obss., 368–71
1290	Miscell. Obss., 142	1342	Miscell. Obss., 371–75
1292	Remarks, 35 (*1*, 582)	1348	Remarks, 36–62 (*1*, 612–25)
1295	Remarks, 390 (*1*, 610)	1349	Miscell. Obss., 406–27
1297	Miscell. Obss., 298–303	1350	Miscell. Obss., 223–57
	Townsend, 214–18	1352	Remarks, 356–67 (*1*, 593–99)
1298	Miscell. Obss., 303–04	1356	Remarks, 62–95 (*1*, 625–41)
	Townsend, 218–19	1358	Miscell. Obss., 428–66
1299	Miscell. Obss., 313–16	1360	Remarks, 367–72 (*1*, 599–601)

APPENDIX B

WATERMARKS IN EDWARDS' EARLY MANUSCRIPTS

T HESE watermarks are introduced in the order in which they first
appear in the early manuscripts and with the same Watermark
(Wm)/countermark (cm) combinations, except where this would necessitate repeating specimens.[1] The watermarks reproduced here are
hand drawn from sheets in the "Miscellanies" or the sermons, with one
exception.[2]

The reproductions are reduced in size, but there is one set of watermarks in full size in Fig. 1, with which they may be compared. No
distinction has been made between the "right" and "wrong" side of the
molds, but the marks have been reproduced from whichever side they
read correctly. The scale below each figure shows the location of the
mark relative to the chain lines. The tiny delta under the scale indicates the center of the half-sheet; some papers can be distinguished by
the location of a mark (e.g. to the right or the left of the center) in the
half-sheet.[3]

Compilers of watermark specimens do not always agree exactly on
the titles to be given the various kinds of marks; I have generally
adopted the designations in Churchill's *Watermarks*. Churchill, Voorn,
and Gravell-Miller[4] were the main sources for identification of the
papermakers' initials and monograms or those of the paper sellers for
whom the paper was manufactured. Such guesses as have been made
are included in the following descriptions:

1. The watermarks in JE's MSS are discussed above, pp. 60–63. A radiograph of a sheet
exhibiting the English/GR^wr watermarks with the chain and wire lines is reproduced in
Fig. 1 (above, p. 64), and a list of the watermarks from which the following illustrations are
taken will be found in Table 1 (above, pp. 71–72).
2. Paper with English-CH marks occurs in JE's first extant sermons and also in his "Natural Philosophy." The two sets of marks are almost identical in appearance but represent two
different sets of molds and almost certainly two separate purchases. Fig. 4 is drawn from the
innermost sheet of the "Natural Philosophy" quire.
3. See above, pp. 71–72.
4. See above, p. 61, nn. 3, 5.

Fig. 4. This English arms has the same content as the one radio-graphed in Fig. 1, except for the cursive CH (possibly CFL or CTL) beneath it. The crowned GR in wreath was the countermark most frequently used with the English Arms. Source: "Natural Philosophy" quire, inside sheet.[5]

Fig. 5. The Vreyheyt was a frequently used Dutch watermark. The kind of horn used in this countermark does not appear in any compilation, so far as I know. Source: Sermon on John 8:34.

Fig. 6. The initials in the countermark have not been identified. Source: "Miscellanies," second Amsterdam/AAB sheet.

Fig. 7. Arms of the Seven Provinces ("United Provinces"), the part of the Netherlands that revolted against Spain in 1581 and achieved independence in 1587. TVH has been taken as the correct reading of the initials because of the shape of the *V*, but if so the cm is in the right half-sheet and the Wm in the left. If the letters are HVT the marks would be in the normal positions with the lion facing left. If the letters are HVT they may have referred to the papermaker H. van Til. Source: the complete Seven Provinces sheet in the "Miscellanies"; the half-sheet that precedes it was made on the same mold.

Fig. 8. Source, with the cm PvL: first sheet of London/PvL paper in the "Miscellanies." The cm GR is taken from the first London/GR sheet in the "Miscellanies." Both cms were frequently used with the London arms, which, in Edwards' papers of this period always had about the same shape and size as the one reproduced here. Other cms used with the London arms in these papers are the initials IV (probably for Jean Villedary) and PD (for P. Dürring [Churchill] or Pieter Dirksz de Jong [Voorn]).

Fig. 9. The cm has been taken as the monogram MvL because of the prominence of the downstroke on the *M* and the fact that M. van Lier was a prominent Dutch papermaker. If the letters are ML they remain unidentified. Source: the one sheet of Amsterdam/MvL paper in the "Miscellanies."

Fig. 10. The initials EYD have not been identified. When they read correctly they are in the left half-sheet, but the Wm is upside down; when the Wm is right side up the cm is still in the left half-sheet but the letters are upside down. Source: the Fleur de lis in the "Miscellanies."

Fig. 11. The cm has not been identified. Source: Sermon on I Pet. 2:9.

---

5. See preceding n. 2.

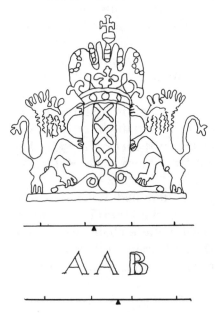

Fig. 4. Wm: English Arms with cursive CH
cm: Crowned GR in wreath

Fig. 5. Wm: Vreyheyt
cm: Horn

Fig. 6. Wm: Amsterdam Arms
cm: AAB

Fig. 7. Wm: Seven Provinces
cm: TVH

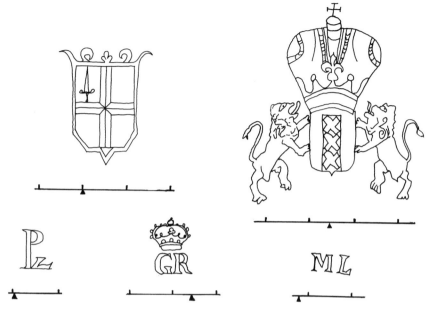

Fig. 8. Wm: London Arms
cm: PvL monogram
cm: Crowned GR

Fig. 9. Wm: Amsterdam Arms
cm: MvL

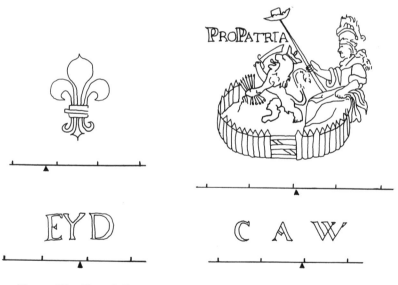

Fig. 10. Wm: Fleur de lis
cm: EYD

Fig. 11. Wm: Maid of Dort (Garden of Hol
land)
cm: CAW

APPENDIX C

THE EVOLUTION OF EDWARDS'
EARLY HANDWRITING

T HE following specimens have been selected to represent successive stages in the development of Edwards' handwriting. While contiguous examples may not seem very different, wider comparisons show
that his hand changed considerably in the decade during which the
"Miscellanies" entries in this volume were written.[1]

1. See the description of JE's handwriting, above, pp. 66–68.

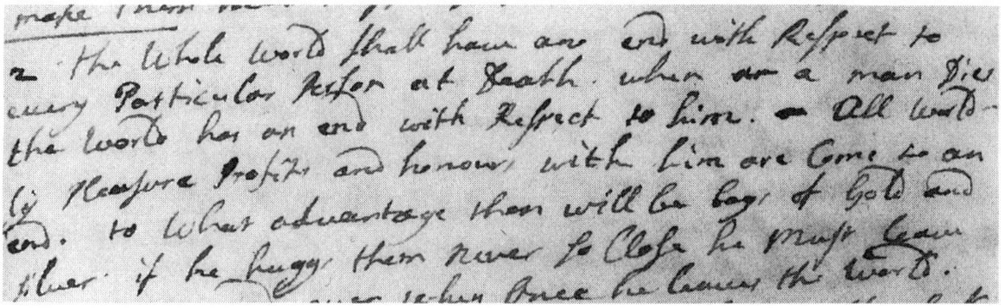

Fig. 12. Vreyheyt sermon on Matt. 16:26 (1721–22)

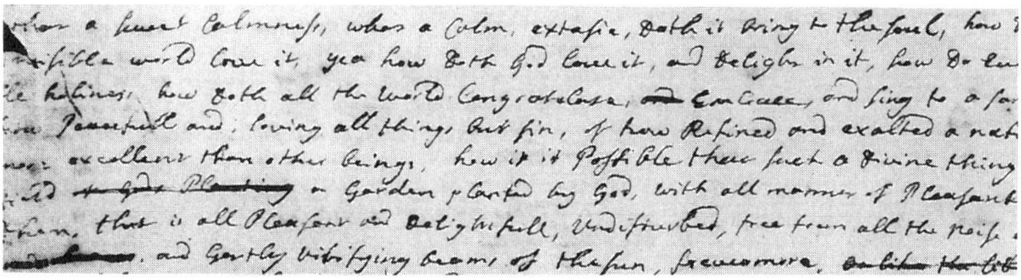

Fig. 13. "Miscellanies" No. a (late 1722)

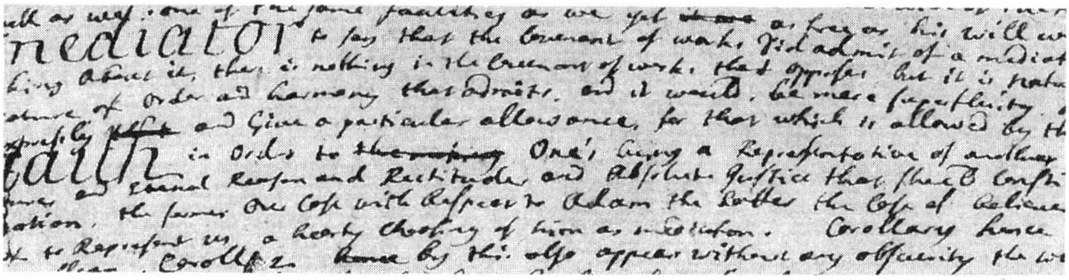

Fig. 14. "Miscellanies" Nos. 32–33 (summer 1723)

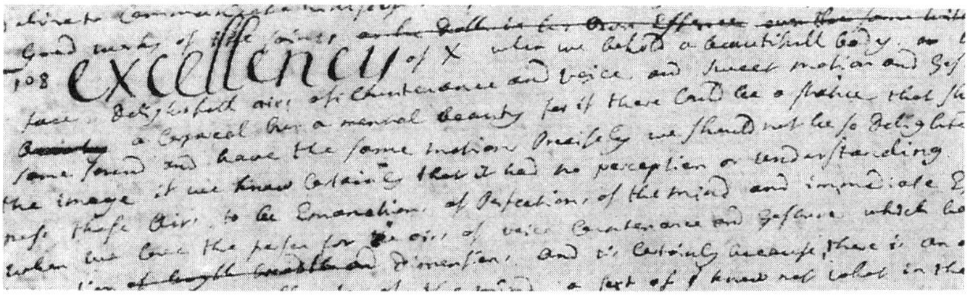

Fig. 15. "Miscellanies" No. 108 (late fall or early winter 1723–24)

Fig. 16. "Miscellanies" No. 126 (fall 1724)

Fig. 17. "Miscellanies" No. 200 (winter 1726)

Fig. 18. "Miscellanies" Nos. 301–302 (fall 1727)

Fig. 19. Sermon on Jer. 6:28–39 (February 1729)

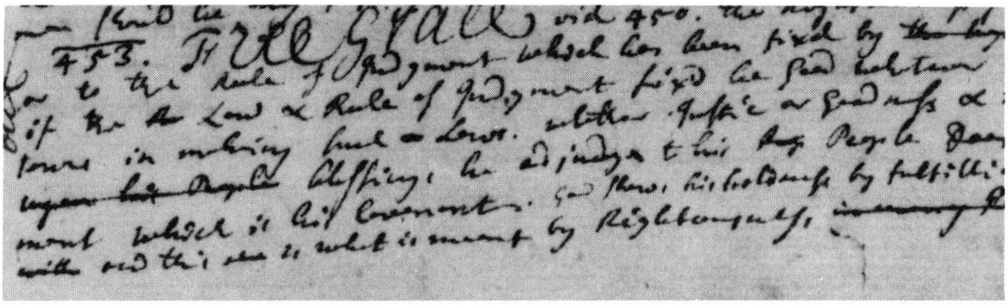

Fig. 20. "Miscellanies" No. 453 (late fall or early winter 1729–30)

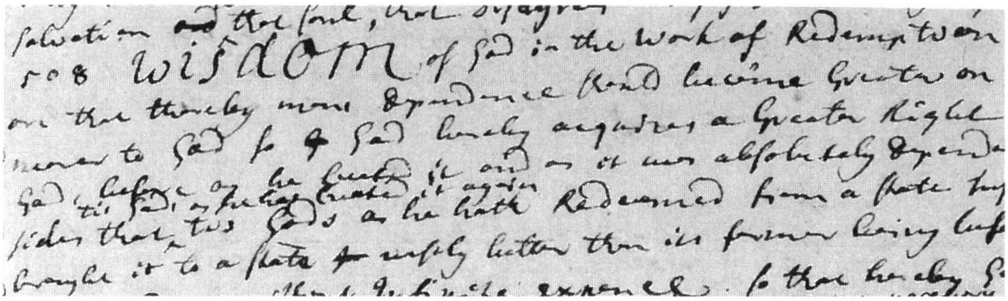

Fig. 21. "Miscellanies" No. 508 (summer 1731)

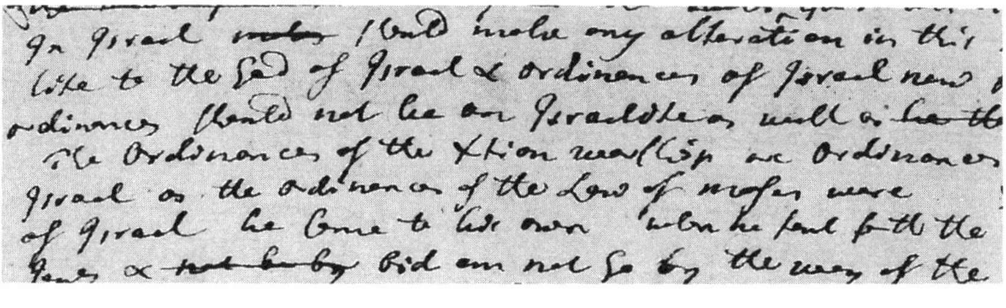

Fig. 22. "Miscellanies" No. 597 (late fall or early winter 1732–33)

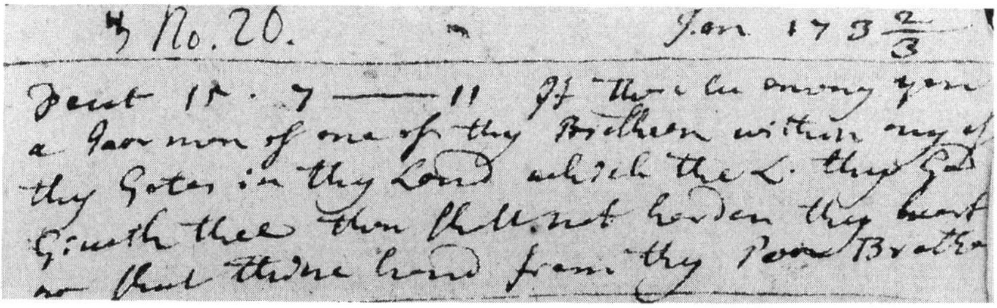

Fig. 23. Sermon on Deut. 15:7–11 (January 1733). The heading at the left is not in Edwards' hand.

APPENDIX D

VARIETIES OF INK TEXTURES IN EDWARDS' EARLY MANUSCRIPTS

U NDER the microscope Edwards' ink often has an appearance far different from what is seen by the naked eye or even with the aid of a reading glass.[1] Many examples would be necessary to demonstrate this fully, but the following photomicrographs exhibit ink textures quite different from one another. Each would seem even more distinctive if the many shades of gray and brown that these ink specimens possess were also visible.[2] Notwithstanding, these six examples explain why ink comparison has been, along with the examination of watermarks, the most useful means for dating Edwards' manuscripts.

Verbal description is very inadequate to convey differences in color, shade, and texture that the eye catches immediately (compare Edwards' distinction between intuitive and notional or even discursive knowledge). Nevertheless, it may be helpful to mention some of the ways in which these ink samples differ from one another.

Fig. 24. This ink appears on the first four entries in the "Miscellanies"; it was somewhat darker on the rest of Edwards' entries in New York and the Amsterdam/AAB sermons he wrote there. It has been considerably exposed to wear and oxidation, yet the pigment remains well attached to the paper.

Fig. 25. This is the same ink as that of Fig. 24 in its somewhat darker shade, but here much heavier and more intense; it occurs on an inside page of a sermon and thus was more shielded from weather and wear. Except for the color, which would have been black, this is probably how the ink must have appeared when first applied.

Fig. 26. Timothy Edwards was using this kind of ink in the 1720s, and Jonathan probably borrowed some while on a visit to Windsor in

---

1. JE's ink is discussed above, pp. 63–66.

2. Black and white photomicrographs at 20× magnification have been used for two reasons. One is that the texture is a more permanent feature of the ink, because exposure to light, moisture, and handling can produce different shades of the same ink, ranging from solid gray to various browns and tans. The other is that it is difficult to reproduce these exact shades in color photography.

the spring or summer of 1726. Its color came almost entirely from the solids held in suspension and deposited on the top of the paper; where these were rubbed or broken off little pigment remained. The result has been described variously as crusty, scabby, or mangy, especially when more of the coating has been broken off.

Fig. 27. Here the solids are better attached to the paper and have rubbed off more uniformly, producing a somewhat fuzzy (in other places more grainy) texture. This specimen is from the first entry on which the ink appears in the "Miscellanies"; it is now a medium shade of brown, in contrast to the grayish "Windsor" ink (like that in Fig. 27) that preceded it. Edwards used this ink for Nos. 152–194 in the first half of 1725.

Fig. 28. Edwards was probably convalescing at home in the winter of 1725–26, for this is a very thin version of Timothy's ink. The liquid itself left only a faint trace, and the scarce solids that remain are those that drifted against paper fibers or the outer edges of the ink line.

Fig. 29. This ink is very much the opposite of that in Fig. 28. It is quite viscous, and it stuck to the paper mostly at points of heavier pressure or on bumps in the paper.

Fig. 24. "Miscellanies"
No. b

Fig. 25. Sermon on Phil.
1:21, second booklet

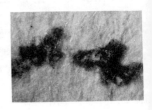

Fig. 26. "Miscellanies"
No. 231

Fig. 27. "Miscellanies"
No. 152

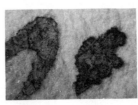

Fig. 28. "Miscellanies"
No. 205

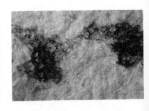

Fig. 29. "Miscellanies"
No. 455

GENERAL INDEX

The abbreviation JE has been used for Jonathan Edwards in this index.

Aaron, 167, 409
Abraham, 22n, 204, 445
Absalom, 204
Adam: fall of, 21–22, 35, 55, 176, 245–46, 323–25, 381, 382–83, 382n, 386–87n, 484–86; covenant with, 22n, 198, 219, 403, 465–66; correspondence between Christ and, 24, 174, 198, 323–24, 403, 450–51, 464–65; human identification with, 39; sin of, 43, 210, 245–46, 324–25, 380, 446–47, 484–87; happiness of, 173–74, 197–98, 540; Eve from rib of, 181; faith of, 218; son of, 302; obedience required from, 319, 450
Afflictions, 286, 351, 474
Aldridge, Alfred O., 59n
Allen, A. V. G., 549
Anderson, Wallace E., 59, 59n
Angels, 186, 232–33, 271, 284–85, 319–20, 326, 490–91; rebellion of, 401–02, 415, 428, 487
Anglican Church (Church of England), 12–13, 79, 207
Antelapsarians, 233n
Antichrist, 54, 185–86, 212n, 414–15, 439, 484
Apocalypse, 191, 319–20
"Apocalypse" notebook, 81n, 142n, 320n
Apollos, 195
Apostles, 240–41, 316–18, 346, 507. *See also* specific apostles
Arianism, 256n, 549
Arminianism, 11, 11n, 13, 14, 22, 27, 29, 37, 132n, 174, 198, 203–04, 216n, 323, 478n, 516–17
Arminius, Jacobus, 11n
Ascension, 343, 480–81
Assurance, 474–75
Atoms, 41–42, 180, 184
Atonement, 48n, 58
Augustine, 40n, 57, 57n, 256n
Authority, 205–08

Baptism, 235, 265, 342, 503, 505
Barth, Karl, 52
Baxter, Richard, 520, 520n

Beasts in Revelation, 191–95
Beauty: and grace, 16; in heaven, 16, 281, 328–29; of God, 31; of natural world, 56n, 177, 278–80, 330–31; of human body, 280
Bedford, Arthur, 191n
Beelzebub. *See* Satan
Being, degree of consent to, 55–56
Being of God, 188, 254–56, 295, 364–65, 394, 410–11, 436, 451–52
Beings, intelligent, 45–48, 56–57, 180, 186, 267
Belief. *See* Faith
Bellamy, Joseph, 48n
Benevolence, 286
Berkeley, George, 47
Bible. *See* Gospel; New Testament; Old Testament; Scriptures
Billings, Edward, 146–47, 147n
Blackmore, Richard, 79
"Blank Bible," 121–22, 123, 274n, 421n, 522n
Bodily worship, 269–70
Body: resurrection of, 178–81, 366; beauty of, 280; of saints, 301; before the fall, 325; sensual appetites of, 388; actions of, and infants, 410–11
Bolton, 13–15, 73n, 76n, 80–82
Bowne, Daniel, 12
Boyle Lectures, 120n
Bushnell, Horace, 548–49

Calamy, Edmund, 12n
Calvinism, 11, 13, 22, 41, 58, 174, 216n, 478n
Casaubon, Meric, 140, 140n
"Catalogue," 4–5, 5n, 10n, 15, 78, 79, 80, 82–83
Catholic Church. *See* Roman Catholic Church
Cerdon, 228
Ceremonies, 206–07, 243–44, 269–70, 393–94
"Chain" lines on paper, 62n, 63, 64
Chain of being, 55
Christ: love of, 17, 212, 247–48, 272–74,

INDEX OF BIBLICAL PASSAGES

NEW TESTAMENT

INDEX OF "MISCELLANIES" NUMBERS

Boldfaced page numbers refer to text of entry.